ILLUSTRATED SERIES™

T0175957

Technology for Success

MICROSOFT® OFFICE 365®
& OFFICE 2019

David W. Beskeen | Jennifer T. Campbell |
Mark Ciampa | Carol M. Cram |
Jennifer Duffy | Steven M. Freund |
Lisa Friedrichsen | Mark Frydenberg |
Ralph E. Hooper | Lisa Ruffolo |
Lynn Wermers

CENGAGE

Australia • Brazil • Canada • Mexico • Singapore • United Kingdom • United States

CENGAGE

Technology for Success and Illustrated Series™ Microsoft® Office 365™ & Office 2019

David W. Beskeen, Jennifer T. Campbell, Mark Ciampa, Carol M. Cram, Jennifer Duffy, Steven M. Freund, Lisa Friedrichsen, Mark Frydenberg, Ralph E. Hooper, Lisa Ruffolo, Lynn Wermers

SVP, GM Skills & Global Product Management: Jonathan Lau

Product Director: Lauren Murphy

Product Assistant: Veronica Moreno-Nestojko

Executive Director, Content Design: Marah Bellegarde

Director, Learning Design: Leigh Hefferon

Associate Learning Designer: Courtney Cozzy

Vice President, Marketing - Science, Technology, and Math: Jason R. Sakos

Senior Marketing Director: Michele McTighe

Marketing Manager: Timothy J. Cali

Director, Content Delivery: Patty Stephan

Content Manager: Grant Davis

Digital Delivery Lead: Laura Ruschman

Designer: Lizz Anderson

Text Designer: Joseph Lee, Black Fish Design

Cover Template Designer: Lisa Kuhn, Curio Press, LLC www.curiopress.com

For product information and technology assistance, contact us at **Cengage Customer & Sales Support, 1-800-354-9706 or support.cengage.com.**

For permission to use material from this text or product, submit all requests online at **www.cengage.com/permissions.**

Library of Congress Control Number: 2019939656

Student Edition ISBN: 978-0-357-02568-0
K12 ISBN: 978-0-357-11974-7
Looseleaf available as part of a digital bundle

Cengage
200 Pier 4 Boulevard
Boston, MA 02210
USA

Cengage is a leading provider of customized learning solutions with employees residing in nearly 40 different countries and sales in more than 125 countries around the world. Find your local representative at **www.cengage.com.**

To learn more about Cengage platforms and services, visit **www.cengage.com.**

Printed at CLDPC, USA, 10-22

Brief Contents

Contents

Technology for Success: Computer Concepts

Word 2019

Getting to Know Microsoft Office Versions

Cengage is proud to bring you the next edition of Microsoft Office. This edition was designed to provide a robust learning experience that is not dependent upon a specific version of Office.

Microsoft supports several versions of Office:

- **Office 365:** A cloud-based subscription service that delivers Microsoft's most up-to-date, feature-rich, modern productivity tools direct to your device. There are variations of Office 365 for business, educational, and personal use. Office 365 offers extra online storage and cloud-connected features, as well as updates with the latest features, fixes, and security updates.

- **Office 2019:** Microsoft's "on-premises" version of the Office apps, available for both PCs and Macs, offered as a static, one-time purchase and outside of the subscription model.

- **Office Online:** A free, simplified version of Office web applications (Word, Excel, PowerPoint, and OneNote) that facilitates creating and editing files collaboratively.

Office 365 (the subscription model) and Office 2019 (the one-time purchase model) had only slight differences between them at the time this content was developed. Over time, Office 365's cloud interface will continuously update, offering new application features and functions, while Office 2019 will remain static. Therefore, your onscreen experience may differ from what you see in this product. For example, the more advanced features and functionalities covered in this product may not be available in Office Online or may have updated from what you see in Office 2019.

For more information on the differences between Office 365, Office 2019, and Office Online, please visit the Microsoft Support site.

Cengage is committed to providing high-quality learning solutions for you to gain the knowledge and skills that will empower you throughout your educational and professional careers.

Thank you for using our product, and we look forward to exploring the future of Microsoft Office with you!

Using SAM Projects and Textbook Projects

SAM and *MindTap* are interactive online platforms designed to transform students into Microsoft Office and Computer Concepts masters. Practice with simulated SAM Trainings and MindTap activities and actively apply the skills you learned live in Microsoft Word, Excel, PowerPoint, or Access. Become a more productive student and use these skills throughout your career.

If your instructor assigns SAM Projects:

1. Launch your SAM Project assignment from SAM or MindTap.
2. Click the links to download your **Instructions file**, **Start file**, and **Support files** (when available).
3. Open the Instructions file and follow the step-by-step instructions.
4. When you complete the project, upload your file to SAM or MindTap for immediate feedback.

To use SAM Textbook Projects:

1. Launch your SAM Project assignment from SAM or MindTap.
2. Click the links to download your **Start file** and **Support files** (when available).
3. Locate the module indicated in your book or eBook.
4. Read the module and complete the project.

 Open the Start file you downloaded.

 Save, close, and upload your completed project to receive immediate feedback.

IMPORTANT: To receive full credit for your Textbook Project, you must complete the activity using the Start file you downloaded from SAM or MindTap.

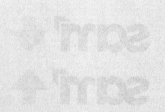

Introduction to Technology for Success: Computer Concepts

You probably use technology dozens of times a day on your phone, computer, and other digital devices to keep in touch with friends and family, research and complete school assignments, shop, and entertain yourself. Even though you use technology every day, understanding how that technology works and how it can work for you will give you the edge you want as you pursue your education and career.

Technology for Success: Computer Concepts will explain the What, Why, and How of technology as it relates to your life, so you can unlock the door to success in the workplace, at home, and at school. It also provides increased skills and safety with the digital devices you use. *Technology for Success: Computer Concepts* will help you master the computer concepts you need to impress at your dream job interview in this age of digital transformation.

Key Features

Based on extensive research and feedback from students today, it has been found that students absorb information more easily if the topics are broken down into smaller lessons that are clearly related to their lives. With this in mind, and to ensure a deeper understanding of technology in the real world, *Technology for Success: Computer Concepts* uses the following approach to helping you understand and apply its contents:

- **Headings** distill key takeaways to help learners understand the big picture and serve as the building blocks of the module designed to help you achieve mastery.

- **Review Questions** help you test your understanding of each topic.

- **Discussion Questions** and **Critical Thinking Activities** help you apply your understanding of the module to the real world.

- **Key Terms** list highlights terms you should know to master the module content.

Digital Learning Experience

The online learning experience includes hands-on trainings, videos that cover the more difficult concepts, and critical thinking challenges that encourage you to problem-solve in a real-world scenario. *Technology for Success: Computer Concepts* is designed to help you build foundational knowledge and integrate it into your daily life with interactive experiences in the MindTap and SAM platforms.

- **Readings** cover focused, concrete content designed to reinforce learning objectives.

- **Videos** complement the reading to reinforce the most difficult concepts.

- **Critical Thinking Challenges** place you in real-world scenarios to practice your problem-solving and decision-making skills.

- **SAM Trainings** are comprised of brief, skills-based videos which are each followed by an assessment. SAM trainings are designed to give you concrete experience with specific technology skills.

- **Module Exams** assess your understanding of how the learning objectives connect and build on one another.

- **In The News RSS Feeds** share the latest technology news to help you understand its impact on our daily lives, the economy, and society. RSS Feeds are currently only available to MindTap users.

Impact of Digital Technology

Fatima looks her best for her profile picture.

submitting her ume online Fatima racticing green mputing.

Fatima has connected her professional social media account to both her laptop and smartphone.

KimSongsak/Shutterstock.com

Fatima Aktar is finishing her degree in social media marketing. During her time at school she has learned about how to use technology for productivity, and specifically how to use technology in social media marketing. Fatima recently visited her school's career counseling center and received a list of tips to use technology to find an entry-level job in her field. She will use the technology with which she is familiar to search for openings, research the companies, schedule and keep track of interviews, and create a professional online presence.

In This Module

- Explain the evolution of society's reliance on technology
- Develop personal uses for technology to help with productivity, learning, and future growth
- Explain the role of technology in the professional world

IN THE COURSE of a day you might use technology to complete assignments, watch a streaming video, flip through news headlines, search for directions, make a dinner reservation, or buy something online. At school, at home, and at work, technology plays a vital role in your activities.

In this module, you will learn how technology has developed over time, explore the ways technology impacts our daily home and work lives, and discover how to choose and prepare for a career in technology.

Explain Society's Reliance on Technology

Over the last quarter century, technology has revolutionized our lives. Because of advances in technology you can more quickly and effectively than ever before access, search for, and share information. You can manage your finances, calendars, and tasks. You can play games and watch videos on your phone or computer for entertainment and relaxation. **Digital literacy** (also called **computer literacy**) involves having a current knowledge and understanding of computers, mobile devices, the web, and related technologies. Being digitally literate is essential for acquiring a job, using and contributing to global communications, and participating effectively in the international community.

A **computer** is an electronic device, operating under the control of instructions stored in its own memory, that can accept data, process the data to produce information, and store the information for future use. **Data** is raw facts, such as text or numbers. A computer includes hardware and software. **Hardware** is the device itself and its components, such as wires, cases, switches, and electronic circuits. **Software** consists of the programs and apps that instruct the computer to perform tasks. Software processes data into meaningful **information**.

Outline the History of Computers

People have relied on tools and machines to count and manipulate numbers for thousands of years. These tools and technologies have evolved from the abacus in ancient times, to the first computing machines in the nineteenth century, to today's powerful handheld devices such as smartphones and tablets.

The first generation of computers used **vacuum tubes** (Figure 1-1), cylindrical glass tubes that controlled the flow of electrons. The ENIAC and UNIVAC are examples of these expensive machines. Their use and availability were limited due to their large size, the amount of power they consumed, the heat they generated, and how quickly they wore out.

Figure 1-1: Electronic digital computer with vacuum tubes

emkaplin/Shutterstock.com

The next generation of computers replaced vacuum tubes with **transistors**, which were smaller, cheaper, and more reliable. These computers contained many components still in use today, including tape and disk storage, memory, operating systems, and stored programs.

In the 1960s, computer engineers developed **integrated circuits**, which packed the equivalent of thousands of vacuum tubes or transistors into a silicon chip about the size of your thumb. In 1971, Ted Hoff and a team of engineers at Intel and IBM introduced the microprocessor. A **microprocessor** is the "brains" of a computer, a chip that contains a central processing unit. Microprocessors were even faster, smaller, and less expensive than integrated circuits. Today, microprocessors are often called processors for short.

In the 1970s and 1980s, computers meant for personal use started to gain popularity. In 1978, Steve Jobs and Steve Wozniak of Apple Computer Corporation introduced the Apple II (**Figure 1-2**), a preassembled computer with color graphics and popular spreadsheet software called VisiCalc.

IBM followed Apple's lead in 1981, introducing its **personal computer (PC)**. Other manufacturers also started making similar machines, and the market grew. Since 1981, the number of PCs in use has grown to the billions. However, many people today use tablets and smartphones in addition to or instead of PCs.

Today's computers have evolved into connected devices that can share data using the Internet or wireless networks. They are smaller, faster, and have far greater capabilities than previous computers. In fact, your smartphone probably has more computing power than the computer that guided the Apollo mission to the moon in 1969!

Explain the Impact of the Internet of Things and Embedded Computers

The **Internet of Things (IoT)** is an environment where processors are embedded in every product imaginable (things), and these things communicate with one another via the Internet or wireless networks. Alarm clocks, coffeemakers, thermostats, streetlights, navigation systems, and much more are enhanced by the growth of IoT. IoT-enabled devices often are referred to as **smart devices** (**Figure 1-3**) because of their ability to communicate, locate, and predict. Smart devices often have associated apps to control and interact with them.

Figure 1-2: Apple II computer

Anton_Ivanov/Shutterstock.com

Figure 1-3: Smart devices use IoT to control home functions, such as a thermostat

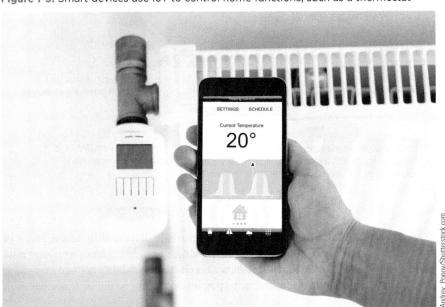

Andrey_Popov/Shutterstock.com

The basic premise of IoT is that objects can be tagged, tracked, and monitored through a local network or across the Internet. Communication technologies such as Bluetooth, RFID tags, near-field communications (NFC), and sensors have become readily available, more powerful, and less expensive. Sensors and tags can transmit data to a server on the Internet over a wireless network at frequent intervals for analysis and storage.

Developments in Big Data have made it possible to efficiently access, store, and process the mountain of data reported by sensors. Mobile service providers offer connectivity to a variety of devices so that transmitting and receiving data can take place quickly.

An **embedded computer** is a computer that functions as one component in a larger product, and which has a specific purpose. Embedded computers usually are small and have limited hardware on their own but enhance the capabilities of everyday devices. Embedded computers perform a specific function based on the requirements of the product in which they reside. For example, an embedded computer in a printer monitors the ink levels, detects paper jams, and determines if the printer is out of paper.

Embedded computers are everywhere. This technology enables computers and devices to connect with one another over the Internet using IoT. You encounter examples of embedded computers multiple times a day, perhaps without being aware of it.

Today's vehicles have many embedded computers. These enable you to use a camera to guide you when backing up, warn you if a vehicle or object is in your blind spot, or alert you to unsafe road conditions. Recently, all new cars were required to include backup cameras and electronic stability control, which can assist with steering the car in case of skidding. All of this technology is intended to make driving safer (**Figure 1-4**).

Figure 1-4: Some of the embedded computers designed to improve safety, security, and performance in today's vehicles

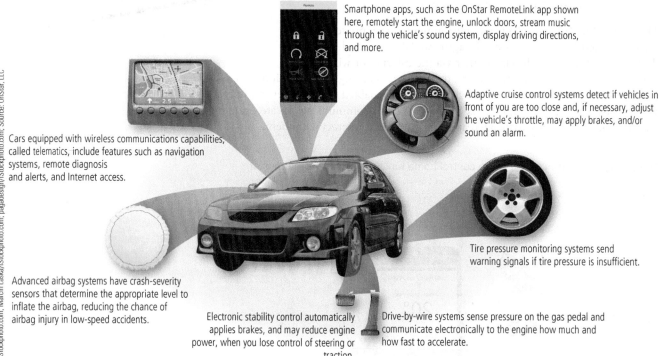

Smartphone apps, such as the OnStar RemoteLink app shown here, remotely start the engine, unlock doors, stream music through the vehicle's sound system, display driving directions, and more.

Adaptive cruise control systems detect if vehicles in front of you are too close and, if necessary, adjust the vehicle's throttle, may apply brakes, and/or sound an alarm.

Cars equipped with wireless communications capabilities, called telematics, include features such as navigation systems, remote diagnosis and alerts, and Internet access.

Tire pressure monitoring systems send warning signals if tire pressure is insufficient.

Advanced airbag systems have crash-severity sensors that determine the appropriate level to inflate the airbag, reducing the chance of airbag injury in low-speed accidents.

Electronic stability control automatically applies brakes, and may reduce engine power, when you lose control of steering or traction.

Drive-by-wire systems sense pressure on the gas pedal and communicate electronically to the engine how much and how fast to accelerate.

Critics of in-vehicle technology claim that it can provide drivers with a false sense of security. If you rely on a sensor while backing up, parking, or changing lanes, you may miss other obstructions that can cause a crash. Reliance on electronic stability control may cause you to drive faster than conditions allow, or to pay less attention to the distance between your vehicle and others.

ATMs and Kiosks

Automated teller machines (ATMs) are one of the more familiar uses of IoT. You can use your ATM card to withdraw cash, deposit checks, and interact with your bank accounts. Recent innovations are improving card security, such as **chip-and-pin technology** that stores data on an embedded chip instead of a magnetic stripe.

ATMs are a type of kiosk. A **kiosk** is a freestanding booth usually placed in a public area that can contain a display device used to show information to the public or event attendees.

Kiosks enable self-service transactions in hotels and airports, for example, to enable users to check in for a flight or room. Healthcare providers also use kiosks for patients to check in and enter information, such as their insurance card number.

IoT at Home

IoT enables you to manage devices remotely in your home, such as to start the washing machine at a certain time, view potential intruders via a webcam, or adjust the room temperature. Personal IoT uses include wearable fitness trackers that record and send data to your smartphone or computer about your exercise activity, the number of steps you take in a day, and your heart rate.

Figure 1-5 shows an example of how IoT can help manage your daily tasks.

Figure 1-5: IoT-enabled devices can help you with daily tasks such as grocery shopping

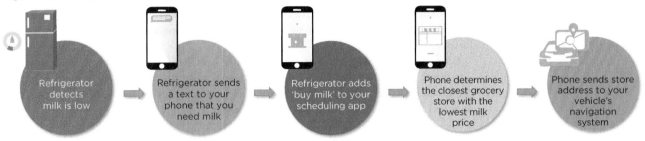

Refrigerator detects milk is low → Refrigerator sends a text to your phone that you need milk → Refrigerator adds 'buy milk' to your scheduling app → Phone determines the closest grocery store with the lowest milk price → Phone sends store address to your vehicle's navigation system

IoT continues to advance its capabilities, and can help you maintain a secure, energy-efficient, connected, voice-activated, remotely accessible home.

IoT in Business

All businesses and areas of business can take advantage of IoT. Manufacturing can use sensors to monitor processes and increase quality of finished goods (Figure 1-6). Retail can use sensors to track inventory or send coupons to customers' phones while they shop. Shipping companies can track mileage and location of their trucks and monitor driving times to ensure the safety of their drivers.

Figure 1-6: Manufacturers can use a tablet to control a robotic arm

Zapp2Photo/Shutterstock.com

A healthcare provider can use IoT to:

- Connect to a patient's wearable blood pressure or glucose monitor
- Send prescription updates and changes to a pharmacy, and alert the patient of the prescription
- Track and store data provided by wearable monitors to determine necessary follow-up care
- Send the patient reminders about upcoming appointments or tests

The uses of IoT are expanding rapidly, and connected devices continue to impact and enhance business practices at all levels.

Discover Uses for Artificial Intelligence

Artificial intelligence (AI) is the technological use of logic and prior experience to simulate human intelligence. AI has a variety of capabilities, such as speech recognition, virtual reality, logical reasoning, and creative responses. Computers with AI can collect information to make decisions, reach conclusions, and combine information in new ways, which is a form of learning.

Computers with AI use machine intelligence rather than human intelligence to make decisions. The goal in creating AI devices is to minimize the gap between what a machine can do and what a human can do. Programmers train the computer to act when presented with certain scenarios by instructing the computer that "if X happens, then do Y."

Explore the Impact of Virtual Reality

Virtual reality (VR) is the use of computers to simulate a real or imagined environment that appears as a three-dimensional (3-D) space. These simulations use 3-D images that enable users to explore and have a sensory experience through visual and sound effects. You use VR in gaming to interact with a virtual environment and digital beings. **Augmented reality (AR)** is a type of VR that uses an image of an actual place or thing and adds digital information to it. A photo of a location overlaid with information about places of interest (**Figure 1-7**) or a football broadcast that shows a first-down marker are examples of AR.

Figure 1-7: Augmented reality combines real images with digital information

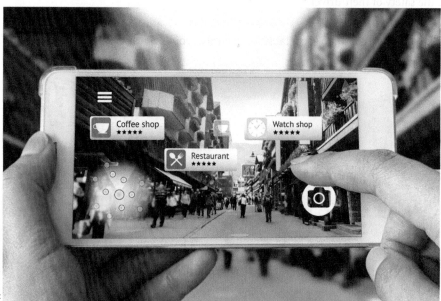

Zapp2Photo/Shutterstock.com

Although VR developers work mostly with digital graphics and animation, they also use AI when creating virtual creatures that make decisions and change their behavior based on interactions with others. A VR developer can create an entire 3-D environment that contains infinite space and depth.

The Digital Divide

All of this technology has many uses for both personal and business needs. However, it is not available to everyone. The **digital divide** is the gap between those who have access to technology and its resources and information, especially on the Internet, and those who do not. Socioeconomic and demographic factors contribute to the digital divide, which can impact individuals, households, businesses, or geographic areas.

Imagine the educational opportunities when you have access to high-speed, unfiltered Internet content; your own laptop, tablet, or smart device; and software to create, track, and process data and information. Then compare these opportunities with the opportunities available to students who live in countries where the government restricts access to Internet content, and economics prevent them from owning their own devices and the software or apps used on them. These inequalities affect learning, knowledge, and opportunities and can have a lasting impact on the future of those affected.

Corporations, non-profits, educational institutions, and governments are working on solutions to narrow the digital divide so that all learners can become digitally literate.

Develop Personal Uses for Technology

You can use technology to help with productivity, learning, and future career growth. In your daily life you interact with embedded computers in stores, public transportation, your car or truck, and more. Assistive technologies help people with disabilities to use technology. Green computing practices reduce the impact of electronic waste on the planet.

Just as any society has rules and regulations to guide its citizens, so does the digital world. As a **digital citizen**, you should be familiar with how to use technology to become an educated and productive member of the digital world. This section covers several areas with which you should be familiar in order to be a digital citizen.

Explore Personal Uses for Technology

Technology can enable you to more efficiently and effectively access and search for information; share personal ideas, photos, and videos with friends, family, and others; communicate with and meet other people; manage finances; shop for goods and services; play games or access other sorts of entertainment; network with other business professionals to recruit for or apply for jobs; keep your life and activities organized; and complete business activities. Artificial intelligence and robotics increase your productivity.

Artificial Intelligence

Some of the practical uses of AI include strategic gaming, military simulations, statistical predictions, and self-driving cars. For example, meteorologists use AI to analyze weather data patterns to create a list of possible outcomes for an upcoming weather event. The predictions made by the AI software then need to be interpreted, reviewed, and prioritized by people.

Some of the ways you might interact with AI on a daily basis include:
- Virtual assistants, which use voice recognition and search engines to answer, react, or reply to user requests
- Social media and online ads, which track your data, such as websites visited, and provide ads targeted to your personal interests
- Video games that provide information to your virtual opponents based on your skill level and past actions
- Music and media streaming services, which recommend options based on your past listening and viewing choices
- Smart cars, which automate many driving tasks such as managing speed and avoiding collisions
- Navigation apps, which provide you with information about traffic and the best routes, along with preferred stops along your way
- Security, such as using your fingerprint to access your phone, or facial recognition and motion-detection cameras that alert you to unusual or unauthorized visitors

Another use of AI is natural language processing. **Natural language processing** is a form of data input in which computers interpret and digitize spoken words or commands. In some cases, users must train the software to recognize the user's speech patterns, accent, and voice inflections. **Digital assistants** like Amazon's Alexa or Apple's Siri use natural language processing to respond to your verbal commands or questions, using search technology to provide answers or perform a task, such as adding an item to a grocery list (**Figure 1-8**).

Figure 1-8: Smart devices provide you with assistance, answers, and more

Use Robotics and Virtual Reality

Robotics is the science that combines engineering and technology to create and program robots. Robots are useful in situations where it is impractical, dangerous, or inconvenient to use a human, such as cleanup of hazardous waste and materials, domestic uses such as vacuuming, and agricultural and manufacturing uses (**Figure 1-9**).

Figure 1-9: Robot used to detect weeds and spray chemicals

Robots can also assist surgeons. A robotic arm or instrument can be more precise, flexible, and controlled than a human hand. 3-D cameras enable the surgeon to see inside the body. Robotic surgeries often take less time to heal and can prevent risk of infection because they require a smaller incision site. However, robots require a surgeon to control and direct the operation. Surgeons must not only be trained medically, but also to use the robot.

Self-driving cars use cameras to change speed due to traffic. They rely on GPS to navigate the best and fastest route. The proponents say that they reduce dangers related to human error. One of the biggest concerns about self-driving cars is that they may contribute to accidents caused by distracted driving.

Outside of gaming, science and medicine use VR for training and research. For example, medical students can use VR to practice their emergency medicine skills. NASA uses VR to simulate space flight and the environments of other planets. Other commercial uses include enabling potential home buyers to move through a home's various rooms, or construction companies to show a preview of the completed building.

When you make a decision based on observation, or answer a question, your brain and senses prompt you to use your past experiences, knowledge base, and visual and other sensory clues to come up with a response. AI and other technologies that mimic human action use some of the same processes. Computers learn from past interactions to predict likely outcomes or responses. They use databases and Internet searches to come up with answers to questions. Cameras can read faces and analyze voices to recognize users.

Utilize Technology in Daily Life

Imagine your life without technology and the Internet. You probably use the Internet daily to find information, connect with social media, make purchases, and more. Your devices can help you connect to the Internet to perform these tasks. The following are examples of how you might interact with technology, including embedded computers and the Internet, in your daily life.

The sound of the alarm you asked your smart speaker to set last night wakes you up. You can smell the coffee brewing from the coffee maker you programmed to go off five minutes before your alarm. Once you leave for work, your thermostat will adjust by five degrees, and then readjust to a more comfortable temperature by the time you arrive home.

On your way to and from work, you check the public transportation app on your phone (**Figure 1-10**) to locate and get directions to the nearest subway station. Once there, you scan your phone to pay your fare and access the terminal. A screen in the station displays

Figure 1-10: You can use apps to find information about public transit options

Rawpixel.com/Shutterstock.com

an alert when the train is incoming. As the subway speeds towards the next station, it relies on sensors to determine any oncoming traffic and report delays, changes in routes, and the next available stop.

After work, you decide to take your car and go shopping. You program your vehicle's GPS to take you to the nearest mall. As you drive, your car senses the space between you and the car ahead and slows your speed to keep a safe distance. Outside the mall, you use a parking app to locate a parking spot near the front door and use your car's cameras to safely navigate into the spot.

Before heading into the store, you decide to check your balance on your debit card. Your banking app tells you how much money is in your checking account. You tap to transfer $40 to your smartphone's payment app, then you head to the store.

You walk into a clothing store, searching for a new sweater. You talk to a sales associate, who uses her tablet to look up your personal profile, including past purchases, based on your phone number. The sales associate tells you what size you wear, and what colors you have bought in the past few years. Together, you find a sweater that fits and that you don't currently have anything like in your wardrobe. Before using the store's self-checkout, you check your store loyalty app on your smartphone to see what coupons are available.

Use Technology to Assist Users with Disabilities

The ever-increasing presence of computers in everyone's lives has generated an awareness of the need to address computing requirements for those with limitations, such as learning disabilities, mobility issues, and hearing and visual disabilities.

The **Americans with Disabilities Act (ADA)** requires any company with 15 or more employees to make reasonable attempts to accommodate the needs of physically challenged workers. The **Individuals with Disabilities Education Act (IDEA)** requires that public schools purchase or acquire funding for adaptive technologies. These laws were put in place to ensure that people with disabilities can access resources, information, and services using the appropriate technology.

Users with visual disabilities can change screen settings, such as increasing the size or changing the color of the text to make the words easier to read. Changing the color of text also can address the needs of users with certain types of color blindness. Instead of using a monitor, blind users can work with voice output. That is, the computer speaks out loud the information that appears on a screen. A Braille printer prints information on paper in Braille (**Figure 1-11**).

Figure 1-11: A Braille printer

Andy Shell/Shutterstock.com

Screen reader technology uses audio output to describe the contents of the screen. Screen readers can read aloud webpages and documents or provide narration of the computer or device's actions. **Alternative text (alt text)** is descriptive text added to an object, such as a picture or drawing (Figure 1-12). A screen reader will read the alt text aloud so that the user understands the image and its purpose. Webpages and documents should include alt text for all images. Alt text can be as simple as the name of a famous individual shown in a photograph, or more complex, such as interpreting the results of a chart or graph. Productivity applications such as Microsoft Office and webpage creation apps prompt users to add alt text, and sometimes provide suggested alt text content.

Figure 1-12: Screen readers use alt text to describe an image

Alt text

Colorful hot air balloons flying over champagne vineyards at sunset, Montagne de Reims, France

Miki Studio/Shutterstock.com

Users with a hearing disability can instruct programs or apps to display words or other visual clues instead of sounds, such as for a notification from an app. Captioning software displays scrolling text for dialogue in a video. Cameras can interpret sign language gestures into text.

Mobility issues can impact a user's ability to interact with hardware, such as a keyboard or a mouse. Users with limited hand mobility can use an on-screen keyboard, a keyboard with larger keys, or a hand-mounted pointer to control the pointer or insertion point. Alternatives to mouse buttons include a hand pad, a foot pedal, a receptor that detects facial motions, or a pneumatic instrument controlled by puffs of air. Users with conditions that cause hands to move involuntarily can purchase input devices such as a keyboard or mouse that are less sensitive to accidental interaction due to trembling or spasms.

Users with learning disabilities might struggle with reading words on a screen, handwriting, or retaining information. Technologies that help these users learn or perform tasks include:

- **Speech recognition programs** so the user can input data or information verbally
- **Graphic organizers** to enable a user to create an outline or structure of information
- **Audio books** to read information aloud to the user instead of reading on a printed page or on the screen

The basic premise of assisted technology is to improve accessibility for all users and provide the same opportunities to learn, work, and play, no matter what limitations a user has.

Apply Green Computing Concepts to Daily Life

People use, and often waste, resources such as electricity and paper while using technology. The practice of **green computing** involves reducing electricity consumed and environmental waste generated when using computers, mobile devices, and related technologies.

Figure 1-13: Look for the Energy Star logo when purchasing appliances or devices

Personal computers, displays, printers, and other devices should comply with guidelines of the ENERGY STAR program (**Figure 1-13**). The United States Department of Energy (DOE) and the United States Environmental Protection Agency (EPA) developed the ENERGY STAR program to help reduce the amount of electricity used by computers and related devices. This program encourages manufacturers to create energy-efficient devices. For example, many devices switch to sleep or power save mode after a specified amount of inactive time.

Electronic waste and trash has a negative effect on the environment where it is discarded. You can avoid electronic waste by not replacing devices every time a new version comes out, and recycling devices and products such as ink and toner when they no longer provide value.

Your personal green computing efforts should include:

- Purchasing and using products with an ENERGY STAR label
- Shutting down your computers and devices overnight or when not in use
- Donating computer equipment
- Using paperless communication
- Recycling paper, toner and ink cartridges, computers, mobile devices, and printers
- Telecommuting and using video conferencing for meetings

Organizations can implement a variety of measures to reduce electrical waste, such as:
- Consolidating servers
- Purchasing high-efficiency equipment
- Using sleep modes and other power management features for computers and devices
- Buying computers and devices with lower power consumption processors and power supplies
- Using outside air, when possible, to cool the data center or computer facility
- Allowing employees to telecommute to save gas and reduce emissions from vehicles

Green computing practices are usually easy to implement and can make a huge impact on the environment.

Enterprise Computing

A large business with many employees is known as an enterprise. **Enterprise computing** refers to the use of technology by a company's employees to meet the needs of a large business. Each department of a company uses technology specific to its function. **Table 1-1** shows some of the uses of technology for different functional units.

Table 1-1: Enterprise functional units

Functional unit	Technology uses
Human resources	Track employees' personal data, including pay rates, benefits, and vacation time
Accounting	Keep track of income and spending
Sales	Manage contacts, schedule meetings, log customer interactions, and process orders
Information technology	Maintain and secure hardware and software
Engineering and product development	Develop plans for and test new products
Manufacturing	Monitor assembly of products and manage inventory of parts and products
Marketing	Create and track success of marketing campaigns that target specific demographics
Distribution	Analyze and track inventory and manage shipping
Customer service	Manage customer interactions

Explain the Role of Technology in the Professional World

Nearly every job requires you to interact with technology to complete projects, exchange information with coworkers, and meet customers' needs. Whether you are looking for a job in a technology field or other area, you can use technology to prepare for and search for a job.

List the Ways that Professionals Might Use Technology in the Workplace

Technological advances, such as the PC, enabled workers to do their jobs more efficiently while at their desks. Today's workers can use smartphones, the Internet, the cloud, and more to work remotely, whether they are **telecommuting** (working from home), or traveling halfway around the world.

An **intelligent workplace** uses technology to enable workers to connect to the company's network, communicate with each other, use productivity software and apps, meet via web conferencing, and more. Some companies provide employees with computers and devices that come with the necessary software and apps, network connectivity, and security. Other workplaces have a **BYOD (bring your own device)** policy, enabling employees to use their personal devices to conduct business. Companies use online collaborative productivity software to allow employees to share documents such as reports or spreadsheets and to make edits or comments.

Technology in K-12 Education

Schools use social networking tools to promote school events, work cooperatively on group projects, and teach concepts such as anti-bullying. Online productivity software enables students to work collaboratively on projects and send the finished assignment to the teacher using email, reducing the need for paper printouts. These factors and more create an **intelligent classroom**, in which technology is used to facilitate learning and communication.

Technology in Higher Education

A college or university might use a **learning management system (LMS)** to set up web-based training sites where students can check their progress in a course, take practice tests, and exchange messages with the instructor or other students. Students also can view instructor lectures online and take classes or earn a degree online. Ebooks let students read and access content from their tablet or device, and access digital assets like videos associated with the content.

Technology in Healthcare

Physicians use computers to monitor patients' vital signs and research symptoms and diagnoses. The **mobile health (mHealth)** trend refers to healthcare professionals using smartphones or tablets to access health records stored in the cloud, and patients using digital devices to monitor their conditions and treatments, reducing the need for visits to the doctor's office. For example, mHealth apps can track prescription information, text reminders to take medication, or refill the prescription. Medical monitoring devices, such as electronic bracelets, collect vital signs and send the data to a specialist. Patients can ingest smart pills that contain sensors to monitor medication or contain tiny cameras to enable a physician to view the patient's internal organs without invasive procedures. Healthcare also uses 3-D printers to manufacture skin for burn patients, and prosthetic devices and casts.

Technology in the Transportation Industry

Transportation workers use handheld computers to scan codes on packages or containers of products before loading them on a vehicle, train, ship, or plane. You then can track the progress of your package as it makes its way to you. Computers find an efficient route for the packages and track their progress (**Figure 1-14**). Drivers use GPS to navigate quickly and safely, avoiding traffic and hazardous conditions. Soon, self-driving trucks will use robotics for mechanical control. Automated vehicles increase independent transportation options for people with disabilities.

Figure 1-14: The transportation industry uses code scanning to track packages

Technology in Manufacturing

Manufacturers use **computer-aided manufacturing (CAM)** to streamline production and ship products more quickly. With CAM, robots perform work that is too dangerous, detailed, or monotonous for people. In particular, they play a major role in automotive manufacturing. For example, robots typically paint the bodies of cars because painting is complex, difficult, and hazardous. Pairing robotic systems with human workers also improves quality, cost efficiency, and competitiveness. Computers and mobile devices make it possible to order parts and materials from the warehouse to assemble custom products. A company's computers monitor assembly lines and equipment using **machine-to-machine (M2M)** communications.

Explore Technology Careers

The technology field provides opportunities for people of all skill levels and interests, and demand for computer professionals continues to grow. The following sections describe general technology career areas.

Software and Apps

The software and apps field consists of companies that develop, manufacture, and support programs for computers, the web, and mobile devices. Some companies specialize in a certain area, such as productivity software or gaming. Other companies sell many types of software that work with both computers and mobile devices and may use the Internet to sync data and use collaborative features.

Technology Equipment

The technology equipment field consists of manufacturers and distributors of computers, mobile devices, and other hardware. In addition to the companies that make the finished products, this field includes companies that manufacture the internal components such as chips, cables, and power supplies.

IT Departments

Most medium and large businesses and organizations have an **Information Technology (IT) department**. IT staff are responsible for ensuring that all the computer operations, mobile devices, and networks run smoothly. They also determine when and if the organization requires new hardware, mobile devices, or software. IT jobs typically are divided into the areas shown in **Table 1-2**.

Table 1-2: IT responsibilities

IT area	Responsibilities
Management	Directs the planning, research, development, evaluation, and integration of technology
Research and software development	Analyzes, designs, develops, and implements new information technology and maintains existing systems
Technical support	Evaluates and integrates new technologies, administers the organization's data resources, and supports the centralized computer operating system and servers
Operations	Oversees the centralized computer equipment and administers the network
Training and support	Teaches employees how to use the information system and answers user questions
Information security	Develops and enforces policies that are designed to safeguard an organization's data and information from unauthorized users

Technology Service and Repair

The technology service and repair field provides preventative maintenance, component installations, and repair services to customers. Some technicians receive training and certifications from manufacturers to become specialists in devices from that manufacturer. Many technology equipment manufacturers include diagnostic software with their computers and devices that assist technicians in identifying problems. Technicians can use the Internet to diagnose and repair software remotely, by accessing the user's computer or device from a different location.

Technology Sales

Technology salespeople must possess a general understanding of technology, as well as specific knowledge of the product they are selling. Strong people skills, including listening and communicating, are important. Some salespeople work directly for a technology equipment or software manufacturer, while others work for resellers of technology, including retail stores.

Technology Education, Training, and Support

Schools, colleges, universities, and companies all need qualified educators to provide technology-related education and training. Instructors at an educational institution typically have a background and degree related to the technology they are teaching. Corporate trainers teach employees how to use the technology specific to the business or industry. Help desk specialists provide support by answering questions from employees to help them troubleshoot problems.

IT Consulting

An IT consultant typically has gained experience in one or more areas, such as software development, social media, or network configuration. IT consultants provide technology services to clients based on their specific areas of expertise. Sometimes a company will hire a large group of IT consultants to work together on a specific task, such as building a new network infrastructure or database.

System Development

System developers analyze and create software, apps, databases, websites and web-based development platforms, cloud services, and networks. Developers identify the business requirements and desired outcomes for the system, specify the structure and security needed, and design and program the system.

Web Marketing and Social Media

Careers in web marketing require you to be familiar not only with marketing strategies, but also with web-based platforms and social media apps. Web marketers create social media plans, including the content and timing of marketing campaigns, posts, and emails. Search engine optimization (SEO) knowledge helps to create web content and layout that enhances the content's results when users search for content.

Data Storage, Retrieval, and Analysis

Employees in this field must be knowledgeable about collecting, analyzing, storing, and reporting data from databases or the web. Data scientists use analytics to compile statistics on data to create strategies or analyze business practices. Web analytics experts measure Internet data, such as website traffic patterns and ads (**Figure 1-15**). Digital forensics examiners use evidence found on computers, networks, and devices to help solve crimes.

Figure 1-15: Web analytic data measures web site traffic patterns

Information and Systems Security

Careers in information and systems security require you to be knowledgeable about potential threats to a device or network, including viruses and hacking. Security specialists need to know tools and techniques to prevent against and recover from digital attacks.

Explore How You Might Prepare for a Career in Technology

You can use both social media and job search websites to learn about technology careers and to promote yourself to potential employers. By creating a profile on a career networking site or creating a personal website or blog that showcases your talents, hiring managers can learn more about you beyond what you can convey in a traditional, one-page paper resume.

Professional Online Presence

Recommended strategies for creating a professional online presence include:
- Do not use humorous or informal names for your account profiles, blog, or domain name.
- Include a photo that shows your best self.
- Upload a PDF of your resume.
- Include links to videos, publications, or digital content you have created.

- Proofread your resume, blog, website, or profile carefully to avoid spelling and grammar mistakes.
- Enable privacy settings on your personal social media accounts, and never post anything online that you would not want a potential employer to see.

Online social networks for professionals can help you keep up with past coworkers, instructors, potential employers, and others with whom you have a professional connection. You can use these networks to search for jobs, learn about a company before interviewing, join groups of people with similar interests or experiences, share information about your career, and communicate with contacts. LinkedIn (**Figure 1-16**) and other professional networking websites also offer online training courses to keep your skills up-to-date.

Figure 1-16: LinkedIn is a career-based social networking site

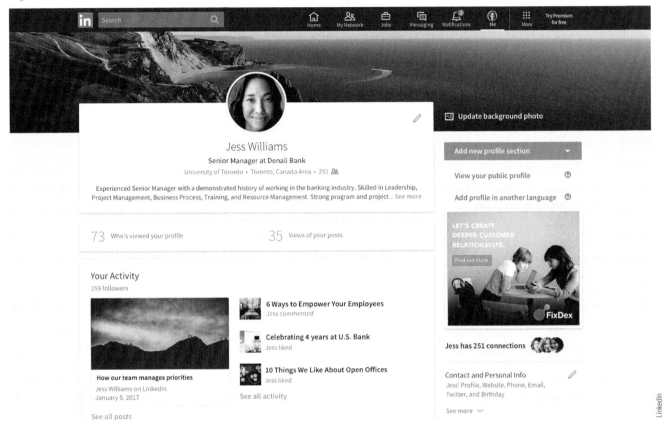

Certifications

Some technology careers require you to have certain certifications. A certification demonstrates your knowledge in a specific area to employers and potential employers. Online materials and print books exist to help you prepare for a certification exam. Most certifications do not require coursework assignments, but instead require you to pass an exam that demonstrates your proficiency in the area. Tests typically are taken at an authorized testing center. Some tests are multiple choice, while others are skills-based. You likely will have to pay a fee to take the exam. Some areas that offer certifications include:

- Application software
- Data analytics, database, and web design
- Hardware
- Networking
- Operating systems
- Programming
- Cybersecurity

Obtaining a certification requires you to spend time and money. Certifications demonstrate your commitment to your chosen area and can help you land a job.

Summary

Computers impact your daily life in many ways, including the use of embedded computers in vehicles, ATMs, and stores, and the "Internet of Things" that allows smart home appliances and other devices to communicate over the Internet or a wireless network.

Computers have evolved from large, inefficient, and expensive devices that used technology such as vacuum tubes to smaller, more powerful connected devices such as PCs, smartphones, and more.

Artificial intelligence, virtual reality, and augmented reality use logic and simulations to make predictions, educate, and entertain. Users with limitations or disabilities can use many different devices and software that enable them to access and use technology. There are many ways you can employ green computing practices to help reduce your impact on the environment.

Technology has had a large impact on the professional world, including intelligent workplaces. Education, transportation, healthcare, and manufacturing all use technology to reduce costs and increase safety and efficiency.

There are many careers available to you in the technology field, including IT, security, software development, and more. To prepare for a career in technology, you should create a professional online presence and take advantage of certification options.

Review Questions

1. (True or False) A microprocessor is the "brains" of a computer.

2. (True or False) Embedded computers are standalone products that have many functions.

3. The basic premise of _____ is that objects can be tagged, tracked, and monitored through a local network, or across the Internet.
   a. intelligent workspaces
   b. the digital divide
   c. the Internet of Things
   d. artificial intelligence

4. (True or False) Computers with AI use human intelligence to make decisions.

5. (True or False) A digital citizen uses technology to be productive and efficient.

6. (True or False) A kiosk is a freestanding booth usually placed in a public area that can contain a display device used to show information to the public or event attendees.

7. _____ are smart devices that respond to a user's verbal commands by using search technology to provide an answer to a question or perform a task.
   a. ATMs
   b. Green computers
   c. Integrated circuits
   d. Digital assistants

8. _____ text is descriptive text added to an object.
   a. Associative
   b. Alternative
   c. Accessible
   d. Assistive

9. (True or False) The ENERGY STAR program encourages manufacturers to reduce the amount of electricity used by computers and related devices.

10. BYOD stands for Bring Your Own _____.
    a. Device
    b. Daily planner
    c. Database
    d. Data

11. (True or False) An intelligent classroom is one in which technology is used to facilitate learning and communication.

12. Colleges use _____ management systems (LMSs) to set up web-based training sites where students can check their progress in a course, take practice tests, and exchange messages with the instructor or other students.
    a. learning
    b. linked
    c. locational
    d. live

13. (True or False) Automated vehicles decrease independent transportation options for people with disabilities.

14. (True or False) The mobile health (mHealth) trend refers to doctors and nurses using smartphones or tablets to access health records stored on mobile devices.

15. A company's computers monitor assembly lines and equipment using _____ communications.
    a. CAM
    b. AI
    c. IT
    d. M2M

16. A company's _____ department oversees the centralized computer equipment and administers the network.
    a. operations
    b. management
    c. technical support
    d. information security

17. (True or False) When looking for a job, you should use humorous or informal names for your account profiles, blog, or domain name to make yourself stand out.

Discussion Questions

1. How have embedded computers and the IoT impacted your daily life? What additional uses can you see yourself using? What security or other risks might you encounter with IoT?

2. How do the following technologies help you in your quest to become a digital citizen: kiosks, enterprise computing, natural language processing, robotics, and virtual reality?

3. What additional uses of technology can you see in the workplace? List ways technology impacts other careers not discussed in this module, such as finance, government, non-profits, and agriculture.

Critical Thinking Activities

1. You work in the educational software industry. Your boss asks you to give a brief lecture to other employees about the digital divide. Create a one-page document in which you define and give examples of the impact of the digital divide, and list ways your company can work to narrow the gap between students without reliable access to educational software, the Internet, and the hardware on which to run both. Discuss the ethical ramifications of not addressing the digital divide—what is your role as a company?

2. You and your roommate decide to reduce your environmental impact by recycling more, going paperless, and using environmentally safe cleaning products. You know you also can use green computing tactics to reduce electronic waste, minimize power use, and more. Create a list of five reasons why you should add green computing to your efforts. List 10 ways you can apply green computing to your daily life.

3. Research the trend of BYOD in workplaces. Compare the advantages to any potential disadvantages. Do you think more companies should adopt this policy? Why or why not?

Key Terms

alternative text (alt text)
Americans with Disabilities Act (ADA)
artificial Intelligence (AI)
audio books
augmented reality (AR)
BYOD (bring your own device)
chip-and-pin technology
computer
computer literacy
computer-aided manufacturing (CAM)
data
digital assistant
digital citizen
digital divide
digital literacy

embedded computer
enterprise computing
graphic organizer
green computing
hardware
Individuals with Disabilities Education Act (IDEA)
information
Information Technology (IT) department
integrated circuits
intelligent classroom
intelligent workplace
Internet of Things (IoT)
kiosk

learning management system (LMS)
machine-to-machine (M2M)
microprocessor
mobile health (mHealth)
natural language processing
personal computer (PC)
robotics
screen reader
smart device
software
speech recognition program
telecommuting
transistor
vacuum tube
virtual reality (VR)

The Web

On his daily commute to school, Jalen uses the time to find the online information he needs to complete his assignments.

alen uses the web throughout the day o collaborate with his classmates, post pdates to his blog, conduct research t educational websites, read sports nd news articles, and check his social etworks such as Instagram and Twitter.

WAYHOME studio/Shutterstock.com

Jalen Washington is a power user of the web, even as he commutes to school. Connecting to the cloud with his mobile phone, he stores, retrieves, and shares files. He opens the Google Chrome browser to check his grades, watch required video lectures on YouTube, and gather content for class projects from reliable online resources. He completes assignments using web apps, compares deals on headphones at e-commerce websites, and buys and sells sports memorabilia on eBay.

In This Module

- Explain the role of the web in daily life
- Describe websites and webpages
- Use e-commerce
- Search the web
- Conduct online research

YOU PROBABLY USE the web dozens or hundreds of times a day to find a place for lunch, keep track of scores, shop for a new phone, post a comment on a blog or message board, and search for photos you need to complete a project at school or work. As a vast library of content, the web is where you go for entertainment, bargains, news, and information of all kinds. To find what you need on the web, you should understand the types of resources the web provides.

In this module, you examine the role of the web in daily life. You explore the components of websites, webpages, and e-commerce and learn how to search the web to find information you can trust.

Explain the Role of the Web in Daily Life

Since its introduction, the **web**, originally known as the **World Wide Web**, has changed the way people access information, conduct business transactions, and communicate, as shown in **Figure 2-1**. Almost everyone can use the web because it is part of the **Internet**, a global collection of millions of computers linked together to share information worldwide. Today, more than 3.2 billion people use the Internet and the web. The more you know about the web and how to access its contents, the more you can get out of it.

Figure 2-1: The web in daily life

Access information

Communicate with others

The web is part of the Internet

Conduct transactions

PopTika/Shutterstock.com

Define Web Browsing Terms

When you use a mobile phone or other device to access the web, you are accessing a collection of webpages located on computers around the world, connected through the Internet. A **webpage** like the one shown in **Figure 2-2** is an electronic document that can contain text, graphics, sound, video, and links to other webpages.

The content of most webpages makes them visually appealing. The links make it possible to pursue information in a nonlinear fashion, following a route that looks more like a web than a straight line.

A collection of webpages (often shortened to "pages") makes up a **website**. A company, organization, institution, group, or person creates and maintains a website. In general, websites focus on a specific topic, business, or purpose.

When you visit a website for the first time, figure out its purpose so you know what type of content to expect and which actions are appropriate. For example, the purpose of the ESPN website shown in **Figure 2-3** is to provide sports news and entertainment, while the Sports Reference website provides statistics only. Both websites are dedicated to sports, but each has a different purpose.

Figure 2-2: Webpage

Graphic ———

Webpage text ———

Link to another
webpage ———

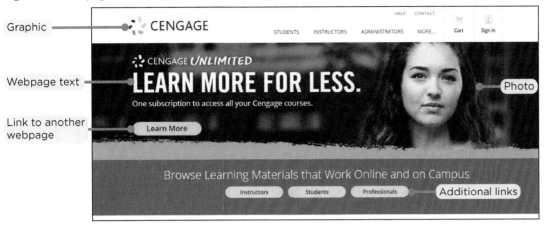

Photo

Additional links

Figure 2-3: Comparing websites

Video to play on
the webpage ———

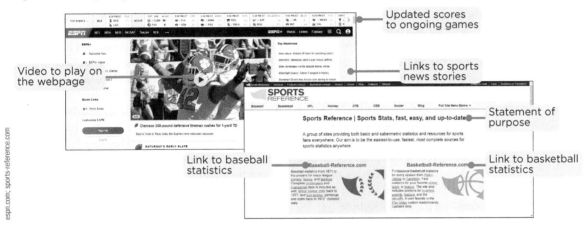

Updated scores
to ongoing games

Links to sports
news stories

Statement of
purpose

Link to baseball
statistics

Link to basketball
statistics

Use a Browser

To access the web, you open a **browser**, an app designed to display webpages. For example, Google Chrome, Apple Safari, and Microsoft Edge are browsers. You use the tools in a browser to **navigate** the web, or move from one webpage to another.

The webpage that appears when you open a browser is called the **home page** or **start page**. (The main page in a website is also called the home page. For example, the webpage shown in Figure 2-2 is the home page on the Cengage website.) To display a different webpage, you use links, short for **hyperlinks**, words or graphics you can click to display a webpage or other resource on the Internet, such as a file.

Keep Track of Webpages

To keep track of billions of webpages, the Internet assigns each one a **uniform resource locator (URL)**, an address that identifies the location of the page on the Internet. A URL can consist of the parts shown in **Figure 2-4**.

Figure 2-4: Parts of a URL

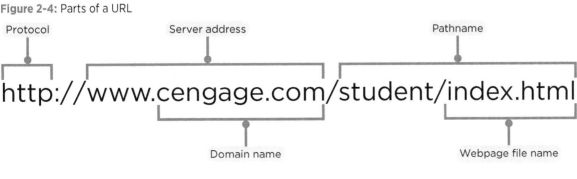

Protocol   Server address   Pathname

http://www.cengage.com/student/index.html

Domain name   Webpage file name

If you can interpret a URL, you can learn about the sponsor, origin, and location of the webpage and catch a glimpse of how the web works. **Table 2-1** defines each part of a URL.

Table 2-1: URL parts

URL Part	Definition
Protocol	A standardized procedure computers use to exchange information
Server address	The address of the server storing the webpage
Pathname	The address to the folder containing the webpage
File name	The name of the webpage file

When the URL for a webpage starts with http://, the browser uses the **Hypertext Transfer Protocol (HTTP)**, the most common way to transfer information around the web, to retrieve the page.

A server is a powerful networked computer that provides resources to other computers. A **web server** delivers webpages to computers requesting the pages through a browser. In the server address www.cengage.com, the www indicates that the server is a web server, cengage is the name the Cengage company chose for this website, and .com means that a commercial entity runs the web server.

The server address in a URL corresponds to an Internet Protocol (IP) address, which identifies every computer on the Internet. An **IP address** is a unique number that consists of four sets of numbers from 0 to 255 separated by periods, or dots, as in 69.32.132.255. Although computers can use IP addresses easily, they are difficult for people to remember, so domain names were created. A **domain name** identifies one or more IP addresses, such as cengage.com. URLs use the domain name in the server address part of the URL to identify a particular website.

In addition, each file stored on a web server has a unique pathname, just like files stored on a computer. The pathname in a URL includes the names of the folders containing the file, the file name, and its extension. A common file name extension for webpages is .html, sometimes shortened to .htm. For example, the pathname might be student/index.html, which specifies a file named index.html stored in a folder named student.

Not all URLs include a pathname. If you don't specify a pathname or file name in a URL, most web browsers open a file named index.html or index.htm, which is the default name for a website's main page.

Navigate the Web

A browser displays the URL for the current webpage in its **address bar**, as shown in **Figure 2-5**. You can also use the address bar to type the URL of the webpage you want to display.

Figure 2-5: Navigating the web with a browser

As you navigate websites, your browser keeps a copy of each page you view in a **cache**, so that the next time you go to a webpage, it loads more quickly. The browser also keeps track of pages you have viewed in sequence by tracking **breadcrumbs**—the path you followed to display a webpage. The **navigation bar** in a browser includes buttons such as Back and Forward that you can use to revisit webpages along the breadcrumb path.

Explain the Purpose of a Top-Level Domain

In a web address, the three-letter extension after the period indicates a **top-level domain (TLD)**, such as the "com" in "cengage.com". The TLD identifies the type of organization associated with the domain. As you visit websites, you might notice some that have TLDs other than .com, such as .edu for educational institutions and .gov for U.S. government agencies. The TLD provides a clue about the content of the website.

An organization called Public Technical Identifiers (PTI) approves and controls TLDs, such as those in **Table 2-2**, which lists popular TLDs in the United States. For websites outside the United States, the suffix of the domain name often includes a two-letter country code TLD, such as .au for Australia and .uk for the United Kingdom.

Table 2-2: Popular TLDs in the United States

TLD	Generally used for
.biz	Unrestricted use, but usually identifies businesses
.com	Most commercial sites that sell products and services
.edu	Academic and research sites such as schools and universities
.gov	U.S. government organizations
.int	International treaty organizations
.mil	Military organizations
.mobi	Sites optimized for mobile devices
.net	Network providers, ISPs, and other Internet administrative organizations
.org	Organizations such as political or not for profit (any website can have the .org TLD but, traditionally, only professional and nonprofit organizations such as churches and humanitarian groups use it)
.pro	Licensed professionals

Describe Internet Standards

Have you ever wondered who is in charge of the web? Who maintains the webpages? Who makes sure all the parts of the complex system work together? One organization is the **Internet Engineering Task Force (IETF)**. This group sets standards that allow devices, services, and applications to work together across the Internet. For example, the IETF sets standards for IP addresses. Other standards set rules for routing data, securing websites, and developing guidelines for responsible Internet use.

Another leading organization is the **World Wide Web Consortium (W3C)**, which consists of hundreds of organizations and experts that work together to write web standards. The W3C publishes standards on topics ranging from building webpages, to technologies for enabling web access from any device, to browser and search engine design.

Describe Websites and Webpages

People around the world visit websites and webpages to accomplish the types of online tasks shown in **Figure 2-6**.

In addition, you can use websites to play games; access news, weather, and sports information; download or read books; participate in online training; attend classes; and more.

Figure 2-6: Tasks you can accomplish on websites

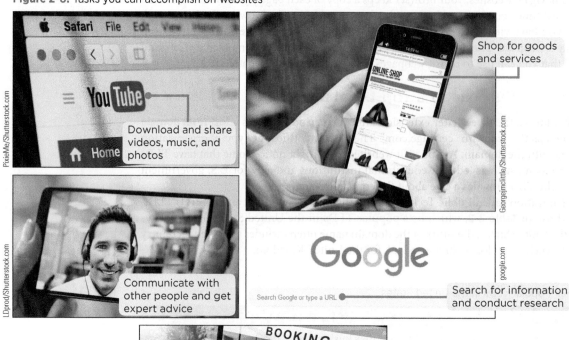

Download and share videos, music, and photos

Shop for goods and services

Communicate with other people and get expert advice

Search for information and conduct research

Make reservations

Identify the Types of Websites

What do you want to do on the web today? Chances are, a certain type of website provides exactly what you're looking for. Most websites fall into one or more of the following categories:

banking and finance	entertainment	portals
blogs	government or organization	retail and auctions
bookmarking	health and fitness	science
business	information and research	search sites
careers and employment	mapping	travel and tourism
content aggregation	media sharing	website creation and management
e-commerce	news, weather, sports, and other mass media	web apps and software as a service (SaaS)
educational	online social networks	wikis and collaboration

Besides displaying information and other content, websites let you interact with it. You can contribute ideas, comments, images, and videos to an online conversation through interactive community pages, social media sites, and **blogs**, which are informal websites with time-stamped articles, or posts, in a diary or journal format.

A **content aggregator** site such as News360 or Flipboard gathers, organizes, and then distributes web content. As a subscriber, you choose the type of content you want and receive updates when new content is available.

An educational website such as ed2go, shown in **Figure 2-7**, offers formal and informal teaching and learning. The web contains thousands of tutorials where you can learn how to build a website or cook a meal. For a more structured learning experience, companies provide online training to employees, and colleges offer online classes and degrees.

Figure 2-7: Educational website

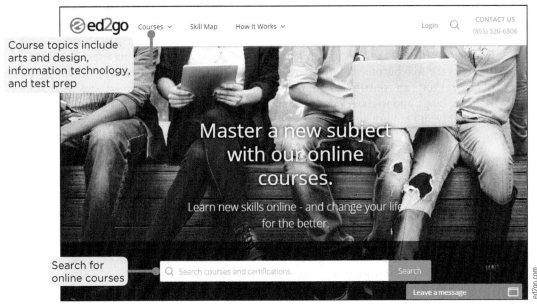

On entertainment websites, you can view or discuss activities ranging from sports to videos. For example, you can cast a vote on a topic for a television show.

With a **media sharing site**, such as YouTube or Flickr, you can manage media such as photos, videos, and music and share them with other site members. Use a media sharing site to post, organize, store, and download media.

An **online social network**, also called a social networking site or social media site, is a website that encourages members to share their interests, ideas, stories, photos, music, and videos online with other registered users. In many online social networks, you can communicate through text, voice, and video chat, and play games with other members. Facebook, Twitter, Whatsapp, Instagram, Pinterest, and Tumblr are some websites classified as online social networks. As shown in **Figure 2-8**, you interact with an online social network through a website or mobile app on your computer or mobile device.

Figure 2-8: Online social networking websites

A **web portal**, or **portal**, is a website that combines pages from many sources and provides access to those pages. Most web portals are customized to meet your needs and interests. For example, your bank might create a web portal that includes snapshots of your accounts and access to financial information.

Using a search site such as Google, you can find websites, webpages, images, videos, news, maps, and other information related to a specific topic. Search sites use **search engines**, software designed to find webpages based on your search criteria. You also can use a search engine to solve mathematical equations, define words, find flights, and more.

General-purpose search sites such as Google, Yahoo!, and Bing help you locate web information when you don't know an exact web address or are not seeking a specific website.

As the web becomes more interactive, an increasing amount of content is supplied by users. You can contribute comments and opinions to informational sites such as news sites, blogs, and wikis. A **wiki** is a collaborative website where you and your colleagues can modify and publish content on a webpage. Wikis are especially useful for group projects.

Explain the Pros and Cons of Web Apps

In addition to using a browser to visit websites and display webpages, you can use it to access **web apps**, which are apps you can run entirely in a browser. (An **app**, short for **application**, is software you use to perform a task.) A web app resides on a server on the Internet, rather than on your computer or mobile device. For example, Microsoft Office provides Excel, PowerPoint, and Word as web apps, shown in **Figure 2-9**. Other popular web apps include Slack (for group collaboration), Trello (for project management), and Google Docs (for word processing).

Figure 2-9: Web apps running in a browser

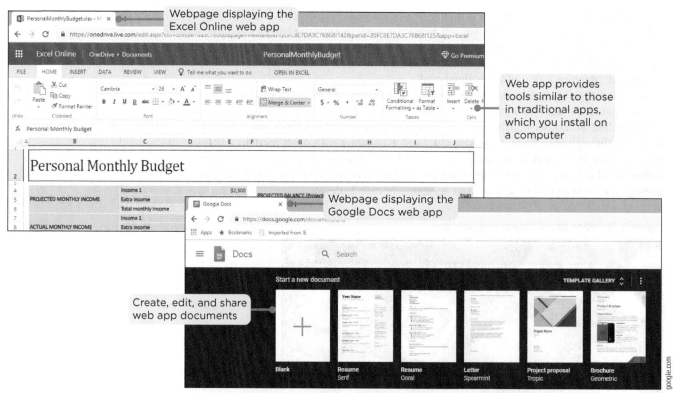

When you use a web app, you usually store your data on the web app's server, or *in the cloud*, a practice known as cloud storage.

You can run many apps as traditional installed apps or as web apps. Examples include Dropbox (which lets you store and exchange files in the cloud) and Skype (which lets you communicate with others using video and voice). Which type of app should you select? To help you decide, **Table 2-3** summarizes the pros and cons of using web apps.

Table 2-3: Pros and cons of web apps

Pros	Cons
Access web apps from any device with a browser and Internet connection.	You must be online to use web apps.
Collaborate with others no matter their location.	Your files are more vulnerable to security and privacy violations.
Store your work on the app's website so you can access it anytime and anywhere.	If the web app provider has technical problems, you might not be able to access your work.
Save storage space on your device.	If the web app provider goes out of business, you can lose your files.
Access the latest version of the app without installing updates.	Web apps often offer fewer features and may run more slowly than installed apps.

Identify the Major Components of a Webpage

Webpages typically include five major areas: header or banner, navigation bar or menu, body, sidebar, and footer. **Figure 2-10** identifies these areas on a webpage. Each area can include text, graphics, links, and media such as audio and video. If you are familiar with these components, you'll know where to find the information you might be seeking.

- **Header**: Located at the top of a webpage, the header or banner usually includes a logo to identify the organization sponsoring the webpage and a title to indicate the topic or purpose of the webpage. Headers and navigation bars can also provide a Search tool for searching the website.
- **Navigation bar**: A bar or menu lists links to other major parts of the website.
- **Body**: The body is the main content area of the webpage, and can provide text, images, audio, and video.

Figure 2-10: Parts of a webpage

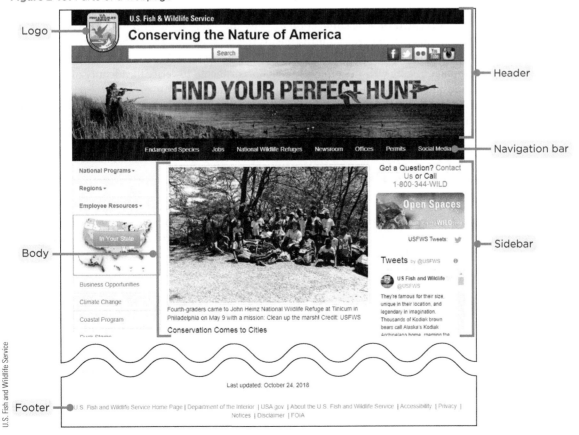

- **Sidebar**: A column on the left or right of the webpage provides supplemental material, including social networking feeds, ads, and links. A current trend is to omit the sidebar to let the body span the full width of the webpage, especially if the body contains images.
- **Footer**: Located at the bottom of a webpage, the footer contains links to other parts of the website and lists information about the webpage, such as when it was last updated.

Identify Secure and Insecure Websites

Before you make a payment on a website or provide sensitive information such as a credit card number, make sure the website is secure. Otherwise, an unauthorized web user could intercept the payment or information and steal your funds or identity. **Figure 2-11** shows how you can identify a secure website.

Figure 2-11: Secure website

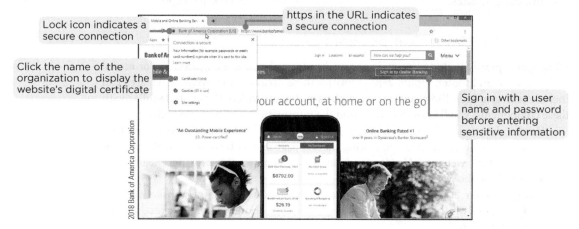

A secure website uses encryption to safeguard transmitted information. **Encryption** is a security method that scrambles or codes data as it is transmitted over a network so it is not readable until it is decrypted.

An encrypted website connection displays https instead of http in the URL. The "s" in https stands for "secure," so https means **Hypertext Transfer Protocol Secure**. Websites such as banks and retail stores use the https protocol to make a secure connection to your computer. Secure websites often use a **digital certificate** to verify the identity of the organization and vouch for the authenticity of the website.

An insecure website does not include indicators such as a lock icon. In addition, the URL starts with "http," indicating an unprotected protocol for transmitting information. The address bar in the Chrome browser identifies such websites as "Not secure."

Use E-commerce

E-commerce, short for electronic commerce, refers to business transactions on an electronic network such as the Internet. If you have bought or sold products such as clothing, electronics, music, tickets, hotel reservations, or gift certificates, you have engaged in e-commerce. **Table 2-4** describes three types of e-commerce websites.

Table 2-4: Three types of e-commerce websites

Type of E-commerce	Description	Example
Business-to-consumer (B2C)	Involves the sale of goods and services to the general public	Shopping websites
Consumer-to-consumer (C2C)	Occurs when one consumer sells directly to another	Online auctions
Business-to-business (B2B)	Consists of businesses providing goods and services to other businesses	Market research websites

Explain the Role of E-commerce in Daily Life

Consumers use e-commerce because it's convenient, and businesses use e-commerce because it can increase revenue. In fact, e-commerce is so popular, it has reshaped the modern marketplace. Business analysts say that physical retail stores are in decline, while e-commerce websites such as Amazon are more popular than ever.

You should understand the advantages and risks of using e-commerce to make your online transactions satisfying and safe. Table 2-5 outlines the pros and cons of e-commerce for consumers.

Table 2-5: E-commerce pros and cons for consumers

Pros	Explanation
Variety	You can choose goods from any vendor in the world. Websites have more models, sizes, and colors, for example, than a physical store.
Convenience	You can shop no matter your location, time of day, or conditions, such as bad weather. You save time by visiting websites instead of stores.
Budget	By searching effectively and comparing prices online, you can find products that meet your budget.
Cons	**Explanation**
Security	At insecure e-commerce sites, you risk unauthorized users intercepting your credit card information and other personal data.
Fraud	Some shopping websites are fraudulent, designed to look legitimate while accessing your account information.
Indirect experience	You cannot experience a product directly to verify its color, quality, or texture. You lose the social interaction that is a natural part of shopping at a physical retailer.

Use E-commerce in Business Transactions

B2B e-commerce involves transferring goods, services, or information between businesses. In fact, most e-commerce is actually between businesses. B2B services include advertising, technical support, and training. B2B products include raw materials, tools and machinery, and electronics. Figure 2-12 shows the Livingston International website, which helps businesses ship goods from other countries.

Figure 2-12: B2B website

Track shipments

Clear business orientation

Sign in for clients only

Request a quote rather than purchase items immediately

Livingston International

The more you know about B2B websites, the more valuable you can be to your employer. For example, B2B websites are different from B2C websites. For consumers, shopping websites offer fixed, consistent pricing. For B2B purchases, pricing can vary based on the level of service provided, negotiated terms, and other factors.

At B2C websites, the consumer is the decision maker. In a B2B transaction, a team of people often need to review and make a purchasing decision. They usually have to follow company procedures, which can lengthen or complicate the transaction.

Use E-commerce in Personal Transactions

You can purchase just about any product or service at a B2C e-commerce website. Doing so is sometimes called e-retail (short for electronic retail). To purchase online, you visit an **electronic storefront**, which contains product descriptions, images, and a shopping cart to collect items you want to purchase. When you're ready to complete the sale, you enter personal data and the method of payment, which should be through a secure Internet connection.

A B2C website tracks your selected items using **cookies**, small text files generated by a web server that act like a storage bin for the items you place in your shopping cart. Cookies store shopping cart item numbers, saved preferences, and other information.

As shown in **Figure 2-13**, B2C websites are usually designed to be easy to use so you can find what you want fast. They include reviews from other customers to help you make purchasing decisions, special offers for web customers only, and wish lists to encourage you to return to the site. Many B2C websites let you research online and then pick up the purchased item in a physical store.

Figure 2-13: B2C website

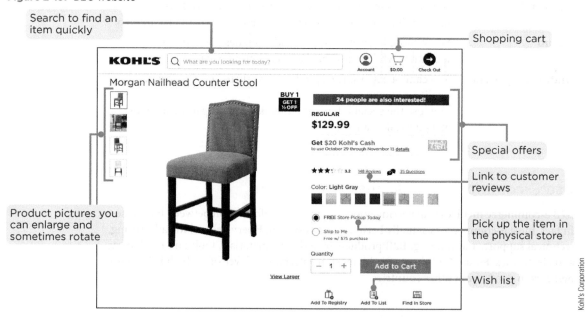

Search to find an item quickly

Shopping cart

Product pictures you can enlarge and sometimes rotate

Special offers

Link to customer reviews

Pick up the item in the physical store

Wish list

Kohl's Corporation

Online classified ads and online auctions are examples of C2C e-commerce websites. An online auction works much like a real-life auction or yard sale. You bid on an item being sold by someone else. The highest bidder at the end of the bidding period purchases the item. eBay is one of the more popular online auction websites.

C2C sites have many sellers promoting the goods, rather than a single merchant hosting a B2C site. Many C2C sites use email forwarding, which hides real email identities, to connect buyer with seller and still protect everyone's privacy. You pay a small fee to the auction site if you sell an item.

Make Secure E-commerce Payments

To make e-commerce payments in a B2C transaction, you can provide a credit card number. Be sure the B2C website uses a secure connection. **3D Secure** is a standard protocol for securing credit card transactions over the Internet. Using both encryption and digital certificates, 3D Secure provides an extra layer of security on a website. Sites that use Verified by Visa, MasterCard SecureCode, and American Express SafeKey use the added 3D Secure protocol.

Besides the https protocol, e-commerce sites also use **Transport Layer Security (TLS)** to encrypt data. This helps protect consumers and businesses from fraud and identity theft when conducting commerce on the Internet.

To provide an alternative to entering credit card information online, some shopping and auction websites let you use an online payment service, such as PayPal, Square Cash, Venmo, and Zelle. To use an online payment service, you create an account that is linked to your credit card or funds at a financial institution. When you make a purchase, you use your online payment service account, which manages the payment transaction without revealing your financial information.

You can also use smartwatches and smartphones to make e-commerce payments. Apple-Pay and Google Wallet are two of several mobile payment and digital wallet services available on smartphones. Scan the watch or phone over a reader, often available in stores, to make the electronic payment.

Another payment method is to use a one-time or virtual account number, which lets you make a single online payment without revealing your actual account number. These numbers are good only at the time of the transaction; if they are stolen, they are worthless to thieves.

Find E-commerce Deals

You can find online deals in at least two ways: visiting comparison shopping sites and using digital deals.

Websites such as BizRate, NexTag, and PriceGrabber are comparison shopping websites that save you time and money by letting you compare prices from multiple vendors.

Digital deals come in the form of gift certificates, gift cards, and coupons. Groupon and NewEgg are examples of deal-of-the-day websites, which help you save money on restaurant meals, retail products, travel, and personal services. Digital coupons consist of promotional codes that you enter when you check out and pay for online purchases. Sites such as RetailMeNot and browser extensions such as Honey provide coupon codes and offer alerts for discounts, as shown in **Figure 2-14**.

Figure 2-14: Digital deals and coupons

Some websites provide digital deals and coupons

Redemption rates are high with mobile phones because consumers carry them when they shop

4 Girls 1 Boy/Shutterstock.com

Apply Information Literacy Skills to Web Searches

You can find virtually any information you want on the Internet; all you need to do is to search for it. Search engines let you enter search criteria and then do the legwork for you, compiling a list of webpages that match your criteria. Of the billions of webpages you can access using Google or another search site, some are valuable and some are not. Telling the difference is a skill you need to succeed in work and life.

Define Information Literacy

How you find, evaluate, use, and communicate online information depends on your **information literacy**. If you have information literacy, you can do the following:

- Navigate many sources of information, including the Internet, online libraries, and popular media sites.
- Select the right tool for finding the information you need.
- Recognize that not all information is created equal.
- Evaluate whether information is misleading, biased, or out of date.
- Manage information to become a knowledgeable decision maker.

You become information literate by understanding and selecting the tools, techniques, and strategies for locating and evaluating information, as shown in **Figure 2-15**.

Figure 2-15: Search tools, techniques, and strategies

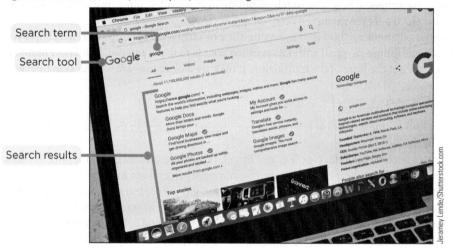

Search term

Search tool

Search results

Jeramey Lende/Shutterstock.com

Explain How Search Engines Work

Suppose you're working on a presentation about mobile phone technology and need to know about current innovations. How can you find this information quickly?

You'd probably start a **general search engine** such as Google, Bing, or Yahoo! and enter a search term or phrase such as *mobile phone innovations*. Within seconds, the first page of search results lists a dozen webpages that might contain the information you need.

How does a general search engine choose the results you see? When you perform a search, a general search engine does not search the entire Internet. Instead, it compiles a database of information about webpages. It uses programs called **spiders** or **crawlers**, software that combs the web to find webpages and add new data about them to the database. These programs build an **index** of terms and their locations.

When you enter a search term, or **query**, a general search engine refers to its database index and then lists pages that match your search term, ranked by how closely they answer your query.

Each search engine uses a different method to retrieve webpage information from an index and create a ranked list of results. The ranking depends on how often and where a search term appears on the webpage, how long the webpage has been published, and the number of other webpages that link to it.

Use Search Tools and Strategies

A **search tool** finds online information based on criteria you specify or selections you make. Search tools include search engines and search boxes on webpages. The more effectively you use search tools, the more quickly you can find information and the more relevant that information will be.

Another type of search tool is a **web directory**, or **subject directory**, an online guide to subjects or websites, usually arranged in alphabetic order, as shown in **Figure 2-16**.

Figure 2-16: Library subject directory

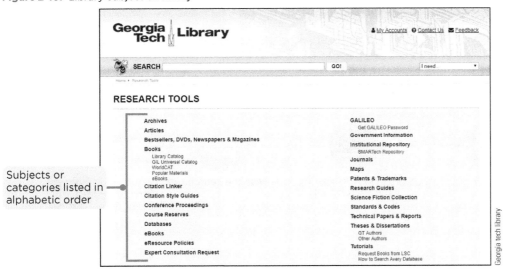

Subjects or categories listed in alphabetic order

Search engines and web directories take different approaches to searching for information. Instead of using an index created by digital spiders, a human editor creates the index for a web directory, selecting categories that make sense for the information the web directory provides. The editor usually reviews sites that are submitted to the directory and can exclude those that do not seem credible or reliable. For this reason, a web directory is often a better choice than a search engine if you are conducting research online.

Specialized search tools concentrate on specific resources, such as scholarly journals or the United States Congress. Examples include the Directory of Open Access Journals, Congress.gov Legislative Search, and Google Books. If you need to research the latest academic studies or look up the status of a bill, using a specialized search tool is more efficient than using a general search engine such as Google.

To get the most out of a web search, develop a search strategy, which involves performing the following tasks before you start searching:
- State what kind of information you are seeking, as specifically as possible.
- Phrase the search term as a question, as in "How do businesses use augmented reality?"
- Identify the keywords or phrases that could answer the question.
- Select an appropriate search tool.

Next, perform the search. For example, if you want to know about how businesses use augmented reality, you could search using *augmented reality* as the **keywords**, the words that best describe what you want to find and produce a list of results that include the words or phrase. If you find the results you need, you can stop searching.

If the term you use is too general, you are likely to find millions of webpages that mention the term. If the term you use is too specific, you might miss useful webpages related to your term. In either case, you need to refine the web search to narrow or broaden the results. **Figure 2-17** summarizes an online search strategy.

Refine Web Searches

Suppose you are interested in the next generation of the mobile Internet, called 5G Internet, and how it can make you more productive when you're on the go. Enter *5G internet* in a search engine, and the results could include millions of webpages about 5G products, news, definitions, and research.

To find the information you're seeking, learn from the search engine results page (SERP) by using the features your search tool provides, as shown in **Figure 2-18**.

Figure 2-17: Search strategy

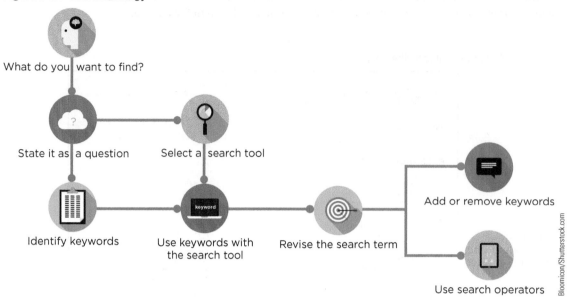

What do you want to find?

State it as a question

Select a search tool

Identify keywords

Use keywords with the search tool

Revise the search term

Add or remove keywords

Use search operators

Bloomicon/Shutterstock.com

Figure 2-18: Learning from the SERP

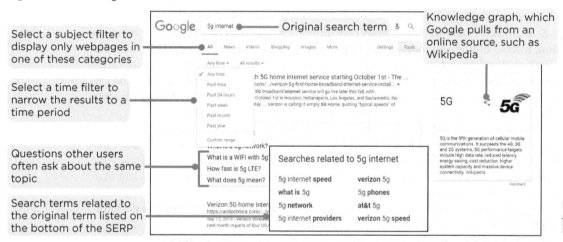

Select a subject filter to display only webpages in one of these categories

Select a time filter to narrow the results to a time period

Questions other users often ask about the same topic

Search terms related to the original term listed on the bottom of the SERP

Original search term

Knowledge graph, which Google pulls from an online source, such as Wikipedia

google.com

In addition to the features shown in Figure 2-18, many search engines follow practices when listing search results:

- Search engines list the most relevant results, or **hits**, on the first page.
- Results labeled as an "Ad" or "Sponsored link" are from advertisers.
- Each type of filter offers related features. For example, if you filter Google search results to show only images, you can filter the images by size, color, and **usage rights**, which indicate when you can use, share, or modify the images you find online.
- In addition to listing related links at the bottom of the SERP, Google displays a "People also search for" list below a link you visited.

You can also refine a web search by using **search operators**, also called **Boolean operators**, which are characters, words, or symbols that focus the search. **Table 2-6** lists common search operators.

Now you're ready to try a new search. **Table 2-7** lists examples of keywords you might use to find information on buying used Android smartphones.

Many search sites have advanced search operators, which are special terms followed by a colon (:). For example, *site:* means to search only the specified site, as in *site: www.cengage.com sam*, which finds information about SAM on the cengage.com website. You can find the advanced search operators by referring to the site's help pages.

Table 2-6: Common search operators

Operator	Means	Example
" " (quotation marks)	Find webpages with the exact words in the same order	"augmented reality" in business
| (vertical bar)	OR	augmented | virtual
- (hyphen)	NOT	augmented reality -virtual
*	**Wildcard** (placeholder for any number of characters)	augment* reality
#..#	Find webpages within a range of numbers	augmented reality 2017..2022

Table 2-7: Examples of web searches

Keywords	Possible results	Suggested change
Looking for a used smartphone	A list of all used phones; returns too many hits	Add the word "Android."
Looking for a used Android smartphone	Still too many hits	Remove common words such as "the" and "an"; remove verb.
Used Android smartphone	Results still include other smartphones	Search for an exact phrase by entering it in quotation marks.
Used "Android smartphone"	List of used Android smartphones	

To broaden a search, you can use a **word stem**, which is the base of a word. For example, instead of using *businesses* as a keyword, use *business*. You can also combine the word stem with an asterisk (*), as in *tech** to find technology, technician, and technique.

Conduct Online Research

When you need to conduct online research for an assignment or project, look beyond general search engines such as Google and Bing. Using search engines designed for research yields more reliable results, saving you time and effort.

Use Specialty Search Engines

Where do you go to find academic information for your research? Try using a **specialty search engine**, which lets you search databases, news providers, podcasts, and other online information sources that general search engines do not always access.

Searching databases is usually a good idea when conducting research, because much of the information on the web is stored in databases. To access this database information, you need to use a special search form and may need to enter a user name and password. For example, Google Scholar searches scholarly literature from many disciplines and includes articles, books, theses, and abstracts.

Other specialty search tools let you find information published on certain types of sites. For example, use Google News or Alltop to find news stories and Podcast Search Service to search podcasts.

Table 2-8 lists additional search tools. Some of these sites help you refine research topics, while others help you find media such as images and videos.

Table 2-8: Additional search tools

Search tool	What it does
Wolfram Alpha	Answers factual questions directly, without listing webpages that might contain the answer
RhythmOne	Finds videos or other multimedia; uses speech recognition to match the audio part of a video with your search term
Ask a Librarian	Connects you to librarians at the Library of Congress and other libraries; allows you to engage in an online chat or submit your question in an online form
TinEye	Does a reverse search for submitted images, rather than key-words, to locate the original image and match it with other indexed images

Evaluate Online Information

On the Internet, anyone can publish anything to a website, a blog, or a social media site, regardless of whether the information is true. How can you tell if a website is worth your time? In general, look for sites from trusted, expert institutions or authors. Avoid sites that show bias or contain outdated information.

If you use the Internet for research, be skeptical about the information you find online. Evaluate a webpage before you use it as an information source. One way to evaluate a web-page is to use the CARS checklist and determine whether the online information is credible, accurate, reasonable, and supportable.

Credibility: When someone is providing you information face to face, you pay attention to clues such as body language and voice tone to determine whether that information is credible, or believable. Obviously, you can't use that same technique to evaluate the credibility of a webpage.

To determine the credibility of a website:
- Identify the author of the webpage and check their credentials. This information is often listed on the Contact Us page or the About page.
- If you find biographical information, read it to learn whether the author has a degree in a field related to the topic.
- Use a search engine such as Google or the professional networking site LinkedIn to search for the author's name and see whether the author is an expert on the subject.

Accuracy: You're attending a classmate's presentation on the history of the personal computer, and he mentions that Bill Gates invented the first PC for home use in 1980, citing an online resource. You know it was actually Steve Wozniak and Steve Jobs in 1976. That inaccuracy makes you doubt the quality of the rest of the presentation.

To check the accuracy of a website:
- Verify its facts and claims. Consult an expert or use fact-checking sites such as snopes. com and factcheck.org to find professionally researched information.
- Evaluate the information source. Be wary of web addresses that contain slight modifi-cations of legitimate sites, use unusual domain names, or have long URLs.
- Find out more about an organization that has no history, physical location, or staff.
- Check to see if the source has a bias and evaluate the information with the bias in mind.
- Check the webpage footer for the date the information was published or updated. For many topics, especially technology, you need current information.

Reasonableness: Along with credibility and accuracy, consider how reasonable an online information source is. Reasonable means fair and sensible, not extreme or excessive.

To check how reasonable a website is:
- Identify the purpose of the webpage. Is the page designed to provide facts and other information, sell a product or service, or express opinions?
- Evaluate whether the webpage offers more than one point of view.

- Emotional, persuasive, or biased language is often a sign that the author is not being fair or moderate. Even opinions should be expressed in a moderate tone.
- Look for a conflict of interest. For example, if the page reviews a certain brand of smartphone and the author sells those types of phones, he or she has a conflict of interest.

Support: Suppose a webpage refers to a study concluding that most people consider computer professionals to be highly ethical. But the page doesn't link to the study itself or mention other sources that support this claim. The page is failing the final criterion in the CARS checklist: support.

To evaluate a webpage's support:

- Look for links or citations to reputable sources or authorities. Test the links to make sure they work.
- Check other webpages and print material on the topic to see if they cite the same sources.
- Look for quotations from experts.
- For photos or other reproduced content, a credit line should appear somewhere on the page that states the source and any necessary copyright information.

Gather Content from Online Sources

As you conduct research online, you gather content from webpages, including text, photos, and links to resources. Follow ethical guidelines and be aware of ownership rights to avoid legal, academic, and professional sanctions and be a responsible member of the online community.

If you copy a photo from the Internet and use it in a report, you might be violating the photographer's **intellectual property rights**, which are legal rights protecting those who create works such as photos, art, writing, inventions, and music.

A **copyright** gives authors and artists the legal right to sell, publish, or distribute an original work. A copyright goes into effect as soon as the work exists in physical form.

If you want to use a photo in your report, you need to get permission from the photo's owner. Contact the photographer by email, and explain what you want to use and how you plan to use it. If a copyright holder gives you permission, keep a copy of the message or document for your records. The holder may also tell you how a credit line should appear. Acquiring permission protects you from potential concerns over your usage and protects the copyright holder's intellectual property rights.

Some online resources, such as e-books, newspapers, magazines, and journals, are protected by **digital rights management (DRM)**, which are techniques such as authentication, copy protection, or encryption that limit access to proprietary materials. It is a violation of copyright law to circumvent these protections to obtain and then use the materials. To avoid legal trouble, only use materials to which you have legal access, and then follow accepted usage laws for any information you obtain.

Some work is in the **public domain**, which means that the item, such as a photo, is available and accessible to the public without requiring permission to use, and therefore not subject to copyright. This applies to material for which the copyright has expired and to work that has been explicitly released to the public domain by its owner. Many websites provide public domain files free for you to download. Much information on U.S. government sites is in the public domain, as shown in **Figure 2-19**, although you must attribute the information and be aware that the sites might contain other copyrighted information.

For any online source, if you don't see a copyright symbol, look for a statement that specifically defines the work as being in the public domain. For quotations and other cited material, the United States **fair use doctrine** allows you to use a sentence or paragraph of text without permission if you include a citation to the original source.

If the discussion about rights and legal trouble makes you nervous, you're not alone. Clearly, it can be hard to know what is acceptable to use and what's not. Most people are not legal experts, so how can you know what you can use and how you can use it? If you make your writing, photographs, or artwork available online, how do you specify to others how they can use that content?

Figure 2-19: Copyright information on the U.S. Department of Agriculture site

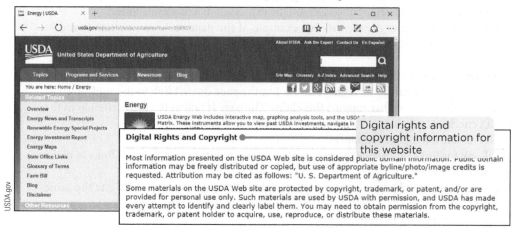

Creative Commons (CC) is a nonprofit organization that helps content creators keep copyright to their materials while allowing others to use, copy, or distribute their work. As a creator, you select a CC license that explains how others can use your work. For example, you can choose whether to allow commercial use of your poem, or allow derivative works, such as translations or adaptations. People who use content that carries a Creative Commons license must follow CC license rules on giving credit for works they use and displaying copyright notices.

CC licenses are based on copyright law and are legal around the world. The CC organization is helping to build a large and ever-growing digital commons, shown in Figure 2-20, a collection of content that users can legally copy, distribute, and expand.

Figure 2-20: Creative Commons website

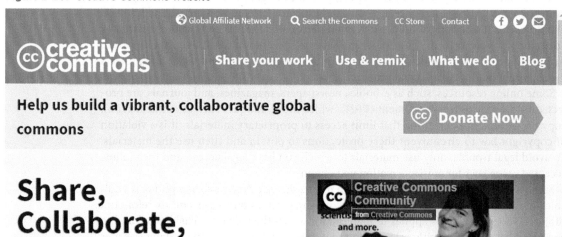

Apply Information Literacy Standards

Part of information literacy involves the ethical use of the information you find on the web. When you use the Internet for research, you face ethical decisions. **Ethics** is the set of moral principles that govern people's behavior. Many schools and other organizations post codes of conduct for computer use, which can help you make ethical decisions while using a computer.

Ethically and legally, you can use other people's ideas in your research papers and presentations as long as you cite the source for any information that is not common knowledge. A **citation** is a formal reference to a source, such as a published work.

Thorough research on technology and other topics usually involves books, journals, magazines, and websites. Each type of information source uses a different **citation style**. Instructors often direct you to use a particular citation style, such as MLA, APA, or Chicago. You can find detailed style guides for each style online. Some software, such as Microsoft Word, helps you create and manage citations and then produce a bibliography, which is an alphabetical collection of citations, as shown in **Figure 2-21**.

Figure 2-21: Citing sources in Microsoft Word

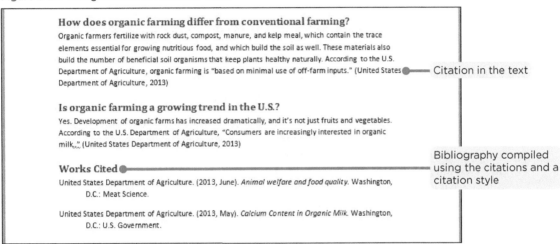

If you use the content from a Wikipedia article but change some of the words, do you have to cite the source for that material? Yes, you do. Otherwise, you are guilty of **plagiarism**, which is using the work or ideas of someone else and claiming them as your own.

To avoid plagiarism, cite your sources for statements that are not common knowledge. Even if you **paraphrase**, which means to restate an idea using words different from those used in the original text, you are still trying to claim someone else's idea as your own. Cite sources when you borrow ideas or words to avoid plagiarism.

Summary

In this module, you learned that the web is part of the Internet, a global collection of millions of computers linked together to share information worldwide. A webpage is an electronic document that can contain text, graphics, sound, video, and links to other webpages, while a website is a collection of webpages. You use a browser to display webpages and enter web addresses, or URLs, which identify the location of webpages on the Internet.

In a URL, the three-letter extension after the period indicates a top-level domain (TLD), which identifies the type of organization associated with the domain. The TLD provides a clue about the content of the website. For example, .com is for commercial enterprises, .edu is for educational institutions, and .gov is for U.S. government agencies.

Nonprofit organizations set the rules for the Internet, such as the names of top-level domains. The IETF sets standards for IP addresses. The W3C publishes standards for websites and webpages.

Websites can be classified into one or more categories, such as blogs, content aggregators, or entertainment sites. A web portal combines pages from many sources and provides access to those pages. Search sites use search engines, software designed to find webpages based on your search criteria.

In addition to using a browser to visit websites and display webpages, you can use it to access web apps, which are apps you run in a browser. A web app offers the advantages of convenience and portability, but involves risks to security and privacy.

Webpages typically include five major areas: header or banner, navigation bar or menu, body, sidebar, and footer. Each area is designed to display specific types of content.

A secure website uses encryption to safeguard transmitted information. Signs of a secure website are a lock icon and the https protocol in the address bar. In an insecure website, the URL starts with "http," indicating an unprotected protocol for transmitting information.

E-commerce refers to business transactions on an electronic network such as the Internet. The three types of e-commerce are business-to-business (B2B), business-to-consumer (B2C), and consumer-to-consumer (C2C). For consumers, e-commerce websites provide the benefits of variety, convenience, and cost, but have the drawbacks of reduced security, fraud, and indirect experience.

B2B e-commerce involves transferring goods, services, or information between businesses. Most e-commerce is actually between businesses. To make a purchase at a B2C website, you visit an electronic storefront, collect items in a shopping cart, and then enter personal data and the method of payment to complete the purchase.

To make secure online payments, use e-commerce websites with the 3D Secure or TLS protocol. You can also use an online payment service such as PayPal, an app such as ApplePay to scan your mobile phone or smartwatch, or a virtual account number.

To find deals for goods and services online, visit comparison shopping sites and use digital deals. Websites such as BizRate, NexTag, and PriceGrabber let you compare prices from multiple vendors. Digital deals come in the form of gift certificates, gift cards, and coupons at websites such as Groupon and RetailMeNot and with browser extensions such as Honey.

How you find, evaluate, use, and communicate online information depends on your information literacy. You become information literate by understanding and selecting the tools, techniques, and strategies for locating and evaluating information.

When you perform an online search, a general search engine compiles a database of information about webpages. The search engine refers to its database index when you enter a search term and then lists pages that match the term, ranked by how closely they answer your query.

A search tool finds online information based on criteria you specify or selections you make. Search tools include search engines, search boxes on webpages, and web directories, which are online guides to subjects or websites, usually arranged in alphabetic order.

If an online search produces too many results or irrelevant results, refine the search by using search operators, characters, words, or symbols that focus the search. To broaden a search, you can use a word stem, which is the base of a word. For example, instead of using *businesses* as a keyword, use *business*.

To find academic information for research, you can use a specialty search engine, which lets you search databases, news providers, podcasts, and other online information sources that general search engines do not always access. Specialty search engines include Wolfram Alpha, Blinkx, and Google Scholar.

When evaluating online information, look for sites from trusted, expert institutions or authors. Avoid sites that show bias or contain outdated information. Evaluate a website using the CARS (credibility, accuracy, reliability, supportability) checklist.

As you gather content from webpages, follow ethical guidelines and be aware of ownership rights to avoid legal, academic, and professional sanctions. Observe intellectual property rights and copyrights to be a responsible member of the online community.

When you use the Internet for research, you face ethical decisions. Ethics is the set of moral principles that govern people's behavior. Ethically and legally, you can use other people's ideas in your research papers and presentations as long as you cite the source for any information that is not common knowledge.

Review Questions

1. Each webpage is assigned a(n) _____, an address that identifies the location of the page on the Internet.
   a. Internet Protocol (IP)
   b. uniform resource locator (URL)
   c. top-level domain (TLD)
   d. Hypertext Transfer Protocol (HTTP)

2. In the web address www.microsoft.com, the ".com" is the _____ meaning _____.
   a. web server name; World Wide Web
   b. pathname; location of the webpage
   c. top-level domain (TLD); commercial enterprise
   d. domain name; name of the organization

3. (True or False) The Internet Engineering Task Force (IETF) sets standards for webpage design.

4. A(n) _____ website gathers, organizes, and then distributes web content.
   a. content aggregator
   b. media sharing
   c. entertainment
   d. search engine

5. (True or False) You must be online to use web apps.

6. On a webpage, a _____ provides supplemental material such as social networking feeds and ads.
   a. navigation bar
   b. header
   c. footer
   d. sidebar

7. Which of the following indicates a secure website connection?
   a. https in the URL
   b. http in the URL
   c. the message "secure website" in the address bar
   d. a shield icon in the address bar

8. Which of the following is *not* an advantage of e-commerce for consumers?
   a. You save time by visiting websites instead of stores.
   b. You have little risk of having your credit card number intercepted.
   c. You can choose goods from any vendor in the world.
   d. You can shop no matter your location, time of day, or conditions.

9. Which of the following describes business-to-business (B2B) e-commerce purchases?
   a. The consumer is the decision maker.
   b. Pricing can vary for each customer.
   c. Customers bid on items being sold by other customers.
   d. Customers can pick up the purchased item in a physical store.

10. A business-to-consumer (B2C) website tracks the items you place in a shopping cart using _____.
    a. an electronic wallet
    b. the Transport Layer Security (TLS) protocol
    c. crawlers
    d. cookies

11. (True or False) A digital coupon provides a promotional code you enter when you check out and pay for online purchases.

12. If you have _____, you can evaluate whether information is misleading, biased, or out of date.
    a. information protocols
    b. technical proficiency
    c. information security
    d. information literacy

13. (True or False) When you perform a search, a general search engine searches the entire Internet.

14. Who or what creates the index for a web directory?
    a. a digital spider
    b. a human editor
    c. a wiki
    d. a search operator

15. Which search operator would you use to locate webpages containing the exact phrase *augmented reality*, with words in the same order?
    a. augmented + reality
    b. – augmented reality
    c. "augmented reality"
    d. ~augmented reality~

16. Which of the following is an example of a specialty search engine?
    a. Bing
    b. Wolfram Alpha
    c. Google
    d. NexTag

17. Checking a website author's credentials is one way to establish a site's _____.
    a. copyright
    b. information literacy
    c. credibility
    d. security

18. Which of the following lets you use a sentence or paragraph of text without permission if you include a citation to its source?
    a. fair use doctrine
    b. Creative Commons
    c. CARS checklist
    d. citation style

19. Plagiarism is best defined as _____.
    a. moral principles that govern our behavior
    b. the act of citing sources
    c. using another's work and claiming it as your own
    d. rights belonging to a work's creator

Discussion Questions

1. How does the web affect your daily life?

2. Media sharing websites let you post photos and videos to share with other people. What are the benefits and drawbacks of using these websites?

3. Business analysts say that physical retail stores are in decline, while e-commerce websites such as Amazon are more popular than ever. Do you agree? Why or why not?

4. Your browser uses a cache to keep track of the websites you visit and businesses use cookies to track your online activities. Do you think these practices invade your privacy? Why or why not?

5. On the Internet, anyone can publish anything to a website, a blog, or a social media site, regardless of whether the information is true. Recent years have seen a spike in misleading or false "news" and hoaxes that are shared as fact on social media. How can you tell fake news stories from real ones?

Critical Thinking Activities

1. Yasmin Hamid is a first-year college student. Knowing she will often research topics using her mobile phone and laptop, she wants a fast, secure browser that is also easy to use. Evaluate and compare reviews of three browsers, at least one of them a mobile browser. Consider Google Chrome, Microsoft Edge, Apple Safari, Mozilla Firefox, Opera, and others you might find in your research. Recommend two browsers: one for when Yasmin uses her laptop, and one for when she uses her mobile phone. Discuss your experiences with these browsers and mention speed, security, and features in your recommendation.

2. Marco Suarez is starting a new job in the Sales and Marketing Department of a financial services company. He is part of a team redesigning the company's website and wants to become better acquainted with current website design principles. Search for this year's best website designs and then examine the sample webpages. What are the current trends in website design? What principles should Marco use to suggest changes to his company's website?

3. Emma Jackson is thinking of starting a retail business with two friends who have extensive experience in sales and business organization. They want to determine whether they should run the business as an e-commerce website or a brick-and-mortar store. Research the pros and cons of e-commerce for businesses and recommend an option to Emma.

4. Ken Chao is a veteran returning to school after six years in the military. After an injury that affected his sight, he finds it difficult to read text on computer screens. However, many of his classes require online research. How can Ken complete his search assignments effectively? How can search engines become more accessible for people with low vision like Ken?

5. You have been putting off writing a research paper, and now it's due in two days. You have gathered a few notes, but fear you will not complete the assignment on time. You are considering purchasing a paper from a website that produces research papers on any topic, though you are concerned the content might not be original. Should you take a chance and purchase the research paper? Is using the website's services even ethical?

Key Terms

3D Secure
address bar
app
application
blog
Boolean operator
breadcrumb
browser
business-to-business (B2B)
business-to-consumer (B2C)
cache
citation
citation style
consumer-to-consumer (C2C)
content aggregator
cookie
copyright
crawler
Creative Commons (CC)
digital certificate
digital rights management (DRM)
domain name
e-commerce
electronic storefront
encryption

ethics
fair use doctrine
general search engine
hit
home page
hyperlink
Hypertext Transfer Protocol (HTTP)
Hypertext Transfer Protocol Secure
   (HTTPS)
index
information literacy
intellectual property rights
Internet
Internet Engineering Task Force (IETF)
IP address
keyword
media sharing site
navigate
navigation bar
online social network
paraphrase
plagiarism
portal
protocol
public domain

query
search engine
search operator
search tool
specialized search tool
specialty search engine
spider
start page
subject directory
top-level domain (TLD)
Transport Layer Security (TLS)
uniform resource locator (URL)
usage right
web
web app
web directory
web portal
web server
webpage
website
wiki
wildcard
word stem
World Wide Web
World Wide Web Consortium (W3C)

Computer Hardware

Staff working together on an all-in-one computer

Mobile devices, such as laptops, are used to easily transport work between locations

iStock.com/PeopleImages

Savannah Montero is an intern at a small graphic design firm with ten employees in Denver, Colorado. In addition to Savannah learning about designing professional graphics for large corporations worldwide, she will also be responsible for learning about and maintaining the staff's computers and mobile devices. Each employee uses a desktop computer, a laptop they can bring home to work on projects, and a tablet that can be used to present work to potential and current customers.

In This Module

- Categorize the various types of computer hardware
- Demonstrate familiarity with input and output devices
- Maintain hardware components

IF YOU USE a smartphone, tablet, or computer, you depend on computer hardware, the physical components that allow your device to operate properly. Computer hardware can include internal components that you can't see, or they can be externally connected devices. In this module you will learn about the many different types of computer hardware, and how to choose and maintain computer hardware that will best meet your needs.

Categorize the Various Types of Computer Hardware

Computers include a variety of hardware types, including the central processing unit, RAM, ROM, and peripheral devices. This section covers the various components of computer hardware, how computers represent data, several storage solutions that are available, the different types of computers, and what to consider when shopping for a new computer.

Define Each Component of Computer Hardware

Computers contain various types of hardware such as memory, storage devices, a central processing unit, input and output devices, and communication devices. When using a computer or requesting help, you should understand how the hardware works and how components interact with one another. Components of a computer include the central processing unit (CPU), memory, storage devices, input devices, and output devices.

The **central processing unit (CPU)** is a complex integrated circuit consisting of millions of electronic parts and is primarily responsible for converting input (data) into meaningful output (information). Data travels in and out of the CPU through embedded wires called a **bus**. **Figure 3-1** illustrates the approximate locations of CPUs in various types of computers and mobile devices.

Figure 3-1: Central processing units

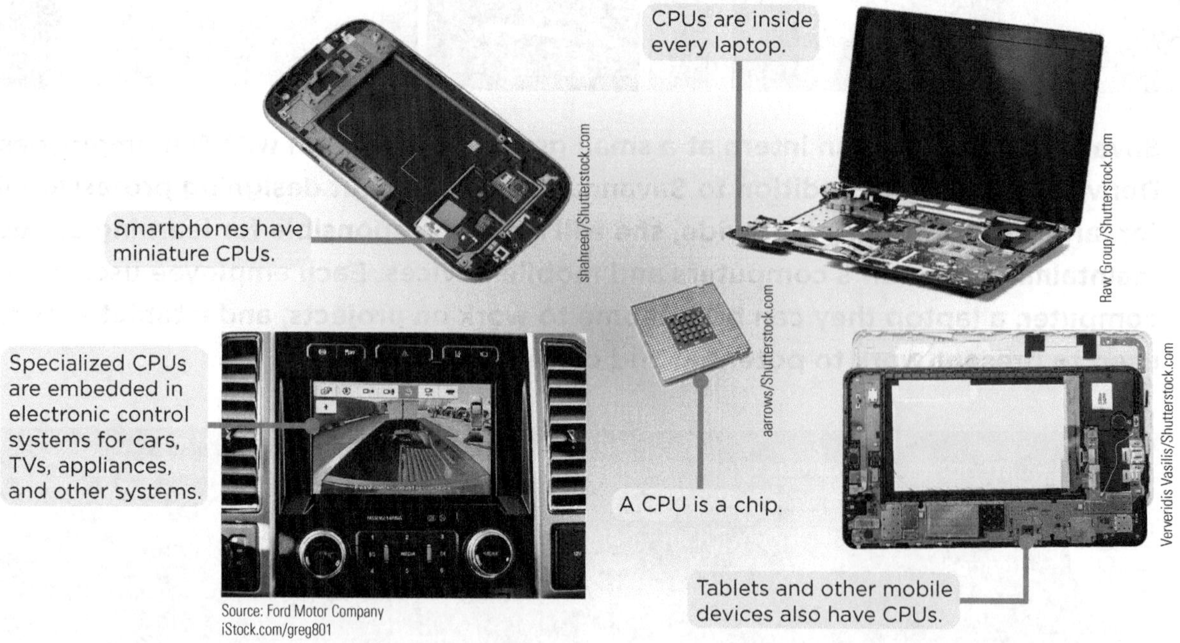

CPUs are inside every laptop.

Smartphones have miniature CPUs.

Specialized CPUs are embedded in electronic control systems for cars, TVs, appliances, and other systems.

A CPU is a chip.

Tablets and other mobile devices also have CPUs.

Source: Ford Motor Company
iStock.com/greg801

shahreen/Shutterstock.com

aarrows/Shutterstock.com

Raw Group/Shutterstock.com

Ververidis Vasilis/Shutterstock.com

When you purchase a computer, you might notice that processors can be advertised as having one or more cores. A processor core is a unit on the processor with the circuitry necessary to execute instructions. Processors with more cores typically perform better and are more expensive than processors with fewer cores. Processors with multiple cores are referred to as **multi-core processors**.

If a processor uses specific data frequently it can store that data in a processor cache. A **processor cache** stores this data next to the processor so that it can easily and quickly be retrieved.

When a CPU executes instructions as it converts input into output, it does so with the control unit and the arithmetic logic unit. The **control unit** manages the flow of instructions within the processor, and the **arithmetic logic unit (ALU)** is responsible for performing arithmetic operations. Instructions executed by the CPU go through a series of four steps, often referred to as a machine cycle or an instruction cycle. This cycle includes the steps the CPU completes to run programmed instructions, make calculations, and make decisions. The four steps in the machine cycle include fetching, decoding, executing, and storing. The fetching and decoding instructions are performed by the control unit, while the executing and storing instructions are performed by the ALU (**Figure 3-2**).

Computer memory is responsible for holding data and programs as they are being processed by the CPU. Different types of memory exist, including random access memory, read-only memory, and virtual memory.

Random access memory (RAM) is stored on one or more chips connected to the main circuit board of the computer (also referred to as the **motherboard**), and temporarily stores data needed by the operating system and apps you use. When you start an app on your computer, the app's instructions are transferred from the hard drive to RAM. Although accessing an app's instructions from RAM results in increased performance, the contents of RAM are lost when power is removed. Memory that loses its contents when power is removed is said to be **volatile**. Memory that is **nonvolatile** does not lose its contents when power is removed.

Read-only memory (ROM) is permanently installed on your computer and is attached to the motherboard. The ROM chip contains the BIOS, which tells your computer how to start. The BIOS also performs a **power-on self test (POST)**, which tests all computer components for proper operation. The ROM also provides the means of communication between the operating system and hardware devices. Computer manufacturers often update the instructions on the ROM chip, which are referred to as **firmware**. These updated instructions, or firmware version, can enable your computer to perform additional tasks or fine-tune how your computer communicates with other devices.

When you run your operating system and other apps on your computer, the operating system and each app will require a certain amount of RAM to function properly. As you run more apps simultaneously, more RAM will be required. If your computer runs low on RAM, it may need to swap the contents of RAM to and from the hard drive. When this takes place, your computer is said to be using **virtual memory**. The area of the hard drive temporarily used to store data that cannot fit in RAM is called a **swap file** or **paging file**. Depending on the type of hard drive installed on your computer, using virtual memory may decrease your computer's performance. **Figure 3-3** illustrates how your computer might use virtual memory.

Figure 3-2: Machine cycle

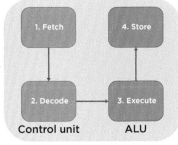

Control unit   ALU

CPU

Figure 3-3: How a computer might use virtual memory

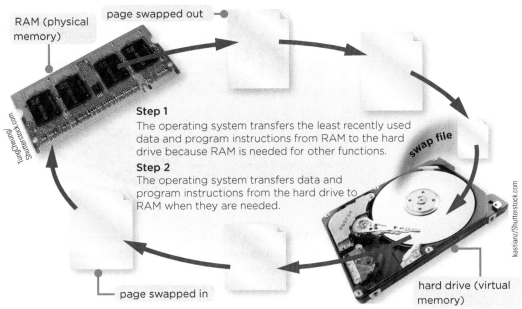

RAM (physical memory)

page swapped out

swap file

Step 1
The operating system transfers the least recently used data and program instructions from RAM to the hard drive because RAM is needed for other functions.

Step 2
The operating system transfers data and program instructions from the hard drive to RAM when they are needed.

page swapped in

hard drive (virtual memory)

In addition to the components residing within your computer, you will also use input and output devices to provide data to the computer and to receive information from the computer. An **input device** communicates instructions and commands to a computer. On a computer, the most common input device might be a keyboard, which can communicate text and instructions. On a mobile phone, the most common input device might be its touchscreen. Additional types of input devices include, but are not limited to, a mouse, stylus, scanner, webcam, microphone, and game controller.

An **output device** conveys information from the computer to the user. On a computer or mobile device, the most common output device might be its display device. Other types of output devices include speakers, headphones, projectors, and printers.

Visually Identify Types of Computer Hardware

Various types of random access memory exist, and the different types vary in cost, performance, and whether or not they are volatile. **Table 3-1** describes common types of RAM. **Figure 3-4** shows different types of computer memory.

Table 3-1: Types of RAM

Type of RAM	Description	Volatile or nonvolatile
Dynamic RAM (DRAM)	Memory needs to be constantly recharged or contents will be erased	Volatile
Static RAM (SRAM)	Memory can be recharged less frequently than DRAM, but can be more expensive than DRAM	Volatile
Magnetoresistive RAM (MRAM)	Memory uses magnetic charges to store contents, and can retain its contents in the absence of power	Nonvolatile
Flash memory	Fast type of memory that typically is less expensive than some other types of RAM, and can retain its contents in the absence of power	Nonvolatile

Figure 3-4: Computer memory

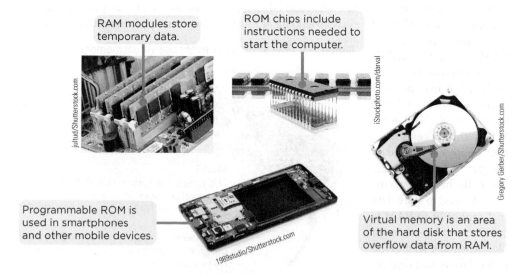

RAM modules store temporary data.

ROM chips include instructions needed to start the computer.

Programmable ROM is used in smartphones and other mobile devices.

Virtual memory is an area of the hard disk that stores overflow data from RAM.

jultud/Shutterstock.com

iStockphoto.com/darval

Gregory Gerber/Shutterstock.com

1989studio/Shutterstock.com

While RAM is used to temporarily store instructions used by apps, storage devices are designed to store data and information for extended periods of time. The type and amount of data you want to store will help you determine the most appropriate storage device to use. Some examples of storage devices include internal and external hard drives, solid state drives, and optical media (**Figure 3-5**).

Figure 3-5: Storage devices

Internal hard drive for a laptop   **External hard drive**   **Memory cards**   **USB flash drive**

Various types of storage devices exist, each with advantages and disadvantages discussed throughout this module. For example, if you want to completely back up the contents of your computer, you might store those contents on an external hard drive or in cloud storage. However, your internal hard drive might store your operating system and apps you currently are using. Businesses might back up their data using a tape drive, which is a storage device that stores data on magnetic tapes. If you want to move several files from one computer to another, consider using a USB flash drive. Finally, you might use a DVD or other type of optical disc to store a movie.

Explain How Computers Represent Data

Most computers are digital and use a binary system to operate. A **binary system** is a number system that has two digits, 0 and 1. The digit 0 indicates the absence of an electronic charge, and a 1 indicates the presence of an electronic charge. These electronic charges (or absence thereof), when grouped together, represent data. Each 0 or 1 is called a bit. A **bit** (short for binary digit) is the smallest unit of data a computer can process. When 8 bits are grouped together, they form a **byte**. A byte can represent a single character in the computer or mobile device. **Figure 3-6** illustrates various bytes, their corresponding bits, and what they represent.

Figure 3-6: Eight bits grouped together as a unit are called a byte

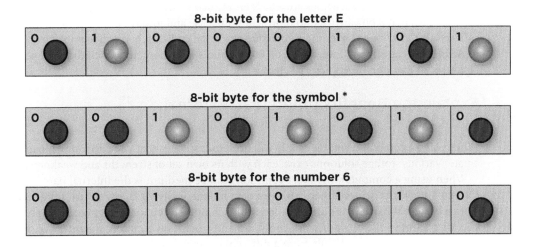

When you type numbers, letters, and special characters on your keyboard, the computer translates them into the corresponding bits and bytes that it can understand. This translation spares you from having to manually type the bits for each number, letter, or special character. When you display text on an output device such as a computer monitor, the computer translates the various bits back to numbers, letters, and special characters that you can understand. **Figure 3-7** shows how a letter is converted to binary form and back.

Figure 3-7: Converting a letter to binary form and back

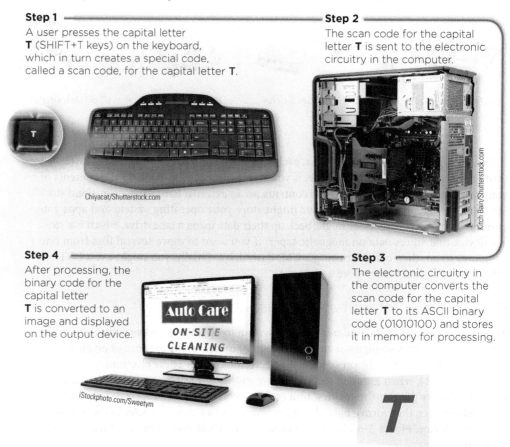

Step 1

A user presses the capital letter **T** (SHIFT+T keys) on the keyboard, which in turn creates a special code, called a scan code, for the capital letter **T**.

Chiyacat/Shutterstock.com

Step 2

The scan code for the capital letter **T** is sent to the electronic circuitry in the computer.

Kitch Bain/Shutterstock.com

Step 4

After processing, the binary code for the capital letter **T** is converted to an image and displayed on the output device.

iStockphoto.com/Sweetym

Step 3

The electronic circuitry in the computer converts the scan code for the capital letter **T** to its ASCII binary code (01010100) and stores it in memory for processing.

When a computer translates a character into bits and bytes, it uses a text coding scheme. Two popular text coding schemes are ASCII and Unicode. **ASCII** is an 8-bit coding scheme, which means that 8 bits are used to represent uppercase and lowercase letters, mathematical operators, and logical operations. **Unicode** is a 16-bit coding scheme that is an extension of ASCII and can support more than 65,000 symbols and characters, including Chinese, Japanese, Arabic, and other pictorial characters.

Explain the Benefits of Internal, External, and Cloud-Based Storage Solutions

When using a computer, you inevitably will need to store files that you either download or create. Various storage solutions exist, each with its own set of strengths and weaknesses.

When using a computer, the most common storage medium is the internal **hard drive** (**Figure 3-8**). Hard drives either can store data magnetically, or they can use solid state storage. Internal hard drives are installed in the computer you are using. For example, if you are creating a file on your work computer and store it on an internal hard drive, you will not be able to access the file from a different computer unless you copy the file to the other computer either by using an external hard drive, USB flash drive, or sending it electronically. Magnetic hard disk drives (HDDs) typically have greater storage capacity and are less expensive than their solid state equivalents, but have several moving parts, making it inadvisable to move the computer while they are running. A **solid state drive (SSD)** is a hard drive without moving parts, and is faster and more durable than magnetic drives (**Figure 3-9**). Solid state drives often are used on mobile devices such as laptops and tablets and come in various physical sizes.

Figure 3-8: Internal magnetic hard drive

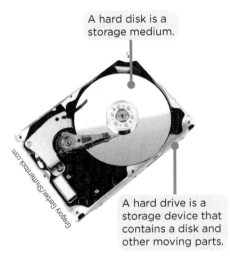

A hard disk is a storage medium.

A hard drive is a storage device that contains a disk and other moving parts.

Gregory Gerber/Shutterstock.com

Figure 3-9: Solid state drive (SSD)

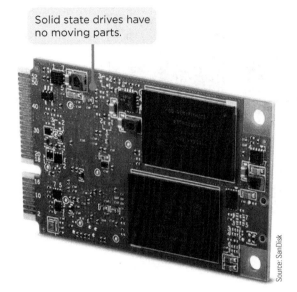

Solid state drives have no moving parts.

Source: SanDisk

In addition to storing data and information on an internal hard drive, you also can store it on an external hard drive. **External hard drives** can add storage capacity to your computer, are housed in a separate case, and typically connect to your computer using a USB cable (**Figure 3-10**). Similar to internal hard drives, external hard drives can use either magnetic or solid state technology. External hard drives also can be transported from one computer to another, so if you are working on a file and save it to the external hard drive, you can connect the drive to a different computer to continue working on that same file.

Optical media include CDs, DVDs, and Blu-ray discs (BDs), but their use as storage media is declining. Optical media were once widely used to distribute installation files for programs and apps, but saving files to optical media required special software or capabilities within the operating system. While optical media is easy to transport, if the discs get damaged, you might not be able to access your stored files. Instead of optical discs, many individuals now use USB flash drives, external hard drives, and cloud storage to transport files.

Cloud storage involves storing electronic files on the Internet, not on a local computer, a practice called storing data "in the cloud." Cloud storage enables you to store your files remotely on servers that could be in a different city, state, or part of the world. Storing files to and retrieving files from cloud storage typically requires only a computer or mobile device with an Internet connection (**Figure 3-11**). With cloud storage, you might not require as much storage on your computer because you can store your files remotely. Examples of cloud storage include Google Drive, Microsoft OneDrive, and Dropbox.

Explain the Pros and Cons of Using Different Types of Computers, Including All-in-Ones, Tablets, Mobile Devices, and Desktop Computers

Various types of computers exist, including desktop computers, all-in-one computers, tablets, and other mobile

Figure 3-10: External hard drive

External hard drive

iStock.com/greg801

Figure 3-11: Cloud storage

iStock.com/Lvcandy

Figure 3-12: Typical desktop computer

iStock.com/kostsov

Figure 3-13: Typical all-in-one computer

iStock.com/Bongkarn Thanyakij

devices. A **desktop computer**, pictured in **Figure 3-12**, typically consists of the system unit, monitor, keyboard, and mouse. Because desktop computers consist of multiple separate components, they are not very portable. However, these computers often can be more powerful and contain more storage than their mobile equivalents such as laptops and tablets. Hardware components such as the hard drive and RAM can be more easily upgraded in desktop computers than in other types of computers. You might use a desktop computer at an office where users do not need the ability to move their computer from place to place.

An **all-in-one computer** is similar to a desktop computer, but the monitor and system unit are housed together (**Figure 3-13**). All-in-one computers take up less space than a desktop computer and are easier to transport, but are typically more difficult to service or upgrade because the components are housed in a very limited space. All-in-one computers sometimes are more expensive than a desktop computer with equivalent hardware specifications.

A **mobile device** is a portable or handheld computing device, such as a smartphone or a tablet, with a screen size of 10.1 inches or smaller. A **tablet** is a small, flat computer with a touch-sensitive screen that accepts input from a digital pen, stylus, or your fingertip (**Figure 3-14**). Tablets often are less powerful than other types of computers, but provide an easy, convenient way to browse the web, read and respond to emails, and create simple documents. Tablets are also easy to transport, making them ideal to take to classes and meetings to take notes. Tablets are used in a variety of professions, such as the medical profession, to easily collect data from patients for storage in their permanent medical records. While the primary method of input on a tablet is by using a digital pen, stylus, or fingertip, you also may be able to connect a wireless Bluetooth keyboard to make it easier to type. It often is not possible to upgrade a tablet; if your tablet's performance begins to deteriorate or cannot keep up with the latest operating systems and apps, it may be necessary to replace the device.

Figure 3-14: Typical tablet

iStock.com/shapecharge

Determine Which Hardware Features Are Personally Necessary to Consider When Purchasing a Computer

When purchasing a computer, understanding your needs will help you to select the most appropriate device. For example, if you plan to use the computer to check your email and browse the web, the type of computer you purchase might be different from one you might purchase for creating and editing video content. When choosing a computer, you should select one with the platform, hardware, form factor, and add-on devices that best meet your needs. Table 3-2 identifies factors to consider when buying a computer, as well as questions that will help lead you to making the most appropriate choices.

Table 3-2: Factors to consider in buying a computer

Consideration	Questions
Platform	• Do I need to use software that requires a specific platform? • Does the computer need to be compatible with other devices I own that use a particular platform?
Hardware	• Do I require specific hardware to perform intended tasks? • How much data and information do I plan to store on the computer?
Hardware specifications	• Will the tasks I perform or software I want to run require certain hardware specifications?
Form factor	• Will I be using this computer in one location, or will I need to be mobile?
Add-on devices	• What additional devices will I need to perform my intended tasks?

A computer's **platform** refers to the software, or operating system, it uses. When two computers use the same platform, it typically is easier to transfer files between the computers. If you are purchasing a computer to do schoolwork, for example, consider purchasing one that uses the same operating system as the computers at your school. If you have a job and want the ability to do some work both on your office and home computer, consider purchasing a computer that uses the same operating system as your work computer. The operating systems used elsewhere in your home, both on computers and mobile devices, also might play a role in the selection. For example, if you own an iPhone or iPad, you might choose to purchase an Apple computer for maximum compatibility between the devices. Two of the most common operating systems on today's computers are Windows and macOS (**Figure 3-15**). Chromebooks are types of laptops that run the ChromeOS operating system. While these are budget friendly, they often do not have the same features and support the same apps as computers running Windows or macOS. Other operating systems include UNIX, Linux, Google Android, and Apple iOS.

When you buy a computer, you should review the computer's hardware specifications so that you purchase one that meets your needs. Computers are available in a variety of brands. Each brand might include models that have varying types of processors, amounts of memory, storage devices, and form factors. You can find specifications about a computer on the computer's packaging, on signage next to the computer's display in a store, or on the manufacturer's or retailer's website (**Figure 3-16**).

Figure 3-15a: Windows operating system

Figure 3-15b: macOS

Courtesy of Apple Inc.

Figure 3-16: Computer specifications found on a retailer's website

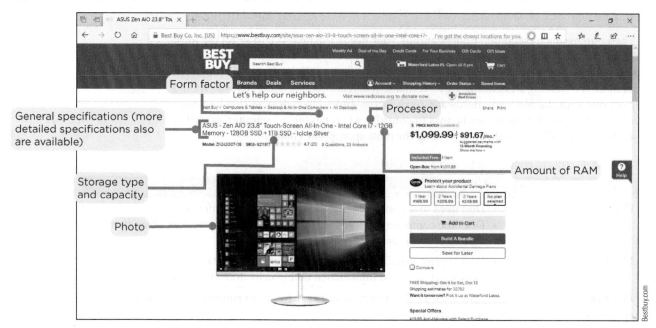

Depending on how you plan to use the computer, you also may have additional requirements such as a certain number of USB ports, touchscreen, Bluetooth compatibility, or an optical drive. When reviewing hardware specifications online, you may need to explore the product's webpage to identify all hardware specifications. In Figure 3-16, for example, general specifications are listed at the top of the product page. However, scrolling the page will reveal additional features and more detailed hardware specifications (**Figure 3-17**).

Figure 3-17: Detailed hardware specifications

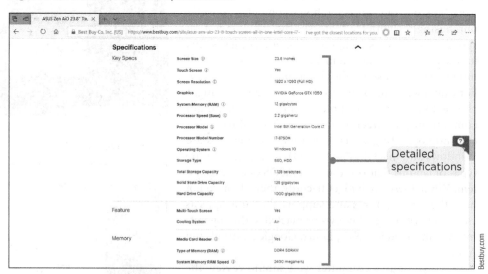

Your budget will play a big role in the computer you purchase, but as you will see, there may be many computers available in the same price range. For example, one computer available for $1,000 might have a great processor and a mediocre hard drive, but another computer at the same price might have a mediocre processor and a great hard drive. It is important to evaluate what each computer has to offer so that you can select the device that best meets your needs.

As mentioned previously, understanding your needs and requirements will help you select the best computer. If you plan to use the computer to create and edit video content, you might select a desktop computer with a large monitor and the best available processor. However, if you plan to use a computer just to check your email messages and perform research on the Internet, you might select a laptop with a lower-end processor. The processor most affects a computer's speed.

A great way to determine the required hardware specifications for your computer is to evaluate the minimum hardware requirements, also called system requirements, for the software you plan to use. For example, if you plan to use a software suite such as Microsoft Office, Microsoft's website outlines the minimum processor, operating system (platform), amount and type of RAM, and storage capacity required to properly run the software (**Figure 3-18**).

Figure 3-18: System requirements for Microsoft Office

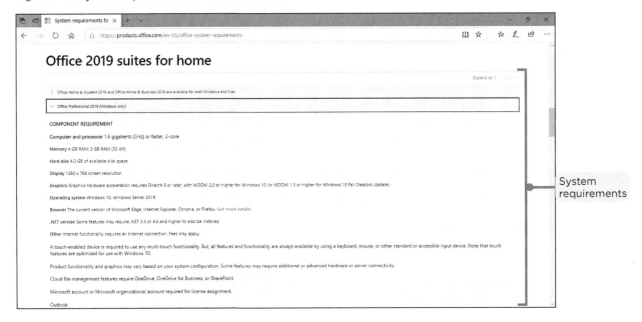

It is likely that you will want to use more than one program or app on your computer, and you will find that each program or app has its own system requirements. The system requirements for one program or app might conflict with the system requirements of the other(s), so you will need to select the computer with the hardware specifications that can accommodate both programs or apps. **Table 3-3** describes how to evaluate conflicting system requirements.

Table 3-3: Evaluating system requirements

Specification	Recommended solution
Different processor requirements	Identify the program or app with the greater processor requirement and select a computer with a processor that meets or exceeds the requirement.
Different memory requirements	Identify the program or app with the greater memory requirement and select a computer with a memory type and capacity that meets or exceeds this requirement.
	Computers with as little as 4 GB of memory are great for basic web browsing and very basic productivity tasks, while computers with as much as 32 GB are often used for virtual reality applications, high-end gaming, and other intensive tasks.
Different storage requirements	Add the storage requirements for each program or app you want to use, and select a computer with the storage capacity that exceeds the sum of all storage requirements.
Other differing hardware requirements	In most cases, identify the program or app with the greater requirement and select a computer that at least meets or exceeds this requirement.

Although following these guidelines will help you select an appropriate computer, keep in mind that you may want the computer to meet your needs for the next three to five years. If you select a computer that exactly meets the system requirements for the present software you intend to use, you might not be able to install or use additional programs or apps in the future. In addition, you should purchase a computer that not only has enough storage capacity for the programs and apps you want to use, but also for the files you intend to store on the computer (homework, photos, videos, important documents, etc.). It is important to note that while purchasing the most expensive computer you can afford might meet your needs, you might not ever use all available resources. For example, if the system requirements for the programs and apps you want to use call for 12 gigabytes (GB) of memory, it might be reasonable to select a computer with 16 GB of memory, but it could be a waste of money to purchase a computer with 32 GB of memory. If you intend to use a computer to play games, you might consider a computer built specifically for gaming applications. These computers typically have a large amount of RAM, as well as other supporting hardware to support an immersive gaming experience. Evaluate your options carefully and seek advice from professionals if you are unsure of your exact needs.

After you have determined the platform and hardware requirements for the computer you want to purchase, you will select a form factor. The **form factor** refers to the shape and size of the computer. Not all form factors may support the hardware you need. For example, a tablet might not contain adequate hardware specifications for editing videos. The three main types of computer form factors are desktops, laptops, and tablets.

As mentioned previously, a desktop computer is a personal computer designed to be in a stationary location, where all of its components fit on or under a desk or table. Components that typically occupy space outside of a desktop include peripheral devices such as a keyboard, mouse, webcam, speakers, and printer. Depending on the form factor, it may also require an external monitor. Towers and all-in-one desktops are two types of desktop form factors, both of which can vary in size (**Figure 3-19**).

Figure 3-19: Desktop and all-in-one form factors

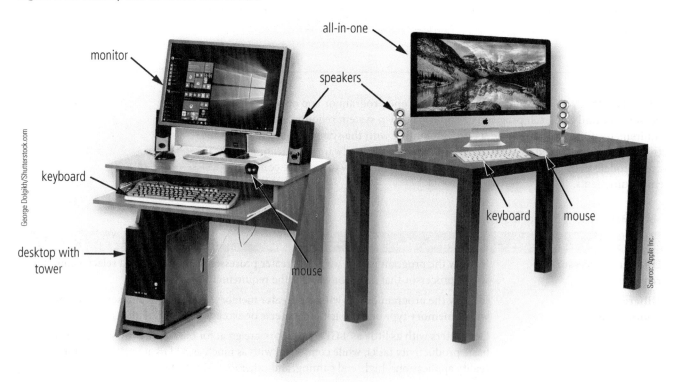

A **laptop**, also called a notebook, is a portable computer that is smaller than the average briefcase and light enough to carry comfortably. Laptops have input devices, such as a keyboard, touchpad, and webcam; output devices, such as a screen and speakers; one or more storage devices, such as a hard drive; and communication capabilities. Many of today's laptops also have touchscreens. **Figure 3-20** shows a traditional laptop and an ultrathin laptop.

Figure 3-20: Laptop form factors

traditional laptop

ultrathin laptop

Julia Nikitina/Shutterstock.com

Source: Apple Inc.

Ultrathin laptops weigh less than traditional laptops and usually are less powerful. Ultrathin laptops have fewer parts to minimize the thickness of the device, but may also have a longer battery life and be more expensive.

As mentioned previously, a tablet is a thin, lighter-weight mobile computer that has a touchscreen. Two popular form factors of tablets are slate and convertible (**Figure 3-21**). A slate tablet resembles a letter-sized pad and does not contain a physical keyboard. A convertible tablet is a tablet that has a screen in its lid and a keyboard in its base, with the lid and base connected by a swivel-type hinge. You can use a convertible tablet like a traditional laptop, or you can rotate the display and fold it down over the keyboard so that it looks like a slate tablet. Tablets are useful especially for taking notes in class, at meetings, at conferences, and in other forums where the standard laptop is not practical. Most tablets might not be as powerful as desktop or laptop computers, but are extremely mobile and convenient to use.

Figure 3-21: Slate and convertible tablets

magnetic keyboard cover

slate tablet in stand

stylus

convertible tablet

iStock.com/Rasslava

An add-on device, also referred to as a **peripheral device**, is a device such as a keyboard, mouse, printer, or speakers that can connected to and extend the capability of a computer. For example, if you need to share hard copies of documents you create, you should purchase a printer. If you plan to work in a quiet location but still would like to hear audio, you might consider purchasing a headset or earbuds. If you will need to regularly bring files from one computer to another, you might purchase an external storage device that you can connect to various computers. Peripheral devices can be used for input, output, or a combination of both.

Figure 3-22: USB hub

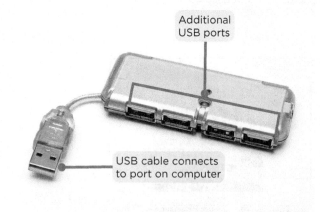

Additional USB ports

USB cable connects to port on computer

iStock.com/jordanchez

When purchasing a peripheral device for your computer, you should make sure that the device is compatible. A peripheral device, for example, may only be compatible with a specific operating system such as Windows. In addition to making sure that the device is compatible with the software on your computer, you also should make sure you have the necessary ports to connect the device. A **port** is a slot on the computer where you can attach a peripheral device. For example, if a peripheral device is designed to connect to a USB port on the computer, you should make sure that you have an available USB port. If all USB ports on your computer are in use, you might consider purchasing a USB hub. A **USB hub** is an external device that contains many USB ports (**Figure 3-22**). Finally, consider purchasing an extended warranty or service plan if one is available.

Demonstrate Familiarity with Input and Output Devices

Input and output devices are necessary to provide information to and receive information from a computer. This section describes the various types of input and output devices, as well as how to install computer hardware.

Figure 3-23: Typical computer keyboard

iStock.com/TARIK KIZILKAYA

Figure 3-24: Typical mouse

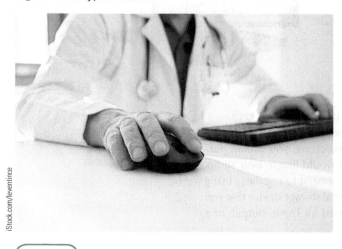

iStock.com/leventince

Experiment with Input Devices

As mentioned previously, an input device is used to communicate instructions or commands to a computer. Various types of input devices are available such as keyboards, pointing devices, touchscreens, microphones, cameras, scanners, and game controllers.

A **keyboard** is an input device that contains keys you can press to enter letters, numbers, and symbols (**Figure 3-23**). Desktop computers have keyboards connected either wired or wirelessly, and laptop computers have a keyboard built-in. Mobile devices such as tablets and smartphones typically have an on-screen keyboard; that is, an image of a keyboard displays on the screen, and you touch the appropriate keys to enter letters, numbers, and symbols.

Another widely used type of input device is a pointing device. A **pointing device** is used to point to and select specific objects on the computer screen. Examples of pointing devices include a mouse, touchpad, and trackball. Pointing devices can be used to select objects, move objects, and position or draw items on the screen.

The **mouse** is the most common pointing device used with computers. A mouse fits under your hand and can connect to your computer either with a wire or wirelessly (**Figure 3-24**). Moving the mouse on a flat surface, such as a desk, moves a pointer on the screen. When the pointer is positioned over an object you want to select, you can press a button on the mouse to select the object. This action is referred to as clicking the mouse.

A touchpad is a pointing device that is commonly used on laptops. A **touchpad** is a flat surface that is touch-sensitive, and you move your finger around the touchpad to move the pointer on the screen (**Figure 3-25**). When the pointer is over an item on the screen you wish to select, you can tap the touchpad with your finger to select the object.

A **trackball** is a stationary pointing device with a ball anchored inside a casing, as well as two or more buttons (**Figure 3-26**). Moving the ball moves the pointer on the screen, and pressing the buttons issues the commands to the computer.

A **touchscreen** is a display that lets you touch areas of the screen to interact with software. In addition to responding to the touch of your fingers, touchscreens also may be able to respond to a stylus or digital pen to enter commands. Tablets and smartphones typically have touchscreens. **Multitouch screens** can respond to multiple fingers touching the screen simultaneously. This is useful when you are performing a gesture such as pinching or stretching an object to resize it.

Pen input is used to make selections or draw on a touchscreen with more precision than a finger. Common pen input devices include a stylus and a digital pen. A **stylus** is a small device, shaped like a pen, that you can use to draw, tap icons, or tap keys on an on-screen keyboard. A **digital pen** is similar to a stylus, but is more capable because it has programmable buttons. Some digital pens can also capture your handwriting as you write on paper or on the screen (**Figure 3-27**).

An option for issuing instructions to your computer without using your hands is using your voice. A **microphone** is used to enter voice or sound data into a computer. Examples of activities that might require a microphone include video conferencing, voice recognition, and recording live music. Many laptops and tablets have built-in microphones, but you can connect a microphone to other types of computers either using a wire or wirelessly. Using a microphone, you can record audio, issue commands to the computer, or speak while the computer translates your words to text in a document. Microphones are also essential if you are using the computer to have an audio or video conversation with one or more other people.

Cameras are input devices because they support you adding pictures or videos to a computer. Most computers come with built-in cameras called **webcams**, which primarily are used for videoconferencing, chatting, or online gaming (**Figure 3-28**). If the computer does

Figure 3-25: Typical touchpad

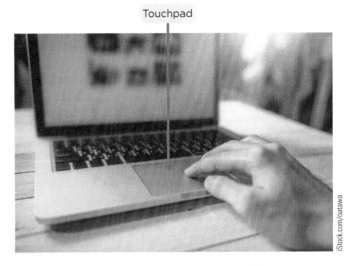

Touchpad

iStock.com/oatawa

Figure 3-26: Typical trackball

iStock.com/pengpeng

Figure 3-27: Digital pen

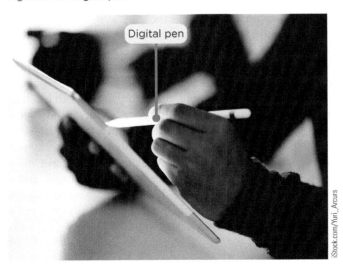

Digital pen

iStock.com/Yuri_Arcurs

Figure 3-28: Webcam

Webcam

iStock.com/innovatedcaptures

not have a built-in webcam, or you would like to connect a different type of camera to your computer, you can do so either via a wired or wireless connection.

A **scanner** is an input device that converts an existing paper image into an electronic file that you can open and work with on your computer. For example, if you want to convert a printed logo to digital form so that you can edit and duplicate it, you could use a scanner to convert the printed logo to a format a computer can understand. In addition to scanning printed materials such as logos and documents, 3-D scanners can scan three-dimensional objects, which then can be manipulated and possibly printed on a 3-D printer (discussed later in this module). You can also use a scanner to scan a printed document so that you can edit it using an app on your computer.

A **game controller** is an input device you use when playing a video game. Various types of game controllers exist such as joysticks, gamepads, dance pads, wheels, and motion-sensing controllers.

- A **joystick** is a handheld vertical lever, mounted on a base, that you move in different directions to control the actions of the simulated vehicle or player.
- A **gamepad** is held in both hands and controls the movement and actions of players or objects. On gamepads, users press buttons with their thumbs or move sticks in various directions to trigger events (**Figure 3-29**).
- A **dance pad** is a flat, electronic device divided into panels that users press with their feet in response to instructions from the video game.
- A **wheel** is a type of game controller that mirrors the functionality of a steering wheel in an automobile. Turning the wheel will turn the vehicle you are driving in the game.
- A **motion-sensing controller** allows users to guide on-screen elements with air gestures.

Figure 3-29: Gamepad

Gamepad

iStock.com/Pekic

Experiment with Output Devices

Recall that an output device conveys information from the computer to its user, or performs an action based on a command. Commonly used output devices include display devices, speakers, headphones, printers, projectors, and voice output.

Computers use display devices as output devices to communicate information to the users. Display devices are connected to desktop computers via a cable, while all-in-one computers, laptops, tablets, and smartphones have built-in display devices. Display devices come in a variety of sizes. If you are simply using a computer to browse the web and check your email, you might consider a smaller display device. However, if you are working with graphics or large spreadsheets, you might use a larger display device. If you want to present to a group of individuals, you might consider using a projector.

Speakers are used to convey audio output, such as music, voice, sound effects, or other sounds. While speakers often are built into computers, tablets, and smartphones, you can also connect speakers via a wired or wireless connection. For example, if you want to play music in a small office setting and would like others to hear it, you might connect a separate speaker to your computer so that it can play more loudly. If you prefer to listen to audio in a public space without disturbing others, consider using headphones. **Headphones** consist of a pair of small listening devices that fit into a band placed over your ears. As an alternative to headphones, **earbuds** are speakers that are small enough to place in your ears. If you prefer a device that provides audio output while being able to accept voice input, consider a headset. **Headsets** include one or more headphones for output, and a microphone for input.

A **printer** creates hard copy output on paper, film, and other media. A printer can be connected to a computer via a cable, a network, or wirelessly. **Table 3-4** describes the various types of printers.

Table 3-4: Types of printers

Type of printer	Description
Ink-jet printer	Prints by spraying small dots of colored ink onto paper
Laser printer	Uses a laser beam and toner to print on paper
Multifunction device (MFD)	Also called an all-in-one printer; can serve as an input device by copying and scanning, as well as an output device by faxing and printing
Mobile printer	Small, lightweight printer that is built into or attached to a mobile device for mobile printing
Plotter	Large-format printer that uses charged wires to produce high-quality drawings for professional applications such as architectural blueprints; plotters draw continuous lines on large rolls of paper
3-D printer	Creates objects based on computer models using special plastics and other materials

Projectors can display output from a computer on a large surface such as a wall or screen (**Figure 3-30**). Projectors are often used in classroom or conference room environments where individuals give presentations. Projectors are connected to computers using a cable or wirelessly, and can either duplicate what is on your computer's monitor or act as an extension of the monitor (your monitor might display one thing while the projector displays another). Some projectors are small and easy to transport, while others are larger and may be permanently mounted in a room.

In addition to output being displayed or printed, computers can also provide voice output. A **voice synthesizer** converts text to speech. Some apps and operating systems have a built-in voice synthesizer. For example, Windows has a Narrator app that can read the contents of the screen. In addition to this form of output being convenient for some, it is also helpful for those with visual impairments.

Figure 3-30: Projector and screen

iStock.com/EricFerguson

Projector

Screen

Explain How to Install Computer Hardware

When you purchase a computer, you should determine an ideal location to use the computer. Select an area that is free from clutter, is not subject to extreme temperatures or water, and is comfortable for you to work. Before you turn on your computer for the first time, you should make sure that all necessary components are included. You should also inspect the computer to make sure it is free from damage.

If you are installing a desktop or all-in-one computer, carefully unpack all components from the box and place them in their desired locations. Connect all components and accessories, such as your keyboard and mouse, and then connect the power. Finally, you can turn on the computer and follow all remaining steps on the screen. Most computer manufacturers include installation instructions with their computers, so be sure to follow any additional steps included in those instructions.

If you are installing a laptop, carefully unpack the laptop and place it in a location next to a power source. It is a good idea to fully charge the laptop's battery before using the device for the first time.

Figure 3-31: Technician repairing a computer

iStock.com/tommaso79

In addition to installing a computer, you might buy peripheral devices, such as a printer or scanner, to connect to the computer. These peripheral devices communicate with the computer through a port. Some devices, called **plug-and-play** devices, will begin functioning properly as soon as you connect them to your computer. Other devices might require that you manually install special software, called a device driver, to work properly. A **device driver** is a program that controls a device attached to your computer, such as a printer, monitor, or video card. If you have to install a program or app for your device to work, make sure you are signed in to the computer with a user account that has the necessary permission to install programs and apps. Some components must be installed inside your computer. If you are uncomfortable or inexperienced in opening a computer and installing or replacing components, contact a professional (**Figure 3-31**).

Devices can also connect to a computer wirelessly. To connect a wireless device to your computer, follow the installation instructions that come with the device.

Maintain Hardware Components

After purchasing a computer, you will want to make sure it runs optimally and is well maintained to guarantee proper performance. This section discusses measuring the performance of computer hardware, troubleshooting problems with hardware and peripherals, and maintaining the hardware and software on your computer.

Measure the Performance of Computer Hardware

When searching for a computer to purchase, you should be able to evaluate the hardware specifications so that you can select the computer that best meets your needs. If you are using a computer for basic tasks such as browsing the web or checking your email, you might not require the same specifications as a user who uses a computer for more compute-intensive tasks such as graphic design or other media development. The processor's **clock speed** measures the speed at which it can execute instructions. Clock speed can be measured in either megahertz (MHz) or gigahertz (GHz). Megahertz specifies millions of cycles per second, while gigahertz specifies billions of cycles per second. A **cycle** is the smallest unit of time a process can measure. The efficiency of a CPU is measured by instructions per cycle (IPC).

The bus speed and width is another factor that affects a computer's performance. As mentioned earlier, a bus is an electronic channel that allows the CPU and various devices inside or attached to a computer to communicate. The **bus width** determines the speed at which data travels, and is also referred to as the **word size**. The wider the bus, the more data that can travel on it. A 64-bit bus, for example, transfers data faster than a 32-bit bus. If you have a fast CPU but the bus speed is slow, that can cause a condition called bottlenecking.

While computer manufacturers advertise performance factors such as clock speed and bus speed, there are other factors that can affect processor performance. For this reason, you should research benchmark test results for the processor(s) you are considering. A **benchmark** is a test run by a laboratory or other organization to determine processor speed and other performance factors. Benchmarking tests compare similar systems performing identical tasks. You typically can find benchmarking information online.

Explain How to Troubleshoot Problems with Hardware and Peripherals

At some point you probably will experience a technology problem with your computer or mobile device that requires troubleshooting. Technology problems that remain unresolved may impact your ability to use your device.

Table 3-5 outlines some common problems you might experience with a computer or mobile device, as well as some recommended solutions.

Table 3-5: Troubleshooting computer hardware problems

Problem	Desktop	Laptop	Tablet	Phone	Recommended solution(s)
Computer or device does not turn on	X	X	X		The computer might be in sleep or hibernate mode; to wake up the computer, try pressing a key on the keyboard, pressing the power button, or tapping the touchscreen if applicable. Unplug the computer and plug it in again.
	X				Make sure power cables are plugged securely into the wall and the back of the computer.
		X	X	X	Make sure the battery is charged if the computer or device is not connected to an external power source. If the battery is charged, connect the external AC adapter and attempt to turn on the computer or device. If the computer or device still does not turn on, the problem may be with the computer or device.
	X	X	X	X	If none of the above options resolves the issue, the power supply or AC adapter might be experiencing problems; contact a professional for assistance.
Battery does not hold a charge or drains very quickly		X	X	X	Verify that the AC adapter used to charge the battery is working properly. If the mobile computer or device can run from the AC adapter without a battery installed, the AC adapter most likely is working properly. If the AC adapter works, it may be time to replace the battery.
Computer issues a series of beeps when turned on	X	X			Refer to your computer's documentation to determine what the beeps indicate, as the computer hardware may be experiencing a problem.
Computer or device turns on, but operating system does not run	X	X	X	X	Disconnect all nonessential peripheral devices, remove all storage media, and then restart the computer or device. Restart the computer or device; if the problem persists, the operating system might need to be restored. If restoring the operating system does not work, the hard drive might be failing.

Table 3-5 Troubleshooting computer hardware problems (*Continued*)

Problem	Desktop	Laptop	Tablet	Phone	Recommended solution(s)
Monitor does not display anything	X				Verify that the monitor is turned on. Verify that the video cable is connected securely to the computer and monitor. Make sure the power cables are plugged securely into the wall and the back of the monitor. Make sure the monitor is set to the correct input source. Restart the computer. If you have access to a spare monitor, see if that monitor will work. If so, your original monitor might be faulty. If not, the problem may be with your computer's hardware or software configuration.
Screen does not display anything		X	X	X	Restart the device. Make sure the device is plugged in or the battery is sufficiently charged.
Keyboard or mouse does not work	X	X	X		Verify that the keyboard and mouse are connected properly to the computer or device. If the keyboard and mouse are wireless, make sure they are turned on and contain new batteries. If the keyboard and mouse are wireless, attempt to pair them again with the computer or wireless receiver. If you have access to a spare keyboard or mouse, see if it will work. If so, your original keyboard or mouse might be faulty. If not, the problem may be with your computer's hardware or software configuration.
		X			Make sure the touchpad is not disabled

Problem	Desktop	Laptop	Tablet	Phone	Recommended solution(s)
Wet keyboard no longer works	X	X			Turn the keyboard upside down to drain the liquid, dab wet areas with a cotton swab, and allow the keyboard to dry.
Speakers do not work	X	X	X	X	Verify that headphones or earbuds are not connected. Make sure the volume is not muted and is turned up on the computer or mobile device.
	X	X			Verify that the speakers are turned on. Make sure the speakers are connected properly to the computer. If necessary, verify that the speakers are plugged in to an external power source.
Hard drive makes noise	X	X			If the computer is not positioned on a flat surface, move it to a flat surface. If something has impacted the hard drive, it might have caused the hard drive to fail. If the problem persists, contact a professional.
Fan contains built-up dust/does not work	X	X			If possible, open the system unit and use a can of compressed air to blow the dust from the fan and away from the system unit.
	X				Remove obvious obstructions that might be preventing the fan from functioning. Verify that the fan is connected properly to the motherboard. If the fan still does not work, it may need to be replaced.

Table 3-5 Troubleshooting computer hardware problems (*Continued*)

Problem	Desktop	Laptop	Tablet	Phone	Recommended solution(s)
Computer or device is too hot	X	X			Verify that the fan or vents are not obstructed. If the fan or vents are obstructed, use a can of compressed air to blow the dust from the fan or vent and away from the computer or device or remove other obstructions.
		X			Purchase a cooling pad that rests below the laptop and protects it from overheating.
			X	X	Exit apps running in the background. Search for and follow instructions how to clear the tablet or phone's cache memory. Run an app to monitor the tablet's or phone's battery performance, and exit apps that require a lot of battery power. Decrease the brightness of the display.
Cannot read from optical disc	X	X			Clean the optical disc and try reading from it again. Try reading from another optical disc. If the second optical disc works, the original disc is faulty. If the second disc does not work, the problem may be with the optical disc drive.
External drive (USB flash drive, optical disc drive, or external hard drive) is not recognized	X	X	X		Remove the drive and insert it into a different USB port, if available. Remove the drive, restart the computer, and insert the drive again. Try connecting the drive to a different computer. If you still cannot read from the drive, it may be faulty.
Program or app does not run	X	X	X	X	Restart the computer or device and try running the program or app again. If feasible, uninstall the program or app, reinstall it, and then try running it again. If the problem persists, the problem may be with the operating system's configuration.

Problem	Desktop	Laptop	Tablet	Phone	Recommended solution(s)
Computer or device displays symptoms of a virus or other malware	X	X	X	X	Make sure your antivirus software is up to date, and then disconnect the computer or device from the network and run antivirus software to attempt to remove the malware. Continue running scans until no threats are detected and then reconnect the computer to the network. If you do not have antivirus software installed, obtain and install a reputable antivirus program or app and then scan your computer in an attempt to remove the malware. You should have only one antivirus program or app installed on your computer or mobile device at one time. If you are unable to remove the malware, take your computer to a professional who may be able to remove the malicious program or app.
Computer or device is experiencing slow performance	X	X	X		Defragment the hard disk.
	X	X			Uninstall programs and apps that you do not need. Verify that your computer or device meets the minimum system requirements for the operating system and software you are running. If possible, purchase and install additional memory (RAM). Run the Optimize Drives feature to maximize free space on your hard drive.
Screen is damaged physically	X	X	X	X	Contact a professional to replace the screen; if the computer or device is covered under a warranty, the repair may be free. Replacing a broken screen on a computer or device might be more costly than replacing the computer or device; consider your options before replacing the screen.

Table 3-5 Troubleshooting computer hardware problems (*Continued*)

Problem	Desktop	Laptop	Tablet	Phone	Recommended solution(s)
Touchscreen does not respond	X	X	X	X	Clean the touchscreen. Restart the computer or device.
Computer or device is wet		X	X	X	Turn off the computer or device, remove the battery, and dry off visible water with a cloth. Fill a plastic bag or box with uncooked rice, submerge the computer or device and battery into the rice so that it is surrounded completely, and then do not turn on the computer or device for at least 24 hours. If the computer or device does not work after it is dry, contact a professional for your options.
Computer or device does not connect to a wireless network	X	X	X	X	Verify that you are within range of a wireless access point. Make sure the information to connect to the wireless network is configured properly on the computer or device. Make sure the wireless capability on the computer or device is turned on. Make sure your router or modem is turned on properly.
Computer or device cannot synchronize with Bluetooth accessories	X	X	X	X	Verify that the Bluetooth device is turned on. Verify that the Bluetooth functionality on your computer or device is enabled. Verify that the computer or device has been paired properly with the accessory. Make sure the Bluetooth device is charged.
Device continuously has poor mobile phone reception			X	X	Restart the device. If you have a protective case, remove the case to see if reception improves. If you are using the device inside a building, try moving closer to a window or open doorway. Contact your wireless carrier for additional suggestions.

Problem	Desktop	Laptop	Tablet	Phone	Recommended solution(s)
Printer does not print	X	X	X	X	Verify that the printer is plugged in and turned on. Verify that the printer is properly connected to the computer either via a wired or wireless connection. Verify that there is paper in the paper tray. Verify that there is sufficient ink or toner.

If you are uncomfortable performing any of the recommended solutions or the solutions are not solving the problem(s), you should consult a professional (independent computer repair company, technical support department, or computer or mobile device manufacturer) for further assessment and resolution. If the problem you are experiencing is not listed, you can perform a search on the Internet to identify potential solutions.

Before attempting to resolve computer or mobile device problems on your own, be sure to follow all necessary safety precautions. Contact a professional if you require additional information.

Explain the Necessary Steps to Maintain Computer Hardware

You should perform tasks periodically to keep your computer hardware in good condition and the software functioning properly. Failure to properly maintain a computer can result in decreasing its lifespan and/or its performance.

Hardware maintenance involves performing tasks to keep the computer's physical components in good working order. Before performing hardware maintenance, you should properly turn off the computer and remove it from its power source. If you are performing hardware maintenance on a laptop, if possible you should remove the battery. Failure to do so might result in damaging the computer's physical components. Recommendations that will help keep your computer functioning properly include:

- Use a damp cloth to clean the screen gently. Do not use any special cleaners to clean the display.
- If the computer has a keyboard, use a can of compressed air to free the keyboard from any dirt and debris. Always hold the can of compressed air upright to avoid damaging the keyboard.
- If the computer has an air vent where a fan removes heat, make sure the vent is free of dust and debris. If the air vent is dirty, contact a trained professional to have it cleaned properly. Do not attempt to clean the air vent yourself, as it is possible that dirt and debris can enter the computer.
- Make sure any media you insert into the computer is clean and free from debris.
- Computers should be used in regulated environments with controlled temperatures and humidity levels. Extreme temperatures or humidity can damage the electronics. As a rule of thumb, if you are uncomfortable because of temperatures that are too high or low, your computer likely should not be operating in that location.
- Computers should not be subject to power fluctuations such as power spikes or power surges. To protect from power fluctuations, consider purchasing and connecting an uninterruptable power supply (UPS) or a surge suppressor. An **uninterruptable power supply (UPS)** is a short-term battery backup that comes on automatically in case of power loss. A **surge suppressor** is a device that prevents power fluctuations from damaging electronic components.

Figure 3-32: Removable media should be in protective cases for transporting

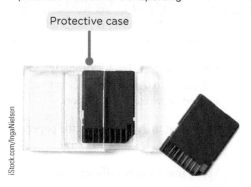

Protective case

- Make sure you have enough free space on your hard drive. When computers run low on available hard drive space, performance can quickly deteriorate. If you are unable to free enough space on your hard drive for the computer to run properly, consider deleting files, purchasing an additional internal hard drive, or purchasing an external hard drive.
- Keep your computer away from dusty or cluttered areas.
- Regularly back up the data on your hard drive, and keep your hard drive away from extreme temperatures.
- Handle removable media with care and, if possible, use protective cases when transporting the media (**Figure 3-32**).

Explain How to Restore a Device and Its Associated Hardware and Software

If you are experiencing a problem with your computer, you might need to take corrective actions such as restoring the operating system, correcting display problems, or updating device drivers.

Figure 3-33: Windows includes a feature to restore your operating system

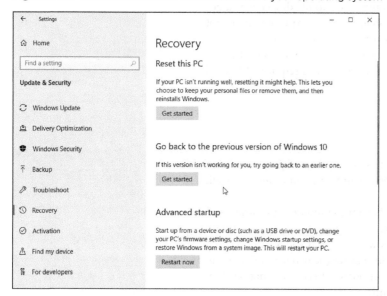

If you are experiencing a problem with your operating system, often characterized by programs and apps not properly starting, persistent error messages, or slow performance, you should consider restoring the operating system. Before you attempt to restore the operating system, you should copy all personal files to a separate storage device such as a USB flash drive or external hard drive. When you **restore** an operating system, you are reverting all settings back to their default, or migrating back to the operating system's previous version. To restore your operating system, review the help documentation and follow the specified steps (**Figure 3-33**). If you want to reinstall Windows but keep your files, use the Reset this PC command. You should still back up your files as a preventative measure.

If you experience problems with your display device, such as it not displaying video output properly, consider trying the following steps to resolve the problem(s):

1. If you are using a desktop computer, make sure the monitor is properly connected to the system unit and to a power source.
2. If the monitor is properly connected to power and the system unit, try connecting a different monitor to the system unit to determine whether the problem is with the monitor or the system unit.
3. If both monitors do not work, try using different power and video cables to see if the original cables were problematic.
4. If you still experience problems, there might be a problem with the video card. The **video card** is a circuit board that processes image signals. Consider taking the computer to a professional for repair.

If you are experiencing issues with other accessories or peripheral devices, you may need to update the device driver. There are two ways to locate and install updated device drivers:

1. Run the update feature within your operating system. When the update is complete, restart the computer to determine whether the device starts functioning properly.
2. Navigate to the device manufacturer's website, and then search for and download the latest software or device drivers for the malfunctioning device. Start the software and follow the instructions on the screen to complete the update.

Summary

In this module, you have learned to categorize the various types of computer hardware. Computer hardware components include the central processing unit (CPU), memory, input devices, and output devices. You also learned how to identify the different types of memory such as random access memory, read-only memory, and virtual memory. In addition, you learned about processor logic and the four steps in the machine cycle: fetching, decoding, executing, and storing. You learned that computers represent data using binary, which consists of 0s and 1s.

Various types of computers exist, including all-in-ones, tablets, mobile devices, and desktop computers. This module reviewed the pros and cons of using each of these types of computers. The benefits of different types of storage, including internal, external, and cloud-based storage, were also discussed. You learned about hardware features that are necessary to consider when purchasing a computer for yourself, such as hardware requirements, selecting a form factor, selecting a platform, and buying add-on devices.

Input and output devices are common types of computer hardware. Types of input devices discussed in this module include keyboards, pointing devices, touchscreens, pen input devices, cameras, scanners, game controllers, and microphones. Types of output devices discussed in this module include monitors, speakers, headphones, projectors, printers, and voice output. In addition to learning about these devices, you also learned the proper steps to install these devices.

Finally, this module has discussed the steps required to maintain and protect hardware components for various types of computers and mobile devices. You can measure the performance of computer hardware by determining a computer's clock speed, bus speed, and bus width. You also learned about benchmarking, and how that can be a fairly accurate representation of how a computer performs. This module also discussed how to restore devices and solve common problems including restoring an operating system, solving display problems, and updating device drivers.

Review Questions

1. (True or False) Flash memory is a type of volatile memory.
2. (True or False) Volatile memory loses its contents when power is removed.
3. (True or False) In an 8-bit coding scheme, 8 bits can represent one character.
4. Which of the following storage devices requires an Internet connection?
   a. internal hard drive
   b. cloud storage
   c. solid state drive
   d. flash memory
5. In which of the following types of computers is the system unit in separate housing from the monitor?
   a. desktop computer
   b. all-in-one computer
   c. laptop computer
   d. tablet
6. (True or False) In general, a high-powered processor is not necessary for a computer that will be used primarily to check email and browse the web.
7. All of the following are pointing devices except:
   a. trackball
   b. touchpad
   c. mouse
   d. touchpointer
8. (True or False) Plotters are small, lightweight printers that easily can be connected to mobile devices.

9. Which of the following tells your computer how to connect to devices you might connect?
   a. device manager
   b. device driver
   c. configuration manager
   d. communication manager
10. (True or False) The speed at which data travels on a bus is referred to as the word size.
11. Under which of the following circumstances might you be most likely to contact a professional to repair your computer or mobile device?
    a. screen is broken
    b. computer cannot synchronize with Bluetooth accessories
    c. computer or device is too hot
    d. printer will not print
12. (True or False) Uninterruptable power supplies and surge suppressors will help protect your computer from power outages.
13. If you are experiencing display problems on your computer, which of the following troubleshooting techniques might you attempt first?
    a. Contact a professional for assistance.
    b. Replace the cables.
    c. Check to see that all cables are properly connected.
    d. Purchase a new monitor.

Discussion Questions

1. When individuals are purchasing a computer, they sometimes might get the most expensive computer they can afford. Why might this not be a good idea?

2. What types of input and output devices would be ideal for a college student completing his or her coursework?

3. Despite how well you might take care of your computer, problems can always arise. When troubleshooting problems you encounter, at what point should you engage a professional for assistance? Why? At what point might you consider purchasing a new computer?

Critical Thinking Activities

1. Wendy Patel is entering college and plans to take the necessary classes to obtain a degree in architecture. Research the programs and apps that Wendy might use in her degree program and recommend a computer with sufficient hardware specifications to adequately support her through the degree program. Provide a link to the computer you locate and justify why you feel the computer will best meet her needs. Why did you choose the central processing unit? Why did you choose the amount of RAM? Why did you choose the storage device?

2. Jason Diaz is a financial advisor who works in an open office with coworkers nearby. Jason advises clients both in person and over the phone, as well as by using videoconferencing.

What types of input and output devices might Jason require on his computer to do his job? Which input and output devices do you feel are necessary, and which ones do you feel would be nice to have? Given the sensitive nature of the information Jason might be displaying and using, are there any other hardware components you might recommend to make sure Jason's clients' information is protected? Justify your answers.

3. You are working part time providing computer support for a veterinarian's office. When you arrive to work one morning, the receptionist informs you that the computer monitor is not displaying anything. List at least three steps you will perform to troubleshoot the problem, and list three possible causes.

Key Terms

all-in-one computer	headphones	projector
arithmetic logic unit (ALU)	headset	random access memory (RAM)
ASCII	input device	read-only memory (ROM)
benchmark	joystick	restore
binary system	keyboard	scanner
bit	laptop	solid state drive (SSD)
bus width	microphone	speakers
byte	mobile device	stylus
camera	motherboard	surge suppressor
central processing unit (CPU)	motion-sensing controller	swap file
clock speed	mouse	tablet
cloud storage	multi-core processor	touchpad
control unit	multitouch screen	touchscreen
cycle	nonvolatile	trackball
dance pad	optical media	Unicode
desktop computer	output device	uninterruptible power supply (UPS)
device driver	paging file	USB hub
digital pen	peripheral device	video card
earbuds	platform	virtual memory
external hard drive	plug-and-play	voice synthesizer
firmware	pointing device	volatile
form factor	port	webcam
game controller	power-on self test (POST)	wheel
gamepad	printer	word size
hard drive	processor cache	

Operating Systems and File Management

When he works outside he adjusts the screen's brightness to avoid glare.

The laptop's operating system controls how Javier accesses the wireless network.

The operating system enables Javier to save files to his laptop and the cloud.

AshTproductions/Shutterstock.com

Javier Esperanza has an internship with an accounting firm, which has provided him with a laptop. The laptop runs Windows 10 as its operating system. Javier uses the apps and utilities provided with Windows to manage the files he stores on his laptop, as well as to share documents with others on OneDrive. Javier has made modifications to the Windows settings to personalize it so that he can work more efficiently.

In This Module

- Explain the pros and cons of different types of operating systems
- Explain how an operating system works
- Personalize a computer operating system, as well as its software and hardware, to increase productivity
- Manage files and folders

IS YOUR COMPUTER or device quick to respond to your instructions? Is it reliable? Do you have tools that enable you to work productively and efficiently? What type of file storage does your computer or device have? The answers to these questions depend on your system software, specifically your operating system.

In this module, you will learn about different types of operating systems and compare options of each type. You will begin to understand how an operating system works to help your computer or device function. You will explore methods to personalize your operating system and program settings to increase your productivity. Lastly, you will learn how to manage the files and folders you store on your computer or device so that you can access them easily.

Compare Operating Systems

Without system software, could you keep track of files, print documents, connect to networks, and manage hardware and other programs? If you answered No, you are correct! When you start your computer or device, system software starts running in the background. Most computers and devices come preloaded with system software, including an operating system. The operating system is critical to using your computer or device.

Differentiate Between an Operating System and System Software

System software is the software that runs a computer, including the operating system and utilities. The operating system and utility programs control the behind-the-scenes operations of a computer or mobile device. An **operating system (OS)** is a program that manages the complete operation of your computer or mobile device and lets you interact with it. An operating system also is called a **platform**. Most programs and apps you run on your computer come in versions specific to your operating system and are optimized to take advantage of the operating system's features.

Suppose you are writing a report and want to save the document to your hard drive. **Table 4-1** shows the role the OS plays as you perform this task.

Table 4-1: Interacting with the operating system

Your task	Role of the operating system
Start a word processing program and open a document	• Starts the word processing program • Provides tools for you to open the document file
Add information to the document	• Manages memory so the computer can run • Saves your unsaved work to temporary storage
Save the document on the hard drive	• Finds the hard drive • Makes sure the hard drive has enough storage space • Saves the document • Stores the location and file name so that you can access the document later

Most operating systems come installed on your computer or device, although it is possible to run an operating system from another medium, such as from a flash drive. You also can run multiple operating systems on some devices.

Differentiate Between Operating Systems

Every computer and device has an operating system. Regardless of the size of the computer or device, most operating systems provide similar functions. Some operating systems also allow users to control a network or administer security. You should be familiar with the functions of your system so that you can take advantage of them to increase your productivity. Standard operating system functions include:

- Starting and shutting down a computer or device
- Managing programs
- Managing memory
- Coordinating tasks
- Configuring devices
- Establishing an Internet connection
- Monitoring performance
- Providing file management
- Updating operating system software
- Monitoring security
- Controlling network access

An operating system also provides a **graphical user interface (GUI)**, which is a collective term for all the ways you interact with the device. A GUI controls how you interact with menus, programs and apps, and visual images such as icons by touching, pointing, tapping, or clicking buttons and other objects to issue commands.

Operating systems also provide **utilities**, which enable you to perform maintenance-type tasks related to managing the computer or device. Utilities are the tools that you use to manage files, search for content or programs, view images, install and uninstall programs and apps, compress and back up files, and maintain the computer or device. Screen savers are another type of utility.

To identify an operating system, you typically state its name and version number, such as Windows 10. Some software manufacturers are doing away with version numbers, and instead offering Software as a Service. **Software as a Service (SaaS)** is software that is distributed online for a monthly subscription or an annual fee. Instead of releasing a new complete version of the program to purchase, the company will provide updates to its subscribers that include fixes for issues or additional functionality. For example, Windows 10 is the last version of Windows that Microsoft plans to release as a standalone version before switching to an SaaS-only model.

Desktop Operating Systems

An operating system installed on a single computer is called a **personal computer (PC) operating system**, or a **desktop operating system** (Table 4-2). Most are single-user operating systems, because only one user interacts with the OS at a time.

Table 4-2: Desktop operating systems

OS	Available for	Notable features
Windows	Desktop computers, laptops, and some tablets	Supports the Cortana virtual assistant, touchscreen input, HoloLens headsets, and built-in apps such as the Microsoft Edge browser
macOS	Macintosh desktop computers and laptops	Includes the Siri virtual assistant, coordination with Apple mobile devices, and cloud file storage
UNIX	Most computers and devices	Multitasking operating system with many versions, as the code is licensed to different developers
Linux	Desktop computers, laptops, and some tablets	Distributed under the terms of a General Public License (GPL), which allows you to copy the OS for your own use, to give to others, or to sell
Chrome OS	Chromebook laptops	Based on Linux, uses the Google Chrome browser as its user interface, and primarily runs **web apps** (an app stored on an Internet server that can be run entirely in a web browser)

If you receive a laptop or access to a computer through your school or workplace, you likely will not have a choice in operating system. However, if you purchase one for yourself, there are several factors to consider in your decision. When selecting an operating system, users compare factors such as available programs and apps, hardware and software support, and security. Depending on the computer or device you select, you may not have a choice in operating systems. Certain computers and devices only run operating systems designed specifically for the computer or device. Before selecting an operating system, be sure to read reviews by experts, as well as user feedback. Determine your needs and priorities to choose the operating system that will help you be productive. Always choose the most updated version of an operating system to take advantage of any new features as well as security settings and fixes.

Another determination when choosing an operating system is open vs. closed source. **Closed source** programs keep all or some of the code hidden, enabling developers to control and profit from the program they create. Closed source programs have standard features and can only be customized using the operating system's tools. Microsoft Windows and macOS are examples of closed source operating systems. **Open source** programs and apps (including operating systems) have no restrictions from the copyright holder regarding modification and redistribution. Users can add functionality and sell or give away their versions to others. Linux is an example of an open source operating system. Proponents of open source programs state that because the code is public, coders can examine, correct, and enhance programs. Some have concerns about unscrupulous programmers adding malicious code that can damage a user's system or be used to gather data without the user's knowledge. Whether you are choosing an open or closed source operating system, program, or app, be sure to research carefully and read reviews to ensure you are getting the highest quality program.

Server Operating Systems

A **server operating system** (Table 4-3) is a multiuser operating system because it controls a single, centralized server computer that supports many users on networked computers. A server operating system manages the network. It also controls access to network resources, such as network printers. Although desktop operating systems include network capability, server operating systems are designed specifically to support all sizes of networks. Many also enable virtualization. **Virtualization** is the practice of sharing computing resources, such as servers or storage devices, among computers and devices on a network. Unless you are a network administrator, you likely will not knowingly interact with a server operating system, but you should be familiar with the capabilities of the operating system being used for this purpose.

Table 4-3: Server operating systems

OS	Notable features
Windows Server	The server version of Windows. It includes advanced security tools and a set of programs called Internet Information Services that manage web apps and services.
macOS Server	Supports all sizes of networks and servers. One unique feature is that it lets authorized users access servers using their iPhones or other Apple devices.
UNIX	A multipurpose operating system that can run on a desktop PC or a server. Many **web servers**, which are Internet computers that store webpages and deliver them to your computer or device, use UNIX because it is a powerful, flexible operating system.

Mobile Operating Systems

Smartphones, tablets, and other mobile devices use a **mobile operating system**. A mobile operating system has features similar to those of a desktop operating system, but is focused on the needs of a mobile user and the capabilities of the device. A mobile operating system works especially well with mobile device features such as touchscreens, voice recognition, and Wi-Fi networks. They also are designed to run using the limited memory of most mobile devices, and the display works with smaller screen sizes.

Mobile devices are optimized to perform functions common to mobile users. These include having video and photo cameras, media players, speech recognition, GPS, wireless capabilities, rotating screen displays that adjust when you switch orientation of your device's screen, and text messaging. You likely use all of these features on a frequent basis for entertainment, travel, and communication. **Table 4-4** shows popular mobile operating systems, and **Figure 4-1** shows examples of smartphones running Android and iOS.

Table 4-4: Mobile operating systems

OS	Notable features
Android	Developed by Google based on Linux, and designed to be run on many types of smartphones and tablets
iOS	Runs only on Apple devices, including the iPhone, iPad, and iPod; derived from macOS

Figure 4-1: Smartphones running iOS and Android operating systems

iStockPhoto.com/Borchee, iStockPhoto.com/gece33

Identify Desktop Components

All operating systems include similar features. The main workspace is called the **desktop** (**Figure 4-2**). The desktop contains icons for programs and files, as well as toolbars, taskbars, menus, and buttons you can use to start programs and apps. A notification area displays the date and time, as well as shortcuts to utilities such as audio controls and network connections.

Figure 4-2: Windows 10 and macOS desktops

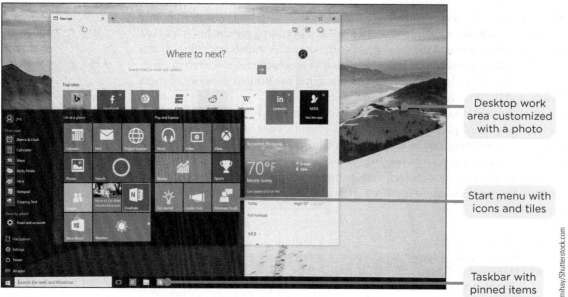

Desktop work area customized with a photo

Start menu with icons and tiles

Taskbar with pinned items

omihay/Shutterstock.com

Windows

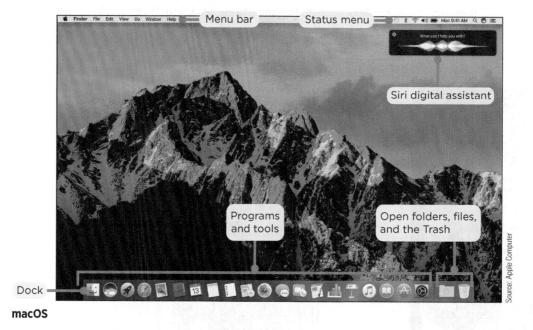

Menu bar

Status menu

Siri digital assistant

Programs and tools

Open folders, files, and the Trash

Dock

Source: Apple Computer

macOS

In any operating system, a **window** is a rectangular-shaped work area that displays an app or a collection of files, folders, and tools. Every time you open a new program or file, a new window opens. You can switch between windows to access different information or resources.

How do you make a computer do what you want it to do? One way is to use a menu. A **menu** is a list of related items, including folders, applications, and commands. Many menus organize commands on submenus. Another feature that enables you to make choices is a dialog box. **Dialog boxes** are windows with controls that let you tell the operating system how you want to complete a command. Menus and dialog boxes enable you to access a program or app's features.

A **file** is a collection of information stored on your computer, such as a text document, spreadsheet, photo, or song. Files can be divided into two categories: data and executable. A **data file** contains words, numbers, and pictures that you can manipulate. For example, a spreadsheet, a database, a presentation, and a word processing document all are data files. An **executable file** contains the instructions your computer or device needs to run programs and apps. Unlike a data file, you cannot open and read an executable file. You run it to perform a task, such as opening a program or app.

File format refers to the organization and layout of data in a file. The file format determines the type or types of programs and apps that you can use to open and display or work with a file. Some files only can be opened in the program with which they were created. Others, such as graphics files, can be opened in multiple programs or apps. A **file extension** is three- or four-letter sequence, preceded by a period, at the end of a file name that identifies the file as a particular type of document, such as .docx (Microsoft Word document), or .jpg (a type of graphic file). When you save a file, the program or app assigns the file extension. Table 4-5 shows some common file extensions by file type.

Table 4-5: Common file extensions

File type	Extensions
Microsoft Office	.docx (Word), .xlsx (Excel), .pptx (PowerPoint)
Text file	.txt, .rtf
Webpage	.htm or .html, .xml, .asp or .aspx, .css
Graphics	.jpg, .png, .tif

Files are stored in folders. A **folder** is a named location on a storage medium that usually contains related documents. You can think of a digital folder as similar to a physical file folder in which you store paper documents. You name the folder so that you know what it contains, and in the folder you store related files. An operating system comes with tools to manage files and folders. These tools allow you to create new, named folders; choose the location of folders; move files between folders; and create a folder hierarchy that includes subfolders (Figure 4-3). Every file you save will have a destination folder—by choosing the correct folder, or adding new folders, you can help keep your files accessible and organized.

A **library** is a special folder that catalogs specific files and folders in a central location, regardless of where the items are actually stored on your device. Library files might include pictures, music, documents, and videos. Your operating system most likely comes with a few libraries. You can customize your libraries to add additional folders, and include files from the Internet or a network. Libraries are helpful to find all files of a certain type, no matter where they are located on your computer or device.

Figure 4-3: Creating a folder hierarchy helps keep files and folders organized

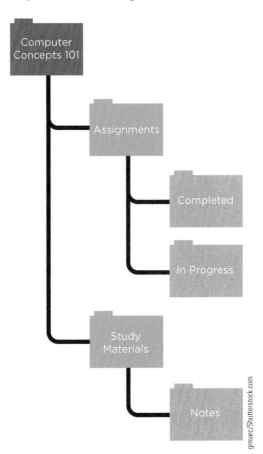

gmarc/Shutterstock.com

Explain How an Operating System Works

An operating system takes care of the technical tasks of running the computer or device while you work on school or professional projects, watch videos, connect with friends, or play games. The operating system is the essential software or app on your computer or device. Operating systems process data, manage memory, control hardware, and provide a user interface. You interact with the operating system to start programs, manage files, get help, customize the user interface, and work with hardware.

The Purpose of an Operating System

The operating system is responsible for coordinating the resources and activities on a computer. It is the go-between for you and the computer—it accepts your instructions and data, and provides information from the system to you. The operating system also manages interactions between hardware and software. For example, if you want to print a flyer you created in your word processing program, the operating system establishes a connection to the printer, sends the flyer document to the printer, and lets other software know the printer is busy until it finishes printing the flyer. During this process, the operating system directs internal components such as the processor, RAM, and storage space to manage and complete its task.

How an Operating System Manages Memory

The purpose of memory management is to optimize the use of a computer or device's internal memory to allow the computer or device to run more efficiently. **Memory** consists of electronic components that store instructions waiting to be executed by the processor, data needed by those instructions, and the results of processing the data into information. A byte is the basic storage unit in memory. Computers and devices contain two types of memory: volatile and nonvolatile. **Volatile memory** is temporary, and loses its contents when the power is turned off. **Nonvolatile memory** is permanent, and its contents remain on the computer or device even when it is turned off.

RAM is the most common type of volatile memory. **RAM (random access memory)** is the storage location that temporarily stores open apps and document data while a computer or device is on. The operating system assigns data and instructions to an area of memory while they are being processed. It carefully monitors the contents of memory, and releases items when the processor no longer requires them. Frequently used instructions and data are stored in a **cache**, which is a temporary storage area designed to help speed up processing time.

Every program or app, including the operating system, requires RAM. The more RAM a device has, the more efficiently it runs. If several programs or apps are running simultaneously, your computer or device might use up its available RAM. When this happens, the computer or device may run slowly. The operating system can allocate a portion of a storage medium, such as a hard disk, to become virtual memory to function as additional RAM.

Virtual memory is the capability of an operating system to temporarily store data on a storage medium until it can be "swapped" into RAM. The area of the hard drive used for virtual memory is thus called a swap file because it swaps data, information, and instructions between memory and storage. A page is the amount of data and program instructions that can swap at a given time. The technique of swapping items between memory and storage is called paging. Paging is a time-consuming process. When an operating system spends more of its time paging instead of executing apps, the whole system slows down and it is said to be thrashing. You may be able to adjust the settings on your operating system to free up memory in order to enable your computer or device to run more quickly.

ROM and flash memory are two common types of nonvolatile memory. **ROM (read-only memory)** refers to memory chips that store permanent data and instructions. The data on most ROM chips cannot be modified. In addition to computers and mobile devices, many peripheral devices, such as printers, contain ROM. **Flash memory** is a type of nonvolatile memory that can be erased electronically and rewritten. Flash memory chips also store data and programs on many mobile and peripheral devices, such as smartphones and digital cameras. Most laptops and desktop computers have the option to add memory and storage. To increase the memory on a smartphone, you can add flash memory in the form of microSD cards. This is something many users take advantage of, especially ones who take lots of high-resolution photos and videos for professional or personal use.

Steps in the Boot Process

To start an operating system, you simply turn on the computer or device. Before you can interact with the operating system, the computer or device goes through the **boot process**, which triggers a series of steps and checks as the computer loads the operating system. The boot process includes the following steps:

1. The computer or device receives power from the power supply or battery, and sends it to the circuitry.

2. The processor begins to run the bootstrap program, which is a special built-in startup program.

3. The **bootstrap program** executes a series of tests to check the components, including the RAM, keyboard, and storage, and identifies connected devices and checks their settings.

4. Once the tests are completed successfully, the computer or device loads the operating system files into RAM, including the kernel. The **kernel** is the core of an operating system. It manages memory, runs programs, and assigns resources.

5. The computer or device loads the system configuration information, prompts you for user verification if necessary, and loads all startup programs, such as antivirus programs or apps.

The boot process starts automatically when you turn on your computer or device. You cannot use the computer or device until the boot process is complete. Depending on your operating system, you may be able to instruct that certain programs or apps you frequently use be started at the same time as your operating system.

How Operating Systems Manage Input and Output

Input is any data and instructions entered into the memory of a device. You can input data and instructions in many ways, including interacting with your touchscreen, or using a keyboard. **Figure 4-4** shows examples of input devices.

Other input devices include:
- Card readers and data collection devices
- Game controllers and motion input devices
- Microphones and webcams
- Scanners
- Touch pads or a mouse

Once data is in memory, the computer or device interprets it, and the system software executes instructions to process the data into information. Instructions used for processing data can be in the form of a program or app, commands, and user responses. The information processed into a useful form is referred to as **output**. Output formats include text, graphics, audio, video, or any combination of these. For example, a webpage typically combines text and graphics, and may include audio and video as well. Output displays on a screen, or can be printed. Other output methods include speakers, headphones, and interactive whiteboards. Do you want to print the processed information? Post it to social media or a website? Send it electronically as an attachment? Think of output as the goal of input. This will help you determine the program, device, or display on which you enter input and instruct the operating system where to direct the output. **Figure 4-5** shows examples of output devices.

Figure 4-4: Card readers, game controllers, and headsets with microphones all are examples of input devices

Figure 4-5: Screen displays, printers, and speakers all are examples of output devices

If a computer or device is slow in accepting or providing input or output, the operating system uses buffers. A **buffer** is an area of memory that stores data and information waiting to be sent to an input or output device. Placing data into a buffer is called **spooling**. An example of spooling is when a document is sent to the buffer while it waits for the printer to be available. By sending data to a buffer, the operating system frees up resources to perform other tasks while the data waits to be processed.

Personalize an Operating System to Increase Productivity

When you start using a computer or device, the operating system and related software and hardware have default settings. **Default settings** are standard settings that control how the screen is set up and how a document looks when you first start typing. As you continue to work with your computer or device, you may decide to customize the settings to be more productive.

Customize System Software

Every operating system has its own tools for customization. For example, Windows uses the Windows Settings dialog box. Operating systems allow you to make adjustments such as:

- Changing the brightness of the screen
- Adding a desktop theme, which is a predefined set of elements such as background images and colors
- Adjusting the screen resolution, which controls how much content you can see on a screen without scrolling
- Adding a sound scheme, which associates sounds such as a bell chime with an event, such as closing a window
- Pinning frequently used apps to the taskbar for easy access
- Selecting items to appear in the Notification area

You also can use these tools to link your smartphone to your computer, uninstall apps, add accounts, manage your network connections, and adjust privacy settings.

On a Windows machine, you use the Settings dialog box. To open the Settings dialog box, click the Start button on the Windows taskbar, and then click the Settings icon. In the Windows Settings dialog box (**Figure 4-6**), click an option to access further options. For example, if you click System, you can adjust settings such as the display, sounds, power, battery, storage, and more.

Figure 4-6: Windows Settings dialog box

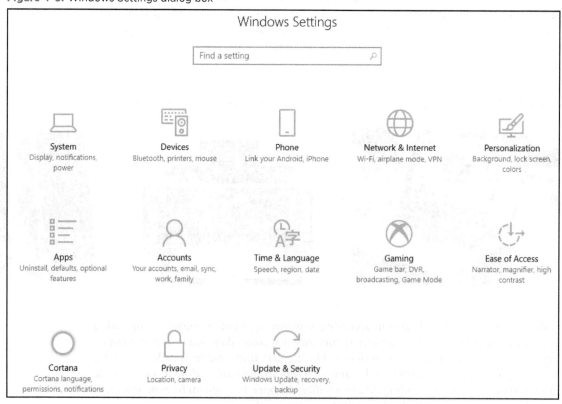

You also can customize the desktop by moving the taskbar, creating and organizing icons for apps and files, and more. In addition, you can create links to files and apps called **shortcuts**. Shortcuts do not place the actual file, folder, or app on the desktop—it still remains in the location where it is saved on your computer or device. A shortcut merely allows you to access the object from the desktop without going through a file manager or a program menu such as the Start menu.

Customize Hardware Using System Software

A **pointing device** is a hardware device that lets you interact with your computer by controlling the movement of the pointer on your computer screen; examples include a mouse, trackball, touchpad, pointing stick, on-screen touch pointer, tablet, or for touch-enabled devices, your hand or finger. You can change the settings of your pointing device. For example, you can switch the mouse buttons if you are left-handed, or adjust the sensitivity of your touchpad. Windows enables you to change these options in the Settings dialog box (**Figure 4-7**).

Figure 4-7: Changing the settings of a pointing device

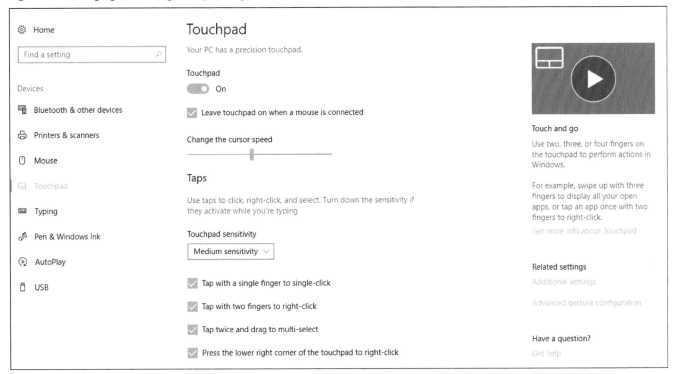

On a desktop computer or laptop, the keyboard is the main input device. A **keyboard** contains not only characters such as letters, numbers, and punctuation, but also keys that can issue commands. You can adjust the keyboard settings to change the commands associated with certain keys, and other modifications, including:

- Controlling the pointing device with the keyboard by using the arrow and other keys
- Changing the language or dialect associated with the keyboard
- Creating new keyboard shortcuts to commands, or enabling sticky keys, which allow you to press keyboard shortcuts one key at a time instead of simultaneously
- Adjusting the settings for toggle keys, for example the CAPS LOCK key, which turn a feature on or off each time a user clicks or presses it

Manage Desktop Windows

When you open an app, file, or folder, it appears on the desktop in a window. Most windows share common elements (**Figure 4-8**):

- The center area of the window displays its contents.
- The title bar at the top displays the name of the app, file, or folder shown in the window.
- A **Maximize button** and **Minimize button** on the title bar enable you to expand a window so that it fills the entire screen or reduce a window so that it only appears as an icon on the taskbar. A **Close button** closes the open window, app, or document. The **Restore Down button** reduces a window to its last non-maximized size.
- Some windows include a ribbon, toolbar, or menu bar that contains text, icons, or images you select to perform actions and make selections.
- Windows also can include vertical and horizontal scroll bars that you drag to display contents currently out of view.

Figure 4-8: Common window elements

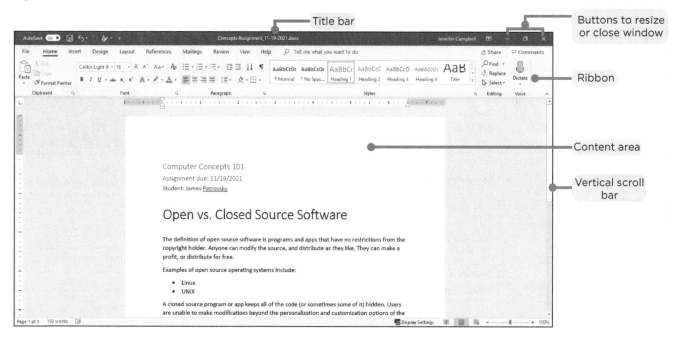

When you have multiple windows, files, and apps open at a time, the windows can appear side-by-side or stacked. Most mobile devices only display stacked windows. The **active window** is the window you are currently using, which appears in front of any other open windows. The steps to switch between windows depends on the type of device or operating system you are running.

- On a mobile device, you might have a button near the Home button that displays all open windows in a stack. When you select it, it displays the stack of open windows and apps. You can select a window to make it the active window, close individual windows, or close all open windows.

Figure 4-9: Apple Dock

Icons on the Dock

Source: Apple Computer

macOS

- On a computer, you can click an icon on the Windows taskbar or the Dock on an Apple computer (**Figure 4-9**). You also can use keyboard shortcuts to cycle through thumbnails of open windows.

You can use two types of windows on a desktop: a **program window** displays a running program; a **folder window** displays the contents of a folder, drive, or device. To start a Windows program, you click the Start button on the taskbar, and then click the program name. To start a Mac program, click the Launchpad (rocket) icon on the dock, then click the app icon. Or, for either Mac or Windows, you can click a shortcut to the app on the desktop. To open a folder window, open your system's folder management tool, such as File Explorer or Finder, and then navigate to the folder you want. To close any type of window, tap or click its Close button.

You can rearrange windows on a computer's desktop to work effectively and to access other items on the desktop. To move a window, point to its title bar, and then drag the window to its new location. To resize a window to display more or less of its content, point to a border or corner of the window, then drag the resizing pointer to make it smaller or larger. Windows and other desktop operating systems allow you to drag a window to the left or right side of the screen., where it "snaps" to fill that half of the screen and displays remaining open windows as thumbnails you can click to fill the other half of the screen.

Use Administrative Tools

An operating system controls your computer by managing its **resources**, which are the components required to perform work, such as the processor, RAM, storage space, and connected devices. The operating system tracks the names and locations of files, as well as empty storage areas where you can save new files. It alerts you if it detects a resource problem, such as too many programs or apps are open for the memory to handle, or the printer is not turned on, or if your hard drive is out of space. To manage RAM resources, an operating system keeps track of the apps, processes, and other tasks the system performs. Microsoft Windows, for example, displays this information in the Windows Task Manager dialog box (**Figure 4-10**). You can open your computer or device's version of the task manager to view running programs and see the percentage of RAM being used. You can shut down programs and apps in the task manager to free up RAM.

GUIs are based on graphical objects, where each object represents a task, command, or object. To interact with a GUI, you tap, click, double-click, or perform some action with tiles, buttons, and icons (**Figure 4-11**).

Figure 4-10: Task Manager

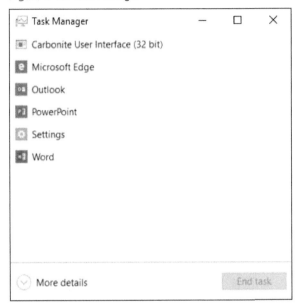

- A **tile** is a shaded rectangle, such as on the Windows Start menu, that represents an app or other resource.
- An **icon** is a small picture that represents a program, file, or hardware device.
- A **button** is a graphic that you click to execute commands you need to work with an app, such as on a toolbar, taskbar, or the ribbon.

Figure 4-11: Windows tiles, buttons, and icons

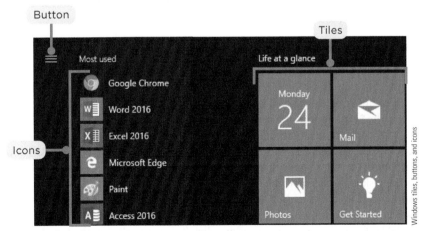

Adjust Power Settings

You may keep your computer or device running constantly, or you may choose to shut it down, either to save power or prevent it being shut down suddenly and unexpectedly, such as by a thunderstorm or battery issue. Operating systems provide shut down options so that you can close programs and processes properly. You can instruct the device to completely shut down, which closes all files and apps, and turns off the power. Some operating systems have a Sleep option to use low power instead of shutting down. Sleep stores the current state of open programs and files, saving you time when you resume using your device.

Since you tend to keep your desktop computer or laptop plugged in while in use, battery life is a bigger concern with mobile devices. You can switch to a low power mode, which limits data usage, dims the screen brightness, and makes other adjustments to slow down battery usage. You also can purchase a replacement battery to switch when your battery power gets low or a portable charger you can plug in with a USB cord to charge your device.

Use Utilities

Regardless of the operating system you're using, if your computer starts to slow down or act erratically, you can use a utility to diagnose and repair the problem. A common solution for Windows desktop systems is to run a **disk cleanup utility**, which finds and removes unnecessary files, such as temporary Internet files or files in the Recycle Bin. Disk optimization utilities free up disk space by reorganizing data.

The Recycle Bin, or Trash folder, is another type of disk utility. This folder stores files you designate to be deleted. When you move a file to the Recycle Bin or Trash, it still takes up storage space, but no longer appears in the folder or location where it was created. The file only is permanently deleted when you empty the folder or run a disk cleanup utility. To avoid wasting time searching for files you have saved, or to manage file locations and sizes, you can use file utilities. **Table 4-6** lists examples of file utilities.

Table 4-6: File management tools

Tool	Purpose
File management	Gives you an overview of stored files and lets you open, rename, delete, move, and copy files and folders
Search tool	Finds files that meet criteria you specify, such as characters in a file name, or the saved date
File compression	Reduces the size of a file to take up less storage space; compressed files often have a .zip file extension and need to be decompressed or unzipped before they can be opened

Customize an Operating System

You can make adjustments to your operating system to make it look and work the way you want to. In Windows, you use the Settings app and Control Panel. **Control Panel** is collection of utility programs that determine how Windows appears and performs on your computer. The **Settings app** contains touch-friendly categories of the most commonly used Windows settings; more advanced settings are found in the Control Panel. Many settings can be adjusted using either tool, for example, changing the desktop background to a picture, pattern, or color. You can change the properties or characteristics of other objects, such as the taskbar, Start menu, and more.

Figure 4-12: A menu

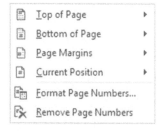

Windows includes menus that enable you to access commands. Menus are organized into categories that are easily identifiable, including File, Print, View, Help, and more (**Figure 4-12**). To open a menu in a window, click it on the toolbar at the top of the window. If a menu includes sub-items, you will see a triangle. Point to the triangle to view sub-items. To instruct the computer or device to complete an action, click it on the menu. Another type of menu is a shortcut menu. A **shortcut menu** is a list of frequently used commands that relate to an object, typically displayed by right-clicking; the commands on a shortcut menu are related to the item you right-clicked.

Some menu commands open a dialog box in which you can select options. For example, when you save or open a file, a dialog box opens (**Figure 4-13**). Dialog box controls include:

- Option buttons: round buttons that present one choice. Also called a radio button.
- Check boxes: square boxes that present a yes/no choice and displays a check mark or x when selected.
- List boxes: lists of options that appear when you click arrows in a dialog box. Some list boxes allow you to make multiple selections.

Figure 4-13: A dialog box

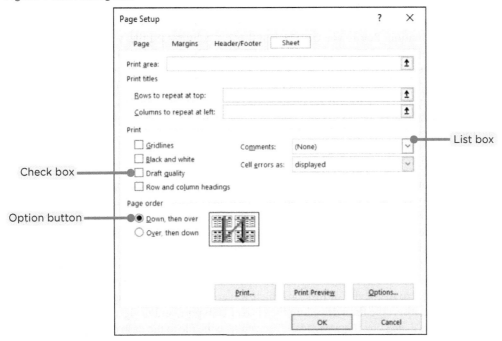

Run More than One Operating System

A **virtual machine** enables a computer or device to run another operating system in addition to the one installed. You might want to enable a virtual machine if you have an app that is incompatible with your current operating system, or to run multiple operating systems on one computer. To run a virtual machine, you need a program or app that is specifically designed to set up and manage virtual machines. You also will need access to installation files for the operating system you want to run on the virtual machine. The virtual machine runs separately in a section of the hard disk called a partition. You can only access one partition of a hard disk at a time.

Manage User Accounts

User accounts identify the resources, such as apps and storage locations, a user can access when working with the computer. User accounts protect your computer against unauthorized access. A user account includes information such as the user name or ID, and a password. You can set preferences for each user account on your computer or device, as well as set permissions to certain folders or files. A standard user account is designed for the everyday user, who will be using the computer or device for work or recreation. An **administrator account** provides full access to the computer. Additional responsibilities associated with an administrator account include installing programs and apps, adjusting security settings, and managing network access. On a computer you use at your home, you likely will not have a separate administrator account—the main user account will have administrator capabilities. On a networked computer, such as at your school or workplace, you will not have access to the administrator account.

Manage Files and Folders

There are many ways to manage files and folders on your computer or device. You can change or view the properties of a file, compress a file to save storage space, move or rename a file or folder, and more.

Compress and Uncompress Files

File size is usually measured in **kilobytes (KB)** (thousands of bytes of data), **megabytes (MB)** (millions of bytes of data), or **gigabytes (GB)** (billions of bytes of data). The more data, the larger the file, and the more storage space it takes up.

You often need to compress files and folders before you share or transfer them. For example, by attaching a compressed file to an email message the smaller file travels faster to its destination. Before you can open and edit a compressed file, you need to extract or uncompress it. Desktop operating systems offer tools to compress and uncompress files. Mobile operating systems do not always include these by default, but you can install them.

To compress a file or folder, select it in your operating system's file management tool, and then instruct the tool to zip or compress the file. To uncompress, double-click the file in the file management tool, and either drag selected files to another folder, or instruct the tool to extract all files into a new folder.

Save Files to Folders and File Systems

The first time you save a file, you need to name it. In Windows, instructing the computer to save a new file opens the Save As dialog box or screen, depending on the program or app. Save As includes controls that let you specify where to store the file, and what file name to use. Navigate to the correct folder on your computer or device, or to another location such as a flash drive or cloud folder. Type the file name, select the file extension if necessary, and then click Save.

The advantage of using a flash drive is that you can remove it from your computer or device, and then use it on a different computer or device. Saving a file to a flash drive means you are not saving it to the device or disk on which you are creating or editing it. To save a file to a flash drive, insert the flash drive into the correct USB port, and navigate to the flash drive in the Save As dialog box (**Figure 4-14**). Once you save the file to the flash drive, you can remove the flash drive, and then insert it into a new device or computer and make any edits you like.

Figure 4-14: Save As dialog box

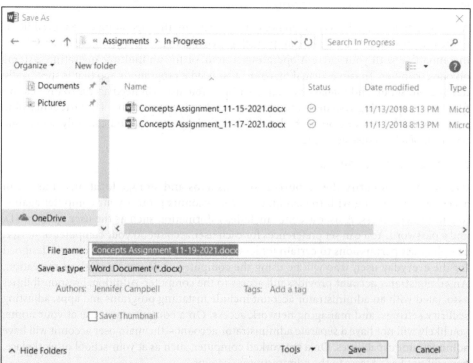

Besides saving files to your hard drive or on a flash drive, you can save them in the cloud. The **cloud** is a storage area located on a server that you access through the Internet or a network. You can upload files to cloud storage to share them with others or to back up your files to a secure, offsite location. You can access files stored on the cloud from any device connected to the Internet. To access a cloud storage location, you may need to download an app, or create an account. Popular cloud storage apps include Dropbox, Microsoft OneDrive, Google Drive, and iCloud. You can save a file to OneDrive from within any Microsoft Office program if you have the right permissions.

If you are creating or editing a file saved to your computer, you should save it frequently so that you don't lose your work. Files you work on using a web app, such as Google Docs or Office 365, save changes as you make them. To save a file with the same name, use the Save command. To save a file with a new name or in a new location, use the Save As or Save a Copy command to reopen the Save As or Save a Copy dialog box, where you can edit the file name or choose a new location to which to save the file.

Determine File Properties

Every file has properties such as its name, type, location, and size (**Figure 4-15**). File properties also include the dates when the file was created, modified, and last accessed. The modified date is useful If you have several versions of a file and want to identify the most recent version. The operating system assigns some properties to files, such as type or format, and updates other properties, such as date, size, and location. Some file types have unique properties. For example, an image might contain information about the dimensions (size) of the image, while a song or media file might include the artist(s) names.

Figure 4-15: Viewing file properties

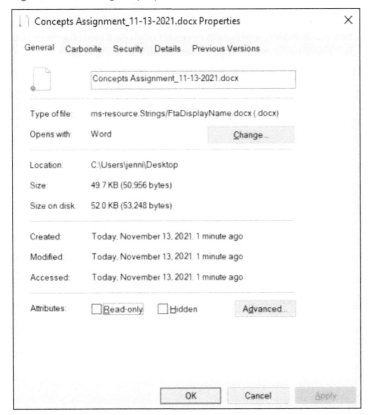

You can view a file's properties to determine information not shown in the file manager, such as the original creation date, the program used to create the file, and more.

Manage File Names and File Placement

Every file on a computer or device has a name. When you save a file, you must give it a name that follows rules called file-naming conventions. Each operating system has its own file-naming conventions. For example, Windows file-names contain up to 255 characters, but cannot include some symbols, such as asterisks or slashes. Only the colon (:) is a prohibited character in macOS.

Most file names contain an extension that tells about its contents, such as the type of platform or app on which the file can be used. File name extensions are added automatically when you save a file, but you can change the extension in some cases. While you can have many files on your computer or device that have the same name, each folder can only include one file with the same name of the same type. To differentiate a version of a file without overwriting the original, you could add additional characters such as numbers, the date, or the initials of the person who modified the file. In general, you should be specific when naming files. A file name should identify the content and purpose of the file, as well as any other information, such as whether the file is a draft or final.

If you want to copy or move files from one location to another, you must first select the files. You can select them from a file management tool, the desktop, or another location. You can select multiple files at once, or just a single file. One method of copying or moving files is to use the **Clipboard**, which is a temporary Windows storage area that holds the selections you copy or cut so you can use them later. The Clipboard saves the file or folder from the source file or folder until you paste it into the destination file or folder. You also can drag files and folders between or within file management tool windows.

You open a saved file using the same techniques as when saving the file, except you use a different dialog box or window. You can locate a file in Windows using File Explorer, or the Finder in macOS. From within a program or app, you can use the Open dialog box to navigate to the folder where a file you want to open is stored.

To open a saved file, make sure you have access to its location. If it is not located on your computer or device, insert the flash drive where it is stored, or connect to a network to access a cloud folder. Navigate to the file's location using the file manager or using the Open dialog box from within a program or app. Locate the folder, and double-click it or select it and click the Open button. When you double-click a file, the file opens.

Manage Folder Names and Folder Placement

You can create a new folder in a file manager such as File Explorer or Finder. For example, you might want to add a folder to your Pictures folder for photos you took during spring break (**Figure 4-16**).

Figure 4-16: Creating a new folder

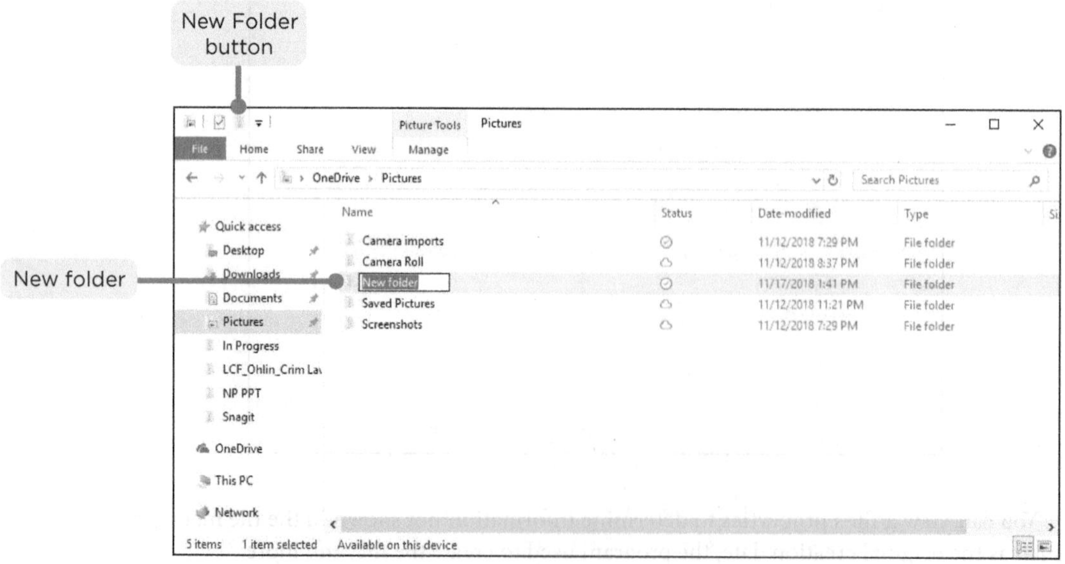

To create a folder, click the New folder button in your file manager. The folder name by default is "New folder." To rename the folder something meaningful, select the folder and click it again to make it editable. Type the new name, then press ENTER or click away from the folder. Folder names should identify the content and purpose of the folder, as well as any other relevant information.

Within your file manager, you can move, copy, and delete folders. Moving or copying a folder affects all of the contents of the folder. To move a folder, select it and drag it to its new location. To copy a folder, use a keyboard shortcut (such as CTRL+C) to create a new copy, or press and hold a key (CTRL or COMMAND) and then drag it to its new location. To delete a selected folder, press DELETE. Deleting a folder moves it to the Recycle Bin or Trash folder, where you can permanently delete it or restore it to its original location if you change your mind.

Organize Files Using File Management Tools

You can use a file manager to reorder, move, or navigate between folders. The Windows 10 file manager is called File Explorer (**Figure 4-17**), and the macOS file manager is called the Finder. When you open the file manager you have access to frequently or recently opened files and folders, favorite files and folders, and the main folders on your computer or device. You can use the search tool to locate files and folders by file name, content, date, and more. To navigate to a folder, you need to locate it using the search tool or by opening a main folder, then opening subfolders until you get to the folder in which the file(s) you need are located. By giving your files descriptive names and putting like subfolders together in a folder, you can more easily locate the files and folders you need.

Figure 4-17: Windows File Explorer

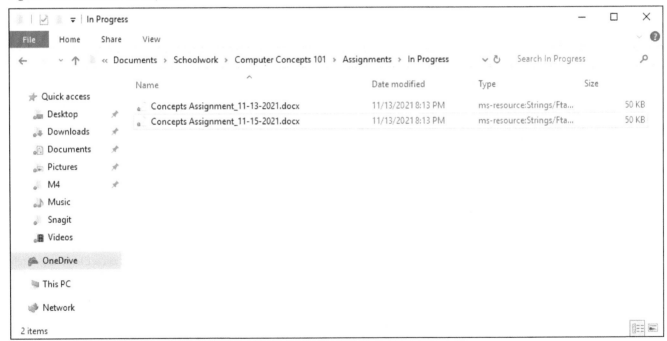

Summary

In this module you have learned that system software is the software that runs a computer, including the operating system and utilities. The operating system manages the complete operation of your computer or device and lets you interact with it. Operating systems come in three basics types: desktop operating systems, server operating systems, and mobile operating systems.

Every program or app requires RAM, which is the volatile and temporary storage for open apps and data. An operating system uses buffers to manage the process of turning input into output.

You can customize elements of system software, including the brightness or resolution of the screen and adding a theme. You also can use the operating system to customize hardware, such as the keyboard or pointing device, and to manage and work with windows.

An operating system controls the system resources, such as the processor, storage space, and connected devices. User accounts identify the resources a user can access.

You can compress files to save space or make them easier to send via email. You can save files to your hard disk, a flash drive, or the cloud. Every file has properties, such as its name, type, location, and size. Within your file manager, you can move, copy, and delete folders.

Review Questions

1. (True or False) An operating system is a program that manages the complete operation of your computer or mobile device and lets you interact with it.

2. GUI stands for _____ user interface.
   a. Google
   b. graphical
   c. government
   d. general

3. (True or False) A data file contains the instructions your computer or device needs to run programs and apps.

4. (True or False) The operating system manages interactions between hardware and software.

5. Which of the following is NOT true about RAM?
   a. Every program and app requires RAM.
   b. The system can assign virtual memory to function as RAM.
   c. RAM is nonvolatile memory.
   d. RAM stores open apps and document data while a computer or device is on.

6. (True or False) The kernel is the core of an operating system.

7. _____ is any data and instructions entered into the memory.
   a. Input
   b. Information
   c. Output
   d. Objection

8. (True or False) A shortcut icon puts the actual file, folder, or app on the desktop, removing it from the location where it is saved on your computer or device

9. (True or False) CAPS LOCK is a sticky key.

10. The _____ window is the window you are currently using, which appears in front of any other open windows.
    a. active
    b. forward
    c. native
    d. default

11. (True or False) When you move a file to the Recycle Bin or Trash, it is permanently deleted.

12. Which of the following units measure millions of bytes of data?
    a. kilobytes
    b. megabytes
    c. gigabytes
    d. terabytes

13. (True or False) When you work on a file using a web app, changes are saved as you make them.

14. (True or False) File properties are the same no matter what type of file.

15. What is the temporary Windows storage area that holds items you copy or cut called?
    a. the cloud
    b. the buffer
    c. the Library
    d. the Clipboard

16. (True or False) Moving or copying a folder affects all of the contents of the folder.

17. (True or False) When you open the file manager you have access to frequently or recently opened files and folders, favorite files and folders, and the main folders on your computer or device.

Discussion Questions

1. What characteristics are common among operating systems? List types of operating systems, and examples of each. How does the device affect the functionality of an operating system?

2. Discuss how an operating system manages the computer's memory. Why is this important?

3. What types of customizations have you or would you make to your operating system, and why?

4. What can you determine about a file by looking at its properties?

Critical Thinking Activities

1. Sarah Jones is a coder who is working with a team to create a new mobile operating system. At their last meeting, the team discussed whether to make the code open source or closed source. What are benefits to each for the developer and for the user? What responsibility does the developer have to ensure the quality of an open source program?

2. You are a teaching assistant for an introductory computer concepts course at your local community college. The instructor asks you to prepare a lecture on input and output. What is the role of the operating system to manage and work with each?

3. Jeremy Aronoff has purchased a new laptop. He wants to customize the operating system to meet his needs. What types of tools should he use, and what can he do with each?

4. You work with a lot of different documents in your internship with a software development company. What kinds of actions can you take to keep your files and folders organized? Discuss the importance of file naming, folder names, and folder structure in keeping yourself organized.

Key Terms

active window
administrator account
Android
boot process
bootstrap program
buffer
button
cache
Chrome OS
Clipboard
Close button
closed source
cloud
Control Panel
data file
default settings
desktop
desktop operating system
dialog box
disk cleanup utility
executable file
file
file extension
file format
flash memory
folder

folder window
gigabyte (GB)
graphical user interface (GUI)
icon
input
iOS
kernel
keyboard
kilobyte (KB)
library
Linux
macOS
macOS Server
Maximize button
megabyte (MB)
memory
menu
Minimize button
mobile OS
nonvolatile memory
open source
operating system (OS)
output
personal computer (PC)
    operating system
platform

pointing device
program window
RAM (random access memory)
resource
Restore Down button
ROM (read-only memory)
server OS
Settings app
Shortcut
Shortcut menu
Software as a Service (SaaS)
spooling
system software
tile
UNIX
user account
utility
virtual machine
virtual memory
virtualization
volatile memory
web app
web server
window
Windows
Windows Server

Software and Apps

Using spreadsheet software, Rachel can graph her income and expenses.

Because her files are stored in the cloud, Rachel can use mobile apps to access the same information on her smartphone or tablet.

Foxy burrow/Shutterstock.com

Rachel Matthews is starting her own interior design firm. She will need to use software and apps to create presentations and drawings for customers and graphics for her firm's website; she will write work proposals and contracts using word processing software and manage her firm's income and expenses in a spreadsheet. She needs to track her customers in a database. Rachel is planning to offer a mobile app to allow customers to take photos of their space and visualize it with different furnishings.

In This Module

- Explain how you can use apps as part of your daily routine

- Use common features of productivity apps (word processing, spreadsheet, presentation, and database) and graphics apps (paint, drawing, image editing, and video and audio editing)

EVERYTHING YOU DO with your smartphone, computer, or tablet requires an app or software. Whether you are sending messages, watching videos, browsing the web, or checking the news, software and apps help you accomplish these tasks. Businesses and home users use productivity apps to manage documents, spreadsheets, presentations, and databases. With graphics software, you can edit and enhance digital images and videos.

In this module, you will learn about the key types of apps and how they are used in your personal and work life. You will learn about different kinds of productivity apps. You can try your hand at being a digital artist with drawing, paint, video, and photo editing apps. You also will learn about different strategies for building mobile apps.

Explain How to Use Apps as Part of Your Daily Life

Define Application Software

When you are listening to music, writing a paper, searching the web, or checking email, you probably are using application software. **Application software** (or software applications, or **apps**) are programs that help you perform specific tasks when using your computer or smartphone. With apps, you can create documents, edit photos, record videos, read the news, get travel directions, go shopping, make online calls, manage your device, and more (**Figure 5-1**).

Figure 5-1: People use a variety of apps

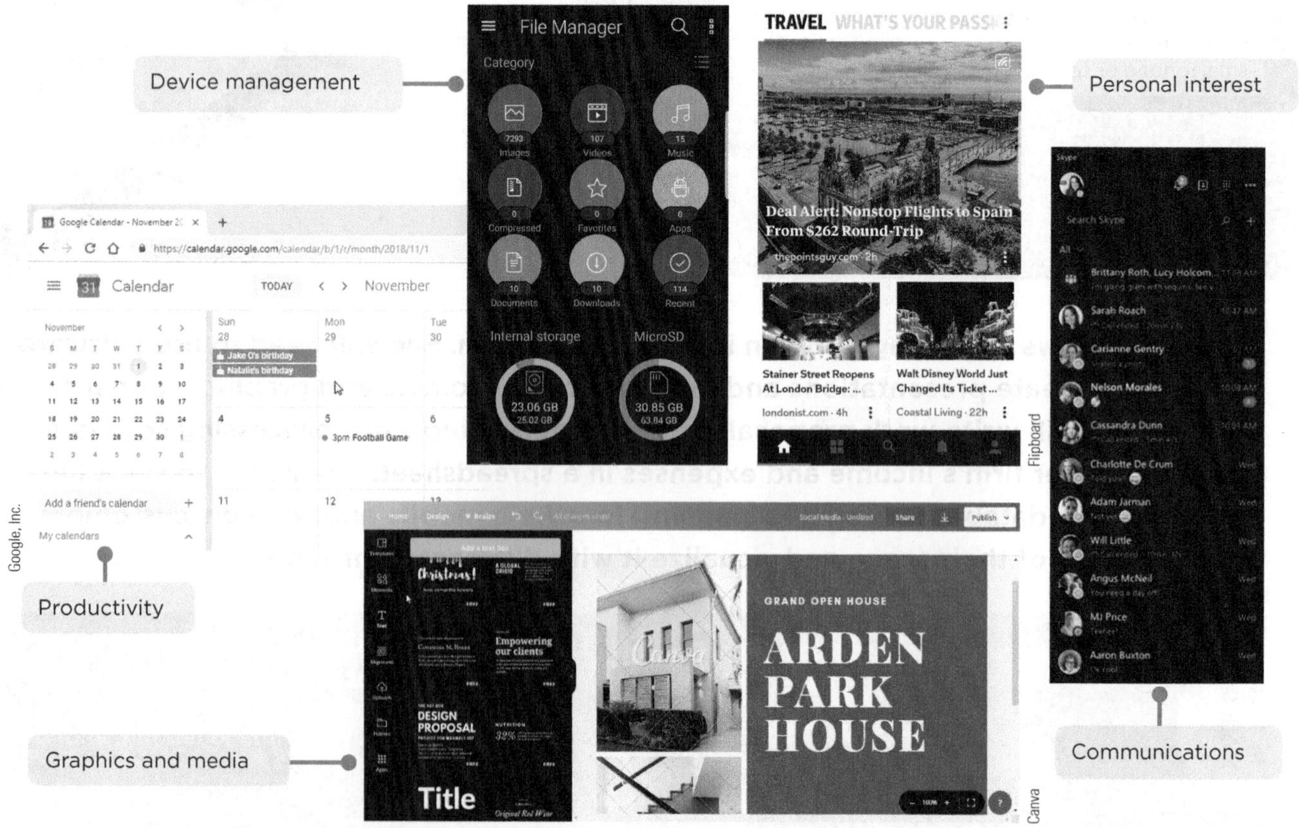

Device management

Personal interest

Productivity

Graphics and media

Communications

Google, Inc.

Describe the Purpose of Each Key Type of App

Productivity apps allow you to create documents for business and personal use. You might use word processing apps to create letters, reports, or documents. With presentation apps, you can create slides that combine text, graphics, images, or video for presentations. You can track your appointments using a digital calendar or scheduling apps; organize your contacts list using contact management apps; and pay your bills, create a budget, or track your expenses using personal finance apps.

Graphics and media apps allow you to interact with digital media. With photo editing apps, you can modify digital images, performing actions such as cropping, applying filters, and adding or removing backgrounds and shapes. With video and audio editing apps, you can arrange recorded movie clips, and add music, titles, or credits to videos. With media player apps, you can listen to audio or music, look at photos, and watch videos.

Personal interest apps give you tools to pursue your interests. You might use travel, mapping, and navigation apps to view maps, obtain route directions, or locate points of interest. News apps gather the day's news from several online sources in one place, based on your preferences. Reference apps provide access to information from online encyclopedias, dictionaries, and databases. Educational apps provide training on a variety of subjects and topics. Entertainment apps include games, movie times, and reviews. Social media apps enable you to share messages, photos, and videos with your friends and colleagues. Shopping apps allow you to make purchases online.

Communications apps provide tools for sharing or receiving information. Using a browser app, you can access webpages; with email apps you can send and receive electronic mail messages. Messaging apps share short messages, videos, and images, usually between mobile phone users. VoIP and video conferencing apps provide the ability to have voice and video conversations over the Internet. FTP apps allow you to transfer files between your computer and a server on the Internet.

Device management apps provide tools for maintaining your computer or mobile device. With a file manager app, you can store, locate, and organize files in your device's storage or in the cloud. A screen saver shows a moving image if no keyboard or mouse activity occurs. Antivirus and antispyware apps will keep your computer or mobile device safe from malicious activity.

Describe Types of Apps

While all apps allow you to accomplish a task, the device on which you access them and the way you obtain the app can determine its capabilities. For example, **local applications** are apps that you install on your computer's hard drive. These programs often have many features and capabilities. For example, Microsoft Office is a suite of applications for word processing, spreadsheets, databases, email, and presentations that you can install locally on your computer.

Portable apps run from a removable storage device such as an external hard drive or flash drive, or from the cloud. When using an external hard drive or flash drive, you connect the storage device to your computer and then run the application. When installed in the cloud, you can access portable apps from a folder in your cloud storage. Portable apps are useful when you have limited storage space on your computer. OpenOffice.org Portable is a portable open source productivity suite offering programs with capabilities like those found in Microsoft Office products.

Web-based applications, or **web apps,** are programs that you access over the Internet, in a browser on your computer or on your mobile device. Because these programs run over the Internet, web apps often offer collaboration features, and store the files or documents you create in the cloud. Microsoft Office 365 and Google's G Suite are web-based productivity applications for creating documents, spreadsheets, presentations, email, and calendars. Microsoft Office Online is a free web-based version offering basic features of word processing, spreadsheets, and presentation software.

Apps that you access on a smartphone or tablet are called **mobile applications**, or **mobile apps.** Usually you download and install these from your device's app store. Many people use mobile apps to increase their personal productivity on the go: using mobile apps, you can check email, maintain an online calendar and contact lists, and obtain maps and travel directions on your mobile device without having to use a desktop or laptop computer. Because screens on mobile devices tend to be small, mobile apps usually focus on a single task, such as checking email, searching the web, or sending a text message. **Figure 5-2** compares mobile and web apps.

Figure 5-2: Mobile and web apps

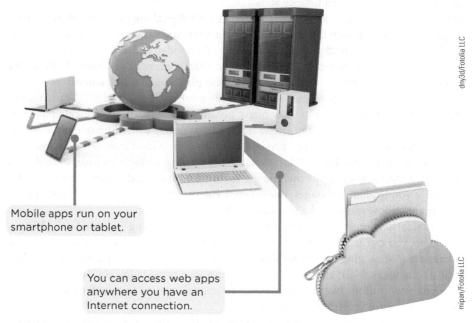

Mobile apps run on your smartphone or tablet.

You can access web apps anywhere you have an Internet connection.

Identify Common Features of Apps

Application software programs and apps have many common features, regardless of whether they run on a computer or mobile device. They:

- are usually represented on your computer's desktop or smartphone's home screen by an icon or tile;
- can be run by double-clicking or tapping the icon or tile;
- open in a window on your desktop or smartphone;
- have menus that give you options to access different features of the program or app;
- have buttons to click or tap to give commands or perform actions.

Some apps are available as both a web app and a mobile app. In this case, you typically can **synchronize** the data and activity between the web app and the mobile app, so your actions and information will be consistent across all your devices. For example, you might look at your Gmail account on your smartphone or tablet, and access Gmail on your computer via its website, as shown in **Figure 5-3**. In both cases, the email messages displayed in your inbox are the same. If you delete an email message using the email app on your mobile device, it will not appear when you check email using the email application on your laptop later.

Figure 5-3: Mail apps synchronize data between mobile and web-based versions

Email app installed from device's app store

Email web app on laptop runs in a browser

Use Mobile Apps

You touch or tap the screen to interact with mobile apps. You also can use an **on-screen keyboard** to enter information in an app on your mobile device, by tapping or swiping over the keys to type. Many on-screen keyboards assist you by predicting words and phrases you might want to type based on context, or by providing automatic corrections. Some on-screen keyboards include voice recognition capabilities, so you can speak the words to be typed. Users who need to type significant amounts of information may opt for a portable keyboard that they can connect to their smartphones using Bluetooth, as shown in **Figure 5-4**.

Figure 5-4: You can enter information in mobile apps using a Bluetooth keyboard or an on-screen keyboard

Many mobile devices come pre-installed with apps for managing email, contacts, calendars, a photo gallery, a web browser, sending and receiving text messages, a camera, a voice recorder, mobile payments, and more. You can organize apps into groups by category, such as Games or Social Media, to make them easier to find. Apps are represented by icons on your screen, as shown in **Figure 5-5**.

Figure 5-5: Your mobile device has a variety of apps

When you download an app, the installation program places an icon on your screen.

Social media apps are grouped together for easy access on this iPad.

Figure 5-6 shows how you might interact with mobile apps throughout your day.

Figure 5-6: Using mobile apps throughout the day

7:30 AM
While taking the bus to work, you use a calendar app to review your schedule for the day.

7:45 AM
You check your email with an email app.

8:00 AM
Walking to your first appointment, you consult a mapping app for directions.

11:00 AM
Your appointment finishes early, so you send a text message to invite a friend to lunch.

12:30 PM
You pay for lunch, using the mobile payment app on your phone.

6:45 AM
You wake up and use a weather app to see if you'll need a coat or umbrella today.

11:00 PM
You use a clock app to set the alarm to wake you at 6:45 am.

6:30 PM
On your way home you see a billboard with a QR code and scan it for more information.

5:00 PM
You go to the gym after work and use a streaming app to listen to your playlists while working out.

12:45 PM
After lunch, you use a camera app to take a selfie with your friend.

vasabii/Shutterstock.com

GaudiLab/Shutterstock.com

Use an App Store to Download and Install Apps

Most of the time you will visit an online store called an **app store** to locate and download apps for your mobile device. App stores offer many free apps; other apps are usually available for between $1 and $5. iPhone users can obtain apps from Apple's App Store; Google Play and Amazon's App Store are popular app stores for Android users.

Developers publish updates to their apps to app stores along with a description of changes made. Your app store can notify you when updates are available. A good practice is to review the individual updates before you download and install them. Many people, however, opt to have their phones or tablets update apps automatically, as updates become available. Usually your mobile device should be charging and connected to Wi-Fi before updating apps. When operating system updates are available, typically your device will send a notification, so you can install it at a convenient time.

Table 5-1 lists common mobile apps and the tasks they can help you accomplish.

Table 5-1: Popular types of mobile apps

Type of app	Helps you to	Examples
Banking and payment	Manage bank accounts, pay bills, deposit checks, transfer money, make payments	Your bank's mobile app, Venmo, PayPal
Calendar	Maintain your online calendar, schedule appointments	Google Calendar, Outlook Calendar
Cloud storage	Store your files in the cloud	Dropbox, OneDrive, Google Drive, iCloud, Amazon Drive
Contact management	Organize your address book	Contacts
Device maintenance	Optimize storage, delete unused or duplicate files, optimize device performance	CCleaner, PhoneClean
Email	Send and receive email messages from your mobile device	Outlook, Gmail
Fitness	Track workouts; set weight-loss goals, review stats from fitness tracking devices	Fitbit, MyFitnessPal
Games	Play games on your mobile device	Words with Friends
Location sharing	Share your location with friends	Find My Friends, Find My Family, Google Maps
Mapping/GPS	View maps; obtain travel directions based on your location	Google Maps, Waze
Messaging	Send text messages, photos, or short videos, or make voice or video calls to your friends	Facebook Messenger, FaceTime, WhatsApp, GroupMe
News and information	Stay up-to-date on current affairs of interest to you	Flipboard, Google News, Weather Channel, CNN
Personal assistant	Search the Internet, set timers, add appointments to your calendar, make hands-free calls by speaking commands	Siri, Cortana, Google Home, Amazon Alexa
Personal productivity	View and make minor edits to documents received by email, or stored on your device or in the cloud	Microsoft Word, PowerPoint, Outlook, Excel, Gmail, Google Docs, Spreadsheets, Slides
Photo and video editing and sharing	Modify photos and videos by cropping, adding filters, adjusting brightness and contrast	Fotor, Canva, Adobe Premiere Clip
Shopping	Make online retail purchases	Amazon.com
Social media	Share status updates, photos, or videos on social networking sites or view friends' posts	Facebook, Instagram, LinkedIn, Twitter
Travel	Make airline, hotel, and restaurant reservations; read and post reviews	Airbnb, Kayak, Priceline, Yelp, TripAdvisor
Web browsing	View websites on your mobile devices	Chrome, Edge, Firefox, Safari

Explain the Differences Between Native Apps and Web Apps

A **native app** is an app written for a specific operating system and installed on a computer or mobile device. Native apps can take advantage of specific features of the devices on which they are installed, such as a smartphone's camera, microphone, or contacts list. You may install native mobile apps by downloading them from an app store. Many native apps require an Internet connection to provide full functionality. Some apps can run offline and will store information on your device until they can synchronize with the cloud.

A **web app** is accessed by visiting a website in a browser. A mobile app is a web app that runs on a mobile device. Mobile web apps often have a **responsive design**, which means the app is optimized for display in a browser on a mobile device, regardless of screen size or orientation. Many app developers prefer web apps because they run on all devices. Web apps rely on HTML5 to display information, JavaScript to manage the app's performance, and CSS (Cascading Style Sheets) to format information.

Some apps are available as both web and native apps. **Figure 5-7** shows native and web versions of Amazon's mobile shopping app. The native app allows you search for an item to purchase by taking a photo of a product or its bar code with your device's camera or tapping the microphone to speak the items to add to your shopping cart. The mobile web app runs in a browser, as shown by the web address in the search bar. Both versions of the app display the same product information.

Figure 5-7: Amazon's native app (left) and web app (right)

A native web app can access your phone's camera or microphone to help you specify items to purchase.

A mobile web app runs in a mobile browser. The web address appears in the address bar.

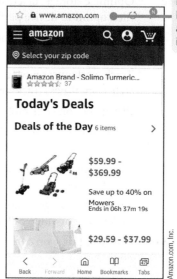

Amazon.com, Inc.

Describe the Pros and Cons of Mobile Apps

Although mobile apps are popular and convenient, they have limitations, as shown in **Table 5-2**.

Table 5-2: Pros and cons of mobile apps

Pros	Cons
Mobile web apps can be created quickly compared to native apps.	Mobile web apps are not as fast and have fewer features than native web apps or desktop apps.
You can access your information on the go.	Poorly designed apps can turn people away.
Voice input and smart on-screen keyboard simplify interactions.	Typing using a small on-screen keyboard can be cumbersome.

Many mobile apps require the ability to connect to the Internet, either over Wi-Fi, or using your carrier's mobile network. Connectivity is crucial to today's mobile user; people want to stay connected to their office, home, and friends all the time, no matter where they are. Files that the apps use or create often are compatible between your desktop or laptop computer and your mobile device.

Most mobile apps are **platform-specific**; that is, if you have an Android phone, you need to install the Android version of your app; if you have an iPhone, you need to download the iPhone version of your app. In most cases, the capabilities of different versions of the same app are comparable; each device's app has a consistent look and feel with that device's user interface and is built to run with that device's mobile operating system.

Summarize Current Trends in App Development

With the growth and popularity of mobile devices, today more people access apps on mobile devices than on laptop or desktop computers. Recent studies found that mobile Internet usage now exceeds desktop usage, and mobile device users now download over 254 billion free mobile apps each year. This increased usage requires designers and developers to design apps with mobile devices in mind first, and to take advantage of the connectivity and new business opportunities that mobile devices enable.

Mobile first design means that designers and developers start building apps to work on mobile devices first because these typically have more restrictions, such as smaller screens. Then, they develop expanded features for a tablet or desktop version. This approach causes app designers and developers to prioritize the most important parts of their websites and apps and implement them first. Mobile first design requires designers to streamline how people interact with their apps by placing content first and providing a simplified user experience.

By using **cross-platform** development tools, developers can build apps that work on multiple platforms, rather than writing different code for Android or iOS devices. iOS developers write apps in Swift or Objective-C, and Android developers write apps in Java. Some cross-platform development tools rely on HTML5, JavaScript, and CSS to create a common web app that runs on multiple platforms. Other cross-platform development tools provide a compiler that can translate code into the different native formats for iOS and Android devices.

The Internet of Things (IoT) refers to objects ("things"), such as a thermostat or coffee maker, that have the capability to send data from attached electronic sensors. As IoT continues to become more relevant, many apps can report data. Fitness trackers have sensors to track your heart rate; digital cameras have sensors for remote controls; "smart" home devices such as your Nest Thermostat have temperature sensors; and your Google Home or Amazon Alexa smart speakers have sensors that detect your voice. All these IoT objects send or receive data that you can examine using apps on your smartphone or tablet.

When you shop online you can use Internet banking in mobile apps. **Mobile commerce**, or **m-commerce**, apps let you use your mobile device to make online purchases of goods and services. Mobile payment capabilities are built into apps such as Uber or Lyft for taxi rides, and online retailers such as Amazon or Walmart.

Use Common Features of Productivity and Graphics Apps

When you are writing a letter or report, maintaining a budget, creating slides for a presentation, or managing the membership list for an organization, you are using productivity apps. Productivity apps include word processing apps for creating documents, spreadsheet apps for creating worksheets, presentation apps for creating slides, and may include email, database, note-taking, and other apps for creating a variety of documents.

To create digital sketches, resize or add special effects to digital photos, or add titles and credits to a video, you will want to use graphics apps. Graphics apps include tools for creating drawings, modeling three-dimensional objects, and editing photos and videos. Graphics apps let you create multimedia to include in letters and reports, presentations, spreadsheets, and other documents.

Many vendors bundle their individual apps into a **productivity suite**, or collection of productivity apps. You can share text, graphics, charts, and other content among projects you create with individual apps and download additional templates for creating specialized projects. For example, you could include a chart created in a spreadsheet app as part of a slide in a presentation, or as a figure in a word processing document.

Several productivity suites provide versions to install on a desktop or laptop computer, to install on a mobile device, and to run in the cloud in a browser. You can install software on your computer by downloading it from a provider's website. After you download the software, you will need to run an installer. The installer will guide you through setting up and configuring the apps. You can install mobile apps from your device's app store. Some productivity suites are free, while others require you to purchase a license or subscription.

When you use a productivity app in a browser as a web app, or on your mobile device, you generally store the documents and files you create in the cloud using the provider's cloud storage service. Storing the files on the cloud makes them available to access them from many devices. You can collaborate with others who can view or edit the same document.

Desktop- or laptop-installed versions of the apps generally provide the most complete and advanced capabilities. Web and mobile versions are often simpler, or lightweight, and contain the most basic and most popular basic features. Some vendors offer versions of their apps for multiple platforms (**Figure 5-8**).

Figure 5-8: Microsoft Word offers versions to install on your computer, run in a browser, or access on a mobile device

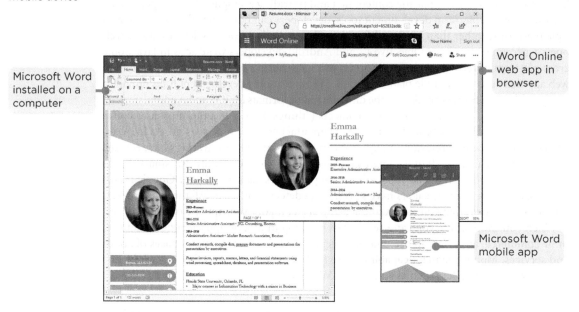

Microsoft Word installed on a computer

Word Online web app in browser

Microsoft Word mobile app

Identify Apps and Productivity Suites Related to Word Processing, Spreadsheet, Presentation, and Database Software

This section summarizes popular productivity suites from Microsoft, Apple, Google, and Apache.

Microsoft Office 365 includes word processing, spreadsheet, and presentation apps, as well as Microsoft Outlook for email, Microsoft OneNote for note taking, and Microsoft Access for databases. Originally developed for computers running Microsoft Windows operating systems, the suite also is available for computers running macOS, and as a collection of web apps in a browser.

Apple iWork is a productivity suite for computers running macOS and iPhones and iPads running the iOS operating system. Users can add illustrations and notes with the Apple Pencil when running these apps on an iPad. iWork includes apps for word processing, spreadsheets, and presentations. iWork for iCloud integrates with Apple's iCloud cloud storage service.

G Suite is a productivity suite from Google available for ChromeOS computers, and computers running other operating systems by accessing them as web apps in a browser. Mobile versions exist for devices running Android and iOS. In addition to Docs, Sheets, and Slides, G Suite products include Google Calendar, Gmail for email, and SketchUp for sketching.

Apache OpenOffice is an open source suite of productivity apps. You can download OpenOffice at no cost from a web server on the Internet and install the apps on your computer. OpenOffice is an alternative to other productivity suites that have a fee to purchase or require a subscription. You can save OpenOffice projects in file formats that you can open with many popular productivity apps. In addition to documents, spreadsheets, and presentations, OpenOffice provides base, an app for creating databases, and math, an app for creating and formatting mathematical equations.

Table 5-3 summarizes popular productivity suites available today.

Table 5-3: Popular productivity suites

	Microsoft Office	Apple iWork	G Suite	OpenOffice
Operating systems supported	Windows, macOS or web apps	macOS, iOS, or web apps	ChromeOS or web apps	Windows, Linux, macOS
Word processor	Microsoft Word	Pages	Google Docs	Writer
Spreadsheet	Microsoft Excel	Numbers	Google Sheets	Calc
Presentation	Microsoft PowerPoint	Keynote	Google Slides	Impress
Database	Microsoft Access			Base
Email	Microsoft Outlook	Apple Mail	Gmail	
Online version	Office Online	iWork for iCloud	G Suite	
Cloud storage	Microsoft OneDrive	iCloud	Google Drive	

In addition to productivity apps that are part of a productivity suite, individual productivity apps are popular as well. For example, Prezi is an online presentation app that you can use to zoom in and out of parts of a canvas to create an online presentation. Zoho writer is an online word processing app with additional features such as posting directly to popular online blogging platforms such as WordPress.

Use Word Processing Software for Basic Word Processing Functions

Word processing software is one of the most widely used types of application software. You can use it to create documents and reports, mailing labels, flyers, brochures, newsletters, resumes, letters, and more. You can change font and font sizes, change the color of text and backgrounds, add photos and shapes, and use provided templates to give a professional appearance to your documents.

Identify the Key Features of Word Processing Software

Although the user interface and features of word processing programs may differ, all word processors share some common key features. The files you create are called **documents**, and each document is a collection of one or more pages. When you open a word processing program, a blank document opens on the screen. The screen displays an **insertion point**, a blinking vertical line to mark your place, and **scroll bars** along the edges that let you navigate to view parts of a document that is too large to fit on the screen all at once. The word processing program offers a variety of commands and options you can use to create and format the document, such as specifying fonts, sizes, colors, and margins.

With some word processing programs, you can speak the text into a microphone connected to your computer or mobile device, and the program will convert your speech to text and type it for you. As you type or speak text, when you reach the end of one line, the word processing software automatically "wraps" words onto a new line. When the text fills the page, the new text automatically flows onto a new page.

Formatting features modify the appearance of a document. Editing, review, reference, and graphics capabilities enhance document content. **Document management tools** protect and organize files, and let you share your document with others.

Word processing programs have both business and personal uses, as summarized in Table 5-4 and Figure 5-9.

Table 5-4: Uses of word processing

Who uses word processing	To create
Business executives, office workers, medical professionals, politicians	Agendas, memos, contracts, proposals, reports, letters, email, newsletters, personalized bulk mailings and labels
Personal users	Letters, greeting cards, notes, event flyers, check lists
Students	Essays, reports, stories, resumes, notes
Conference promoters and event planners	Business cards, postcards, invitations, conference tent cards, name tags, gift tags, stickers
Web designers	Documents for publishing to the web after converting them to HTML

Figure 5-9: Word processing programs have both personal and business uses

Personal uses of word processors include creating, editing, view, printing, publishing, and collaborating on a variety of documents, such as letters, invitations, flyers, reports, and research papers.

Business uses of word processors include creating memos, contracts, invoices, and marketing brochures.

Format Text Using Word Processing Software

With a word processing program, you can highlight important information, and make text easier to read. You **format** text by changing its font type, size, style, color, and special effects such as reflection, shadows, and outlining. Most word processing programs provide tools to make text bold, italic, or underlined; automatically set text to lowercase, uppercase, or capitalize each word in a phrase; or highlight the background of text in color. Table 5-5 summarizes popular text-formatting options.

Table 5-5: Text formatting options

Format option	Description and use	Examples
Font type	Defines what characters look like. Some fonts have rounded letters; others are more angular. Some are formal; others are more casual.	Times New Roman Comic Sans MS **Arial Black**
Font size	Determines the size of the character, measured in *points*; each point is 1/72 of an inch; change the title font to be bigger than the rest of your text or use smaller fonts for footnotes or endnotes.	This text is 12 points This text is 18 points

Table 5-5: (continued)

Format option	Description and use	Examples
Font style	Adds visual effects features to text; bolding text makes it stand out on the page, shadow gives it depth, underlining, italicizing, and highlighting text provide emphasis.	**bold** shadow <u>underline</u> *italics* highlighting
Font color	Determines the color of each character and adds interest; be sure to use font colors that show up well against the document background.	Red text Blue text Green text

Format Documents Using Word Processing Software

Formatting a document improves its appearance and readability. Document formatting features include formatting in multiple columns, adding borders around text, adding a page break to specify a location for a new page to begin, and changing spacing between lines of text. You also can specify a document's margins and the **page orientation** (the direction in which content is printed on the page, portrait or landscape).

To give a document a professional appearance, you can specify styles for a document's title, headings, paragraphs, quotes, and more. A **style** is a named collection of formats that are stored together and can be applied to text or objects. For example, the Heading 1 style for a document might format text using Calibri font, size 16, blue text color, left justified. Any text in the document formatted with the Heading 1 style will have those characteristics. If you modify the characteristics of a style, all the format of text in that style will update to reflect the new characteristics.

Many productivity suites offer built-in templates for creating different kinds of documents. A **template** is a document that has been preformatted for a specific purpose (such as an invitation, a brochure, a flyer, a cover letter, or a resume). You can specify the content of your documents, but you do not have to develop a color scheme or design a layout.

In addition, you might make use of the formatting features shown in **Table 5-6** when creating or editing a document.

Table 5-6 Additional document formatting options

Use this feature	When you want to
Alignment	Align paragraphs at the left margin, right margin, or center of the page
Graphics	Add photos, pictures, logos, charts, or screenshots to your document to add visual appeal
Headers and Footers	Display information such as a document title, author's name, or page number at the top or bottom of each page
Hyperlinks	Direct readers to related documents, email addresses, or websites online
Line Spacing	Specify how much "white space" appears before, between, or after each line of text (measured in points)
Lists	Display a list of items preceded by numbers or a symbol called a bullet
Mail Merge	Create and send customized letters or email messages that are personalized with the recipient's name and other information
Margins	Specify the region of the page where text will appear, measured from the left, right, top, and bottom edges of the page
Reference	Create a bibliography containing citations to reference articles in a research paper
Tables	Organize text in rows and columns

Some word processing features are included in programs and apps for creating different types of documents. **Table 5-7** has several examples.

Table 5-7 Programs and apps for creating different types of documents

Related program	Function	Use to create	Examples
Desktop publishing	Combines word processing with graphics and advanced layout capabilities	Newsletters, brochures, flyers	Quark Xpress, Adobe InDesign, Microsoft Publisher
Text / code editor	Creates webpages using HTML tags	Webpages	iWeb, VSCode, Dreamweaver, WebStorm
Note taking	Stores and accesses thoughts, ideas, and lists	Notes	EverNote, OneNote
Speech recognition	Enters text that you speak, rather than type	Documents	Dragon Naturally Speaking, Windows Speech Recognition

Manage Word Processing Documents

Word processing software offers document management tools to edit, share, protect, and save documents. You also can copy text and graphics from one document (or spreadsheet or database) to another.

By storing documents in the cloud, you can share documents with several people who can read, edit, and comment on the same document at the same time (**Figure 5-10**). If they are unsure of the edits, they can discuss the changes in comments and tracked changes to compare versions, without creating multiple copies of the same file. This process of collaboration is often more efficient than exchanging multiple versions of the same file by email, and then merging each person's changes together. When sharing a document, you can restrict access to a document by providing a **view-only link**, or **read-only access**. A person who has read-only access to the file can read, but not change it.

Figure 5-10: Creating, collaborating, and commenting on a shared document

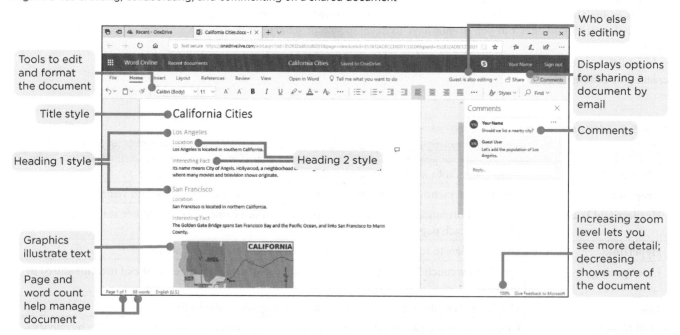

Use Spreadsheet Software to Manage Basic Workbooks

When you want to manipulate numbers or display numerical data, a spreadsheet is the tool you want. Keeping to-do lists, creating a budget, tracking your personal finances, following the performance of your favorite sports teams, and calculating payments on a loan are all tasks you can accomplish using a spreadsheet. Businesses often use spreadsheets to calculate taxes or payroll.

Spreadsheet apps let you interact with numbers, charts, graphics, text, and data. Spreadsheets can perform calculations on data stored in a grid of cells and recalculate values automatically when the data changes. Spreadsheet software originated as an electronic alternative to paper ledgers used by bookkeepers to track sales and expenses. Use of the software expanded to other business departments, such as sales, marketing, and human resources. Spreadsheets are used widely outside of the business world, in science, mathematics, economics, and finance, and by home users, students, and teachers.

Spreadsheets allow you to organize data stored in rows and columns and perform simple or complex calculations on that data.

Define Worksheets and Workbooks

You use spreadsheet software to create, edit, and format worksheets. To create a worksheet, enter values, labels, and formulas into cells. **Worksheets** are laid out in a grid of rows and columns; they use letters or pairs of letters, such as A or AB, to identify each column, and consecutive numbers to identify each row. You can see only a small part of the worksheet on your screen at once. Adjust the scroll bars along the bottom or right side of the spreadsheet app to view other parts of a worksheet. You can insert or delete entire rows and columns.

A **cell** in a worksheet is the location formed by the intersection of a column and a row. For example, cell K11 is located at the intersection of column K and row 11. In **Figure 5-11**, cell K11 contains the number 15,800, which represents the number of total projected production of skateboards in Year 10. You can refer to a cell by its **cell address**, or location in the worksheet. A **workbook** is a collection of related worksheets contained in a single file.

Figure 5-11: Using spreadsheet software

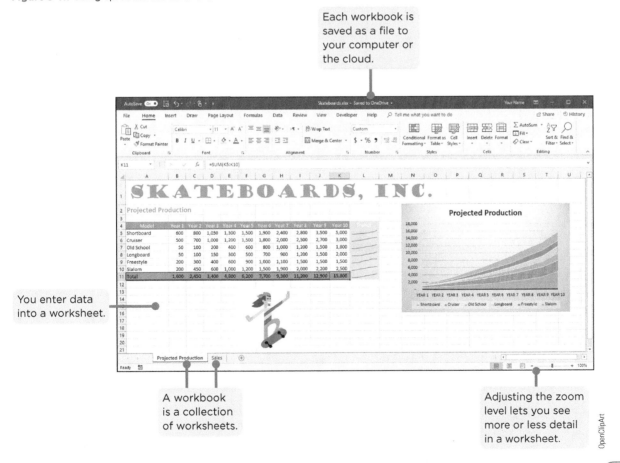

Each workbook is saved as a file to your computer or the cloud.

You enter data into a worksheet.

A workbook is a collection of worksheets.

Adjusting the zoom level lets you see more or less detail in a worksheet.

OpenClipArt

Identify the Key Features of Spreadsheets

Spreadsheet software often includes many additional features, such as:
- Formatting tools to change a worksheet's appearance
- Page layout and view features to change the zoom level, divide a worksheet into panes, or freeze rows or columns, to make large worksheets easier to read
- Printing features to control whether you want to print entire worksheets or only selected areas
- Web capabilities to share workbooks online, add hyperlinks, and save worksheets as webpages
- Developer tools to add customized functions
- Tools to analyze data in a spreadsheet

Define Formulas and Functions

Figure 5-12 shows a worksheet for calculating projected production of skateboards for a skateboard company. Many of the cells contain numbers, or values that can be used in calculations. Other cells contain **formulas**, or computation rules, to calculate values using cell references, numbers, and arithmetic **operators** such as "+", "-", "*", and "/". You can type a formula directly into a cell or in the formula bar above the worksheet. For example, when creating this worksheet, you can type a formula in cell K11 to determine the projected production of all models in Year 10 by calculating the sum of the numeric values in the cells above it (K5 through K10).

Figure 5-12: Basic features of spreadsheet software

Rows are represented by numbers and contain data for individual records. Here each row of data contains a skateboard model and its projected production over several years.

Type formulas into the formula bar to specify calculations for the spreadsheet program to perform.

Trend lines, or spark lines, summarize data changes over time.

Columns are represented by letters and can contain data categories such as a skateboard model, or a projected production for a given year.

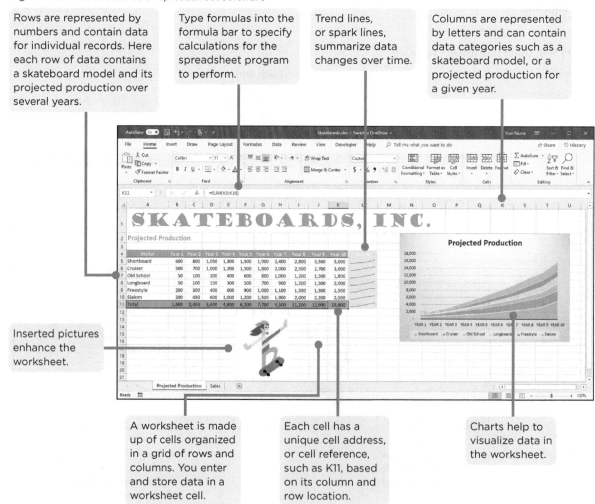

Inserted pictures enhance the worksheet.

A worksheet is made up of cells organized in a grid of rows and columns. You enter and store data in a worksheet cell.

Each cell has a unique cell address, or cell reference, such as K11, based on its column and row location.

Charts help to visualize data in the worksheet.

Spreadsheet formulas always begin with an equal sign ("="). When you type the formula =K5+K6+K7+K8+K9+K10 in cell K11, that cell will display the value 15,800, the result of the calculation. If you later change any of the values in cells K5 through K10, the spreadsheet app will automatically recalculate the value in cell K11 to display the updated sum. Formulas use arithmetic operators and functions to perform calculations based on cell values in a worksheet.

A **function** is a predefined computation or calculation, such as calculating the sum or average of values or finding the largest or smallest value in a range of cells. For example, =SUM(K5:K10) is a formula that uses the SUM function to add all of the numbers in the range of cells K5 through K10. In this formula, SUM is the **name** of the function, and its **argument** (information necessary for a formula or function to calculate an answer), specified in the parentheses after the function's name, are the values in the range of cells K5:K10, to be added. The result is the same as the formula =K5+K6+K7+K8+K9+K10, but using the function is simpler, especially if you are adding values in many cells.

Formula arguments can be values or cell references. An **absolute reference** is a cell reference that does not change when the formula containing that reference is moved to a new location. A **relative reference** is a cell reference that changes when the formula containing that reference is moved to a new location.

Spreadsheet apps contain **built-in functions** to perform financial, mathematical, logical, date and time, and other calculations, as shown in **Table 5-8**. Many spreadsheet apps allow users to write their own custom functions to perform special purpose calculations.

Table 5-8 Common spreadsheet functions

Use these functions	To do this
SUM, AVERAGE, COUNT	Calculate the sum, average, or count of cells in a range
RATE, PMT	Calculate interest rates and loan payments
DATE, TIME, NOW	Obtain the current date, time, or date and time
IF, AND, OR, NOT	Perform calculations based on logical conditions
MAX, MIN	Calculate largest and smallest values in a group of cells
VLOOKUP	Look up values in a table

Analyze Spreadsheet Data

Once you enter data into a worksheet, you can use several tools to make the data more meaningful.

- Use **conditional formatting** to highlight cells that meet specified criteria. For example, in a worksheet containing states and populations, you might use conditional formatting to display all the population values greater than 10,000,000 using bold, red text with a yellow background.
- **Sort** data by values in a column to arrange them in increasing or decreasing order; you might sort sales in decreasing order, so your highest performing sales associates appear at the top of the list
- **Filter** worksheet data to display only the values you want to see, such as sales associates who brought in more than $100,000 in a month.
- Use **what-if analysis** to test multiple scenarios by temporarily changing one or more variables, to see the effect on related calculations. For example, if you cannot afford the monthly payment of $590.48 on a $20,000 car loan at 4% interest for 36 months, you can specify the smaller amount you can afford each month and see how many additional months will be required to pay off the loan.
- Use **trendlines**, or **sparklines**, simple charts to visually summarize changes in values over time with small graphs that appear in cells of the worksheet next to the values they represent.
- Use **pivot tables** to create meaningful data summaries to analyze worksheets containing large amounts of data. For example, if your worksheet contains data about sales

associates, their region, and quarterly sales results, you can use pivot tables to summarize the data with reports of Sales by Quarter, Sales by Region, or Sales by Associate.

- Automate your worksheets with **macros**, small programs you create to perform steps you repeat frequently. For example, if your worksheet contains information for a sales invoice, you can create a macro to save it as a PDF file, centered on the page. By assigning these steps to a macro, you can perform this task with one button click.

Create Charts Using Spreadsheet Software

Charts (sometimes called graphs) represent data using bars, columns, pie wedges, lines, or other symbols. Charts present data visually and make it easier to see relationships among the data. You can visualize data using pie charts, bar graphs, line graphs, and other chart types. A line chart tracks trends over time. A column chart compares categories of data to one another, and a pie chart compares parts (or slices) to the whole. A stacked area chart, shown in **Figure 5-13**, shows how several values (projected production of various models of skateboards) change over time in the same graphic.

Figure 5-13: Working with charts

To create a chart, select a data range, and choose a chart type, layout, and location.

Chart tools help you design visually appealing charts.

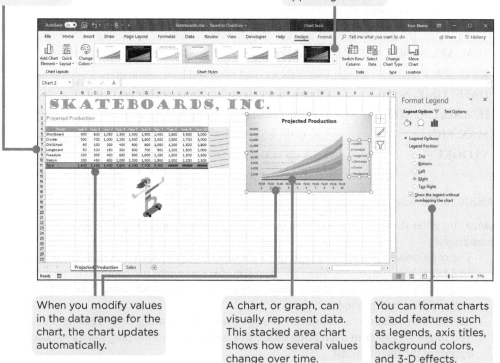

When you modify values in the data range for the chart, the chart updates automatically.

A chart, or graph, can visually represent data. This stacked area chart shows how several values change over time.

You can format charts to add features such as legends, axis titles, background colors, and 3-D effects.

Format Spreadsheets

You can change how a worksheet looks by using formatting features as well as by inserting elements such as graphics. Formatting highlights important data and makes worksheets easier to read; graphic elements enhance a worksheet. When you format a number, the value remains the same, even if the way it appears in a cell changes. **Table 5-9** shows several ways to format a worksheet.

Table 5-9: Formatting a worksheet

Formatting option	Use to	Example
Currency	Identify currency value such as euros, pounds, or dollars	$4.50 or £4.50 or €4.50
Decimal places	Display additional level of accuracy	4.50 4.500, 4.5003
Font types, colors, styles, and effects	Emphasize text and numbers	4.50 4.500, *4.5003*
Alignment	Align text across cells for a title heading; center, or left- or right-align labels or values	Student Scores 75 80 95
Borders and shading	Enhance the worksheet	Student Scores 75 80 95
Cell height and width	Emphasize certain cells	Student Scores 75 80 95 88
Photographs, clip art, shapes, and other graphics	Illustrate a point; can format, reposition, and resize	☺ Student Scores 75 80 95 88
Headers and footers	Create professional reports	Bergen Data Analysis: Fall Report Page 3 of 5

Use Presentation Software to Create and Share Presentations

When you want to display information in a slide show, **presentation software** can help you organize your content and create professional-looking digital slide shows. You might create a presentation for work or school, show slides of photos from your vacation to friends, or create digital signs. Slide shows can be printed; viewed on a laptop, desktop, or mobile device; projected on a wall using a multimedia projector connected to a computer; or displayed on large monitors or information kiosks.

With **presentation apps** you can create slides that visually communicate ideas, messages, and other information. A **presentation** contains a series of slides. Each slide has a specific layout based on its content (such as titles, headings, text, graphics, videos, and charts), and each layout has predefined placeholders for these content items (such as title layout, two-column layout, and image with a caption layout).

Identify the Key Features of Presentation Software

As you work, you can display presentations in different views. Normal view shows thumbnails, or small images of slides, and an editing pane, where you can add or modify content. In Notes view, you can add speaker's notes with talking points for each slide when giving the presentation. You can insert, delete, duplicate, hide, and move slides within your presentation.

You can add main points to a slide as a bulleted list by typing them into a text box on the slide. You also can add graphics or images to illustrate your talking points.

Presentation apps sometimes include a gallery that provides images, photos, video clips, and audio clips to give presentations greater impact. Some presentation apps offer a search tool to help you locate online images or videos to include in your slides. Some presentation apps even offer design ideas to give your slides a more professional appearance, as shown in **Figure 5-14**.

Figure 5-14: Creating a presentation

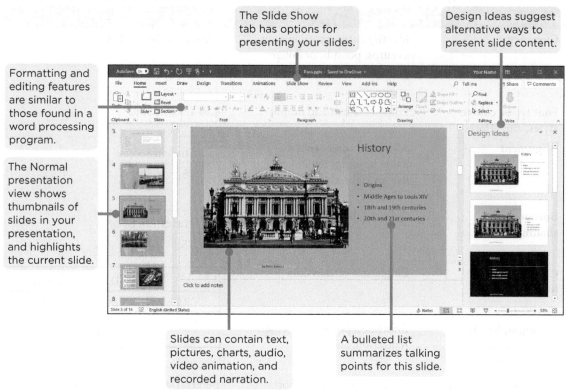

Formatting and editing features are similar to those found in a word processing program.

The Normal presentation view shows thumbnails of slides in your presentation, and highlights the current slide.

The Slide Show tab has options for presenting your slides.

Design Ideas suggest alternative ways to present slide content.

Slides can contain text, pictures, charts, audio, video animation, and recorded narration.

A bulleted list summarizes talking points for this slide.

Presentation apps may also incorporate features such as checking spelling, formatting, researching, sharing, and publishing presentations online.

Format Presentation Content

Slides can contain text, graphics, audio, video, links, and other content, as shown in **Table 5-10**.

Table 5-10: Adding content to slides

Slide content	How to enter	Provides
Text in a paragraph or bulleted list	Click a placeholder and type, or copy and paste text from another file, or insert text from a document file.	Content; most programs offer a variety of bullet styles, including number and picture bullets
Graphics such as line art, photographs, clip art, drawn objects, diagrams, data tables, and screenshots	Click a content placeholder, draw directly on the slide, or copy and paste a graphic from another file.	Illustrations to convey meaning and information for the slide content
Media clips, such as video and audio, including recorded narrations	Click a content placeholder and choose a file, or insert the file directly onto a slide by recording it.	Media content to enhance a slide show
Links	Click content placeholder, copy and paste links from a website or type the link directly.	Links to another slide, another document, or a webpage
Embedded objects	Click menu commands or a content placeholder.	External files in a slide
Charts	Link or embed a worksheet or chart from Excel or create a chart directly within PowerPoint.	Graphic display of data to support your presentation

You also can select the theme, or design, for the entire presentation, by choosing a predefined set of styles for backgrounds, text, and visual designs that appear on each slide, or modifying predefined elements to make them your own.

Other formatting features (**Figure 5-15**) include:

- Formatting text using tools like those in word processing software to choose fonts, sizes, colors, and styles such as bold or italics
- Setting a slide's dimensions, aspect ratio (standard or widescreen), and orientation (portrait or landscape)
- Changing text direction, aligning text on a slide or within a text box, and adding shadows or reflection effects
- Resizing graphics to make them larger or smaller; rotating, mirroring, or cropping images
- Adding SmartArt graphics that display text in predesigned configurations to convey lists, processes, and other relationships
- Formatting charts and worksheets to present numerical data, like those found in spreadsheets
- Moving objects to different locations on a slide, aligning objects, and grouping objects

Figure 5-15: Formatting a presentation

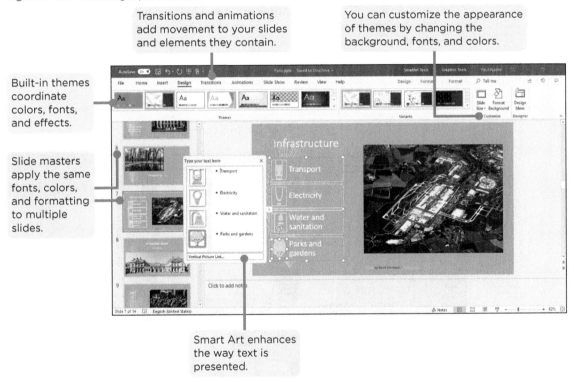

Transitions and animations add movement to your slides and elements they contain.

You can customize the appearance of themes by changing the background, fonts, and colors.

Built-in themes coordinate colors, fonts, and effects.

Slide masters apply the same fonts, colors, and formatting to multiple slides.

Smart Art enhances the way text is presented.

Include Transitions in Presentations

Transitions are visual effects that occur as you move from one slide to another. For example, you can "push" an existing slide off the right edge of the screen as a new one slides in from the left or apply a "cube" effect that will make the new slide appear as if it was on the side of a rotating cube. You can set many options for transitions, such as sound effects, direction, and duration. You can set transitions for individual slides or for the entire presentation, to begin automatically after a preset amount of time, or manually with a screen tap or mouse click.

Include Animations in Presentations

Animations, or effects applied to an object that make the object appear, disappear, or move, can add visual appeal to a presentation when used carefully. Presentation apps offer a variety of animations, such as entrance, exit, and emphasis, each with a variety of options.

A photo can fade in as you display a slide, or an object can fly in from the edge of the slide. You can set animations to begin automatically when you advance a slide, or to start when you click or tap. Animations can move horizontally, vertically, or diagonally across the slide. You can set the order for multiple animations, such as displaying a bulleted list one item at a time, and then float in a graphic from the bottom edge of the slide.

Use Presentation Templates and Masters

Using a presentation template, you can add your content to a predefined design to create common presentations such as calendars, diagrams, and infographics. A **slide master** is an overall template for a presentation formatted with a theme, customized title and text fonts, backgrounds, and other objects that appear on slides in the presentation. Adding headers and footers lets you display the presentation title, slide number, date, logos, or other information on a single slide, or on all slides automatically.

Share and Display Presentations

When giving a presentation to a large group, you often display the slides on a large monitor or project them to a screen as a **slide show**, so everyone can see them (**Figure 5-16**). You might print handouts from your slides so audience members can take notes, or send a link to your slides by email so audience members can follow along during the presentation on their own devices. When presentations are stored in the cloud, others can access them online. You also can share them on a blog or website by copying the HTML embed code provided by the presentation app's share option and pasting it into a blogpost or webpage.

Figure 5-16: Giving a presentation

A presenter can show a presentation on a large screen in a conference room.

If the presenter shares the presentation, attendees can also follow it on their laptops or mobile devices.

iStock.com/lovro77

Design Effective Presentations

When creating a presentation, it is important to communicate the content as clearly as possible. By following these tips, you can design effective presentations.

- Organize your presentation to have a beginning, a middle, and an end. Figure out how to visualize each of your topics.
- Your audience can read a slide faster than you can talk about it. Plan your presentation so you focus on one topic or item at a time. Be careful not to cram too much information

on one slide. When including text on a slide, many people follow the 6 × 6 rule: no more than six bullets or lines of text with no more than six words per line. However, the clarity of your message is more important than word count on a slide.

- Choose appropriate backgrounds, colors, and fonts. Use large fonts (at least 20 point) so the audience can see your text from across the room. Be careful with your choice of font color: many colorblind people cannot see the difference between red or green, so do not use these colors when formatting text to categorize items.
- Use graphics wisely, so they enhance the story your presentation is trying to convey. When searching online for graphics or images, look for public domain or Creative Commons-licensed content that you can modify, adapt, or build upon for use in your presentations. Verify that you have permission to use any image or photo you did not create yourself and provide attribution as necessary.
- Use animations carefully to enhance the presentation; too many transitions or animations can be a distraction. Pick one or two transitions and apply them to the entire presentation. You want your audience to focus on the slide's message, not the elaborate screen effects.
- Use the spelling and grammar features built into your presentation software. If your slides have spelling or grammatical errors, your content will lose credibility.

When delivering a presentation, follow these tips to keep your audience interested and engaged:

- Check your equipment in advance. Be sure your laptop or mobile device is connected to the projector. Perform a sound check if your presentation includes music or other audio to make sure you can hear the audio through any connected speakers.
- Speak loudly and clearly, as if you are having a conversation with the audience. If the room is large, use a microphone so everyone can hear you.
- Don't read your slides when giving a presentation. Use as few words on your slides as possible. Instead, let the slides be reminders for you about what to talk about, and the images on the slide a backdrop as you tell your story and look at the audience.
- If possible, try not to stand behind a podium or only in one place. Moving around the stage or the room and interacting with audience members will keep their attention.
- Consider using technology to enhance your presentation. Use a laser pointer or other pointing device when explaining figures on your slides. Use a wireless remote control to advance your slides so you do not have to stand behind a podium computer. Use a tablet computer so you can write on slides with a stylus.
- Involve your audience. Ask a question and use an interactive polling tool such as Poll-Everywhere (**Figure 5-17**) to invite the audience to respond by sending a text message or visiting a website to indicate their response, using their smartphones. Responses will update in real time for everyone to see.

Figure 5-17: Collecting and displaying live responses during a presentation

Poll Everywhere

Collect live responses

Invite the audience to respond simultaneously by visiting a website or texting a number on their phones.

See instant results

Responses appear in an animated graph or chart embedded in your presentation. Results update live for all to see.

- Do a dry-run beforehand to get a sense of how much time the presentation will take. If you give a short presentation, such as 5 minutes, you might consider creating a presentation with 20 slides and setting the timing so that slides advance automatically at preset intervals, such as 15 seconds apart. This technique allows the speaker to talk to the audience without having to advance the slides manually. It ensures the presentation will end on time, and the slides become a visual backdrop for engaging the audience with your message.

Use Database Software to Manage Basic Databases

You can use database software to keep track of contacts, addresses, collections, and more. Large enterprises use databases to store vast quantities of data that enable us to shop online (**Figure 5-18**), execute web searches, or find friends on social media.

Figure 5-18: Databases

If you shop online, you search databases of products to find what you want.

When you make a purchase, a database stores your transaction information.

Large databases store billions of pieces of data and handle hundreds or thousands of users at a time.

Odua Images/Shutterstock.com

A **database** is a collection of data organized in a manner that allows access, retrieval, and reporting of that data. With database software, you can create, access, and manage a database by adding, updating, and deleting data; filter, sort and retrieve data from the database; and create forms and reports using the data in the database. To create reports from a database, you specify queries, or requests for information from the database.

Databases have many applications:

- Individuals might use database software on a personal computer to track contacts, schedules, possessions, or collections.
- Small businesses might use database software to process orders, track inventory, maintain customer lists, or manage employee records.
- Companies might use databases to store customer relationship management data, such as interactions with customers and their purchases.

Database software provides visual tools to create queries. The database software represents a query in **SQL (Structured Query Language)**, a language that provides a standardized way to request information from a relational database system. Advanced users may type SQL commands directly to interact with a database.

Database software is available as a desktop, server, or web-enabled application. Desktop applications are designed for individual users to run on desktop or laptop computers.

When a database has multiple users accessing it simultaneously, a server solution is usually the best. Products such as Oracle, Microsoft SQL Server, and MySQL allow you to organize large amounts of data, and have many users update it simultaneously.

Databases can be stored in a file on a hard disk, a solid-state drive, an external drive, or in cloud storage. Because many users may need to access a database at the same time, and databases can be quite large, enterprise databases generally run on a shared computer called a **server**. Data can be exported from a database into other programs, such as a spreadsheet program, where you can create charts to visualize data that results from a query. You also can export data from a database to other formats, including HTML, to publish it to the web.

Identify Apps Related to Database Software

A **relational database management system (RDBMS)**, or **relational database**, is a database that consists of a collection of tables where items are organized in columns and rows. A unique key identifies the value in each row. Common values in different tables can be related, or linked, to each other, so that data does not have to be repeated, making it less prone to error.

Microsoft Access is a popular relational database for personal computers. While Microsoft Access is geared toward consumers and small businesses, SQL Server and Oracle provide advanced database solutions for enterprise use.

Identify the Key Features of Database Software

In a relational database, such as Microsoft Access, data is organized into tables of **records** (rows of data) and is stored electronically in a database. After opening a database, you choose options to view tables, create queries, and perform other tasks.

The software displays commands and work areas appropriate to the view for your task. You enter and edit data in some views. You design, modify, and format layouts of reports, forms, tables, and queries in others. You can retrieve data using queries and print reports to see the results.

Use Database Tables

Each piece of data in a database is entered and stored in an area called a **field**, a column containing a specific property for each record, such as a person, place, object, event, or idea. Each field is assigned a **field name**, a column label that describes the field. Fields are defined by their data type, such as text, date, or number. The text data type stores characters that cannot be used in mathematical calculations. Logical data types store yes/no or true/false values. Hyperlinks store data as web addresses.

Tables are a collection of records for a single subject, such as all the customer records, organized in grids of rows and columns, much like worksheets in spreadsheet applications. Tables store data for the database. Columns contain fields; rows contain records. A database can contain one or more tables.

You can sort table data by one or more fields to create meaningful lists. For example, you might sort customer data by the amounts of their purchases in decreasing order, to see the customers with the largest purchases first. Filters let you see only the records that contain criteria you specify, such as purchases over $1000. **Figure 5-19** shows important database elements in an Access database for an animal care center.

Define a Database Query

A **query** extracts data from a database based on specified criteria, or conditions, for one or more fields. For example, you might query a sales database to find all the customers in Connecticut who made purchases of more than $1000 in January and sort the results in decreasing order by the purchase amount. **Figure 5-20** shows a query on the animal care center database that returns the animal names in alphabetical order, with their owner's first and last names.

A query contains the tables and fields you want to search along with the parameters, or pieces of information, you want to find. You can use text criteria or logical operators to specify parameters. The query displays results in a datasheet, which you can view on-screen or print. You can save queries to run later; query results are updated using the current data in the tables each time you run the query.

Figure 5-19: Tables, fields, records, and relationships in a database

Tables are related by common values. The OwnerID in the tblAnimal table refers to the owner information associated with the OwnerID in the tblOwner table.

Records can be sorted in ascending or descending order based on a field's value. In the tblAnimal table, records are sorted in increasing order of Owner ID values.

Field names often describe the field's contents.

A record is the set of field values for a single entity, such as an animal owner.

A table is a collection of records.

Fields can have different data types. The Animal Birth Date field has data type Date/Time; the other fields are have the Short Text data type.

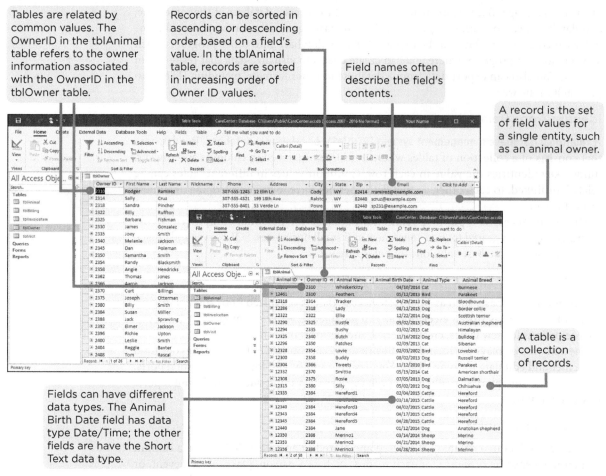

Figure 5-20: Creating and running a database query

Run the query to obtain the results.

The diagram shows the relationship between the tblOwner table and the tblAnimal table. One owner can own one or more animals.

The query results contain each animal's name, sorted alphabetically, followed by its owner's name.

A query can combine data from different tables of a database. This query collects the animal's name from the tblAnimal table, and its owner's name from the tblOwner table, and sorts the results in ascending order by the animal's name.

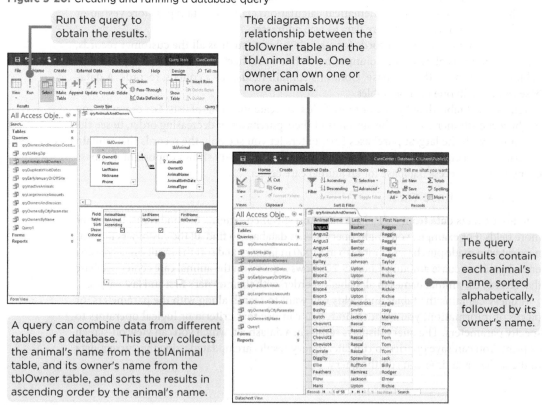

You can build queries using a visual query builder tool, which converts your query specifications to SQL. SQL provides a series of keywords and commands that advanced users might type directly to create and run queries.

Use Database Reports

A **report** is a user-designed layout of database content. Like forms, reports have labels to describe data and other controls that contain values. You might prepare a monthly sales report listing top deals and agents, or an inventory report to identify low-stock items. Reports contain the data along with headers, footers, titles, and sections. You can group data into categories and display totals and subtotals on fields that have numeric data. You can sort and filter data by one or more fields, and add graphics such as charts, diagrams, or a company's logo.

Follow these steps to create a report:

1. Specify the format and layout options for the report.

2. Identify data to include based on a data set or queries using specified criteria.

3. Run the report to populate it with data from the database.

Use Database Forms

A **form** is a screen used to enter data into a database. A form provides an easy-to-use data entry screen that generally shows only one record at a time. Like paper forms, database forms guide users to fill in information in specified formats. A form is made up of **controls**, or elements such as labels, text boxes, list boxes, buttons, and graphics, that specify where content is placed and how it is labeled.

You can use controls to reduce data entry errors. For example, a form might contain a text box in which a database user can type an email address. The form only would accept data that is in the format of a valid email address.

Forms also help users navigate records and find specific information. **Figure 5-21** shows a database report and form for the animal center.

Figure 5-21: A database report and form

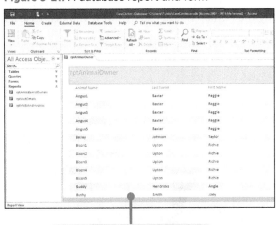

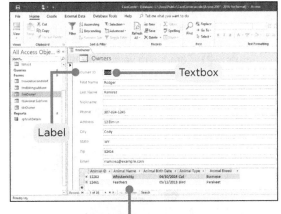

A report contains the query results in an attractive format.

A form contains fields where you can enter values into the database.

Manage Databases

Databases are complex files. Databases with multiple users usually need a database administrator to oversee the database. A database administrator has several important responsibilities, including:

- Controlling access to the database by regulating who can use it and what parts they can see; for example, you do not want all employees to view private salary information
- Ensuring data integrity and minimizing data entry errors by controlling how data is entered, formatted, and stored

- Preventing users from inadvertently changing or deleting important data
- Controlling version issues, which arise when multiple users access the same data at the same time, so that changes are not lost or overwritten
- Managing database backup plans regularly to avoid or recover damaged or lost files
- Establishing and maintaining strict database security to protect susceptible data from hacker attacks

Describe Big Data

When you enter a status update on Facebook or send a tweet on Twitter, or purchase an item on Amazon, or download a song from iTunes, each of these activities is stored in a database. These databases can grow very quickly because of the large volume of data that users generate continuously. **Big Data** refers to data collections so large and complex that it is difficult to process using relational database applications. Amazon, for example, analyzes data from shopping patterns of all its customers to recommend products that you might like to purchase.

New technologies are being developed to manage large quantities of unstructured data such as status updates, Tweets, and online purchases, which do not fit well into rows and columns. Storing very large data sets, such as all the tweets on Twitter or messages on Facebook sent in a day, typically involves distributing these items among several database servers in the cloud. By storing large databases in the cloud, companies easily can increase storage or processing capabilities as needed to store, access, or query the data.

Use Graphics Software

When you need a new banner image for your website, or you want to edit a digital photo, or create a logo for your business, graphics software will accomplish the task. You can create, view, manipulate, and print many types of digital images using graphics programs and apps.

Digital images are stored either in **bitmap**, sometimes called **raster**, or **vector** format. Bitmap images are based on a grid of colored dots called **pixels** (picture elements). A bitmap assigns a color to each pixel in a graphic. The large number and small size of pixels gives your eye the illusion of continuity, and results in a realistic looking image (see **Figure 5-22**). A high-resolution photo can contain thousands of pixels, so bitmap files can be large and difficult to modify. Resizing the bitmap image can distort it and decrease its resolution.

Figure 5-22: Comparing vector and bitmap images

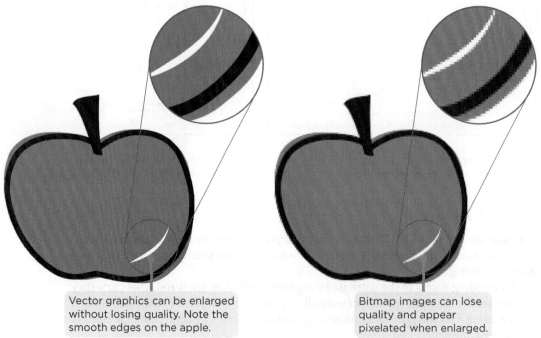

Vector graphics can be enlarged without losing quality. Note the smooth edges on the apple.

Bitmap images can lose quality and appear pixelated when enlarged.

Vector graphics tend to be simple images composed of shapes, lines, and diagrams. Vector graphics use mathematical formulas instead of pixels to define their appearance. Vector graphics are useful for images that can be shrunk or enlarged and still maintain their crisp outlines and clarity. Many company logos are designed as vector graphics, because they need to scale. They must look sharp when shrunk to fit on business cards, as well as when they are enlarged to display on webpages or print on large signs.

Most clip art images are stored as vector graphics. **Clip art** refers to premade pictures and symbols available on the web or included with your application's image gallery. You can include clip art in documents, presentations, or worksheets. Clip art libraries include images that are available sometimes for free, or for a small fee. Clip art is a quick way to add simple graphics to your work.

Identify the Key Features of Graphics Software

Graphics software programs use a variety of drawing and editing tools to create, modify, and enhance images. You can use tools to change the size, crop, rotate, and flip an image. Many programs have features to adjust the brightness, color saturation, and contrast of photos. Many graphics programs allow you to:

- Use a mouse or stylus to draw on the screen using a crayon, pencil, paintbrush, or calligraphy pen, and set the color and thickness
- Use shape tools to create lines, circles, rectangles, arrows, and callouts
- Use color palettes to specify colors for shapes, lines, and borders
- Add filters and effects to provide visual interest, and adjust brightness and contrast
- Add text to graphics using a variety of fonts, colors, sizes, and styles
- Crop or resize an image

When working with a graphics program, you can save images in a variety of file formats, as summarized in Table 5-11. Some of these formats compress images so they require less storage.

Table 5-11: Popular graphics formats

Name	Extension	Description
Bitmap	.bmp	Uncompressed file format that codes a value for each pixel. Files can be large.
TIFF (Tagged Image File Format)	.tiff	Large image format commonly used for print publishing because it maintains quality. Avoid using on webpages because of the large file sizes.
JPEG (Joint Photographic Experts Group)	.jpg	A compressed image file format usually used to save photos taken with digital cameras. Useful for images on webpages and in documents, because they have high quality and small file sizes.
GIF (Graphics Interchange Format)	.gif	A proprietary compressed graphics format that supports images with animation and transparent backgrounds.
PNG (Portable Networks Graphics)	.png	An open compressed format that has replaced GIF in many cases. Supports images with transparent backgrounds. Low resolution images that you can edit without losing quality. Great for use on webpages.
Raw data	.raw	Uncompressed and unprocessed data from a digital camera, usually used by professional photographers.

Describe Paint Apps

Using **paint apps**, you can draw pictures, shapes, and other graphics with various on-screen tools, such as a text tool, pen, brush, eyedropper, and paint bucket (**Figure 5-23**). Most paint programs produce bitmap images. Some programs provide templates for adding

Figure 5-23: Features of paint programs

Text formatting options include font family, size, color, and alignment. Text is stored as vector graphics.

Editing tools let you change colors.

Paint programs feature freehand drawing tools such as pencils, pens, brushes, paints, and colors, as well as tools to draw shapes and lines.

Paint programs include tools to add text annotations.

Placing different elements on layers can help when editing an image.

graphics to popular documents such as greeting cards, mailing labels, and business cards. Some paint apps allow you to create 3D images and diagrams (**Figure 5-24**).

Microsoft Paint and Paint 3D are easy-to-use paint programs. Paint.NET and GIMP are free paint programs you can download, and SumoPaint is a free web-based paint app with many features. Popular drawing programs include Adobe Illustrator, Adobe Fireworks, CorelDraw, Corel DESIGNER, and OpenOffice Draw.

Figure 5-24: With Paint3D you can create and interact with three-dimensional models

The 3D library provides a variety of 3D models with which to create three-dimensional drawings.

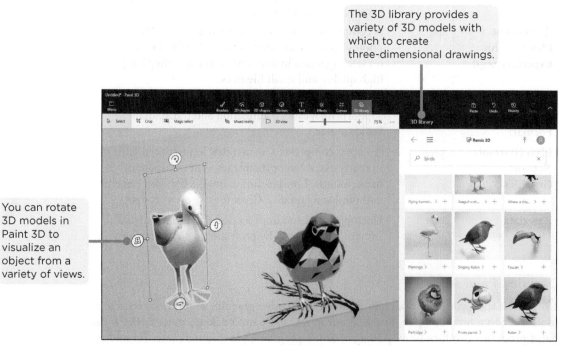

You can rotate 3D models in Paint 3D to visualize an object from a variety of views.

Describe Photo Editing Apps

Photo and image editing apps provide the capabilities of paint apps and let you enhance and modify existing photos and images. Modifications can include adjusting or enhancing brightness, contrast, saturation, sharpness, or tint (**Figure 5-25**).

Figure 5-25: You can enhance a photo using photo editing apps

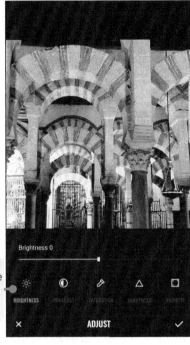 

Options for adjusting a photo's appearance include brightness, contrast, saturation, and sharpness.

Image editing software for the home or small business user provides an easy-to-use interface; includes tools to draw pictures, shapes, and other images; and provides the capability of modifying existing graphics and photos. Word processing, presentation, and other productivity applications usually include basic image editing capabilities.

With photo management apps you can view, organize, sort, search, print, and share digital photos. Some photo management app services such as Google Photos will organize your photos for you based on the date, time, or location where they were taken. They use advanced image recognition techniques to search your photos for particular items, colors, people, or scenes (**Figure 5-26**).

Video editing apps such as FilmoraGo and Adobe Premiere Clip allow you to modify a segment of a video, called a clip. For example, you can reduce the length of a video clip, reorder a series of clips, or add special effects, such as a title at the beginning of the video, or credits that scroll up at the end, as shown in **Figure 5-27**. Video editing software typically includes audio editing capabilities. With audio editing apps, such as Audacity, you can modify audio clips, produce studio-quality soundtracks, and change the playback speed. Most television shows and movies and many online videos are created or enhanced using video and audio editing software. You can record audio or video using your mobile device, and use audio and video editing apps on your phone, tablet, or computer to edit these files.

Figure 5-26: With some photo management apps, you can search your photos based on categories or characteristics

Searching for photos of food returns several delicious results.

Figure 5-27: You can use a video editing app on your phone to enhance videos before posting them online

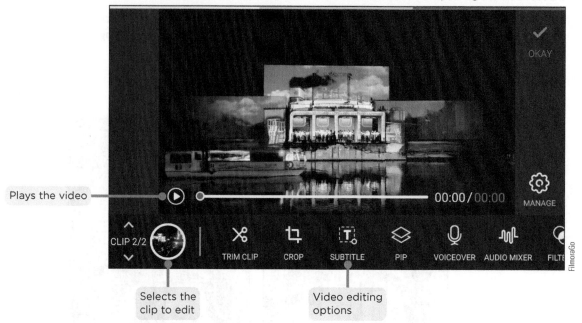

Plays the video

Selects the clip to edit

Video editing options

FilmoraGo

Describe Drawing Apps

Drawing apps let you create simple, two-dimensional images. In contrast to paint apps, drawing apps generally create vector graphics. You can modify and resize vector graphics without changing image quality. Some drawing programs can layer graphics one on top of another to create a unique complex graphic or collage of images.

Drawing programs feature freehand drawing tools such as pens or brushes, as well as tools for drawing lines, shapes, and specifying their colors. You can use drawing programs to create logos, diagrams, blueprints, business cards, flyers, and banner graphics for your website.

MODULE

5

Summary

In this module you learned to name, visually identify, and describe popular productivity apps including word processing, spreadsheet, presentation, and database software and their key features. You also learned to describe different types of application software, including graphics software, drawing apps, paint apps, and photo editing apps.

Productivity apps are used in both personal and business settings. Types of productivity apps discussed in this module include word processing, spreadsheet, presentation, and database software. Many of these apps run on your desktop, in a browser, or on a mobile device or tablet.

With word processing software, you can format text and documents and manage documents. With spreadsheet software, you can create and manage workbooks, analyze data, create charts, and format spreadsheets.

With presentation software, you can create slides, add transitions between slides, use presentation templates, and include animations on elements in slides, to make more effective presentations. You also can format, share, and display presentations.

With database programs, you can create database tables, reports, and forms; create and perform queries; and manage databases.

Review Questions

1. You want to share information about an upcoming event at your school by creating a short promotional video. Which type of app might you use to create the video?
   a. graphics and media
   b. communications
   c. device management
   d. personal interest

2. Which of these is not an option for formatting text?
   a. changing the text's color
   b. changing the text's size
   c. making text bold
   d. copying a region of text

3. Which type of app would most likely NOT be found included in a productivity suite?
   a. word processing
   b. web browser
   c. spreadsheet
   d. presentation

4. To run a productivity app with most complete and advanced capabilities, you would most likely _____.
   a: download it from an app store to your smartphone
   b. run a web app in a web browser
   c. install and run the software on your desktop or laptop computer
   d. update the app online to make sure you have the most recent version

5. Mobile first design is important because _____.
   a. developers must provide simplified user experiences for apps that run on small screens
   b. sales of personal computers have surpassed sales of smartphones
   c. developers can only write apps for one platform
   d. smartphones generally have more processing power than laptops

6. When a value in a worksheet changes, the spreadsheet program will _____.
   a. reformat any cells whose values changed
   b. recalculate any cells whose formulas depend on the value that changed
   c. delete the value
   d. launch a calculator for you to check the calculations

7. When giving a presentation, pushing one slide off the right edge of the screen as another one appears is an example of a(n) _____.
   a. transition
   b. exit
   c. entrance
   d. animation

8. In a relational database, data is organized into rows of data called _____.
   a. fields
   b. tables
   c. records
   d. views

9. When you take a photo with a digital camera, most likely it is saved in _____ format.
   a. TIFF
   b. GIF
   c. PNG
   d. JPG

Discussion Questions

1. Experiment with using apps from any two of the productivity suites listed in Table 5-3. Can you find reasons to choose one over the other?

2. Compare photo or image editing programs that work on your personal computer with similar apps that work on your phone. Which do you find easier or more convenient to use? Why?

3. Read an article about how Big Data enables companies to track large amounts of personal information. What types of information do companies track? Are you concerned about your own privacy online in this age of Big Data?

Critical Thinking Activities

1. Leah Jacobs is starting her own dance studio and wants to create digital media and use productivity software to support her business. She is hiring a graphic artist to create a logo for her business. She wants to use the logo across all visual communications at the company, from business cards to database forms, to websites and social media. What programs and apps should she consider using to run her business?

2. Jason Chang is creating photos of his restaurant for a new website. Some of the photos of the staff have red eye, others are badly lit so that the restaurant looks dark, and some of the food photos have little contrast or are badly composed. He asks your advice about ways to enhance his photos to make them look better for the website. What suggestions might you give? Do you think it is okay to modify photos digitally to improve their appearance, or is that deceiving his customers? Why or why not?

3. Kris Allen runs a pet day care center. She needs to keep track of contact information for her customers, their animals, the services provided (such as walking and grooming), and the staff who are assigned to care for them. She also must send out invoices for payment each month. What features of spreadsheet and/or database software might she use to facilitate her business?

Key Terms

absolute reference
animation
Apache OpenOffice
app
app store
Apple iWork
application software
argument
Big Data
bitmap
built-in function
cell
cell address
chart
clip art
communications apps
conditional formatting
control
cross-platform
database
device management apps
document
document management tools
drawing apps
field
field name
filter
form
format
formula

function
G suite
graphics and media apps
insertion point
local application
macro
m-commerce
Microsoft Office 365
mobile app
mobile commerce
mobile first design
name
native app
on-screen keyboard
operator
page orientation
paint apps
personal interest apps
photo and image editing apps
pivot table
pixel
platform-specific
portable app
presentation
presentation app
presentation software
productivity apps
productivity suite
query
raster

read-only access
record
relational database
relational database management system (RDBMS)
relative reference
report
responsive design
scroll bars
server
slide master
slide show
sort
sparkline
spreadsheet
SQL (Structured Query Language)
style
table
template
transition
trendline
vector
video editing apps
view-only link
web app
web-based application
what-if analysis
word processing software
workbook
worksheet

Security and Safety

Hideo watches for signs of attacks on the school's network and computers.

Hideo writes a newsletter that has news and tips about how to stay safe while using the Internet. He also schedules monthly sessions to demonstrate to students how to protect their computers from attacks.

Hideo is working as an intern at his school's Information Technology department during his final semester before graduation. He helps protect the school's computers and networks from attackers. He monitors the network for any signs of attacks and helps to prevent them from quickly spreading. Hideo also sends out messages warning the school about the latest attacks and writes a weekly newsletter with tips about how to stay secure online. Each month he holds a Lunch-and-Learn session for students who want hands-on instruction in how to keep their computers safe.

In This Module

- Discuss computer safety and health risks
- Use protective measures to safeguard computers and data

YOU LIKELY USE your phone or a computer hundreds of times each day to read messages from friends, search for a new restaurant, work on school assignments, play games, shop for clothes, and check your bank balance. But attackers are always watching for any openings to steal your information or infect your devices. They often trick us into doing things that make it easy for them to steal our data, identities, and more. To stay secure online, you should understand how to defend yourself from these attacks.

In this module, you examine the types of attacks that occur today and how you can protect your computers and other devices and your personal information. You will also explore personal health risks that come from using a computer or smartphone.

Discuss Computer Safety and Health Risks

Warning: Using This Device Could Be Hazardous to Your Safety and Health is a warning label you would never see on a computer. But that doesn't mean that using a computer is entirely safe. There are hazards to using a computer that you might not even be aware of.

Figure 6-1 illustrates the three main types of hazards from computers: to our information, the environment, and our health. The first type of hazard relates to the threat to your data and programs (apps), and comes from attackers who want to steal your information. Hazards to our environment come from the toxic electronic components of computers and other digital devices that are exposed when the devices are discarded. Hazards to our physical bodies include eye strain from viewing the computer screen in poor light, poor posture when using devices, or muscle fatigue that comes from typing on a keyboard.

The more you know about these hazards, the better you can protect your data, the environment, and your own health.

Figure 6-1: Computer hazards can be physical, environmental, or from those who want to steal information

Jada positions her computer screen at the right height and makes sure she does not have a glare from the window that might cause eye strain.

Jada is concerned that the hazardous toxic elements in her computer are properly recycled when her computer is discarded.

Jada is careful to protect the information she enters from attackers.

Determine the Risks to Computer Security and Safety

A *risk* is the possibility something might occur that results in an injury or a loss. You often hear warnings about risks, such as a thunderstorm approaching or that a floor is wet. You probably take some type of action to protect yourself when you become aware of risks, such as going indoors to avoid the storm or walking carefully so that you do not slip and fall. Although we do not often think about it, using our computers can also introduce risks. And as with a storm or wet floor you should take precautions with these computer risks.

Today, one of the more dangerous risks of using a computer is that someone will steal our important information. Although the technical term for these thieves is *threat actor*, a more general and common term used to describe individuals who launch attacks against other users and their computers is simply **attackers**. These attackers may work individually, but more often they belong to organized gangs of young attackers who meet in hidden online "dark web" forums to trade information, buy and sell stolen data and attacker tools, and even coordinate their attacks.

Who are these attackers? **Script kiddies** are individuals who want to attack computers, but lack the knowledge of computers and networks needed to do so. Script kiddies instead do their work by downloading freely available automated attack software (*scripts*) from websites and using it to perform malicious acts. **Hactivists** are attackers who are strongly motivated by principles or beliefs. Attacks by hactivists can involve breaking into a website and changing the contents on the site as a means of making a political statement. **Cyberterrorists** attack a nation's computer networks, like the electrical power grid, to cause disruption and panic among citizens. Instead of using an army to strike at an adversary, governments are now employing state-sponsored attackers to launch computer attacks against their enemies through **nation state actors**. Another serious security threat to companies can come from its own employees, contractors, and business partners, called **insiders**. For example, a healthcare worker upset about being passed over for a promotion might illegally gather health records on celebrities and sell them to the media, or a securities trader who loses billions of dollars on bad stock bets could use her knowledge of the bank's computer security system to conceal the losses through fake transactions.

Once, the reason for launching computer attacks was for the attackers to show off their technology skills (*fame*). Today that is no longer the case. Attackers are more focused on financial gain: to steal personal information so that they can generate income (*fortune*).

These attackers try to steal and then use your credit card numbers, online financial account information, or Social Security numbers. With this information they can pretend to be you and buy expensive items online while charging them to your credit card, or break into your bank account to transfer your money to another account.

Securing Personal Information

For most computer users the greatest risk comes from attackers who want to steal their information for their own financial gain.

The risks you face online when using the Internet or email include:

- Online banking. Attackers try to steal your password to access your online bank account and transfer your money overseas.
- E-commerce shopping. When you enter your credit card number to make an online purchase an attacker can try to intercept your card number as it is transmitted over the network.
- Fake websites. Attackers can set up an "imposter" website that looks just like the site where you pay your monthly credit card bill. This fake website tricks you into entering your username and password, and that information then falls into the hands of the attackers. Because the fake website looks very similar to the real website, it can be hard to identify these unsafe websites.
- Social media sites. Attackers can ask to be a "friend" on your social media site by pretending to be someone you met or went to school with. Once you accept this new friend the attacker may be able to see personal information about you, such as your pet's name or your favorite vacation spot. This information could be used to reset your

password on another website that requires the answer to the security question *What is the name of your pet?* Also, smartphone apps that are linked to social media sites have been known to gather user information without proper notification.

Gathering your personal information is not something that is done only by attackers. Many organizations collect and store your personal information for legitimate means. This information should be accessible only to those who are authorized to use it. But some organizations might secretly share your confidential information without your consent. Table 6-1 lists some of the valid and invalid uses of your personal information by organizations.

Table 6-1: Uses of personal information

Organization	Information	Valid use	Invalid use
School	Telephone number	Call you about an advising appointment	Give to credit card company who calls you about applying for a new credit card
Hospital	Medical history	Can refer to past procedures when you are admitted as a patient	Sell to drug company who sends you information about their drugs
Employer	Personal email address	Will send to you the latest company newsletter	Provides to a local merchant who is having a holiday sale

The total amount of data collected on individuals can be staggering. Many organizations use **data mining**, which is the process of sorting through extremely large sets of data to uncover patterns and establish relationships. Most data mining tools even allow organizations to predict future trends.

Some tips for protecting your personal information that is gathered by legitimate organizations include:

- Give only necessary information when completing an online form or a warranty or rebate card.
- Review the information that online sites such as Google, Facebook, Microsoft, and others have stored about you.
- Request to be removed from mailing lists.
- Create another email account to use when a merchant or website requires an address.
- Do not use your social media account login information to log in to another site (when that option is available).

Figure 6-2: Computer waste can harm the environment

Olivier Le Queinec/Shutterstock.com

Environmental Risks

What happens to computers and other digital devices when they have reached the end of their lives and are no longer needed? Too often they are simply thrown away and end up in a landfill, resulting in large amounts of **e-waste** (electronic waste). According to the Environmental Protection Agency (EPA), Americans generate over 9.4 million tons of e-waste each year.[1] Not only does this increase the need for more and larger landfill sites, but also discarded computer equipment can harm the environment. Computer parts like those shown in **Figure 6-2** contain valuable materials such as gold, palladium, platinum, and copper. However, they also contain other metals that are toxic, such as lead and mercury. These toxic metals may eventually contaminate the ground and water supply, causing harm to the environment.

An initiative called *Sustainable Electronics Management (SEM)* promotes the reduction of e-waste. **Table 6-2** outlines the action steps of SEM. All users should consider how they can reduce their e-waste.

Table 6-2: SEM action steps

Step	Action	Description
1	Buy green	When purchasing new electronic equipment buy only products that have been designed with environmentally preferable attributes.
2	Donate	Donate used but still functional equipment to a school, charity, or non-profit organization.
3	Recycle	Send equipment to a verified used electronics recycling center.

Understand the Risks to Physical, Behavioral, and Social Health

In addition to the hazards related to the safety of your information and hazards to the environment from toxic electronic components, there is another type of hazard. This is the hazard of technology to our physical health as well as our behavioral and social well-being.

Risks to Physical Health

How frequently do you use your smartphone? It's probably more often than you think. Although it varies by age, according to some estimates younger users check their smartphone 86 times each day. And most of the time users are on their smartphones they are doing something else as well. **Table 6-3** lists some of the activities and the percentage of users doing the activities while they are on their phones.

Table 6-3: Percentage of smartphone usage during select activities

Activity	Percentage of users
Shopping	92%
Spending leisure time	90%
Watching television	89%
Talking to family or friends	85%
Eating in a restaurant	81%
Eating at home	78%
Driving	59%
During a business meeting	54%
Walking across a road	44%

Although we might not use a personal computer with the same frequency or in the same way as we do a smartphone, nevertheless the amount of time spent on a computer for most people is measured in the thousands—or even tens of thousands—of hours per year. And any activity at which you spend that much time is very likely to put a strain on your physical body.

Many users of technology devices report aches and pains associated with repeated and long-term usage of the devices, known as **repetitive strain injury (RSI)**. RSI impacts your muscles, nerves, tendons, and ligaments. RSI most often affects the upper parts of the body, including:

- Elbows
- Forearms
- Hands
- Neck
- Shoulders
- Wrists

There are a variety of symptoms for RSI:

- Aching
- Cramp
- Numbness
- Pain
- Stiffness
- Tenderness
- Throbbing
- Tingling
- Weakness

RSI is most often caused by three factors. **Table 6-4** lists the causes, descriptions, and examples of RSI.

Table 6-4: Causes and examples of RSI

Cause	Description	Example
Repetitive activity	Repeating the same activity over a lengthy time period	Typing on a keyboard for multiple hours every day over several years
Improper technique	Using the wrong procedure or posture	Slouching in a chair
Uninterrupted intensity	Performing the same high-level activity without frequent periods of rest	Working at a computer all day with no breaks

Most computer users suffer from RSI that is brought about through using an improper technique for sitting at a computer. **Figure 6-3** illustrates incorrect posture while working on a computer: the user is not sitting up straight in the chair, he is too close to the computer screen, and glare from the window behind him is reflecting off the screen. Being too close to a screen or looking at screens without regular breaks can cause eyestrain.

Figure 6-3: Incorrect posture while working on a computer

Face too close to the screen

Glare from window reflecting off the screen

Not sitting up straight in the chair

Africa Studio/Shutterstock.com

To prevent RSI your workplace should be arranged correctly. **Ergonomics** is an applied science that specifies the design and arrangement of items that you use so that you and the

items interact efficiently and safely. **Figure 6-4** shows the correct ergonomic posture and techniques for working on a computer. These include:

- Arms. The arms are parallel to the floor at approximately a 90-degree angle.
- Eyes. The distance to the screen is 18–28 inches from the eyes, and the viewing angle is downward at about 20 degrees to the center of the screen.
- Feet. The feet are flat on the floor. Use a proper chair with adjustable height and multiple legs for stability.

Figure 6-4: Correct posture while working on a computer

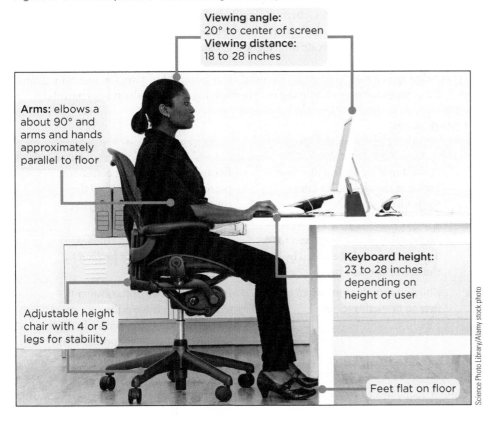

Science Photo Library/Alamy stock photo

Risks to Behavioral Health

Just as there are hazards to physical health from using digital devices, there also are behavioral health hazards. These hazards are sometimes more difficult to observe but are every bit as serious as RSI and other physical hazards.

One behavioral hazard is **technology addiction**. This occurs when a user is obsessed with using a technology device and cannot walk away from it without feeling extreme anxiety. Because near-constant use of technology has become the norm, whether it is a toddler playing a game on a tablet, a teenager locked away in her room tied to her laptop, or an adult buried in his phone at a party, technology addiction can be difficult to identify in a friend or companion, much less in yourself.

In addition to technology addiction, there are other behavioral risks associated with using technology, including:

- Sedentary lifestyle. Too much time spent using a technology device often results in too little time for physical activity and can contribute to an overall sedentary lifestyle.
- Psychological development. Excessive use of technology has been associated with several psychological mental health concerns such as poor self-confidence, anxiety, depression, lower emotional stability, and even lower life satisfaction.
- Social interaction. Users who spend excessive amounts of time using technology often resist face-to-face interaction with others, and this may hinder social skill development or even cause social withdrawal.

Risks to Social Health

The scientific study of how people's thoughts, feelings, and social behaviors are influenced by other people is called social psychology. While there are many positive factors that influence your social behavior and resulting social health, there are negative impacts that can cause serious harm to your social health.

One negative impact that can result in serious emotional harm is cyberbullying. Bullying is one person using his or her strength or influence to intimidate someone else. **Cyberbullying** is bullying that takes place on technology devices like cell phones, computers, and tablets using online social media platforms, public online forums, gaming sites, text messaging, or email. Cyberbullying includes sending, posting, or sharing negative, harmful, mean-spirited, and usually false content about another person. It can even include sharing personal or private information to cause embarrassment or humiliation to that person before others.

Cyberbullying is considered more harmful than general bullying for several reasons. Table 6-5 compares features of bullying to cyberbullying to show why it is so harmful.

Table 6-5: Harmful features of cyberbullying

Feature	Bullying	Cyberbullying
Seems to never end	A child may be bullied at school but once the child goes home the bullying ceases.	Because cyberbullying comments posted online are visible all the time, to the victim the bullying never ends.
Everyone knows about it	Mean-spirited words spoken to a victim may only be heard by those who are nearby.	A cyberbully can post comments online that can be read by everyone.
May follow for a lifetime	Bullying usually stops when the person or victim leave.	Posted cyberbullying comments may remain visible online for years and even follow the victim through life, impacting college admissions and employment.

Another social health risk is cyberstalking. In the animal kingdom *stalking* is often used to describe an animal hunting its prey. Among humans stalking is unwanted and obsessive attention or harassment directed towards another person. **Cyberstalking** involves the use of technology to stalk another person through email, text messages, phone calls, and other forms of communication.

Cyberbullying and cyberstalking are serious intrusions into a person's life. If you suspect that someone you know may be a victim or if you are yourself, you should contact local law enforcement agencies.

Describe Common Cybersecurity Attacks

Attackers have a wide array of tools that they use to attack computers and networks. These tools generally fall into two categories. The first category is malicious software programs that are created by attackers to infiltrate the victims' computers without their knowledge. Once onboard, this software can intercept data, steal information, launch other attacks, or even damage the computer so that it no longer properly functions.

The other category may be overlooked but is equally serious: tricking users into performing a compromising action or providing sensitive information. These attacks take advantage of user confusion about good security practices and deceive them into opening the door for the attacks. Defeating security through a person instead of technology is a low-cost but highly effective approach for the attackers.

Figure 6-5 illustrates the tools that attackers use. It is important that you understand cybersecurity attacks so that you can properly defend yourself and keep your data secure.

Figure 6-5: Cybersecurity attack tools

Attacker is writing malicious software to infect a user's computer to steal information

Attacker is sending an email that pretends to come from a friend of the victim but when opened creates a "backdoor" for the attacker to enter the computer and steal passwords

Andrey_Popov/Shutterstock.com

Attacks Using Malware

Malware is malicious software that can delete or corrupt files and gather personal information. Malware refers to a wide variety of software programs that attackers use to enter a computer system without the user's knowledge or consent and then perform an unwanted and harmful action.

A computer **virus** is malicious computer code that, like its biological counterpart, reproduces itself on the same computer. Almost all viruses "infect" by inserting themselves into a computer file. When the file is opened, the virus is activated.

Another type of malware that attempts to spread is a worm. A **worm** is a malicious program that uses a computer network to replicate (worms are sometimes called *network viruses*). A worm enters a computer through the network and then takes advantage of a vulnerability on the host computer. Once the worm has exploited that vulnerability on one system, it immediately searches for another computer on the network that has the same vulnerability.

According to ancient legend, the Greeks won the Trojan War by hiding soldiers in a large hollow wooden horse that was presented as a gift to the city of Troy. Once the horse was wheeled into the fortified city, the soldiers crept out of the horse during the night and attacked.

A computer **Trojan** is malware that hides inside another program, often one downloaded from the web. It "masquerades" as performing a safe activity but also does something malicious. For example, a user might download what is advertised as a calendar program, yet when it is installed, in addition to installing the calendar it also installs malware that scans the system for credit card numbers and passwords, connects through the network to a remote system, and then transmits that information to the attacker.

One of the fastest-growing types of malware is ransomware. **Ransomware** prevents a user's device from properly and fully functioning until a fee is paid. The ransomware embeds itself onto the computer in such a way that it cannot be bypassed, even by rebooting.

Early ransomware, called *blocker ransomware*, prevented the user from accessing the computer's resources and displayed a special screen pretending to be from a reputable third-party, such as law enforcement. The screen provided a "valid" reason for blocking the user's computer such as performing some illegal action, along with instructions for lifting the block. **Figure 6-6** shows a blocker ransomware message.

Figure 6-6: Blocker ransomware

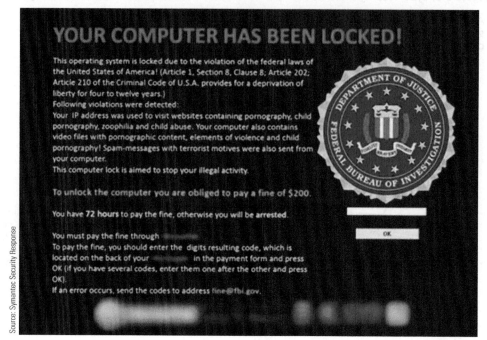

Today, ransomware has evolved so that instead of just blocking the user from accessing the computer, it encrypts all the files on the device so that none of them can be opened. A screen appears telling the victim that his or her files are now encrypted, and a fee must be paid to receive a key to unlock them. In addition, attackers increase the urgency for payment: the cost for the key to unlock the crypto-malware increases every few hours, or a number of the encrypted user files are deleted every few hours, with the number continually increasing. If the ransom is not paid promptly (often within 36 to 96 hours) the key can never be retrieved. **Figure 6-7** is an example of this type of an encrypting ransomware message.

Figure 6-7: Encrypting ransomware

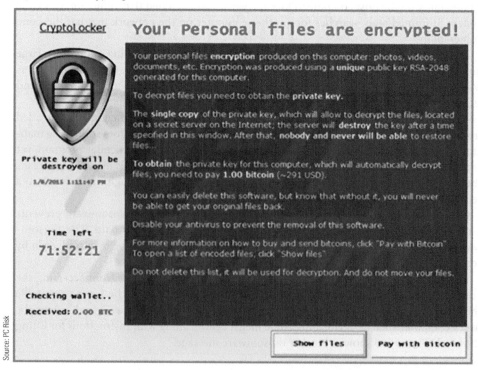

On a computer network each computer has a unique address so that data destined for that computer can be delivered to the correct device. Some attacks will change that address so that the data is instead sent to the attacker's computer, where the attacker can then read the victim's credit card number or password. An attack that changes the device's address is called **address spoofing**.

Attacks Using Social Engineering

Social engineering is a category of attacks that attempts to trick the victim into giving valuable information to the attacker. At its core, social engineering relies on an attacker's clever manipulation of human nature in order to persuade the victim to provide information or take actions. Several basic principles of psychology make social engineering highly effective. These are listed in Table 6-6, with the example of an attacker pretending to be the chief executive officer (CEO) calling the organization's help desk to have a password reset.

Table 6-6: Social engineering principles

Principle	Description	Example
Authority	Directed by someone impersonating authority figure or falsely citing their authority	"I'm the CEO calling."
Intimidation	To frighten and coerce by threat	"If you don't reset my password, I will call your supervisor."
Consensus	Influenced by what others do	"I called last week and your colleague reset my password."
Scarcity	Something is in short supply	"I can't waste time here."
Urgency	Immediate action needed	"My meeting with the board starts in 5 minutes."
Familiarity	Victim well-known and well-received	"I remember reading a good evaluation on you."
Trust	Confidence	"You know who I am."

One of the most common forms of social engineering is phishing. **Phishing** is sending an email or displaying a web announcement that falsely claims to be from a legitimate enterprise in an attempt to trick the user into giving private information. Users are asked to respond to an email or are directed to a website where they are requested to update personal information such as passwords, credit card numbers, Social Security numbers, bank account numbers, or other information. However, the email or website is actually an imposter and is set up to steal what information the user enters.

A few years ago phishing messages were easy to spot with misspelled words and obvious counterfeit images, but that is no longer the case. In fact, one of the reasons that phishing is so successful today is that the emails and the fake websites are difficult to distinguish from those that are legitimate: logos, color schemes, and wording seem to be almost identical. Figure 6-8 illustrates an actual phishing email message that looks like it came from a genuine source.

Attackers can use hoaxes as a first step in an attack. A **hoax** is a false warning, often contained in an email message that pretends to come from a valid source like the company's IT department. The hoax says that there is a "deadly virus" circulating through the Internet and that you should erase specific files or change security configurations, and then

Figure 6-8: Phishing email message

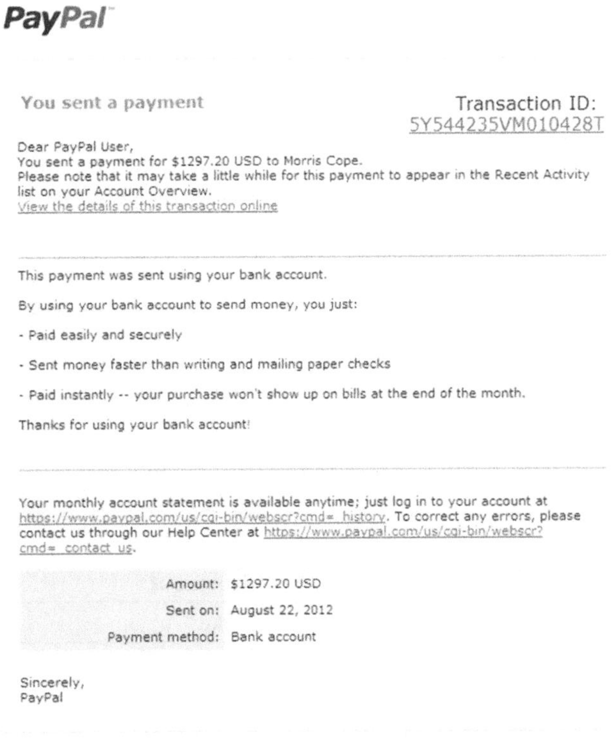

PayPal

You sent a payment   Transaction ID:
                                                      5Y544235VM010428T

Dear PayPal User,
You sent a payment for $1297.20 USD to Morris Cope.
Please note that it may take a little while for this payment to appear in the Recent Activity list on your Account Overview.
View the details of this transaction online

This payment was sent using your bank account.

By using your bank account to send money, you just:

- Paid easily and securely

- Sent money faster than writing and mailing paper checks

- Paid instantly -- your purchase won't show up on bills at the end of the month.

Thanks for using your bank account!

Your monthly account statement is available anytime; just log in to your account at https://www.paypal.com/us/cgi-bin/webscr?cmd=_history. To correct any errors, please contact us through our Help Center at https://www.paypal.com/us/cgi-bin/webscr?cmd=_contact_us.

Amount: $1297.20 USD

Sent on: August 22, 2012

Payment method: Bank account

Sincerely,
PayPal

forward the message to other users. However, changing configurations allows an attacker to break into your computer. Or, erasing files may make the computer unstable, prompting you to call the telephone number in the hoax email message for help, which is actually the phone number of the attacker.

Spam is unwanted email messages sent from an unknown sender to many email accounts, usually advertising a product or service such as low-cost medication, low-interest loans, or free credit reports. Spam continues to flood the email inboxes of Internet users. About 14.5 billion spam emails are sent daily, and if there is only one response for every 12.5 million emails sent, spammers still earn about $3.5 million over the course of one year.[2]

Beyond being annoying and interfering with work productivity as users spend time reading and deleting spam messages, spam can be a security vulnerability. This is because spam can be used to distribute malware. Spam sent with attachments that contain malware is one of the most common means by which attackers distribute their malware. If you open a malicious attachment sent through a spam email. your computer is immediately infected.

Use Protective Measures to Safeguard Computers and Data

Cybersecurity attacks are relentless. Over 11.2 billion data records have been breached since 2005.[3] It is estimated that malicious cyber activity cost the U.S. economy up to $109 billion annually.[4] And the numbers go on and on.

Because attacks are nonstop it is very important that you use protective measures to safeguard your computers and make your data secure from the attackers.

You may be thinking, "All this security stuff is too technical for me to do." However, that's not entirely true. Although some measures to ward off malware are technical, most are just practical common sense to prevent social engineering attacks. That's because social engineering attacks are the focus of attackers: over 93 percent of data breaches start by a phishing attack, and 22 percent of employees have clicked at least one phishing link in the last year.[5] If users can resist phishing attacks—even just a little—it can significantly reduce the number of overall successful attacks and start to make a real dent in cybercrime.

Using protective measures to safeguard your computers and data has never been more important than it is today.

Explain the Steps to Protect Computer Equipment

Protecting a computer from a cyberattack is important. But all that effort is useless if the computer has been damaged by dropping it, by a lightning strike, if the hard drive has failed, or the computer itself is stolen. This means that an overall protection scheme involves the necessary steps to protect the computer equipment.

Protecting Computers from Electrical Problems

Although the electrical power that comes into your home, school, or place of work is generally constant in its "force" (voltage), there may be occasional increases or decreases that can impact sensitive electrical devices, particularly computers. These electrical changes are listed in **Table 6-7**.

Table 6-7: Electrical changes

Electrical change	Explanation
Blackout	Total loss of power
Brownout	Drop in voltage lasting minutes or hours
Spike	Very short duration of voltage increase
Surge	Short duration of voltage increase
Noise	Unwanted high frequency energy

A **surge protector** can defend computer equipment from spikes, surges, and noise. A surge protector lies between the computer and the electrical outlet, and absorbs any electrical change so that it does not reach the computer equipment. **Figure 6-9** shows a surge protector.

While surge protectors can protect from a momentary change they cannot provide power in the event of a blackout or brownout. In this case an **uninterruptible power supply (UPS)** can be used. Like a surge protector, a UPS is positioned between the computer and electrical outlet; however, it contains a battery that maintains power to the equipment for a short time in case of an interruption in the primary electrical power source.

Figure 6-9: Surge protector

jirateep sankote/Shutterstock.com

Protect Computers from Theft

The primary advantage of a mobile device like a laptop computer, tablet, or smartphone is that it can be easily transported from one location to another. However, this mobility is also one of its greatest weaknesses: a thief can easily grab an unattended device. This means that you should always be aware of the risk of theft with your mobile devices.

To prevent laptops from being stolen you can use a cable lock. Most portable devices (as well as many expensive computer monitors) have a special security slot built into the case. A cable lock can be inserted into the security slot and rotated so that the cable lock is secured to the device. The cable can then be connected to an immovable object. A cable lock is illustrated in **Figure 6-10**.

Figure 6-10: Cable lock

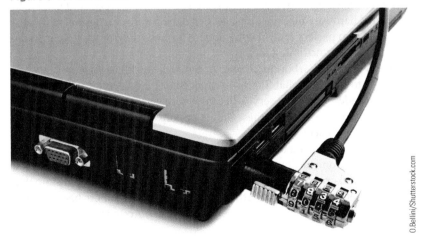

O.Bellini/Shutterstock.com

To reduce the risk of theft or loss:

- Keep mobile devices out of sight when traveling in a high-risk area.
- Avoid becoming distracted by what is on the device so that you can maintain an awareness of your surroundings.
- When holding a device, use both hands to make it more difficult for a thief to snatch.
- Do not use the device on escalators or near transit train doors.
- White or red headphone cords may indicate they are connected to an expensive device; consider changing the cord to a less conspicuous color.
- If a theft does occur, do not resist or chase the thief. Instead, take note of the suspect's description, including any identifying characteristics and clothing, and then call the authorities. Also contact the wireless carrier and change all passwords for accounts accessed on the device.

If a mobile device is lost or stolen, several security features can be used to locate the device to recover it. The device's operating system or an installed third-party app like Prey Project can provide the security features listed in Table 6-8.

Table 6-8: Security features for recovery of a stolen device

Security feature	Explanation
Alarm	The device can generate an alarm even if it is on mute.
Last known location	If the battery is charged to less than a specific percentage, the device's last known location can be indicated on an online map.
Locate	The current location of the device can be pinpointed on a map through the device's GPS.
Remote lockout	The mobile device can be remotely locked and a custom message sent that is displayed on the login screen.
Thief picture	A thief who enters an incorrect passcode three times will have his or her picture taken through the device's on-board camera and emailed to the owner.

If a lost or stolen device cannot be recovered, it might be necessary to perform *remote wiping*, which erases the sensitive data stored on the mobile device. This ensures that even if a thief is able to access the device, no sensitive data will be compromised.

Perform Data Backups

One of the most important steps to protecting computer equipment is frequently overlooked: to create data backups on a regular basis. Creating a **data backup** means copying files from a computer's hard drive that are then stored in a remote location. Data backups can protect against hardware malfunctions, user error, software corruption, and natural disasters. They can also protect against cyberattacks because they can restore infected computers to their properly functioning state.

Online backup services like Carbonite, iDrive, Acronis, or BackBlaze use special software on the computer to monitor what files have changed or have been created; these are then automatically uploaded to a cloud server. Because these backups are performed automatically and stored at a remote location these online backup services provide the highest degree of protection to most users.

However, there are sometimes situations when an online backup service may not be the right choice, such as when only a slow Internet connection is available. In that case you can perform your own backup from the hard drive to another medium and then store that medium in a remote location. Modern operating systems can perform these backups, and third-party software is also available, such as Aoemi Backupper, Acronis True Image, and EaseUS ToDo Backup.

Protect Mobile Devices and Your Privacy

In addition to protecting your mobile device from theft, you should also protect it from attackers who want to steal information stored on it or transmitted to and from the device. You should also protect the privacy of your information.

Protect Mobile Devices

There are several types of attacks directed toward mobile devices. Several of the most common attacks are directed toward wireless networks that support these devices.

Wi-Fi is a wireless data network technology that provides high-speed data connections for mobile devices. This type of network is technically known as a wireless local area network (WLAN). Devices such as tablets, laptop computers, smartphones, and wireless printers that are within range of a centrally located connection device can send and receive information using radio frequency (RF) transmissions at high speeds.

This central connection device needed for a home-based Wi-Fi network combines several networking technologies. These are usually called **wireless routers**. The wireless router acts as the "base station" for the wireless devices, sending and receiving wireless signals between all devices as well as providing the "gateway" to the external Internet (it typically is connected to the user's modem that is in turn connected to an Internet connection). A wireless router is illustrated in **Figure 6-11**.

Figure 6-11: Wireless router

Milosbeo/Shutterstock.com

There are several risks from attacks on Wi-Fi networks, such as:
- Reading wireless transmissions. Usernames, passwords, credit card numbers, and other information sent over the Wi-Fi network could be easily seen by an attacker.
- Viewing or stealing computer data. An attacker who can connect to a home Wi-Fi network could access any folder that has file sharing enabled on any computer on the network. This essentially provides an attacker full access to view or steal sensitive data from all computers on the network.
- Injecting malware. Attackers could inject Trojans, viruses, and other malware onto the user's computer.
- Downloading harmful content. In several instances, attackers have accessed a home computer through an unprotected Wi-Fi network, downloaded child pornography to the computer, and then turned that computer into a file server to distribute the content. When authorities traced the files back to that computer, the unsuspecting owner was arrested and his equipment confiscated.

When using a public Wi-Fi network in a coffee shop, airport, or school campus there are also security concerns. First, these networks are rarely protected (to allow easy access by users), so attackers can read any wireless transmissions sent to and from the user's device. In addition, an attacker may set up an *evil twin*, another computer designed to mimic an authorized Wi-Fi device. A user's mobile device may unknowingly connect to this evil twin instead of the authorized device so that attackers can receive the user's transmissions or directly send malware to the user's computer.

When using any public Wi-Fi, be sure you are connecting to the approved wireless network. Also limit the type of activity you do on public networks to simple web surfing or watching online videos. Accessing online banking sites or sending confidential information that could be intercepted is not a good idea.

Configuring your own Wi-Fi wireless router to provide the highest level of security is an important step. Configuration settings for wireless routers are listed in **Table 6-9**.

Table 6-9: Configuration settings for Wi-Fi wireless routers

Wireless router setting	Explanation	Recommended configuration
Access password	This requires a password to access the configuration settings of the device.	Create a strong password so that attackers cannot access the wireless router and turn off the security settings.
Remote management	Remote management allows the configuration settings to be changed from anywhere through an Internet connection.	Turn off remote management so that someone outside cannot access the configuration settings.
Service Set Identifier (SSID)	The SSID is the "name" of the local wireless network.	Change this from the default setting to a value that does not reveal the identity of the owner or the location of the network (such as *MyWireNet599342*).
Wi-Fi Protected Access 2 (WPA2) Personal	WPA2 encrypts the wireless data transmissions and also limits who can access the Wi-Fi network.	Turn on WPA2 and set a strong pre-shared key (PSK), which must also be entered once on each mobile device.
Wi-Fi Protected Setup (WPS)	WPS simplifies setting up the security on a wireless router.	Turn off WPS due to its security vulnerabilities.
Guest access	Guest access allows temporary users to access the wireless network without any additional configuration settings.	Turn on Guest Access when needed and turn it back off when the approved guests leave.
Disable SSID broadcasts	This prevents the wireless router from "advertising" the wireless network to anyone in the area.	Leave SSID broadcasts on; turning them off only provides a very weak degree of security and may suggest to an attacker that your network has valuable information.

Protect Your Privacy

Privacy is defined as the state or condition of being free from public attention to the degree that you determine. That is, privacy is freedom from attention, observation, or interference, based on your decision. Privacy is the right to be left alone to the level that you choose.

Prior to the current age of technology many individuals generally were able to choose the level of privacy that they desired. Those who wanted to have very open and public lives in which anyone and everyone knew everything about them were able to freely provide that information to others. Those who wanted to live a very quiet or even unknown life could limit what information was disseminated.

However, today that is no longer possible. Data is collected on almost all actions and transactions that individuals perform. This includes data collected through web surfing, purchases (online and in stores), user surveys and questionnaires, and a wide array of other sources. It also is collected on benign activities such as the choice of movies streamed through the Internet, the location signals emitted by a cell phone, and even the path of walking as recorded by a surveillance camera. This data is then aggregated by data brokers. Data brokers hold thousands of pieces of information on hundreds of millions of consumers worldwide. These brokers then sell the data to interested third parties such as marketers or even governments.

To protect important information, consider the following privacy best practices:

- Shred financial documents and paperwork that contains personal information before discarding it.
- Do not carry a Social Security number in a wallet or write it on a check.
- Do not provide personal information either over the phone or through an email message.
- Keep personal information in a secure location in a home or apartment.
- Be cautious about what information is posted on social-networking sites and who can view your information. Show "limited friends" a reduced version of a profile, such as casual acquaintances or business associates.
- Keep only the last three months of the most recent financial statements and then shred older documents instead of tossing them in the trash or a recycling bin. For paper documents that must be retained, use a scanner to create a PDF of the document and then add a strong password to the PDF file that must be entered before it can be read.
- Give cautious consideration before giving permission to a website or app request to collect data.
- Use common sense. Websites that request more personal information than would normally be expected, such as a user name and password to another account, should be avoided.

Use Strong Authentication

Authentication is the process of ensuring that the person requesting access to a computer or other resources is authentic, and not an imposter. There are different types of authentication or proof of genuineness that can be presented.

Use Strong Passwords

In most computer systems, a user logging in would be asked to identify herself. This is done by entering an identifier known as the user name, such as MDenton. Yet because anyone could enter this user name, the next step is for the user to authenticate herself by proving that she actually is MDenton. This is often done by providing information that only she would know, namely, a password. A **password** is a secret combination of letters, numbers, and/or characters that only the user should have knowledge of. Logging in with a user name and password is illustrated in **Figure 6-12**.

Passwords are by far the most common type of authentication today. Yet despite their widespread use, passwords provide only weak protection. The weakness of passwords is due to human memory: you can memorize only a limited number of items. Passwords place heavy loads on human memory in multiple ways:

Figure 6-12: User login

Iurii Stepanov/Shutterstock.com

- The most effective passwords are long and complex. However, these are difficult to memorize and then accurately recall when needed.
- Users must remember multiple passwords for many different accounts. You have accounts for different computers and mobile devices at work, school, and home; multiple email accounts; online banking; Internet site accounts; and so on.
- For the highest level of security, each account password should be unique, which further strains your memory.

- Many security policies require that passwords expire after a set period of time, such as every 45–60 days, when a new one must be created. Some security policies even prevent a previously used password from being used again, forcing you to repeatedly memorize new passwords over and over.

Because of the burdens that passwords place on human memory, most users take shortcuts to help them memorize and recall their passwords. One shortcut is to create and use a **weak password**. Weak passwords use a common word as a password (*princess*), a short password (*football*), a predictable sequence of characters (*abc123*), or personal information (*Braden*) in a password.

Several recent attacks have stolen hundreds of millions of passwords, which are then posted on the Internet. The ten most common passwords are very weak and are listed in in **Table 6-10.**[6]

Table 6-10: Ten most common passwords

Rank	Password
1	123456
2	123456789
3	qwerty
4	password
5	1111111
6	12345678
7	abc123
8	password1
9	1234567
10	12345

Attackers can easily break weak passwords using sophisticated hardware and software tools. They often focus on breaking your passwords because, like the key to a door, once the password is compromised it opens all the contents of your computer or account to the attacker.

It is important that you create and manage secure, strong passwords. A **strong password** is a longer combination of letters, numbers, and/or symbols that unlocks access to protected electronic data. A longer password is always more secure than a shorter password, regardless of complexity. In other words, *Long is strong*. This is because the longer a password is, the more attempts an attacker must make to break it. Most security experts recommend that a secure password should be a minimum of 15-20 characters in length.

Table 6-11 illustrates the number of possible passwords for different password lengths using a standard 95-key keyboard along with the average attempts needed to break a password. Obviously, a longer password takes significantly more time to attempt to break than a short password.

Table 6-11: Number of possible passwords

Password length	Number of possible passwords	Average attempts to break password
2	9025	4513
3	857,375	428,688
4	81,450,625	40,725,313
5	7,737,809,375	3,868,904,688
6	735,091,890,625	367,545,945,313

In addition to having long passwords there are other general recommendations regarding creating passwords:

- Do not use passwords that consist of dictionary words or phonetic words.
- Do not repeat characters (xxx) or use sequences (abc, 123, qwerty).
- Do not use birthdays, family member names, pet names, addresses, or any personal information.

Now, you are wondering, how can I possibly apply all these recommendations and memorize long, complex, and unique passwords for all my accounts? Instead of relying on human memory for passwords, security experts universally recommend that you use a **password manager**, a program installed on your computer or mobile device. With a password manager, you can create and store multiple strong passwords in single user "vault" file that is protected by one strong master password. You can then retrieve individual passwords as needed from the vault file, thus freeing you from the need to memorize multiple passwords. The value of using a password manager is that unique strong passwords such as *WUuAôxB$2aWøBnd&Tf7MfEtm* can be easily created and used for any of your accounts.

Authenticating with Biometrics

In addition to using passwords for authentication based on what you know, another category rests on the features and characteristics of you as an individual. This type of authentication, something you are, is called **biometric security**. Biometric security uses the unique characteristics of your face, hands, or eyes to authenticate you. Some of the different types of biometrics that are used today for authentication include:

- Retina. The retina is a layer at the back of the eye. Each person's retina is unique, even if you have an identical twin. A retinal scanner maps the unique patterns of a retina as you look into the scanner's eyepiece.
- Fingerprint. Your fingerprint consists of a unique pattern of ridges and valleys. A static fingerprint scanner requires you to place your entire thumb or finger on a small oval window on the scanner, which takes an optical "picture" of the fingerprint and compares it with the fingerprint image on file. Another type of scanner is a dynamic fingerprint that requires you to move your finger across a small slit or opening.
- Voice. Voice recognition, using a standard computer microphone, can be used to authenticate users based on the unique characteristics of a person's voice.
- Face. A biometric authentication that is becoming increasingly popular on smartphones is facial recognition. Every person's face has several distinguishable "landmarks" called nodal points, illustrated in **Figure 6-13**. Using a standard computer

Figure 6-13: Facial recognition

metamorworks/Shutterstock.com

webcam, facial recognition software can measure the nodal points and create a numerical code (faceprint) that represents the face.

- Iris. Your iris is a thin, circular structure in the eye. An iris scanner, which can use a standard computer webcam, uses the unique characteristics of the iris for identification.

Add Two Factor Authentication

A growing trend in authentication is to combine multiple types of authentication. This is most often used with passwords (something you know) and the approved user having a specific item in his possession (something you have) that no one else would have. This is called **two factor authentication (2FA)** and it makes authentication stronger.

The most common authentication elements that are combined are passwords and codes sent to a cell phone using a text message. After correctly entering your password a four- to six-digit code is sent to your cell phone. The code must then be entered as the second authentication method. This is seen in **Figure 6-14**.

Figure 6-14: 2FA

selinofoto/Shutterstock.com

Explain the Benefits of Encryption

If you were the only one who had your information, it would be a much easier job to keep it safe. However, our personal information is transmitted and stored on remote servers many times each day. Think about the last time you made an online purchase: your credit card number was transmitted from you to the online retailer to your credit card provider to your bank to your smartphone—and that's just part of the journey. Yet despite the risks to our data there is a technology that we can use to significantly strengthen the security of our information, whether it is sitting on our computer or being transmitted around the world.

Imagine that an attorney had a set of documents that needed to be kept safe. The attorney could hire guards and add outside lighting to deter a thief. But what if the thief were still able to avoid these protections and break into the attorney's office? Now suppose that the attorney had also placed the documents in a safe that required a key to open it. This extra level of protection would thwart even the most sophisticated thief because it would require a very specialized set of skills to even attempt to open a locked safe.

This is the idea behind encryption. **Encryption** is the process of "scrambling" information in such a way that it cannot be read unless the user possesses the "key" to unlock it back to a readable format (**decryption**), a concept illustrated in **Figure 6-15**. This provides an extra level of protection: if an attacker were somehow able to get to the information on your computer, she still could not read the scrambled (encrypted) information because she would not have the key to unlock it.

Figure 6-15: Encryption/decryption key

Andrey_l/Shutterstock.com

And encryption can be applied to data on your hard drive (*data-at-rest*) just as it can be used to protect data being transmitted across the Internet (*data-in-transit*). A company employee traveling to another country carrying a laptop that contains sensitive company information would encrypt that data to protect it in case the laptop was lost or stolen. The employee also would encrypt a signed contract to send over the Internet back to the home office so that nobody else could intercept and read the contract.

It is essential that the key for encryption/decryption be kept secure. If someone were able to access your key they could then read any encrypted documents sent to you. They could also impersonate you by encrypting a false document with your key and sending it in your name. The receiver of the document would assume that you were the sender since they were able to decrypt the document using your key.

A **digital certificate** is a technology used to verify a user's identity and key that has been "signed" by a trusted third party. This third party verifies the owner and that the key belongs to that owner. Digital certificates make it possible to verify the identity of a user and the user's key to prevent an attack from someone impersonating the user.

Discuss Measures to Prevent Identity Theft and Protect Financial Information

Attackers target your personal information because with your information, they can steal your hard-earned money or ruin your ability to receive a loan. In many ways the theft and manipulation of your personal information for financial fraud is one of the most harmful types of attacks.

There are several ways that you can and should prevent your information from falling into the hands of attackers. It is especially important to protect your financial data.

Prevent Identity Theft

Identity theft involves using someone's personal information, such as their name, Social Security number, or credit card number, to commit financial fraud. Using this information to obtain a credit card, set up a cellular telephone account, or even rent an apartment, thieves can make excessive charges in the victim's name. The victim is charged for the purchases and suffers a damaged credit history that can lead to being denied loans for school, cars, and homes.

The following are some of the actions that can be undertaken by identity thieves:

- Produce counterfeit checks or debit cards and then remove all money from the bank account.
- Establish phone or wireless service in the victim's name.
- File for bankruptcy under the person's name to avoid eviction.
- Go on spending sprees using fraudulently obtained credit and debit card account numbers.
- Open a bank account in the person's name and write bad checks on that account.
- Open a new credit card account, using the name, date of birth, and Social Security number of the victim. When the thief does not pay the bills, the delinquent account is reported on the victim's credit report.
- Obtain loans for expensive items such as cars and motorcycles.

Table 6-12 outlines some of the ways in which attackers can steal your personal information.

Table 6-12: How personal information is stolen

Technique	Explanation
Dumpster diving	Discarded credit card statements, charge receipts, and bank statements can be retrieved after being discarded in the trash for personal information.
Phishing	Attackers convince victims to enter their personal information at an imposter website after receiving a fictitious email from a bank.
Change of address form	Using a standard change-of-address form the attackers divert all mail to their post office box so that the victim never sees any charges made.
Pretexting	An attacker who pretends to be from a legitimate research firm asks for personal information.
Stealing	Stolen wallets and purses contain personal information that can be used in identity theft.

One of the growing areas of identity theft involves identity thieves filing fictitious income tax returns with the U.S. Internal Revenue Service (IRS). Identity thieves steal a filer's Social Security number then file a fake income tax return claiming a large refund—often larger than the victim is entitled to—that is sent to the attacker. Because the IRS has been sending refunds more quickly than in the past, thieves can receive the refund and disappear before the victim files a legitimate return and the fraud is detected. According to the IRS, it delivered over $5.8 billion in refund checks to identity thieves who filed fraudulent tax returns in one year, even though it stopped about 3 million fraudulent returns for that year.[7]

Protect Financial Information

Financial information is frequently stolen by online attackers. Avoiding this theft involves two basic steps. The first step is to deter thieves by safeguarding information. This includes:

- Shred financial documents and paperwork that contains personal information before discarding it.
- Do not carry a Social Security number in a wallet or write it on a check.
- Do not provide personal information either over the phone or through an email message.
- Keep personal information in a secure location in a home or apartment.

The second step is to monitor financial statements and accounts by doing the following:

- Be alert to signs that may indicate unusual activity in an account, such as a bill that did not arrive at the normal time or a large increase in unsolicited credit cards or account statements.
- Follow up on calls regarding purchases that were not made.
- Review financial and billing statements each month carefully as soon as they arrive.

There are laws to help U.S. users monitor and protect their financial information that is stored by a credit reporting agency. You can request one free credit report annually to review your credit history and determine if an attacker has secretly taken out a credit card or even a large loan in your name. You can also have a credit "freeze" (as well as a "thaw") put on your credit information so that it cannot be accessed without your explicit permission. These are also free. It is a good idea to monitor your credit information regularly.

Protect Yourself While Online

Like most users, you probably spend most of your time online when you are on your computer or smartphone. Because we spend so much time online, it is good to consider ways you can protect yourself while online. This also includes protecting your online profile while using social media.

Configuring Your Browser's Security

Today all web browsers support dynamic content that can change, such as animated images or customized information. This can be done through web browser additions called extensions, plug-ins, and add-ons.

However, these web browser additions introduce a new means for attackers to exploit security weaknesses and gain access to the user's computer through the web browser. For example, an add-on might allow your computer to download a "script" or series of instructions that commands the browser to perform specific actions. An attacker could exploit a security weakness in the add-on to download and execute malware on the user's computer.

Another weakness of a web browser is cookies. A **cookie** is a file created by a website that stores information on your computer, such as your website preferences or the contents of an electronic shopping cart. When you visit the website in the future, the web server can retrieve this stored information. Cookies can pose both security and privacy risks. Some can be stolen and used to impersonate you, while others can be used to track your browsing or buying habits.

Although all web browsers are different, each can be configured for stronger security through different settings. Some of the important security settings include:

- Cookies. You can accept or deny cookies. Also, you can specify that cookies be deleted once the browser is closed. In addition, exceptions can be made for specific websites, and all existing cookies can be viewed and selectively removed.
- Scripting. Sites can be allowed to run scripting languages or blocked from running them, and exceptions can be made for specific websites.

- Plug-ins. You can block all plug-ins or selective plug-ins. Another option prompts the user when a plug-in requests to run.
- Pop-ups. You can also block all pop-up messages, permit all pop-ups, or selectively choose which sites to run pop-ups.
- Clear browsing data. All accumulated history of web browsing can be cleared from the computer's hard drive.
- Plug-in validation. A plug-in validation will examine the plug-ins that are being used and alert the user to any out-of-date or known vulnerable plug-ins.

Protecting Your Online Profile

Social-networking sites contain a treasure trove of information for attackers. An attacker might view your Facebook page to find answers to security questions that are used for resetting passwords (such as, *What is your mother's maiden name*?). With so much valuable information available, social-networking sites should be at the forefront of security today; sadly, that is not always the case. Social-networking sites have a history of providing lax security, of not giving users a clear understanding of how security features work, and of changing security options with little or no warning.

Several general defenses can be used for any social-networking site. First and foremost, you should be cautious about what information you post. Posting *I'm going to Florida on Friday for two weeks* could be a tempting invitation for a burglar. Other information posted could later prove embarrassing. Asking yourself questions such as *Would my boss approve?* Or *What would my mother think of this?* before posting may provide an incentive to rethink the material before posting.

Second, be cautious regarding who can view your information. Certain types of information could prove to be embarrassing if read by certain parties, such as a prospective employer. Other information should be kept confidential. You should consider carefully who is accepted as a friend on a social network. Once a person has been accepted as a friend, that person will be able to access any personal information or photographs. Instead, it may be preferable to show "limited friends" a reduced version of a profile, such as casual acquaintances or business associates.

Finally, because security settings in social-networking sites are often updated frequently by the site with little warning, pay close attention to information about new or updated security settings. New settings often provide a much higher level of security by allowing you to fine-tune your account profile options.

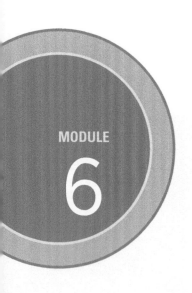

MODULE

6

Summary

In this module, you learned that a risk is the possibility something may occur that results in an injury or a loss. Today, for most users the greatest risk to using computers and smartphones comes from attackers who want to steal their information so that they can use it to generate money for themselves.

Other risks include electronic waste (e-waste) from discarded computer equipment, which increases the need for more and larger landfill sites, and can harm the environment. Repetitive strain injury (RSI) impacts muscles, nerves, tendons, and ligaments, and should be combatted by arranging the workspace according to proper ergonomics. Behavioral hazards include technology addiction, a sedentary lifestyle, restricted psychological development, and less social interaction.

Cyberbullying is bullying that takes place on technology devices, and cyberstalking involves the use of technology to stalk another person through email, text messages, phone calls, and other forms of electronic communication.

Malware (*malicious software*) is the general term that refers to a wide variety of software programs that attackers use to carry out their work. Social engineering is a category of attacks that attempts to trick the victim into giving valuable information to the attacker.

Use a surge protector to prevent damage from spikes, surges, and noise, and an uninterruptible power supply (UPS) to maintain power to the equipment in case of an interruption in the primary electrical power source. You should also protect devices from physical impact.

To prevent laptops from being stolen a cable lock can be used. If a mobile device is lost or stolen, several different security features can be used to locate the device to recover it.

Data backups can protect against hardware malfunctions, cyberattacks, user error, software corruption, and natural disasters. Options include online backup services that automatically upload new or changed files to a cloud server, or copying all files to another medium and storing it in a remote location.

There are several risks from attacks on Wi-Fi networks and the use of web browsers, including loss of privacy and identity theft. Passwords are the most common type of authentication used today, but provide only weak protection. A password manager lets you create and store multiple strong passwords in single user "vault" file. Another type of authentication is biometrics, which uses the unique physical characteristics of your face, hands, or eyes to authenticate you. Two factor authentication (2FA) and it makes authentication stronger. Encryption "scrambles" information so that it cannot be read unless the user possesses the "key." A digital certificate associates a user's identity with their key. Web browsers allow scripts, extensions, plug-ins, add-ons, and cookies that can be security and privacy risks.

Be cautious about what information you post on social-networking sites, and setting who can view your information. Pay close attention to information about new or updated security settings.

Review Questions

1. _____ are attackers who want to attack computers but lack the knowledge needed to do so.
   a. Script kiddies
   b. Hactivists
   c. Cyberterrorists
   d. Nation state actors

2. Each of the following is a factor that causes repetitive strain injury (RSI) except _____.
   a. repetitive activity
   b. improper technique
   c. lack of restful sleep
   d. uninterrupted intensity

3. (True or False) A worm is a malicious program that uses a computer network to replicate.

4. A _____ is a very short duration of a voltage increase that can be absorbed by a surge protector.
   a. spike
   b. surge
   c. blackout
   d. brownout

5. (True or False) Wi-Fi Protected Access 2 (WPA2) Personal encrypts wireless data transmissions and limits who can access the Wi-Fi network.

6. When creating a strong password _____ is the most important element.
   a. length
   b. complexity
   c. repetitiveness
   d. ability to memorize

7. _____ is the process of "scrambling" information in such a way that it cannot be read unless the user possesses the "key."
   a. Decryption
   b. Encryption
   c. Digital signing
   d. Certification

8. (True or False) You have the right to see your credit information.

9. Which of the following is *not* a web browser setting for managing cookies?
   a. Have all cookies automatically expire after 45 days.
   b. Accept or deny cookies.
   c. Delete all cookies when the web browser is closed.
   d. Make exceptions for specific websites.

Discussion Questions

1. How serious are the risks to your computer security?

2. How would you approach a friend that you suspect is addicted to technology?

3. What steps would you take to prevent your tablet from being stolen?

4. Why is it important to protect a Wi-Fi network? What should you do to protect your Wi-Fi network?

Critical Thinking Activities

1. Heinrich Koch is a second-year college student. Last semester his best friend had his laptop stolen. The laptop was an old computer that he planned to replace soon, but the greatest loss was his data: he had not performed a backup and all his data was lost. Heinrich himself does not perform data backups but knows that he needs to do that on a regular basis. He has decided to use an online backup service that will automatically back up his data whenever it changes. Evaluate and compare reviews of online backup services. Consider iDrive, Carbonite, Acronis True Image, BackBlaze, and others you might find in your research. Recommend a service that you consider the best solution for Heinrich. Discuss your reviews and mention speed, security, and features in your recommendation.

2. Aadab Baqri is completing her degree at a community college and intends to transfer to a university next semester. She has kept a Microsoft Word document that lists her account user names and passwords, but she knows that she needs something much more secure to create and manage her passwords and account information. Evaluate and compare reviews of three password managers, at least one of which can be used on a mobile device. Consider KeePass, Bitwarden, Enpass, KeePassXC, and others you might find in your research. Recommend two password managers: one for when Aadab uses her laptop, and one for when she uses her mobile phone. Discuss your experiences with these password managers and mention security and features in your recommendation.

Key Terms

address spoofing
attackers
authentication
biometric security
cookie
cyberbullying
cyberstalking
cyberterrorists
data backup
data mining
decryption
digital certificate
e-waste
encryption

ergonomics
hactivists
hoax
identity theft
insiders
malware
nation state actors
password
password manager
phishing
privacy
ransomware
repetitive strain injury (RSI)
script kiddies

social engineering
spam
strong password
surge protector
technology addiction
Trojan
two factor authentication (2FA)
uninterruptible power
   supply (UPS)
virus
weak password
Wi-Fi
wireless router
worm

References

1. Button, Kimberly, "20 staggering e-waste facts," *Earth911*, Feb. 24, 2016, accessed Nov. 14, 2018, https://earth911.com/eco-tech/20-e-waste-facts/.

2. Bauer, Emily, "15 outrageous email spam statistics that still ring true in 2018," *Propeller*, accessed Nov. 14, 2018, https://www.propellercrm.com/blog/email-spam-statistics.

3. "Data Breaches," *Privacy Rights Clearinghouse*, updated Nov. 14, 2018, accessed Nov. 14, 2018, www.privacyrights.org/data-breaches.

4. "Data breach investigation report," *Verizon*, accessed Nov. 14, 2018, https://enterprise.verizon.com/resources/reports/dbir/.

5. "Data breach investigation report," *Verizon*, accessed Nov. 14, 2018, https://enterprise.verizon.com/resources/reports/dbir/.

6. Hunt, Troy, "86% of passwords are terrible (and other statistics)," *TroyHunt.com*, accessed Nov. 14, 2018, https://www.troyhunt.com/86-of-passwords-are-terrible-and-other-statistics/.

7. Wood, Robert, "IRS paid $5.8 billion in fraudulent refunds, identity theft efforts need work," *Forbes*, Feb. 19, 2015, accessed Nov. 14, 2018, https://www.forbes.com/sites/robertwood/2015/02/19/irs-paid-5-8-billion-in-fraudulent-refunds-identity-theft-efforts-need-work/.

Creating Documents with Word

CASE ▶ You have been hired to work at JCL Talent, Inc., a business support services company that provides employment and recruitment services for employers and job seekers. Shortly after reporting to your new office, Dawn Lapointe, Director of JCL Talent – Technical Careers division, asks you to use Word to create a memo to staff and a tip sheet for job seekers.

Module Objectives

After completing this module, you will be able to:

- Understand word processing software
- Explore the Word window
- Start a document
- Save a document
- Select text
- Format text using the Mini toolbar and the Ribbon
- View and navigate a document
- Cut and paste text
- Copy and paste text
- Format with fonts
- Set document margins
- Add bullets and numbering
- Insert a graphic
- Apply a theme

Files You Will Need

IL_WD_1-1.docx	Support_WD_1-4.docx
Support_WD_1-2.docx	IL_WD_1-5.docx
IL_WD_1-3.docx	Support_WD_1-6.docx

Understand Word Processing Software

Learning
Outcomes
• Identify the
features of Word
• State the benefits
of using a word
processing
program

A **word processing program** is a software program that includes tools for entering, editing, and formatting text and graphics. Microsoft Word is a powerful word processing program that allows you to create and enhance a wide range of documents quickly and easily. FIGURE 1-1 shows the first page of a report created using Word and illustrates some of the Word features you can use to enhance your documents. The electronic files you create using Word are called **documents**. One of the benefits of using Word is that document files can be stored on a hard disk, flash drive, or other physical storage device, or to OneDrive or another Cloud storage place, making them easy to transport, share, and revise.

CASE ▶ *Before beginning your memo, you explore the editing and formatting features available in Word.*

DETAILS

You can use Word to accomplish the following tasks:

- **Type and edit text**

  The Word editing tools make it simple to insert and delete text in a document. You can add text to the middle of an existing paragraph; replace text with other text, undo an editing change, and correct typing; spelling; and grammatical errors with ease.

- **Copy and move text from one location to another**

  Using the more advanced editing features of Word, you can copy or move text from one location and insert it in a different location in a document. You also can copy and move text between documents. This means you don't have to retype text that is already entered in a document.

- **Format text and paragraphs with fonts, colors, and other elements**

  The sophisticated formatting tools in Word allow you to make the text in your documents come alive. You can change the size, style, and color of text, add lines and shading to paragraphs, and enhance lists with bullets and numbers. Creatively formatting text helps to highlight important ideas in your documents.

- **Format and design pages**

  The page-formatting features in Word give you power to design attractive newsletters, create powerful résumés, and produce documents such as research papers, business cards, brochures, and reports. You can change paper size, organize text in columns, and control the layout of text and graphics on each page of a document. For quick results, Word includes preformatted cover pages, pull quotes, and headers and footers, as well as galleries of coordinated text, table, and graphic styles. If you are writing a research paper, Word makes it easy to manage reference sources and create footnotes, endnotes, and bibliographies.

- **Enhance documents with tables, charts, graphics, screenshots, and videos**

  Using the powerful graphics tools in Word, you can spice up your documents with pictures, videos, photographs, screenshots, lines, preset quick shapes, and diagrams. You also can illustrate your documents with tables and charts to help convey your message in a visually interesting way.

- **Use Mail Merge to create form letters and mailing labels**

  The Word Mail Merge feature allows you to send personalized form letters to many different people. You can also use Mail Merge to create mailing labels, directories, email messages, and other types of documents.

- **Share documents securely**

  The security features in Word make it quick and easy to remove comments, tracked changes, and unwanted personal information from your files before you share them with others. You can also add a password or a digital signature to a document and convert a file to a format suitable for publishing on the web.

FIGURE 1-1: A report created using Word

Add headers to every page

Add lines

Insert graphics

Add bullets to lists

Format the size and appearance of text

Create charts

Create columns of text

Create tables

Align text in paragraphs evenly

Add page numbers in footers

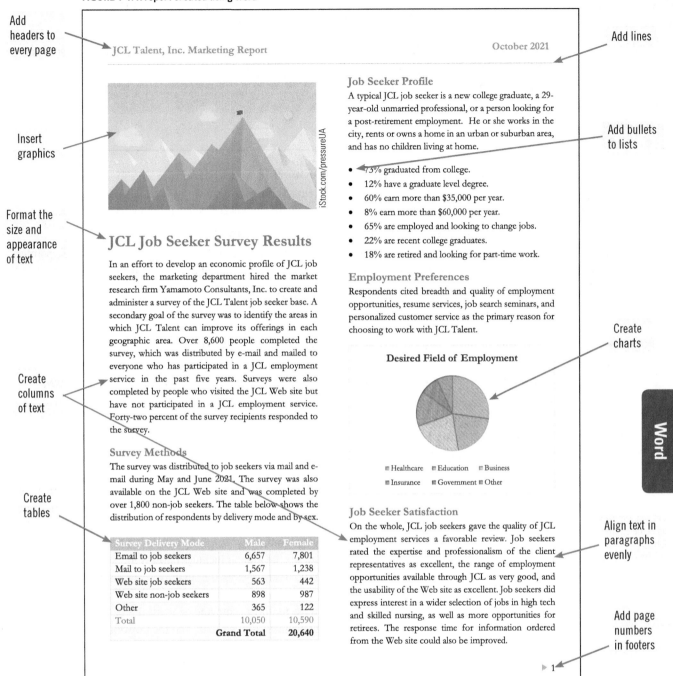

JCL Talent, Inc. Marketing Report   October 2021

Job Seeker Profile

A typical JCL job seeker is a new college graduate, a 29-year-old unmarried professional, or a person looking for a post-retirement employment. He or she works in the city, rents or owns a home in an urban or suburban area, and has no children living at home.

- 73% graduated from college.
- 12% have a graduate level degree.
- 60% earn more than $35,000 per year.
- 8% earn more than $60,000 per year.
- 65% are employed and looking to change jobs.
- 22% are recent college graduates.
- 18% are retired and looking for part-time work.

Employment Preferences

Respondents cited breadth and quality of employment opportunities, resume services, job search seminars, and personalized customer service as the primary reason for choosing to work with JCL Talent.

Desired Field of Employment

Healthcare ∎ Education ∎ Business
∎ Insurance ∎ Government ∎ Other

JCL Job Seeker Survey Results

In an effort to develop an economic profile of JCL job seekers, the marketing department hired the market research firm Yamamoto Consultants, Inc. to create and administer a survey of the JCL Talent job seeker base. A secondary goal of the survey was to identify the areas in which JCL Talent can improve its offerings in each geographic area. Over 8,600 people completed the survey, which was distributed by e-mail and mailed to everyone who has participated in a JCL employment service in the past five years. Surveys were also completed by people who visited the JCL Web site but have not participated in a JCL employment service. Forty-two percent of the survey recipients responded to the survey.

Survey Methods

The survey was distributed to job seekers via mail and e-mail during May and June 2021. The survey was also available on the JCL Web site and was completed by over 1,800 non-job seekers. The table below shows the distribution of respondents by delivery mode and by sex.

Survey Delivery Mode	Male	Female
Email to job seekers	6,657	7,801
Mail to job seekers	1,567	1,238
Web site job seekers	563	442
Web site non-job seekers	898	987
Other	365	122
Total	10,050	10,590
	Grand Total	**20,640**

Job Seeker Satisfaction

On the whole, JCL job seekers gave the quality of JCL employment services a favorable review. Job seekers rated the expertise and professionalism of the client representatives as excellent, the range of employment opportunities available through JCL as very good, and the usability of the Web site as excellent. Job seekers did express interest in a wider selection of jobs in high tech and skilled nursing, as well as more opportunities for retirees. The response time for information ordered from the Web site could also be improved.

▷ 1

iStock.com/pressureUA

Word

Planning a document

Before you create a new document, it's a good idea to spend time planning it. Identify the message you want to convey, the audience for your document, and the elements, such as tables or charts, you want to include. You should also think about the tone and look of your document—are you writing a business letter, which should be written in a pleasant, but serious, tone and have a formal appearance, or are you creating a flyer that must be colorful, eye-catching, and fun to read? The purpose and audience for your document determine the appropriate design. Planning the layout and design of a document involves deciding how to organize the text, selecting the fonts to use, identifying the graphics to include, and selecting the formatting elements that will enhance the message and appeal of the document. For longer documents, such as newsletters, it can be useful to sketch the layout and design of each page before you begin.

Explore the Word Window

When you start Word, the Word start screen opens. It includes a list of recently opened documents and a gallery of templates for creating a new document. **CASE** ▸ *You open a blank document and examine the elements of the Word program window.*

STEPS

1. **sam** ↓ **Start Word, then click** Blank document

   A blank document opens in the **Word program window**, as shown in FIGURE 1-2. The blinking vertical line in the document window is the **insertion point**. It indicates where text appears as you type.

TROUBLE
If the Ribbon is hid-
den, click the Ribbon
Display Options but-
ton on the title bar,
then click Show Tabs
and Commands.

2. **Move the mouse pointer around the Word program window**

   The mouse pointer changes shape depending on where it is in the Word program window. You use pointers to move the insertion point or to select text to edit. TABLE 1-1 describes common pointers in Word.

3. **Place the mouse pointer over a button on the Ribbon**

   When you place the mouse pointer over a button or some other elements of the Word program window, a ScreenTip appears. A **ScreenTip** is a label that identifies the name of the button or feature, briefly describes its function, conveys any keyboard shortcut for the command, and includes a link to associated help topics, if any.

DETAILS

QUICK TIP
If your computer has
touchscreen capa-
bility, your Quick
Access toolbar will
also include a Touch/
Mouse Mode button.

QUICK TIP
To display a different
tab, you simply click
its name on the
Ribbon.

TROUBLE
Click the View tab,
then click the Ruler
check box in the
Show group to
display the rulers if
they are not already
displayed.

Using FIGURE 1-2 **as a guide, find the elements described below in your program window:**

- The **title bar** displays the name of the document and the name of the program. Until you give a new document a different name, its temporary name is Document1. The left side of the title bar contains the **Quick Access toolbar**, which includes buttons for saving a document and for undoing, redoing, and repeating a change. The right side of the title bar contains the **Ribbon Display Options button**, which you use to hide or show the Ribbon and tabs, the resizing buttons, and the program Close button.

- The **File tab** provides access to **Backstage view** where you manage files and the information about them. Backstage view includes commands related to working with documents, such as opening, printing, and saving a document. The File tab also provides access to your account and to the Word Options dialog box, which is used to customize the way you use Word.

- The Ribbon contains the Word tabs. Each **tab** on the Ribbon includes buttons for commands related to editing and formatting documents. The commands are organized in **groups**. For example, the Home tab includes the Clipboard, Font, Paragraph, Styles, and Editing groups. The Ribbon also includes the **Tell Me what you want to do box**, which you can use to find a command or access the Word Help system, the **Share button**, which you can use to save a document to the Cloud, and the **Comment button**, which you use to see comments.

- The **document window** displays the current document. You enter text and format your document in the document window.

- The rulers appear in the document window in Print Layout view. The **horizontal ruler** displays left and right document margins as well as the tab settings and paragraph indents, if any, for the paragraph in which the insertion point is located. The **vertical ruler** displays the top and bottom document margins.

- The vertical and **horizontal scroll bars** are used to display different parts of the document in the document window. The scroll bars include **scroll boxes** and **scroll arrows**, which you use to scroll.

- The **status bar** displays the page number of the current page, the total number of pages and words in the document, and the status of spelling and grammar checking. It also includes the view buttons, the Zoom slider, and the Zoom level button. You can customize the status bar to display other information.

- The **view buttons** on the status bar allow you to display the document in Read Mode, Print Layout, or Web Layout view. The **Zoom slider** and the **Zoom level button** provide quick ways to enlarge and decrease the size of the document in the document window, making it easy to zoom in on a detail of a document or to view the layout of the document as a whole.

FIGURE 1-2: Elements of the Word program window

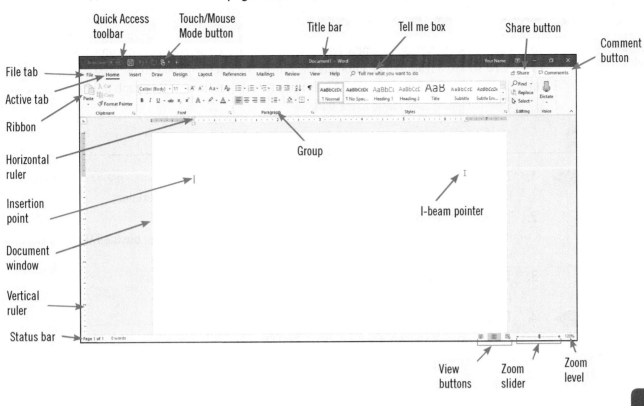

TABLE 1-1: Common mouse pointers in Word

name	pointer	use to
I-beam pointer	I	Move the insertion point in a document or to select text
Click and Type pointers, including left-align and center-align	I≡ I	Move the insertion point to a blank area of a document in Print Layout or Web Layout view; double-clicking with a Click and Type pointer automatically applies the Paragraph formatting (alignment and indentation) required to position text or a graphic at that location in the document
Selection pointer	⌖	Click a button or other element of the Word program window; appears when you point to elements of the Word program window
Right-pointing arrow pointer	⬈	Select a line or lines of text; appears when you point to the left edge of a line of text in the document window
Hand pointer	☝	Open a hyperlink; appears when you point to a hyperlink in a task pane or when you press CTRL and point to a hyperlink in a document
Hide white space pointer	⊣⊢	Hide the white space in the top and bottom margins of a document in Print Layout view
Show white space pointer	⊢⊣	Show the white space in the top and bottom margins of a document in Print Layout view

Start a Document

You begin a new document by simply typing text in a blank document in the document window. Word uses **word wrap**, a feature that automatically moves the insertion point to the next line of the document as you type. You only press ENTER when you want to start a new paragraph or insert a blank line.

CASE ➤ *You type a quick memo to the staff.*

STEPS

1. **Type JCL Talent, then press ENTER twice**
   Each time you press ENTER the insertion point moves to the start of the next line.

2. **Type TO:, then press TAB twice**
   Pressing TAB moves the insertion point several spaces to the right. You can use the TAB key to align the text in a memo header or to indent the first line of a paragraph.

3. **Type JCL Managers, then press ENTER**
   The insertion point moves to the start of the next line.

4. **Type: FROM: TAB TAB Dawn Lapointe ENTER**
       DATE: TAB TAB April 12, 2021 ENTER
       RE: TAB TAB Creative Meeting ENTER ENTER
   Red wavy or blue double lines may appear under the words you typed, indicating a possible spelling or grammar error. Spelling and grammar checking is one of the many automatic features you will encounter as you type. TABLE 1-2 describes several automatic features. You can correct any typing errors you make later.

5. **Type The next creative staff meeting will be held on the 18th of April at 3 p.m. in the conference room on the ground floor., then press SPACEBAR**
   As you type, notice that the insertion point moves automatically to the next line of the document. You also might notice that Word automatically changed "18th" to "18th" in the memo. This feature is called **AutoCorrect**. AutoCorrect automatically makes typographical adjustments and detects and adjusts typing errors, certain misspelled words (such as "taht" for "that"), and incorrect capitalization as you type.

6. **Type Heading the agenda will be the accessibility design of our new Recruitment Tips webpage. The page is scheduled for September.**
   When you type the first few characters of "September," the Word AutoComplete feature displays the complete word in a ScreenTip. **AutoComplete** suggests text to insert quickly into your documents. You can ignore AutoComplete for now. Your memo should resemble FIGURE 1-3.

7. **Press ENTER, then type Anna Jocharz has been hired to draft content. A preliminary content outline is attached. Prior to the meeting, please review the web content accessibility guidelines recommended by the World Wide Web Consortium.**
   When you press ENTER and type the new paragraph, notice that Word adds more space between the paragraphs than it does between the lines in each paragraph. This is part of the default style for paragraphs in Word, called the **Normal style**.

8. **Position the ⌶ pointer after for (but before the space) in the last sentence of the first paragraph, then click to move the insertion point after for**

9. **Press BACKSPACE three times, then type to launch in**
   Pressing BACKSPACE removes the character before the insertion point.

10. **Move the insertion point before staff in the first sentence, then press DELETE six times to remove the word "staff" and the space after it**
    Pressing DELETE removes the character after the insertion point. FIGURE 1-4 shows the revised memo.

FIGURE 1-3: Memo text in the document window

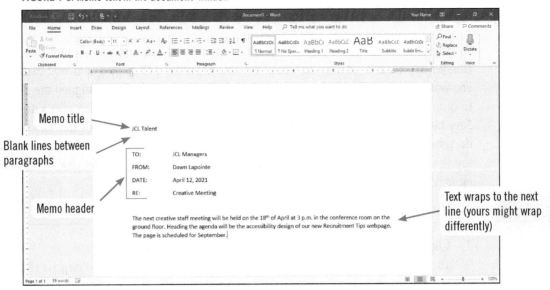

Memo title → JCL Talent

Blank lines between paragraphs

Memo header

Text wraps to the next line (yours might wrap differently)

FIGURE 1-4: Edited memo text

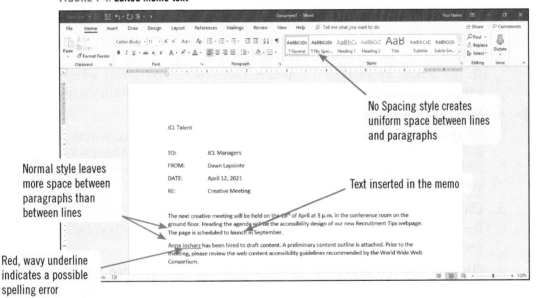

No Spacing style creates uniform space between lines and paragraphs

Normal style leaves more space between paragraphs than between lines

Text inserted in the memo

Red, wavy underline indicates a possible spelling error

TABLE 1-2: Automatic features that appear as you type in Word

feature	what appears	to use
AutoComplete	A ScreenTip suggesting text to insert appears as you type	Press ENTER to insert the text suggested by the ScreenTip; continue typing to reject the suggestion
AutoCorrect	A small blue box appears when you place the pointer over text corrected by AutoCorrect; an AutoCorrect Options button appears when you point to the blue box	Word automatically corrects typos, minor spelling errors, and capitalization, and adds typographical symbols (such as © and ™) as you type; to reverse an AutoCorrect adjustment, click the AutoCorrect Options arrow, then click the option that will undo the action
Spelling and Grammar	A red wavy line under a word indicates a possible misspelling or a repeated word; a blue double line under text indicates a possible grammar error	Right-click red- or blue-underlined text to display a shortcut menu of correction options; click a correction option to accept it and remove the colored underline, or click Ignore to leave the text as is

Save a Document

To store a document permanently so you can open it and edit it at another time, you must save it as a **file**. When you **save** a document you give it a name, called a **filename**, and indicate the location where you want to store the file. Files created in Word 2019 are automatically assigned the .docx file extension to distinguish them from files created in other software programs. You can save a document using the Save button on the Quick Access toolbar or the Save command on the File tab. Once you have saved a document for the first time, you should save it again every few minutes and always before printing so that the saved file is updated to reflect your latest changes. **CASE** ▶ *You save your memo using a descriptive filename and the default file extension.*

STEPS

1. **Click the Save button 🖫 on the Quick Access toolbar**

   The first time you save a document, the Save As screen opens. The screen displays all the places you can save a file to, including OneDrive, your PC (identified as This PC), or a different location.

2. **Click Browse in the Save As screen**

   The Save As dialog box opens, similar to FIGURE 1-5. The default filename, JCL Talent, appears in the File name text box. The default filename is based on the first few words of the document. The default file type, Word Document, appears in the Save as type list box. TABLE 1-3 describes the functions of some of the buttons in the Save As dialog box.

3. **Type IL_WD_1_Memo in the File name text box**

   The new filename replaces the default filename. Giving your documents brief descriptive filenames makes it easier to locate and organize them later. You do not need to type .docx when you type a new filename.

4. **Navigate to the location where you store your Data Files**

   You can navigate to a different drive or folder in several ways. For example, you can click a drive or folder in the Address bar or the navigation pane to go directly to that location. When you are finished navigating to the drive or folder where you store your Data Files, that location appears in the Address bar. Your Save As dialog box should resemble FIGURE 1-6.

5. **Click Save**

   The document is saved to the drive and folder you specified in the Save As dialog box, and the title bar displays the new filename, IL_WD_1_Memo.docx.

6. **Place the insertion point before conference in the first sentence, type large, then press SPACEBAR**

   You can continue to work on a document after you have saved it with a new filename.

7. **Click 🖫**

   Your change to the memo is saved. After you save a document for the first time, you must continue to save the changes you make to the document.

Using keyboard shortcuts

A **shortcut key** is a function key, such as F1, or a combination of keys, such as CTRL+S, that you press to perform a command. For example, instead of using the Cut, Copy, and Paste commands on the Ribbon or the Mini toolbar, you can use the **keyboard shortcuts** CTRL+X to cut text, CTRL+C to copy text, and CTRL+V to paste text. You can also press CTRL+S to save changes to a document instead of clicking the Save button on the Quick Access toolbar or clicking Save on the File tab. Becoming skilled at using keyboard shortcuts can help you quickly accomplish many of the tasks you perform in Word. If a keyboard shortcut is available for a command, then it is listed in the ScreenTip for that command.

FIGURE 1-5: Save As dialog box

Active folder or drive
(yours might differ)

Folders and files in
the active folder or
drive (yours might
differ)

Default filename and file
extension are selected

Click to change
the file type

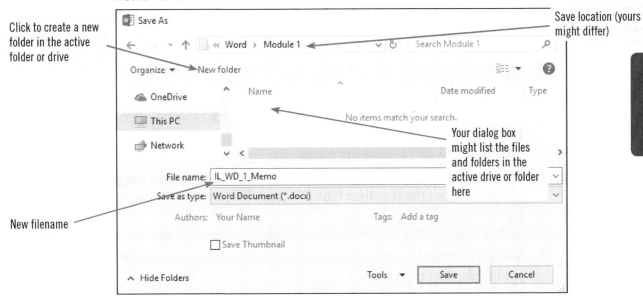

FIGURE 1-6: File to be saved to the Mod 1 folder

Click to create a new
folder in the active
folder or drive

Save location (yours
might differ)

Your dialog box
might list the files
and folders in the
active drive or folder
here

New filename

Word

TABLE 1-3: Save As dialog box buttons

button	use to
Back	Navigate back to the last location shown in the Address bar
Forward	Navigate to the location that was previously shown in the Address bar
Up to	Navigate to the location above the current location in the folder hierarchy
Organize	Open a menu of commands related to organizing the selected file or folder, including Cut, Copy, Delete, Rename, and Properties
New folder	Create a new folder in the current folder or drive
Change your view	Change the way folder and file information is shown in the folder window in the Save As dialog box; click the Change your view button to toggle between views, or click the arrow to open a menu of view options

Creating Documents with Word

WD 1-9

Select Text

Learning
Outcomes
• Select text
• Show and hide
  formatting
• Undo and redo
  actions
• Manage hyperlinks

Before deleting, editing, or formatting text, you must **select** the text. Selecting text involves clicking and dragging the I-beam pointer across the text to highlight it. You can also select words and paragraphs by double-clicking or triple-clicking text, or you can click or double-click in the margin to the left of text with the ⟋ pointer to select whole lines or paragraphs. TABLE 1-4 describes the many ways to select text.

CASE ▶ *You revise the memo by selecting text and replacing it with new text. You also remove a hyperlink from text.*

STEPS

1. **Click the** Show/Hide ¶ button ¶ **in the Paragraph group**

   Formatting marks appear in the document window. **Formatting marks** are special characters that appear on your screen but do not print. Common formatting marks include the paragraph symbol (¶), which shows the end of a paragraph—wherever you press ENTER; the dot symbol (.), which represents a space—wherever you press SPACEBAR; and the arrow symbol (→), which shows the location of a tab stop—wherever you press TAB. Working with formatting marks turned on can help you to select, edit, and format text with precision.

2. **Click before** JCL Managers, **then drag the pointer over the text to select it**

   The words are selected, as shown in FIGURE 1-7. For now, you can ignore the floating Mini toolbar that appears over text when you first select it.

3. **Type** Creative Staff

   The text you type replaces the selected text.

4. **Double-click** Dawn, **type your first name, double-click** Lapointe, **then type your last name**

   Double-clicking a word selects the entire word.

5. **Place the pointer in the margin to the left of the** RE: line **so that the pointer changes to** ⟋, **click to select the line, then type** RE:, **press TAB, press TAB, then type** Recruitment Tips webpage

   Clicking to the left of a line of text with the ⟋ pointer selects the entire line.

6. **Select the sentence** Anna Jocharz has been hired to draft content. **in the second paragraph, then press** DELETE

   Selecting text and pressing DELETE removes the text from the document.

7. **Click after the period at the** end of the second paragraph, **then type** See www.w3.org for more information.

   When you press SPACEBAR after typing the web address, Word automatically formats the web address as a hyperlink. A **hyperlink** is text that when clicked opens a webpage in a browser window. Text that is formatted as a hyperlink appears as colored, underlined text. You want to remove the hyperlink formatting.

8. **Right-click** www.w3.org, **then click** Remove Hyperlink

   Removing a hyperlink removes the link, but the text remains.

9. **Click** ¶, **then click the** Save button 🖫 **on the Quick Access toolbar**

   Formatting marks are turned off, and your changes to the memo are saved. The Show/Hide ¶ button is a **toggle button**, which means you can use it to turn formatting marks on and off. The edited memo is shown in FIGURE 1-8.

FIGURE 1-7: **Text selected in the memo**

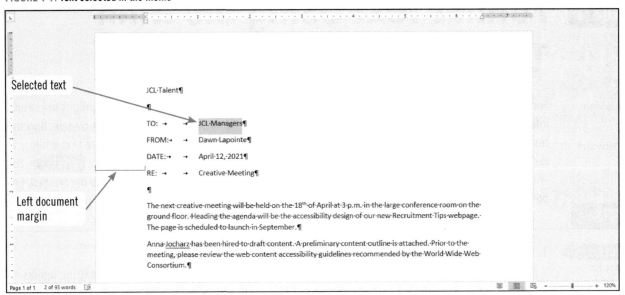

Selected text

Left document margin

FIGURE 1-8: **Edited memo with replacement text**

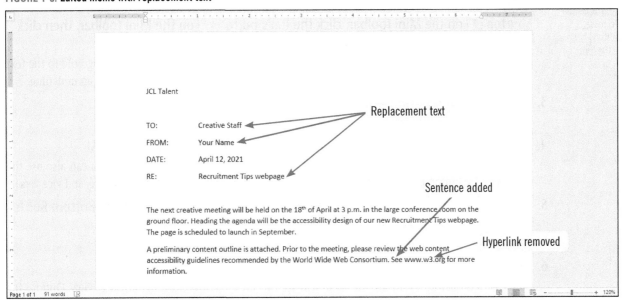

Replacement text

Sentence added

Hyperlink removed

TABLE 1-4: **Methods for selecting text**

to select	use the pointer to
Any amount of text	Drag over the text
A word	Double-click the word
A line of text	Move the pointer to the left of the line, then click
A sentence	Press and hold CTRL, then click the sentence
A paragraph	Triple-click the paragraph or double-click with the pointer to the left of the paragraph
A large block of text	Click at the beginning of the selection, press and hold SHIFT, then click at the end of the selection
Multiple nonconsecutive selections	Select the first selection, then press and hold CTRL as you select each additional selection
An entire document	Triple-click with the pointer to the left of any text; press CTRL+A; or click the Select button in the Editing group on the Home tab, and then click Select All

Word

Format Text Using the Mini Toolbar and the Ribbon

Learning Outcomes
• Modify text formatting
• Print a document
• Modify print settings
• Close a document

Formatting text is a fast and fun way to improve the appearance of a document and highlight important information. You can easily change the font, color, size, style, and other attributes of text by selecting the text and clicking a command on the Home tab. The **Mini toolbar**, which appears above text when you first select it, also includes commonly used text and paragraph formatting commands. **CASE** *You enhance the appearance of the memo by formatting the text using the Mini toolbar. When you are finished, you preview the memo for errors and then print it.*

STEPS

TROUBLE
If the Mini toolbar disappears, right-click the selection to display it again.

1. **Select JCL Talent**

   The Mini toolbar appears over the selected text, as shown in FIGURE 1-9. You click a formatting option on the Mini toolbar to apply it to the selected text. TABLE 1-5 describes the function of the buttons on the Mini toolbar. The buttons on the Mini toolbar are also available on the Ribbon.

QUICK TIP
Click the Decrease Font Size button A˅ to decrease the font size.

2. **Click the Increase Font Size button A˄ on the Mini toolbar six times, click the Bold button B on the Mini toolbar, click the Italic button I on the Mini toolbar, then click the Underline button U on the Mini toolbar**

   Each time you click the Increase Font Size button the selected text is enlarged. Applying bold to the text makes it thicker. Applying Italic to text makes it slanted. Apply an underline to text adds an underline.

3. **Click the Center button ≡ in the Paragraph group on the Home tab**

   The selected text is centered between the left and right margins.

4. **Click the Change Case button Aa˅ in the Font group, then click UPPERCASE**

   The lowercase characters in the selected text are changed to uppercase characters. You can also use the Change Case button to change the case of selected characters from uppercase to lowercase, and vice versa.

5. **Click the blank line between the RE: line and the body text, then click the Bottom Border button ⊞ in the Paragraph group**

   A single line border is added between the heading and the body text in the memo.

6. **Save the document, click the File tab, then click Print**

   Information related to printing the document appears on the Print screen in Backstage view. Options for printing the document appear on the left side of the Print screen and a preview of the document as it will look when printed appears on the right side, as shown in FIGURE 1-10. Before you print a document, it's a good habit to examine it closely so you can identify and correct any problems.

7. **Click the Zoom In button ✚ on the status bar five times, then proofread your document carefully for errors**

   The document is enlarged in print preview. If you notice errors in your document, you need to correct them before you print. To do this, press ESC or click the Back button in Backstage view, correct any mistakes, save your changes, click the File tab, and then click the Print command again to be ready to print the document.

8. **Click the Print button on the Print screen**

   A copy of the memo prints using the default print settings. To change the current printer, change the number of copies to print, select what pages of a document to print, or modify another print setting, you simply change the appropriate setting on the Print screen before clicking the Print button.

9. **Click the File tab, then click Close**

   The document closes, but the Word program window remains open.

FIGURE 1-9: Mini toolbar

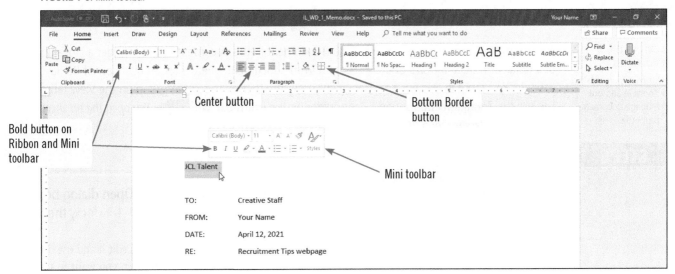

Bold button on Ribbon and Mini toolbar

Center button

Bottom Border button

Mini toolbar

FIGURE 1-10: Preview of the completed memo

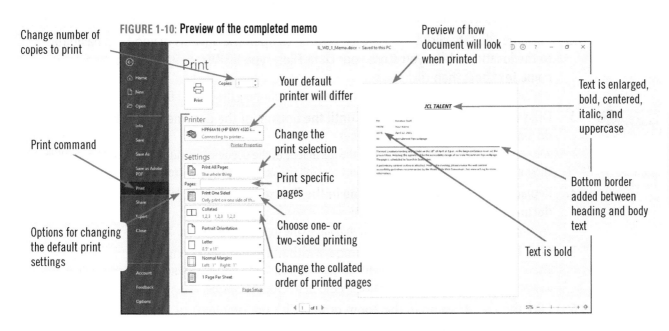

Change number of copies to print

Print command

Options for changing the default print settings

Your default printer will differ

Change the print selection

Print specific pages

Choose one- or two-sided printing

Change the collated order of printed pages

Preview of how document will look when printed

Text is enlarged, bold, centered, italic, and uppercase

Bottom border added between heading and body text

Text is bold

TABLE 1-5: Buttons on the Mini toolbar

button	use to	button	use to
Calibri (Body) ▾	Change the font of text	B	Apply bold to text
11 ▾	Change the font size of text	I	Apply italic to text
A˄	Make text larger	U	Apply an underline to text
A˅	Make text smaller	✐ ˅	Apply colored highlighting to text
✣	Copy the formats applied to selected text to other text	A	Change the color of text
A̲⁄ ˅	Apply a style to text	⁞☰	Apply bullets to paragraphs
		⁝☰	Apply numbering to paragraphs

Creating Documents with Word

Word

View and Navigate a Document

The Zoom feature in Word lets you enlarge a document in the document window to get a close-up view of a detail or reduce the size of the document in the document window for an overview of the layout as a whole. You zoom in and out on a document using the tools in the Zoom group on the View tab or you can use the Zoom level buttons and Zoom slider on the status bar. **CASE** ▶ *You open the tip sheet, save it with a new filename, and then customize a document property for the file.*

STEPS

1. **Click the File tab, click Open, click This PC, click Browse to open the Open dialog box, navigate to the location where you store your Data Files, click IL_WD_1-1.docx, then click Open**
   The document opens in Print Layout view. Once you have opened a file, you can edit it and use the Save or the Save As command to save your changes. You use the **Save** command when you want to save the changes you make to a file, overwriting the stored file. You use the **Save As** command when you want to leave the original file intact and create a duplicate file with a different filename, file extension, or location.

2. **Click the File tab, click Save As, click Browse to open the Save As dialog box, navigate to the location where you store your Data Files, type IL_WD_1_TipSheet in the File name text box, then click Save**
   You can now make changes to the tip sheet file without affecting the original file.

3. **Drag the vertical scroll box down until the bottom of the document is visible in your document window, as shown in FIGURE 1-11**
   You **scroll** to display different parts of the document in the document window. You can also scroll by clicking the scroll arrows above and below the scroll bar, or by clicking the scroll bar.

4. **Replace Your Name with your name in the first sentence of the last paragraph in the document, then press CTRL+HOME**
   Pressing CTRL+HOME moves the insertion point to the top of the document.

5. **Click the View tab, then click the Page Width button in the Zoom group**
   The document is enlarged to the width of the document window. When you enlarge a document, the area where the insertion point is located appears in the document window.

6. **Click the Zoom button in the Zoom group, click the Whole page option button in the Zoom dialog box, then click OK to view the entire document**
   You use the Zoom dialog box to select a zoom level for displaying the document in the document window.

7. **Move the Zoom slider on the status bar to the right until the Zoom percentage is approximately 200%, then click the Zoom Out button ▬ until the zoom level is 120%**
   Dragging the Zoom slider enlarges or reduces a document in the document window. You can also click the Zoom Out and Zoom In buttons to change the zoom level.

8. **Click the File tab**
   The right side of the Info screen in Backstage view shows the document properties for the file. **Document properties** are user-defined details about a file that describe its contents and origin, including the name of the author, the title of the document, and keywords that you can assign to help organize and search your files.

9. **Click the Add a title text box in the Properties section of the Info screen, type Tips, then click outside the text box**
   The new Title property for the document appears in Backstage view as shown in as shown in FIGURE 1-12

10. **Click Back button to return to the Home tab, then save your changes**
    The document appears at 120% zoom in Print Layout view.

FIGURE 1-11: Zoom slider

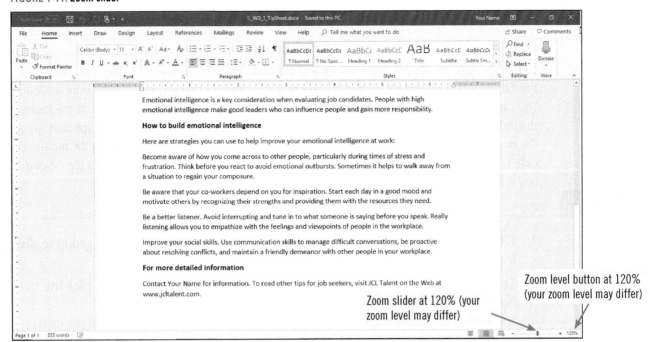

Zoom level button at 120%
(your zoom level may differ)

Zoom slider at 120% (your
zoom level may differ)

FIGURE 1-12: Document properties in Backstage view

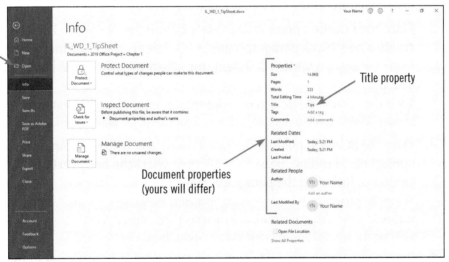

Click to navigate to
and open an existing
document

Title property

Document properties
(yours will differ)

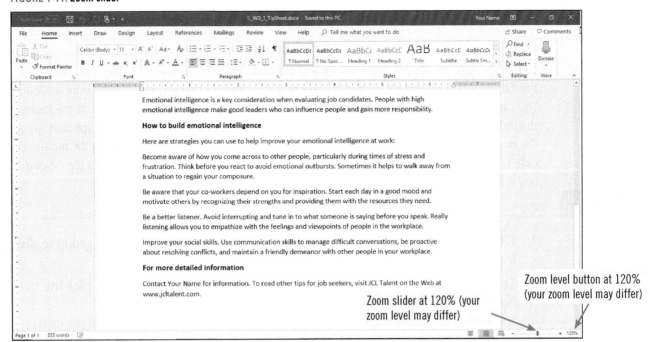

Using Word document views

Document views are different ways of displaying a document in the document window. Each Word view provides features that are useful for working on different types of documents. The default view, **Print Layout view,** displays a document as it will look on a printed page. Print Layout view is helpful for formatting text and pages, including adjusting document margins, creating columns of text, inserting graphics, and formatting headers and footers. Also useful is **Read Mode view,** which displays document text so that it is easy to read on screen. Other Word views are helpful for performing specialized tasks. **Web Layout view** allows you to format webpages or documents that will be viewed on a computer screen. In Web Layout view, a document appears just as it will when viewed with a web browser. Outline view is useful for editing and formatting longer documents that include multiple headings. **Outline view** allows you to reorganize text by moving the headings. Finally, **Draft view,** shows a simplified layout of a document, without margins, headers and footers, or graphics. When you want to quickly type and edit text, it's often easiest to work in Draft view. You switch between views by clicking the view buttons on the status bar or by using the commands on the View tab. Changing views does not affect how the printed document will appear. It simply changes the way you view the document in the document window.

Cut and Paste Text

The editing features in Word allow you to move text from one location to another in a document. Moving text is often called **cut and paste**. When you **cut** text, it is removed from the document and placed on the **Clipboard**, a temporary storage area for text and graphics that you cut or copy from a document. You can then **paste**, or insert, text that is stored on the Clipboard in the document at the location of the insertion point. You cut and paste text using the Cut and Paste buttons in the Clipboard group on the Home tab. You can also move selected text by dragging it to a new location using the mouse. This is called **drag and drop**. **CASE** ▶ *You reorganize the information in the tip sheet using the cut-and-paste and drag-and-drop methods.*

STEPS

1. **Click Home tab, then click the** Show/Hide ¶ button ¶ **in the Paragraph group to display formatting marks**

2. **Select** Tips for Job Seekers **(including the paragraph mark after it), then click the** Cut button **in the Clipboard group**

   The text is removed from the document and placed on the system clipboard. Word uses two different clipboards: the system **clipboard**, which holds just one item and is not visible, and the **Office Clipboard** (the Clipboard), which holds up to 24 items and can be displayed. When you cut-and-paste or copy-and-paste items one at a time, you use the system clipboard.

3. **Place the insertion point immediately before the** Are you... heading, **press** ENTER **to create a new blank paragraph under JCL Talent, place the insertion point in the new blank paragraph under JCL Talent, Inc., then click the** Paste button **in the Clipboard group**

   The text is pasted at the location of the insertion point, as shown in FIGURE 1-13. The Paste Options button appears below text when you first paste it in a document. For now you can ignore the Paste Options button.

4. **Place the insertion point in the** blank paragraph **below the Are you emotionally intelligent... heading, press** DELETE, **then select the body text** Be aware of your own emotions, **including the paragraph mark**

   The entire paragraph of text is selected, including the paragraph mark. Word considers any string of text that ends with a paragraph mark as a paragraph, including titles, headings, and single lines in a list. You will drag the selected text to a new location using the mouse.

5. **Press and hold the mouse button over the selected text, then drag the pointer's vertical line to the beginning of the** Control how you express... **paragraph, as shown in** FIGURE 1-14

   You drag the insertion point to where you want the text to be inserted when you release the mouse button.

6. **Release the mouse button, click to deselect the text, then save your changes**

   The selected text is moved to the location of the insertion point. Text is not placed on the Clipboard when you drag and drop it.

Highlighting text in a document

The Highlight tool allows you to mark and find important text in a document. **Highlighting** is transparent color that is applied to text using the Highlight pointer ⚟. To highlight text, click the Text Highlight Color arrow ✐ ▾ in the Font group on the Home tab, select a color, then use the I-beam part of the pointer to select the text you want to highlight. Click ✐ ▾ to turn off the Highlight pointer. To remove highlighting, select the highlighted text, click ✐ ▾ then click No Color. Highlighting prints, but it is used most effectively when a document is viewed on screen.

FIGURE 1-13: Moved text with Paste Options button

Pasted text   Paste Options button

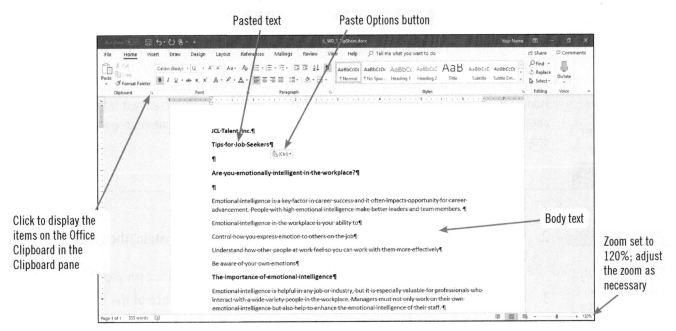

Click to display the items on the Office Clipboard in the Clipboard pane

Body text

Zoom set to 120%; adjust the zoom as necessary

FIGURE 1-14: Dragging and dropping text in a new location

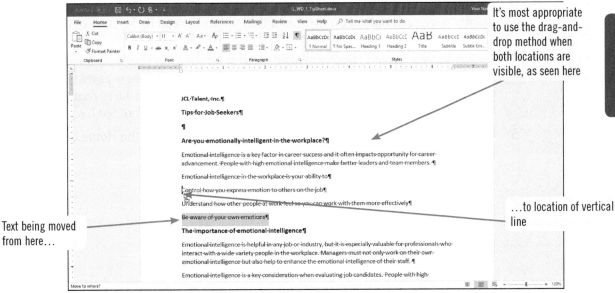

It's most appropriate to use the drag-and-drop method when both locations are visible, as seen here

...to location of vertical line

Text being moved from here...

Using the Undo, Redo, and Repeat commands

Word remembers the editing and formatting changes you make so that you can easily reverse or repeat them. You can reverse the last action you took by clicking the Undo button ↺ on the Quick Access toolbar, or you can undo a series of actions by clicking the Undo arrow ↺▾ and selecting the action you want to reverse. When you undo an action using the Undo arrow, you also undo all the actions above it in the list—that is, all actions that were performed after the action you selected. Similarly, you can keep the change you just reversed by using the Redo button ↻ on the

Quick Access toolbar. The Redo button appears only immediately after clicking the Undo button to undo a change.

If you want to repeat an action you just completed, you can use the Repeat button ↻ on the Quick Access toolbar. For example, if you just typed "thank you," clicking ↻ inserts "thank you" at the location of the insertion point. If you just applied bold, clicking ↻ applies bold to the currently selected text. You also can repeat the last action you took by pressing F4.

Word

Copy and Paste Text

Learning
Outcomes
• Cut, copy, and
  paste text
• Split the window
• Compare and
  combine multiple
  documents

Copying and pasting text is similar to cutting and pasting text, except that the text you **copy** is not removed from the document. Rather, a copy of the text is placed on the Clipboard, leaving the original text in place. You can copy text to the Clipboard using the Copy button in the Clipboard group on the Home tab, or you can copy text by pressing CTRL as you drag the selected text from one location to another. **CASE** ▶ *You continue to edit the tip sheet by copying text from one location to another using the copy-and-paste method.*

STEPS

QUICK TIP
You can also cut
or copy text by
right-clicking the
selected text, and
then clicking the Cut
or Copy command
on the menu that
opens.

1. **Scroll to the bottom of the document**

2. **Select more detailed in the heading For more detailed information, then click the Copy button 🗐 in the Clipboard group**

   A copy of the selected text is placed on the Clipboard, leaving the original text you copied in place.

3. **Place the insertion point before information in the first sentence of the final paragraph, then click the Paste button**

   The text "more detailed" is inserted in the final paragraph, as shown in FIGURE 1-15. Notice that the pasted text is formatted differently than the paragraph in which it was inserted.

4. **Click the Paste Options button 🗋 (Ctrl) ▾ that appears next to the text, move the mouse pointer over each button on the menu that opens to read its ScreenTip, then click the Keep Text Only (T) button**

   The formatting of "more detailed" is changed to match the rest of the paragraph, as shown in FIGURE 1-16. The buttons on the Paste Options menu allow you to change the formatting of pasted text. You can choose to keep the original formatting (Keep Source Formatting), match the destination formatting (Merge Formatting), paste the selection as a graphic object (Picture), or paste as unformatted text (Keep Text Only).

5. **Click the Show/Hide ¶ button ¶ in the Paragraph group on the Home tab to turn off the display formatting marks, then save your changes**

Splitting the document window to copy and move items in a long document

If you want to copy or move items between parts of a long document, it can be useful to split the document window into two panes. This allows you to display the item you want to copy or move in one pane and the destination for the item in the other pane. To split a window, click the Split button in the Window group on the View tab, and then drag the horizontal split bar that appears to the location you want to split the window. Once the document window is split into two panes, you can use the scroll bars in each pane to display different parts of the document. To copy or move an item from one pane to another, you can use the Cut, Copy, and Paste commands, or you can drag the item between the panes. When you are finished editing the document, double-click the split bar to restore the window to a single pane, or click the Remove Split button in the Window group on the View tab.

FIGURE 1-15: Text pasted in document

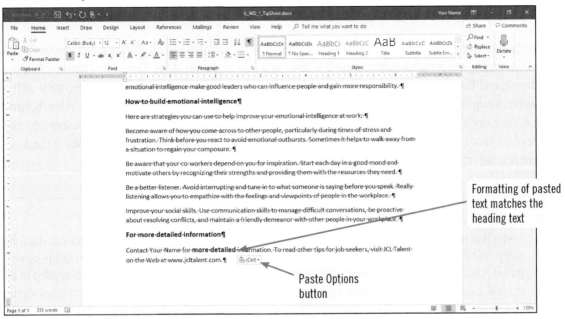

Formatting of pasted text matches the heading text

Paste Options button

FIGURE 1-16: Copied text in document

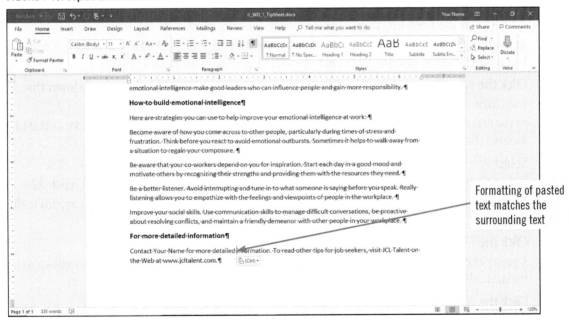

Formatting of pasted text matches the surrounding text

Copying and moving items between documents

You can also use the Clipboard to copy and move items between documents. To do this, open both documents and the Clipboard pane. With multiple documents open, copy or cut an item from one document and then switch to the other document and paste the item. To switch between open documents, point to the Word icon on the taskbar, and then click the document you want to appear in the document window. You can also display more than one document at the same time by clicking the Arrange All button or the View Side by Side button in the Window group on the View tab.

Format with Fonts

Learning
Outcome
• Modify text
formatting

Formatting text with fonts is a quick and powerful way to enhance the appearance of a document. A **font** is a complete set of characters with the same typeface or design. Arial, Times New Roman, Courier, Tahoma, and Calibri are some of the more common fonts, but there are hundreds of others, each with a specific design and feel. Another way to change the appearance of text is to increase or decrease its **font size**. Font size is measured in points. A **point** is 1/72 of an inch. **CASE** *You change the font and font size of the headings in the tip sheet. You select a font and font sizes that enhance the positive tone of the document and help to structure the tip sheet visually for readers.*

STEPS

1. **Press CTRL+HOME**

   Notice that the name of the font used in the document, Calibri, is displayed in the Font list box in the Font group. The word "(Body)" in the Font list box indicates Calibri is the font used for body text in the current theme, the default theme. A **theme** is a related set of fonts, colors, styles, and effects that is applied to an entire document to give it a cohesive appearance. The font size, 11, appears in the Font Size list box in the Font group.

QUICK TIP
There are two types of fonts: **serif fonts** have a small stroke, called a serif, at the ends of characters; **sans serif fonts** do not have a serif.

2. **Select Tips for Job Seekers, then click the Font arrow in the Font group**

   The Font list, which shows the fonts available on your computer, opens as shown in **FIGURE 1-17**. The font names are formatted in the font. Font names can appear in more than one location on the Font list.

3. **Drag the pointer slowly down the font names in the Font list, drag the scroll box to scroll down the Font list, then click Berlin Sans FB Demi**

   As you drag the pointer over a font name, a preview of the font is applied to the selected text. Clicking a font name applies the font. The font of the selected text changes to Berlin Sans FB Demi.

QUICK TIP
You can also type a font size in the Font Size text box.

4. **Click the Font Size arrow in the Font group, drag the pointer slowly up and down the Font Size list, then click 18**

   As you drag the pointer over a font size, a preview of the font size is applied to the selected text. Clicking 18 increases the font size of the selected text to 18 points.

5. **Select Are you emotionally intelligent in the workplace?, click the Font arrow, click Berlin Sans FB Demi in the Recently Used Fonts list, click the Font Size arrow, click 22**

   The title is formatted in 22-point Berlin Sans FB Demi bold. The bold formatting was already applied to the text.

6. **Click the Font Color arrow in the Font group**

   A gallery of colors opens. It includes the set of theme colors in a range of tints and shades as well as a set of standard colors. You can point to a color in the gallery to preview it applied to the selected text.

7. **Click the Blue, Accent 1 color as shown in FIGURE 1-18, then deselect the text**

   The color of the title text changes to blue. The active color on the Font Color button also changes to blue.

TROUBLE
If the mini toolbar closes, select the text again.

8. **Scroll down, select the heading The importance of emotional intelligence, then, using the Mini toolbar, click the Font arrow, click Berlin Sans FB Demi, click the Font Size arrow, click 14, click 🅰, then deselect the text**

   The heading is formatted in 14-point Berlin Sans FB Demi bold with a blue color.

9. **Repeat Step 8 to apply 14-point Berlin Sans FB Demi blue to the How to build emotional intelligence and For more detailed information headings, press CTRL+HOME, then save your changes**

   Compare your document to **FIGURE 1-19**.

FIGURE 1-17: Font list

Font list arrow   Font Size list arrow

Fonts used in the default theme

List of recently used fonts (your list may differ)

Alphabetical list of all fonts on your computer (your list may differ)

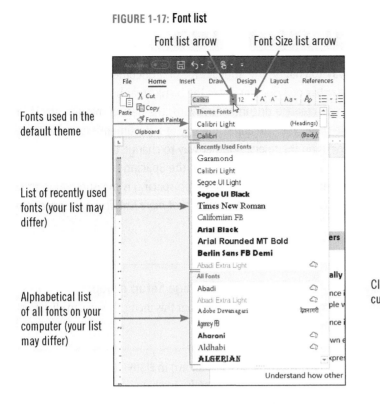

FIGURE 1-18: Font Color Palette

Font Color list arrow   Name of color appears as a ScreenTip

Click to create a custom color

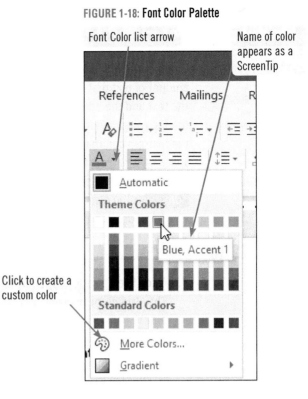

FIGURE 1-19: Document formatted with fonts

Heading formatted in 18-point Berlin Sans FB Demi bold

Title formatted in 22-point Berlin Sans FB Demi bold, blue

Body text formatted in 11-point Calibri

Heading formatted in 14-point Berlin Sans FB Demi bold, blue

JCL Talent, Inc.

Tips for Job Seekers

Are you emotionally intelligent in the workplace?

Emotional intelligence is a key factor in career success and it often impacts opportunity for career advancement. People with high emotional intelligence make better leaders and team members.

Emotional intelligence in the workplace is your ability to

Be aware of your own emotions

Control how you express emotion to others on the job

Understand how other people at work feel so you can work with them more effectively

The importance of emotional intelligence

Emotional intelligence is helpful in any job or industry, but it is especially valuable for professionals who interact with a wide variety people in the workplace. Managers must not only work on their own emotional intelligence but also help to enhance the emotional intelligence of their staff.

Page 1 of 1   334 words

Applying shadows and other text effects to text

The Word Text Effects and Typography feature allows you to add visual appeal to your documents by adding special text effects to text, including outlines, shadows, reflections, and glows. The feature also includes a gallery of preformatted combined text effect styles, called **WordArt**, that you can apply to your text to format it quickly and easily. To apply a WordArt style to text, simply select the text, click the Text Effects and Typography button in the Font group on the Home tab, and select a WordArt style from the gallery. To apply an individual text effect style, such as a shadow, outline, reflection, or glow, select the text, click the Text Effects and Typography button, point to the type of text effect you want to apply, and then select a style from the gallery that opens. Experiment with combining text effect styles to give your text a striking appearance.

If you are unhappy with the way text is formatted, you can use the Clear All Formatting command to return the text to the default format settings—11-point Calibri. Select the text, then click the Clear All Formatting button in the Font group on the Home tab.

Set Document Margins

Learning
Outcomes
• Modify page setup
• Alter line and
paragraph spacing
and indentation

Changing a document's margins is one way to change the appearance of a document and control the amount of text that fits on a page. The **margins** of a document are the blank areas between the edge of the text and the edge of the page. When you create a document in Word, the default margins are 1" at the top, bottom, left, and right sides of the page. You can adjust the size of a document's margins using the Margins command on the Layout tab or using the rulers. Another way to change the amount of open space on a page is to add space before and after paragraphs. You use the Spacing options in the Paragraph group on the Layout tab to change paragraph spacing. Paragraph spacing is measured in points.

CASE ▸ *You reduce the size of the document margins in the tip sheet so that more text fits on the page. You also add space under a paragraph.*

STEPS

1. **Click the Layout tab, then click the Margins button in the Page Setup group**

   The Margins menu opens. You can select predefined margin settings from this menu, or you can click Custom Margins to create different margin settings.

2. **Click Custom Margins**

   The Page Setup dialog box opens with the Margins tab displayed, as shown in FIGURE 1-20. You can use the Margins tab to change the top, bottom, left, or right document margin; to change the orientation of the pages from portrait to landscape; and to alter other page layout settings. **Portrait orientation** means a page is taller than it is wide; **landscape orientation** means a page is wider than it is tall. This tip sheet uses portrait orientation.

3. **Click the Top down four times until 0.6" appears, then click the Bottom down arrow until 0.6" appears**

   The top and bottom margins of the tip sheet will be .6".

QUICK TIP
The minimum allow-
able margin settings
depend on your
printer and the size
of the paper you are
using. Word displays
a warning message if
you set margins that
are too narrow for
your printer.

4. **Press TAB, type .6 in the Left text box, press TAB, then type .6 in the Right text box**

   The left and right margins of the report will also be .6". You can change the margin settings by using the arrows or by typing a value in the appropriate text box.

5. **Click OK**

   The document margins change to .6". The location of each margin (right, left, top, and bottom) is shown on the horizontal and vertical rulers at the intersection of the white and shaded areas.

6. **Place the insertion point in the blank paragraph under Tips for Job Seekers, press DELETE, then place the insertion point in Tips for Job Seekers**

   The paragraph spacing settings for the active paragraph (the paragraph where the insertion point is located) are shown in the Before and After text boxes in the Paragraph group on the Layout tab.

7. **Click the Before up arrow in the Spacing section in the Paragraph group once until 6 pt appears, then click the After up arrow in the Spacing section in the Paragraph group four times until 30 pt appears**

   Six points of space are added before the Tips for Job Seekers paragraph, and 30 points of space are added after, as shown in FIGURE 1-21.

FIGURE 1-20: Margins tab in Page Setup dialog box

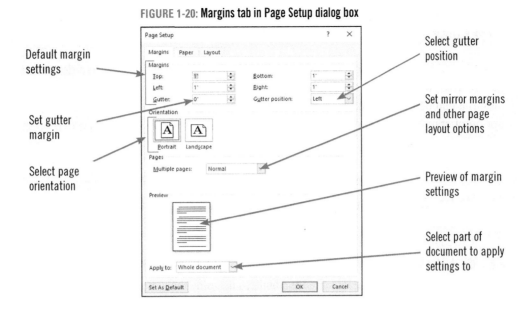

Default margin settings

Set gutter margin

Select page orientation

Select gutter position

Set mirror margins and other page layout options

Preview of margin settings

Select part of document to apply settings to

Ruler shows location of left margin

Ruler shows location of top margin

6 points of space added before paragraph; 30 points of space added after paragraph

Document margins are narrower than the original default margins

FIGURE 1-21: Info sheet with smaller margins and space after a paragraph

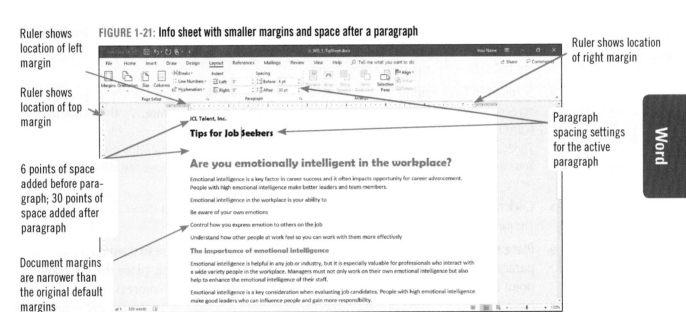

Ruler shows location of right margin

Paragraph spacing settings for the active paragraph

Changing orientation, margin settings, and paper size

By default, the documents you create in Word use an 8 ½" × 11" paper size in portrait orientation with the default margin settings. You can change the orientation, margin settings, and paper size to common settings using the Orientation, Margins, and Size buttons in the Page Setup group on the Layout tab. You can also adjust these settings and others in the Page Setup dialog box. For example, to change the layout of multiple pages, use the Multiple pages arrow on the Margins tab to create pages that use mirror margins, that include two pages per sheet of paper, or that are formatted using a book fold. **Mirror margins** are used in a document with facing pages, such as a magazine, where the margins on the left page of the document are a mirror image of the margins on the right page. Documents with mirror margins have inside and outside margins, rather than right and left margins. Another type of margin is a gutter margin, which is used in documents that are bound, such as books. A gutter adds extra space to the left, top, or inside margin to allow for the binding. Add a gutter to a document by adjusting the setting in the Gutter position text box on the Margins tab. To change the size of the paper used, use the Paper size arrow on the Paper tab to select a standard paper size, or enter custom measurements in the Width and Height text boxes.

Creating Documents with Word

Add Bullets and Numbering

Formatting a list with bullets or numbering can help to organize the ideas in a document. A **bullet** is a character, often a small circle, that appears before the items in a list to add emphasis. Formatting a list as a numbered list helps illustrate sequences and priorities. You can quickly format a list with bullets or numbering by using the Bullets and Numbering buttons in the Paragraph group on the Home tab.

CASE ▸ *You format the lists in your tip sheet with numbers and bullets.*

STEPS

1. **Under "Emotional intelligence in the workplace is your ability to", select the three-line list that begins with "Be aware of your own emotions..."**
   Three single-line paragraphs of text are selected.

2. **Click the Home tab, then click the Bullets button ☷ in the Paragraph group**
   The three paragraphs are formatted as a bulleted list using the most recently used bullet style as shown in FIGURE 1-22.

3. **Click a bullet in the list to select all the bullets, click the Bullets arrow ☷ ˅ in the Paragraph group, click the check mark bullet style, then click the document to deselect the text**
   The bullet character changes to a check mark.

4. **Scroll until the heading How to build emotional intelligence is at the top of your screen, select the four paragraphs that begin with "Become aware...", then click the Numbering arrow ☷ ˅ in the Paragraph group**
   The Numbering Library opens. You use this list to choose or change the numbering style applied to a list. You can drag the pointer over the numbering styles to preview how the selected text will look if the numbering style is applied.

5. **Click the Number alignment : Left numbering style called out in FIGURE 1-23**
   The paragraphs are formatted as a numbered list.

6. **Place the insertion point before times in the first sentence of the first numbered paragraph, type peak, press SPACEBAR to add a space after peak, place the insertion point before Think in the second sentence of the paragraph, then press ENTER**
   Pressing ENTER in the middle of the numbered list creates a new numbered paragraph and automatically renumbers the remainder of the list. Similarly, if you delete a paragraph from a numbered list, Word automatically renumbers the remaining paragraphs.

7. **Click 1 in the list**
   Clicking a number in a list selects all the numbers, as shown in FIGURE 1-24.

8. **Click the Bold button ☐ in the Font group then save your changes**
   The numbers are all formatted in bold. Notice that the formatting of the items in the list does not change when you change the formatting of the numbers. You can also use this technique to change the formatting of bullets in a bulleted list.

FIGURE 1-22: Bullets applied to list

Bullets button

Selected
paragraphs
formatted as
a bulleted list

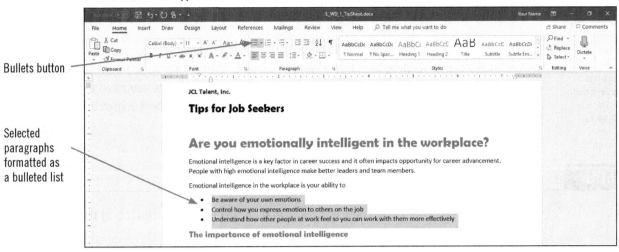

FIGURE 1-23: Numbering library

Numbering
arrow

Choose this num-
bering style (the
location in your
Numbering Library
may differ)

Click to change the
style, format, and
alignment of the
numbers in a list

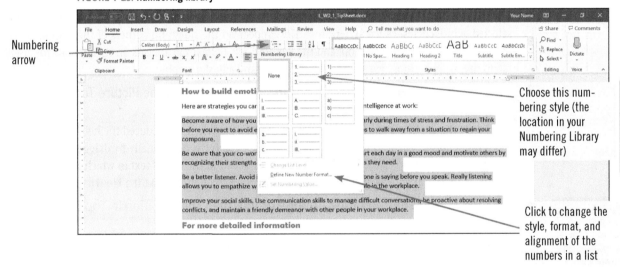

FIGURE 1-24: Numbered list

Numbers
selected in
numbered list

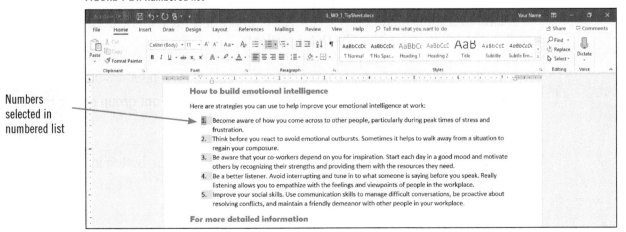

Word

Insert a Graphic

You can insert graphic images, including photos taken with a digital camera, scanned art, and graphics created in other graphics programs, into a Word document. To insert a graphic file into a document, you use the Pictures command in the Illustrations group on the Insert tab. Once you insert a graphic, you can resize it and apply a Picture style to it to enhance its appearance. **CASE** *You insert a picture in the document, resize it, position it, and then add a shadow.*

STEPS

1. **Press CTRL+HOME, click the Insert tab, then click the Pictures button in the Illustrations group**

   The Insert Picture dialog box opens. You use this dialog box to locate and insert graphic files. Most graphic files are **bitmap graphics**, which are often saved with a .bmp, .png, .jpg, .tif, or .gif file extension.

2. **Navigate to the location where you store your Data Files, click the file Support_WD_1-2.jpg, then click Insert**

   The picture is inserted as an inline graphic at the location of the insertion point. When a graphic is selected, white circles, called **sizing handles**, appear on the sides and corners of the graphic, a white **rotate handle** appears at the top, and the Picture Tools Format tab appears on the Ribbon. You use this tab to size, crop, position, wrap text around, format, and adjust a graphic.

3. **Type 2.5 in the Shape Height text box in the Size group on the Picture Tools Format tab, then press ENTER**

   The size of the graphic is reduced, as shown in FIGURE 1-25. When you reduced the height of the graphic, the width reduced proportionally. You can also resize a graphic proportionally by dragging a corner sizing handle. Until you apply text wrapping to a graphic, it is part of the line of text in which it was inserted (an **inline graphic**). To move a graphic independently of text, you must make it a **floating graphic**.

4. **Click the Position button in the Arrange group, then click Position in Top Right with Square Text Wrapping**

   The graphic is moved to the top-right corner of the page and the text wraps around it. Applying text wrapping to the graphic made it a floating graphic. A floating graphic can be moved anywhere on a page. You can also move a floating graphic to a new location by dragging it using the mouse.

5. **Click the Picture Effects button in the Picture Styles group, point to Shadow, move the pointer over the shadow styles in the gallery to preview them in the document, then click Offset Bottom Right in the Outer section**

   A drop shadow is applied to the picture, as shown in FIGURE 1-26. You can use the Picture Effects button to apply other visual effects to a graphic, such as a glow, soft edge, reflection, bevel, or 3-D rotation.

6. **Select Tips for Job Seekers, click the Font Color arrow in the Font group on the Home tab, then click Green, Accent 6**

   The text is formatted in green.

7. **Click to deselect the text, click the View tab, click the One Page button in the Zoom group, then save your changes**

   Next, you will finalize the look of the tip sheet.

Creating Documents with Word

FIGURE 1-25: Inline graphic in document

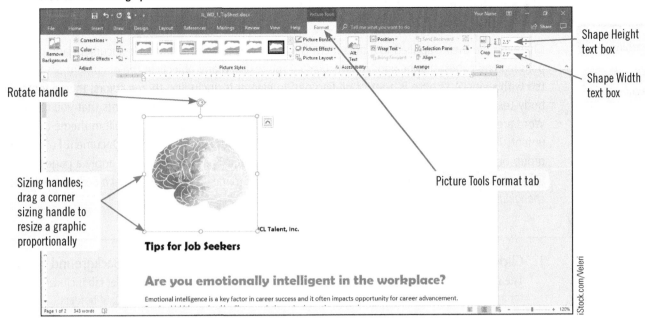

Rotate handle

Shape Height
text box

Shape Width
text box

Picture Tools Format tab

Sizing handles;
drag a corner
sizing handle to
resize a graphic
proportionally

JCL Talent, Inc.

Tips for Job Seekers

Are you emotionally intelligent in the workplace?

Emotional intelligence is a key factor in career success and it often impacts opportunity for career advancement.

FIGURE 1-26: Floating graphic with shadow effect applied

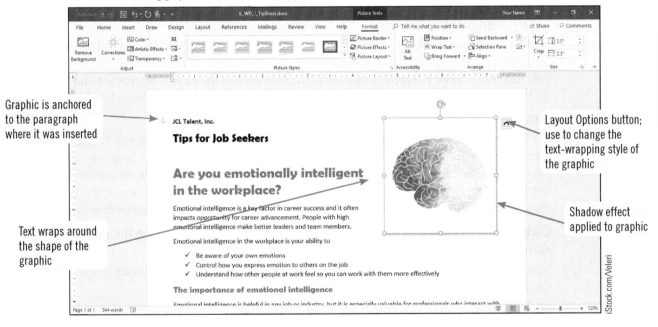

Graphic is anchored
to the paragraph
where it was inserted

Layout Options button;
use to change the
text-wrapping style of
the graphic

Shadow effect
applied to graphic

Text wraps around
the shape of the
graphic

JCL Talent, Inc.

Tips for Job Seekers

Are you emotionally intelligent in the workplace?

Emotional intelligence is a key factor in career success and it often impacts opportunity for career advancement. People with high emotional intelligence make better leaders and team members.

Emotional intelligence in the workplace is your ability to

✓ Be aware of your own emotions
✓ Control how you express emotion to others on the job
✓ Understand how other people at work feel so you can work with them more effectively

The importance of emotional intelligence

Emotional intelligence is helpful in any job or industry, but it is especially valuable for professionals who interact with

Enhancing pictures with styles and effects

A fun way to give a document personality and flair is to apply a style or an effect to a picture. To apply a style, select the picture and then choose from the style options in the Styles group on the Picture Tools Format tab. Styles include a preset mixture of effects, such as shading, borders, shadows, and other settings. The Effects command in the Styles group on the Picture Tools Format tab gives you the power to apply a customized variety of effects to an object, including a shadow, bevel, glow, reflection, soft edge, or 3-D rotation. To apply an effect, select the object,

click the Picture Effects arrow, point to the type of effect you want to apply, and then select from the options in the gallery that opens. To further customize an effect, click the Options command for that type of effect at the bottom of the gallery to open the Format Picture pane. The best way to learn about styles and effects is to experiment by applying them to a picture and seeing what works. To return a picture to its original settings, click the Reset Picture button in the Adjust group on the Picture Tools Format tab.

Apply a Theme

Learning Outcomes
- Change document themes
- Format page background elements

Changing the theme applied to a document is a quick way to set the tone of a document and give it a polished and cohesive appearance, particularly if the text and any objects in the document are formatted with styles. A **theme** is a set of unified design elements, including theme colors, theme fonts for body text and headings, and theme effects for graphics. By default, all documents that you create in Word are formatted with the Office theme, but you can easily apply a different built-in theme to a document. To apply a theme to a document, you use the Themes command in the Document Formatting group on the Design tab. Another way to enhance the look of a document is to apply a page border. **CASE** ▶ *You polish the tip sheet by adding a page border to the document, applying a built-in theme, and changing the theme colors.*

STEPS

1. **Click the Design tab, then click the Page Borders button in the Page Background group**

   The Borders and Shading dialog box opens, as shown in FIGURE 1-27. The Page Border tab includes options for applying a border around each page of a document, and for customizing the look of borders.

2. **Click the Box button on the Page Border tab, then click OK**

   A single line page border is added to the document.

3. **Click the Themes button on the Design tab, move the pointer over each theme in the gallery, then point to Organic**

   A gallery of built-in themes opens. When you point to the Organic theme in the gallery, a preview of the theme is applied to the document, as shown in FIGURE 1-28. Notice that the font colors and the fonts for the body text change when you preview each theme. It's important to choose a theme that not only mirrors the tone, content, and purpose of your document, but also meets your goal for document length.

4. **Scroll down, then click Vapor Trail**

   A complete set of new theme colors, fonts, styles, and effects is applied to the document. Only document content that uses theme colors, text that is formatted with a style (including default body text), and table styles and graphic effects change when a new theme is applied. Notice that while the font of the body text changed, the font you previously applied to the headings remains the same. Changing the document theme does not affect the formatting of text to which individual font formatting has already been applied.

5. **Click the Colors button in the Document Formatting group, then move the pointer over each set of theme colors on the menu that opens**

   When you point to a theme color set in the gallery, a preview of the colors is applied to the document. Changing theme colors changes the colors only. Other theme styles are not affected.

6. **Click Blue**

   The Blue theme colors are applied to the document, as shown in FIGURE 1-29.

7. **sam↑ Save the document, submit the document to your instructor, close the file, then exit Word**

FIGURE 1-27: **Page Border tab in Borders and Shading dialog box**

Choose a line style, color, and weight for the border

Options for customizing a page border

Preview of border settings

Click buttons or edges of preview to apply borders

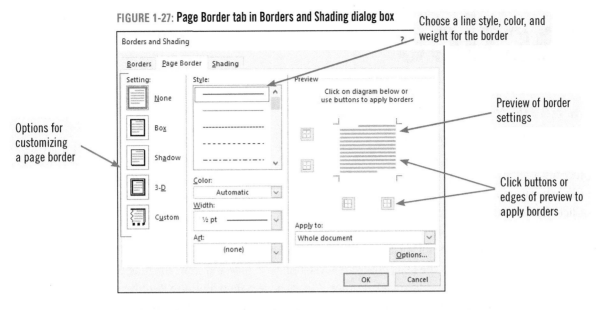

FIGURE 1-28: **Organic theme previewed in document**

Themes gallery

Organic theme

Preview of Organic theme applied to document

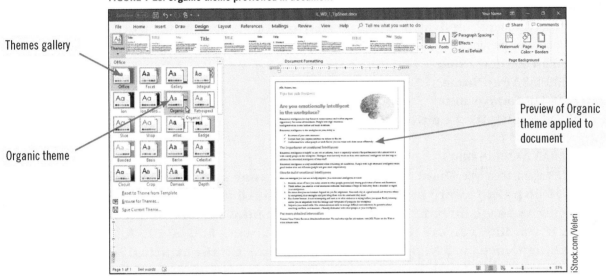

FIGURE 1-29: **Vapor Trail theme and Blue theme colors applied to document**

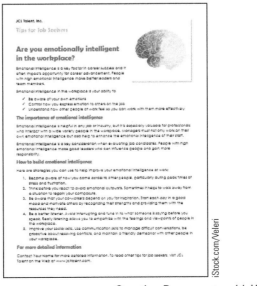

Creating Documents with Word

Practice

Skills Review

1. **Explore the Word program window.**
   a. Start Word and open a new, blank document.
   b. Identify as many elements of the Word program window as you can without referring to the module material.
   c. Click the File tab, then click the Info, New, Open, Save, Save As, Print, Share, and Export commands.
   d. Click the Back button in Backstage view to return to the document window.
   e. Click each tab on the Ribbon, review the groups and buttons on each tab, then return to the Home tab.
   f. Point to each button on the Home tab and read its ScreenTip.
   g. Click the View tab and click the Ruler checkbox several times to hide and show the ruler. Show the ruler.
   h. Click the View buttons to view the blank document in each view, then return to Print Layout view.
   i. Use the Zoom slider to zoom all the way in and all the way out on the document, then return to 120%.

2. **Start a document.**
   a. In a new blank document, type **Health West International** at the top of the page, then press ENTER two times.
   b. Type the following, pressing TAB as indicated and pressing ENTER at the end of each line:
   To: TAB TAB **Matthew Chao**
   From: TAB TAB **Your Name**
   Date: TAB TAB **Today's date**
   Re: TAB TAB **Health West Conference**
   Pages: TAB TAB **1**
   Fax: TAB TAB **212-555-0043**
   c. Press ENTER again, then type **Thank you for confirming your attendance at our upcoming Global Health Conference in February. I have booked your accommodations. Your conference package includes three nights, continental breakfast, and the conference dinner. If you like, you can also purchase the following add-ons: Exhibitor's Kiosk, Networking Lunch, and Night Out in Boston. Please see the attached schedule for conference dates and details.**
   d. Press ENTER, then type **To make a payment, please call me at 617-555-0156 or visit our website at www.healthwest5.com. Payment must be received in full by the 3rd of October to hold your room. We look forward to seeing you!**
   e. Insert **Fireside Chat Social Hour,** before Networking Lunch.
   f. Insert **Insurance** before Conference in the first sentence.
   g. Using the BACKSPACE key, delete 1 in the Pages: line, then type **2**.
   h. Using the DELETE key, delete upcoming in the first sentence of the first paragraph.

3. **Save a document.**
   a. Click the Save button on the Quick Access toolbar.
   b. Save the document as **IL_WD_1-ChaoFax** with the default file extension to the location where you store your Data Files.
   c. After your name, type a comma, press SPACEBAR, then type **Conference Manager**.
   d. Save the document.

4. **Select text.**
   a. Turn on formatting marks.
   b. Select the Re: line, then type **Re:** TAB TAB **Global Health Insurance Conference**

Skills Review (continued)

c. Select three in the third sentence, then type **two**.

d. Select 3rd of October in the second sentence of the last paragraph, type **15th of November**, select **room**, then type **reservation**.

e. Delete the sentence We look forward to seeing you!

f. Turn off the display of formatting marks, then save the document.

5. Format text using the Mini toolbar.

a. Select Health West International, click the Increase Font Size button on the Mini toolbar eight times, apply bold, then click the Decrease Font Size button on the Mini toolbar twice.

b. Center Health West International on the page.

c. Change the case of Health West International to uppercase.

d. Apply a bottom border under Health West International.

e. Apply bold to the following words in the fax heading: To:, From:, Date:, Re:, Pages:, and Fax:.

f. Apply yellow highlighting to 15th of November.

g. Use the Undo, Redo, and Repeat buttons to undo the highlighting, redo the highlighting, undo, repeat, then undo the highlighting again.

h. Underline 15th of November.

i. Italicize the last sentence of the first paragraph.

j. Read the document using the Read Mode view.

k. Return to Print Layout view, zoom in on the document, then proofread the fax.

l. Correct any typing errors in your document, then save the document. Compare your document to FIGURE 1-30.

m. Preview the document in Print Preview, identify each printing options available to you on the Print screen in Backstage view, then print the document only if required to so by your instructor.

n. Return to Print Layout view, save, submit the fax per your instructor's directions, then close the document.

FIGURE 1-30

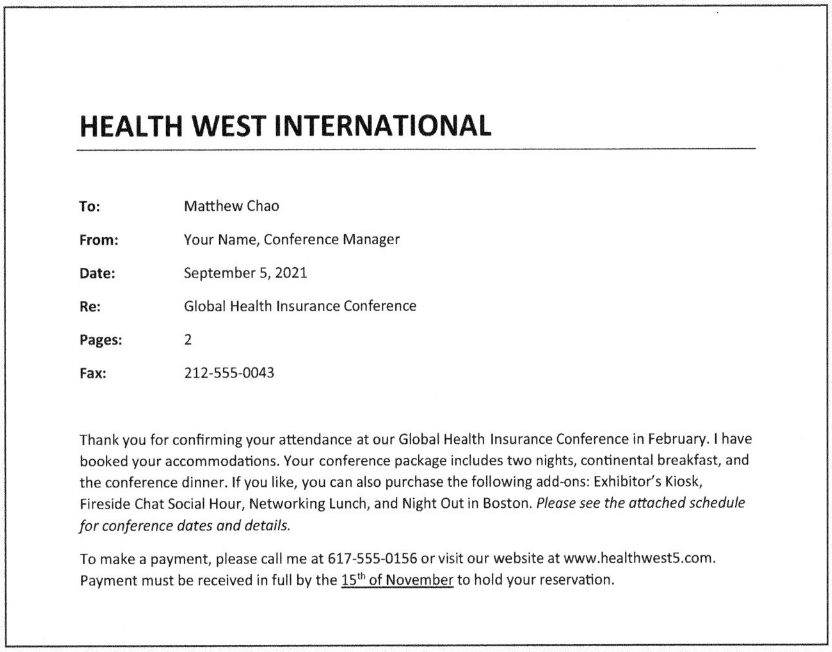

HEALTH WEST INTERNATIONAL

To:	Matthew Chao
From:	Your Name, Conference Manager
Date:	September 5, 2021
Re:	Global Health Insurance Conference
Pages:	2
Fax:	212-555-0043

Thank you for confirming your attendance at our Global Health Insurance Conference in February. I have booked your accommodations. Your conference package includes two nights, continental breakfast, and the conference dinner. If you like, you can also purchase the following add-ons: Exhibitor's Kiosk, Fireside Chat Social Hour, Networking Lunch, and Night Out in Boston. *Please see the attached schedule for conference dates and details.*

To make a payment, please call me at 617-555-0156 or visit our website at www.healthwest5.com. Payment must be received in full by the 15th of November to hold your reservation.

6. View and navigate a document.

a. Open the file IL_WD_1-3.docx from the location where you store your Data Files, then save it as **IL_WD_1_HealthWest** in the File name text box.

b. Switch to Page Width view, then scroll through the document to get a feel for its contents.

c. Use the Zoom dialog box to view the Whole Page.

d. Use the Zoom slider to set the Zoom percentage at approximately 100%.

e. Read the document using the Read Mode view. (*Hint:* Press ESC to leave Read Mode view.)

    f. Return to Print Layout view, zoom in, scroll to the bottom of the document, then replace Your Name with your name in the final sentence.

    g. Add the Title property **Global** to the document properties in the file, return to Print Layout view, change the zoom level to 120%, then save your changes.

7. Cut and paste text

    a. Turn on the display of formatting marks.

    b. Select the first body paragraph that begins We aim… (including the paragraph mark after it), cut it to the clipboard, then paste the paragraph before the heading Experience and expertise across the globe.

    c. Delete the heading The Health West International Difference.

    d. In the list of locations, move the Middle East paragraph after the Europe paragraph.

    e. Move the United States paragraph after the Greater China paragraph.

    f. Move the Southeast Asia paragraph before the United States paragraph.

    g. Move the Greater China paragraph after the Europe paragraph, then save your changes.

8. Copy and paste text

    a. Scroll to the bottom of the document, then remove the hyperlink in the final paragraph.

    b. Select the sentence Get an online quote at www.healthwest5.com, then copy the sentence to the clipboard.

    c. Scroll to the top of the page, add a blank paragraph under the Health West International heading, then paste the sentence at the location of the blank paragraph.

    d. Use the Paste Options button to Keep Source formatting.

    e. Format the pasted sentence in italic, turn off formatting marks, then save your changes.

9. Format with fonts

    a. Format the heading Health West International in 20-point Calibri Light with a Blue, Accent 1 font color.

    b. Format the heading The industry leader in global health benefits in 12-point Calibri Light with a Gold, Accent 4 font color.

    c. Format Experience and expertise across the globe, Global member support, and Clinical expertise in 12-point Calibri Light with a Gold, Accent 4 font color.

    d. Apply bold formatting to the last paragraph in the document, then change the font color to Blue, Accent 1.

    e. Scroll up, select Health West International, click the Text Effects and Typography arrow, preview several WordArt styles applied to the text, then apply one of the styles.

    f. Click the Undo button, add an Offset: Bottom Right shadow to the title, then save your changes.

10. Set Document Margins

    a. Change the left and right margins to 2".

    b. View the document in Multiple Pages view.

    c. Change the left and right margins to 1.5".

    d. Change all four document margins to .7".

    e. Change the zoom level to 120%, then add 24 points of space before the heading The industry leader in global health benefits.

    f. Save your changes.

11. Add Bullets and Numbering

    a. Select the five-line list of locations that begins with Europe and ends with United States, then format it as a bulleted list using the circle bullet symbol.

    b. Change the font color of the bullets to Blue, Accent 1.

    c. Press and hold CTRL to select the headings Experience and expertise across the globe, Global member support, and Clinical expertise, then apply numbering.

    d. Click 1 in the list, then change the font color of the numbers to Blue, Accent 1.

    e. Save your changes.

Skills Review (continued)

12. Insert a Graphic

a. Click in the first body paragraph to move the insertion point to the top of the document, then open the Insert Picture dialog box.

b. Navigate to the location where you store Data Files, then insert the file **Support_ WD_1-4.jpg**.

c. Change the height of the graphic to 1.2 using the Shape Height text box in the Size group on the Picture Tools Format tab.

d. Use the Position command to wrap text around the graphic and position it in the Top Left with Square Text Wrapping.

e. Apply the Double Frame, Black picture style to the graphic.

f. Click the Reset Picture arrow in the Adjust Group on the, reset the picture, then apply the Simple Frame, White picture style.

g. Change the font size of Health West International to 28 point.

h. Click before The industry leader in global health benefits heading, press ENTER, change the font size of the heading to 18 point, then save your changes.

13. Apply a theme

a. Change the view to One Page, click the Design tab, click the Page Border button, then apply a single line box border to the page.

b. Use the Themes feature, preview several different themes applied to the document. Apply a theme, zoom in and out on the document to evaluate its suitability, then apply another theme, zoom in and out, and so forth.

c. Apply the View theme.

d. Change all four document margins to .6" to better fit the text on the page.

e. Zoom in on the bottom of the document, then add 24 points of space above the last paragraph.

f. Change the theme colors to Red.

g. Zoom in on the top of the document, then change the font color of the Get an online quote... paragraph to Brown, Accent 5.

h. Change the font color of the four light brown headings to Orange, Accent 3. Compare your document to FIGURE 1-31.

i. Save your changes, preview the document, submit it per your instructor's directions, then close the document and exit Word.

FIGURE 1-31

Health West International

Get an online quote at www.healthwest5.com.

The industry leader in global health benefits

Our award-winning global health insurance business provides health benefits to more than one million members worldwide. We are world leaders in providing health care benefits with a seventy-five year track record of excellence and expertise. In addition, we have developed world-class health systems for governments, businesses, and health providers around the world. By delivering comprehensive health benefits worldwide, we are committed to helping create a stronger, healthier global community.

More than 1,500 dedicated Health West employees can be found in our global locations, including

- Europe (Madrid, London, and Berlin)
- Greater China (Shanghai and Hong Kong)
- Middle East (Dubai, Cairo, and Abu Dhabi)
- Southeast Asia (Singapore, Manila, and Jakarta)
- United States (Hartford and nationally)

We aim to be the global leader in delivering world-class health solutions. Our goals are to make quality health care more accessible to empower people to live healthier lives. Our strengths include

1. **Experience and expertise across the globe**

With nearly a century of experience in health care, we've specialized in international health benefits insurance for more than 55 years. Our global footprint reaches wherever our members travel. Our prestigious awards include "Best International Health Insurance Provider" and "International Health Insurer of the Year."

2. **Global member support**

Our professional Member Service representatives are trained to assist you, 24 hours a day, 365 days a year. We can help locate health care services wherever you are, arrange for reimbursement in more than 180 currencies, and answer your questions about claims, benefit levels, and coverage—in ten languages with the ability to communicate in more than 160 languages through interpretation services.

3. **Clinical expertise**

You can depend on our clinical knowledge and experience for help with pre-trip planning, which is especially important if you have a chronic health condition. We can also coordinate medical care, obtain prescription medications and medical devices, and handle medical emergency or evacuation services.

Looking for international health insurance? Get an online quote at www.healthwest5.com. For more information, contact Your Name at 860-555-0035.

iStock.com/bubaone

Word

Independent Challenge 1

You work at the Riverwalk Medical Clinic, a large outpatient medical facility staffed by family physicians, specialists, nurses, and other allied health professionals. Your boss has drafted an information sheet to help seasonal allergy sufferers and asks you to edit and format it so that it is eye catching and attractive.

a. Open the file IL_WD_1-5.docx from the drive and folder where you store your Data Files, save it as **IL_WD_1_AllergyInfo**, then read the document to get a feel for the content. FIGURE 1-32 shows how you will format the info sheet.

b. Show the rulers in your document window if they are not already visible.

c. Accept or ignore all suggested spelling and grammar changes in the document.

d. Insert the Riverwalk Medical Clinic logo file Support_IL_WD_1-6.jpg at the top of the document. Change the height of the logo to 1", then position the logo in the bottom right with square text wrapping. (*Hint*: Zoom in and out on the document as necessary. If an anchor symbol appears in the margin, you can ignore it.)

e. Center the first two lines of text in the document.

f. Change the font of Riverwalk Medical Clinic to Arial Black. Change the font size to 18 point. Change the font color to Orange, Accent 2. Apply an Offset: Bottom Right shadow text effect.

g. Format Advice for Seasonal Allergy Sufferers in 28-point Arial Black with a Blue, Accent 1 font color. Apply an Offset Bottom Right shadow text effect.

FIGURE 1-32

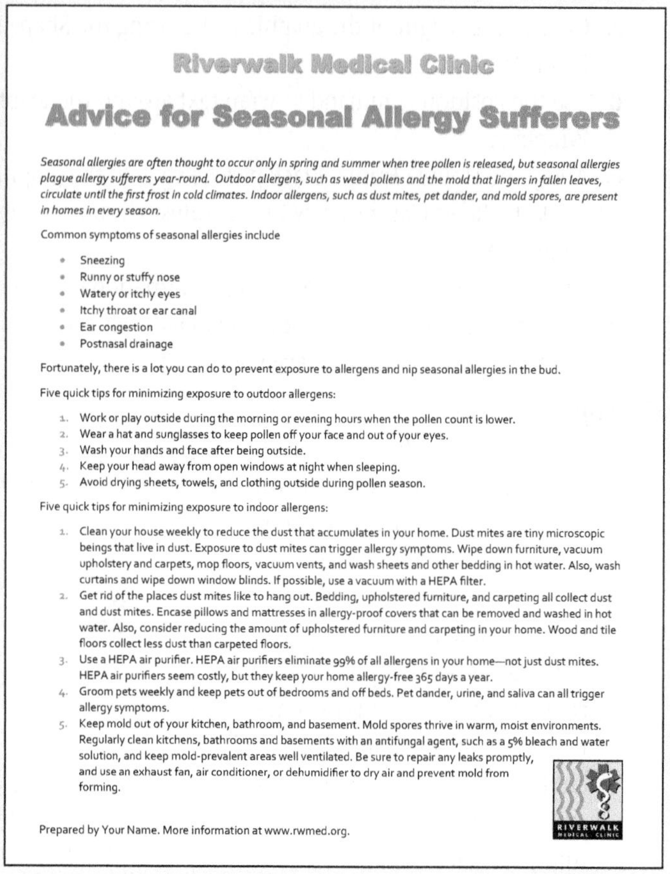
Riverwalk Medical Clinic

Advice for Seasonal Allergy Sufferers

Seasonal allergies are often thought to occur only in spring and summer when tree pollen is released, but seasonal allergies plague allergy sufferers year-round. Outdoor allergens, such as weed pollens and the mold that lingers in fallen leaves, circulate until the first frost in cold climates. Indoor allergens, such as dust mites, pet dander, and mold spores, are present in homes in every season.

Common symptoms of seasonal allergies include

- Sneezing
- Runny or stuffy nose
- Watery or itchy eyes
- Itchy throat or ear canal
- Ear congestion
- Postnasal drainage

Fortunately, there is a lot you can do to prevent exposure to allergens and nip seasonal allergies in the bud.

Five quick tips for minimizing exposure to outdoor allergens:

1. Work or play outside during the morning or evening hours when the pollen count is lower.
2. Wear a hat and sunglasses to keep pollen off your face and out of your eyes.
3. Wash your hands and face after being outside.
4. Keep your head away from open windows at night when sleeping.
5. Avoid drying sheets, towels, and clothing outside during pollen season.

Five quick tips for minimizing exposure to indoor allergens:

1. Clean your house weekly to reduce the dust that accumulates in your home. Dust mites are tiny microscopic beings that live in dust. Exposure to dust mites can trigger allergy symptoms. Wipe down furniture, vacuum upholstery and carpets, mop floors, vacuum vents, and wash sheets and other bedding in hot water. Also, wash curtains and wipe down window blinds. If possible, use a vacuum with a HEPA filter.
2. Get rid of the places dust mites like to hang out. Bedding, upholstered furniture, and carpeting all collect dust and dust mites. Encase pillows and mattresses in allergy-proof covers that can be removed and washed in hot water. Also, consider reducing the amount of upholstered furniture and carpeting in your home. Wood and tile floors collect less dust than carpeted floors.
3. Use a HEPA air purifier. HEPA air purifiers eliminate 99% of all allergens in your home—not just dust mites. HEPA air purifiers seem costly, but they keep your home allergy-free 365 days a year.
4. Groom pets weekly and keep pets out of bedrooms and off beds. Pet dander, urine, and saliva can all trigger allergy symptoms.
5. Keep mold out of your kitchen, bathroom, and basement. Mold spores thrive in warm, moist environments. Regularly clean kitchens, bathrooms and basements with an antifungal agent, such as a 5% bleach and water solution, and keep mold-prevalent areas well ventilated. Be sure to repair any leaks promptly, and use an exhaust fan, air conditioner, or dehumidifier to dry air and prevent mold from forming.

Prepared by Your Name. More information at www.rwmed.org.

h. Apply italic to the first body paragraph.

i. Change all four document margins to .5", then reduce the font size of Advice for Seasonal Allergy Sufferers by 2 points.

j. Format the six-line list of common symptoms (beginning with Sneezing) as a bulleted list, then apply the Blue, Accent 1 font color to the bullets.

k. Format the five-line list of tips for minimizing exposure to outdoor allergens (beginning with Work or play outside) as a numbered list. (*Hint*: If you make a mistake, click the Undo button and try again.)

l. Format the five-paragraph list of tips for minimizing exposure to indoor allergens, beginning with Clean your house weekly, as a numbered list.

m. Apply bold to the numbers in each numbered list, and change the font color of the numbers to Blue, Accent 1.

n. In the second numbered list, select paragraph 2, cut it, place the insertion point before Groom in the new paragraph 3, then paste the text.

o. Change the document theme to Basis, then change the theme colors to Blue Green.

p. Add a Shadow page border to the document.

q. Increase the font size of **Riverwalk Medical Clinic** to 22, then add 12 points of space after **Advice for Seasonal Allergy Sufferers**.

r. Zoom in on the bottom of the document. Replace Your Name in the final line with your name, remove the hyperlink from www.rwmed.org, and add 24 points of space before the final line paragraph.

s. Zoom out, examine the document carefully for formatting errors, and make any necessary adjustments so that all the text fits on one page.

t. Save the document, submit it per your instructor's directions, then close the file and exit Word.

Independent Challenge 2

Yesterday you interviewed for a job as the administrative assistant in the Business Department at Jericho College. You spoke with several people at the college, including Sonia Alvarado, director of human resources, whose business card is shown in FIGURE 1-33. You need to write a follow-up letter to Ms. Alvarado, thanking her for the interview and expressing your interest in the college and the position. She also asked you to send her some samples of your work as evidence of your Word skills.

a. Start Word and save a new blank document as **IL_WD_1_AlvaradoLetter** to the location where you store your Data Files.

b. Begin the letter by clicking the No Spacing button in the Styles group. You use this button to apply the No Spacing style to the document so that your document does not include extra space between paragraphs.

c. Type a personal letterhead for the letter that includes your name, address, telephone number, email address, and webpage or LinkedIn address, if you have one. Remove any hyperlinks. Accept or undo any automatic corrections. (*Note: Format the letterhead after you finish typing the letter.*)

d. Three lines below the bottom of the letterhead, type today's date.

e. Four lines below the date, type the inside address, referring to FIGURE 1-33 for the information. Include the recipient's title, college name, and full mailing address.

f. Two lines below the inside address, type **Dear Ms. Alvarado:** for the salutation.

g. Two lines below the salutation, type the body of the letter according to the following guidelines:
   - In the first paragraph, thank her for the interview. Then restate your interest in the position and express your desire to work for the college. Add any specific details you think will enhance the power of your letter.
   - In the second paragraph, note that you are enclosing three samples of your work, and explain something about the samples you are enclosing.
   - Type a short final paragraph.

h. Two lines below the last body paragraph, type a closing, then four lines below the closing, type the signature block. Be sure to include your name in the signature block.

i. Two lines below the signature block, type an enclosure notation. (*Hint*: An enclosure notation usually includes the word "Enclosures" or the abbreviation "Enc." followed by the number of enclosures in parentheses.)

j. Edit your letter for clarity and precision. Move sentences if necessary, replace words with more precise words, and correct any spelling or grammar errors.

k. Change the font of the letter to a serif font, such as Times New Roman, Garamond, or something similar. Adjust the font size so the letter can be read easily.

l. Format the letterhead using fonts, font colors, text effects, borders, themes, paragraph spacing, paragraph alignment, change case, and other formatting features. Be sure the design of your letterhead reflects your personality and is suitable for a professional document.

m. Change the Title document property to **Letter**.

n. Save your changes, preview the letter, submit it per your instructor's directions, then close the document and exit Word.

FIGURE 1-33

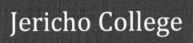

Jericho College

SONIA ALVARADO
Director of Human Resources

JERICHO COLLEGE
783 Valley View Highway
Concord, CA 94520

925-555-0100

sonia_alvarado@jericho.edu
www.jerichocollege.edu

Word

Visual Workshop

Create the letter shown in FIGURE 1-34. Before beginning to type, click the No Spacing button in the Styles group on the Home tab. Type the letter before formatting the letterhead and applying the theme. To format the letterhead, change the font size of the first line of text to 40 point and apply the Gradient Fill: Blue, Accent 5, Reflection WordArt style. Change the font color of the address line to Blue, Accent 5. Add the bottom border to the letterhead. When the letterhead is formatted, change the font size of the body text to 12 point, apply the Organic theme, then change the font color of the letterhead text to Green, Accent 1. Save the document as **IL_WD_1-SakuraDoksa** to the location where you store your Data Files, submit the letter to your instructor, then close the document and exit Word.

FIGURE 1-34

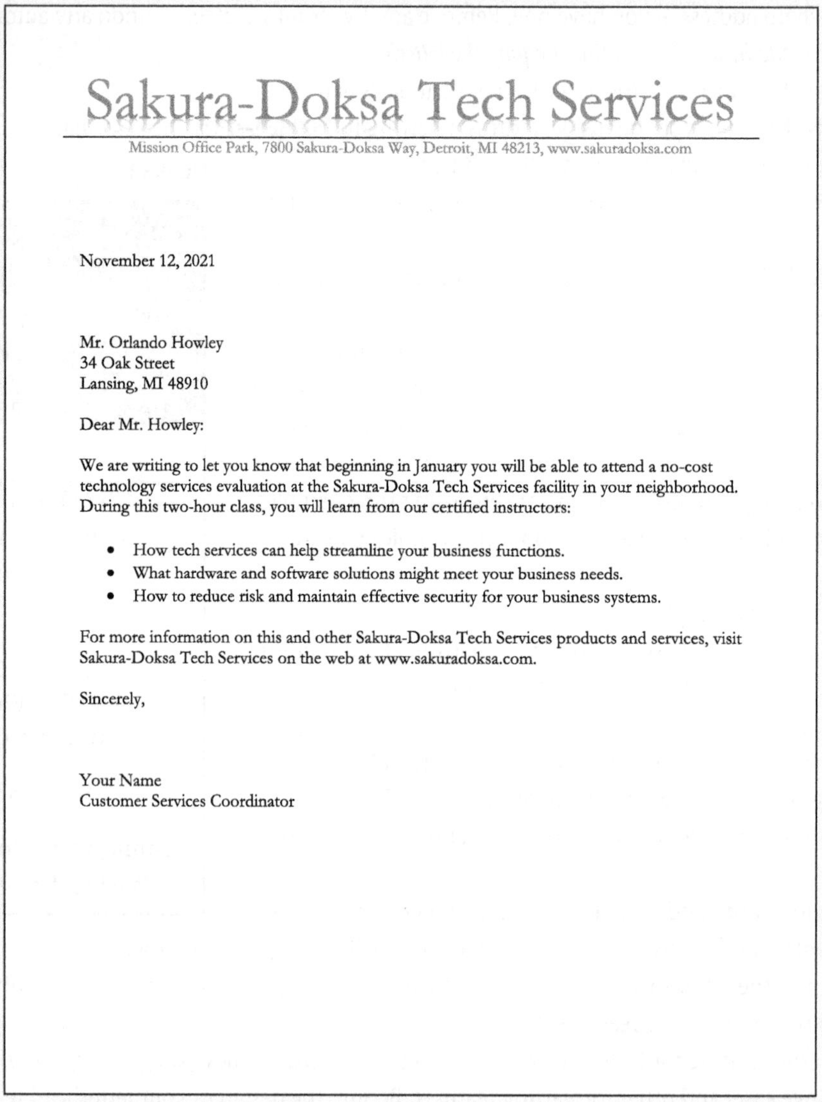

Sakura-Doksa Tech Services

Mission Office Park, 7800 Sakura-Doksa Way, Detroit, MI 48213, www.sakuradoksa.com

November 12, 2021

Mr. Orlando Howley
34 Oak Street
Lansing, MI 48910

Dear Mr. Howley:

We are writing to let you know that beginning in January you will be able to attend a no-cost technology services evaluation at the Sakura-Doksa Tech Services facility in your neighborhood. During this two-hour class, you will learn from our certified instructors:

- How tech services can help streamline your business functions.
- What hardware and software solutions might meet your business needs.
- How to reduce risk and maintain effective security for your business systems.

For more information on this and other Sakura-Doksa Tech Services products and services, visit Sakura-Doksa Tech Services on the web at www.sakuradoksa.com.

Sincerely,

Your Name
Customer Services Coordinator

Editing and Formatting Documents

CASE You have been asked to edit and format a research report on job growth in the tech sector. After editing the report and applying styles to format the text, you plan to add page numbers, a header, footnotes, and a bibliography to the report. Finally, before distributing the report file electronically, you will strip the file of private information.

Module Objectives

After completing this module, you will be able to:

- Insert comments
- Find and replace text
- Check spelling and grammar
- Research information
- Change line spacing and indents
- Apply styles to text

- Insert page numbers and page breaks
- Add headers and footers
- Add footnotes and endnotes
- Insert citations
- Create a bibliography
- Inspect a document

Files You Will Need

IL_WD_2-1.docx	IL_WD_2-3.docx
IL_WD_2-2.docx	IL_WD_2-4.docx

Insert comments

You can collaborate on documents with colleagues in different ways. One way is to insert comments into a document when you want to ask questions or provide information to other reviewers. A **comment** is text contained in a comment balloon that appears along the right side of your document in Print Layout view when All Markup view is active. Shading appears in the document at the point where you inserted the comment. A line connects the comment mark and the comment balloon. Each reviewer is assigned a unique color automatically, which is applied to the comment shading, bar, and balloon. **CASE** ▸ *Your colleague, Dawn Lapointe, read the draft of the report and inserted comments. You open the report to review and respond to Dawn's comments. You add, edit, delete, and resolve comments.*

STEPS

1. **sam** ↓ **Start Word, open the file IL_WD_2-1.docx from the location where you store your Data Files, save it as IL_WD_2_TechJobs, change the zoom level to 100%, then click the Review tab**

   Simple Markup is the default option in the Display for Review box in the Tracking group on the Review tab. With this option, comments appear in comment balloons along the right side of the page. If you see comment balloons and no comment wording, then click a comment balloon to read the comment. If you want to see all comments, click the Show Comments button in the Comments group.

2. **Click the Display for Review arrow in the Tracking group, then click All Markup**

   The comments that Dawn inserted appear to the right of the document. The text "job" is shaded in a color and a dotted line goes from the text to the comment, indicating the text is associated with the comment.

3. **Select the word Sector in the title (the first line), then click the New Comment button 🗩 in the Comments group**

   The word "Sector" is shaded, and a comment balloon appears in the right margin. Your name or the name assigned to your computer appears in the box.

4. **Type This title is approved by the web team.**

   Your comment appears as shown in FIGURE 2-1.

5. **Click Dawn's first comment balloon (starts with "This is…"), click the Reply button 🗩 in the comment, type I am compiling a list., then click anywhere in the document text**

   Your response appears indented under the original comment. You can also click the New Comment button to insert an indented reply to a comment.

6. **Click Dawn's second comment balloon ("Great!"), then click the Delete Comment button 🗩 in the Comments group**

   The comment is removed from the document.

7. **Click after "list." in the "I am compiling a list." comment you inserted in Step 5, then type I will send it to you.**

   You edit a comment by clicking in the comment box and typing. When you click in a comment box, its colored outline appears.

8. **Scroll down, click Dawn's comment balloon containing the text "Please add citations…", click the Resolve button 🗩 in the comment, then click anywhere in the document text**

   The comment is marked as resolved and is dimmed, as shown in FIGURE 2-2. You can reopen a comment that has been marked as resolved by clicking the comment and then clicking the Reopen button in the comment.

9. **Click All Markup in the Tracking group, click No Markup, then save your changes**

   Selecting No Markup hides the comments. Hiding the comments does not remove them from the document. It simply hides them from view on the screen. You will keep the comments hidden while you format the document.

FIGURE 2-1: **New comment in document**

New Comment button

Delete Comment button

Display for Review arrow

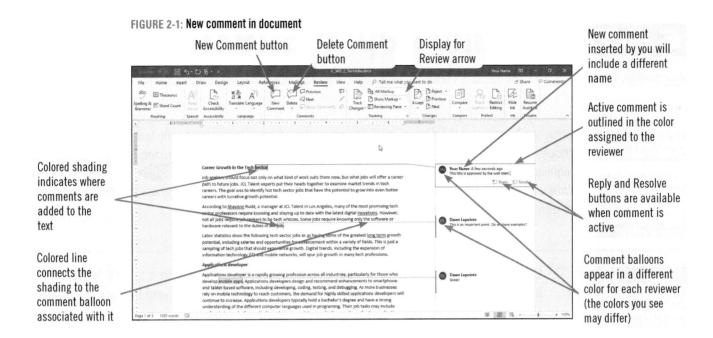

New comment inserted by you will include a different name

Active comment is outlined in the color assigned to the reviewer

Reply and Resolve buttons are available when comment is active

Comment balloons appear in a different color for each reviewer (the colors you see may differ)

Colored shading indicates where comments are added to the text

Colored line connects the shading to the comment balloon associated with it

FIGURE 2-2: **Resolved comment in document**

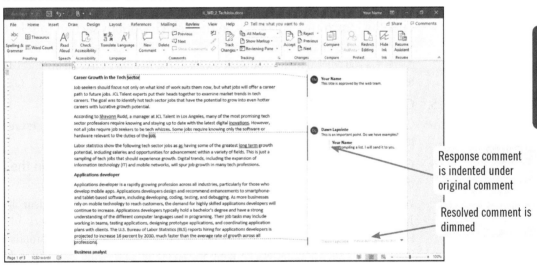

Response comment is indented under original comment

Resolved comment is dimmed

Inking comments in Word

If you are working in Touch mode on a touch-enabled device, you can draw or write comments using your finger, a digital pen, or a mouse. The type of inking features available to you will depend on your device. To begin, click the Ink Comment button in the Comments group on the Review tab to create an ink comment, and then use your finger, stylus, or mouse to draw or write in the comment box. On some devices, you can change the color and type of pen stroke to use for inking by using the Pen button in the Comments group. You can also erase a comment by using the Ink Comment Eraser button in the Comments group. When you are finished inking a comment, click anywhere in the document. Note: To switch your device to Touch mode and be able to use the full range of inking features available in Word, you need to click the Touch/Mouse Mode button on the Quick Access toolbar, and then click Touch. This button will only be available if you are working on a touch-enabled device.

Find and Replace Text

Learning Outcomes
- Find and replace text and formatting
- Search for text
- Move to a specific location in a document

The Find and Replace feature in Word allows you to automatically search for and replace all instances of a word or phrase in a document. For example, you might need to substitute "position" for "job". To manually locate and replace each instance of "job" in a long document would be very time-consuming. Using the Replace command, you can find and replace all occurrences of specific text at once, or you can choose to find and review each occurrence individually. Using the Find command, you can locate and highlight every occurrence of a specific word or phrase in a document. **CASE** *You notice the word "talent" is used to describe job qualifications that are actually skills in the report. You use the Replace command to search the document for all instances of "talent" and replace them with "skill".*

STEPS

1. **Change the zoom level to 120%, press CTRL+HOME, click the Home tab, click the Replace button in the Editing group, then click More in the Find and Replace dialog box**

   The Find and Replace dialog box opens and expands, as shown in FIGURE 2-3.

2. **Type talent in the Find what text box**

   The text "talent" is the text that will be replaced.

3. **Press TAB, then type skill in the Replace with text box**

   The text "skill" will replace the text "talent".

4. **Click the Match case check box in the Search Options section to select it**

   Selecting the Match case check box tells Word to find only exact matches for the uppercase and lowercase characters you entered in the Find what text box. You want to replace all instances of "talent" in the body text of the report. You do not want to replace "Talent" in the proper name "JCL Talent".

5. **Click Replace All**

   Clicking Replace All changes all occurrences of "talent" to "skill" in the press release. A message box reports eight replacements were made.

6. **Click OK to close the message box, then click the Close button in the Find and Replace dialog box**

   Word replaced "talent" with "skill" in eight locations but did not replace "Talent" in the company name. To find or replace text that is formatted a certain way, click the Find arrow, click Advanced Find, click the Format button in the Find and Replace dialog box, and then select the appropriate format options. To find or replace special characters, click the Special button in the Find and Replace dialog box.

7. **Click the Find button in the Editing group**

   Clicking the Find button opens the Navigation pane, which is used to browse a longer document by headings, by pages, or by specific text. The Find command allows you to quickly locate all instances of text in a document. You use it to verify that Word did not replace "Talent" in JCL Talent.

8. **Type Talent in the search text box in the Navigation pane**

   The word "Talent" is highlighted and selected in the document, as shown in FIGURE 2-4.

9. **Click the Close button in the Navigation pane**

   The highlighting is removed from the text when you close the Navigation pane.

10. **Press CTRL+HOME, then save the document**

FIGURE 2-3: Find and Replace dialog box

Replace only exact matches of uppercase and lowercase characters

Find only complete words

Use wildcards (*) in a search string

Find words that sound like the Find what text

Find and replace all forms of a word

Find or replace text that is formatted with certain settings

Find or replace special characters and formatting marks

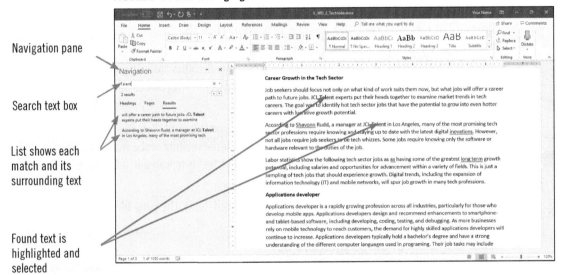

FIGURE 2-4: Found text highlighted in document

Navigation pane

Search text box

List shows each match and its surrounding text

Found text is highlighted and selected

Navigating a document using the Navigation pane and the Go to command

Rather than scrolling to move to a different place in a longer document, you can use the Navigation pane to quickly move the insertion point to a specific page, a specific heading, or specific text. One way to open the Navigation pane is by clicking the Page number button on the status bar, then clicking the link in the Navigation pane for the type of item, headings or pages, you want to use to navigate the document.

To move to a specific page, section, line, table, graphic, or other item in a document, you use the Go To tab in the Find and Replace dialog box. On the Go To tab in the Find and Replace dialog box, select the type of item you want to find in the Go to what list box, enter the relevant information about that item, and then click Next to move the insertion point to the item.

Check Spelling and Grammar

While you are working on or after you finish typing and revising a document, you can use the Spelling and Grammar command to search the document for misspelled words and grammar errors. The Spelling and Grammar checker flags possible mistakes and writing style issues, suggests correct spellings, and offers remedies for grammar errors such as subject–verb agreement, repeated words, and punctuation.

CASE ▶ *You use the Spelling and Grammar checker to search the report for errors. Before beginning the search, you select to ignore words you know are spelled correctly, such as Shavonn, a proper noun.*

STEPS

TROUBLE
If Shavonn is not flagged as misspelled, skip to Step 3.

1. **Right-click Shavonn in the second body paragraph**

   A menu that includes suggestions for correcting the spelling of "Shavonn" opens. You can correct individual spelling and grammar errors by right-clicking text that is underlined with a red wavy line (a possible misspelling), a blue double underline (a possible grammar error), or gold dotted line (a possible writing style issue), and then selecting a correction. Although "Shavonn" is not in the Word dictionary, it is a proper name that is spelled correctly in the document.

QUICK TIP
To change the language used by the Word proofing tools, click the Language button in the Language group on the Review tab, click Set Proofing Language, select the language you prefer in the dialog box that opens, then click OK.

2. **Click Ignore All**

   Clicking Ignore All tells Word not to flag "Shavonn" as misspelled.

3. **Press CTRL+HOME, click the Review tab, then click the Spelling & Grammar button in the Proofing group**

   The Editor pane opens, as shown in FIGURE 2-5. The pane identifies "inovations" as misspelled and suggests possible corrections for the error. The first word selected in the Suggestions box is the correct spelling.

4. **Click innovations in the Suggestions box**

   Word replaces the misspelled word with the correctly spelled word. You can also use the arrow next to a suggested correction to hear the word read aloud, to hear the spelling of the word, or to change all instances of the error in a document. Next, the pane indicates that "as" is repeated in a sentence.

QUICK TIP
To add a word to the Dictionary so it is not flagged as misspelled, click Add to Dictionary.

5. **Click Delete Repeated Word in the Editor pane**

   Word deletes the second occurrence of the repeated word. Next, the pane identifies a grammar error. The phrase "long-term" is missing the hyphen.

6. **Click long-term in the Suggestions box**

   Word adds a hyphen between "long" and "term". Next, the pane identifies a potential subject-verb disagreement. The verb used with the subject in the sentence is not an error.

TROUBLE
If the Editor pane does not close, continue to correct spelling and grammar errors in your document.

7. **Click Ignore Once**

   Word ignores the flagged verb, the Editor pane closes, and a message box opens. The Editor identifies many common errors, but you cannot rely on it to find and correct all spelling and grammar errors in your documents, or to always suggest a valid correction. Always proofread your documents carefully.

8. **Click OK to complete the spelling and grammar check, press CTRL+HOME, then save the document**

Using Smart Lookup

The Smart Lookup feature gives you quick access to information about document text, including definitions, images, and other material from online sources. For example, you might use Smart Lookup to see the definition of a word used in a document or to hear the word pronounced. To use Smart Lookup, select the text you want to look up in your document, right-click it, then click Smart Lookup. You can also select text, then click the Smart Lookup button in the Research group on the References tab. The Insights pane opens and includes the Explore and Define tabs. The Explore tab includes images and web links related to the selected text. The Define tab includes a dictionary definition of the selected text and a link you can click to hear the selected text pronounced.

FIGURE 2-5: Editor pane

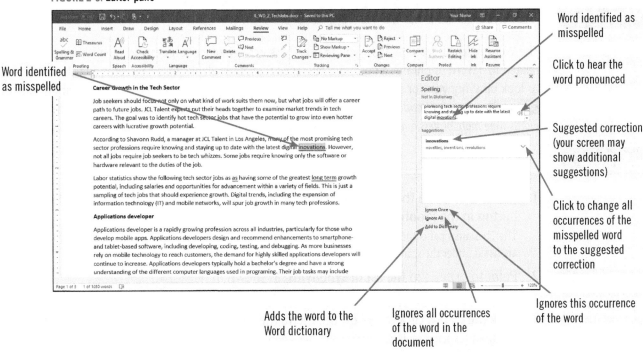

Word identified as misspelled

Click to hear the word pronounced

Suggested correction (your screen may show additional suggestions)

Click to change all occurrences of the misspelled word to the suggested correction

Word identified as misspelled

Adds the word to the Word dictionary

Ignores all occurrences of the word in the document

Ignores this occurrence of the word

Inserting text with AutoCorrect

As you type, AutoCorrect automatically corrects many commonly misspelled words. By creating your own AutoCorrect entries, you can set Word to insert text that you type often, such as your name or contact information, or to correct words you misspell frequently. For example, you could create an AutoCorrect entry so that the name "Mary T. Watson" is automatically inserted whenever you type "mtw" followed by a space. You create Auto-Correct entries and customize other AutoCorrect and AutoFormat options using the AutoCorrect dialog box. To open the Auto-Correct dialog box, click the File tab, click Options, click Proofing in the Word Options dialog box that opens, and then click AutoCorrect Options. On the AutoCorrect tab in the AutoCorrect dialog box, type the text you want to be corrected automatically in the Replace text box (such as "mtw"), type the text you want to be inserted in its place automatically in the With text box (such as "Mary T. Watson"), and then click Add. The AutoCorrect entry is added to the list. Click OK to close the AutoCorrect dialog box, and then click OK to close the Word Options dialog box. Word inserts an AutoCorrect entry in a document when you press SPACEBAR or a punctuation mark after typing the text you want Word to correct. For example, Word inserts "Mary T. Watson" when you type "mtw" followed by a space. If you want to remove an AutoCorrect entry you created, simply open the AutoCorrect dialog box, select the AutoCorrect entry you want to remove in the list, click Delete, click OK, and then click OK to close the Word Options dialog box.

Research Information

Learning Outcomes
- Find synonyms
- Check the word count

The Word Research features allow you to quickly search reference sources and the web for information related to a word or phrase. Among the reference sources available are a thesaurus, which you can use to look up synonyms for awkward or repetitive words, as well as dictionary and translation sources.

CASE ▶ *After proofreading your document for errors, you decide the report would read better if several words were more professional. You use the Thesaurus to find synonyms.*

STEPS

1. **Select whizzes in the third line of the second body paragraph, then click the Thesaurus button in the Proofing group on the Review tab**

   The Thesaurus pane opens. "Whizzes" appears in the search text box, and possible synonyms for "whizzes" are listed under the search text box.

QUICK TIP

To look up synonyms for a different word, type the word in the search text box, then click the search button.

2. **Point to experts in the list of synonyms, as shown in FIGURE 2-6.**

   A shaded box containing an arrow appears around the word.

3. **Click the arrow, click Insert on the menu that opens, then close the Thesaurus pane**

   The word "experts" replaces "whizzes" in the report.

4. **Right-click relevant in the fourth line of the second body paragraph, point to Synonyms on the menu that opens, then click pertinent**

   The word "pertinent" replaces "relevant" in the report.

5. **Select the three paragraphs of body text under the "Career Growth..." title, then click the Word Count button in the Proofing group**

   The Word Count dialog box opens, as shown in FIGURE 2-7. The dialog box lists the number of pages, words, characters, paragraphs, and lines included in the selected text. Notice that the status bar also displays the number of words included in the selected text and the total number of words in the entire document. If you want to view the page, character, paragraph, and line count for the entire document, make sure nothing is selected in your document, and then click Word Count in the Proofing group.

6. **Click Close, then save the document**

Reading a document aloud using Word

The Word Read Aloud feature reads a document aloud for you. Reading a document aloud can help you hear grammar errors, discover missing words, or notice other writing issues you might not notice when proofreading a document on screen. As Word reads the document aloud, each word is highlighted on the screen as it is pronounced. To read a document aloud using Word, move the insertion point to the beginning of the document, then click the Read Aloud button in the Speech group on the Review tab. A toolbar of playback controls opens at the top of the document window and Word begins to read aloud. You can use the Setting button on the playback controls toolbar to change the reading speed or the reading voice. The Previous, Next, Pause, and Play buttons allow you to pause and resume the reading, or to navigate through the document paragraph by paragraph. When you are finished reading the document aloud using Word, click the Stop button on the playback controls toolbar.

FIGURE 2-6: **Thesaurus pane**

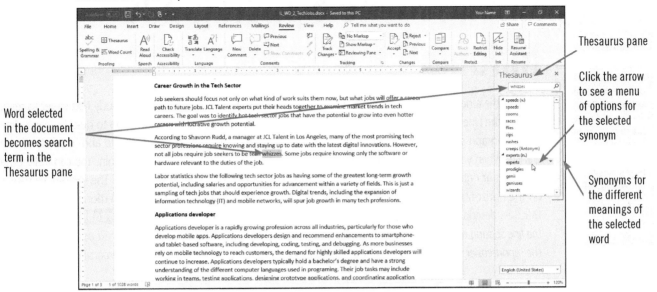

Word selected in the document becomes search term in the Thesaurus pane

Thesaurus pane

Click the arrow to see a menu of options for the selected synonym

Synonyms for the different meanings of the selected word

FIGURE 2-7: **Word Count dialog box**

Word Count	?	✕
Statistics:		
Pages		1
Words		181
Characters (no spaces)		915
Characters (with spaces)		1,096
Paragraphs		3
Lines		12
☑ Include textboxes, footnotes and endnotes		
	Close	

Using a add-ins for Word

Add-ins are small programs embedded in Word that allow you to access information on the web without having to leave Word. For example, you can look up something on Wikipedia, insert an online map in one of your documents, or access dictionaries and other reference sources, all from within Word using an add-in. To find and install an add-in, click the Get Add-ins button in the Add-ins group on the Insert tab to open the Office Add-ins gallery. The Store tab in the Office Add-ins gallery includes a searchable list of the add-ins available to you, which you can also browse by category. Some add-ins are free, and some require purchase.

To install an add-in, click the Add button next to it on the Store tab. To use an add-in after you have installed it, click the My Add-ins button on the Insert tab to open the Office Add-ins gallery with the My Add-ins tab displayed. Select the Add-in you want to use on this tab, and then click Add. A new button for the add-in may be added to your ribbon. When you no longer need an add-in you have installed, you can remove it by right-clicking the add-in on the My Add-in tab in the Office Add-ins gallery, and then clicking Remove.

Editing and Formatting Documents

Word

Change Line Spacing and Indents

Learning
Outcomes
• Alter line and
  paragraph spacing
  and indentation
• Set line and para-
  graph spacing and
  indentation
• Set paragraph
  pagination and
  formatting options

Altering the amount of space between lines and paragraphs in a document can make body text easier to read. You use the Line and Paragraph Spacing arrow in the Paragraph group on the Home tab to quickly change line and paragraph spacing. Indenting paragraphs can also make a document easier to read and understand at a glance. When you **indent** a paragraph, you move its edge in from the left or right margin. You can indent the entire left or right edge of a paragraph, just the first line, or all lines except the first line. The **indent markers** on the horizontal ruler indicate the indent settings for the paragraph in which the insertion point is located. TABLE 2-1 describes different types of indents and some of the methods for creating each. **CASE** ▸ *You increase the line spacing of the report, remove space under a paragraph, and create indents for body text paragraphs to make the report easier to read. You work with formatting marks turned on, so you can see the paragraph marks (¶).*

STEPS

1. **Press CTRL+HOME, click the Home tab, click the Show/Hide ¶ button ¶ in the Paragraph group, press CTRL+A to select the entire document, then click the Line and Paragraph Spacing arrow ⌶≡⌄ in the Paragraph group**
   The Line Spacing list opens. This list includes options for increasing the space between lines. Both line and paragraph spacing are measured in points.

2. **Click 2.0, then click the document to deselect the text**
   The space between the lines in the document increases to 2.

3. **Place the insertion point in the first body paragraph under the title, click ⌶≡⌄ then click 1.15**
   The space between the lines in the paragraph decreases to 1.15. Notice that you do not need to select an entire paragraph to change its paragraph formatting; simply place the insertion point in the paragraph.

4. **Select the next two paragraphs of body text, click ⌶≡⌄, then click 1.15**
   The line spacing between the selected paragraphs changes to 1.15. To change the paragraph-formatting features of more than one paragraph, you must select the paragraphs.

5. **Click before Job at the beginning of the first body paragraph, then press TAB**
   The first line of the paragraph is indented ½", as shown in FIGURE 2-8. Notice the First Line Indent marker is located at the ½" mark on the horizontal ruler. The ruler shows the indent settings for the paragraph in which the insertion point is located. Pressing TAB is a quick way to indent the first line of a paragraph ½".

6. **Place the insertion point in the second body paragraph, then drag the First Line Indent marker ▽ right to the ½" mark on the horizontal ruler**
   FIGURE 2-9 shows the First Line Indent marker being dragged. The first line of the second body paragraph is indented 1/2". Dragging the First Line Indent marker indents only the first line of a paragraph.

7. **Place the insertion point in the third body paragraph, then drag the Hanging Indent marker △ right to the ½" mark on the ruler**
   Take care to drag the Hanging Indent marker and not the Left Indent marker. FIGURE 2-10 shows the Hanging Indent marker being dragged. The lines under the first line of the third body paragraph are indented ½". Dragging the Hanging Indent marker indents the subsequent lines of a paragraph more than the first line.

8. **Place the insertion point in the first body paragraph, click ⌶≡⌄, click Remove Space After Paragraph, then save your changes**
   The space between the first and second body paragraphs is eliminated. Using the Line and Paragraph Spacing arrow is a quick way to add or remove space between paragraphs. You can also change the paragraph spacing settings for the active paragraph using the Spacing Before and After text boxes in the Paragraph group on the Layout tab.

FIGURE 2-8: First line indent

First Line Indent marker

Hanging Indent marker

Left Indent marker   First line indented ½"

Right Indent marker

Line spacing is 1.15

FIGURE 2-9: Dragging the First Line Indent marker

First Line Indent marker being dragged to the 1/2" mark

Dotted line shows position of First Line Indent marker as it is being dragged

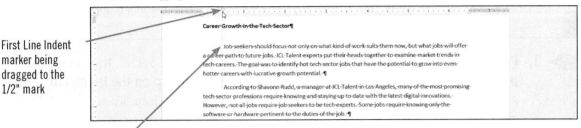

FIGURE 2-10: Dragging the Hanging Indent marker

Hanging Indent marker being dragged to the 1/2" mark

Dotted line shows position of Hanging Indent marker as it is being dragged

Hanging indent

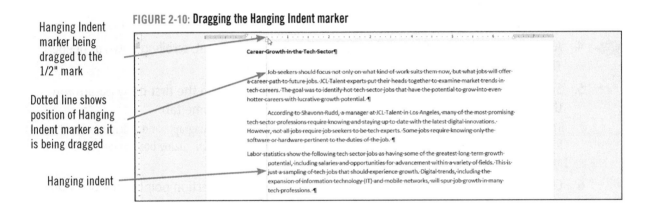

TABLE 2-1: Types of indents

indent type: description	to create
Left indent: The left edge of a paragraph is moved in from the left margin	Drag the Left Indent marker ▢ on the ruler to the right to the position where you want the left edge of the paragraph to align; when you drag the left indent marker, all the indent markers move as one
Right indent: The right edge of a paragraph is moved in from the right margin	Drag the Right Indent marker △ on the ruler to the left to the position where you want the right edge of the paragraph to align
First line indent: The first line of a paragraph is indented more than the subsequent lines	Drag the First Line Indent marker ▽ on the ruler to the right to the position where you want the first line of the paragraph to begin; or activate the First Line Indent marker ▽ in the tab indicator, and then click the ruler at the position where you want the first line of the paragraph to begin
Hanging indent: The subsequent lines of a paragraph are indented more than the first line	Drag the Hanging Indent marker △ on the ruler to the right to the position where you want the hanging indent to begin; or activate the Hanging Indent marker △ in the tab indicator, and then click the ruler at the position where you want the second and remaining lines of the paragraph to begin; when you drag the hanging indent marker, the left indent marker moves with it
Negative indent (or Outdent): The left edge of a paragraph is moved to the left of the left margin	Drag the Left Indent marker ▢ on the ruler left to the position where you want the negative indent to begin; when you drag the left indent marker, all markers move as one

Apply Styles to Text

Learning
Outcomes
• Apply built-in
styles to text
• Modify existing
styles

Applying a style to text allows you to apply multiple format settings to text in one easy step. A **style** is a set of format settings, such as font, font size, font color, paragraph spacing, and alignment, that are named and stored together. Word includes many **Style sets**—groups of related styles that share common fonts, colors, and formats, and are designed to be used together in a document to give it a polished and cohesive look. Each Style set includes styles for a title, subtitle, several heading levels, body text, and other text elements. By default, all text is formatting using the Normal style. **CASE** *You apply title and heading styles to the report to make the report easier to read. You also modify the Normal style that is applied to body text.*

STEPS

1. **Press CTRL+HOME, select the title** Career Growth in the Tech Sector, **then move the pointer over the** styles **in the Styles gallery in the Styles group on the Home tab**
   As you move the pointer over a style in the gallery, a preview of that style is applied to the selected text.

2. **Click** Title
   The Title style is applied to the selected text. All other paragraphs are formatted with the Normal style.

3. **Select** Applications developer, **click** Heading 1 **in the Styles group, then click the heading to deselect the text**
   The Heading 1 style is applied to the Applications developer heading, as shown in FIGURE 2-11.

4. **Apply the** Heading 1 **style to each bold heading in the document, scrolling down as needed**
   The Heading 1 style is applied to nine headings in total in the document.

5. **Scroll to the top of the document, place the insertion point in the first body paragraph, then click the** Launcher ▣ **in the Paragraph group on the Home tab**
   The Indents and Spacing tab in the Paragraph dialog box shows the line, paragraph, and indentation settings for the active paragraph, as shown in FIGURE 2-12. You can use the Paragraph dialog box to check or change any paragraph setting.

6. **Click** OK **to close the paragraph dialog box, then, with the insertion point in the first body paragraph, right-click** Normal **in the Styles group, click** Update Normal to Match Selection
   The format of each paragraph formatted with the Normal style in the document is changed to match the first body paragraph. The title and headings are indented now, too because the Heading 1 and Title styles are based on the Normal style. When the Normal style changed, the styles based on the Normal style changed, too.

7. **Right-click** Heading 1 **in the Styles group, click** Modify, **click the** Style based on arrow **in the Modify Style dialog box, click** (no style), **then click** OK
   The Heading 1 style is now based on no style and the indent is removed from the headings in the document. You can use the Modify Style dialog box to change any format setting in a style.

8. **Right-click** Title **in the Styles group, click** Modify, **click the** Style based on arrow **in the Modify Style dialog box, click** (no style), **then click** OK
   The Title style is now based on no style and the indent is removed from the title in the document.

9. **Select the** Career Growth... title, **click the** Increase Font Size button Aˆ **in the Font group, click the** Font Color arrow ▲ ˅ , **click** Blue, Accent 1, Darker 25%, **click the** Line and Paragraph Spacing arrow ⌄ **in the Paragraph group, click** Add Space After Paragraph, **deselect the title, then save your changes**
   The font size of the title is increased, the font color changes to dark blue, and extra space is added after the title paragraph, as shown in FIGURE 2-13. You can modify the format of text to which a style has been applied without changing the style itself.

FIGURE 2-11: **Styles applied to the report**

Title style applied

Styles group shows style applied to paragraph where insertion point is located

Line spacing is decreased to 1.15

Heading 1 style applied

Line spacing is 2

FIGURE 2-12: **Indents and Spacing tab in Paragraph dialog box**

Active paragraph includes a ½" First Line indent

Spacing above and below active paragraph is 0

Line spacing of active paragraph is 1.15

Preview of selected settings

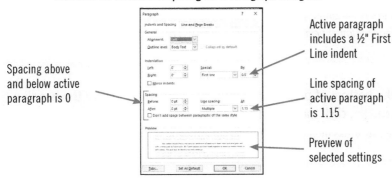

FIGURE 2-13: **Modified styles applied to the document**

Modified Title style applied text; text is also blue, is larger, and has space added under the title

Modified Normal style applied to body text

Modified Heading 1 style applied to text

Changing the style set

Changing the style set applied to a document is a quick way to give a document a different look and design. Style sets include font and paragraph settings for headings and body text. When you change the Style set, a complete set of new fonts and colors is applied to the entire document. All the body text and all the headings that have been formatted with a style change to the format settings for the active style set. To change the style set, you click one of the style sets available in the Document Formatting group on the Design tab. You can also change the color scheme or font used in the active Style set by clicking the Colors or Fonts buttons in the Document Formatting group and then selecting from the available color schemes or font options.

You can also save a group of font and paragraph settings as a new style set. To do this, click the More button in the Document Formatting group, and then click Save as a New Style Set. If you want to return a document to its original style set, click the More button, and then click Reset to the Default Style Set.

Insert Page Numbers and Page Breaks

Learning
Outcomes
• Insert page,
  section, and
  column breaks
• Insert page
  numbers

As you type text in a document, Word inserts an **automatic page break** (also called a soft page break) when you reach the bottom of a page, allowing you to continue typing on the next page. You can also force text onto the next page of a document by using the Breaks command to insert a **manual page break** (also called a hard page break). If you want to number the pages of a multiple-page document, you can insert a page number field to add a page number to each page. A **field** is a code that serves as a placeholder for data that changes in a document, such as a page number or the current date. When you use the Page Number button on the Insert tab to add page numbers to a document, you insert the page number field at the top, bottom, or side of any page, and Word automatically numbers all the pages in the document for you.

CASE ▸ *You insert a manual page break where you know you want to begin a new page of the report, and then you add a page number field so that page numbers will appear at the bottom of each page in the document.*

STEPS

QUICK TIP
Pressing
CTRL+ENTER is a fast
way to insert a man-
ual page break.

1. **Scroll to the bottom of page 1, place the insertion point before the heading** Customer service manager, **click the** Layout tab, **then click the** Breaks button **in the Page Setup group**
   You also use the Breaks menu to insert page, column, and text-wrapping breaks. See TABLE 2-2.

2. **Click** Page
   Word inserts a manual page break before "Customer service manager" and moves all the text following the page break to the beginning of the next page, as shown in FIGURE 2-14.

QUICK TIP
To delete a page
break, select it and
then press DELETE.
Page breaks are
only visible when
formatting marks are
turned on.

3. **Scroll down, place the insertion point before the heading** Intelligence analyst **on page 2, press and hold** CTRL, **then press** ENTER
   The heading is forced to the top of the third page.

4. **Press** CTRL+HOME, **click the** Insert tab, **then click the** Page Number button **in the Header & Footer group**
   Use the Page Number menu to select the position for the page numbers. If you choose to add a page number field to the top, bottom, or side of a document, a page number will appear on every page in the document.

QUICK TIP
To change the loca-
tion or formatting
of page numbers,
click the Page Num-
ber button, point
to a page number
location, then select
a format from the
gallery.

5. **Point to** Bottom of Page
   A gallery of formatting and alignment options for page numbers at the bottom of a page opens.

6. **Click** Plain Number 2 **in the Simple section**
   A page number field containing the number 1 is centered in the Footer area at the bottom of page 1 of the document, as shown in FIGURE 2-15. The document text is gray, or dimmed, because the Footer area is open. Text that is inserted in a Footer area appears at the bottom of every page in a document.

7. **Double-click the** document text
   The page number is now dimmed because it is located in the Footer area, which is no longer the active area. When the document is printed, the page numbers appear as normal text.

QUICK TIP
To remove page
numbers from a
document, click
the Page Number
button, then click
Remove Page
Numbers.

8. **Press** CTRL+HOME, **click the** View tab, **click the** Multiple Pages button **in the Zoom group, then save the document**
   Word numbered each page of the report automatically, and each page number is centered at the bottom of the page, as shown in FIGURE 2-16.

FIGURE 2-14: **Manual page break in document**

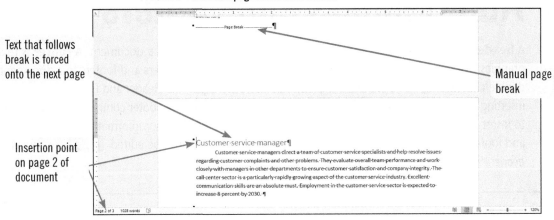

Text that follows break is forced onto the next page

Manual page break

Insertion point on page 2 of document

FIGURE 2-15: **Page number in document**

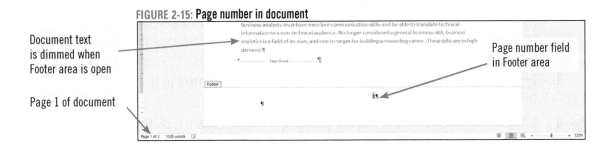

Document text is dimmed when Footer area is open

Page number field in Footer area

Page 1 of document

FIGURE 2-16: **Pages 1, 2, and 3**

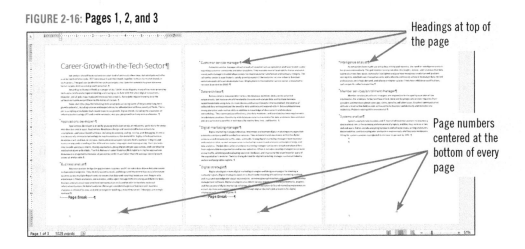

Headings at top of the page

Page numbers centered at the bottom of every page

TABLE 2-2: **Types of breaks**

break	function
Page	Forces the text following the break to begin at the top of the next page
Column	Forces the text following the break to begin at the top of the next column
Text Wrapping	Forces the text following the break to begin at the beginning of the next line

Editing and Formatting Documents

Add Headers and Footers

Learning Outcomes
• Insert headers and footers
• Manage headers and footers

A **header** is text or graphics that appears at the top of every page of a document. A **footer** is text or graphics that appears at the bottom of every page. You can add headers and footers to a document by double-clicking the top or bottom margin of a document to open the Header and Footer areas, and then inserting text and graphics into them. You can also use the Header or Footer command on the Insert tab to insert predesigned headers and footers that you can modify with your information. When the header and footer areas are open, the document text is dimmed and cannot be edited. **CASE** *You create a header that includes the name of the report.*

STEPS

1. **Click the** Page Width button **in the Zoom group on the View tab, click the** Insert tab, **then click the** Header button **in the Header & Footer group**
   A gallery of built-in header designs opens.

2. **Scroll down the gallery to view the header designs, scroll up the gallery, then click** Blank
   The Header area opens and the Header & Footer Tools Design tab opens and is the active tab, as shown in FIGURE 2-17. This tab is available whenever the Header and Footer areas are open. The [Type Here] **content control** is selected in the Header area. You replace a content control with your own information.

3. **Type** Career Growth in the Tech Sector **in the content control in the Header area**
   This text will appear at the top of every page in the document.

QUICK TIP
You can also use the Insert Alignment Tab button in the Position group to left-, center-, and right-align text in the Header and Footer areas.

4. **Select the** header text **(but not the paragraph mark below it), click the** Home tab, **click the** Font Color button **A in the Font group, click the** Center button **≡ in the Paragraph group, click the** Bottom Border button **⊞ ⌄, then click in the Header area to deselect the text**
   The text is the same blue used in the document and is centered in the Header area with a bottom border.

5. **Click the** Header & Footer Tools Design tab, **then click the** Go to Footer button **in the Navigation group**
   The insertion point moves to the Footer area, where a page number field is centered in the Footer area.

6. **Select the** page number field **in the footer, click the** Font Color button **A on the Mini toolbar, then click in the** Footer area **to deselect the text and field**
   The footer text (the page number) is the same color blue as the headings.

7. **Click the** Close Header and Footer **button in the Close group, then scroll down until the bottom of page 1 and the top of page 2 appear in the document window**
   The Header and Footer areas close, and the header and footer text is dimmed, as shown in FIGURE 2-18.

8. **Press** CTRL+HOME
   The report already includes the report title at the top of the first page, making the header information redundant.

QUICK TIP
To remove headers or footers from a document, click the Header or Footer button, and then click Remove Header or Remove Footer.

9. **Position the pointer over the** header **text at the top of page 1, double-click the** header **to open the Header area, click the** Different First Page check box **in the Options group on the Header and Footer Tools Design tab, then click the** Close Header and Footer button
   The header and footer text is removed from the Header and Footer areas on the first page.

10. **Click** Show/Hide ¶ button **¶ in the Paragraph group on the Home tab, click the** View tab, **click the** Multiple Pages button **in the Zoom group, then save your changes**
    The headers and footers and all the pages in the document are shown in FIGURE 2-19.

FIGURE 2-17: Header area

Header area is open

Content control

Header & Footer Tools Design tab active

Document text is dimmed

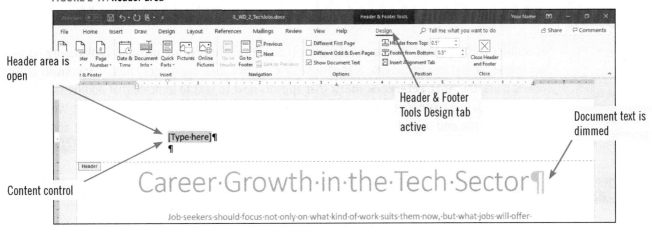

FIGURE 2-18: Header and footer in document

Header text is blue and appears centered in the header on every page

Page number is blue and appears in footer on every page

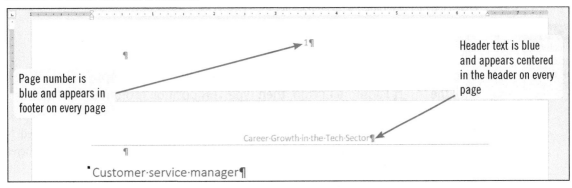

FIGURE 2-19: Header and footer on pages 2 and 3

Header and footer are blank on page 1

Header and footer appear on pages 2 and 3

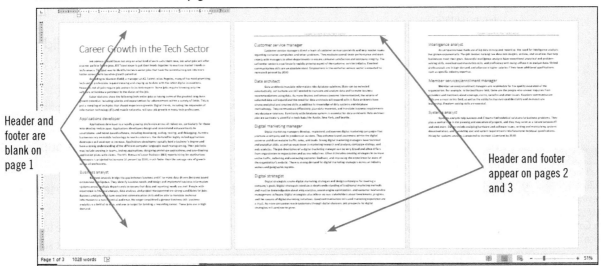

Word

Add Footnotes and Endnotes

Learning
Outcomes
• Insert footnotes
  and endnotes
• Modify footnote
  and endnote
  properties

Footnotes and endnotes are used in documents to provide further information, explanatory text, or references for text in a document. A **footnote** or **endnote** is an explanatory note that consists of two linked parts: the **note reference mark** that appears next to text to indicate that additional information is offered in a footnote or endnote, and the corresponding footnote or endnote text. Word places footnotes at the end of each page and endnotes at the end of the document. You insert and manage footnotes and endnotes using the tools in the Footnotes group on the References tab. **CASE** *You add several footnotes to the report.*

STEPS

1. **Click the** 100% button **in the Zoom group, scroll until the Business analyst heading is at the top of your screen, place the insertion point at the end of the last body paragraph (after "demand."), click the** References tab, **then click the** Insert Footnote button **in the Footnotes group**

    A note reference mark, in this case a superscript 1, appears after "demand.", and the insertion point moves below a separator line at the bottom of the page. A note reference mark can be a number, a symbol, a character, or a combination of characters.

2. **Type** Job growth is strong in Seattle, Austin, and Boston.

    The footnote text appears below the separator line at the bottom of page 1.

3. **Scroll up, place the insertion point at the end of the heading** Applications developer, **click the** Insert Footnote button, **then type** This position is often called "mobile applications developer."

    The footnote text appears at the bottom of the first page, above the first footnote you added. Notice that when you inserted a new footnote above an existing footnote, Word automatically renumbered the footnotes, as shown in FIGURE 2-20.

4. **Place the insertion point at the end of the paragraph under the Applications developer heading, click the** Insert Footnote button, **then type** Many hold a master's degree.

    The footnote text appears between the text for footnotes 1 and 3 at the bottom of the page.

5. **Click the** Launcher 🔲 **in the Footnotes group**

    The Footnotes and Endnotes dialog box opens. You can use this dialog box to change the location of footnote and endnote text, to convert footnotes to endnotes, and to change the formatting of the note reference marks.

6. **Click the** Number format arrow **in the Format section, click** A, B, C,..., **then click** Apply

    The note reference marks in the document change from 1, 2, 3 format to an A, B, C format, as shown in FIGURE 2-21.

7. **Click the** Undo button 🔄 **on the Quick Access toolbar**

    Clicking the Undo button restores the 1,2,3 numbering format.

8. **Press** CTRL+HOME, **then click the** Next Footnote button **in the Footnotes group**

    The insertion point moves to the "1" reference mark in the document.

9. **Click the** Next Footnote button, **press** DELETE **to select the number 2 reference mark, press** DELETE **again, then save your changes**

    The second reference mark and associated footnote are deleted from the document and the footnotes are renumbered automatically. You must select a reference mark to delete a footnote; you cannot simply delete the footnote text itself.

FIGURE 2-20: Renumbered footnotes in the document

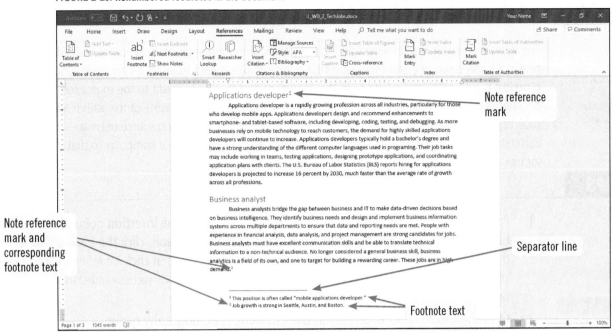

Note reference mark

Note reference mark and corresponding footnote text

Separator line

Footnote text

FIGURE 2-21: Note reference marks in new format

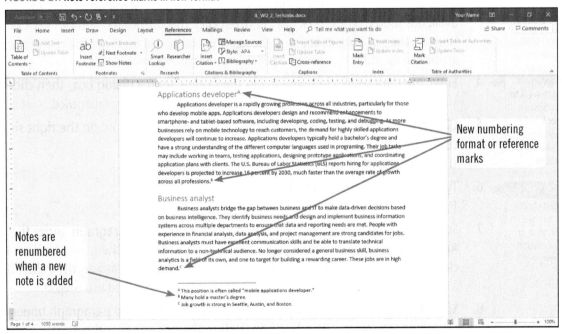

New numbering format or reference marks

Notes are renumbered when a new note is added

Word

Insert Citations

Learning Outcomes
- Add a source to a document
- Insert a citation
- Edit a citation

The Word References feature allows you to keep track of the reference sources you consult when writing research papers, reports, and other documents, and makes it easy to insert a citation in a document. A **citation** is a parenthetical reference in the document text that gives credit to the source for a quotation or other information used in a document. Citations usually include the name of the author and, for print sources, a page number. When you insert a citation you can use an existing source or create a new source. Each time you create a new source, the source information is saved on your computer so that it is available for use in any document. **CASE** ▶ *You add several citations to the report.*

STEPS

1. **Press CTRL+HOME, change the zoom level to 120%, place the insertion point after "job" but before the period at the end of the second body paragraph, click the Style arrow in the Citations & Bibliography group on the References tab, then click MLA Seventh Edition**
   You will format the sources and citations in the report using the style recommended by the Modern Language Association (MLA).

QUICK TIP
When you create a new source for a document, it appears automatically in the bibliography when you generate it.

2. **Click the Insert Citation button in the Citations & Bibliography group**
   A list of the sources (one) already used in the file opens. You can choose to cite this source, create a new source, or add a placeholder for a source. When you add a new citation to a document, the source is added to the list of master sources stored on the computer. The new source is also associated with the document.

QUICK TIP
Only sources that you associate with a document stay with the document when you move it to another computer. The master list of sources remains on the computer where it was created.

3. **Click Add New Source, click the Type of Source arrow, scroll down to view the available source types, click Report, then click the Corporate Author check box**
   You select the type of source and enter the source information in the Create Source dialog box. The fields available in the dialog box change, depending on the type of source selected.

4. **Enter the data shown in FIGURE 2-22 in the Create Source dialog box, then click OK**
   The citation (JCL Talent) appears at the end of the paragraph before the final period.

5. **Click the citation to select it, click the Citation Options arrow on the right side of the citation, then click Edit Citation**
   The Edit Citation dialog box opens, as shown in FIGURE 2-23.

QUICK TIP
You can also choose to add or remove the author, year, or title from a citation.

6. **Type 15 in the Pages text box, then click OK**
   The page number 15 is added to the citation.

7. **Scroll down, place the insertion point at the end of the paragraph under the Applications developer heading (before the period), click the Insert Citation button, click Add New Source, enter the information shown in FIGURE 2-24, then click OK**
   A citation for the Web publication that the data was taken from is added to the report.

8. **Scroll to page 2, place the insertion point at the end of the paragraph under the Customer service manager heading (before the period) click the Insert Citation button, then click U.S. Bureau of Labor Statistics in the list of sources**
   The citation (U.S. Bureau of Labor Statistics) appears at the end of the paragraph.

9. **Press CTRL+END, then repeat Step 8 to insert a U.S. Bureau of Labor Statistics citation at the end of the last paragraph in the document**

10. **Scroll up to page 2, place the insertion point at the end of the paragraph under the Data architect heading (before the period) click the Insert Citation button, click Add New Placeholder, type NYT, click OK, then save your changes**
    You added a citation placeholder for a source that you still need to add to the document.

FIGURE 2-22: **Creating a report source**

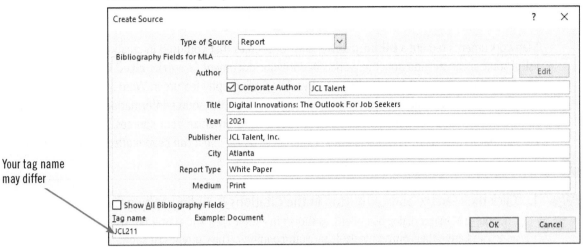

Your tag name
may differ

FIGURE 2-23: **Edit Citation dialog box**

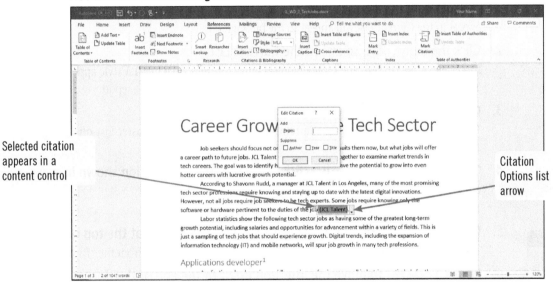

Selected citation
appears in a
content control

Citation
Options list
arrow

FIGURE 2-24: **Adding a Web publication source**

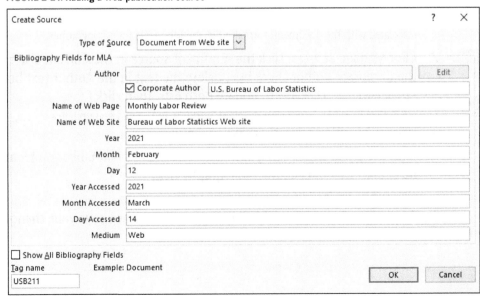

Create a Bibliography

Learning
Outcomes
• Add and delete
  sources
• Edit a source
• Insert a bibliogra-
  phy field

Many documents require a **bibliography**, a list of sources that you used in creating the document. The list of sources can include only the works cited in your document (a **works cited** list) or both the works cited and the works consulted (a bibliography). The Bibliography feature in Word allows you to generate a works cited list or a bibliography automatically, based on the source information you provide for the document. The Source Manager dialog box helps you to organize your sources. **CASE** *You add a bibliography to the report. The bibliography is inserted as a field and it can be formatted any way you choose.*

STEPS

1. **Click the** Manage Sources button **in the Citations & Bibliography group**

   The Source Manager dialog box opens, as shown in FIGURE 2-25. The Master List shows the two sources you added and any other sources available on your computer. The Current List shows the sources available in the current document, as well as the NYT placeholder you added. A check mark next to a source indicates the source is cited in the document. You use the tools in the Source Manager dialog box to add, edit, and delete sources from the lists, and to copy sources between the Master and Current Lists. The sources that appear in the Current List will appear in the bibliography.

2. **Click the** Singh, Riya **source in the Current List**

   A preview of the citation and bibliographical entry for the source in MLA style appears in the Preview box. You do not want this source to be included in your bibliography for the report.

3. **Click** Delete

   The source is removed from the Current List but remains on the Master List on the computer where it originated.

4. **Click** NYT **in the Current List, click** Edit**, enter the information shown in** FIGURE 2-26**, then click** OK

   The Pappas source is added to the Current List.

5. **Click** Close**, then scroll until the heading Data Architect is at the top of your screen**

   The NYT placeholder citation has been replaced with the information from the "Pappas" source.

6. **Press** CTRL+END **to move the insertion point to the end of the document, click the** Bibliography button **in the Citations & Bibliography group, then click** Bibliography **in the Built-in gallery**

   A Bibliography field is added at the location of the insertion point. The bibliography includes all the sources associated with the document, formatted in the MLA style for bibliographies.

7. **Click** Manage Sources**, click the** JCL Talent **source in the Current List, click** Edit**, deselect the** Corporate Author **check box, delete the text in the Author text box, type** Shavonn Rudd**, click** OK**, click** Yes **to update both lists, then click** Close

   The source is edited to include a different author name. When you update a source, you need to update the Bibliography field to include the revised information.

8. **Click the** Bibliography field**, click** Update Citations and Bibliography **at the top of the field, then click outside the Bibliography field**

   The updated Bibliography is shown in FIGURE 2-27.

9. **Press** CTRL+END**, press** ENTER**, type your name, then save your changes**

Editing and Formatting Documents

FIGURE 2-25: **Source Manager dialog box**

Your Master List will contain the two sources you added, and either no additional sources or different additional sources

Preview of the citation and bibliography entry for the selected source in MLA style (as defined by Word)

List of sources associated with the document

Sources with a check mark have a citation in the document

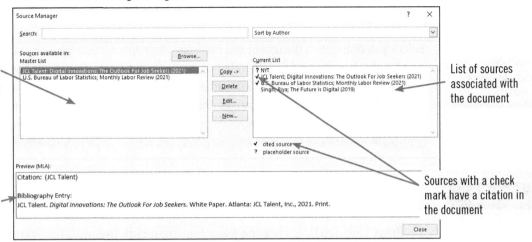

FIGURE 2-26: **Adding a Periodical source**

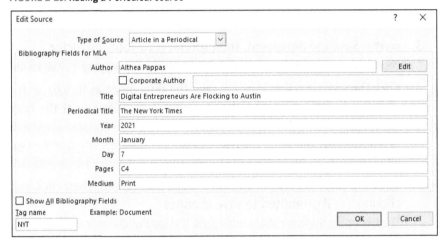

FIGURE 2-27: **Bibliography field in document**

Finding and citing sources with the Word Researcher

The Word Researcher tool helps you find citable sources, quotations, images, and other material for a research paper. Using Researcher, you can search for journal articles and websites that relate to a topic, add information from those sources into a document, automatically create a citation for the source, and automatically create and update a bibliography—all without having to manually enter the source information. To begin, click the Researcher button in the Research group on the References tab to open the Researcher pane. Type a keyword for your topic in the search box, press ENTER, and then explore the list of sources related to your topic. When you find a source that is useful to you, you can select text (or an image) from it and add the selection to your document, choosing to add text only or to add the text and a citation. When you add a citation, Word automatically creates a bibliography that is updated each time you add additional material to the document. To avoid plagiarism, be sure to paraphrase text that is not a quote, and always include citations giving credit for any content that is not your original work. Also, always verify that the bibliographies you create using Word are formatted in the most up-to-date MLA, APA, Chicago, or other style.

Editing and Formatting Documents

Inspect a Document

Learning Outcomes
- Edit document properties
- Remove document properties
- Modify advanced document properties

Before you distribute a document electronically to people outside your organization, it's wise to make sure the file does not include embedded private or confidential information. The Info screen in Backstage view includes tools for stripping a document of sensitive information, for securing its authenticity, and for guarding it from unwanted changes once it is distributed to the public. One of these tools, the Document Inspector, detects and removes unwanted private or confidential information from a document. **CASE** ▶ *Before share the report with the public, you remove all identifying information from the file.*

STEPS

1. Press CTRL+HOME, click the View tab, then click the Multiple Pages button

The completed document is shown in FIGURE 2-28.

2. Click the Review tab, click No Markup, then click All Markup

The comments you hid in the first lesson are now visible in the document.

3. sam?▲ Save the document, then submit it to your instructor

You will save the document with a new file name before stripping it of all identifying information.

QUICK TIP

To recover unsaved changes to a file, click Manage Document on the Info screen, then click Recover Unsaved Documents.

4. Click the File tab, click Save As, save the document as IL_WD_2_TechJobs_Inspected, click the File tab, then click the Show All Properties link at the bottom of the Info screen

The left side of the Info screen in Backstage view includes options related to stripping the file of private information. See TABLE 2-3. The right side of the Info screen displays the expanded document property information. You want to remove this information from the file before you distribute it electronically.

QUICK TIP

A document property, such as author name, might appear automatically in a content control in a document. Stripping a file of document properties does not remove information from a content control.

5. Click the Check for Issues button on the Info screen, then click Inspect Document, clicking Yes if prompted to save changes

The Document Inspector dialog box opens. You use this dialog box to indicate which private or identifying information you want to search for and remove from the document.

6. Make sure all the check boxes are selected, then click Inspect

After a moment, the Document Inspector dialog box indicates the file contains comments and document properties, as shown in FIGURE 2-29. You want to remove this information from the file.

7. Click Remove All next to Comments, click Remove All next to Document Properties and Personal Information, then click Close

The comments and document property information are removed from the report file, but the change will not be reflected on the Info screen until you reopen it.

8. Click the Back button on the Info screen, save your changes to the document, then click the File tab

The comments have been removed from the file. Info screen shows the document properties have been removed from the file.

9. Submit the document to your instructor, close the file, then exit Word

FIGURE 2-28: Formatted document

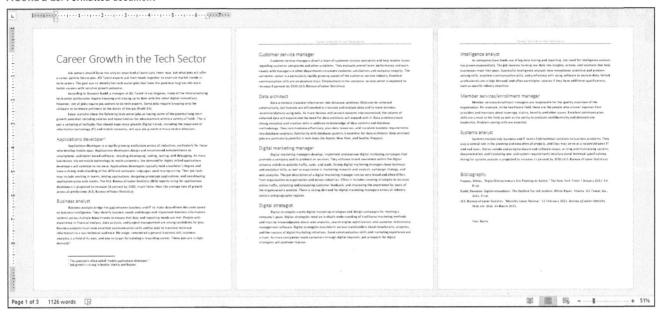

FIGURE 2-29: Results after inspecting document

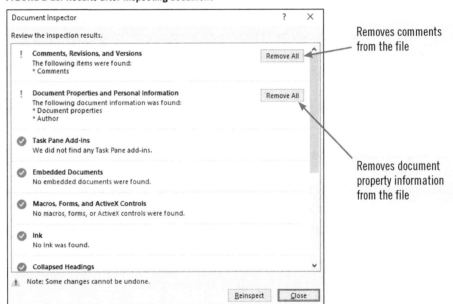

Removes comments from the file

Removes document property information from the file

TABLE 2-3: Options on the Info screen

option	use to
Protect Document	Mark a document as final so that it is read-only and cannot be edited; encrypt a document so that a password is required to open it; restrict what kinds of changes can be made to a document and by whom; restrict access to editing, copying, and printing a document and add a digital signature to a document to verify its integrity
Check for Issues	Detect and remove unwanted information from a document, including document properties and comments; check for content that people with disabilities might find difficult to read; and check the document for features that are not supported by previous versions of Microsoft Word
Manage Document	Browse and recover draft versions of unsaved files

Practice

Skills Review

1. Insert comments

  a. Start Word, open the file IL_WD_2-2.docx from the location where you store your Data Files, save it as **IL_WD_2_Zone**.

  b. Using the All Markup option on the Review tab, show all the comments in the document.

  c. Select Studio in the title, then insert a new comment with the text **I will change this to "Zone" throughout.**

  d. Reply to Judith's first comment with the text **OK.**

  e. Navigate to Judith's next comment and mark the comment resolved.

  f. Navigate to Judith's previous comment and add the sentence **I will add a footnote.**

  g. Navigate to the final comment in the document, then delete the comment.

  h. Save your changes, hide the comments in the document, then press CTRL+HOME.

2. Find and replace text.

  i. Using the Replace command, replace all instances of "2017" with **2019**.

  j. Replace all instances of "Studio" with **Zone**, taking care to match the case when you perform the replace.

  k. Replace all instances of "course" with **class,** taking care to replace whole words only when you perform the replace. (*Hint*: Deselect Match case if it is selected.) Replace each instance of "course" individually rather than replacing all instances at once.

  l. Open the Navigation pane, then view all instances of "zone" in the document to make sure no errors occurred when you replaced Studio with Zone.

  m. Click the Pages link in the Navigation pane, click the thumbnail for each page to scroll through the document, click the thumbnail for page 1, close the Navigation pane, then save your changes.

3. Check spelling and grammar and research information.

  a. Switch to the Review tab.

  b. Move the insertion point to the top of the document, then use the Spelling & Grammar command to search for and correct any spelling and grammar errors in the document.

  c. Use the Thesaurus to replace "helpful" in the first body paragraph with a different suitable word, then close the Thesaurus pane.

  d. Check the word count of the document.

  e. Proofread your document, correct any errors, then save your changes.

4. Change line spacing and indents.

  a. Change the line spacing of the entire document to 1.5.

  b. Change the line spacing of the first body paragraph to 1.15.

  c. Indent the first line of the first body paragraph .3". (*Hint*: Use the Paragraph dialog box.)

  d. Remove the paragraph space under the first body paragraph, then save your changes.

5. Apply styles to text.

  a. Apply the Title style to the title "The Global Fitness Zone".

  b. Apply the Subtitle style to the subtitle "A Health, Fitness, and Rehabilitation Facility".

  c. Apply the Heading 1 style to each red heading in the document.

  d. Apply the Heading 2 style to each green heading in the document.

  e. With the insertion point in the first body paragraph, update the Normal style to match the first body paragraph.

Skills Review (continued)

f. Modify the Title style to be based on no style.

g. Modify the Subtitle, Heading 1, and Heading 2 styles to be based on no style.

h. Change the theme of the document to Metropolitan. (*Hint*: Use the Design tab.)

i. Select the title, change the font size to 36, change the font color to Aqua, Accent 1, Darker 25%, then apply bold.

j. Select the subtitle, change the font size to 14, then add 24 points of space after the paragraph.

k. Select the heading "Welcome...", add 6 points of space after the paragraph, then update the Heading 1 style to match the selection

l. Select the heading "Benefits of Exercise", add 6 points of space before the paragraph, and 3 points of space after the paragraph, then update the Heading 2 style to match the selection.

m. Scroll to the bottom of page 1, click the first item in the bulleted list, add 6 points of space before the paragraph, then save your changes.

6. Insert page numbers and page breaks.

a. Scroll to the bottom of page 2, then insert a manual page break before the heading "Facilities and Services". (*Hint*: The page break will appear at the bottom of page 2.)

b. Insert page numbers in the document at the bottom of the page. Select the Accent Bar 1 page number style from the gallery.

c. Close the Footer area, scroll through the document to view the page number on each page.

d. Turn on formatting marks, delete the manual page break at the bottom of page 2, then save your changes to the document.

7. Add headers and footers.

a. Double-click the Footer area, then use the Go to Header button to move the insertion point to the Header area.

b. Click the Header button, scroll down the gallery of built-in header designs, then select the Filigree header.

c. Click the Document title content control in the header, then type **The Global Fitness Zone**.

d. Replace the text in the Author content control with your name, press END to move the insertion point out of the content control, then press SPACEBAR. (*Note*: If your name does not appear in the header, right-click the Author content control, click Remove Content Control, then type your name in the header.)

e. Close headers and footers, then scroll to view the header and footer on each page.

f. Open headers and footers, select the text in the Header area, including the paragraph mark after your name, change the alignment of the selected text to left, then remove the first line indent. (*Hint*: You can use drag the indent marker on the ruler or use the Paragraph dialog box to remove the first line indent.)

g. Remove the header and footer from the first page of the document, close headers and footers, then save your changes.

8. Add footnotes and endnotes.

a. Press CTRL+HOME, scroll down, place the insertion point at the end of the first body paragraph, insert a footnote, then type **Active people live longer and feel better!**

b. Place the insertion point at the end of the first paragraph under the Getting Started heading, insert a footnote, then type **Each day is 1,440 minutes. We help you set aside 30 of them for physical activity.**

c. Place the insertion point at the end of the Getting Started heading, insert a footnote, type **Always consult a physician before beginning an exercise program.**

d. Change the number format of the footnotes to ***, +, #,** then save your changes.

9. Insert citations.

a. Place the insertion point at the end of the second paragraph under the Benefits of Exercise heading (after "down from 52% in 2019" but before the period), then be sure the style for citations and bibliography is set to MLA Seventh Edition.

b. Insert a citation, add a new source, enter the source information shown in the Create Source dialog box in FIGURE 2-30, then click OK.

Skills Review (continued)

c. Place the insertion point at the end of the second paragraph under the Getting Started heading, insert a citation, then select Shree, Maxine from the list of sources.

d. Edit the citation to include the page number **22**.

e. Scroll to page 2, place the insertion point at the end of the "Be a morning exerciser" paragraph in the bulleted list, but before the ending period, insert a citation for WebMD, then save your changes.

FIGURE 2-30

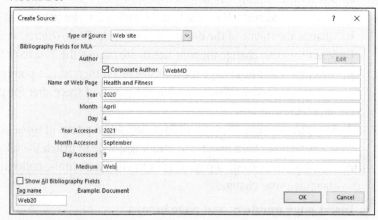

10. Create a bibliography.

a. Press CTRL+END, then insert a bibliography labeled **Works Cited**.

b. Open the Source Manager dialog box.

c. Delete the National Heart/Lung Health Institute source from the Current list.

d. Select the source Health, National Institute of: ... in the Current List, click Edit, click the Corporate Author check box, edit the entry so it reads **National Institute of Health**, click OK, then click Close.

e. Update the bibliography field.

f. With the bibliography field selected, click the Bibliographies button, then select Bibliography.

g. Click the Bibliographies button again, select References, then save your changes. Pages 1 and 3 of the formatted document are shown in FIGURE 2-31.

h. Save your changes to the document, then submit it to your instructor without closing the document.

FIGURE 2-31

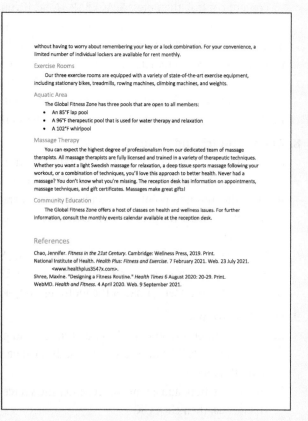

Editing and Formatting Documents

Skills Review (continued)

11. Inspect a document

    a. Save a copy of the document as **IL_WD_2_Zone_Inspected** to the drive and folder where you store your Data Files.

    b. Open the Navigation pane, click the Headings link, click the headings listed in the Navigation pane to scroll through the document, then close the Navigation pane.

    c. Use the Go To command to move the insertion point to the top of page 1.

    d. Use the Find and Replace dialog box to find all em dashes in the document, but do not replace the em dashes. (*Hint*: Scroll through the document using the Find Next button.)

    e. Use the Find and Replace dialog box to find text formatted with the Heading 2 style, but do not replace the text.

    f. Select a word in the document, look it up using the Smart Lookup button, then close the Smart Lookup pane.

    g. Show the comments in the document, then, using the Review tab, delete all the comments in the document.

    h. Use the Check for Issues command to run the Document Inspector.

    i. Remove all document property and personal information data from the document, then save your changes.

    j. Submit a copy of the document to your instructor, close the document, then exit Word.

Independent Challenge 1

The Riverwalk Medical Clinic publishes a variety of newsletters and information reports related to health and wellness for patients. Your colleague has drafted a newsletter about staying healthy while travelling and forwarded the file to you. The file includes comments with instructions for finalizing the document. You need to add citations and footnotes and format the newsletter for distribution to patients.

    a. Start Word, open the file IL_WD_2-3.docx from the drive and folder where you store your Data Files, save it as **IL_WD_2_Newsletter**, then read the document to get a feel for its contents.

    b. Show the comments in the document, scroll through the comments, reply to or resolve each comment, add a comment, then delete all comments from the document.

    c. Format the newsletter using styles. Apply the Title style to the orange text, the Heading 1 style to the blue text, and the Heading 2 style to the green text. (You will format the masthead after formatting the body of the document.)

    d. Apply a theme to the document. Choose a theme that suits the purpose and audience for the document. You can change the theme colors or style set if you wish.

    e. Change the font size of the title so that the title fits on one line.

    f. Modify the Heading 1 and Heading 2 styles so that the font, font size, font color, and paragraph spacing of the headings gives the newsletter an attractive and cohesive look.

    g. Using styles, format the first three lines of the document as a masthead for the newsletter. The masthead for this document should be attractive, but should not compete with the title of the document for attention. After applying styles, apply other formats, such as font size, font color, text effects, paragraph alignment, and borders to customize the look of the masthead.

    h. Add a header to the document using the Filigree header style. Type **Riverwalk Medical Clinic** in the Document title content control, then type your name in the Author content control. (*Hint*: If the Author content control shows different text, replace that text with your name.)

    i. Add a page number to the bottom of each page using the page number style of your choice.

    j. Remove headers and footers from the first page of the document.

    k. Use the Find command or the Navigation pane to find the text specified in the table below, then add a footnote at each location, using the footnote text specified in the table.

Independent Challenge 1 (continued)

Find text	Footnote text
behavior and health of the traveler	**Behavior is a critical factor. For example, going outdoors in a malaria-endemic area could result in becoming infected.**
public health	**It is best to consult a travel medicine specialist.**
tweezers	**Pack these items in checked luggage.**
Sunscreen	**SPF 15 or greater.**

l. Change the Citations and Bibliography style to MLA. Use the Find command or the Navigation pane to find the text specified in the table below, then add a citation at each location, using the source specified in the table. Some citations include a page number. Remember to insert the citation before the period at the end of a sentence.

Find text	Citation source	Citation page number
people travel	World Tourism Organization	15
consequences	World Health Organization	
Source:	Johnson, Margaret	50
prevalent in sub-Saharan Africa	Centers for Disease Control and Prevention	
pregnancy	Clinton, Edmund	92

m. Press CTRL+END, then add a bibliography to the newsletter.

n. Check the document for spelling and grammar errors, then use the thesaurus to replace a words with a synonym.

o. View the document in Multiple pages view, then make any formatting adjustments necessary so that the document flows smoothly between pages and is easy to read. **FIGURE 2-32** shows a sample first page of the newsletter.

p. Save the document, submit a copy to your instructor, close the document, then exit Word.

FIGURE 2-32

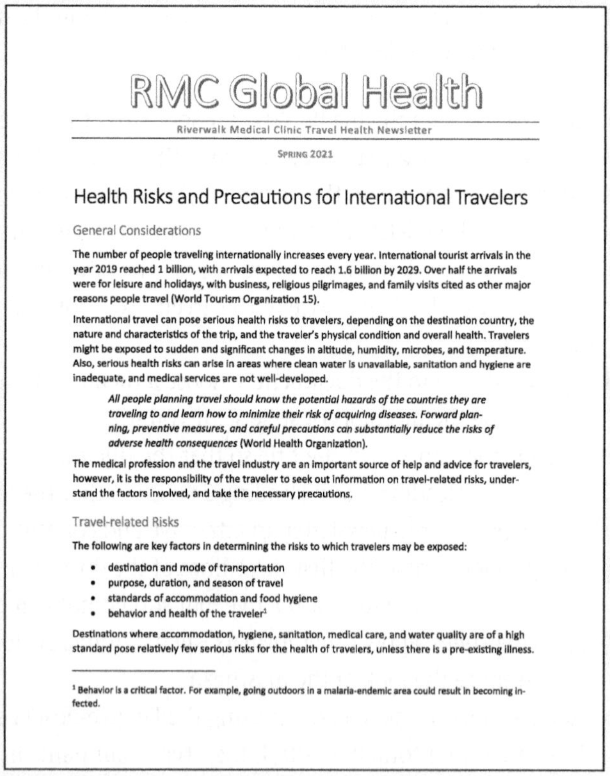
RMC Global Health

Riverwalk Medical Clinic Travel Health Newsletter

Spring 2021

Health Risks and Precautions for International Travelers

General Considerations

The number of people traveling internationally increases every year. International tourist arrivals in the year 2019 reached 1 billion, with arrivals expected to reach 1.6 billion by 2029. Over half the arrivals were for leisure and holidays, with business, religious pilgrimages, and family visits cited as other major reasons people travel (World Tourism Organization 15).

International travel can pose serious health risks to travelers, depending on the destination country, the nature and characteristics of the trip, and the traveler's physical condition and overall health. Travelers might be exposed to sudden and significant changes in altitude, humidity, microbes, and temperature. Also, serious health risks can arise in areas where clean water is unavailable, sanitation and hygiene are inadequate, and medical services are not well-developed.

All people planning travel should know the potential hazards of the countries they are traveling to and learn how to minimize their risk of acquiring diseases. Forward planning, preventive measures, and careful precautions can substantially reduce the risks of adverse health consequences (World Health Organization).

The medical profession and the travel industry are an important source of help and advice for travelers, however, it is the responsibility of the traveler to seek out information on travel-related risks, understand the factors involved, and take the necessary precautions.

Travel-related Risks

The following are key factors in determining the risks to which travelers may be exposed:

- destination and mode of transportation
- purpose, duration, and season of travel
- standards of accommodation and food hygiene
- behavior and health of the traveler[1]

Destinations where accommodation, hygiene, sanitation, medical care, and water quality are of a high standard pose relatively few serious risks for the health of travelers, unless there is a pre-existing illness.

[1] Behavior is a critical factor. For example, going outdoors in a malaria-endemic area could result in becoming infected.

Independent Challenge 2

As an administrative assistant at a community college, you frequently format the research papers written by the members of your department. The format recommended by the *MLA Handbook for Writers of Research Papers*, a style guide that includes information on preparing, writing, and formatting research papers, is the standard format used by many schools, colleges, and universities. In this independent challenge, you will research the MLA guidelines for formatting a research paper and use the guidelines you find to format the pages of a research report.

a. Use your favorite search engine to search the web for information on the MLA guidelines for formatting a research report. Use the keywords **MLA Style** and **research paper format** to conduct your search.

FIGURE 2-33

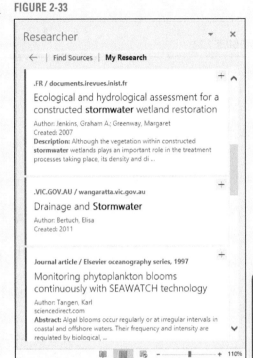

b. Look for information on the proper formatting for the following aspects of a research paper: paper size, margins, title page or first page of the report, line spacing, paragraph indentation, and page numbers. Also find information on proper formatting for citations and a works cited page. Print the information you find.

c. Start Word, open the file IL_WD_2-4.docx from the drive and folder where you store your Data Files, then save it as **IL_WD_2_Research**. Using the information you learned, format this document as a research report.

d. Correct spelling and grammar errors in the document. If possible, add "stormwater" to the Word dictionary.

e. Adjust the margins, set the line spacing, and add page numbers to the document in the format recommended by the MLA. Use **Stormwater Management: A Case Study** as the title for your sample report, use your name as the author name, and use the name of the course you are enrolled in currently as well as the instructor's name for that course. Make sure to format the title page exactly as the MLA style dictates.

f. Format the remaining text as the body of the research report. Indent the first line of each paragraph rather than use quadruple spacing between paragraphs.

g. Create five sources and insert five citations in the document—including at least one journal article and one website. If possible, use the Researcher tool to add sources and citations. FIGURE 2-33 shows the Researcher pane with sample sources. You can also make up sources. (*Note*: For this practice document, you are allowed to make up sources. Never make up sources for real research papers.)

h. Add two citation placeholders to the document.

i. Create a works cited page, following MLA style. If necessary, edit the format of the citations and works cited page to conform to MLA format.

j. Save the document, submit a copy to your instructor, close the document, then exit Word.

Visual Workshop

Use a blank document to create the Works Cited page shown in FIGURE 2-34, then save the document as **IL_WD_2_WorksCited**. Use 12-point Times New Roman for the text, double-space the lines in the document, and apply a hanging indent to the paragraphs in the list. Format "Works Cited" with the Heading 1 style and center the heading at the top of the document. Add your name and a page number to the header, then format the header text in 12-point Times New Roman. Correct spelling and grammar errors, remove the document property information from the file, then submit a copy to your instructor.

FIGURE 2-34

Works Cited

Harper, Maxine. "Landing the Perfect Job." *eHow,* www.ehow.com/landing-32980-the-perfect-job.html.

Khatri, Jamaica. "Data Analyst." *The Vintage Book of Contemporary Professions,* edited by Roger Mendez, Vintage, 2019, pp. 204-07.

Lu, Maya C. *Business and Environmentalism.* Reed Publishers, 2020.

Patel, Simon. "10 Tips for Job Seekers." *Working: Business Careers for the Digital World,* 20 Aug. 2020, example.com/article/working. Accessed 14 June 2021.

Formatting Text and Graphics

CASE You have been asked to finalize a report on the activities of the Technology department that will be distributed to other departments at JCL Talent. After formatting the headings in the report, you use tabs and create tables to organize the information so that it is easy to understand. Finally, you illustrate the report with images, shapes, and SmartArt.

Module Objectives

After completing this module, you will be able to:

- Use the Format Painter
- Work with tabs
- Add borders and shading
- Insert a table
- Insert and delete rows and columns
- Apply a table style
- Insert online pictures
- Size and scale a graphic
- Draw and format shapes
- Arrange graphic objects
- Create SmartArt graphics

Files You Will Need

IL_WD_3-1.docx	IL_WD_3-3.docx
IL_WD_3-2.docx	IL_WD_3-4.docx

Use the Format Painter

Learning Outcomes
- Apply formatting using the Format Painter
- Clear formatting
- Insert special characters

You can dramatically change the appearance of text by applying different font styles, font effects, and character-spacing effects. When you are satisfied with the formatting of specific text, you can quickly apply the same formats to other text in the document using the Format Painter. The **Format Painter** is a powerful Word feature that allows you to copy all the format settings applied to selected text to other text that you want to format the same way. **CASE** ▶ *You enhance the appearance of the text in the report on the activities of the Technology department by applying different font styles and text effects. You also insert the date and a copyright symbol in the document.*

STEPS

1. **sam ✦ Start Word, open the file** IL_WD_3-1.docx **from the location where you store your Data Files, save it as** IL_WD_3_Update, **then drag the** Zoom slider **to 100**

2. **Select the title** Update: JCL Technical Careers Division, **click the** Text Effects and Typography button A ˅ **in the Font group on the Home tab, click the** Fill: Blue; Accent color 1; Shadow style **(the second WordArt style in the first row), click the** Font Size arrow, **click** 24, **click the** Font Color arrow A ˅, **then click** Green, Accent 6, Darker 25%
The title is formatted in 24-point WordArt style, green.

3. **Select the heading** Career Connections Webinar Series **to display the Mini toolbar, click the** Font Size arrow, **click** 14, **click the** Bold button B, **click the** Italic button I, **click the** Font Color arrow A ˅, **click the** Blue, Accent 1, Darker 25% color **in the theme colors, then deselect the text**
The heading is formatted in 14-point bold, italic, and blue.

4. **Select** Career Connections Webinar Series, **then click the** Format Painter button **in the Clipboard group on the Home tab**
The pointer changes to 📋I.

5. **Scroll down, drag** 📋I **to select the heading** Social Media Advertising Campaign, **then deselect the text**
The heading is formatted in 14-point bold, italic, and blue, as shown in FIGURE 3-1.

6. **Select** Social Media Advertising Campaign **again, then double-click the** Format Painter button
Double-clicking the Format Painter button allows the Format Painter to remain active until you turn it off. By keeping the Format Painter active, you can apply formatting to multiple items.

7. **Scroll down, select the headings** Upcoming Conferences **and** Technical Careers Division Personnel, **then click the** Format Painter button **to turn off the Format Painter**
The headings are formatted in 14-point bold, italic, and blue.

8. **Press** CTRL+END, **type** Prepared by, **type your name followed by a comma, press** SPACEBAR, **click the** Insert tab, **then click the** Insert Date and Time button 📅 **in the Text group**
The Date and Time dialog box opens with available formats for inserting the date and time.

9. **Select the third format in the list, click** OK **to insert the current date at the insertion point, press** ENTER, **then click the** Symbol button **in the Symbols group**
A gallery of commonly used symbols opens, as shown in FIGURE 3-2. You can insert a symbol from this gallery or click More Symbols to open a larger gallery of symbols.

10. **Click the** copyright symbol © **in the gallery, press** SPACEBAR, **type** JCL Talent, **click the** Home tab, **press** CTRL+HOME, **then save your changes**
The copyright symbol is inserted before the JCL Talent.

FIGURE 3-1: Formats copied and applied using the Format Painter

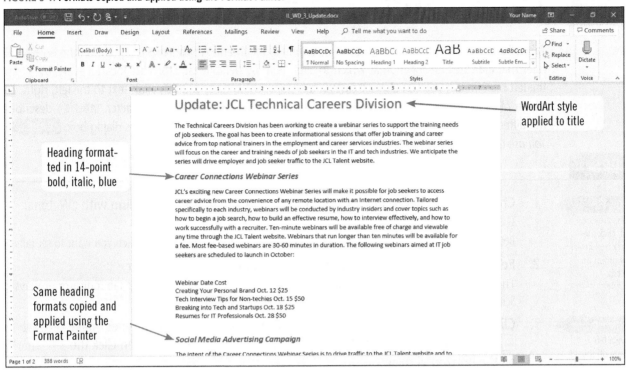

WordArt style applied to title

Heading formatted in 14-point bold, italic, blue

Same heading formats copied and applied using the Format Painter

FIGURE 3-2: Symbol gallery

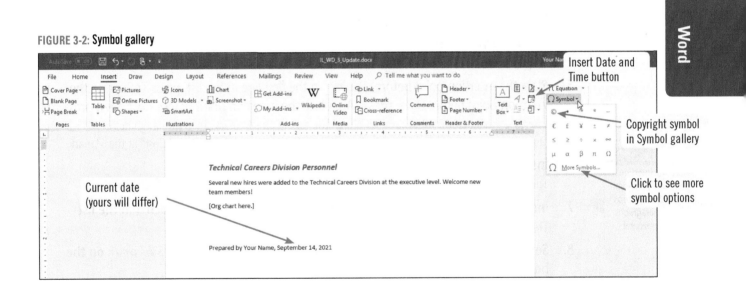

Insert Date and Time button

Copyright symbol in Symbol gallery

Click to see more symbol options

Current date (yours will differ)

Clearing formatting from text

If you are unhappy with the way text is formatted, you can use the Clear All Formatting command to return the text to the default format settings. The default format includes font and paragraph formatting: text is formatted in 11-point Calibri, and paragraphs are left-aligned with 1.08 point line spacing, 8 points of space after, and no indents. To clear formatting from text and return it to the default format, select the text you want to clear, and then click the Clear All Formatting button in the Font group on the Home tab. If you prefer to return the text to the default font and remove all paragraph formatting, making the text 11-point Calibri, left-aligned, single spaced, with no paragraph spacing or indents, select the text and then simply click the No Spacing button in the Styles group on the Home tab.

Work with Tabs

Tabs allow you to align text at a specific location in a document. A **tab stop** is a point on the horizontal ruler that indicates the location at which to align text. By default, tab stops are located every 1/2" from the left margin, but you can also set custom tab stops. Using tabs, you can align text to the left, right, or center of a tab stop, or you can align text at a decimal point or insert a bar character. TABLE 3-1 describes the different types of tab stops. You set tabs using the horizontal ruler or the Tabs dialog box. **CASE** ▶ *You use tabs to format the detailed information on webinars so it is easy to read.*

STEPS

1. **Change the zoom level to 120, then select the five-line list beginning with "Webinar Date Cost"**

   Before you set tab stops for existing text, you must select the paragraphs for which you want to set tabs.

2. **Point to the tab indicator L at the left end of the horizontal ruler**

   The icon in the tab indicator indicates the active type of tab; pointing to the tab indicator displays a ScreenTip naming the active tab type. By default, left tab is the active tab type.

3. **Click the tab indicator to see each of the available tab and indent types, make Left Tab L the active tab type, click the 1" mark on the horizontal ruler, then click the 3¾" mark on the horizontal ruler**

   Clicking the horizontal ruler inserts a tab stop of the active type for the selected paragraph or paragraphs. A left tab stop is inserted at the 1" mark and the 3¾" mark.

4. **Click the tab indicator twice so the Right Tab icon ◢ is active, then click the 5" mark on the horizontal ruler**

   A right tab stop is inserted at the 5" mark on the horizontal ruler, as shown in FIGURE 3-3.

5. **Place the insertion point before Webinar in the first line in the list, press TAB, place the insertion point before Date, press TAB, place the insertion point before Cost, then press TAB**

   Inserting a tab before "Webinar" left-aligns the text at the 1" mark, inserting a tab before "Date" left-aligns the text at the 3¾" mark, and inserting a tab before "Cost" right-aligns "Cost" at the 5" mark.

6. **Insert a tab at the beginning of each remaining line in the list**

   The paragraphs left-align at the 1" mark.

7. **Insert a tab before each Oct. in the list, then insert a tab before each $ in the list**

   The dates left-align at the 3¾" mark. The prices right-align at the 5" mark.

8. **Select the five lines of tabbed text, drag the right tab stop to the 5½" mark on the horizontal ruler, then deselect the text**

   Dragging the tab stop moves it to a new location. The prices right-align at the 5½" mark.

9. **Select the last four lines of tabbed text, click the Launcher ▣ in the Paragraph group, then click the Tabs button at the bottom of the Paragraph dialog box**

   The Tabs dialog box opens, as shown in FIGURE 3-4. You can use the Tabs dialog box to set tab stops, change the position or alignment of existing tab stops, clear tab stops, and apply tab leaders to tabs. **Tab leaders** are lines that appear in front of tabbed text.

10. **Click 3.75" in the Tab stop position list box, click the 2 option button in the Leader section, click Set, click 5.5" in the Tab stop position list box, click the 2 option button in the Leader section, click Set, click OK, deselect the text, then save your changes**

    A dotted tab leader is added before each 3.75" and 5.5" tab stop in the last four lines of tabbed text, as shown in FIGURE 3-5.

Formatting Text and Graphics

FIGURE 3-3: Left and right tab stops on the horizontal ruler

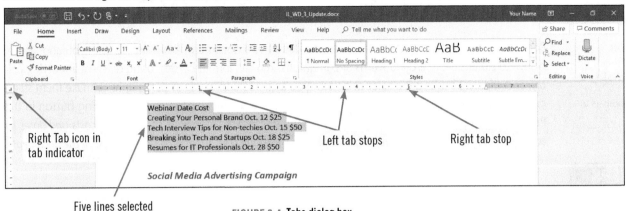

Right Tab icon in tab indicator

Five lines selected

Left tab stops

Right tab stop

Webinar Date Cost
Creating Your Personal Brand Oct. 12 $25
Tech Interview Tips for Non-techies Oct. 15 $50
Breaking into Tech and Startups Oct. 18 $25
Resumes for IT Professionals Oct. 28 $50

Social Media Advertising Campaign

FIGURE 3-4: Tabs dialog box

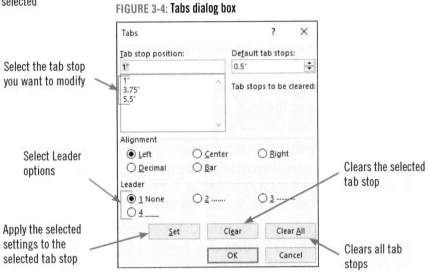

Select the tab stop you want to modify

Select Leader options

Apply the selected settings to the selected tab stop

Clears the selected tab stop

Clears all tab stops

FIGURE 3-5: Tab leaders

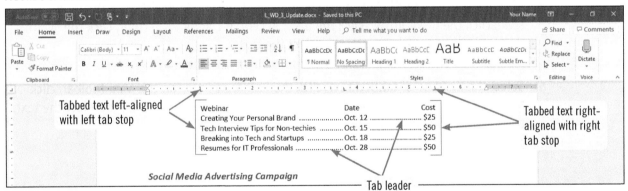

Tabbed text left-aligned with left tab stop

Tabbed text right-aligned with right tab stop

Webinar	Date	Cost
Creating Your Personal Brand	Oct. 12	$25
Tech Interview Tips for Non-techies	Oct. 15	$50
Breaking into Tech and Startups	Oct. 18	$25
Resumes for IT Professionals	Oct. 28	$50

Social Media Advertising Campaign

Tab leader

TABLE 3-1: Types of tabs

tab	use to
Left tab	Set the start position of text so that text runs to the right of the tab stop as you type
Center tab	Set the center align position of text so that text stays centered on the tab stop as you type
Right tab	Set the right or end position of text so that text moves to the left of the tab stop as you type
Decimal tab	Set the position of the decimal point so that numbers align around the decimal point as you type
Bar tab	Insert a vertical bar at the tab position

Add Borders and Shading

Learning Outcomes
• Apply shading to text
• Apply borders to text

Borders and shading can add color and artistic design to a document. **Borders** are lines you add above, below, to either side, or around words or paragraphs. You can format borders using different line styles, colors, and widths. **Shading** is a color or pattern you apply behind words or paragraphs to make them stand out on a page. You apply borders and shading using the Borders button and the Shading button in the Paragraph group on the Home tab. **CASE** *You enhance the tabbed text for webinar costs and dates by adding shading to it. You also apply a border around the tabbed text to set it off from the rest of the document.*

STEPS

1. **Select the** five paragraphs **of tabbed text, click the** Shading arrow 🖎 **in the Paragraph group on the Home tab, click the** Blue, Accent 1, Lighter 80% color, **then deselect the text**
   Light blue shading is applied to the five paragraphs. Notice that the shading is applied to the entire width of the paragraphs, from the left to the right margin.

2. **Select the** five paragraphs, **drag the** Left Indent marker ▢ **to the ¾" mark on the horizontal ruler, drag the** Right Indent marker △ **to the 5¾" mark, then deselect the text**
   The shading for the paragraphs is indented from the left and right, as shown in FIGURE 3-6.

3. **Select the** five paragraphs, **click the** Bottom Border arrow ⊞ ˅ **in the Paragraph group, click** Outside Borders, **then deselect the text**
   A black outside border is added around the selected text. The style of the border added is the most recently used border style, in this case the default, a thin black line.

4. **Select the** five paragraphs, **click the** Outside Borders arrow ⊞ ˅, **click** No Border, **click the** No Border arrow ⊞ ˅, **then click** Borders and Shading
   The Borders and Shading dialog box opens, as shown in FIGURE 3-7. You use the Borders tab to change the border style, color, and width, and to add boxes and lines to words or paragraphs.

5. **Click the** Box icon **in the Setting section, scroll down the Style list, click the** double-line style, **click the** Color arrow, **click the** Blue, Accent 1, Darker 25% color, **click the** Width arrow, **click** ¾ pt, **click** OK, **then deselect the text**
   A ¾-point dark blue double-line border is added around the tabbed text.

6. **Select the** first line **of tabbed text, click the** Bold button 🅱 **on the Mini toolbar, click the** Font Color arrow 🄰 ˅, **click the** Blue, Accent 1, Darker 25% color, **deselect the text, then save your changes**
   The Webinar, Date, and Cost text changes to bold dark blue, as shown in FIGURE 3-8.

Underlining text

Another way to call attention to text and to enhance the appearance of a document is to apply an underline style to words you want to highlight. The Underline arrow in the Font group displays straight, dotted, wavy, dashed, and mixed underline styles, along with a gallery of colors to choose from. To apply an underline to text, simply select it, click the Underline arrow, and then select an underline style from the list. For a wider variety of underline styles, click More Underlines in the list, and then select an underline style in the Font dialog box. You can change the color of an underline at any time by selecting the underlined text, clicking the Underline arrow, pointing to Underline Color, and then choosing from the options in the color gallery. If you want to remove an underline from text, select the underlined text, and then click the Underline button.

FIGURE 3-6: Shading applied to the tabbed text

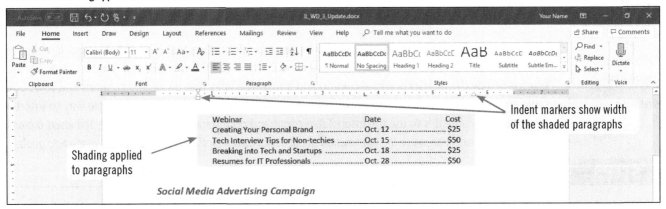

Indent markers show width of the shaded paragraphs

Shading applied to paragraphs

Webinar	Date	Cost
Creating Your Personal Brand	Oct. 12	$25
Tech Interview Tips for Non-techies	Oct. 15	$50
Breaking into Tech and Startups	Oct. 18	$25
Resumes for IT Professionals	Oct. 28	$50

Social Media Advertising Campaign

FIGURE 3-7: Borders tab in Borders and Shading dialog box

Choose a line style

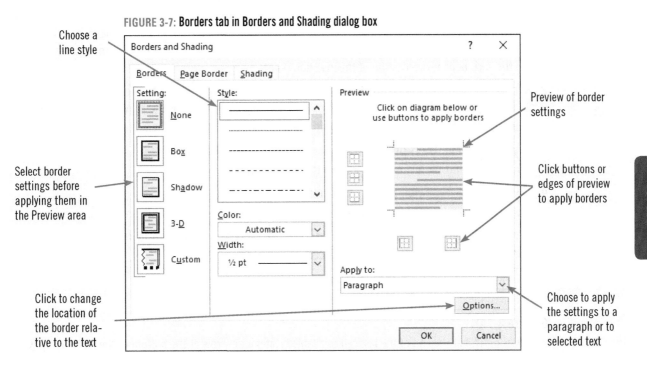

Preview of border settings

Select border settings before applying them in the Preview area

Click buttons or edges of preview to apply borders

Click to change the location of the border relative to the text

Choose to apply the settings to a paragraph or to selected text

FIGURE 3-8: Borders and shading applied to the document

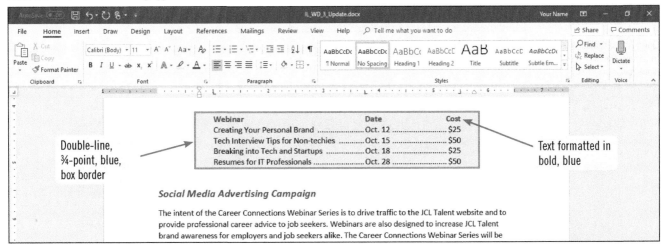

Double-line, ¾-point, blue, box border

Webinar	Date	Cost
Creating Your Personal Brand	Oct. 12	$25
Tech Interview Tips for Non-techies	Oct. 15	$50
Breaking into Tech and Startups	Oct. 18	$25
Resumes for IT Professionals	Oct. 28	$50

Text formatted in bold, blue

Social Media Advertising Campaign

The intent of the Career Connections Webinar Series is to drive traffic to the JCL Talent website and to provide professional career advice to job seekers. Webinars are also designed to increase JCL Talent brand awareness for employers and job seekers alike. The Career Connections Webinar Series will be

Insert a Table

Learning
Outcomes
• Insert a table
• Select and enter
  table data

Adding a table to a document is a useful way to illustrate information that is intended for quick reference and analysis. A **table** is a grid of columns and rows that you can fill with text and graphics. A **cell** is the box formed by the intersection of a column and a row. The lines that divide the columns and rows of a table and help you see the grid-like structure of the table are called **borders**. A simple way to insert a table into a document is to use the Insert Table command on the Insert tab. **CASE** *You insert a blank table and add text to organize the information about social media platforms and JCL Talent marketing goals.*

STEPS

1. **Scroll down, place the insertion point in the blank paragraph above the Upcoming Conferences heading, click the Insert tab, then click the Table button in the Tables group**

   The Table menu opens. It includes a grid for selecting the number of columns and rows you want the table to contain, as well as commands for inserting a table. TABLE 3-2 describes these commands. As you move the pointer across the grid, a preview of the table with the specified number of columns and rows appears in the document at the location of the insertion point.

2. **Point to the second box in the fourth row to select 2x4 Table, then click**

   A table with two columns and four rows is inserted in the document, as shown in FIGURE 3-9. Black borders surround the table cells. The insertion point is in the first cell in the first row.

3. **Type Platform, then press TAB**

   Pressing TAB moves the insertion point to the next cell in the row.

4. **Type Marketing Goal, press TAB, then type Facebook**

   Pressing TAB at the end of a row moves the insertion point to the first cell in the next row.

5. **Press TAB, type Follower count, press TAB, then type the following text in the table, pressing TAB to move from cell to cell**

Instagram	Brand awareness
LinkedIn	Website traffic/Conversions

6. **Press TAB**

   Pressing TAB at the end of the last cell of a table creates a new row at the bottom of the table, as shown in FIGURE 3-10. The insertion point is located in the first cell in the new row.

TROUBLE
If you pressed TAB
after the last row,
click the Undo
button 🔄 on the
Quick Access toolbar
to remove the new
blank row.

7. **Type the following, pressing TAB to move from cell to cell and to create a new row**

WhatsApp	Website traffic
Twitter	Promoted tweets

8. **Save your changes**

   The completed table is shown in FIGURE 3-11.

FIGURE 3-9: **Blank table**

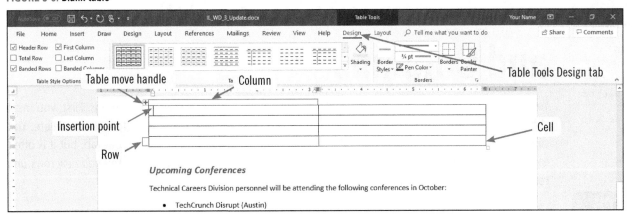

FIGURE 3-10: **New row in table**

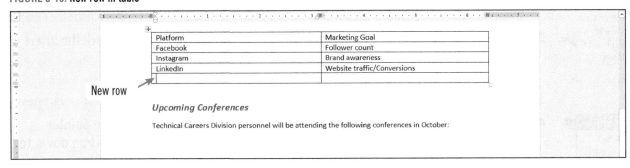

FIGURE 3-11: **Text in the table**

TABLE 3-2: **Table menu commands**

command	use to
Insert Table	Create a table with any number of columns and rows and select an AutoFit behavior
Draw Table	Create a complex table by drawing the table columns and rows
Convert Text to Table	Convert text that is separated by tabs, commas, or another separator character into a table
Excel Spreadsheet	Insert a blank Excel worksheet into the document as an embedded object
Quick Tables	Insert a preformatted table template and replace the placeholder data with your own data

Insert and Delete Rows and Columns

Learning
Outcomes
• Insert and delete
rows and columns

You can easily modify the structure of a table by adding and removing rows and columns. First, you must click or select an existing row or column in the table to indicate where you want to insert or delete. You can select any element of a table using the Select command on the Table Tools Layout tab, but it is often easier to select, add, and delete rows and columns using the mouse. **CASE** *You add new rows and columns to the social media platform table, and delete unnecessary rows.*

STEPS

QUICK TIP

You can also insert a row by right-clicking a row, clicking the Insert button on the Mini toolbar, and then clicking Insert Above or Insert Below.

1. **Click the Home tab, click the Show/Hide ¶ button ¶ in the Paragraph group to display formatting marks, then move the pointer up and down the left edge of the table**
   An end of cell mark appears at the end of each cell and an end of row mark appears at the end of each row. When you move the pointer to the left of two existing rows, an Insert Control appears outside the table.

2. **Move the pointer to the left of the border above the Twitter row, then click the Insert Control**
   A new row is inserted directly above the Twitter row, as shown in FIGURE 3-12.

3. **Click the first cell of the new row, type Snapchat, press TAB, then type Brand awareness**

QUICK TIP

If the end of row mark is not selected, you have selected only the text in the row, not the row itself.

4. **Place the pointer in the margin to the left of the Instagram row until the pointer changes to ⬧, click to select the row, press and hold the mouse button, drag down to select the LinkedIn row, then release the mouse button**
   The Instagram and LinkedIn rows are selected, including the end of row marks.

5. **Click the Table Tools Layout tab, then click the Insert Below button in the Rows & Columns group**
   Two new rows are added below the selected rows. To insert multiple rows, you select the number of rows you want to insert before inserting the rows, and then click an Insert Control or use the buttons on the Ribbon.

QUICK TIP

If you select a row and press DELETE, you delete only the contents of the row, not the row itself.

6. **Click the WhatsApp row, click the Delete button in the Rows & Columns group, click Delete Rows, select the two blank rows, click the Delete button on the Mini toolbar, then click Delete Rows**
   The WhatsApp row and the two blank rows are deleted.

7. **Place the pointer over the top border of the Marketing Goal column until the pointer changes to ↓, then click to select the entire column**

QUICK TIP

To select a cell, place the pointer near the left border of the cell, then click.

8. **Click the Insert Right button in the Rows & Columns group, then type Cost Basis**
   A new column is inserted to the right of the Marketing Goal column, as shown in FIGURE 3-13.

9. **Place the pointer over the border between the Marketing Goal and Cost Basis columns at the at the top of the table, click the Insert Control, then type Budget in the first cell of the new column**
   A new column for Budget is added between the Marketing Goal and Cost Basis columns.

QUICK TIP

You can use the arrow keys or press TAB to move the insertion point from cell to cell.

10. **Press DOWN ARROW to move the insertion point to the next cell in the Budget column, click the Home tab, click ¶ to turn off the display of formatting marks, enter the text shown in FIGURE 3-14 in each cell in the Budget and Cost Basis columns, then save your changes**
    Compare your table to FIGURE 3-14.

FIGURE 3-12: Inserted row

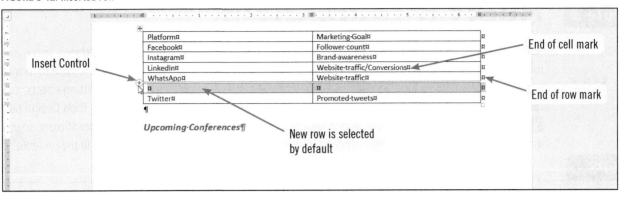

Insert Control

End of cell mark

End of row mark

New row is selected by default

FIGURE 3-13: Inserted column

New column

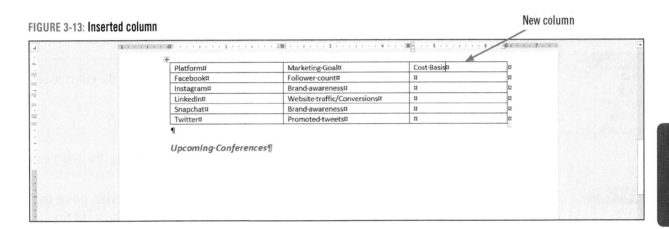

FIGURE 3-14: Text in Budget and Cost Basis columns

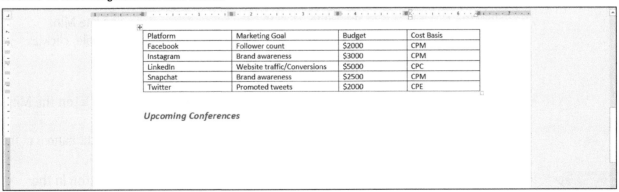

Platform	Marketing Goal	Budget	Cost Basis
Facebook	Follower count	$2000	CPM
Instagram	Brand awareness	$3000	CPM
LinkedIn	Website traffic/Conversions	$5000	CPC
Snapchat	Brand awareness	$2500	CPM
Twitter	Promoted tweets	$2000	CPE

Upcoming Conferences

Formatting Text and Graphics

Apply a Table Style

Learning
Outcomes
• Apply a table style

Adding shading and other design elements to a table can help give it a polished appearance and make the data easier to read. Word includes predefined, built-in table styles that you can apply to a table to format it quickly. Table styles include borders, shading, fonts, alignment, colors, and other formatting effects. You can apply a table style to a table using the buttons in the Table Styles group on the Table Tools Design tab.
CASE *You want to enhance the appearance of the table with shading, borders, and other formats, so you apply a table style to the table. Before applying a style, you adjust the width of the columns to fit the contents.*

STEPS

QUICK TIP
The insertion point must be in the table for the Table Tools tabs to be active.

1. **Click the** Table Tools Layout tab, **click the** AutoFit button **in the Cell Size group, then click** AutoFit Contents
The width of the table columns is adjusted to fit the text.

2. **Click the** Table Tools Design tab
The Table Tools Design tab includes buttons for applying table styles and for adding, removing, and customizing borders and shading in a table.

QUICK TIP
The number after the word "Table" in the Table style name is the row identifier in the gallery of table styles.

3. **Click the** More button ⊡ **in the Table Styles group**
The gallery of table styles opens, as shown in **FIGURE 3-15**. You point to a table style in the gallery to preview the style applied to the table.

4. **Move the pointer over the styles in the gallery, then click the** Grid Table 5 Dark – Accent 1 style
The Grid Table 5 Dark – Accent 1 style is applied to the table, as shown in **FIGURE 3-16**. This style makes the data easier to read, but the dark colors are heavy for the tone of your document.

QUICK TIP
Click Clear in the gallery of table styles to remove all borders, shading, and other style elements from a table.

5. **Click the scroll arrows in the Table Styles group to scroll the gallery of styles, point to several styles to see each style applied to the table, click the** More button ⊡ **in the Table Styles group, then click the** Grid Table 2 – Accent 3 style
The Grid Table 2 – Accent 3 style is applied to the table. This style makes the table data easier to read.

6. **In the Table Style Options group, click the** Banded Rows check box **to clear it**
The shading is removed from alternating rows in the table. When the banded columns or banded rows setting is active, the odd columns or rows are formatted differently from the even columns or rows to make the table data easier to read.

7. **Select the** first column **of the table, click the** Font Color arrow ⊿⁃ **on the Mini toolbar, click** Green, Accent 6, Darker 25%, **select the** first row **of the table, click** ⊿⁃, **then click** Blue, Accent 1, Darker 25%
The text in the first column is green and the text in the header row is blue.

8. **Select the** Budget **and** Cost Basis **columns, then click the** Center button ☰ **on the Mini toolbar**
The text in the Budget and Cost Basis columns is center-aligned. You can also use the buttons in the Alignment group on the Table Tools Layout tab to change the alignment of text in cells.

QUICK TIP
You can also use the Select button in the Table group on the Table Tools Layout tab to select a table, row, column, or cell.

9. **Click the** table move handle ⊞, **click the** Home tab, **click the** Center button **in the Paragraph group on the Ribbon, then deselect the table**
Clicking the table move handle selects the entire table. Clicking the Center button with the entire table selected centered the table between the margins, as shown in **FIGURE 3-17**.

10. **Press CTRL+HOME, then save your changes**

FIGURE 3-15: Gallery of table styles

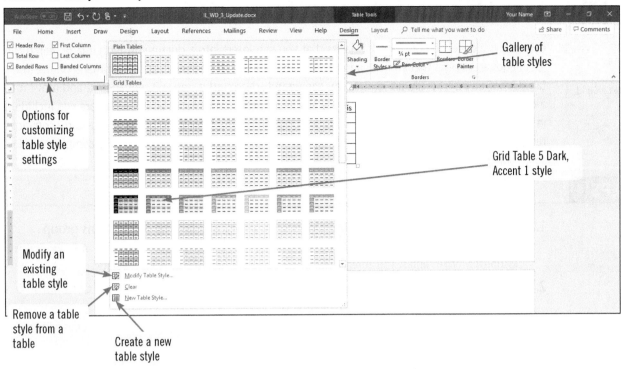

Options for customizing table style settings

Gallery of table styles

Grid Table 5 Dark, Accent 1 style

Modify an existing table style

Remove a table style from a table

Create a new table style

FIGURE 3-16: Grid Table 5 Dark – Accent 1 style applied to table

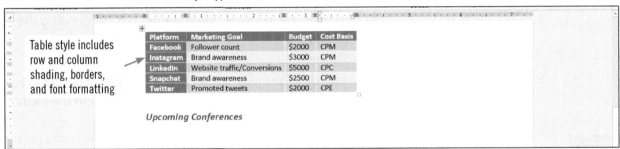

Table style includes row and column shading, borders, and font formatting

Platform	Marketing Goal	Budget	Cost Basis
Facebook	Follower count	$2000	CPM
Instagram	Brand awareness	$3000	CPM
LinkedIn	Website traffic/Conversions	$5000	CPC
Snapchat	Brand awareness	$2500	CPM
Twitter	Promoted tweets	$2000	CPE

Upcoming Conferences

FIGURE 3-17: Completed table

Heading row text is blue

Column text is green

Table is centered between the margins

Text is centered in Budget and Cost Basis columns

Platform	Marketing Goal	Budget	Cost Basis
Facebook	Follower count	$2000	CPM
Instagram	Brand awareness	$3000	CPM
LinkedIn	Website traffic/Conversions	$5000	CPC
Snapchat	Brand awareness	$2500	CPM
Twitter	Promoted tweets	$2000	CPE

Upcoming Conferences

Word

Insert Online Pictures

Learning Outcomes
• Insert pictures
• Wrap text around objects

Clip art is a collection of graphic images that you can insert into a document. Bing image search clip art images are images that you can add to a document using the Online Pictures command on the Insert tab. Once you insert a clip art image, you can wrap text around it, resize it, enhance it, and move it to a different location. Always carefully review any license requirements for an image before you include it in a document. Images licensed under Creative Commons can be used by the public but carry copyright restrictions. **CASE** *You illustrate the document with an online clip art image.* Note: To complete this lesson, your computer must be connected to the Internet.

STEPS

1. **Click the Insert tab, then click the Online Pictures button in the Illustrations group**

   The Online Pictures window opens. You can search for images related to a keyword. A **keyword** is a descriptive word or phrase you enter to obtain an image described by the word or phrase.

2. **Type meeting in the search text box, press ENTER, then click the Creative Commons only check box if it is not already selected**

   Images that have the keyword "meeting" associated with them appear in the Online Pictures window, as shown in **FIGURE 3-18**.

TROUBLE
Select a different clip if the clip shown in **FIGURE 3-18** is not available to you.

3. **Click the clip called out in FIGURE 3-18, then click Insert**

   The clip is inserted as an inline graphic at the location of the insertion point, as shown in **FIGURE 3-19**. Until you apply text wrapping to an inline graphic, it is part of the line of text in which it was inserted. Sizing handles appear on the square edges of the graphic when it is selected. Notice the graphic includes a credit line. This inter-departmental report does not require that you retain the credit line, so you will remove it.

4. **Click the word Unknown in the credit line, click the border of the box surrounding the credit line to select it, then press DELETE**

   The credit line box is removed from the image.

5. **Click the Picture Tools Format tab, click the Color button in the Adjust group, click Blue, Accent color 1 Light in the Recolor section, click the Picture Border button in the Picture Styles group, click Blue, Accent 1, then deselect the graphic,**

   The color of the image changes from black to blue, and a blue picture border is added. To move a graphic independently of the line of text in which it was inserted, you must make it a floating graphic.

QUICK TIP
To position a graphic anywhere on a page, you must apply text wrapping to it even if there is no text on the page.

6. **Click the image to select it, click the Layout Options button ⌐ on the side of the image, then click the Square button ⌐ in the With Text Wrapping section**

   The text wraps around the square sides of the graphic, making the graphic a floating object. Notice the anchor that appears in the upper-left corner of the photo. The anchor indicates the floating graphic is **anchored** to the nearest paragraph, so that the graphic moves with the paragraph if the paragraph is moved. The anchor is a nonprinting symbol that appears when an object is selected.

QUICK TIP
To position a graphic using precise measurements, click the Position button, click More Layout Options, then adjust the settings on the Position tab in the Layout dialog box.

7. **Position the pointer over the graphic, when the pointer changes to ⛶, drag the graphic down, using the green guidelines that appear, so its top aligns with the first paragraph of body text and its left aligns with the left margin, as shown in FIGURE 3-20, then release the mouse button**

   The graphic is positioned below the title on the left side of the page.

8. **Deselect the graphic, then save your changes.**

FIGURE 3-18: Online Pictures window

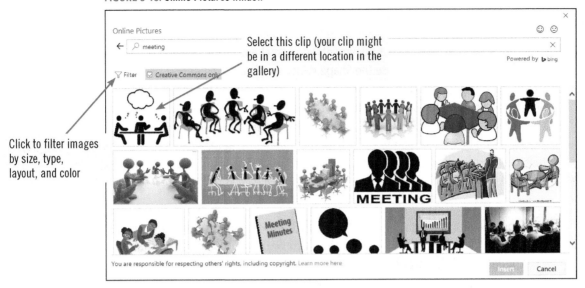

Click to filter images by size, type, layout, and color

Select this clip (your clip might be in a different location in the gallery)

FIGURE 3-19: Inline graphic

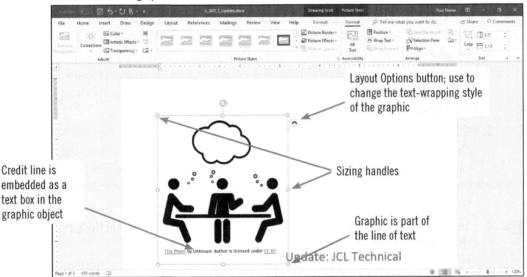

Layout Options button; use to change the text-wrapping style of the graphic

Credit line is embedded as a text box in the graphic object

Sizing handles

Graphic is part of the line of text

FIGURE 3-20: Graphic being moved to a new location

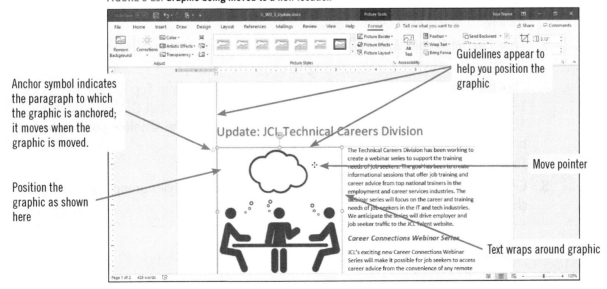

Anchor symbol indicates the paragraph to which the graphic is anchored; it moves when the graphic is moved.

Position the graphic as shown here

Guidelines appear to help you position the graphic

Move pointer

Text wraps around graphic

Size and Scale a Graphic

Learning Outcomes
• Format objects
• Scale a graphic

Once you insert a graphic into a document, you can change its shape or size. You can use the mouse to drag a sizing handle, you can use the Shape Width and Shape Height text boxes in the Size group on the Picture Tools Format tab to specify an exact height and width for the graphic, or you can change the scale of the graphic using the Size tab in the Layout dialog box. Resizing a graphic with the mouse allows you to see how the image looks as you modify it. Using the text boxes in the Size group or the Size tab in the Layout dialog box allows you to set precise measurements. **CASE** *You reduce the size of the graphic that you inserted in the JCL document.*

STEPS

1. **Double-click the graphic to select it and activate the Picture Tools Format tab, place the pointer over the middle-right sizing handle, when the pointer changes to ⟺, drag to the left until the graphic is about 2" wide**

   Refer to the ruler as you drag. When you release the mouse button, the image is taller than it is wide. Dragging a side, top, or bottom sizing handle changes only the width or height of a graphic.

2. **Click the Undo button ↶ on the Quick Access toolbar, place the pointer over the lower-right sizing handle, when the pointer changes to ⤡, drag up and to the left until the graphic is about 2" high and 2" wide, then release the mouse button**

   The image is smaller. Dragging a corner sizing handle resizes the graphic proportionally so that its width and height are reduced or enlarged by the same percentage. TABLE 3-3 describes ways to resize objects using the mouse.

3. **Click the Launcher ⟲ in the Size group**

   The Layout dialog box opens with the Size tab active, as shown in FIGURE 3-21. The Size tab allows you to enter precise height and width measurements for a graphic or to scale a graphic by entering the percentage you want to reduce or enlarge it by. When a graphic is sized to **scale** (or scaled), its height to width ratio remains the same.

4. **Select the measurement in the Height text box in the Scale section, type 50, then click the Width text box in the Scale section**

   The scale of the width changes to 50% and the Absolute measurements in the Height and Width sections decrease proportionally.

5. **Click OK**

   The image is reduced to 50% of its original size.

6. **Type 1 in the Shape Width text box in the Size group, then press ENTER**

   The image is reduced to be 1" wide and 1" high.

7. **Click the Position button in the Arrange group, click Position in Top Right with Square Text Wrapping, click the Position button again, click More Layout Options, click the Absolute position button in the Vertical section, type .6 in the Absolute position text box, then click OK**

   The graphic is positioned below the title on the right side of the page.

8. **Click the Reflected Rounded Rectangle style in the Picture Styles group, then save your changes**

   A style is applied to the image, as shown in FIGURE 3-22.

FIGURE 3-21: Size tab in the Layout dialog box

Set specific
height and width
measurements
(yours may differ)

Change the scale
of an object

Select to keep
height and width
proportional

Select to make scaled
measurements relative
to the original size

Click to reset
image to its
original size

Original size
of image

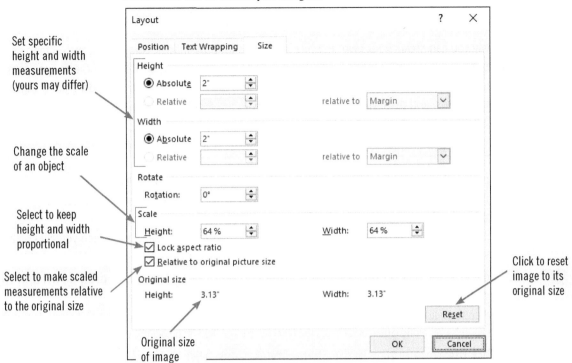

FIGURE 3-22: Style applied to resized image

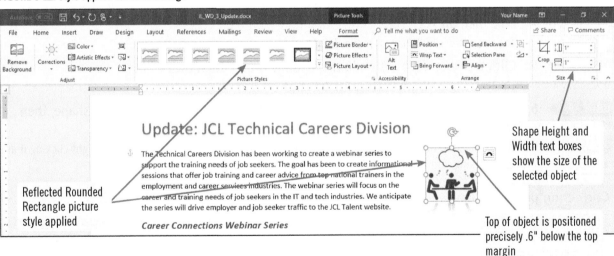

Reflected Rounded
Rectangle picture
style applied

Shape Height and
Width text boxes
show the size of the
selected object

Top of object is positioned
precisely .6" below the top
margin

TABLE 3-3: Methods for resizing an object using the mouse

do this	to
Drag a corner sizing handle	Resize a clip art or bitmap graphic and maintain its proportions
Press SHIFT and drag a corner sizing handle	Resize any graphic object and maintain its proportions
Press CTRL and drag a side, top, or bottom sizing handle	Resize any graphic object vertically or horizontally while keeping the center position fixed
Press CTRL and drag a corner sizing handle	Resize any graphic object diagonally while keeping the center position fixed
Press SHIFT+CTRL and drag a corner sizing handle	Resize any graphic object while keeping the center position fixed and maintaining its proportions

Draw and Format Shapes

One way you can create your own graphics in Word is to draw shapes. **Shapes** are the rectangles, ovals, lines, callouts, block arrows, stars, and other drawing objects you can create using the Shapes command in the Illustrations group on the Insert tab. Once you draw a shape, you can add colors, borders, fill effects, shadows, and three-dimensional effects to it. **CASE** ▶ *You use the Shapes feature to draw shapes in the Update document.*

STEPS

1. **Scroll until the Career Connections... heading is at the top of your screen, click the Insert tab, click the Shapes button in the Illustrations group, then click the Cloud icon in the Basic Shapes section of the Shapes menu**

   The Shapes menu contains categories of shapes and lines that you can draw. When you click a shape in the Shapes menu, the pointer changes to ┼. You draw a shape by clicking and dragging with this pointer.

2. **Position the ┼ pointer over JCL in the first line of body text, then drag down and to the right to create a cloud that is approximately 1" high and 2" wide**

   When you release the mouse button, sizing handles appear around the cloud to indicate it is selected, as shown in FIGURE 3-23. Notice the cloud covers the text. In Front of Text is the default wrapping style for a shape.

3. **Click the More button in the Shape Styles group, click Colored Fill - Green Accent 6, click the Shape Effects button, point to Preset, then click Preset 5**

   The color of the cloud changes to green and the image is formatted with a bevel and shadow style.

4. **Type .8 in the Height text box in the Size group, press TAB, type 1.2 in the Width text box, then press ENTER**

   The size of the cloud shape is reduced.

5. **Click the Wrap Text button in the Arrange group, then click Tight**

   The text wraps to the curved shape of the image.

6. **Right-click the cloud shape, click Add Text, type Great idea!, deselect the shape, then save your document**

   Text is added to the cloud, as shown in FIGURE 3-24. You can add text to any shape by right-clicking it and then clicking Add Text or Edit Text.

Correcting pictures, changing colors, and applying artistic effects

The Corrections command in the Adjust group allows you to adjust a picture's relative lightness (**brightness**), alter the difference between its darkest and lightest areas (**contrast**), and change the sharpness of an image. To make these adjustments, select the image and then click the Corrections button to open a gallery of preset percentages applied to the selected picture. Point to an option in the gallery to preview it in the document; click an option in the gallery to apply it. You can also fine-tune brightness, contrast, or sharpness by clicking Picture Corrections Options in the Corrections gallery, and then using the sliders in the Picture Corrections section of the Format Picture pane to adjust the percentage.

The Color command in the Adjust group is used to change the vividness and intensity of color in an image (**color saturation**), and to change the "temperature" of a photo by bringing out the cooler blue tones or the warmer orange tones (**color tone**). The Color command is also used to recolor a picture to give it a stylized effect, such as sepia tone, grayscale, or duotone (using theme colors). To make changes to the colors in a picture, select it, click the Color button, and then select one of the color modes or variations in the gallery that opens, or click Picture Color Options to fine tune color settings using the Picture Format pane.

The Artistic Effects command in the Adjust group allows you to make a photo look like a drawing, a painting, a photocopy, a sketch, or some other artistic medium. To experiment with applying an artistic effect, select a photo, click the Artistic Effects button, and then point to each effect to preview it applied to the photo.

After you adjust a picture, you can undo any changes by clicking the Reset Picture button in the Adjust group. This command discards all formatting changes made to a picture, including size, cropping, borders, and effects.

FIGURE 3-23: Shape in document

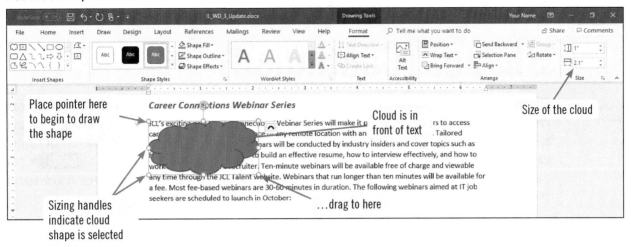

Place pointer here to begin to draw the shape

Size of the cloud

Sizing handles indicate cloud shape is selected

Cloud is in front of text

...drag to here

FIGURE 3-24: Text added to shape

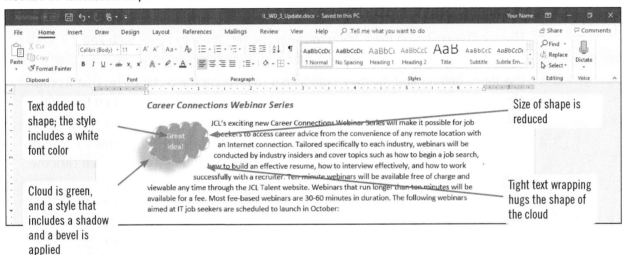

Text added to shape; the style includes a white font color

Cloud is green, and a style that includes a shadow and a bevel is applied

Size of shape is reduced

Tight text wrapping hugs the shape of the cloud

Adding alt text and checking documents for accessibility issues

It's important to design documents so that they are accessible to people of all abilities. The Alt Text command allows you to add a text description of a graphic image to a document so that people who are visually impaired and using a screen reader can access the content of the image. The alt text associated with an image should serve the same purpose and convey the same essential information as the image so that no information or functionality is lost for readers who are visually impaired. To add alt text to an image, select the image, click the Alt Text command in the Accessibility group on the Picture Tools Format tab, and then type the alternative text description in the text box on the Alt Text pane. When

you are finished, close the Alt Text pane. You can edit alt text at any time by right-clicking an image and then clicking Edit Alt Text.

The Accessibility Checker locates elements of a document that might be a potential problem for readers with disabilities, and it offers suggestions on how to resolve each issue. For example, the Accessibility Checker might flag a graphic that does not include alt text, or it might issue a warning about formatting that makes text hard to read. To check a document for accessibility issues, click the File tab, click Check for Issues on the Info screen, and then click Check Accessibility. The results of the inspection appear in the Accessibility Checker pane.

(Continued)

Word

Draw and Format Shapes (Continued)

Learning
Outcomes
• Use the Format
  Painter
• Change and
  modify shapes

Shapes when used appropriately, can enhance any document. The shape features in Word let you can create a document that works well to present ideas using visual cues to facilitate your message. You can change an existing shape to a different one to see which works best for the document. The Format Painter can apply similar styles to different shapes to create a cohesive design in the document. **CASE** ▸ *You continue to use the Shapes feature to add additional shapes and try different shape styles that include text in the document.*

STEPS

1. **Scroll down until the Social Media... heading is at the top of your screen, click the** Insert tab, **click the** Shapes button **in the Illustrations group, click the** Rectangle icon **in the Rectangles section, then use the** ＋ **pointer to draw a rectangle below the Social Media... heading**

2. **Use the Size group on the Ribbon to resize the rectangle to be .6" high and 1.2" wide, right-click the** rectangle shape, **click** Add Text, **then type** Genius!

3. **Use the** ⬚ **pointer and the green guidelines to position the rectangle so that its top aligns with the top of the Social Media... heading and the right side is on the right margin, as shown in** FIGURE 3-25, **then release the mouse button**

4. **Scroll up until both shapes are visible in the document window, select the** cloud, **click the** Home tab, **click the** Format Painter button **in the Clipboard group, then click the edge of the rectangle shape with the** 🖌I
   Clicking the rectangle with the Format Painter copied the formatting settings applied to the cloud shape— green, bevel, shadow, and tight text wrapping—to the rectangle shape.

5. **With the rectangle selected, click the** Drawing Tools Format tab, **click the** Edit Shape button 🖵 **in the Insert Shapes group, point to** Change Shape, **then click the** Cloud icon **in the Basic Shapes section**
   The rectangle changes to a cloud. Notice that changing the object shape does not change the text or the format settings applied to the object.

6. **Select the** Great idea! cloud, **click the** Edit Shape button, **point to** Change Shape, **then click the** Thought Bubble: Cloud icon **in the Callouts section**
   The cloud changes to a thought bubble cloud.

TROUBLE ▸
Do not be concerned
if your cloud shape
does not match the
figure exactly.

7. **Position the pointer over the** yellow adjustment handle **on the thought bubble cloud, drag the handle down and left, similar in** FIGURE 3-26, **then release the mouse button**
   Dragging the adjustment handle modifies the shape of the thought bubble cloud.

8. **Save your changes**

FIGURE 3-25: Positioning the rectangle

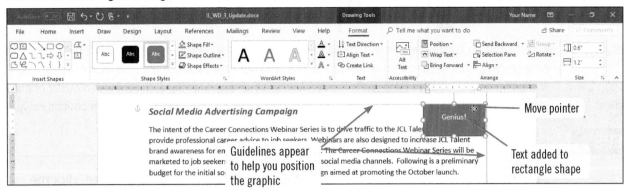

FIGURE 3-26: Cloud shapes in document

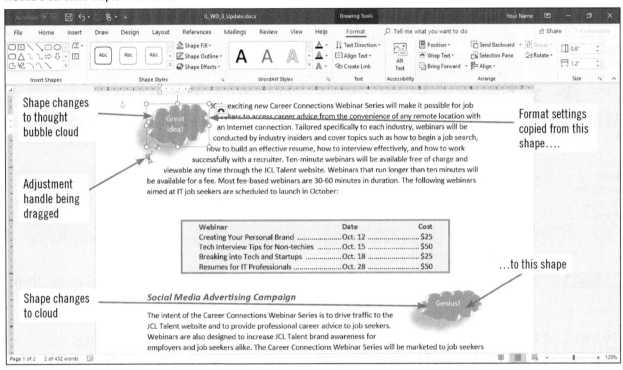

Enhancing graphic objects with styles and effects

Another way to make a document fun and visually appealing for the reader is to apply a style or an effect to a graphic object. To apply a style, select the object and then choose from the style options in the Styles group on the active Format tab for that type of object. Styles include a preset mixture of effects, such as shading, borders, shadows, and other settings. The Effects command in the Styles group on the active Format tab gives you the power to apply a customized variety of effects to an object, including

a shadow, bevel, glow, reflection, soft edge, or 3-D rotation. To apply an effect, select the object, click the Effects command for that type of object, point to the type of effect you want to apply, and then select from the options in the gallery that opens. To further customize an effect, click the Options command for that type of effect at the bottom of the gallery to open the Format Shape pane. The best way to learn about styles and effects is to experiment by applying them to an object and seeing what works.

WD 3-21

Arrange Graphic Objects

Another way to create graphics in Word is to create objects that are composed of multiple shapes. The Arrange group on the Picture Tools Format tab includes commands you can use to layer, rotate, flip, align, and group graphic objects. **CASE** ▶ *You decide to illustrate page 2 of the document with a cluster of small stars. You edit, rotate, and adjust the stars before grouping them into one object that you can position easily.*

STEPS

1. **Scroll until the heading** Upcoming Conferences **is at the top of your screen, click the** Insert tab, **click the** Shapes button **in the Illustrations group, click the** Star: 5 Points icon **in the Stars and Banners section of the Shapes menu, then click a blank area of page 2**

   A 1" square star shape is inserted in the document.

2. **Press** CTRL+C **to copy the star, press** CTRL+V **to paste a copy of the star, then press** CTRL+V **again to paste another copy of the star**

   Two stars are pasted for a total of three overlapping stars. These pasted objects have the same text wrapping style as the source object—In Front of Text. To paste an object as an inline graphic, click the Paste Options button below a pasted object, then click the Picture (P) option.

3. **Drag each star to position them in a non-overlapping horizontal line**

4. **Select the first** star, **click the** Shape Fill arrow **in the Shape Styles group, click** Green, Accent 6, **select the second** star, **click the** Shape Fill arrow, **click** Gold, Accent 4

   One star is blue, one star is green, and one star is gold, as shown in in FIGURE 3-27.

5. **Select the** green star, **position the pointer over the yellow** adjustment handle, **drag the handle up about** 1/8", **select the** gold star, **then drag the** adjustment handle **down about** 1/8"

   The Adjustment handle changed the internal proportions. The green star becomes wider and the gold star becomes narrower.

6. **Select the** green star, **drag the** rotate handle **left about** 1/4", **select the** blue star, **then drag the** rotate handle **right about** 1/4"

   The green star is rotated left and the blue star is rotated right.

7. **Position the three stars so that they overlap each other, similar to** FIGURE 3-28

   The stars are stacked in layers. Don't be concerned if the layering of your stars is different.

8. **Select the** gold star, **click the** Bring Forward arrow **in the Arrange group, then click** Bring to Front

   The gold star becomes the front layer of the stack of objects. You use the Bring Forward and Send Backward arrows to shift the order of the layers in a stack of graphic objects.

9. **Press and hold** CTRL, **click the** blue star, **click the** green star **so that all three stars are selected, click the** Group button **in the Arrange group, then click** Group

   The three star objects become a single object with sizing handles around a surrounding border. Any formatting applied will affect all the objects within the grouped object.

10. **Type** 1 **in the Shape Height text box in the Size group, type** 1.2 **in the Shape Width text box, press** ENTER, **click the** Position button **in the Arrange group, click** Position in Top Right with Square Text Wrapping, **deselect the object, then save your changes**

    The size of the grouped object is reduced to 1" high and 1.2" wide, and the object is positioned in the top-right corner of the page, as shown in in FIGURE 3-29.

Formatting Text and Graphics

FIGURE 3-27: Stars with fill color applied

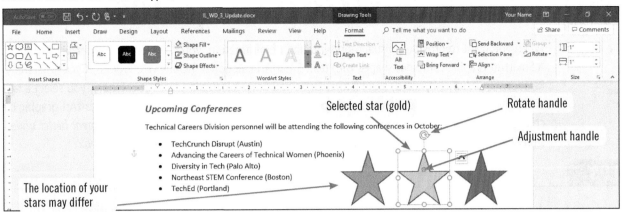

FIGURE 3-28: Stars layered in document

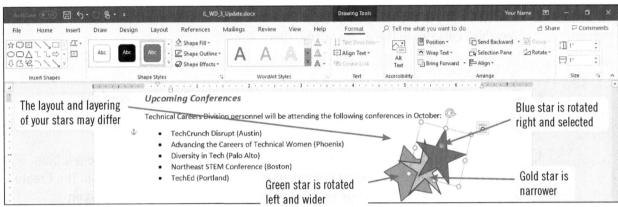

FIGURE 3-29: Grouped and resized object positioned in top corner

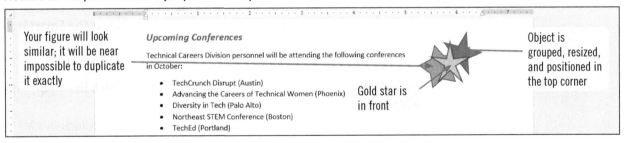

Creating an illustration in a drawing canvas

A **drawing canvas** is a workspace for creating your own graphics. It provides a frame-like boundary between an illustration and the rest of the document so that the illustration can be sized, formatted, and positioned like a single graphic object. If you are creating an illustration that includes multiple shapes, such as a flow chart, it is helpful to create the illustration in a drawing canvas. To draw shapes or lines in a drawing canvas, click the Shapes button in the Illustrations group on the Insert tab, click New Drawing Canvas to open a drawing canvas in the document, and then create and format your illustration in the drawing canvas. When you are finished, right-click the border of the drawing canvas and then click Fit to resize the drawing canvas to fit the illustration. You can then resize the illustration by dragging a border of the drawing canvas. Once you have resized a drawing canvas, you can wrap text around it and position it. By default, a drawing canvas has no border or background so that it is transparent in a document, but you can add fill and borders to it if you wish.

Word

Create SmartArt Graphics

When you want to provide a visual representation of information, you can create a **SmartArt graphic**. A SmartArt graphic combines shapes with text. SmartArt categories include List, Process, Cycle, Hierarchy, Relationship, Matrix, Pyramid, and Picture. Once you have selected a SmartArt category, you select a layout and then type text in the SmartArt shapes or text pane. You can further modify a SmartArt graphic by changing fill colors, shape styles, and layouts. **CASE** *To help recipients of this document better understand the executive structure at JCL Talent, you create an organizational chart SmartArt graphic.*

STEPS

1. **Scroll down, select [Org chart here.] under the Technical Careers... heading, click the Insert tab, then click SmartArt in the Illustrations group**

   The Choose a SmartArt Graphic dialog box opens. You use it to select the category of diagram you want to create and the layout and design for the diagram. The right pane shows a preview of the selected diagram layout.

2. **Click Hierarchy in the left pane, select the Name and Title Organization Chart style (first row, third column) in the middle pane, then click OK**

   An organization chart SmartArt object is inserted in the document and the SmartArt Tools Design tab becomes active.

3. **Click [Text] in the top blue box, type Dawn LaPointe, click the border of the white box just beneath Dawn's box to select the box, then type Director**

   As you type, the font size adjusts so that the text fits in each text box.

4. **Click the blue box below and to the left to select it, press DELETE, click the left blue box in the bottom row to select it if necessary, click the Add Shape arrow in the Create Graphic group, click Add Shape Below, then click the Add Shape button again**

   A shape is added to the right of the shape you just inserted. The Add Shape menu provides options for adding more shapes below, above, before, and after to your SmartArt graphic. You can also add an Assistant shape. New shapes will be added depending upon which box is currently selected in the SmartArt graphic.

5. **Click the Change Colors button in the SmartArt Styles group, select Colorful – Accent Colors (first selection in the Colorful section), click the More button ⬇ in the SmartArt Styles group, then click Polished (first selection in the 3-D section)**

   Colors and a SmartArt style are applied to the organizational chart.

6. **Click the orange box to select it, click the SmartArt Tools Format tab, click the Shape Fill arrow in the Shape Styles section, then click Green, Accent 6**

   The orange box changes to green. You can also format each element of a SmartArt graphic individually.

7. **Type the text shown in FIGURE 3-30 in each box the SmartArt graphic, click outside the object to deselect it, then save your changes**

8. **Click the View tab, click Multiple Pages in the Zoom group**

   The completed document is shown in FIGURE 3-31.

9. **sam'⬆ Submit the document to your instructor, close the file, then exit Word**

FIGURE 3-30: Organizational chart

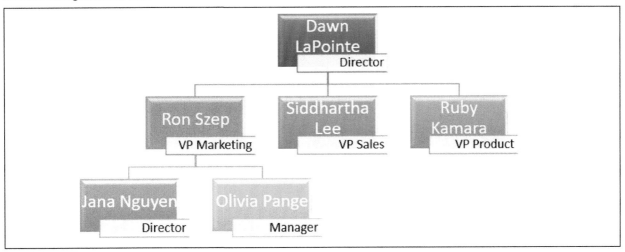

FIGURE 3-31: Completed document

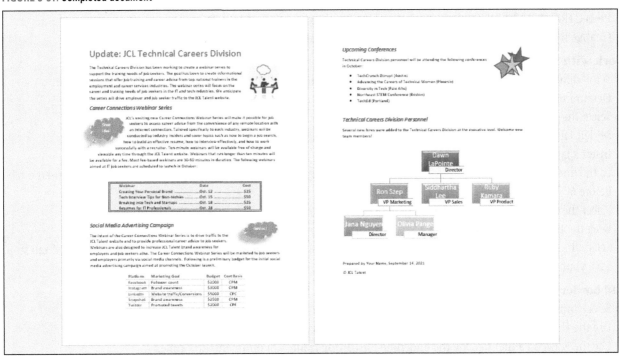

Formatting Text and Graphics

WD 3-25

Word

Practice

Skills Review

1. Use the Format Painter

   a. Start Word, open the file IL_WD_3-2.docx from the location where you store your Data Files, save it as **IL_WD_3_Appointments**.

   b. Format the title "East Mountain Counseling Center" in any WordArt style.

   c. Change the font size of the title to 28.

   d. Change the WordArt style of the title to the second style in the third row.

   e. Format the subtitle in 14-point italic.

   f. Format the heading "Our policy" in 14-point bold, italic with a Gray, Accent 3 font color.

   g. Use the Format Painter to copy the format of the Our policy heading to the following headings: Five-step approach to scheduling appointments, Determining the time required for an appointment, and Processing new clients.

   h. Press CTRL+END to go to the end of the document, type **Last revised**, insert the current date using the format MM-DD-YYYY, type **by**, then type your name.

   i. Type **East Mountain Counseling is an affiliate of PRG Health.**, then insert a trademark symbol (™) after Health.

   j. Press CTRL+HOME, click the Design tab, then change the theme colors to Red Orange.

   k. Change the font color of the title to Red, Accent 3, then save your changes.

2. Work with tabs.

   a. Scroll down to the bottom of page 1, format "Appointment Time," the first line in the six-line list under the Determining... heading, in bold with a Red, Accent 3 font color.

   b. Select the six-line list of appointment time information.

   c. Set left tab stops at the 1½" mark, the 3¾" mark, and the 5" mark.

   d. Insert a tab at the beginning of each line in the list.

   e. In the first line, insert a tab before Time. In the second line, insert a tab before 90. In the remaining lines, insert a tab before 60 or 90.

   f. Select the six lines of tabbed text, then drag the second tab stop to the 4" mark on the horizontal ruler.

   g. Drag the third tab stop at the 5" mark off the ruler to remove it.

   h. Select the last five lines of tabbed text, open the Tabs dialog box, then apply a dotted line tab leader to the 4" tab stop.

   i. Save your changes to the document.

3. Add borders and shading.

   a. Select "Appointment," then apply an underline.

   b. Use the Underline arrow in the Font group to change the color of the underline to Dark Gray, Text 2.

   c. Use the Format Painter to copy the underline formatting from "Appointment" to "Time."

   d. Click the heading Determining..., add 6 points of space after the paragraph, then open the Borders and Shading dialog box.

   e. Use the Border tab to apply a ½-point width, Dark Gray, Text 2 colored border below the heading.

   f. Use the Format Painter to apply the same paragraph and border settings to the other headings in the report: Our policy, Five-step approach..., and Processing new clients.

   g. Scroll to the end of the document, click in the Last revised... paragraph, then center the paragraph.

   h. Apply Dark Gray, Text 2, Lighter 80% shading to the paragraph.

   i. Add a ½ -point, dotted line, Dark Gray, Text 2 box border around the paragraph.

   j. Save your changes.

4. Insert a table.

a. Turn on formatting marks, click in the middle blank paragraph above the Processing new clients heading, then insert a table that contains two columns and three rows.

b. Type the text shown below, pressing TAB to add rows as necessary.

S. Beran	10-2
M. Kurosawa	1-5
C. Foth	2-7
M. Smith	2-4
P. Eriksen	12-6
F. Janda	10-3

c. Save your changes.

5. Insert and delete rows and columns.

a. Insert a row above the S. Beran row, type **Counselor** in the first cell, they type **Availability** in the second cell.

b. Delete the M. Smith row.

c. Insert a column to the left of the Counselor column, then type **Day** in the first cell.

d. Type the days of the work week, begin with Monday and end with Friday, in each empty cell in the new column.

e. Save your changes.

6. Apply a table style.

a. Select the table, then use the AutoFit command to fit the table to the contents.

b. Click the Table Tools Design tab, preview table styles applied to the table, and then apply an appropriate style.

c. Apply the List Table 4 – Accent 3 style to the table, then remove the style and from Banded Rows and First Column.

d. Center the text in the Availability column.

e. Center the table between the margins, then save your changes.

7. Insert online pictures. (*Note:* To complete these steps, your computer must be connected to the Internet.)

a. Press CTRL+HOME, then open the Online Pictures window.

b. Search using Bing Image Search to find images related to the keyword **mountain**. Click the Filter link in the Online Pictures window, select Clip Art on the Filter menu to filter the search results, then verify the Creative Commons checkbox is selected.

c. Insert the mountain with orange sky image shown in FIGURE 3-32. (*Note:* Select a different image if this one is not available to you. It is best to select an image that is similar in shape to the image shown in FIGURE 3-32.)

d. Scroll down, click Unknown in the credit line, select the box that surrounds the credit line, then delete the credit line box.

e. Use the Shape Width text box in the Size group on the Picture Tools Format tab to change the width of the image to 3".

f. Use the Position command to position the image in the top right with square text wrapping.

g. Apply a 1-point Black, Text 1 color picture border, then change the color of the image to Gold, Accent color 5 Light.

h. Use the Reset Picture arrow to reset the picture (but not the size).

i. Use the Artistic Effects button to apply the Glow Diffused artistic effect to the image.

j. Use the Color button to change the color tone to Temperature: 11200K.

k. Use the Corrections button to adjust the brightness and contrast to Brightness 0% (Normal) Contrast −40%, then save your changes.

FIGURE 3-32

Formatting Text and Graphics

8. **Size and scale a graphic.**
   a. Resize the image proportionally so that it is about **1"** high and **1.5"** wide.
   b. Drag the image so its top is aligned with the first line of body text and its left side is aligned with the left margin.
   c. Resize the image so that it is precisely **1.18"** high and **1.78"** wide.
   d. Position the image so it Horizontal absolute position is 0" to the right of the margin and its Vertical absolute position is 1" below the margin.
   e. Add ¼-point Black, Text 1 picture border around the image, then save your changes.

9. **Draw and format shapes.**
   a. Scroll until the Five-step approach... heading is at the top of your screen.
   b. Click the Shapes button, click the Star: 7 Points shape, then click in the numbered list below the Five-step... heading.
   c. Resize the shape to be **1"** high and **1.5"** wide.
   d. Right-click the shape, click Add Text, type **New!**, select the text, then apply bold.
   e. Fill the shape with Intense Effect – Gold, Accent 2, then apply the Preset 1 shape effect.
   f. Change the shape of the object to Explosion: 8 Points (Stars and Banners section).
   g. Apply square text wrapping, then position the shape so it aligns with the right margin and the first line of body text under the Five-step...heading. (*Hint*: Make sure the shape is under the border.)
   h. Draw a rectangle shape over the numbered list, then resize it to **.5"** high and **.8"** wide.
   i. Select the explosion shape, then use the Format Painter to copy the format of the explosion shape to the rectangle shape.
   j. Change the shape of the rectangle to Star: 4 Points.
   k. Position the Star: 4 Points shape to the left of the tabbed text at the bottom of page 1, so that it aligns with the left margin, then save your changes.

10. **Arrange Graphic Objects**
    a. Select the Star: 4 Points shape, copy it, then paste two copies.
    b. Drag the two pasted copies of the star shape to a blank area of the page.
    c. Change the fill color of one star to be Red, Accent 3.
    d. Position the two stars so that they overlap each other slightly, then use the Bring Forward arrow to bring the gold star to the front.
    e. Select the two stars, use the Group arrow to group them into a single object.
    f. Position the grouped object in the bottom right of the page with square text wrapping.
    g. Select the single gold star on the left side of the page, rotate the shape 90 degrees to the left, then save your changes.

11. **Create SmartArt Graphics**
    a. Scroll the end of the document, click in the middle blank paragraph above the Last revised...shaded paragraph, then click the SmartArt button.
    b. Select Process in the list of SmartArt types, select the Accent Process style, then click Insert.
    c. Change the colors of the SmartArt object to the Colorful Range – Accent Colors 5 to 6 style.
    d. Enter text in the SmartArt object so that the process diagram appears as shown in FIGURE 3-33.
    e. Resize the SmartArt object to be **3.2"** high, then save your changes.
    f. Adjust the size or position of objects as needed to so that your document resembles the document shown in the figure. View your document in two-page view and compare it to the document shown in FIGURE 3-34.
    g. Save your changes to the document, submit it to your instructor, close the file, and then exit Word.

FIGURE 3-33

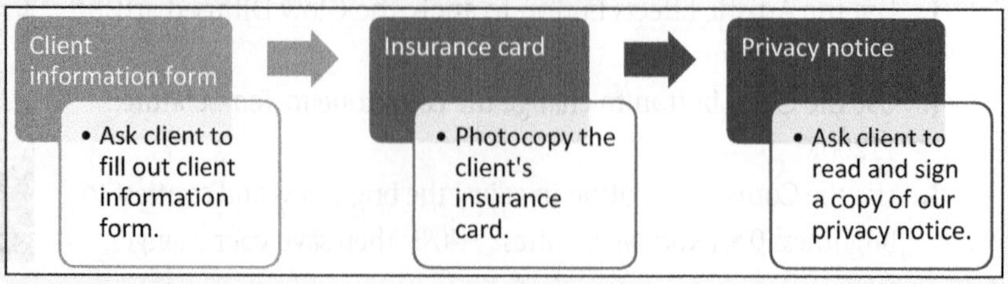

Skills Review (continued)

FIGURE 3-34

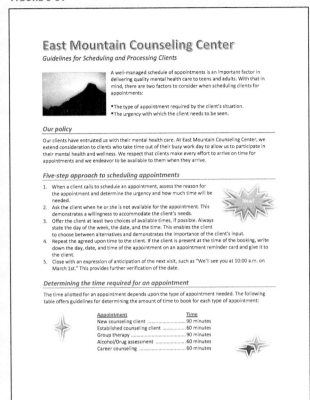

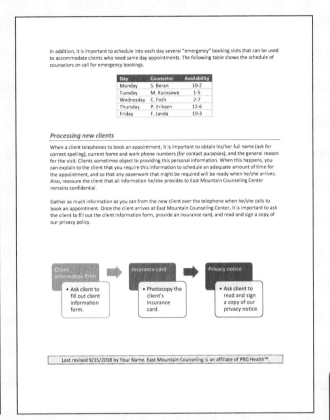

Independent Challenge 1

The Riverwalk Medical Clinic publishes a variety of helpful tips and information sheets related to health issues. Your colleague has assembled a "Fast Facts" sheet on Lyme disease and has asked you to format it so it highlights the important information regarding the disease. Design and formatting elements will make the document attractive to readers.

   a. Start Word, open the file IL_WD_3-3.docx from the drive and folder where you store your Data Files, save it as **IL_WD_3_FastFacts**, then read the document to get a basic understanding of its contents.

   b. Select the entire document, then change the font to 10-point Garamond.

   c. Change all four document margins to Narrow .5.

   d. Change the theme colors to Orange Red. (*Hint*: Use the Theme Colors button on the Design tab.)

   e. Change the font size of the first line, "Riverwalk Medical Clinic—Fast Facts", to 14.

   f. Change the font size of the second line, the title "Lyme Disease...", to 20.

   g. Change the font size of the heading "How ticks spread the disease" to 14, apply bold, then add a bottom border.

   h. Use the Format Painter to copy the format of the "How ticks spread the disease" heading to the following headings in the tip sheet: Tick habitat and distribution, Symptoms and signs, Treatment and prognosis, and Protection from tick bites.

   i. Insert an online picture that is a photograph. Select a photograph that is appropriate to the content. (*Hint*: Use the Filter link in the Online Pictures window to filter for photographs.)

   j. Remove the credit line box from the image, if necessary.

   k. Resize the image proportionally so that it is 2.5" wide, wrap text around the image, then position the photograph to the left of the "How ticks spread the disease" heading the page. FIGURE 3-35 shows a sample layout.

   l. Enhance the photograph with corrections, colors, artistic effects, borders, or styles.

Independent Challenge 1 (continued)

m. Using circle and cross shapes, create a medical symbol similar to the one shown in **FIGURE 3-35**. Apply red fill to the circle and white fill to the cross.

n. Use the adjustment handle to alter the shape of the cross if necessary. Group the two shapes in to a single object, then position the medical symbol graphic in the top-right corner on the first page.

o. Apply font colors to the document that work with the photograph you selected, then adjust the color and style of the borders as necessary.

FIGURE 3-35

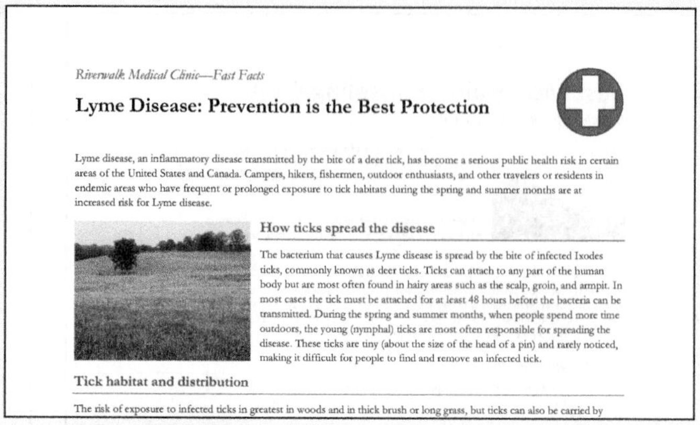

Riverwalk Medical Clinic—Fast Facts

Lyme Disease: Prevention is the Best Protection

Lyme disease, an inflammatory disease transmitted by the bite of a deer tick, has become a serious public health risk in certain areas of the United States and Canada. Campers, hikers, fishermen, outdoor enthusiasts, and other travelers or residents in endemic areas who have frequent or prolonged exposure to tick habitats during the spring and summer months are at increased risk for Lyme disease.

How ticks spread the disease

The bacterium that causes Lyme disease is spread by the bite of infected Ixodes ticks, commonly known as deer ticks. Ticks can attach to any part of the human body but are most often found in hairy areas such as the scalp, groin, and armpit. In most cases the tick must be attached for at least 48 hours before the bacteria can be transmitted. During the spring and summer months, when people spend more time outdoors, the young (nymphal) ticks are most often responsible for spreading the disease. These ticks are tiny (about the size of the head of a pin) and rarely noticed, making it difficult for people to find and remove an infected tick.

Tick habitat and distribution

The risk of exposure to infected ticks in greatest in woods and in thick brush or long grass, but ticks can also be carried by

p. Add your name to the footer, then examine the document carefully for formatting errors, and make any necessary adjustments. Adjust the size and placement of the photograph if necessary so that all the text fits on a single page.

q. Save the flyer, submit it to your instructor, then close the file and exit Word.

Independent Challenge 2

The business services firm where you work has been contracted by the city of Lincoln to redesign a report published by the Economic Development Authority. The client would like the report to include graphics, tables, and other elements that make the report visually interesting. The report must also be accessible to people who are visually impaired and using a screen reader. You design the report to highlight the important information, and add Alt Text so that readers of all abilities can access the content of the graphic images.

a. Start Word, open the file IL_WD_3-4.docx from the drive and folder where you store your Data Files, then save it as **IL_WD_3_Lincoln**.

b. Read the document to get a basic understanding of the contents, use CTRL+A to select all the text in the document, then clear all formatting from the text.

c. Determine the font and font sizes you will use for the body text, title, subtitle, and headings.

d. Select all the text again, change the style to No Spacing, then apply the font you intend to use for the body text to all the text in the report.

e. Format the title and subtitle using a font, font size, and font color of your choice.

f. Format the heading Mission using a font, font size, and font color of your choice, then, use the Format Painter to copy the formatting of the Mission heading to the Lincoln Advantage and Issues headings.

g. Format the subheading Services using a font, font size, and font color of your choice, then use the Format Painter to copy the formatting of the Services heading to the following headings: Project Finance, Real Estate Development, Business Loans, Technology/Innovation, Arts/Creativity, and Geography.

h. Scroll to the bottom of the document. Above the final paragraph, insert a table with two columns and three rows, then enter the following text.

Years	Population Growth
2020–2040	18%
2040–2060	32% (projected)

i. Autofit the table to the content, apply an appropriate table style to the table, adjust the formatting, then center the table between the margins.

Independent Challenge 2 (continued)

j. Scroll to the top of the document. Using shapes, create a graphic to illustrate the document. The graphic should be composed of two or more shapes. For example, you might draw city buildings, an abstract design, or something else you think will represent the content.

k. Format the shapes with fills, outlines, and effects. Use the adjustment and rotate handles to alter the shapes as necessary.

l. Position the shapes so that they overlap, use the Bring Forward and Send Backward buttons to adjust the layers, then group the shapes into a single object.

m. Resize the grouped object, wrap text around it, and position it in the document.

n. Create a SmartArt graphic similar to FIGURE 3-36. Use the Alternating Hexagons SmartArt style (List group), then format the SmartArt graphic using colors, styles, and effects.

o. Resize the SmartArt graphic and position it in the document.

p. Use the Multiple Pages button to view both pages of the document, then adjust the size and position of the graphics.

q. Select the shapes graphic you created in steps j–m, use the Alt Text button to open the Alt Text pane, then mark the shapes graphic as decorative.

r. Select the SmartArt graphic, then type a description of the SmartArt graphic in the Alt Text pane.

s. Use the Check for Issues button on the File tab to check the document for accessibility issues.

t. Add your name to the footer, save your changes to the document, submit it to your instructor, close the file, and then exit Word.

FIGURE 3-36

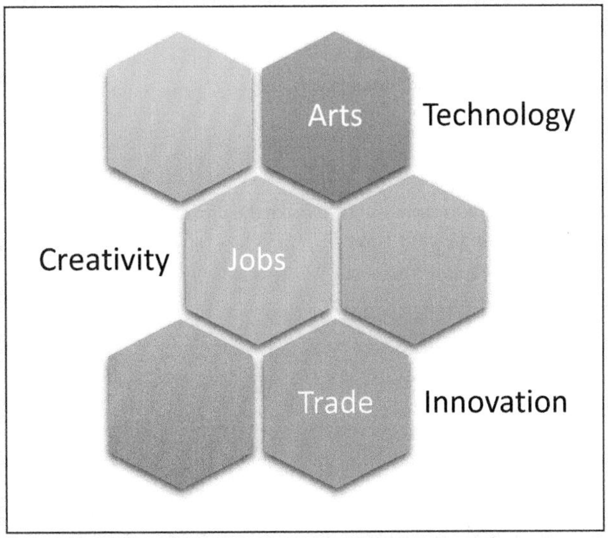

Visual Workshop

Open the file IL_WD_3-5.docx from the location where you store your Data Files, then save the document as **IL_WD_3_ClaimFlyer**. Create the one-page flyer shown in FIGURE 3-37. Use 12-point Calibri for the body text, 36-point Calibri for the title, 16-point Calibri for the subtitle, and 18-point Calibri for the headings. To create the SmartArt graphic object, use the Staggered Process style from the Process group. Add a registered trademark symbol ® after "Springfield" in each instance of "Springfield Mobile App". Add your name to the footer, then submit a copy of the flyer to your instructor.

FIGURE 3-37

Filing a claim

With Springfield Insurance Company

We're here to help you

Filing a claim is simple. Springfield Insurance is here to help you every step of the way. Our team will help to make your claims experience as simple and convenient as possible. With 24/7 claims support, we'll work to help you get back to normal quickly. You can file your claim online quickly and easily by logging in to My Account. Once you're logged in, you can start your claim and track its progress.

Start your claim using the Springfield® Mobile app.

More ways to file a claim

- Access 24/7 claims service by calling 1-800-555-0100.
- Start your claim using the Springfield® Mobile app.
- Report your claim by contacting your agent.

What to expect during the claims process

Knowing what to expect when you file a claim can help make the process easier to navigate. Most Springfield claims follow the same basic steps.

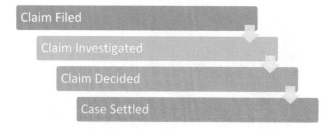

Staying organized can help you keep track of your claim. Write your claim number on important documents and use our claim worksheets to help you keep everything straight. When you have questions, contact your Springfield agent.

Agent: Your Name

Getting Started with Excel

CASE You have been hired as an assistant at JCL Talent, a company that provides recruitment services for employers and job seekers. You report to Dawn LaPointe, the director of technical careers. As Dawn's assistant, you create worksheets to analyze data from various company offices to help her make sound decisions on company expansion, investments, and new recruiting opportunities.

Module Objectives

After completing this module, you will be able to:

- Explore Excel
- Enter data
- Edit data
- Copy and move cell data
- Enter formulas and use AutoSum
- Copy formulas with relative cell references

- Copy formulas with absolute cell references
- Enter a formula with multiple operators
- Insert a function
- Switch worksheet views
- Choose print options

Files You Will Need

IL_EX_1-1.xlsx   IL_EX_1-4.xlsx
IL_EX_1-2.xlsx   IL_EX_1-5.xlsx
IL_EX_1-3.xlsx

Explore Excel

Learning
Outcomes
• Define key
  spreadsheet terms
• Open and save an
  Excel file
• Identify Excel
  window elements

Microsoft Excel is an **electronic spreadsheet program**, a computer program used to perform calculations and analyze and present numeric data. An Excel file, a **workbook**, is a collection of related worksheets contained within a single file with the file extension xlsx. A workbook is made up of one or more worksheets. A **worksheet** contains a grid of columns and rows where you can enter and manipulate data, perform calculations with data, and analyze data. **CASE** *You decide to review the distribution of technical postings in JCL's North American offices, to learn more about where and when these types of jobs have been posted.*

STEPS

1. **sam** ↓ Click the Start button ⊞ on the Windows taskbar, type Excel, click Excel, click Open, navigate to the location where you store your Data Files, click IL_EX_1-1.xlsx, then click Open

2. Click the File tab, click Save As on the navigation bar, click Browse, navigate to the location where you store your Data Files if necessary, type IL_EX_1_Postings in the File name box, then click Save

   Using FIGURE 1-1 as a guide, identify the following items:

   • The **Name box** is the box to the left of the formula bar that shows the cell reference or name of the active cell. "A1" appears in the Name box.
   • The **formula bar** is the area above the worksheet grid where you enter or edit data in the active cell.
   • The **worksheet window** is an area of the program window that displays part of the current worksheet, which can contain a total of 1,048,576 rows and 16,384 columns. The columns and rows intersect to form cells, where you can enter and manipulate text, numbers, formulas, or a combination of all three. Every cell has its own unique location or **cell address**, a cell's location, expressed by its column letter and row number such as A1.
   • The **cell pointer** is a dark rectangle that outlines the active cell in a worksheet. In the figure, the cell pointer outlines cell A1, so A1 is the active cell.
   • By default, a workbook file contains one worksheet named Sheet1—but you can have as many sheets as your computer's memory allows in a workbook. The New sheet button to the right of Sheet1 allows you to add worksheets to a workbook. **Sheet tab scrolling buttons** are triangles that let you navigate to additional sheet tabs when available; they're located to the left of the sheet tabs.
   • You can use the scroll bars to move around in a worksheet that is too large to fit on the screen at once.
   • The status bar provides a brief description of the active command or task in progress. The **mode indicator** on the left end of the status bar indicates the program's status, such as the Edit mode in Excel. You are in Edit mode any time you are entering or changing the contents of a cell. You can use the Zoom In and Zoom Out buttons in the status bar to increase or decrease the scale of the displayed worksheet.
   • You can use the **Tell me box** on the ribbon to find a command or access the Excel Help system.
   • The AutoSave button on the Quick Access Toolbar is on if you are working on a file saved on OneDrive. When AutoSave is on, your file will be automatically saved as you make changes.

3. **Click cell B4**

   Cell B4 becomes the active cell. To activate a different cell, you can click the cell or press the arrow keys on your keyboard to move to it.

4. **Click cell B4, drag ⊹ to cell B11, then release the mouse button**

   You selected a group of cells and they are highlighted, as shown in FIGURE 1-2. A series of two or more adjacent cells in a column, row, or rectangular group of cells, notated using the cell address of its upper-left and lower-right corners, such as B4:B11, is called a **range**; you select a range when you want to perform an action on a group of cells at once, such as moving them or formatting them.

FIGURE 1-1: **Open workbook**

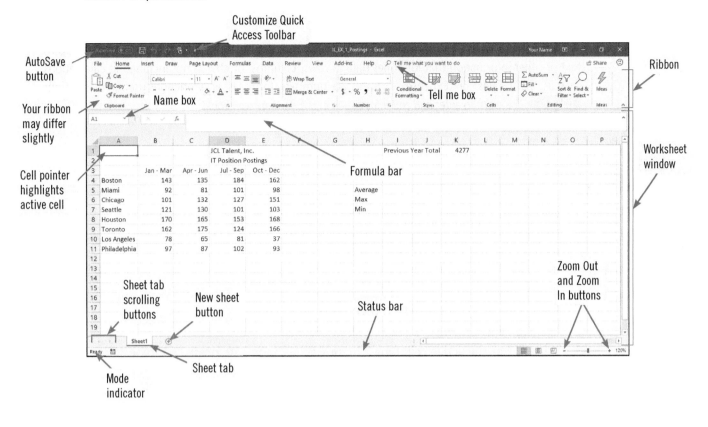

Customize Quick
Access Toolbar

AutoSave
button

Your ribbon
may differ
slightly

Name box

Cell pointer
highlights
active cell

Formula bar

Tell me box

Ribbon

Worksheet
window

Zoom Out
and Zoom
In buttons

Sheet tab
scrolling
buttons

New sheet
button

Status bar

Mode
indicator

Sheet tab

FIGURE 1-2: **Selected range**

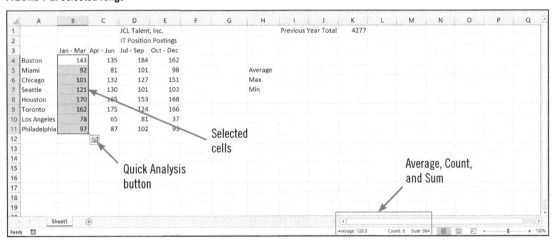

Selected
cells

Quick Analysis
button

Average, Count,
and Sum

Navigating a worksheet

With over a million cells available in a worksheet, it is important to know how to move around in, or navigate, a worksheet. You can use the arrow keys on the keyboard ↑, ↓, →, or ← to move one cell at a time, or press PAGE UP or PAGE DOWN to move one screen at a time. To move one screen to the left, press ALT+PAGE UP; to move one screen to the right, press ALT+PAGE DOWN.

You can also use the mouse pointer to click the desired cell. If the desired cell is not visible in the worksheet window, use the scroll bars or use the Go To command by clicking the Find & Select button in the Editing group on the Home tab on the ribbon. To quickly jump to the first cell in a worksheet, press CTRL+HOME; to jump to the last cell, press CTRL+END.

Excel

Enter Data

To enter content in a cell, you can type in the formula bar or directly in the cell itself. **Labels** are descriptive text or other information that identifies data in rows, columns, or charts, not included in calculations, such as "2021 Sales" or "Expenses". **Values** are numbers, formulas, and functions used in calculations.

CASE ▸ *You want to enter and edit information in the Postings workbook.*

STEPS

1. **Click cell F3, type Total, then click the Enter button ✓ on the formula bar**

   Clicking the Enter button accepts the entry without moving the cell pointer to a new location. The new text is left-aligned in the cell because labels are left-aligned by default. Excel recognizes an entry as a value if it is a number or it begins with one of these symbols: +, –, =, @, #, or $. When a cell contains both text and numbers, Excel recognizes it as a label.

2. **Click cell A12, type Vancouver, then press TAB**

   Pressing TAB accepts the entry and moves the active cell to the right, to cell B12.

3. **With B12 as the active cell, type 120, press TAB, type 130, press TAB, type 117, press TAB, type 130, then press TAB**

   The quarterly data is displayed for the Vancouver office, as shown in FIGURE 1-3. The numbers are right-aligned because values are right-aligned by default. You want to replace the monthly labels in row 3 with quarter labels.

4. **Click cell B3, then press DEL**

   You can delete each cell entry individually or delete a range of cells.

5. **Click cell C3, press and hold the mouse button, drag ✛ to cell E3, release the mouse button, then press DEL**

6. **Click cell B3, type Quarter 1, then click ✓ on the formula bar**

   You could continue to type quarter labels into columns C, D, and E, but it is easier to use Auto Fill to enter these labels. **Auto Fill** lets you drag a fill handle to copy a cell's contents or continue a selected series into adjacent cells.

7. **Click cell B3, position the pointer on the lower-right corner of the cell (the fill handle) so that the pointer changes to ✛, drag ✛ to cell E3, then release the mouse button**

   Dragging the fill handle across a range of cells copies the contents of the first cell into the other cells in the range or completes a data series. In this case, since Excel detected a data pattern in the selected cells, it filled the remaining selected cells with a series of annual quarters.

8. **Click the Auto Fill Options button ▦**

   Options for filling the selected range include Fill Series, which is selected, as shown in FIGURE 1-4. The other available options allow you to change to copying cells, fill the cells with formatting only, or fill the cells without formatting.

9. **Save your work**

FIGURE 1-3: Vancouver data entered

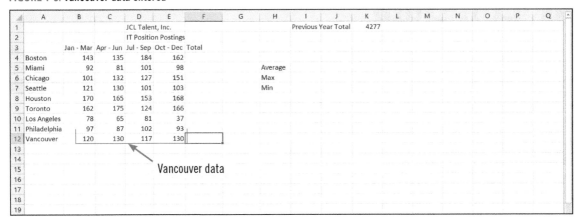

FIGURE 1-4: Auto Fill options

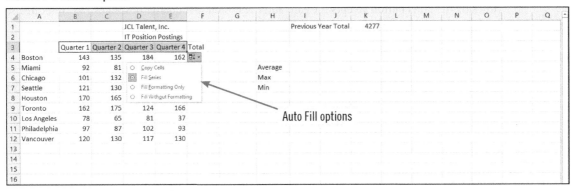

Inserting and deleting selected cells

As you add formulas to your workbook, you may need to insert or delete cells. To insert cells, click the Insert arrow in the Cells group on the Home tab, then click Insert Cells. The Insert dialog box opens, asking if you want to insert a cell and move the current active cell down or to the right of the new one. To delete one or more selected cells, click the Delete arrow in the Cells group, click Delete Cells, and in the Delete dialog box, indicate which way you want to move the adjacent cells. When using this option, be careful not to disturb row or column alignment that may be necessary to maintain the accuracy of cell references on the worksheet. You can also click the Insert button or Delete button in the Cells group to insert or delete a single cell. Excel automatically adjusts cell references within the formulas of any moved cells to reflect their new locations.

Using Auto Fill and Flash Fill

Auto Fill is an Excel feature that lets you drag a fill handle to copy a cell's contents or continue a series into adjacent cells. This can be used to enter the months of the year, days of the week, and custom lists of a series. Flash Fill, although similar to Auto Fill, isn't used to fill in a series of data. It is an Excel feature that looks for patterns in the data you enter and automatically fills or formats data in remaining cells based on those patterns. The filled data must be adjacent to the example data. Flash Fill often detects the pattern as you enter data and shows the new data in a light font. Pressing ENTER accepts the suggestion and enters the data. If Excel doesn't detect a pattern automatically, you can click the Flash Fill button in the Data Tools group on the Data tab to fill in the data.

Edit Data

Learning Outcomes
• Edit cell entries in the formula bar
• Edit cell entries in the cell

You can change, or edit, the contents of an active cell at any time. To do so, double-click the cell, and then click in the formula bar or just start typing. Excel switches to Edit mode when you are making cell entries. Different pointers, shown in TABLE 1-1, guide you through the editing process. **CASE** *You noticed some errors on the worksheet and want to make corrections.*

STEPS

QUICK TIP

On some keyboards, you might need to press F-LOCK to enable the function keys.

1. **Click cell B4, then click to the left of 4 in the formula bar**

   As soon as you click in the formula bar, a blinking vertical line called the **insertion point** appears on the formula bar at the location where new text will be inserted. See FIGURE 1-5.

2. **Press DEL, type 3, then click the Enter button ☑ on the formula bar**

   Clicking the Enter button accepts the edit, and the Boston first quarter posting is 133. You can also press ENTER to accept an edit. Pressing ENTER to accept an edit moves the cell pointer down one cell.

3. **Click cell B6, then press F2**

   Excel switches to Edit mode, and the insertion point blinks in the cell. Pressing F2 activates the cell for editing directly in the cell instead of the formula bar. Whether you edit in the cell or the formula bar is simply a matter of preference; the results on the worksheet are the same.

QUICK TIP

If you notice a mistake *after* confirming a cell entry, click the Undo button ↺ on the Quick Access toolbar. The Undo button allows you to reverse up to 100 previous actions, one at a time. If you mistakenly undo an action, you can click the Redo button ↻ on the Quick Access toolbar.

4. **Press BACKSPACE, type 9, then press ENTER**

   The value in the cell changes from 101 to 109, and cell B7 becomes the active cell.

5. **Click cell H6, then double-click the word Max in the formula bar**

   Double-clicking a word in a cell selects it. When you selected the word, the Mini toolbar automatically opened.

6. **Type Maximum, then press ENTER**

   When text is selected, typing deletes it and replaces it with the new text.

7. **Double-click cell H7, click to the right of n, type imum, then click ☑**

   Double-clicking a cell activates it for editing directly in the cell. Compare your screen to FIGURE 1-6.

8. **Save your work**

Recovering unsaved changes to a workbook file

You can use Excel's AutoRecover feature to automatically save (Autosave) your work as often as you want. This means that if you suddenly lose power or if Excel closes unexpectedly while you're working, you can recover all or some of the changes you made since you saved it last. (Of course, this is no substitute for regularly saving your work; it's just added insurance.) To customize the AutoRecover settings, click the File tab, click Options, then click Save. AutoRecover lets you decide how often and into which location it should Autosave files. When you restart Excel after losing power, you will see a new section, Recovered files, above the listing of recent files. You can click Show Recovered Files to access the saved and Autosaved versions of files that were open when Excel closed.

FIGURE 1-5: Worksheet in Edit mode

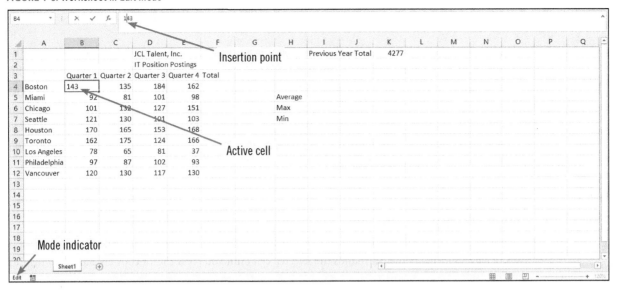

FIGURE 1-6: Edited worksheet

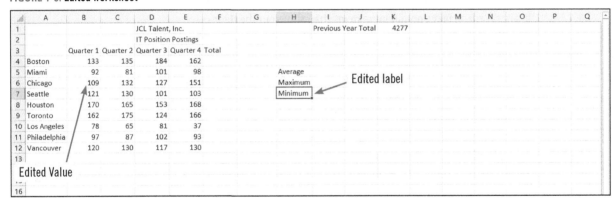

TABLE 1-1: Common pointers in Excel

name	pointer	use to	visible over the
Normal	✛	Select a cell or range; indicates Ready mode	Active worksheet
Fill handle	✚	Copy cell contents or series to adjacent cells	Lower-right corner of the active cell or range
I-beam	I	Edit cell contents in active cell or formula bar	Active cell in Edit mode or over the formula bar
Move	⁺↖	Change the location of the selected cell(s)	Perimeter of the active cell(s)
Copy	↖⁺	Create a duplicate of the selected cell(s)	Perimeter of the active cell(s) when CTRL is pressed
Column resize	↔	Change the width of a column	Border between column heading indicators

Excel

Copy and Move Cell Data

Learning Outcomes
• Copy cell data to the Clipboard
• Paste a Clipboard entry
• Move a range

You can copy or move the contents in cells and ranges from one location to another using several methods, including the Cut, Copy, and Paste buttons on the Home tab on the ribbon, the fill handle of the active cell or range, or the drag-and-drop feature. When you copy cells, the original data remains in its original location; when you cut or move cells, the original data is deleted from its original location. You can copy and move cells or ranges within a worksheet or from one worksheet to another. **CASE** *You want to show totals and statistical information for each quarter in your worksheet, so you decide to copy and move selected cells to speed up your task.*

STEPS

1. **Click cell F3, then click the Copy button 🗐 in the Clipboard group on the Home tab**

   The cell data is copied to the **Clipboard**, a temporary Windows storage area that holds the selections you copy or cut. A moving border surrounds the selected cell until you press ESC or copy an additional item to the Clipboard.

2. **Click the dialog box launcher 🖻 in the Clipboard group**

   The Office Clipboard opens in the Clipboard task pane, as shown in FIGURE 1-7. When you copy or cut an item, it is cut or copied both to the Clipboard provided by Windows and to the Office Clipboard. The Office Clipboard can hold up to 24 of the most recently cut or copied items from any Office program. Your Clipboard task pane may contain more items than shown in the figure.

3. **Click cell A13, then click the Paste button 🖺 in the Clipboard group**

   A copy of the contents of cell F3 is pasted into cell A13. Notice that the information you copied remains in the original cell F3; if you had cut instead of copied, the information would have been deleted from its original location once it was pasted. You can also paste an item by clicking it in the Office Clipboard.

4. **Click the Paste Options button 🖺 (Ctrl) ▾**

   The Paste Options open, as shown in FIGURE 1-8. These options allow you to determine what you want pasted and how you want the pasted data to appear on the worksheet. Review the three categories, Paste, Paste Values, and Other Paste Options. The current pasted data doesn't need any change in formatting.

5. **Press ESC twice, then click the Close button ⊠ on the Clipboard task pane**

6. **Select the range H5:H7, point to any edge of the selected range until the pointer changes to ⬉, drag the range to cell A15, then release the mouse button**

   The move pointer displays an outline of the range you are dragging. When you release the mouse button, you "drop" the selection to the range A15:A17. When pasting an item from the Clipboard, you only need to specify the upper-left cell of the range where you want to paste the selection. If you press and hold CTRL while dragging and dropping, the information is copied instead of moved.

Getting Started with Excel

FIGURE 1-7: Copied data in Office Clipboard

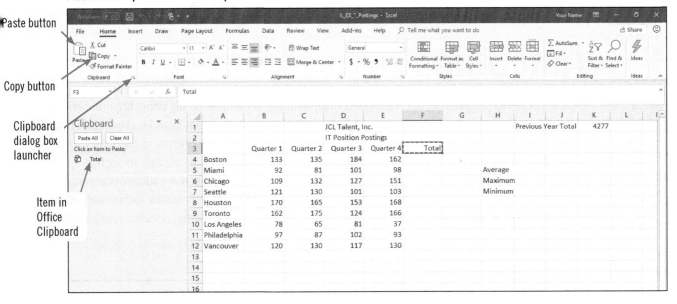

Paste button

Copy button

Clipboard dialog box launcher

Item in Office Clipboard

FIGURE 1-8: Paste options

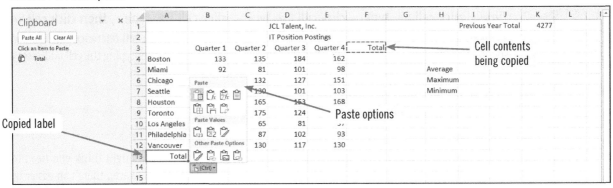

Cell contents being copied

Copied label

Paste options

Using Paste Options and Paste Preview

You can selectively paste copied or cut formulas, values, or other data by using the Paste Options button that opens on the worksheet after you paste data or the Paste arrow in the Clipboard. The Paste Preview feature shows how the current selection will look when pasted. When you click the Paste Options button (or simply press [Ctrl] or the Paste arrow, a gallery of paste option icons opens, organized by category. The Paste category includes pasting formulas, pasting formulas and number formatting, pasting using the source formatting, pasting with no borders (to remove any borders around pasted cells), pasting with the source

column widths, and pasting transposed data so that column data appears in rows and row data appears in columns. The Paste Values category includes pasting values only (without formatting), pasting values and number formatting, and pasting values with source formatting. The Other Paste Options category includes pasting formatting, links, pictures, and linked pictures. Clicking Paste Link in this category creates a link to the source data so that in the future, changes to the copied data update the pasted data. Clicking Picture in this category pastes the data as a picture where the picture tools can be used to format it, resize it, or move it.

Enter Formulas and Use AutoSum

Learning
Outcomes
• Use cell references
  to create a formula
• Build formulas
  with the AutoSum
  button

Excel is a powerful program because cells can contain formulas rather than simply values like numbers and text. A **formula** is a mathematical statement that calculates a value. Formulas in an Excel worksheet start with the equal sign (=), also called the **formula prefix**, followed by cell addresses, range names, values, and **arithmetic operators**, which are symbols that perform mathematical calculations such as +, −, *, and /. See TABLE 1-2 for a list of commonly used arithmetic operators. Formulas are automatically recalculated when worksheet data changes. For this reason, use cell references in formulas, rather than values, whenever possible. **CASE** *You want to create formulas in the worksheet that calculate yearly totals for each location.*

STEPS

1. **Click cell F4**

   This is the first cell where you want to insert a formula. To calculate the yearly total for the Boston location, you need to add the quarterly totals.

2. **Type =, click cell B4, type +, click cell C4, type +, click cell D4, type +, then click cell E4**

   Compare your formula bar to FIGURE 1-9. The blue, red, purple, and green cell references in cell F4 correspond to the color of the cells. When entering a formula, clicking cells rather typing the cell addresses helps avoid typing errors.

3. **Click the Enter button ✓ on the formula bar**

   The result of the formula =B4+C4+D4+E4, 614, appears in cell F4.

4. **Click cell B13**

   You want this cell to total first quarter positions for all the locations. You might think you need to create a formula that looks like this: =B4+B5+B6+B7+B8+B9+B10+B11+B12. However, there's an easier way to achieve this result.

5. **On the ribbon, click the AutoSum button Σ in the Editing group on the Home tab**

   The SUM function is inserted in the cell, and a suggested range appears in parentheses. A **function** is a predefined procedure that returns a value; it includes the **arguments** (the information necessary to calculate an answer) as well as cell references and other unique information. Clicking the AutoSum button sums the adjacent range (that is, the cells next to the active cell) above or to the left, although you can adjust the range if necessary by selecting a different range before accepting the cell entry. Using the SUM function is quicker than entering a formula, and using the range B4:B12 is more efficient than entering individual cell references.

6. **Click ✓ on the formula bar**

   Excel calculates the total contained in cells B4:B12 and displays the result, 1082, in cell B13. The cell actually contains the formula =SUM(B4:B12), but it displays the result. Compare your screen to FIGURE 1-10.

7. **Save your work**

FIGURE 1-9: Entering a formula

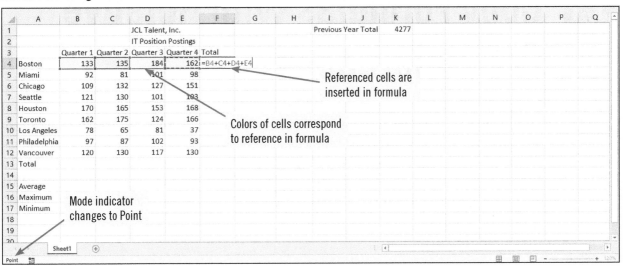

FIGURE 1-10: SUM function in a worksheet

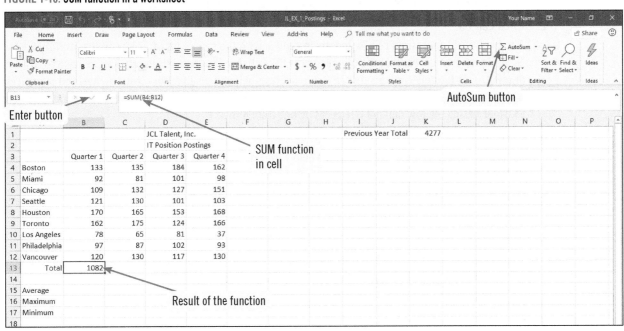

TABLE 1-2: Excel arithmetic operators

operator	purpose	example
+	Addition	=A5+A7
–	Subtraction or negation	=A5–10
*	Multiplication	=A5*A7
/	Division	=A5/A7
%	Percent	=35%
^ (caret)	Exponent	=6^2 (same as 6^2)

Copy Formulas with Relative Cell References

Learning Outcomes
- Copy formulas with relative cell references
- Use the fill handle to copy formulas

As you work in Excel, you may want to reuse formulas by copying them. When you copy formulas, Excel automatically adjusts any cell addresses in the formula so they remain consistent relative to the formula's new location. For example, if you copy a formula containing a cell reference down a column, the row number in each copied formula increases by one. This type of cell reference in a formula is called a **relative cell reference**, because it changes to reflect the new formula's new location; it's the default type of addressing used in Excel worksheets. **CASE** ▶ *You want to reuse a formula you created, so you will copy it to other cells.*

STEPS

1. **Click cell F4, then drag the fill handle down to cell F12**

   The formula for calculating the total for all four quarters is copied into the range F5:F12.

2. **Click cell F5**

   A copy of the formula from cell F4 appears in cell F5, with the new result of 372, as shown in **FIGURE 1-11**. Notice in the formula bar that the cell references have changed so that cells in row 5 are referenced instead of row 4. This formula contains relative cell references, which tells Excel to substitute new cell references within the copied formulas as necessary. In this case, Excel adjusted the cell references in the formula in cell F5 by increasing the row number references by one from 4 to 5.

3. **Click cell F6**

   Because the location of this cell is two rows below the original formula, Excel adjusted the cell references in the copied formula by increasing the row number references by two from 4 to 6.

4. **Click cell B13, then drag the fill handle to the right to cell F13**

   A formula similar to the one in cell B13 now appears in the range C13:F13.

5. **Click cell C13**

   In copying the formula one cell to the right, the cell references in the formula bar are adjusted by increasing the column letter references by one from B to C. Compare your worksheet to **FIGURE 1-12**.

6. **Save your work**

FIGURE 1-11: Formula copied using the fill handle

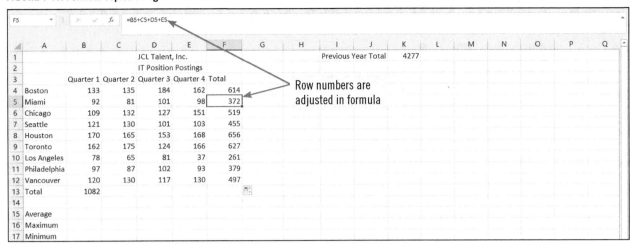

FIGURE 1-12: Formula column references changed

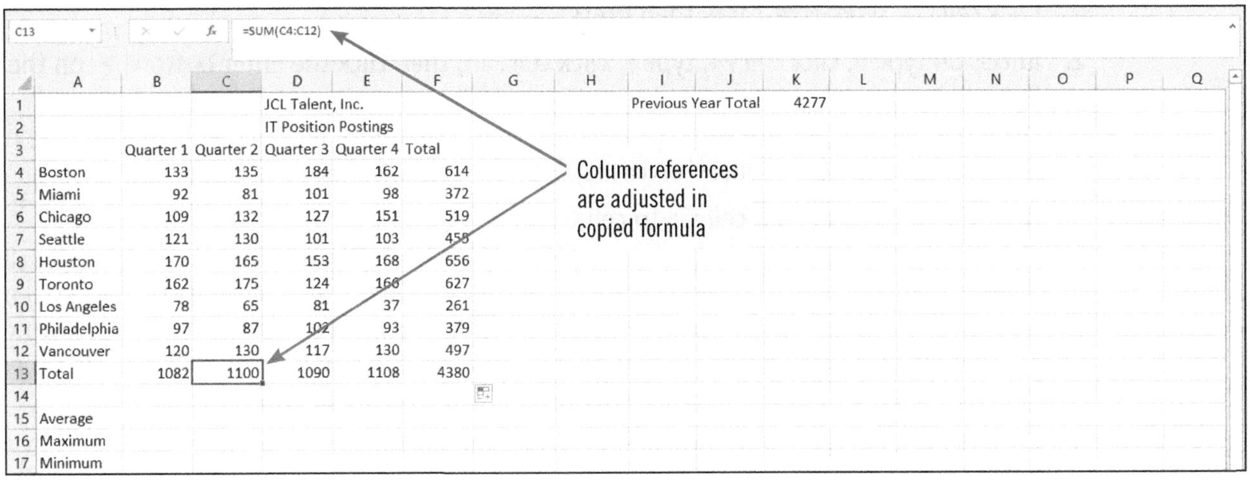

Inserting functions into formulas

You can insert a function on its own or as part of another formula. For example, you have used the SUM function on its own to add a range of cells—for example, =SUM(B5:B9). You could also use the SUM function within a formula that adds a range of cells and then multiplies the total by a decimal—for example, =SUM(B5:B9)*.5.

Excel

Learning
Outcomes
• Create an absolute
  cell reference
• Use the fill handle
  to copy absolute
  cell references

Copy Formulas with Absolute Cell References

When copying formulas, you might want one or more of the cell references in the formula to remain unchanged. For example, you might have a price in a specific cell that you want to use in all the copied formulas, regardless of their location. If you use relative cell referencing, the formula results would be incorrect, because the formula would reference a different cell every time you copy it. In this situation, you need to use an **absolute cell reference**, which refers to a specific cell and does not change when you copy the formula. Absolute cell references display a dollar sign ($) before the column letter and row number of the address (for example, $A$1). You can either type the dollar sign when typing the cell address in a formula, or you can select a cell address on the formula bar and then press F4, and the dollar signs are added automatically. When copying a formula, absolute cell references remain fixed in the copied formulas. **CASE** *You decide to calculate each location's percentage of the total postings.*

STEPS

1. **Click cell G3, type % of Total, then press ENTER**

2. **In cell G4 type =, click cell F4, type /, click cell F13, then click the Enter button ✓ on the formula bar**

   The result, 14.02%, appears in cell G4. This value represents the total positions for Boston (in cell F4) divided by the total for all locations (in cell F13). You want to calculate this percentage for each location.

   QUICK TIP

   Before you copy or move a formula, always check to see if you need to use an absolute cell reference.

3. **Drag the fill handle from cell G4 to cell G12**

   The resulting values in the range G5:G12 are the error messages #DIV/0!. Because you used relative cell addressing in the formula in cell G4, the copied formula adjusted so that the formula in cell G5 is =F5/F14; because there is no value in cell F14, the result is a division by 0 error. You need to use an absolute reference for cell F13 in the formula to keep the denominator from adjusting in a relative way as the formula is copied. That way, the denominator will always reference the total for all locations in cell F13.

   QUICK TIP

   When changing a cell reference to an absolute reference, make sure the reference is selected or the insertion point is to the left of the reference you want to change before pressing F4.

4. **Click cell G4, press F2 to change to Edit mode, then press F4**

   When you press F2, the range finder outlines the arguments of the equation in blue and red. The insertion point appears next to the F13 cell reference in cell G4. When you press F4, dollar signs are inserted in the F13 cell reference, making it an absolute reference. See **FIGURE 1-13**.

5. **Click ✓, then drag the fill handle from cell G4 to cell G12**

   Because the formula correctly contains an absolute cell reference, the correct percentage values appear for each location in cells G5:G12. Compare your worksheet to **FIGURE 1-14**.

6. **Save your work**

FIGURE 1-13: **Absolute reference created in formula**

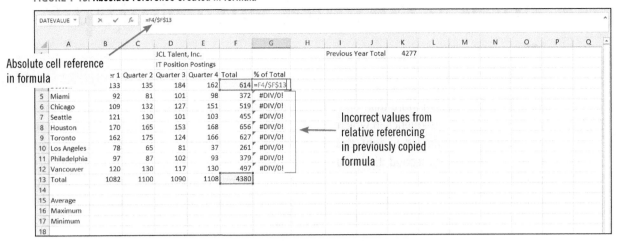

Absolute cell reference
in formula

FIGURE 1-14: **Correct percentages calculated**

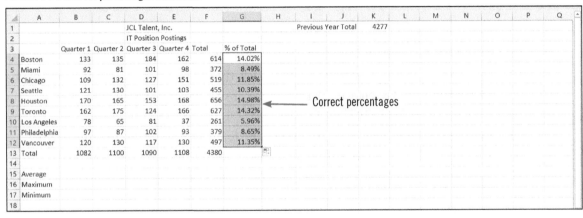

Using a mixed reference

Sometimes when you copy a formula, you want to change the row reference, but keep the column reference the same. This type of cell referencing, where one factor remains constant and the other one varies, is a **mixed reference**. For example, when copied, a formula containing the mixed reference C$14 would change the column letter relative to its new location, but not the row number. In the mixed reference $C14, the column letter would not change, but the row number would be updated relative to its location. Like an absolute reference, a mixed reference can be created by pressing F4 with the cell reference selected. With each press of the F4 key, you cycle through all the possible combinations of relative, absolute, and mixed references (C14, $C$14, C$14, and $C14).

Enter a Formula with Multiple Operators

Learning Outcomes
- Understand the order of operations
- Create a formula with multiple operators

Formulas often contain more than one arithmetic operator. In these formulas, Excel follows the **order of operations**, the sequence in which operators are applied in a mathematical calculation. Instead of calculating simply from left to right, this order calls for calculations in parentheses to be performed first, exponent calculations second, then multiplication and division, and finally addition and subtraction. If there are multiple occurrences of an operation, such as two multiplication operations, they are calculated from left to right. If your formula requires addition or subtraction to be calculated before multiplication or division, you can change the calculation order using parentheses around the addition or subtraction. For example, the formula to average the numbers 100, 200, and 300 is (100+200+300)/3 to make sure the numbers are totaled before the division operation. TABLE 1-3 shows more examples of how calculations are performed in Excel. **CASE** *You need to analyze the percentage increase of this year's total for the North American locations from last year's total.*

STEPS

1. **Click cell J3, type This Year, then click the Enter button ✓ on the formula bar**

   You will enter this year's total using the calculation in cell F13.

2. **Click cell K3, type =, click cell F13, then click the Enter button ✓ on the formula bar**

   The value in cell F13 is copied to cell K3. You entered a cell reference rather than the value, so if any worksheet data is edited you won't have to reenter this total.

3. **Click cell J5, type % Increase, then click the Enter button ✓ on the formula bar**

   You want the formula to calculate the percentage increase of this year's total postings over last year. Percentage increase is calculated by subtracting the old value from the new value and dividing that difference by the old value, or (new − old)/old.

4. **Click cell K5, type =, type (, click cell K3, type -, click cell K1, then type)**

   In this first part of the formula, you are finding the difference in totals between this year and last year. You enclosed this calculation with parentheses so it will be performed before any other calculations, because calculations in parentheses are always calculated first. Compare your screen to FIGURE 1-15.

5. **Type /, click cell K1, then click the Enter button ✓ on the formula bar**

   The second part of this formula divides the difference in yearly totals by the total for the previous year to find the percentage of the growth. Because you enclosed the subtraction calculation in parentheses, it was calculated before the division calculation. The value in cell K5 is in decimal format. You want to display this value as a percentage with two decimal places.

6. **Click the Percent Style button % in the Number group on the Home tab, then click the Increase Decimal button in the Number group twice**

   The percentage increase in cell K5 is 2.41%, as shown in FIGURE 1-16.

7. **Save your work**

FIGURE 1-15: Formula with parentheses

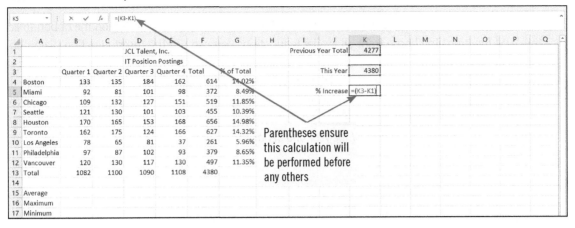

Parentheses ensure
this calculation will
be performed before
any others

FIGURE 1-16: Formula with percentage increase

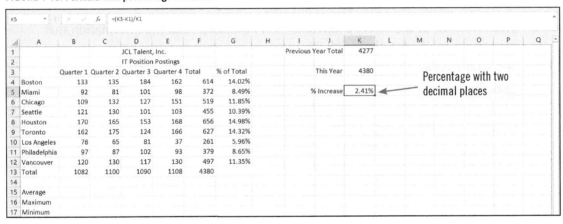

Percentage with two
decimal places

TABLE 1-3: Calculation results in Excel formulas

formula	result
10+20+40/2	50
(10+20+40)/2	35
10+5*2	20
(10+5)*2	30
20–10/2	15
(20–10)/2	5

Excel

Insert a Function

Learning Outcomes
- Use the Insert Function button
- Select a range for use in a function
- Insert a function by typing
- Use AutoComplete to enter formulas

You can insert functions in several ways. So far, you have used the AutoSum button on the ribbon to add the SUM function. To choose from all available functions you can use the Insert Function dialog box. This is especially valuable if you're not sure of the name of the function you need, because functions are organized into categories, such as Financial, Date & Time, and Statistical, and you are guided through the process. Other ways to insert a function include manually typing it in a cell and using the AutoSum arrow to insert commonly used functions. **CASE** *You need to calculate the average, maximum, and minimum location postings for the first quarter of the year and decide to use functions to do so.*

STEPS

1. **Click cell B15, then click the** Insert Function button *fx* **on the formula bar**

   An equal sign (=) is inserted in the active cell, and the Insert Function dialog box opens, as shown in FIGURE 1-17. In this dialog box, you specify the function you want to use by clicking it in the Select a function list of recently used functions, clicking the Or select a category arrow to choose a desired function category, or typing the function name, or its description, in the Search for a function field.

2. **Click** AVERAGE **in the Select a function list if necessary, read the information that appears under the list, then click** OK

   The Function Arguments dialog box opens, as shown in FIGURE 1-18.

3. **Click the** Collapse button ▲ **in the Number1 field of the Function Arguments dialog box, select the range B4:B12 on the worksheet, then click the** Expand button 🔽 **in the Function Arguments dialog box**

   Clicking the Collapse button minimizes the dialog box so that you can select cells on the worksheet. When you click the Expand button, the dialog box is restored. You can also begin dragging on the worksheet to automatically minimize the dialog box; after you select the desired range, the dialog box is restored.

4. **Click** OK

   The Function Arguments dialog box closes, and the calculated value is displayed in cell B15. The average postings per location for Quarter 1 is 120.222.

5. **Click cell B16, type =, then type m**

   Because you are manually typing this function, you must manually type the opening equal sign (=). Once you type an equal sign in a cell, each letter you type acts as a trigger to activate the Excel **Formula Auto-Complete**, a feature that automatically suggests text, numbers, or dates to insert based on previous entries. Because you entered the letter *m*, this feature suggests a list of function names beginning with "M."

6. **Double-click** MAX **in the list, select the range B4:B12, then click the** Enter button ✓ **on the formula bar**

   The result, 170, appears in cell B16. When you completed the entry, the closing parenthesis was automatically added to the formula.

7. **Click cell B17, type =, type m, double-click** MIN **in the list of function names, select the range B4:B12, then press** ENTER

   The result, 78, appears in cell B17.

8. **Select the range B15:B17, drag the** fill handle **to the range C15:E17, then save your work**

   The average, maximum, and minimum values for all the quarters appear in the selected range, as shown in FIGURE 1-19.

FIGURE 1-17: Insert Function dialog box

Search for a
function field

Your list of
recently used
functions may
differ

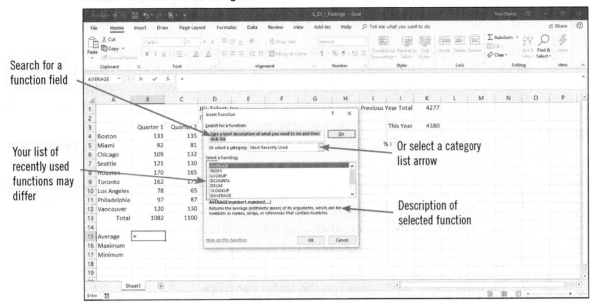

Or select a category
list arrow

Description of
selected function

FIGURE 1-18: Function Arguments dialog box

Insert Function
button

Argument

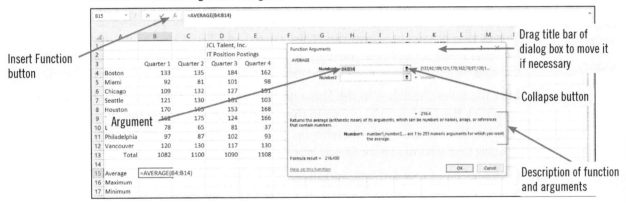

Drag title bar of
dialog box to move it
if necessary

Collapse button

Description of function
and arguments

FIGURE 1-19: Completed AVERAGE, MAX, and MIN functions

	A	B	C	D	E	F	G	H	I	J	K	L	M	N	O	P
1				JCL Talent, Inc.					Previous Year Total		4277					
2				IT Position Postings												
3		Quarter 1	Quarter 2	Quarter 3	Quarter 4	Total	% of Total		This Year		4380					
4	Boston	133	135	184	162	614	14.02%									
5	Miami	92	81	101	98	372	8.49%		% Increase		2.41%					
6	Chicago	109	132	127	151	519	11.85%									
7	Seattle	121	130	101	103	455	10.39%									
8	Houston	170	165	153	168	656	14.98%									
9	Toronto	162	175	124	166	627	14.32%									
10	Los Angeles	78	65	81	37	261	5.96%									
11	Philadelphia	97	87	102	93	379	8.65%									
12	Vancouver	120	130	117	130	497	11.35%									
13	Total	1082	1100	1090	1108	4380										
14																
15	Average	120.222	122.222	121.111	123.111											
16	Maximum	170	175	184	168											
17	Minimum	78	65	81	37											
18																

Excel

Switch Worksheet Views

You can change your view of the worksheet window at any time, using either the View tab on the ribbon or the View buttons on the status bar. Changing your view does not affect the contents of a worksheet; it just makes it easier for you to focus on different tasks, such as preparing a worksheet for printing. The View tab includes a variety of viewing options, such as View buttons, zoom controls, and the ability to show or hide worksheet elements such as gridlines. The status bar offers fewer View options but can be more convenient to use. **CASE** ▶ *You want to review your worksheet before sharing it with your colleagues.*

STEPS

1. **Click cell A1, verify that the zoom level in the Zoom area of the status bar is 120%, click the View tab on the ribbon, then click the 100% button in the Zoom group**

   The worksheet zooms to 100%. Another way to change the zoom level is to use the Zoom slider on the status bar.

2. **Click the Zoom in button ⊞ on the status bar twice**

   The worksheet zooms in 10% at a time, to 120%.

3. **Click the Page Layout button in the Workbook Views group on the View tab**

   The view switches from the default view, Normal, to Page Layout view. **Normal view** shows the worksheet without including certain features like headers and footers; it's ideal for creating and editing a worksheet but may not be detailed enough when you want to put the finishing touches on a document. **Page Layout view** provides an accurate view of how a worksheet will look when printed, including headers and footers, as shown in **FIGURE 1-20**. Above and to the left of the page are rulers. A page number indicator on the status bar tells you the current page and the total number of pages in this worksheet.

4. **Click the Ruler check box in the Show group on the View tab to remove the checkmark, then click the Gridlines check box in the Show group to remove the checkmark**

   Removing the checkmarks hides the rulers and gridlines. By default, gridlines in a worksheet do not print, so hiding them gives you a more accurate image of your final document.

5. **Click the Page Break Preview button ▦ on the status bar**

   Your view changes to Page Break Preview, which displays a reduced view of each page of your worksheet, along with page break indicators that you can drag to include more or less information on a page.

6. **Drag the pointer ↕ from the bottom page break indicator to the bottom of row 20, as shown in FIGURE 1-21**

   When you're working on a large worksheet with multiple pages, sometimes you need to adjust where pages break; in this worksheet, however, the information all fits comfortably on one page.

7. **Click the Page Layout button in the Workbook Views group, click the Ruler box in the Show group, then click the Gridlines box in the Show group**

   Adding checkmarks to the check boxes displays the rulers and gridlines. You can show or hide View tab items in any view.

8. **Click the Normal button in the Workbook Views group, then save your work**

FIGURE 1-20: **Page Layout view**

Turns ruler on/off

If header is added,
it appears here

Workbook
Views group

Turns
gridlines
on/off

Horizontal ruler

Add header

Vertical
ruler

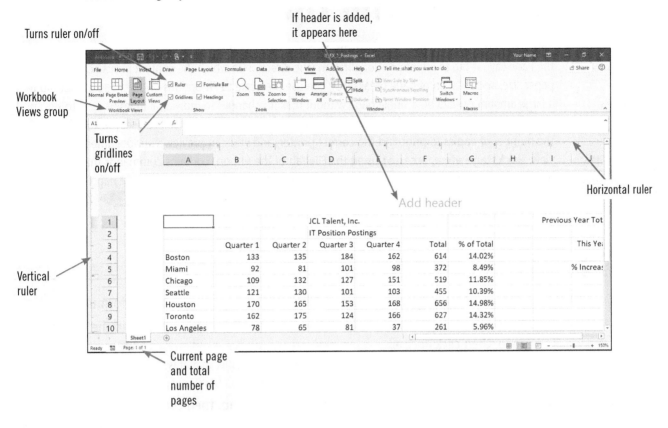

	Quarter 1	Quarter 2	Quarter 3	Quarter 4	Total	% of Total		
JCL Talent, Inc.							Previous Year Tot	
IT Position Postings								
Boston	133	135	184	162	614	14.02%	This Yea	
Miami	92	81	101	98	372	8.49%	% Increas	
Chicago	109	132	127	151	519	11.85%		
Seattle	121	130	101	103	455	10.39%		
Houston	170	165	153	168	656	14.98%		
Toronto	162	175	124	166	627	14.32%		
Los Angeles	78	65	81	37	261	5.96%		

Current page
and total
number of
pages

FIGURE 1-21: **Page Break Preview**

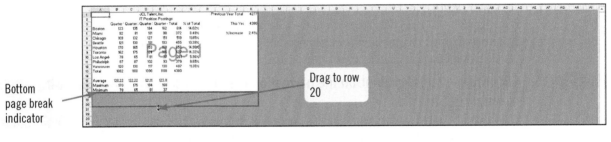

Drag to row
20

Bottom
page break
indicator

Getting Started with Excel

Choose Print Options

Learning Outcomes
- Change the page orientation
- Print gridlines
- Center a worksheet on a page
- Preview and print a worksheet

Before printing a document, you may want to make final adjustments to the output. You can use tools on the Page Layout tab to adjust print orientation (the direction in which the content prints across the page), paper size, and location of page breaks. You can use the Scale to Fit options on the Page Layout tab to fit a large amount of data on a single page without making changes to individual margins, and to turn gridlines and column/row headings on and off. When you are ready to print, you can set print options such as the number of copies to print and the correct printer, and you can preview your document in Backstage view. **Backstage view**, accessed using the File tab of the ribbon, contains commands that allow you to manage files and options for the program such as print settings. You can also adjust page layout settings in Backstage view and immediately see the results in the document preview. **CASE** *You are ready to prepare your worksheet for printing.*

STEPS

1. **Click cell A20, type your name, then click the Enter button ☑ on the formula bar**

2. **Click the Page Layout tab on the ribbon, click the Orientation button in the Page Setup group, then click Portrait**

   The orientation changes to **portrait**, so the printed page is taller than it is wide. You can see from the vertical dotted line, indicating a page break, that all columns don't fit on one page in this orientation.

3. **Click the Orientation button in the Page Setup group, then click Landscape**

   The paper orientation returns to **landscape**, so the printed page is wider than it is tall. Now all the content fits on one page.

4. **Click the Gridlines Print box in the Sheet Options group on the Page Layout tab, then save your work**

   Printing gridlines makes the data easier to read, but the gridlines will not print unless the Gridlines Print box is selected. You can also print row numbers and column letters by clicking the Headings Print box. If you don't want to print gridlines or headings, make sure these boxes are not selected.

5. **Click the File tab, click Print on the navigation bar, then select an active printer if necessary**

   The Print tab in Backstage view displays a preview of your worksheet exactly as it will look when it is printed. To the left of the preview, you can also change a number of document settings and print options. Compare your screen to FIGURE 1-22. You can print from this view by clicking Print, or you can return to the worksheet without printing by clicking the Back button ⊙.

6. **Click the Page Setup link in the Settings list, click the Margins tab in the Page Setup dialog box, click the Horizontally check box in the Center on page section, click the Vertically check box in the Center on page section, then compare your screen to FIGURE 1-23**

   The printed worksheet will be centered on the page.

7. **Click OK, then click Print**

   One copy of the worksheet prints.

8. **sam↟ Save your workbook, submit your work to your instructor as directed, click File, click Close, then click the Close button ▨ on the title bar**

FIGURE 1-22: **Worksheet in Backstage view**

Click to return
to worksheet

Click to change
number of
copies

Print button

Active printer;
yours will be
different

Click arrows or
enter values to
specify which
pages to print

Click to zoom
in or out on
the page

Click to
select scaling
options

Click to
change
paper size

Click to print
entire workbook
or selection

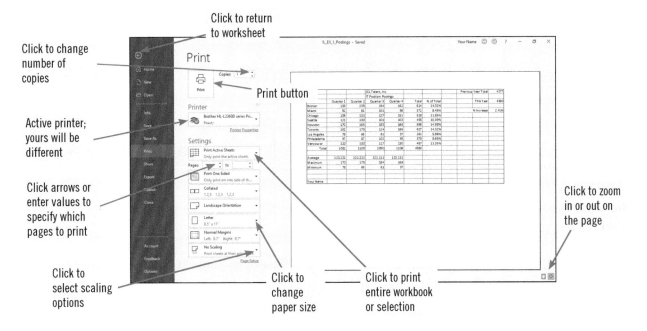

FIGURE 1-23: **Page Setup dialog box**

Margins tab

Click to center
on printed page

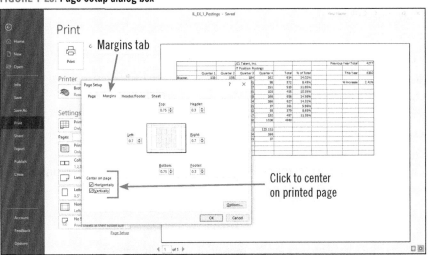

Excel

Setting a print area

If you want to print a selected worksheet area repeatedly, it's best to define a **print area**, so that the Quick Print feature prints only that portion of the worksheet area. To define a print area, select the range you want to print on the worksheet, click the Page Layout tab on the ribbon, click the Print Area button in the Page Setup group, then click Set Print Area. A print area can consist of one contiguous range of cells, or multiple ranges in different parts of a worksheet. To clear a print area, click the Page Layout tab on the ribbon, click the Print Area button in the Page Setup group, then click Clear Print Area.

Scaling to fit

If you have a large amount of data that you want to fit to a single sheet of paper, you can control how much of your work to print on a single sheet by clicking the No Scaling arrow in the Settings list in the Print screen in Backstage view, then clicking Fit Sheet on One Page, Fit All Columns on One Page, or Fit all Rows on One Page. Another method for fitting worksheet content onto one page is to click the Page Layout tab on the ribbon, then change the Width and Height settings in the Scale to Fit group to 1 page each. You can also click the Page Setup link in the Print screen in Backstage view, click the Page tab if necessary in the Page Setup dialog box, click the Fit to option button, then enter 1 in the page(s) wide by and tall fields.

Practice

Skills Review

1. Explore Excel.
a. Start Excel.
b. Open IL_EX_1-2.xlsx from the location where you store your Data Files, then save it as **IL_EX_1_Travel**.
c. Locate the Name box, formula bar, worksheet window, cell pointer, sheet tab scrolling buttons, mode indicator, and Tell me box.

2. Enter data.
a. Click cell B3, type **Jan**, then confirm the entry.
b. Click cell D7, type **202497**, then conform the entry.
c. Activate cell B3, then use Auto Fill to enter the months **Feb** and **Mar** in the range C3:D3.
d. Save your changes to the file.

3. Edit data.
a. Use F2 to correct the spelling of Maimi in cell A6 (the correct spelling is Miami).
b. Click cell C7, then use the formula bar to change the value to **188270**.
c. Click cell A17, then enter your name.
d. Save your changes.

4. Copy and move cell data.
a. Select the range G4:G6.
b. Copy the selection to the Clipboard.
c. Open the Clipboard task pane, then paste the selection to cell A10.
d. Delete the labels in the range G4:G6.
e. Close the Clipboard task pane, then activate cell A8.
f. Use the drag-and-drop method to copy the contents of cell A8 to cell E3. (*Hint*: Press and hold CTRL while dragging.)
g. Save your work.

5. Enter formulas and use AutoSum.
a. Activate cell E4, then enter a formula that adds cells B4, C4, and D4.
b. Use AutoSum to enter the total expenses for the month of January in cell B8.
c. Save your changes.

6. Copy formulas with relative cell references.
a. Activate cell E4, then use the fill handle to copy the formula in cell E4 to the range E5:E7.
b. Activate cell B8, then use the fill handle to copy the formula in cell B8 to the range C8:E8.
c. Save your work.

7. Copy formulas with absolute cell references.
a. Enter **% of Total** in cell F3.
b. In cell F4, create a formula that divides the value in cell E4 by the value in cell E8 using an absolute reference to cell E8.
c. Use the fill handle to copy the formula in cell F4 to the range F5:F7.
d. Save your work.

Skills Review (continued)

8. Enter a formula with multiple operators.

  a. Enter a formula in cell B10 that calculates the average travel expenses for the month of January. Use a formula that contains cell references and not a function. (*Hint*: The formula is =(B4+B5+B6+B7)/4.)

  b. Review the use of the parentheses in the formula.

  c. Save your work.

9. Insert a function.

  a. Use the Insert Function button to create a formula in cell B11 that calculates the maximum travel expense for January.

  b. In cell B12, enter a function to calculate the minimum travel expenses for January.

  c. Select the range B10:B12, then use the fill handle to copy the functions into the range C10:D12.

  d. Save your work.

10. Switch worksheet views.

  a. Click the View tab on the ribbon, then switch to Page Layout view.

  b. Verify that the Ruler and Gridlines check boxes contain checkmarks.

  c. Switch to Page Break view and adjust the page break so it comes at the bottom of row 20.

  d. Switch to Normal View, use a button in the Zoom group of the View tab to zoom the worksheet to 100%, then use the Zoom buttons in the Status bar to zoom the worksheet back to 120%.

  e. Save your changes.

11. Choose print options.

FIGURE 1-24

  a. Use the Page Layout tab to change the orientation to Portrait.

  b. Turn on gridlines for printing using a check box in the Sheet Options group of the Page Layout tab.

  c. Preview the worksheet in Backstage view, then use the Page Setup dialog box to center the worksheet vertically and horizontally on the page. (*Hint*: The commands are located on the Margins tab.) Compare your screen to FIGURE 1-24.

  d. Save your changes, submit your work to your instructor as directed, close the workbook, then exit Excel.

	Reed & Allen Legal Services				
	Travel Expenses				
	Jan	Feb	Mar	Total	% of Total
New York	220,125	187,012	240,185	647,322	24.26%
Los Angeles	289,134	302,184	219,750	811,068	30.39%
Miami	157,368	207,305	257,217	621,890	23.30%
Chicago	197,516	188,270	202,497	588,283	22.04%
Total	864,143	884,771	919,649	2,668,563	
Average	216,036	221,193	229,912		
Maximum	289,134	302,184	257,217		
Minimum	157,368	187,012	202,497		
Your Name					

Independent Challenge 1

The CFO at Riverwalk Medical Clinic has hired you to help him analyze departmental insurance reimbursements. He also would like to see what quarterly revenues would look like with a 20% increase in quarterly reimbursements. You've been given a worksheet for this project that contains some but not all of the data.

  a. Open IL_EX_1-3.xlsx from the location where you store your Data Files, then save it as **IL_EX_1_Reimbursements**.

  b. Enter the data shown in TABLE 1-4 in the range E4:E11.

  c. Type your name in cell A17.

  d. Move the label in cell F2 to cell A15.

Excel

Independent Challenge 1 (continued)

e. Use the Clipboard to copy and paste the label in cell F3 to cell A12.

f. Use the formula bar to correct the spelling error in the label in cell A6. (*Hint*: The correct spelling is Immunology.)

g. Edit cell A8 to correct the spelling error in the label. (*Hint*: The correct spelling is Ophthalmology.)

h. Type **Quarter 1** in cell B3, then use Auto Fill to enter Quarter 2, Quarter 3, and Quarter 4 in the range C3:E3.

i. Create a formula in cell F4 that uses cell references and totals the quarterly reimbursements for the Cardiology department.

j. Use the fill handle to copy the formula in cell F4 to the range F5:F11.

k. Using AutoSum, create a formula in cell B12 that totals the first quarter reimbursements for all the departments.

l. Copy the formula in cell B12 to the range C12:E12.

m. Enter a formula in cell B14 to calculate a 20% increase in the first quarter reimbursement total in cell B12. (*Hint:* You need to add B12 to B12 multiplied by .20. Use parentheses if necessary to follow the order of operations.)

n. Enter a function, using the help of AutoComplete, in cell B15 that calculates the average first quarter reimbursement amount for the departments.

o. Copy the formulas in the range B14:B15 to the range C14:E15.

p. Switch to Page Break view and adjust the page break to the bottom of row 18.

q. Switch to Normal View, then zoom the worksheet to 120%.

r. Turn on gridlines for printing.

s. Change the page orientation to landscape.

t. Preview the worksheet in Backstage view, then use the Page Setup dialog box to center the worksheet horizontally and vertically on the page. Compare your screen to FIGURE 1-25.

u. Submit your work to your instructor as directed.

v. Close the workbook, then exit Excel.

TABLE 1-4

cell address	value
E4	67247.90
E5	45581.20
E6	43000.60
E7	48539.20
E8	38125.00
E9	28909.50
E10	39216.90
E11	71189.10

FIGURE 1-25

	Quarter 1	Quarter 2	Quarter 3	Quarter 4	Total
Riverwalk Medical Clinic					
Insurance Reimbursements					
	Quarter 1	Quarter 2	Quarter 3	Quarter 4	Total
Cardiology	61,762.00	61,738.20	72,076.60	67,247.90	262,824.70
Dermatology	36,109.90	40,214.60	44,374.00	45,581.20	166,279.70
Immunology	43,877.60	44,719.80	46,702.10	43,000.60	178,300.10
Neurology	41,321.00	45,897.40	46,790.60	48,539.20	182,548.20
Ophthalmology	51,827.70	30,045.20	36,611.20	38,125.00	156,609.10
Orthopedics	15,682.50	26,103.00	27,650.20	28,909.50	98,345.20
Pediatrics	33,715.00	36,561.40	83,403.50	39,216.90	192,896.80
Psychology	72,950.60	66,427.60	73,403.60	71,189.10	283,970.90
Total	357,246.30	351,707.20	431,011.80	381,809.40	
20% increase	428,695.56	422,048.64	517,214.16	458,171.28	
Average	44,655.79	43,963.40	53,876.48	47,726.18	
Your Name					

1 of 1

Independent Challenge 2

As the assistant to the Dean of STEM (science, technology, engineering, and mathematics) at West Shore Community College, it is your responsibility to review the budgets for the departments in the division and help with a budget forecast for the upcoming academic year. You've decided to use Excel formulas and functions to help with this analysis.

a. Open IL_EX_1-4.xlsx from the location where you store your Data Files, then save it as **IL_EX_1_Budgets**.

b. Move the labels in the range A6:A11 to the range A5:A10.

c. Enter **Total** in cell A11, then use AutoSum to calculate the total 2020 expenses for all departments in cell B11.

d. Enter **Average** in cell A12, then use the AutoSum arrow to enter a function in cell B12 that calculates the average 2020 expenses for all departments. (*Hint*: make sure you include only the department data.)

e. Use the fill handle to copy the formulas in the range B11:B12 to the range C11:C12.

f. Using cell references, enter a formula in cell D5 that calculates the 2022 Budget for the engineering department, using the increase shown in cell F2 over the 2021 expenses in cell C5. Use absolute cell references where necessary. (*Hint*: Multiply the percentage in cell F2 by the 2021 expenses in cell C5, then add that amount to the 2021 expenses in cell C5.)

g. Use the fill handle to copy the formula in cell D5 to the range D6:D10.

h. Use the fill handle to copy the formulas in the range C11:C12 to the range D11:D12.

i. Enter a formula in cell F5 that calculates the percentage increase in total expenses from 2020 to 2021. (*Hint*: The 2020 total is in cell B11 and the 2021 total is in cell C11.)

j. Change the page orientation to landscape, then turn on gridlines for printing.

k. Enter your name in cell A14.

l. Preview the worksheet in Backstage view. Compare your screen to FIGURE 1-26.

m. Save your work, then submit the worksheet to your instructor as directed.

n. Close the workbook and exit Excel.

FIGURE 1-26

West Shore Community College				2022 Budget Increase	
STEM Division				2.15%	
Departmental Budgets					
Department	2020 Expenses	2021 Expenses	2022 Budget	% Increase in Expenses 2020 to 2021	
Engineering	$50,124.17	$52,457.65	$53,585.49	6.01%	
Computer Science	$45,287.23	$55,214.98	$56,402.10		
Biology	$36,784.98	$36,799.88	$37,591.08		
Chemistry	$58,214.78	$59,847.47	$61,134.19		
Physics	$61,002.27	$62,178.78	$63,515.62		
Math	$37,512.32	$39,781.33	$40,636.63		
Total	$288,925.75	$306,280.09	$312,865.11		
Average	$48,154.29	$51,046.68	$52,144.19		
Your Name					

Visual Workshop

Open IL_EX_1-5.xlsx from the location where you store your Data Files, then save it as **IL_EX_1_Royalties**. Complete the worksheet shown in FIGURE 1-27 using the skills you learned in this module. Use functions to calculate the values in B8:B11 and C11. The values in column C are calculated by multiplying the gross revenues in column B by the percentage in cell E2. Adjust your zoom level as necessary to match the figure. Enter your name in cell A14. Submit your work to your instructor as directed.

FIGURE 1-27

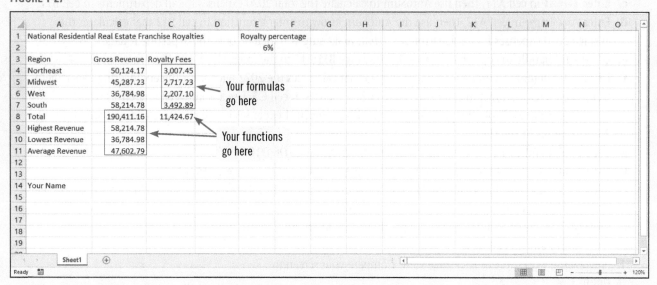

Formatting a Worksheet

CASE Cheri McNeil, the manager of the Boston office at JCL Talent, has gathered data from all JCL recruiters on technology position postings for the first quarter of the year. Cheri has created a worksheet listing this information, and she asks you to format the worksheet to make it easier to read and understand.

Module Objectives

After completing this module, you will be able to:

- Format values
- Change font and font size
- Change font styles and alignment
- Adjust column width
- Insert and delete rows and columns

- Apply colors, borders, and documentation
- Apply conditional formatting
- Rename and move a worksheet
- Check spelling

Files You Will Need

IL_EX_2-1.xlsx   IL_EX_2-4.xlsx
IL_EX_2-2.xlsx   IL_EX_2-5.xlsx
IL_EX_2-3.xlsx

Format Values

Learning
Outcomes
• Format a number
• Format a date
• Increase/decrease
  decimals

When you **format** a cell, you enhance the appearance of information by changing its font, size, color, or alignment. Formatting changes only the appearance of a value or label; it does not alter the actual data in any way. To format a cell or range, first you select it, then you apply the formatting using the ribbon, Mini toolbar, or a keyboard shortcut. You can apply formatting before or after you enter data in a cell or range.

CASE ▶ *Cheri has provided you with a worksheet that details technology postings, and you're ready to improve its appearance. You start by formatting some cells to better reflect the type of information they contain, such as currency, percentages, and dates.*

STEPS

1. **sam** ↓ **Start Excel, open** IL_EX_2-1.xlsx **from the location where you store your Data Files, then save it as** IL_EX_2_Tech

   This worksheet is difficult to interpret because all the information is crowded and looks the same. In some columns, such as D, the contents appear cut off because there is too much data to fit given the current column width. You decide not to widen the columns yet, because the other changes you plan to make might affect column width and row height.

2. **Select the range** G3:G15, **then click the** Accounting Number Format button $ **in the Number group on the Home tab**

   A **number format** is applied to values to express numeric concepts, such as currency, date, and percent-age. The default Accounting number format adds dollar signs and two decimal places to the expense data, as shown in **FIGURE 2-1**.

3. **Select the range** H3:H15, **then click the** Comma Style button **in the Number group**

   The values in column H display the Comma Style format, which does not include a dollar sign but can be useful for some types of accounting data.

4. **Click cell** M1, **click the** Number Format arrow, **click** Percentage, **then click the** Increase Decimal button **in the Number group**

   The revenue rate is now formatted with a percent sign (%) and three decimal places. The Number Format arrow lets you choose from popular number formats and shows an example of what the selected cell or cells would look like (when multiple cells are selected, the example is based on the first cell in the range). Each time you click the Increase Decimal button, you add one decimal place; clicking the button twice would add two decimal places.

5. **Click the** Decrease Decimal button **in the Number group three times**

   All three decimal places are removed from the revenue rate value.

6. **Select the range** C3:C15, **then click the** launcher **in the Number group**

   The Format Cells dialog box opens with the Date category already selected on the Number tab.

7. **Click the** 14-Mar **format in the Type list box, as shown in** FIGURE 2-2, **then click** OK

   The dates in column C appear in the 14-Mar format.

8. **Select the range** I3:J15, **right-click the range, click** Format Cells **on the shortcut menu, in the Category list click** Currency, **in the Decimal places box type** 2 **if necessary, then click** OK

   This number format looks similar to the Accounting format but aligns currency symbols and decimal points slightly differently. Compare your worksheet to **FIGURE 2-3**.

9. **Select the range** G3:I15, **click the** Decrease Decimal button **in the Number group twice, press** CTRL+HOME, **then save your work**

   The cell values in this range now use a custom format that doesn't display decimal places. This format is applied to all cells in the range, including the cells in column H that display the $ symbol.

FIGURE 2-1: Accounting number format applied to range

Number Format
list arrow

Accounting Number
Format button

Increase Decimal
button

Decrease Decimal
button

Cells formatted
with Accounting
number format

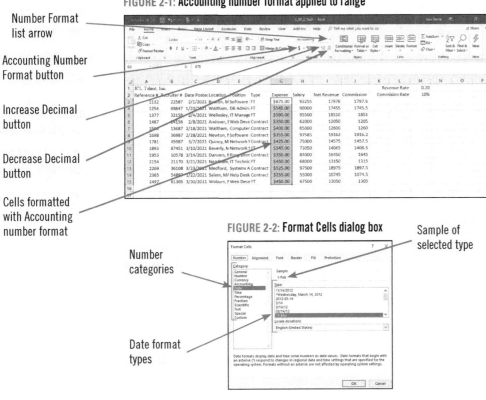

FIGURE 2-2: Format Cells dialog box

Sample of
selected type

Number
categories

Date format
types

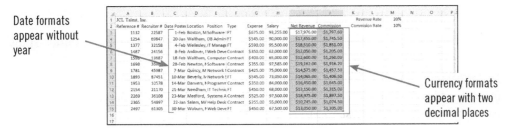

FIGURE 2-3: Worksheet with formatted values

Date formats
appear without
year

Currency formats
appear with two
decimal places

Excel

Working with online pictures, other images, and symbols

You can illustrate your worksheets using online pictures and
other images. To add a picture to a worksheet, click the Online
Pictures button in the Illustrations group on the Insert tab. The
Online Pictures dialog box opens. Here you can search for online
pictures from the Bing search engine or OneDrive, as shown in
FIGURE 2-4. To search, type one or more keywords in the search
box, then press ENTER. When you double-click an image in the
Search Results window, the image is inserted at the location of
the active cell. Clicking an image selects it and adds resizing
handles. To resize an image proportionally, drag any corner
sizing handle. If you drag an edge sizing handle, the image will
be resized nonproportionally. You can add alternative text to an
image by right-clicking it, clicking Edit Alt Text on the shortcut
menu, then entering the text in the Alt Text pane. To move an
image, point inside the image until the pointer changes to ,
then drag it to a new location. To delete a picture, select it,
then press DEL. To work with an image it must be selected. You

FIGURE 2-4: Results of Online Picture search

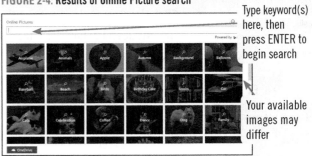

Type keyword(s)
here, then
press ENTER to
begin search

Your available
images may
differ

can select an image, or any object, by clicking it. To work with
multiple images at once, hold CTRL while clicking each image.
You can insert a symbol in a worksheet by clicking the Insert
tab, clicking the Symbols button in the Symbols group, clicking
Symbol, clicking a symbol from the Symbols tab in the Symbol
dialog box, clicking Insert, then clicking Close to close the Symbol dialog box.

Change Font and Font Size

Learning
Outcomes
• Change a font
• Change a font size

A **font** is the appearance and shape of the letters, numbers, and special characters and is usually designed with a font name, such as Calibri or Times New Roman. The **font size** is the size of characters, measured in units called points. A **point** is a unit of measure used for font size and row height; one point is equal to ¹⁄₇₂ of an inch. The default font and font size in Excel is 11-point Calibri. TABLE 2-1 shows examples of several fonts in different font sizes. You can change the font and font size of any cell or range using the Font and Font Size arrows. The Font and Font Size arrows are located on the Home tab on the ribbon and on the Mini toolbar, which opens when you right-click a cell or range. To save time, you can also use a **cell style**, a pre-designed combination of font, font size, and font color that you can apply to a cell. **CASE** *You want to change the font and font size of the labels and the worksheet title, so this information stands out.*

STEPS

1. **Click the Font arrow in the Font group on the Home tab, scroll down in the Font list to see an alphabetical listing of the fonts available on your computer, then click Calibri, as shown in FIGURE 2-5**

   The font in cell A1 changes to Calibri to match the rest of the worksheet.

2. **Click the Font Size arrow in the Font group, then click 20**

   The worksheet title is formatted in 20-point Calibri, and the Font and Font Size boxes on the Home tab display the new font and font size information.

3. **Click the Cell Styles button in the Styles group, then click Heading 1 under Titles and Headings**

   The title is formatted in the Heading 1 cell style.

4. **Select the range A2:J2, click the Cell Styles button, then click Heading 2 under Titles and Headings**

   Notice that some of the column labels are now too wide to appear fully in the column. Excel does not automatically adjust column widths to accommodate cell formatting; these column widths must be adjusted manually. You'll learn to do this in a later lesson.

5. **Click cell L1, hold SHIFT, then click cell L2**

   Holding SHIFT while clicking a cell selects that cell and any cells between it and the cell first selected. In this case there are only two cells selected.

6. **Click the Cell Styles button, then click Heading 4 under Titles and Headings**

   The revenue and commission rate labels are now formatted consistently. Compare your worksheet to FIGURE 2-6.

7. **Save your work**

TABLE 2-1: Examples of fonts and font sizes

font name	12 point	24 point
Calibri	Excel	Excel
Playbill	Excel	Excel
Comic Sans MS	Excel	Excel
Times New Roman	Excel	Excel

FIGURE 2-5: Font list

Font list arrow

Active cell displays preview of selected formatting change

Font size list arrow

Click a font to apply it to the selected cell

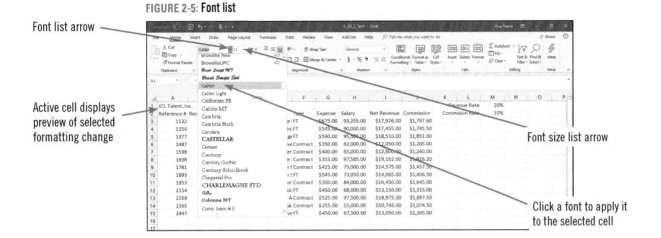

FIGURE 2-6: Worksheet with formatted headings and column labels

Cell Styles

Title formatted in Heading 1 cell style

Rate labels are formatted in Heading 4 cell style

Column labels are formatted in Heading 2 cell style

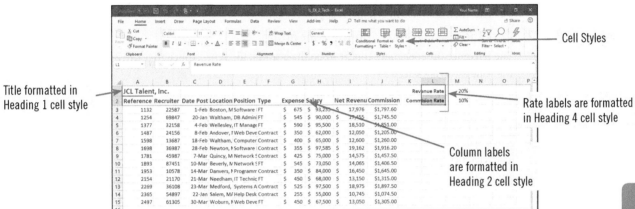

Working with cell styles

You can modify any style in the Cell Styles gallery. In the Cell Styles gallery, right-click the cell style that you want to modify, on the shortcut menu shown in **FIGURE 2-7**, click Modify, select the style options from the Style Includes list in the Style dialog box, click the Format button to choose new customized formatting, then click OK twice. To create a new cell style, click New Cell Style at the bottom of the Cell Styles gallery, enter a name in the Style name box, select style options from the Style Includes list, click the Format button to choose customized formatting for your style, then click OK twice. You can merge styles from a different workbook by opening the workbook that contains the cell styles that you want to copy, clicking Merge Styles at the bottom of the Cell Styles gallery, clicking the workbook

FIGURE 2-7: Shortcut menu in Cell Styles gallery

in the Merge styles from list, then clicking OK. If styles in the workbooks have the same name, you will be asked if you want to merge those styles.

Excel

Change Font Styles and Alignment

Learning
Outcomes
• Apply formatting
• Use the Format
  Painter
• Change cell
  alignment

Font styles are formats that indicate how characters are emphasized, such as bold, underline, and italic. You have seen font styles applied with cell styles, and you can also apply them individually. You can change the **alignment**, the placement of cell contents in relation to a cell's edges, such as left or centered, of labels and values in cells. See TABLE 2-2 for a description of common font style and alignment buttons that are available on the Home tab. Once you have formatted a cell the way you want it, you can "paint" or copy the cell's formats to other cells by using the Format Painter button in the Clipboard group on the Home tab. This is similar to using copy and paste, but instead of copying cell contents, it copies only the cell's formatting. **CASE** ▶ *You want to further enhance the worksheet's appearance by adding bold and underline formatting and centering some of the labels.*

STEPS

QUICK TIP
You can use the Underline button [U] to underline cell contents. You can also use the Mini toolbar to format text by right-clicking selected cells.

1. **Select the range A3:A15, then click the Bold button [B] in the Font group on the Home tab**
   The reference numbers in column A appear in bold.

2. **Click the Italic button [I] in the Font group**
   The reference numbers now appear in boldface and italic type. Notice that the Bold and Italic buttons in the Font group are selected.

3. **Click the Italic button [I] to deselect it**
   The italic font style is removed from the reference numbers but the bold font style remains.

4. **Click the Center button [≡] in the Alignment group**
   The reference numbers are centered within their cells.

QUICK TIP
To format a selected cell or range using keyboard shortcuts, you can press CTRL+B to bold, CTRL+I to italicize, and CTRL+U to underline.

5. **Click the Format Painter button [🖌] in the Clipboard group, then select the range B3:B15**
   The formatting in column A is copied to the recruiter number data in column B. To paint the formats to more than one selection, double-click the Format Painter button to keep it activated until you turn it off. You can turn off the Format Painter by pressing ESC or by clicking [🖌].

6. **Click cell A1, select the range A1:J1, then click the Merge & Center button [▦] in the Alignment group**
   The Merge & Center button creates one cell out of the ten cells across the row, then centers the text in that newly created, merged cell. The title "JCL Talent, Inc." is centered across the 10 columns you selected. To split a merged cell into its original components, select the merged cell, then click the Merge & Center button [▦] to deselect it. Occasionally, you may find that you want cell contents to wrap within a cell. You can do this by selecting the cells containing the text you want to wrap, then clicking the Wrap Text button [ab↵] in the Alignment group on the Home tab on the ribbon.

QUICK TIP
To clear all formatting from a selected range, click the Clear button [◇] in the Editing group on the Home tab, then click Clear Formats.

7. **Compare your screen to FIGURE 2-8, then save your work**

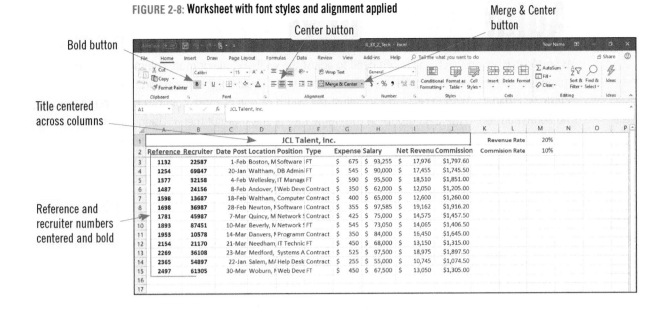

FIGURE 2-8: Worksheet with font styles and alignment applied

Bold button

Center button

Merge & Center button

Title centered across columns

Reference and recruiter numbers centered and bold

TABLE 2-2: Common font style and alignment buttons

button	description
B	Bolds cell content
I	Italicizes cell content
U	Underlines cell content
	Centers content across columns; also merges two or more selected, adjacent cells into one cell; also unmerges previously merged cells
	Aligns content at the left edge of the cell
	Centers content horizontally within the cell
	Aligns content at the right edge of the cell
ab c	Wraps long text into multiple lines to fit within a column
	Aligns content at the top of a cell
	Aligns content at the bottom of a cell
	Aligns content in the middle of a cell

Rotating and indenting cell entries

In addition to applying fonts and font styles, you can rotate or indent data within a cell. To rotate text within a cell, click the Home tab, select the cells you want to modify, then click the dialog box launcher ⌐ in the Alignment group to open the Alignment tab of the Format Cells dialog box. Click a position in the Orientation box or type a number in the Degrees box to rotate text from its default horizontal orientation, then click OK. You can indent cell contents by clicking the Increase Indent button ⌐= in the Alignment group, which moves cell contents to the right one space, or the Decrease Indent button ⌐=, which moves cell contents to the left one space.

Adjust Column Width

Learning Outcomes
• Change a column width by dragging
• Resize a column with AutoFit
• Change the width of multiple columns

As you format a worksheet, you might need to adjust the width of one or more columns to accommodate changes in the amount of text, the font size, or font style. The default column width is 8.43 characters, a little less than 1". With Excel, you can adjust the width of one or more columns by using the mouse, the Format button in the Cells group on the Home tab, or the shortcut menu. Using the mouse, you can drag or double-click the right edge of a column heading. The Format button and shortcut menu include commands for making more precise width adjustments. TABLE 2-3 describes common column formatting commands. **CASE** *You have noticed that some of the labels in columns A through L don't fit in the cells. You want to adjust the widths of the columns so that the labels appear in their entirety.*

STEPS

1. **Position the pointer on the line between the column C and column D headings until it changes to ↔**

   See FIGURE 2-9. A **column heading** is a box that appears above each worksheet column and identifies it by a letter. You positioned the mouse pointer here because in order to adjust column width using the mouse, you need to position the pointer on the right edge of the column heading for the column you want to adjust.

2. **Click and drag ↔ to the right until the column fully displays the column label Date Posted (approximately 12.71 characters or 94 pixels)**

   As you change the column width, a ScreenTip opens listing the column width.

3. **Position the pointer on the line between columns D and E until it changes to ↔, then double-click**

   Column D automatically widens to fit the widest entry. Double-clicking the right edge of a column heading activates **AutoFit**. This feature adjusts column width or row height to accommodate its widest or tallest entry.

4. **Use AutoFit to resize columns E, F, G, H, and L**

5. **Position the pointer in the column heading area for column I until it changes to ↓, then drag to select columns I and J**

6. **Click the Format button in the Cells group, then click Column Width**

   The Column Width dialog box opens. Column width measurement is based on the number of characters that will fit in the column when formatted in the Normal font and font size (in this case, 11-point Calibri).

7. **Type 14 in the Column width box, then click OK**

   The widths of columns I and J change to reflect the new setting. See FIGURE 2-10.

8. **Click cell A1, then save your work**

FIGURE 2-9: Preparing to change the column width

Resize pointer

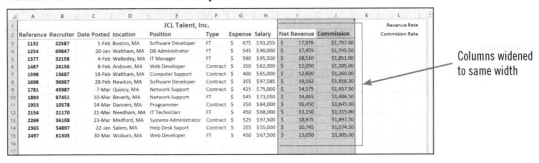

FIGURE 2-10: Worksheet with column widths adjusted

Columns widened to same width

TABLE 2-3: Common column formatting commands

command	description	available using
Column Width	Sets the width to a specific number of characters	Format button; shortcut menu
AutoFit Column Width	Fits to the widest entry in a column	Format button; mouse
Hide & Unhide	Hides or displays selected column(s)	Format button; shortcut menu
Default Width	Resets column to worksheet's default column width	Format button

Changing row height

Changing row height is as easy as changing column width. Row height is calculated in points, the same unit of measure used for fonts. The row height must exceed the size of the font you are using. Normally, you don't need to adjust row height manually, because row heights adjust automatically to accommodate font size changes. If you format something in a row to be a larger point size, Excel adjusts the row to fit the largest point size in the row. However, you have just as many options for changing row height as you do column width. Using the mouse, you can place the ✛ pointer on the line dividing a row heading from the heading below it, and then drag to the desired height; double-clicking the line AutoFits the row height where necessary. You can also select one or more rows, then use the Row Height command on the shortcut menu, or click the Format button on the Home tab, then click the Row Height or AutoFit Row Height command.

Excel

Insert and Delete Rows and Columns

Learning
Outcomes
• Use the Insert
  dialog box
• Use column and
  row heading
  buttons to insert
  and delete

As you modify a worksheet, you might find it necessary to insert or delete rows and columns to keep your worksheet current. For example, you might need to insert rows to accommodate new inventory products or remove a column of yearly totals that are no longer necessary. When you insert a new row, the row is inserted above the cell pointer and the contents of the worksheet shift down from the newly inserted row. When you insert a new column, the column is inserted to the left of the cell pointer and the contents of the worksheet shift to the right of the new column. To insert multiple rows, select the same number of row headings as you want to insert before using the Insert command. **CASE** *You want to improve the overall appearance of the worksheet by inserting a row between the company name and the column labels. Also, you have learned that row 9 and column K need to be deleted from the worksheet.*

STEPS

1. **Right-click cell F2, then click Insert on the shortcut menu**

   The Insert dialog box opens. See **FIGURE 2-11**. You can choose to insert a single cell and shift the cells in the active column to the right, insert a single cell and shift the cells in the active row down, or insert an entire column or a row.

2. **Click the Entire row option button, then click OK**

   A blank row appears between the company name and the column labels, visually separating the worksheet data, and the Insert Options button opens next to cell F3.

3. **Click the Insert Options button, then review your choices**

   This menu lets you format the inserted row in Format Same As Above (the default setting, already selected), Format Same As Below, or Clear Formatting.

4. **Click to close the menu without making changes, then click the row 9 heading**

   All of row 9 is selected, as shown in **FIGURE 2-12**.

5. **Click the Delete button in the Cells group; do not click the Delete arrow**

   Excel deletes row 9, and all rows below it shift up one row. You must use the Delete button or the Delete command on the shortcut menu to delete a row or column; pressing DEL on the keyboard removes only the *contents* of a selected row or column.

6. **Click the column K heading**

   The column is empty and isn't necessary in this worksheet.

7. **Click the Delete button in the Cells group**

   Excel deletes column K. The remaining columns to the right shift left one column.

8. **Save your work**

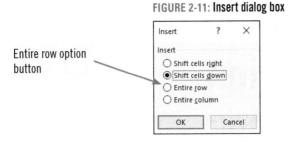

FIGURE 2-11: **Insert dialog box**

Entire row option button

FIGURE 2-12: **Worksheet with row 9 selected**

Delete button

Row 9 heading

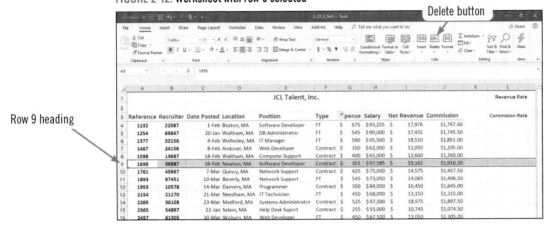

Hiding and unhiding columns and rows

When you don't want data in a column or row to be visible, but you don't want to delete it, you can hide the column or row. To hide a selected column, click the Format button in the Cells group on the Home tab, point to Hide & Unhide, then click Hide Columns. A hidden column is indicated by a dark green vertical line in its original position. This green line is removed when you click elsewhere on the worksheet, but a thin double line remains

between the column heading to remind you that one or more columns are hidden. You can display a hidden column by selecting the column headings on either side of the hidden column, clicking the Format button in the Cells group, pointing to Hide & Unhide, then clicking Unhide Columns. (To hide or unhide one or more rows, substitute Hide Rows and Unhide Rows for the Hide Columns and Unhide Columns instructions.)

Create and apply a template

A **template** is a predesigned, preformatted Office file that contains default text formats, themes, placeholder text, headers and footers, and graphics that you can replace with your own information for hundreds of purposes, including budgets, flyers, and resumes. Template files have a file extension of .xltx. You can create your own template to provide a model for creating a new workbook by saving a workbook with this extension. To use a template, you apply it, which means you create a workbook based on the template. A workbook based on a template has the same content, formulas, and formatting defined in the template, but is saved in the standard workbook format, .xlsx. The template file itself remains unchanged. To save a file as a template, click the File tab, click Save As, click This PC if necessary, click More options, click the Save as type arrow, click Excel Template in the list of file types, as shown

FIGURE 2-13: **Save menu file types**

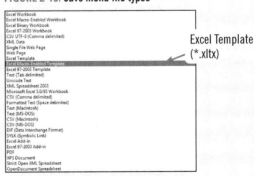

Excel Template (*.xltx)

in **FIGURE 2-13**, type a name for the new template in the File name box (the default save location is the Custom Office Templates folder), then click Save.

Apply Colors, Borders, and Documentation

Learning
Outcomes
• Change text and
fill color
• Apply a border to
a cell
• Add a header
and footer to a
worksheet

You have seen how you can use cell styles to add predesigned formatting, including colors and borders to a worksheet. If a cell style doesn't capture the formatting you need for a worksheet, you can add this formatting individually. Color options are based on the worksheet theme. A **theme** is a predefined, coordinated set of colors, fonts, graphical effects, and other formats that can be applied to a spreadsheet to give it a consistent, professional look. In Excel, applying a theme to one sheet applies it to all other sheets in that workbook. You can also add a **header** and/or a **footer** to provide useful text, date and other information, including a graphic, along the top or bottom of every page of a worksheet. A header prints above the top margin of the worksheet, and a footer prints below the bottom margin. **CASE** *You want to add a border and color to the reference numbers on the worksheet to make them stand out from the other information. You also want to add information about the worksheet in a header and footer.*

STEPS

QUICK TIP
Themes can be
changed by clicking
the Page Layout tab,
clicking the Themes
button, and selecting a Theme from
the Themes gallery.

1. **Select the range** A4:A15, **click the** Fill Color arrow ⬚ **in the Font group, then click the** Blue-Gray, Text 2, Lighter 80% **color (second row, fourth column from the left)**
   The color is applied to the background (or fill) of this range. When you change fill or font color, the color on the Fill Color or Font Color button changes to the last color you selected.

2. **Click the** Borders arrow ⬚ **in the Font group, review the Borders menu, as shown in** FIGURE 2-14, **then click** Right Border
   You can use the options at the bottom of the Borders menu to draw a border or to change a border line color or style.

3. **Click the** Font Color arrow ⬚ **in the Font group, then click the** Blue-Gray, Text 2 color **(first row, fourth column from the left)**
   The new color is applied to the labels in the selected range. This color will make the first column reference numbers stand out.

QUICK TIP
You can use the settings in the Options
group on the Header
& Footer Tools
Design tab to set a
different header or
footer for the first
page of a worksheet.
You can also use an
option in this group
to set different headers or footers for odd
and even worksheet
pages.

4. **Click the** Insert tab, **click the** Text button, **then click the** Header & Footer button
   The header is divided into three sections, as shown in FIGURE 2-15, where you can enter or edit text. The Header & Footer Tools Design tab includes elements and options for customizing the header or footer.

5. **Click the** Sheet Name button **in the Header & Footer Elements group on the Header & Footer Tools Design tab**
   The & [Tab] code is added, which will display the current sheet name in this location. Using codes instead of manually typing the information ensures this information is always up to date.

6. **Click the** Go to Footer button **in the Navigation group, enter your name in the center footer section, click any cell on the worksheet, click the** Normal button ⬚ **in the status bar, then press** CTRL+HOME
   The header and footer are only visible in Page Layout view and Print Preview.

7. **Click** File, **then click** Print
   Your header and footer will provide useful information to others viewing the worksheet.

8. **Click the** Back button ⬚ **to return to your worksheet, then save your work**

FIGURE 2-14: Borders menu

Borders menu

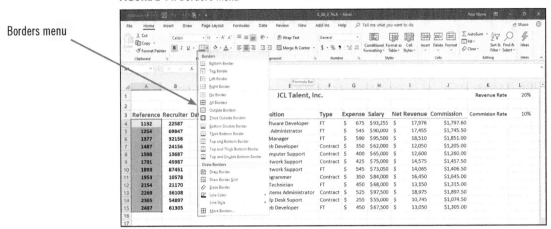

FIGURE 2-15: Header & Footer Tools Design tab

Go To Footer button

Options for header

Three sections of header

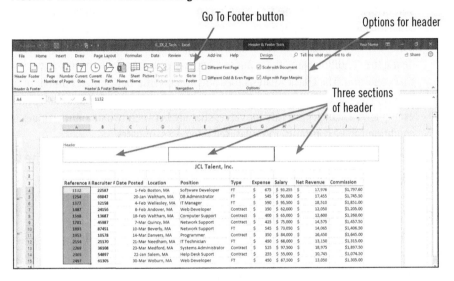

Checking worksheet accessibility

Part of successfully formatting your worksheets includes checking to see if any format presents accessibility problems. **Accessibility** is the quality of removing barriers that may prevent individuals with disabilities from interacting with data or an app. You can check for accessibility issues by clicking File, clicking the Check for Issues arrow in the Info window, then clicking Check Accessibility. The Accessibility Checker pane opens and displays an Inspection Results Warnings listing is displayed, as shown in FIGURE 2-16. You can click the warnings to see additional information below the Warnings list and directions on how to fix the issue.

FIGURE 2-16: Accessibility Checker pane

Warnings

Excel

Apply Conditional Formatting

Learning
Outcomes
• Create a Data Bars
 rule
• Create a Highlight
 Cells rule

So far, you've used formatting to change the appearance of different types of data, but you can also use **conditional formatting**, special formatting that is applied if values meet specified criteria. **CASE** ▶ *Cheri is concerned about hiring expenses exceeding the yearly budget. You decide to use conditional formatting to highlight certain trends and patterns in the data so that it's easy to compare net revenue and spot the highest expenses.*

STEPS

> **QUICK TIP**
>
> You can create a custom data bar rule by clicking the Conditional Formatting button, clicking New Rule, clicking the Format Style arrow, clicking Data Bar, adjusting the options in the New Formatting Rule dialog box, then clicking OK.

1. **Select the range I4:I15, click the** Conditional Formatting button **in the Styles group on the Home tab, point to** Data Bars, **then click** Blue Data Bar **under Gradient Fill (first row, first column)**

    Data bars are colored horizontal bars that visually illustrate differences between values in a range of cells.

2. **Select the range G4:G15, click the** Quick Analysis button 📄 **that opens next to the selection, then click the** Greater Than button **on the Formatting tab**

    The Greater Than dialog box opens, displaying an input box you can use to define the condition and a default format (Light Red Fill with Dark Red Text) selected for cells that meet that condition. You can define the condition using the input box and assigning the formatting you want to use for cells that meet that condition. The Quick Analysis tool offers a powerful but limited number of options. To set more conditions, you can click the Highlight Cells Rules option on the Conditional Formatting menu instead. For example, you can create a rule for values that are between two amounts. Values used in input boxes for a condition can be constants, formulas, cell references, or dates.

> **QUICK TIP**
>
> You can highlight duplicate values in a selected range by clicking the Conditional Formatting button in the Styles group, pointing to Highlight Cells Rules, clicking Duplicate Values, then selecting a formatting option.

3. **Type** 500 **in the Format cells that are GREATER THAN box, click the** with list arrow, **click** Light Red Fill, **compare your settings to** FIGURE 2-17, **then click** OK

    All cells with values greater than $500 in column G appear with a light red fill.

4. **Click cell** G4, **type** 499, **then press** ENTER

    Because of the rule you created, the appearance of cell G4 changes because the new value no longer meets the condition you set. Compare your results to FIGURE 2-18.

5. **Press** CTRL+HOME, **then save your work**

Formatting data with icon sets

Icon sets are a conditional format in which different icons are displayed in a cell based on the cell's value. In one group of cells, for example, upward-pointing green arrows might represent the highest values, while downward-pointing red arrows represent the lower values. To add an icon set to a data range, select a data range, click the Conditional Formatting button in the Styles group, point to Icon Sets, then click an icon set. You can customize the values that are used as thresholds for color scales and icon sets by clicking the Conditional Formatting button in the Styles group, clicking Manage Rules, clicking the rule in the Conditional Formatting Rules Manager dialog box, clicking Edit Rule, entering new values, clicking OK, clicking Apply, then clicking OK to close the dialog box.

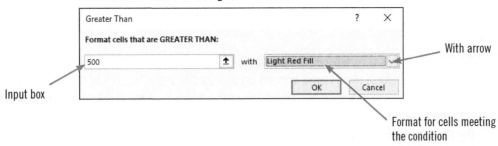

FIGURE 2-17: Greater Than dialog box

Input box

With arrow

Format for cells meeting the condition

FIGURE 2-18: Worksheet with conditional formatting

	A	B	C	D	E	F	G	H	I	J	K	L
1					JCL Talent, Inc.						Revenue Rate	20%
2												
3	Reference	Recruiter	Date Posted	Location	Position	Type	Expense	Salary	Net Revenue	Commission	Commision Rate	10%
4	1132	22587	1-Feb	Boston, MA	Software Developer	FT	$ 499	$93,255	$ 18,152	$1,815.20		
5	1254	69847	20-Jan	Waltham, MA	DB Administrator	FT	$ 545	$90,000	$ 17,455	$1,745.50		
6	1377	32158	4-Feb	Wellesley, MA	IT Manager	FT	$ 590	$95,500	$ 18,510	$1,851.00		
7	1487	24156	8-Feb	Andover, MA	Web Developer	Contract	$ 350	$62,000	$ 12,050	$1,205.00		
8	1598	13687	18-Feb	Waltham, MA	Computer Support	Contract	$ 400	$65,000	$ 12,600	$1,260.00		
9	1781	45987	7-Mar	Quincy, MA	Network Support	Contract	$ 425	$75,000	$ 14,575	$1,457.50		
10	1893	87451	10-Mar	Beverly, MA	Network Support	FT	$ 545	$73,050	$ 14,065	$1,406.50		
11	1953	10578	14-Mar	Danvers, MA	Programmer	Contract	$ 350	$84,000	$ 16,450	$1,645.00		
12	2154	21170	21-Mar	Needham, MA	IT Technician	FT	$ 450	$68,000	$ 13,150	$1,315.00		
13	2269	36108	23-Mar	Medford, MA	Systems Administrator	Contract	$ 525	$97,500	$ 18,975	$1,897.50		
14	2365	54897	22-Jan	Salem, MA	Help Desk Suport	Contract	$ 255	$55,000	$ 10,745	$1,074.50		
15	2497	61305	30-Mar	Woburn, MA	Web Developer	FT	$ 450	$67,500	$ 13,050	$1,305.00		
16												

Managing conditional formatting rules

If you create a conditional formatting rule and then want to change a condition, you don't need to create a new rule; instead, you can edit the rule using the Rules Manager. Click the Conditional Formatting button in the Styles group, then click Manage Rules. The Conditional Formatting Rules Manager dialog box opens, as shown in **FIGURE 2-19**, listing any rules you have set. Use the Show Formatting rules for arrow to see rules for other parts of a worksheet or for other sheets in the workbook. Select the rule you want to edit, click Edit Rule, then modify the settings in the Edit the Rule Description area in the Edit Formatting Rule dialog box. To change the formatting for a rule, click the Format button in the Edit the Rule Description area, select the formatting styles you want the cells to have, then click OK three times to close the Format Cells dialog box, the Edit Formatting Rule dialog box, and the Conditional Formatting Rules Manager dialog box. To delete a rule, select the

FIGURE 2-19: Conditional Formatting Rules Manager dialog box

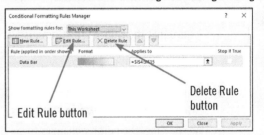

Edit Rule button

Delete Rule button

rule in the Conditional Formatting Rules Manager dialog box, then click the Delete Rule button. You can quickly clear conditional formatting rules by clicking the Conditional Formatting button in the Styles group, pointing to Clear Rules, then clicking Clear Rules from Selected Cells or Clear Rules from Entire Worksheet.

Rename and Move a Worksheet

Learning Outcomes
• Rename a sheet
• Apply color to a sheet tab
• Reorder sheets in a workbook

By default, an Excel workbook initially contains one worksheet named Sheet1, although you can add sheets anytime. Each sheet name appears on a sheet tab at the bottom of the worksheet. To move from sheet to sheet, you can click any sheet tab at the bottom of the worksheet window. The **sheet tab scrolling buttons** let you navigate to additional sheet tabs when available; they are located to the left of the sheet tabs and are useful when a workbook contains too many sheet tabs to display at once. To make a workbook more accessible, you can rename worksheets with descriptive names. Worksheets are easier to identify if you add color to the tabs. You can also organize worksheets in a logical order. **CASE** *In the current worksheet, Sheet1 contains detailed information about technical job postings in the Boston office. Sheet2 contains commission information, and Sheet3 contains no data. You want to rename these sheets to reflect their contents. You also want to add color to a sheet tab to easily distinguish one from the other and change their order.*

STEPS

1. **Click the Sheet2 sheet tab**

   Sheet2 becomes active, appearing in front of the Sheet1 tab; this worksheet contains the commission information. See **FIGURE 2-20**.

2. **Click the Sheet1 tab**

   Sheet1, which contains the detailed job posting data, becomes active again.

3. **Double-click the Sheet2 tab, type Commission, then press ENTER**

   The new name for Sheet2 automatically replaces the default name on the tab. Worksheet names can have up to 31 characters, including spaces and punctuation.

4. **Right-click the Commission tab, point to Tab Color on the shortcut menu, then click the Blue, Accent 5, Darker 25% color (fifth row, second column from the right), as shown in FIGURE 2-21**

5. **Right-click the Sheet1 tab, click Rename on the shortcut menu, type Boston Tech, then press ENTER**

   Notice that the color of the Commission tab changes depending on whether it is the active tab; when the Boston Tech tab is active, the color of the Commission tab changes to the blue tab color you selected. You decide to rearrange the order of the sheets so that the Commissions tab is to the right of the Sheet3 tab.

6. **Click the Commissions tab, hold down the mouse button, drag it to the right of the Sheet3 tab, as shown in FIGURE 2-22, then release the mouse button**

   As you drag, the pointer changes to ▯, the sheet relocation pointer, and a small black triangle just above the tabs shows the position where the moved sheet will be when you release the mouse button. The last sheet in the workbook is now the Commission sheet. See **FIGURE 2-23**. You can move multiple sheets by pressing and holding SHIFT while clicking the sheets you want to move, then dragging the sheets to their new location.

7. **Right-click the Sheet3 tab, click Delete on the shortcut menu, press CTRL+HOME, then save your work**

   The sheet is deleted.

FIGURE 2-20: Sheet tabs in workbook

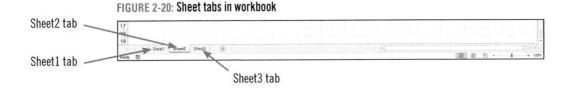

Sheet2 tab

Sheet1 tab

Sheet3 tab

FIGURE 2-21: Tab Color palette

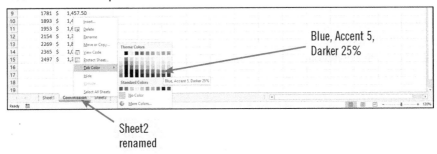

Blue, Accent 5,
Darker 25%

Sheet2
renamed

FIGURE 2-22: Moving the Commission sheet

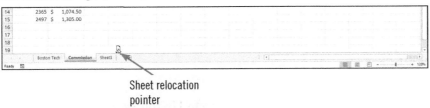

Sheet relocation
pointer

FIGURE 2-23: Reordered sheets

Commission sheet
is the last sheet

Copying, adding, and deleting worksheets

There are times when you may want to copy a worksheet. For example, a workbook might contain a sheet with Quarter 1 expenses, and you want to use that sheet as the basis for a sheet containing Quarter 2 expenses. To copy a sheet within the same workbook, press and hold CTRL, drag the sheet tab to the desired tab location, release the mouse button, then release CTRL. A duplicate sheet appears with the same name as the copied sheet followed by "(2)" indicating that it is a copy. You can then rename the sheet to a more meaningful name. To copy a sheet to a different workbook, both the source and destination workbooks must be open. Select the sheet to copy or move, right-click the sheet tab, click Move or Copy in the shortcut menu, then complete the information in the Move or Copy dialog box. Be sure to click the Create a copy check box if you want to copy rather than move the worksheet. Carefully check your calculation results whenever you move or copy a worksheet. You can add multiple worksheets quickly by pressing and holding SHIFT, clicking the number of existing worksheet tabs that correspond with the number of sheets you want to add, clicking the Insert arrow in the Cells group on the Home tab, then clicking Insert Sheet. You can delete multiple worksheets from a workbook by clicking the Home tab on the ribbon, pressing and holding SHIFT, clicking the sheet tabs of the worksheets you want to delete, clicking the Delete arrow in the Cells group, then clicking Delete Sheet.

Check Spelling

Learning Outcomes
- Change the spelling using a suggestion
- Replace text using Find & Select

Excel includes a spell checker to help you ensure that the words in your worksheet are spelled correctly. The spell checker scans your worksheet, displays words it doesn't find in its built-in dictionary, and suggests replacements when they are available. To check all the sheets in a multiple-sheet workbook, you need to display each sheet individually and run the spell checker for each one. Because the built-in dictionary cannot possibly include all the words that anyone needs, you can add words to the dictionary, such as your company name, an acronym, or an unusual technical term. Once you add a word or term, the spell checker no longer considers that word misspelled. Any words you've added to the dictionary using Word, Access, or PowerPoint are also available in Excel. **CASE** ▶ *Before you share this workbook with Cheri, you want to check the spelling.*

STEPS

1. **Click the Boston Tech sheet tab, click the Review tab on the ribbon, then click the Spelling button in the Proofing group**

   The Spelling: English (United States) dialog box opens, as shown in FIGURE 2-24, with "Commision" selected as the first misspelled word on the worksheet, and with "Commission" selected in the Suggestions list as a possible replacement. For any word, you have the option to Ignore this case of the flagged word, Ignore All cases of the flagged word, Change the word to the selected suggestion, Change All instances of the flagged word to the selected suggestion, or Add to Dictionary to add the flagged word to the dictionary.

2. **Click Change**

   Next, the spell checker finds the word "Suport" and suggests "Support" as an alternative.

3. **Verify that the word "Support" is selected in the Suggestions list, then click Change**

   When no more incorrect words are found, Excel displays a message indicating that the spell check is complete.

4. **Click OK**

5. **Click the Home tab, click Find & Select in the Editing group, then click Replace**

   The Find and Replace dialog box opens. You can use this dialog box to replace a word or phrase. It might be a misspelling of a proper name that the spell checker didn't recognize as misspelled, or it could simply be a term that you want to change throughout the worksheet.

6. **Type Contract in the Find what text box, press TAB, then type Temp in the Replace with text box**

   Compare your dialog box to FIGURE 2-25.

7. **Click Replace All, click OK to close the Microsoft Excel dialog box, then click Close to close the Find and Replace dialog box**

   Excel made six replacements, changing each instance of "Contract" on the worksheet to "Temp."

8. **Click the File tab, click Print on the navigation bar, click the Custom Scaling setting in the Settings section on the Print tab, then click Fit Sheet on One Page**

9. **sam↑ Click the Back button ⊙ to return to your worksheet, save your work, submit it to your instructor as directed, close the workbook, then close Excel**

   The completed worksheet is shown in FIGURE 2-26.

Translating text

You can translate text in a worksheet by clicking the Review tab, clicking the Translate button in the Language group, then, if necessary, clicking Turn on when asked if you want to use intelligent services. The Translator pane opens and allows you to select the From language and the To language from menus of world languages. The translated text appears in the To language box.

FIGURE 2-24: Spelling: English (United States) dialog box

Misspelled word

Suggested
replacements for
misspelled word

Spelling: English (United States)   ?   ✕

Not in Dictionary:
Commision   [Ignore Once]

                                                   [Ignore All]

                                                   [Add to Dictionary]

Suggestions:
Commission   [Change]
Commissions
                                                   [Change All]

                                                   [AutoCorrect]

Dictionary language: English (United States) ▼

[Options...]   [Undo Last]   [Cancel]

Click to ignore all
occurrences of
misspelled word

Click to add word
to dictionary

FIGURE 2-25: Find and Replace dialog box

Find and Replace   ?   ✕

Find   Replace

Find what: Contract   ▼

Replace with: Temp   ▼

                                          [Options >>]

[Replace All] [Replace] [Find All] [Find Next] [Close]

FIGURE 2-26: Completed worksheet

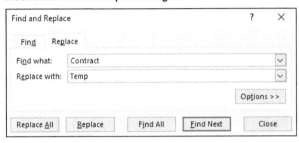

										Revenue Rate	20%

JCL Talent, Inc.

Reference #	Recruiter #	Date Posted	Location	Position	Type	Expense	Salary	Net Revenue	Commission	Commission Rate	10%
1132	22587	1-Feb	Boston, MA	Software Developer	FT	$ 499	$ 93,255	$ 18,152	$1,815.20		
1254	69847	20-Jan	Waltham, MA	DB Administrator	FT	$ 545	$ 90,000	$ 17,455	$1,745.50		
1377	32158	4-Feb	Wellesley, MA	IT Manager	FT	$ 390	$ 95,500	$ 18,510	$1,851.00		
1487	24156	8-Feb	Andover, MA	Web Developer	Temp	$ 350	$ 62,000	$ 12,050	$1,205.00		
1598	13687	18-Feb	Waltham, MA	Computer Support	Temp	$ 400	$ 65,000	$ 12,600	$1,260.00		
1781	45987	7-Mar	Quincy, MA	Network Support	Temp	$ 425	$ 75,000	$ 14,575	$1,457.50		
1893	87451	10-Mar	Beverly, MA	Network Support	FT	$ 545	$ 73,050	$ 14,065	$1,406.50		
1953	10578	14-Mar	Danvers, MA	Programmer	Temp	$ 350	$ 84,000	$ 16,450	$1,645.00		
2154	21170	21-Mar	Needham, MA	IT Technician	FT	$ 450	$ 68,000	$ 13,150	$1,315.00		
2269	36108	23-Mar	Medford, MA	Systems Administrator	Temp	$ 525	$ 97,500	$ 18,975	$1,897.50		
2365	54897	22-Jan	Salem, MA	Help Desk Support	Temp	$ 255	$ 55,000	$ 10,745	$1,074.50		
2497	61305	30-Mar	Woburn, MA	Web Developer	FT	$ 450	$ 67,500	$ 13,050	$1,305.00		

Using Find & Select features

You can navigate to a specific place in a workbook by clicking the Find & Select button in the Editing group on the Home tab, clicking Go To, typing a cell address, then clicking OK. Clicking the Find & Select button also allows you to quickly go to comments, formulas, constants, data validation, and conditional formatting in a worksheet. You can use the Go to Special dialog box to navigate to cells with special elements such as different types of formulas or objects. Some Go to Special commands also appear on the Find & Select menu. Using this menu, you can also change the mouse pointer shape to the Select Objects pointer so you can quickly select drawing objects when necessary. To return to the standard Excel pointer, press ESC.

Excel

Practice

Skills Review

1. Format values.
a. Start Excel, open IL_EX_2-2.xlsx from the location where you store your Data Files, then save it as **IL_EX_2_Investments**.
b. Format the range B3:B7 using the Accounting number format.
c. Change the format of the date in cell B9 so it appears as 18-Jun.
d. Increase the number of decimals in cell D1 to 1, using a button in the Number group on the Home tab.
e. Save your work.

2. Change font and font size.
a. Select the range A3:A7.
b. Change the font of the selection to Calibri.
c. Increase the font size of the selection to 11 point.
d. Increase the font size of the label in cell A1 to 11 point.
e. Save your changes.

3. Change font styles and alignment.
a. Apply the Heading 2 cell style to cell A1.
b. Use the Merge & Center button to center the label in cell A1 over columns A and B.
c. Apply the italic and bold font formats to the label in cell C1.
d. Use the Format Painter to copy the format in cell C1 to the label in cell A9.
e. Change the alignment of cell B2 to Align Right using a button in the Alignment group on the Home tab.
f. Save your changes.

4. Adjust column width.
a. Resize column C to a width of 21.00 characters.
b. Use the AutoFit feature to automatically resize both columns A and B at the same time.
c. Change the text in cell B2 to **Total Managed Assets**.
d. Adjust the width of column B to display all of the content in cell B2.
e. Save your changes.

5. Insert and delete rows and columns.
a. Use the Insert dialog box to insert a new row between rows 1 and 2.
b. Use a column heading button to insert a new column between columns B and C.
c. Type **Fee** in cell C3 and center the label in the cell.
d. Create a formula in cell C4 that calculates the fee for the Boston office by multiplying the total managed assets in cell B4 by the annual fee percentage in cell E1. (*Hint*: Make sure you use the correct type of cell references in the formula.)
e. Copy the formula in cell C4 to the range C5:C8.
f. Use a row heading button to delete the Philadelphia row from the worksheet.
g. Save your changes.

6. Apply colors, borders, and documentation.
a. Add an outside border around the range A3:C7.
b. Apply the Green, Accent 6, Lighter 80% fill color (second row, last column) to the range D1:E1.
c. Change the color of the font in the range A9:B9 to Green, Accent 6, Darker 50% (last row, last column under Theme Colors).
d. Add a header in the center section of the worksheet that contains the sheet name.

Skills Review (continued)

e. Enter your name in the center section of the worksheet footer.

f. Save your changes.

7. **Apply conditional formatting.**

a. Select the range C4:C7, then create a Highlight Cells rule that changes cell contents to green fill with dark green text if the value is greater than 50000.

b. Select the range B4:B7, then apply Gradient Fill green data bars. (*Hint*: Click Green Data Bar in the Gradient Fill section.)

c. Open the Conditional Formatting Rules Manager dialog box and view the conditional formatting rules for the worksheet. (*Hint*: Click Manage Rules on the Conditional Formatting menu, then click the Show formatting rules for arrow.)

d. Review the rules for the worksheet, making sure your rules are correct, then close the dialog box.

e. Save your changes.

8. **Rename and move a worksheet.**

a. Rename the Sheet1 tab to **Active Management** and rename the Sheet2 tab to **Passive Management**.

b. Add a sheet to the workbook, then name the new sheet **Total Fees**.

c. Change the Active Management tab color to Green, Accent 6, Darker 50%.

d. Change the Passive Management tab color to Blue, Accent 5, Darker 50%.

e. Reorder the sheets so that the Total Fees sheet comes before (to the left of) the Active Management sheet.

f. Delete the Total Fees sheet.

g. Activate the Active Management sheet, then save your work.

9. **Check spelling.**

a. Move the cell pointer to cell A1.

b. Use the Find & Select feature to replace the word "Boston" with **New York**.

c. Use the Spelling tool to check the spelling on the worksheet and correct any spelling errors, using suggestions as appropriate.

d. Save your changes, then compare your Active Management sheet to FIGURE 2-27.

e. Preview the Active Management sheet in Backstage view, submit your work to your instructor as directed, then close the workbook and close Excel.

FIGURE 2-27

▲	A	B	C	D	E	F
1	CGS Investments			*Annual Fee Percentage*	1.1%	
2						
3	Office	Total Managed Assets	Fee			
4	New York	$ 5,426,324.35	$ 59,689.57			
5	Los Angeles	$ 4,895,714.77	$ 53,852.86			
6	Cincinnati	$ 3,415,981.19	$ 37,575.79			
7	Indianapolis	$ 4,213,257.23	$ 46,345.83			
8						
9	*Report date:*	18-Jun				
10						

Independent Challenge 1

As an accountant for Riverwalk medical clinic, you have been asked to review the expenses for the emergency room. You've organized the data in an Excel workbook, and now you want to format the data to improve its readability and highlight trends in expenses.

a. Start Excel, open IL_EX_2-3.xlsx from the location where you store your Data Files, then save it as **IL_EX_2_Riverwalk**.

b. Format the values in the Total column in the Accounting number format with two decimal places.

c. Format the values in the % of Total column as Percent format with two decimal places.

d. Format the values in the Inv. Date column with the Date format 14-Mar.

Independent Challenge 1 (continued)

e. Apply bold formatting to the column labels and increase the font size of the labels to 12.

f. Italicize the inventory Type items in column A.

g. Change the font of the Sales Tax label in cell K1 to Calibri.

h. Apply the Title cell style to cell A1.

i. Delete column I, then delete row 13.

j. Merge and center the title in cell A1 over columns A1:I1.

k. Resize column widths as necessary, using AutoFit or by dragging, so that all columns are wide enough to display the data and labels.

l. Use the Format Painter to copy the date format in the Inv. Date column to the values in the Inv. Due column.

m. Change the fill color of the sales tax information in the range J1:K1 to the Light Turquoise, Background 2 color (first row, third column from the left).

n. Change the font color of the sales tax information in the range J1:K1 to the Dark Teal, Text 2 color (first row, fourth column from the left).

o. Add a bottom border to the column labels.

p. Use conditional formatting to apply blue gradient data bars to the Total column data. Do not include the total in cell H38 at the bottom of the column.

q. Add the 3 Arrows (Colored) (first set in the Directional group) icon set to the Quantity column to illustrate the relative differences between quantities. Do not include the total in cell E38 at the bottom of the column in this format.

r. Rename Sheet3 to **Budget** and rename Sheet1 to **Actual**. Change the color of the Budget sheet to Red in the Standard colors. Change the color of the Actual sheet to Purple in the Standard colors.

s. Move Sheet2 to the right of the Budget sheet.

t. Activate the Actual Sheet and spell check the worksheet. Correct any spelling errors.

u. Using Find and Select, replace all instances of Maxi on the worksheet with ACE.

v. Delete Sheet2, enter your name in the center section of the Actual worksheet header, enter the sheet name in the center section of the worksheet footer, then save the file.

w. Preview the Actual worksheet in Backstage view. Compare your worksheet to FIGURE 2-28.

x. Submit your work to your instructor as directed, close the workbook, then close Excel.

FIGURE 2-28

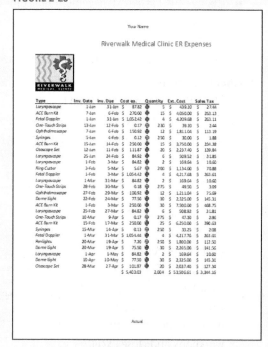

Independent Challenge 2

You are assisting the head of business operations at First Financial Services. You have been asked to format a worksheet showing the first-quarter business services for the company's five branches. As part of this effort, you want to illustrate service trends among the branches.

   a. Start Excel, open IL_EX_2-4.xlsx from the location where you store your Data Files, then save it as **IL_EX_2_FinancialServices**.

   b. Enter a formula in cell B8 for the Main total, then copy the formula to the range C8:F8.

   c. Enter a formula in cell G3 for the Credit card processing total, then copy the formula to the range G4:G8.

   d. Apply the Title cell style to cell A1, apply the Heading 4 cell style to the column headings in row 2, and apply the Total cell style to the range A8:G8.

   e. Merge and center the title in cell A1 across the range A1:G1.

   f. Format the range B3:G8 using the Accounting number format. AutoFit the widths of all columns and format the range with no decimal places.

   g. Format the date in cell B9 using the first 14-Mar-12 date format.

   h. Rotate the label in cell A2 up by 45 degrees. Copy this rotated format to the other column headings.

   i. Format the range A9:B9 with a Blue-Gray, Text 2, Lighter 80% (second row, fourth column from the left) fill.

   j. Format the range A9:B9 with a Blue, Accent 1, Darker 50% (last row, fifth column from the left, under Theme Colors) font color.

   k. Create a conditional format in the range G3:G8 so that entries less than 25,000,000 appear in light red fill with dark red text.

   l. Create a conditional format in the range B8:F8 to add the 3 Stars Ratings icon set. Widen the columns as necessary to fully display the data and formatting.

   m. Use the Spelling tool to check spelling in the sheet.

   n. Rename Sheet1 to **First Quarter**. Copy the First Quarter sheet and rename the copied sheet **Second Quarter**. Move the Second Quarter sheet if necessary so it is to the right of the First Quarter sheet.

   o. On the Second Quarter sheet, delete the data in the range B3:F7 and delete the date in cell B9.

   p. Activate the First Quarter sheet. Compare your worksheet to FIGURE 2-29.

   q. Enter your name in the center header section, change the worksheet orientation to landscape, then save your work.

   r. Preview the worksheet, make any final changes you think are necessary, then submit your work to your instructor as directed.

   s. Close the workbook, then close Excel.

FIGURE 2-29

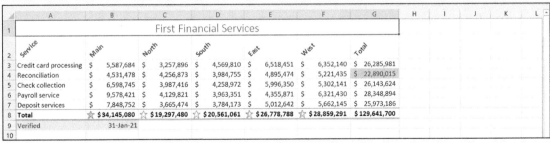

Visual Workshop

Open IL_EX_2-5.xlsx from the location where you store your Data Files, then save it as **IL_EX_2_EngineeringServices**. Use the skills you learned in this module to format the worksheet so it looks like the one shown in FIGURE 2-30. (Note that cell A1 is selected in the figure.) Use the blue gradient fill for the data bars in the Total column. Use the Title cell style for the company name in cell A1, the Heading 1 cell style for the column labels in row 2, and the Total cell style for the total values in the last row. The font color for the service packages listed in column A is Dark Blue in the standard colors. (*Hint*: A row has been deleted from the worksheet.) Enter your name in the upper-left section of the header, check the spelling on the worksheet, save your changes, then submit your work to your instructor as directed.

FIGURE 2-30

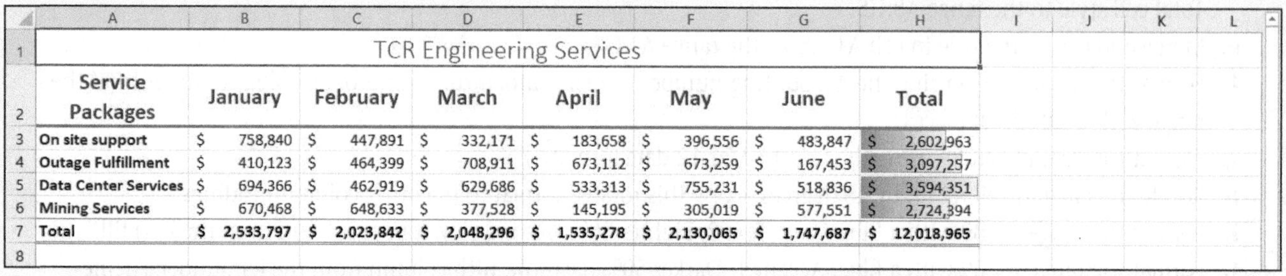

	A	B	C	D	E	F	G	H	I	J	K	L
1				TCR Engineering Services								
2	Service Packages	January	February	March	April	May	June	Total				
3	On site support	$ 758,840	$ 447,891	$ 332,171	$ 183,658	$ 396,556	$ 483,847	$ 2,602,963				
4	Outage Fulfillment	$ 410,123	$ 464,399	$ 708,911	$ 673,112	$ 673,259	$ 167,453	$ 3,097,257				
5	Data Center Services	$ 694,366	$ 462,919	$ 629,686	$ 533,313	$ 755,231	$ 518,836	$ 3,594,351				
6	Mining Services	$ 670,468	$ 648,633	$ 377,528	$ 145,195	$ 305,019	$ 577,551	$ 2,724,394				
7	Total	$ 2,533,797	$ 2,023,842	$ 2,048,296	$ 1,535,278	$ 2,130,065	$ 1,747,687	$ 12,018,965				
8												

Formatting a Worksheet

Analyzing Data Using Formulas

CASE ▶ Ellie Schwartz, the vice president of Finance at JCL, wants to know how North American revenues have performed compared to last year and relative to projected targets. She asks you to prepare a worksheet that summarizes and analyzes this revenue data.

Module Objectives

After completing this module, you will be able to:

- Enter a formula using the Quick Analysis tool
- Build a logical formula with the IF function
- Build a logical formula with the AND function
- Round a value with a function
- Build a statistical formula with the COUNTA function
- Enter a date function
- Work with equation tools
- Control worksheet calculations

Files You Will Need

IL_EX_3-1.xlsx   IL_EX_3-4.xlsx
IL_EX_3-2.xlsx   IL_EX_3-5.xlsx
IL_EX_3-3.xlsx

Learning
Outcomes
• Create a formula
using the Quick
Analysis tool
• Create a formula
to find a percent-
age increase

Enter a Formula Using the Quick Analysis Tool

So far, you have used the AutoSum button on the ribbon to quickly add simple formulas that sum and average selected data. You can also add formulas using the Quick Analysis tool, which opens when you select a range of cells. This tool allows you to quickly format, chart, or analyze data by calculating sums, averages, and other selected totals. **CASE** *To help Ellie evaluate revenues at JCL, you want to calculate yearly revenue totals for each North American office and compare the yearly performance of each office to the previous year.*

STEPS

1. **sam** ⬇ **Start Excel, open IL_EX_3-1.xlsx from the location where you store your Data Files, then save it as IL_EX_3_Revenue**

2. **Select the range B3:E12, click the Quick Analysis button ⬛ that appears below the selection, then click the Totals tab**

   The Totals tab in the Quick Analysis tool displays commonly used functions, as shown in **FIGURE 3-1**. This tab includes two Sum buttons, one that inserts the SUM function in a row beneath the selected range, and one that inserts the SUM function in the column to the right of the range.

QUICK TIP
Clicking the first AutoSum button enters totals in a row below a selected range.

3. **Click the Sum button displaying the gold column**

   The newly calculated totals display in the column to the right of the selected range, in cells F3:F12.

4. **Click cell H3, type =(, click cell F3, type -, click cell G3, then type)**

   This first part of the formula finds the difference in total revenue from the previous year to this year. You enclosed this operation in parentheses to make sure this difference is calculated first.

5. **Type /, then click cell G3**

   The second part of this formula divides the difference in revenue by the total revenue for the previous year, to calculate the increase or decrease.

6. **Click the Enter button ✓ on the formula bar**

   The result, .75405003, appears in cell H3. The column isn't wide enough to fully display this value but the number of decimal places will be adjusted in the next formatting step.

7. **Click the Percent Style button % in the Number group, then click the Increase Decimal button ⬛ in the Number group twice**

   The formatted percentage, 75.41%, appears in cell H3.

8. **Drag the fill handle from cell H3 to cell H12, then save your work**

   The percentage changes in annual revenue for each office appear in column H, as shown in **FIGURE 3-2**.

FIGURE 3-1: **Quick Analysis tool**

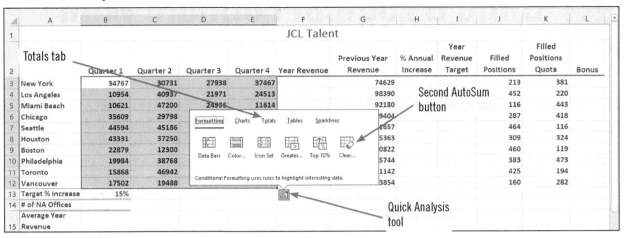

FIGURE 3-2: **Percentage changes**

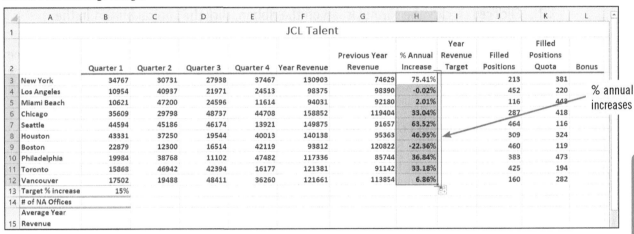

Excel

Build a Logical Formula with the IF Function

Learning
Outcomes
• Build a logical
formula using the
IF function
• Apply comparison
operators in a
logical test

You can build a formula in a worksheet using a **logical function** that returns a different value depending on whether the given condition is true or false. An **IF function** is a logical function that assigns a value to a cell based on a logical test. A **logical formula** makes calculations based on criteria that you create, called **stated conditions**. For example, you can build a formula to calculate bonuses based on a person's performance rating, where the stated condition is 5. If a person is rated a 5 on a scale of 1 to 5, he or she receives an additional 10% of his or her salary as a bonus; otherwise, there is no bonus. The IF function has three parts, including the **logical test**, which is the first part of the function. This test is a condition that can be answered with a true or false response. If the logical test is true, then the second part of the function is applied; if it is false, then the third part of the function is applied. When entering the logical test portion of an IF statement, you often use some combination of the comparison operators listed in TABLE 3-1.

CASE ▶ *Ellie asks you to calculate whether each office met or missed its revenue target for the year.*

STEPS

1. **Click cell I3, click the Formulas tab on the ribbon, click the Logical button in the Function Library group, then click IF**

   The Function Arguments dialog box opens, displaying three boxes for the three parts of a logical function: the Logical_test, which in this case tests if the annual increase is greater than or equal to the target increase; the Value_if_true box, which tells what to do if the test results are true; and the Value_if_false box, which tells what to do if the test results are false.

2. **With the insertion point in the Logical_test box click cell H3, type > =, click cell B13, press F4, then press TAB**

   The symbol (>) represents "greater than." B13 needs to be formatted as an absolute reference because it is a fixed value in a formula that will be copied into other cells. So far, the formula reads, "If the annual increase is greater than or equal to the target increase..."

3. **With the insertion point in the Value_if_true box type MET, then press TAB**

   This part of the function tells Excel to display the text MET if the annual increase equals or exceeds the target increase of 15%. Quotation marks are automatically added around the text you entered.

4. **Type MISSED in the Value_if_false box, then click OK**

   This part tells Excel to display the text MISSED if the results of the logical test are false—that is, if the increase does not equal or exceed the target. The function is complete, and the result, MET, appears in cell I3, as shown in FIGURE 3-3.

5. **Drag the fill handle to copy the formula in cell I3 into the range I4:I12**

   Compare your results with FIGURE 3-4. Most offices met their target increase but four offices did not.

6. **Save the workbook**

FIGURE 3-3: Worksheet with IF function

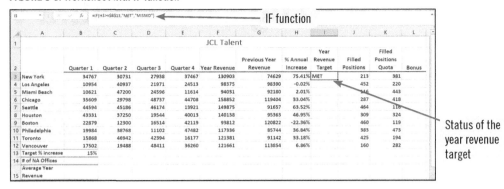

IF function

Status of the
year revenue
target

FIGURE 3-4: Worksheet showing yearly revenue status

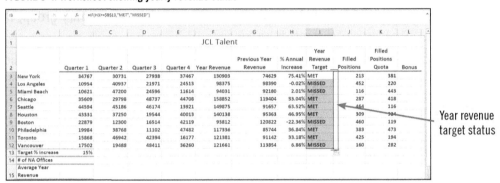

Year revenue
target status

TABLE 3-1: Comparison operators

operator	meaning	operator	meaning
<	Less than	<=	Less than or equal to
>	Greater than	>=	Greater than or equal to
=	Equal to	<>	Not equal to

Nesting IF functions

You can nest IF functions to test several conditions in a formula. A nested IF function contains IF functions inside other IF functions to test these multiple conditions. To create a nested IF function, enter the second IF statement in the value_if_false argument of the first IF statement. For example, the nested statement =IF(H3<0%,"Warning",IF(H3<50%,"No Bonus","Bonus")) tests whether a warning should be issued based on the percentage increases for an office. Assuming the percentage increase of an office is in cell H3, the nested IF statement first checks to see if the increase was less than 0. If that first test is true, the text "Warning" will display. If the first test is false, a second test will be performed to check to see if the increase is less than 50%. If that second test is true (values are less than 50%), the text "No Bonus" will display. If that second test is false, the text "Bonus" will display.

Excel

Learning
Outcomes
• Build a logical
  formula using the
  AND function
• Apply logical tests

Build a Logical Formula with the AND Function

You can also build a logical function using the AND function. The AND function evaluates all of its arguments and returns, or displays, TRUE if every logical test in the formula is true. The AND function returns a value of FALSE if one or more of its logical tests is false. The AND function arguments can include text, numbers, or cell references. **CASE** ▶ *JCL awards bonuses to offices that meet targets for both annual revenue and filled positions. Now that you've determined which offices met their revenue goal, you need to see which offices are eligible for a bonus by meeting both this target and the filled positions target.*

STEPS

1. **Click cell L3, click the Logical button in the Function Library group, then click AND**
   The Function Arguments dialog box opens.

2. **With the insertion point in the Logical1 box, click cell J3, type >=, click cell K3, then press TAB**
   This part of the formula reads, "If the number of filled positions is greater than or equal to the filled positions quota..."

3. **With the insertion point in the Logical2 box, click cell I3, then type = "MET"**
   This part of the formula reads, "If the revenue goal was met..."

TROUBLE
If you get a formula error, check to be sure that you typed the quotation marks around MET.

4. **Click OK**
   The function is complete, and the result, FALSE, appears in cell L3, as shown in FIGURE 3-5, because both stated conditions were not met. Although the revenue target was met, the number of filled positions was not greater than or equal to the quota.

5. **Drag the fill handle to copy the formula in cell L3 into the range L4:L12**
   Compare your results with FIGURE 3-6.

QUICK TIP
You can place one function, such as an AND function, inside a formula containing another function, such as an IF function. For example, you could replace the formulas in cell I3 and L3 with one formula in L3 that reads =IF(AND(H3>=$B$13, J3>=K3), "TRUE", "FALSE").

6. **Enter your name in the center section of the footer, preview the worksheet, then save your work**

Using the OR and NOT logical functions

The OR logical function follows the same syntax as the AND function, but rather than returning TRUE if every argument is true, the OR function will return TRUE if any of its arguments are true. It will only return FALSE if all of its arguments are false. The NOT logical function reverses the value of its argument. For example, NOT(TRUE) reverses its argument of TRUE and returns FALSE. You might want to use this function in a worksheet to ensure that a cell is not equal to a particular value. See TABLE 3-2 for examples of the AND, OR, and NOT functions.

FIGURE 3-5: **Worksheet with AND function**

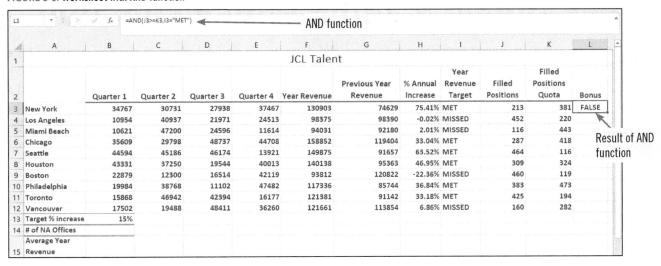

FIGURE 3-6: **Worksheet with bonus status evaluated for all offices**

	A	B	C	D	E	F	G	H	I	J	K	L
1						JCL Talent						
2		Quarter 1	Quarter 2	Quarter 3	Quarter 4	Year Revenue	Previous Year Revenue	% Annual Increase	Year Revenue Target	Filled Positions	Filled Positions Quota	Bonus
3	New York	34767	30731	27938	37467	130903	74629	75.41%	MET	213	381	FALSE
4	Los Angeles	10954	40937	21971	24513	98375	98390	-0.02%	MISSED	452	220	FALSE
5	Miami Beach	10621	47200	24596	11614	94031	92180	2.01%	MISSED	116	443	FALSE
6	Chicago	35609	29798	48737	44708	158852	119404	33.04%	MET	287	418	FALSE
7	Seattle	44594	45186	46174	13921	149875	91657	63.52%	MET	464	116	TRUE
8	Houston	43331	37250	19544	40013	140138	95363	46.95%	MET	309	324	FALSE
9	Boston	22879	12300	16514	42119	93812	120822	-22.36%	MISSED	460	119	FALSE
10	Philadelphia	19984	38768	11102	47482	117336	85744	36.84%	MET	383	473	FALSE
11	Toronto	15868	46942	42394	16177	121381	91142	33.18%	MET	425	194	TRUE
12	Vancouver	17502	19488	48411	36260	121661	113854	6.86%	MISSED	160	282	FALSE
13	Target % increase	15%										
14	# of NA Offices											
15	Average Year Revenue											

Bonus status

Excel

TABLE 3-2: **Examples of AND, OR, and NOT functions (cell A1=10, cell B1=20)**

function	formula	result
AND	=AND(A1>5,B1>25)	FALSE
OR	=OR(A1>5,B1>25)	TRUE
NOT	=NOT(A1=0)	TRUE

Round a Value with a Function

Learning Outcomes
- Build a function using the ROUND function
- Use Formula AutoComplete to insert a function

You have used formatting to increase and decrease the decimal places of numbers displayed on a worksheet. In this case, only the formatting of these numbers changes. Their values, when used in future worksheet calculations, remain the same as they originally appeared on the worksheet. You can round a value or formula result to a specified number of decimal places by using the **ROUND function**; the resulting rounded value is then used instead of the original value in future worksheet calculations. **CASE** *In your worksheet, you want to find the average yearly revenue and round that calculated value to the nearest integer.*

STEPS

1. **Click cell B15, click the AutoSum arrow $\Sigma \cdot$, then click Average**

2. **Select the range F3:F12, then click the Enter button ✓ on the formula bar**
   The result, 122636.4, appears in cell B15.

3. **Click to the right of = in the formula bar**
   You want to position the ROUND function here, at the beginning of the formula.

4. **Type RO**
   Formula AutoComplete displays a list of functions beginning with RO beneath the formula bar.

5. **Double-click ROUND in the functions list**
   The new function and an opening parenthesis are added to the AVERAGE function, as shown in **FIGURE 3-7**.

6. **Press END, then type ,0)**
   The comma separates the arguments within the formula, and 0 indicates that you don't want any decimal places to appear in the calculated value. You may have also noticed that the parentheses at either end of the formula briefly became bold, indicating that you entered the correct number of open and closed parentheses so the formula is balanced.

7. **Click the Enter button ✓ on the formula bar**

8. **Compare your worksheet to FIGURE 3-8, then save your work**

FIGURE 3-7: ROUND function added to an existing function

ScreenTip indicates needed arguments

ROUND function and opening parenthesis inserted in formula

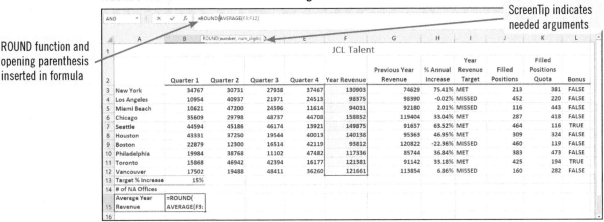

FIGURE 3-8: Rounded year average

Round function surrounds average formula

Calculated value with no decimals

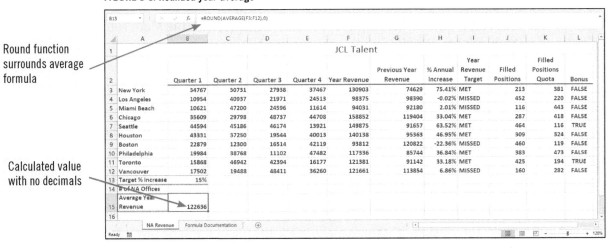

Using Excel rounding functions

You can use other rounding functions besides ROUND to fine-tune the rounding results you want to see. The **MROUND function** rounds a number to the nearest multiple of another number. The syntax is: MROUND(number, multiple). For example, MROUND(14,3) returns the value 15 because 15 is the nearest multiple of 3 to 14. The **ROUNDDOWN function** works like the ROUND function except that rather than rounding a number to the

next closest value, it always rounds down. The syntax is ROUNDDOWN(number, num_digits). For example, =ROUNDDOWN(15.778, 2) returns a value of 15.77 because this is the nearest two-digit number below 15.778. The **ROUNDUP function** works similarly but rounds a number up. The syntax is ROUNDUP(number, num_digits). For example, =ROUNDUP(15.778, 2) returns a value of 15.78.

Excel

Build a Statistical Formula with the COUNTA function

When you select a range, a count of cells in the range that are not blank appears in the status bar. For example, if you select the range A1:A5 and only cells A1, A4, and A5 contain data, the status bar displays "Count: 3." To count nonblank cells more precisely, or to incorporate these calculations in a worksheet, you can use the COUNT and COUNTA functions. The **COUNT function** tallies the number of cells in a range that contain numeric data, including numbers, dates, and formulas. The **COUNTA function** tallies how many cells in a specified range contain any entries (numbers, dates, or text). For example, the formula =COUNT(A1:A5) returns the number of cells in the range that contain numeric data, and the formula =COUNTA(A1:A5) returns the number of cells in the range that are not empty. **CASE** ▶ *In your worksheet, you want to calculate the number of offices in the North America region. You also want to format some worksheet values using a custom format, so that the data looks exactly the way you want.*

STEPS

1. **Click cell B14, click the Formulas tab on the ribbon, click the More Functions button, then point to Statistical**

   A gallery of statistical functions opens, as shown in FIGURE 3-9.

2. **Scroll down the list of functions if necessary, then click COUNTA**

   The Function Arguments dialog box opens.

3. **With the insertion point in the Value1 box select the range A3:A12, then click OK**

   The number of offices, 10, appears in cell B14.

4. **Select the range H3:H12, click the Home tab on the ribbon, click the Format button in the Cells group, then click Format Cells**

   Currently, the negative values in this range are difficult to distinguish from the positive values.

5. **Click Custom in the Category menu, click after % in the Type box, type ;[Red](0.00%) as shown in FIGURE 3-10, then click OK**

   The negative percentages in cells H4 and H9 now appear in red with parentheses.

6. **Select the range B3:G12, press and hold CTRL, then click cell B15**

   Holding CTRL allows you to select multiple ranges and cells.

7. **Click the Accounting Number Format button $\boxed{\$}$ in the Number group, then click the Decrease Decimal button $\boxed{\tiny{.00 \atop +.0}}$ twice**

   Formatting these revenue figures makes them easier to read. Compare your worksheet to FIGURE 3-11.

FIGURE 3-9: **Statistical functions**

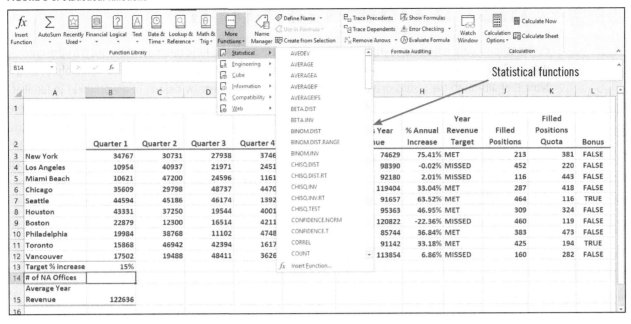

FIGURE 3-10: **Custom number format**

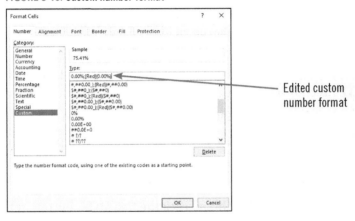

Edited custom
number format

FIGURE 3-11: **Formatted worksheet**

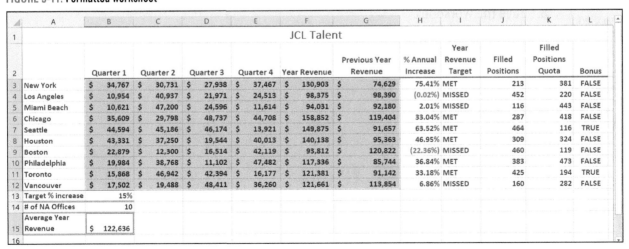

Enter a Date Function

Learning Outcomes
• Enter a date using the TODAY function
• Enter a date using the DATE function

Excel includes date functions to make it easy to calculate date and time related results, such as the current date or the time between events. See TABLE 3-3 for some of the available Date and Time functions in Excel. Note that although the results of all date and time functions appear by default in a worksheet in familiar-looking date and time formats, Excel actually stores them as sequential serial numbers and uses these numbers in calculations. January 1, 1900 is assigned serial number 1 and dates are represented as the number of days following that date. You can see the serial number of a date by using the **DATEVALUE function** or by applying the Number format to the cell. For example, to see the serial number of January 1, 2021 you would enter =DATEVALUE("1/1/2021"). The result would be the serial number 44197. **CASE** ▶ *To help document your work on this report, you decide to use a date function.*

STEPS

1. **Click cell A2, click the Formulas tab on the ribbon, then click the Date & Time button in the Function library**

   A list of date and time functions opens, as shown in FIGURE 3-12.

2. **Click TODAY, then click OK in the dialog box**

   The **TODAY function** displays the current date and updates each time a worksheet is opened. However, you want the workbook to show the date it was completed, rather than the date the workbook is opened.

3. **Press DEL, click the Date & Time button in the Function Library, then click DATE**

   The **DATE function** uses three arguments, year, month, and day, to enter a date.

4. **With the insertion point in the Year box type 2021, then press TAB**

5. **With the insertion point in the Month box type 2, then press TAB**

6. **Type 24 in the Day box, then click OK**

   The function is complete, and the result, 2/24/2021, appears in cell A2.

7. **Click the Home tab on the ribbon, click the Cell Styles button in the Styles group, then click 20% Accent1 in the Themed Cell Styles group**

   Compare your worksheet to FIGURE 3-13.

8. **Save the workbook**

FIGURE 3-12: Date & Time functions

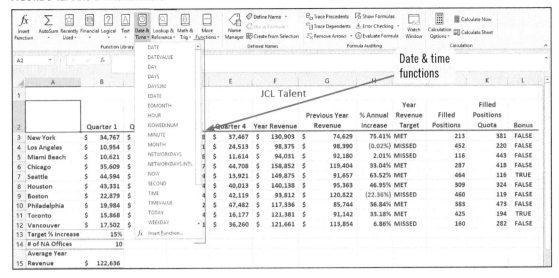

FIGURE 3-13: Formatted date

Formatted date

TABLE 3-3: Date and Time functions

function	calculates	example formula	example result
DAY	The day of the month using a date serial number	=DAY(44197)	1
NOW	The current date and time	=NOW()	1/1/2021 10:00
MONTH	The month number using a date serial number	=MONTH(44197)	1
TIME	A serial number in time format from hours, minutes, and seconds	=TIME(5,12,20)	0.216898
TIMEVALUE	A serial time in text format	=TIMEVALUE("5:15:24")	.219028
YEAR	The year portion of a date	=YEAR(44197)	2021
HOUR	The hour portion of a time	=HOUR("6:45:21 PM")	18
MINUTE	The minute portion of a time	=MINUTE("6:45:21 PM")	45
SECOND	The second portion of a time	=SECOND("6:45:21 PM")	21
WEEKDAY	The day of the week from a serial date (1 =Sunday, 2 = Monday…)	=WEEKDAY("6/21/2021")	2
WORKDAY	A serial number in date format after a certain number of working days	=WORKDAY(44198,5)	44204 (When formatted as a date: 1/8/2021

Excel

Work with Equation Tools

**Learning
Outcomes**
• Select an equation
  structure
• Enter an equation
  using the equation
  tools

Excel's equation tools allow you to insert many common equations, such as the area of a circle and the Pythagorean theorem, in a worksheet. The worksheet does not display the results of these expressions, it simply displays them with the correct syntax and structure. This can be helpful to illustrate the thinking behind a formula or to share mathematical information with others, such as algebraic formulas. You can also compose your own equations and formulas using structures such as fractions, exponents, radicals, and matrices along with many available mathematical symbols. **CASE** ▶ *Before sending the workbook to Ellie, you want to document the process you used to determine the revenue percentage increase. You have started this process on a separate worksheet in the workbook.*

STEPS

1. **Click the** Formula Documentation sheet tab, **click the** Insert tab **on the ribbon, click the** Symbols button **if necessary, then click the** Equation button **in the Symbols group**
   The Equation Tools Design tab opens and the Drawing Tools Format tab becomes available. An equation placeholder that reads, "Type equation here," is added to the worksheet.

2. **With the Equation Tools Design tab active, click the** Fraction button **in the Structures group, then click the** Stacked Fraction button **(first row, first column)**
   The structure of a fraction is placed on the worksheet with a blank numerator and denominator, as shown in FIGURE 3-14.

3. **Click the** upper box **(the numerator), then type** (Year Revenue – Previous Year Revenue)

4. **Click the** lower box **(the denominator), then type** Previous Year Revenue

5. **Select the** equation **if necessary, place the** Move pointer ⁺↖ **on the edge of the equation, drag the** equation **so the upper left corner is in cell** A9, **then click cell** A1

6. **Compare your worksheet to** FIGURE 3-15, **then save your work**

FIGURE 3-14: **Fraction structure added to worksheet**

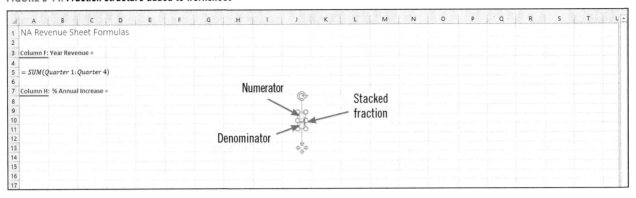

FIGURE 3-15: **Completed equation**

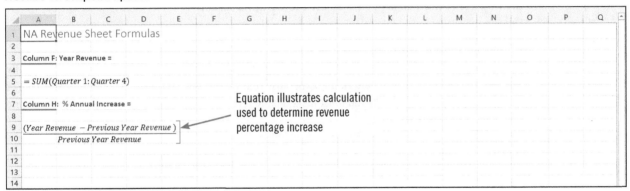

Using Draw tools

On a touch-enabled device you can use your mouse, a stylus, or even your finger to draw or write. If your device is touch-enabled, the Touch/Mouse Mode button appears on the Quick Access toolbar and the Draw tab automatically becomes available on the ribbon. You can add or remove the Touch/Mouse Mode button by clicking the Customize Quick Access Toolbar button ⬚, then clicking Touch/Mouse Mode. Touch mode adds space between the buttons on the ribbon, making them easier to access with your fingertip. You can manually turn on the Draw tab by clicking the File tab, clicking Options, clicking Customize Ribbon in the Excel Options dialog box, selecting the Draw box in the Main Tabs list, then clicking OK.

Clicking the Draw button in the Tools group of the Draw tab allows you to select a pen, pencil, or highlighter. If you click

the selected instrument you can change its thickness and color. As you work, you can correct drawing mistakes using the Eraser tool, also in the Tools group. Clicking the Ink to Shape button in the Convert group before beginning to draw converts your completed drawing to a geometric shape. The Ink to Shape feature works with pens and pencils but not highlighters. The Convert group includes an Ink to Math button that converts a handwritten mathematical expression to text. If you wish to see the steps followed in creating drawings on the worksheet, use the Ink Replay button in the Replay group to replay each step.

To modify an ink shape, you must select it, either by using the Lasso Select button in the Tools group to enclose it or by clicking the shape. Once a shape is selected, you can move, copy, rotate, and format it using the Drawing Tools Format tab.

Excel

Control Worksheet Calculations

Learning
Outcomes
• Control formula
calculations
• Calculate work-
sheet formulas

Whenever you change a value in a cell, Excel automatically recalculates all the formulas on the worksheet based on that cell. This automatic calculation is efficient unless you create a worksheet so large that the recalculation process slows down data entry and screen updating. Worksheets with many formulas, data tables, or functions may also recalculate slowly. In these cases, you might want to apply the **manual calculation** option to turn off automatic calculation of worksheet formulas, allowing you to selectively determine if and when you want Excel to perform calculations. When you turn on the manual calculation option, Excel stops automatically recalculating all open worksheets. **CASE** ▶ *Because you have added several formulas to the worksheet, you decide to review the formula settings in the workbook and see whether changing from automatic to manual calculation improves performance.*

STEPS

1. **Click the NA Revenue sheet tab, click the File tab on the ribbon to open Backstage view, click Options, then click Formulas on the Options screen**

   The options related to formula calculation and error checking appear, as shown in FIGURE 3-16.

2. **Under Calculation options, click the Manual option button**

   When you select the Manual option, the Recalculate workbook before saving check box automatically becomes active and contains a check mark. Because the workbook will not recalculate until you save or close and reopen the workbook, you must make sure to recalculate your worksheet before you print it and after you finish making changes.

3. **Click OK**

   Ellie informs you that the first quarter revenue for the New York office is incorrect and needs updating.

4. **Click cell B3**

   Before proceeding, notice that in cell F3 the year revenue for the New York office is $130,903.

5. **Type 34305, then click the Enter button ☑ on the formula bar**

   Notice that the year revenue in cell F3 does not adjust to reflect the change in cell B3. The word "Calculate" appears in the status bar to indicate that a specific value on the worksheet did indeed change and remind-ing you that the worksheet must be recalculated.

6. **Click the Formulas tab, click the Calculate Sheet button in the Calculation group, click cell A1, then save the workbook**

   The year revenue in cell F3 is now $130,441. The other formulas on the worksheet affected by the value in cell B3 changed as well, as shown in FIGURE 3-17. Because this is a relatively small worksheet that recalcu-lates quickly, you decide that the manual calculation option is not necessary.

7. **Click the Calculation Options button in the Calculation group, then click Automatic**

   Now Excel will automatically recalculate the worksheet formulas any time you make changes.

8. **sam̄ ⬆ Save your changes, activate cell A1, submit the workbook to your instructor as directed, close the workbook, then close Excel**

FIGURE 3-16: **Excel formula options**

Click to select
manual calculation
of worksheet formulas

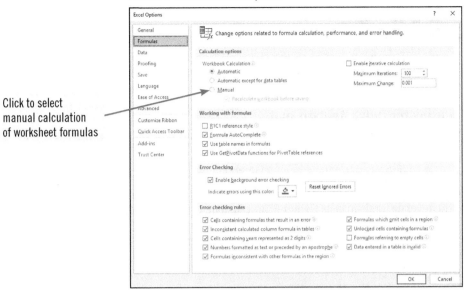

FIGURE 3-17: **Worksheet with updated values**

	A	B	C	D	E	F	G	H	I	J	K	L
1						JCL Talent						
2	2/24/2021	Quarter 1	Quarter 2	Quarter 3	Quarter 4	Year Revenue	Previous Year Revenue	% Annual Increase	Year Revenue Target	Filled Positions	Filled Positions Quota	Bonus
3	New York	$ 34,305	$ 30,731	$ 27,938	$ 37,467	$ 130,441	$ 74,629	74.79%	MET	213	381	FALSE
4	Los Angeles	$ 10,954	$ 40,937	$ 21,971	$ 24,513	$ 98,375	$ 98,390	(0.02%)	MISSED	452	220	FALSE
5	Miami Beach	$ 10,621	$ 47,200	$ 24,596	$ 11,614	$ 94,031	$ 92,180	2.01%	MISSED	116	443	FALSE
6	Chicago	$ 35,609	$ 29,798	$ 48,737	$ 44,708	$ 158,852	$ 119,404	33.04%	MET	287	418	FALSE
7	Seattle	$ 44,594	$ 45,186	$ 46,174	$ 13,921	$ 149,875	$ 91,657	63.52%	MET	464	116	TRUE
8	Houston	$ 43,331	$ 37,250	$ 19,544	$ 40,013	$ 140,138	$ 95,363	46.95%	MET	309	324	FALSE
9	Boston	$ 22,879	$ 12,300	$ 16,514	$ 42,119	$ 93,812	$ 120,822	(22.36%)	MISSED	460	119	FALSE
10	Philadelphia	$ 19,984	$ 38,768	$ 11,102	$ 47,482	$ 117,336	$ 85,744	36.84%	MET	383	473	FALSE
11	Toronto	$ 15,868	$ 46,942	$ 42,394	$ 16,177	$ 121,381	$ 91,142	33.18%	MET	425	194	TRUE
12	Vancouver	$ 17,502	$ 19,488	$ 48,411	$ 36,260	$ 121,661	$ 113,854	6.86%	MISSED	160	282	FALSE
13	Target % increase	15%										
14	# of NA Offices	10										
15	Average Year Revenue	$ 122,590										

Updated values

Excel

Showing and printing worksheet formulas

Sometimes you need to show or keep a record of all the formulas in a worksheet. You might want to do this to show exactly how you came up with a complex calculation, so you can explain it to others. To display formulas rather than results in a worksheet, first open the workbook. Click the Formulas tab on the ribbon, then click the Show Formulas button in the Formula Auditing group to select it. When the Show Formulas button is selected, formulas rather than resulting values are displayed on the worksheet, and any entered values appear without number formatting. You can print the worksheet to save a record of all the formulas. The Show Formulas button is a toggle: click it again to show the values, rather than the formulas, on the worksheet.

Practice

Skills Review

1. **Enter a formula using the Quick Analysis tool.**
   a. Start Excel, open IL_EX_3-2.xlsx from the location where you store your Data Files, then save it as **IL_EX_3_Labs**.
   b. On the First Quarter worksheet, select the range B3:D9, then use the Quick Analysis tool to enter the first quarter revenue totals in column E.
   c. In cell G3, use the revenue totals in cells E3 and F3 to calculate the percent increase in revenue from the previous quarter to the first quarter.
   d. Format the value in cell G3 using the percent style with two decimal places.
   e. Copy the formula in cell G3 into the range G4:G9.

2. **Build a logical formula with the IF function.**
   a. In cell H3, use the Function Arguments dialog box to enter the formula **=IF(G3>=$B$10,"Met","Missed")**.
   b. Copy the formula in cell H3 into the range H4:H9.
   c. Save your work.

3. **Build a logical formula with the AND function.**
   a. In cell J3, use the Function Arguments dialog box to enter the formula **=AND(H3="Met",I3>=4)**.
   b. Copy the formula in cell J3 into the range J4:J9.
   c. Enter your name in the center section of the footer for the First Quarter sheet.
   d. Save your work.

4. **Round a value with a function.**
   a. In cell B12, use the AutoSum list arrow to enter a function to average the first quarter revenue values in column E.
   b. Use Formula AutoComplete to edit this formula to include the ROUND function showing zero decimal places.
   c. Correct any errors in the formula.
   d. Save your work.

5. **Build a statistical formula with the COUNTA function.**
   a. In cell B11, use a statistical formula to calculate the number of lab locations in column A.
   b. Create a custom format for the percentages in column G so that the negative values appear in red with parentheses.
   c. Format the revenue values in the range B3:F9 and in cell B12 using the Accounting Number Format with no decimal places.
   d. Save your work.

6. **Enter a date function.**
   a. In cell D12, enter **Report Date**.
   b. In cell E12, use the TODAY function to enter today's date.
   c. Delete the TODAY function in cell E12, then use the DATE function to enter the date 4/3/2021.
   d. Use the Cell Style Rose, 20% - Accent 1 (the first row and first column in the Themed Cell Styles group) to format the range D12:E12.
   e. Activate cell A1, then save your work.

7. **Work with equation tools.**
   a. Activate the Formula Documentation sheet.
   b. Add a stacked fraction to the worksheet.
   c. Enter **(First Quarter Revenue – Previous Quarter Revenue)** as the numerator.
   d. Enter **Previous Quarter Revenue** as the denominator.

Skills Review (continued)

e. Move the equation to place its upper left corner in cell A9.

f. Activate cell A1, then save your work.

8. Control worksheet calculations.

a. Activate the First Quarter sheet.

b. Open the Formulas category of the Excel Options dialog box.

c. Change the worksheet calculations to manual.

d. Change the value in cell B3 to **72000**.

e. Recalculate the worksheet manually.

f. Change the worksheet calculation back to automatic using the Calculation Options button on the Formulas tab of the ribbon, then save the workbook.

g. Preview the worksheet in Backstage view. Compare your screen to FIGURE 3-18.

h. Save your changes, submit your work to your instructor as directed, close the workbook, then close Excel.

FIGURE 3-18

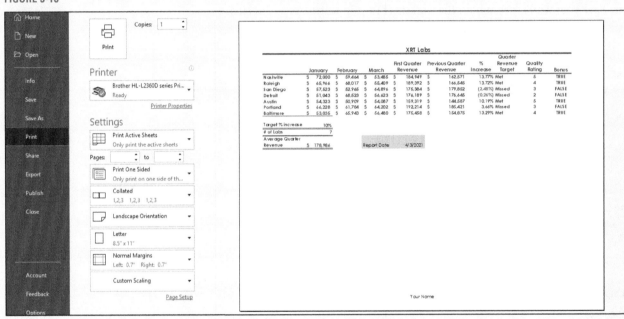

Independent Challenge 1

The manager at Riverwalk Medical Clinic has hired you to analyze patient accounts and insurance reimbursements for their Boston imaging facility. He would like you to flag overdue accounts and calculate the average procedure amount.

a. Open IL_EX_3-3.xlsx from the location where you store your Data Files, then save it as **IL_EX_3_Accounts**.

b. Use the DATE function to return the date 5/18/2021 in cell B3.

c. Enter a formula in cell C5 that calculates the statement age by subtracting the statement date in cell B5 from the report date in cell B3. (*Hint*: The formula needs to use an absolute reference for the report date in cell B3 so this cell address doesn't change when copied.)

d. Copy the formula in cell C5 to the range C6:C11.

Independent Challenge 1 (continued)

e. In cell F5, enter an IF function that calculates the patient responsibility. (*Hint*: The Logical_test should check to see if the procedure amount is greater than the insurance payment, the Value_if_true should calculate the procedure amount minus the insurance payment, and the Value_if_false should be 0.)

f. Copy the IF function in cell F5 to the range F6:F11.

g. In cell G5, enter an AND function to find accounts that are past due. Accounts are past due if a patient is responsible for a balance due and the statement age is over 30 days. (*Hint*: The Logical1 condition should check to see if the statement age is more than 30, and the Logical2 condition should check if the patient responsibility is greater than 0.)

h. Use the fill handle to copy the AND function in cell G5 into the range G6:G11.

i. In cell B13, enter a COUNTA function to calculate the number of accounts in column A.

j. Enter a function in cell B14 that averages the procedure amounts in column D.

k. Use Formula AutoComplete to enter a function to round the average in cell B14 to zero decimal places.

l. Enter your name in the center section of the footer.

m. Preview the worksheet in Backstage view. Compare your screen to FIGURE 3-19.

n. Save your work, then submit the worksheet to your instructor as directed.

o. Close the workbook and Excel.

FIGURE 3-19

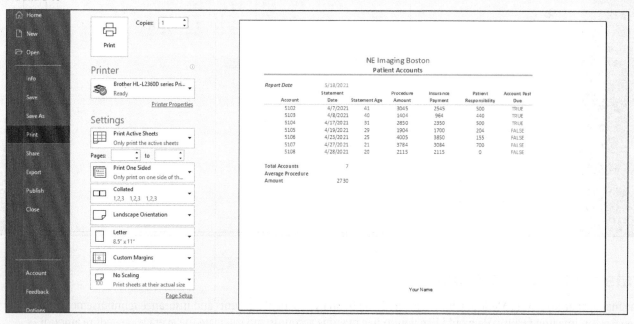

Independent Challenge 2

As the senior loan officer at North Shore Bank, one of your responsibilities is reviewing the quarterly loan portfolios for the four branches. This includes adding statistics including total loan amounts, average total loans, and the growth in loans issued at each branch. You are preparing a portfolio review for the 4th quarter, which you plan to issue on December 31.

a. Open IL_EX_3-4.xlsx from the location where you store your Data Files, then save it as **IL_EX_3_Loans**.

b. Use the TODAY function to enter today's date in cell B12. Verify today's date is displayed.

c. Delete the date in cell B12 and replace it with the date 12/31/2021 using the DATE function.

d. Use the Quick Analysis button to enter totals in the range F4:F7 and B8:E8. (*Hint*: You need to use two buttons on the Totals tab to accomplish this.)

e. Enter a formula in cell H4 to find the percentage increase for the total 4th quarter loans over the 3rd quarter total for the Main Street branch. Format the percentage increase using the percent style with two decimal places.

f. Copy the percentage increase formula in cell H4 to the range H5:H7.

g. In cell J4, enter an AND function to determine if the Main Street branch is eligible for a bonus. To be eligible, the 4th quarter percentage increase must be over 10% and the customer ratings must be higher than 85%.

h. Use the fill handle to copy the AND function in cell J4 into the range J5:J7.

i. Enter a function in cell B10 that averages the total 4th quarter loan amounts in column F, then round the average to zero decimal places.

j. In cell B11, enter a function to calculate the number of branches in column A.

k. Create a custom format for the percentages in column H so that the negative values appear in red with parentheses.

l. Format the loan values in the ranges B4:G7, B8:E8, and cell B10 using the Accounting Number Format with no decimals. Widen the columns as necessary to fully display all of the worksheet data.

m. Activate the Documentation tab and use a stacked fraction to document the 4th quarter % increase formula in cell A3.

n. Activate the 4th Quarter Report sheet. Switch to manual calculation for formulas. Change the personal loan amount for the Main Street branch in cell B4 to **1306500**. Calculate the worksheet formula manually. Turn on automatic calculation again.

o. Enter your name in the center footer section.

p. Preview the worksheet in Backstage view. Compare your screen to FIGURE 3-20.

q. Save your work, then submit the worksheet to your instructor as directed.

r. Close the workbook and Excel.

Excel

FIGURE 3-20

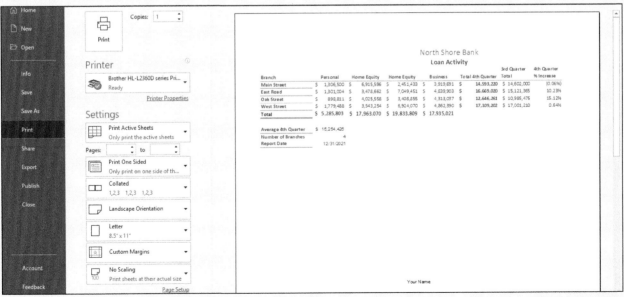

Visual Workshop

Open IL_EX_3-5.xlsx from the location where you store your Data Files, then save it as **IL_EX_3_Freight**. Use the skills you learned in this module to complete the worksheet so it looks like the one shown in FIGURE 3-21. To build the formulas in column G, calculate the percentage increase of the second quarter revenue over the first quarter revenue. (*Hint*: The percentage increases in column G must be calculated before calculating the average increase in cell B10.) To build the formulas in column I, a warning should be issued if the percentage increase is less than the average increase shown in cell B10 AND the on-time delivery is less than 75%. (*Hint*: Remember to use an absolute cell reference where necessary.) When you are finished, enter your name in the center footer section, then submit your work to your instructor as directed.

FIGURE 3-21

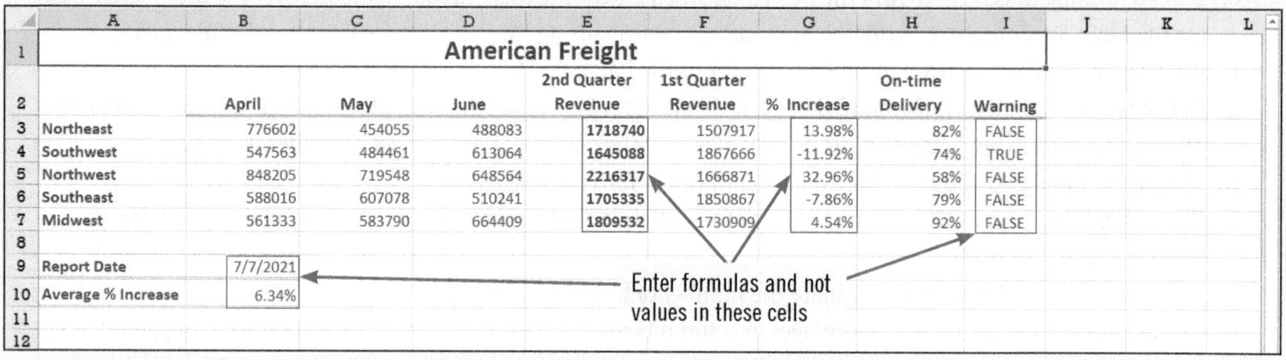

	A	B	C	D	E	F	G	H	I
1					**American Freight**				
2		April	May	June	2nd Quarter Revenue	1st Quarter Revenue	% Increase	On-time Delivery	Warning
3	Northeast	776602	454055	488083	1718740	1507917	13.98%	82%	FALSE
4	Southwest	547563	484461	613064	1645088	1867666	-11.92%	74%	TRUE
5	Northwest	848205	719548	648564	2216317	1666871	32.96%	58%	FALSE
6	Southeast	588016	607078	510241	1705335	1850867	-7.86%	79%	FALSE
7	Midwest	561333	583790	664409	1809532	1730909	4.54%	92%	FALSE
8									
9	Report Date	7/7/2021							
10	Average % Increase	6.34%							
11									
12									

Enter formulas and not values in these cells

Working with Charts

CASE At the upcoming annual meeting, Ellie Schwartz, the vice president of finance, wants to review expenses at JCL Talent's U.S. offices. She asks you to create charts showing the expense trends in these offices over the past four quarters.

Module Objectives

After completing this module, you will be able to:

- Plan a chart
- Create a chart
- Move and resize a chart
- Change the chart design
- Change the chart layout

- Format a chart
- Create a pie chart
- Summarize data with sparklines
- Identify data trends

Files You Will Need

IL_EX_4-1.xlsx   IL_EX_4-4.xlsx
IL_EX_4-2.xlsx   IL_EX_4-5.xlsx
IL_EX_4-3.xlsx

Plan a Chart

The process of creating a chart involves deciding which data to use and what type of chart best highlights the trends or patterns that are most important, such as steady increases over time or stellar performance by one sales rep compared to others in the same division. Understanding the parts of a chart makes it easier to evaluate specific elements to make sure the chart effectively illustrates your data. **CASE** ▶ *In preparation for creating the charts for Ellie's presentation, you review the purpose of the charts and decide how to organize the data.*

DETAILS

Use the following guidelines to plan the chart:

• **Determine the purpose of the chart, and identify the data relationships you want to graphically communicate**
You want to create a chart that shows quarterly expenses for JCL U.S. offices. You also want to illustrate whether the quarterly expenses for each office increased or decreased from quarter to quarter.

• **Determine the results you want to see, and decide which chart type is most appropriate**
Different chart types display data in distinctive ways. For example, a pie chart compares parts of a whole, whereas a line chart is best for showing trends over time. To choose the best chart type for your data, first decide how you want your data to be interpreted. **FIGURE 4-1** shows the available chart types in Excel, listed by category on the All Charts tab of the Insert Chart dialog box. **TABLE 4-1** describes several of these charts. Because you want to compare JCL expenses in multiple offices over a period of four quarters, you decide to use a column chart.

• **Identify the worksheet data you want the chart to illustrate**
Sometimes you use all the data in a worksheet to create a chart, while at other times you may need to select a range within the sheet. The worksheet from which you are creating your chart contains expense data for each of the past four quarters and the totals for the past year. To create a column chart, you will need to use all the quarterly data except the quarterly totals.

• **Understand the elements of a chart**
The chart shown in **FIGURE 4-2** contains basic elements of a chart. In the figure, JCL offices are on the category axis and expense dollar amounts are on the value axis. The **category axis**, also called the *x*-axis, is the horizontal axis in a chart, usually containing the names of data categories. The **value axis**, also called the vertical axis, contains numerical values. In a 2-dimensional chart, it is also known as the *y*-axis. (Three-dimensional charts contain a **z-axis**, for comparing data across both categories and values.) The area inside the horizontal and vertical axes that contains the graphical representation of the data series is the **plot area**. **Gridlines**, the horizontal and vertical lines, make a chart easier to read. Each individual piece of data plotted in a chart is a **data point**. In any chart, a **data marker** is a graphical representation of a data point, such as a bar or column. A set of values represented in a chart is a **data series**. In this chart, there are four data series: Quarter 1, Quarter 2, Quarter 3, and Quarter 4. Each is made up of columns of a different color. To differentiate each data series, information called a **legend** or a legend key identifies how the data is represented using colors and/or patterns.

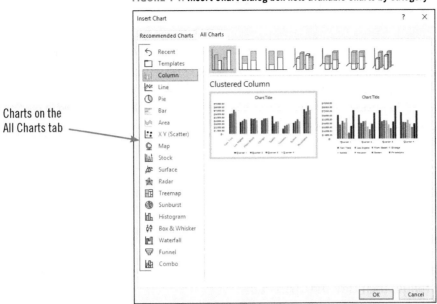

FIGURE 4-1: Insert Chart dialog box lists available charts by category

Charts on the
All Charts tab →

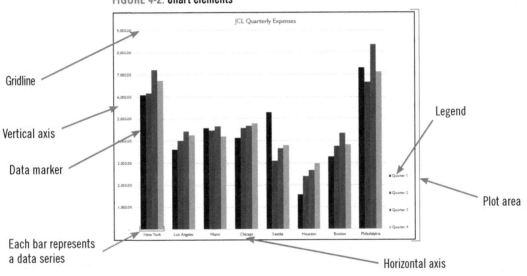

FIGURE 4-2: Chart elements

Gridline

Vertical axis

Data marker

Each bar represents
a data series

Legend

Plot area

Horizontal axis

TABLE 4-1: Common chart types

type	description
Column	A chart that displays data values as columns; column height represents its value
Line	A chart or visualization that displays data as separate lines across categories
Pie	A chart in the shape of a circle divided into slices like a pie, which shows data values as percentages of the whole
Bar	A column chart turned on its side so that the length of each bar is based on its value
Area	Shows how individual volume changes over time in relation to total volume
Line with Markers	Compares trends over time by showing data markers that represent worksheet data values

Excel

Create a Chart

Learning
Outcomes
• Create a chart
• Add a title to a chart

To create a chart in Excel, you first select the worksheet range or ranges containing the data you want to chart. Once you've selected a range, you can use the Quick Analysis tool or the Insert tab on the ribbon to create a chart based on the data in that range. **CASE** ▶ *Using the worksheet containing the quarterly expense data, you create a chart that shows how the expenses in each office varied in relation to each other, across all four quarters of the year.*

STEPS

1. **saṁ ⬇ Start Excel, open IL_EX_4-1.xlsx from the location where you store your Data Files, then save it as IL_EX_4_USQuarterlyExpenses**
   You want the chart to include the quarterly office expenses values, as well as quarter and office labels, but not any totals.

2. **Select the range A4:E12, click the Quick Analysis button 🖾 in the lower-right corner of the range, then click the Charts tab**
   The Charts tab on the Quick Analysis tool recommends commonly used chart types based on the range you have selected. It also includes a More Charts button for additional chart types.

3. **On the Charts tab, verify that Clustered Column is selected, as shown in FIGURE 4-3, then click Clustered Column**
   A clustered column chart is inserted in the center of the worksheet. **Clustered column charts** display data values in side-by-side columns. Two contextual Chart Tools tabs, Design and Format, become available on the ribbon. On the Design tab, which is currently active, you can quickly change the chart layout and chart style, and you can swap how the columns and rows of data in the worksheet are represented in the chart or select a different data range for the chart. In Normal view, three tools open to the right of the chart: the Chart Elements button 🞢 lets you add, remove, or change chart elements; the Chart Styles button 🖌 lets you set a style and color scheme; and the Chart Filters button 🍥 lets you filter the results shown in a chart. Currently, the offices are charted along the horizontal *x*-axis, with the quarterly expense dollar amounts charted along the vertical *y*-axis. This lets you easily compare the quarterly expenses for each office.

4. **Click the Switch Row/Column button in the Data group on the Chart Tools Design tab**
   The quarters are now charted along the x-axis. The expense amounts per office are charted along the y-axis, as indicated by the updated legend. See FIGURE 4-4.

5. **Click the Undo button 🔄 on the Quick Access Toolbar**
   The chart returns to its original data configuration.

6. **Click the Chart Title placeholder, type JCL Quarterly Expenses, click the Enter button ✓ then click anywhere in the chart to deselect the title**
   Adding a title helps identify the chart. The border around the chart, along with the **sizing handles**, the small circles at the corners and the edges, indicates that the chart is selected. See FIGURE 4-5. Your chart might be in a different location on the worksheet and may look slightly different; you will move and resize it in the next lesson. Any time a chart is selected, as it is now, a blue border surrounds the worksheet data range on which the chart is based, a purple border surrounds the cells containing the category axis labels, and a red border surrounds the cells containing the data series labels. This chart is known as an **embedded chart** because it is displayed as an object in the worksheet. Embedding a chart in the current sheet is the default selection when creating a chart, but you can also embed a chart on a different sheet in the workbook, or on a newly created chart sheet. A **chart sheet** is a separate sheet in a workbook that contains only a chart that is linked to the workbook data.

7. **Save your work**

FIGURE 4-3: Charts tab in Quick Analysis tool

Charts tab selected

Quick Analysis tool

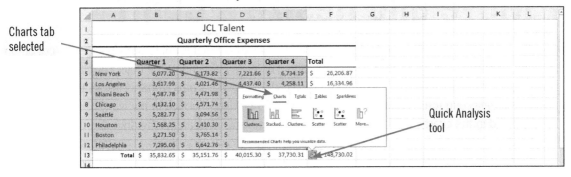

Undo button

Chart Tools tabs

Switch Row/ Column button

Chart title placeholder

Click to change chart elements

Click to change style and color schemes

Click to filter results

Legend

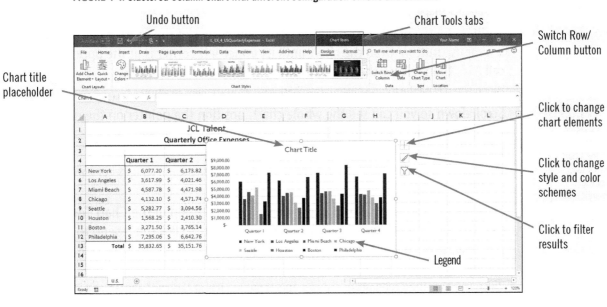

Excel

Column labels (data series labels)

Row labels (category axis labels)

Selected chart object

Legend

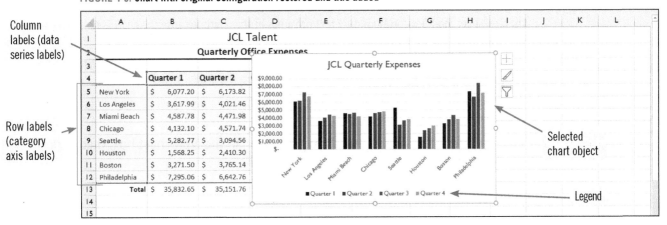

Move and Resize a Chart

Learning Outcomes
• Reposition a chart
• Resize a chart

A chart is an **object**, an independent element on a worksheet that is not located in a specific cell or range and can be moved and resized. You can select an object by clicking it; the object displays sizing handles to indicate it is selected. You can move a selected chart anywhere on a worksheet or to another worksheet without affecting formulas or data in the worksheet. Any data changed in the worksheet is automatically updated in the chart. You can resize a chart to improve its appearance by dragging its sizing handles. Dragging a corner sizing handle resizes the chart proportionally. Dragging a side, top, or bottom handle resizes it horizontally or vertically. **CASE** ▸ *You want the chart to be bigger and more noticeable.*

STEPS

QUICK TIP
To delete a selected chart, press DEL.

1. **Make sure the chart is still selected, then position the pointer over the chart**
   The pointer shape ⁺↖ indicates that you can move the chart.

2. **Position ↖ on a blank area near the upper-left corner of the chart, press and hold the left mouse button, drag the chart until its upper-left corner is at the upper-left corner of cell A16, then release the mouse button**
   When you release the mouse button, the chart appears in the new location.

QUICK TIP
To resize a selected chart to an exact size, click the Chart Tools Format tab, then enter the desired height and width in the Size group.

3. **Scroll down so you can see the whole chart, position the pointer on the right-middle sizing handle until it changes to ↔, then drag the right border of the chart to the right edge of column G**
   The chart is widened. See **FIGURE 4-6**. You can also use the ↕ pointer on an upper or lower sizing handle to increase the chart size vertically.

4. **Click the Quick Layout button in the Chart Layouts group of the Chart Tools Design tab, click Layout 1 (in the upper-left corner of the palette), click the legend to select it, press and hold SHIFT, drag the legend down using ↖ to the bottom of the plot area, then release SHIFT**
   When you click the legend, sizing handles appear around it and "Legend" appears as a ScreenTip when the pointer hovers over the object. As you drag, a dotted outline of the legend border appears. Pressing and holding SHIFT holds the horizontal position of the legend as you move it vertically.

5. **Scroll up if necessary, click cell A7, type Miami, then click the Enter button ✓ on the formula bar**
   The axis label changes to reflect the updated cell contents, as shown in **FIGURE 4-7**. Changing any data in the worksheet modifies corresponding text or values in the chart. Because the chart is no longer selected, the Chart Tools tabs no longer appear on the ribbon.

QUICK TIP
You can also use the Copy and Paste buttons in the Clipboard group of the Home tab to copy a selected chart and paste it on a different worksheet.

6. **Click the chart to select it, click the Chart Tools Design tab, then click the Move Chart button in the Location group**
   The Move chart dialog box shows options to move a chart to a new sheet or as an object in an existing worksheet, as shown in **FIGURE 4-8**.

7. **Click the New sheet option button, type Column in the New sheet box, then click OK**
   The chart is placed on its own chart sheet, named Column.

FIGURE 4-6: **Moved and resized chart**

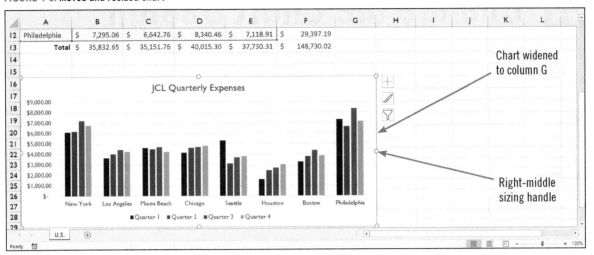

Chart widened to column G

Right-middle sizing handle

FIGURE 4-7: **Worksheet with modified legend and label**

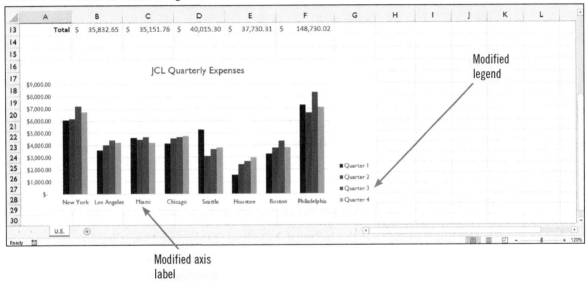

Modified legend

Modified axis label

FIGURE 4-8: **Move Chart dialog box**

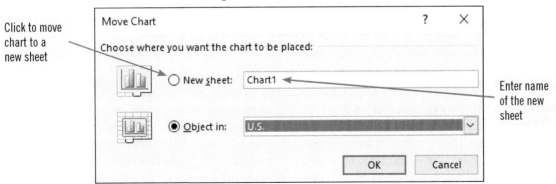

Click to move chart to a new sheet

Move Chart

Choose where you want the chart to be placed:

New sheet: Chart1

Object in: U.S.

OK   Cancel

Enter name of the new sheet

Change the Chart Design

You can change the type of an existing chart, modify the data range and column/row configuration, apply a different chart style, and change the layout of objects within it. The layouts in the Chart Layouts group on the Chart Tools Design tab arrange multiple objects in a chart at once, such as its legend, title, and gridlines; choosing one of these layouts is a quick alternative to manually changing each object one at a time. **CASE** *You've discovered that the data for Boston's third quarter is incorrect. You also want to see if using different chart types and layouts helps make the trends and patterns easier to spot.*

STEPS

1. **Click the U.S. sheet tab, click cell D11, type 4775.20, press ENTER, then click the Column sheet tab**

   In the chart, the Quarter 3 data marker for Boston reflects the adjusted expense figure. See FIGURE 4-9.

2. **Select the chart, if necessary, by clicking a blank area within the chart border, click the Chart Tools Design tab on the ribbon, click the Quick Layout button in the Chart Layouts group, then click Layout 3**

   The legend moves to the bottom of the chart. You prefer the original layout.

3. **Click the Undo button ⟲ on the Quick Access Toolbar, then click the Change Chart Type button in the Type group**

   The Change Chart Type dialog box opens, as shown in FIGURE 4-10. The left side of the dialog box lists available categories, and the right side shows the individual chart types. A pale gray border surrounds the currently selected chart type.

4. **Click Bar in the list of categories on the left, confirm that the first Clustered Bar chart type is selected on the right, then click OK**

   The column chart changes to a Clustered Bar chart. See FIGURE 4-11. You decide to see how the data looks in a 3-D column chart.

5. **Click the Change Chart Type button in the Type group, click Column on the left side of the Change Chart Type dialog box, click 3-D Clustered Column (fourth from the left in the top row), verify that the leftmost 3-D chart is selected, then click OK**

   A three-dimensional column chart appears. You notice that the three-dimensional column format gives you a sense of volume, but it is more crowded than the two-dimensional column format.

6. **Click the Change Chart Type button in the Type group, click Clustered Column (first from the left in the top row), then click OK**

7. **Click the Style 3 chart style in the Chart Styles group**

   The columns change to lighter shades of color. You prefer the previous chart style's color scheme.

8. **Click ⟲ on the Quick Access Toolbar, then save your work**

Creating a combo chart

A **combo chart** presents two or more chart types in one—for example, a column chart with a line chart. Combo charts are useful when charting dissimilar but related data. For example, you can create a clustered column–line combination chart based on both home price and home size data, showing home prices in a clustered column chart and related home sizes in a line chart. Here, a secondary axis (such as a vertical axis on the right side of the chart) would supply the scale for the home sizes. To create a combo chart, select all the data you want to plot, click the Insert Combo chart button in the Charts group in the Insert tab, click a suggested type or Create Custom Combo Chart, supply additional series information if necessary, then click OK.

FIGURE 4-9: Chart with modified data

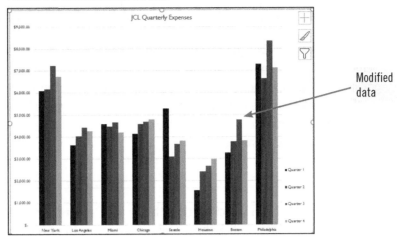

Modified
data

FIGURE 4-10: Change Chart Type dialog box

Chart type
categories

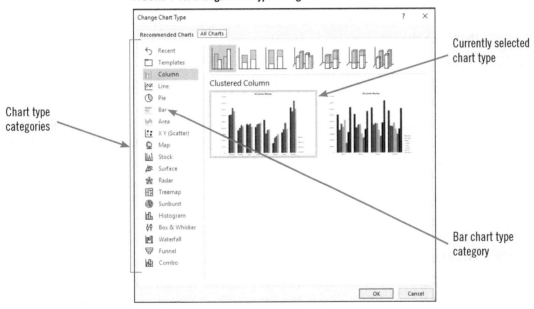

Currently selected
chart type

Bar chart type
category

FIGURE 4-11: Column chart changed to bar chart

Click More button
to see additional
chart styles

Change
Chart Type
button

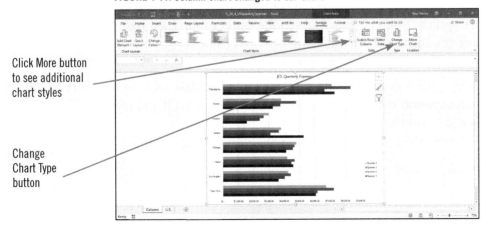

Change the Chart Layout

Learning
Outcomes
• Change the grid-
lines display
• Add axis titles
• Add a data table

While the Chart Tools Design tab contains preconfigured chart layouts you can apply to a chart, the Chart Elements button makes it easy to add, remove, and modify individual chart objects such as a chart title, gridlines, or legend. Using options on this shortcut menu, you can also add a **data table**, a grid containing the chart data, to the chart. **CASE** ▸ *You want to change the layout of the chart by creating titles for the horizontal and vertical axes. Because the chart is on its own sheet, you also want to add a data table to provide more detailed information.*

STEPS

1. **With the chart still selected, click the Chart Elements button ⊞ in the upper-right corner of the chart, click the Gridlines arrow on the Chart Elements fly-out menu, click Primary Major Horizontal to deselect it, then click ⊞ to close the menu**
   The gridlines that extend across the chart's plot area are removed, as shown in FIGURE 4-12.

2. **Click ⊞, click the Axis Titles check box to add a checkmark, click ⊞ to close the Chart Elements fly-out menu, with the vertical axis title on the chart selected type Expenses, then click the Enter button ✓**
   Descriptive text on the category axis helps readers understand the chart.

3. **Click the horizontal axis title on the chart, type U.S. Offices, then click ✓**
   The horizontal axis labels are added, as shown in FIGURE 4-13.

4. **Right-click the horizontal axis labels ("New York," "Los Angeles," etc.), click Font on the shortcut menu, click the Latin text font arrow in the Font dialog box, scroll down the font list, click Times New Roman, select 9 in the Size box, type 12, then click OK**
   The font of the horizontal axis labels changes to Times New Roman, and the font size increases, making the labels easier to read.

5. **With the horizontal axis labels still selected, click the Home tab on the ribbon, click the Format Painter button in the Clipboard group, then click the area within the vertical axis labels**

6. **Right-click the chart title (JCL Quarterly Expenses), click Format Chart Title on the shortcut menu, click Border in the Format Chart Title pane to display the options if necessary, then click the Solid line option button in the pane**
   A solid border in the default blue color appears around the chart title.

7. **Click the Effects button ◻ in the Format Chart Title pane, click Shadow, click the Presets arrow, click Offset: Bottom Right in the Outer group (first row, first from the left), then close the Format Chart Title pane**
   A border with a drop shadow surrounds the title.

8. **Click ⊞, click the Data Table check box to add a data table to the chart, in the list of chart elements click the legend check box to deselect it and remove the original legend, then save your work**
   A data table with a legend shows the chart data. Compare your work to FIGURE 4-14.

FIGURE 4-12: Gridlines removed from chart

Chart Tools
Design tab

Chart without
gridlines

Chart Elements
button

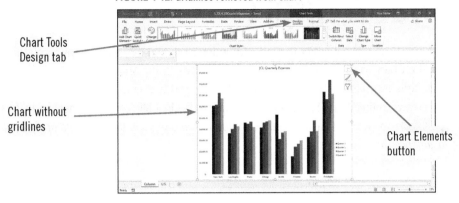

FIGURE 4-13: Axis titles added to chart

Vertical
axis title

Horizontal
axis labels

Vertical
axis labels

Horizontal axis title

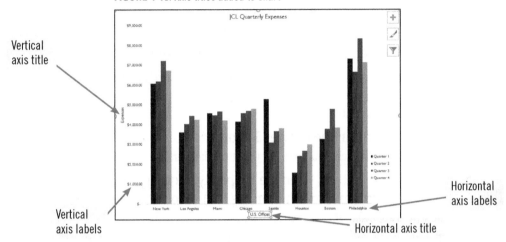

FIGURE 4-14: Enhanced chart

Border and shadow
added to chart title

Data table with
a legend

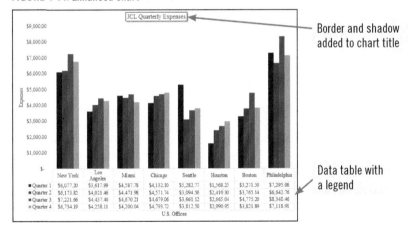

Working with chart axes

You can change both the number format and text formatting of a chart's axes. For example, you may want to change the starting and ending values of an axis. You can do this by right-clicking the axis, selecting Format Axis from the shortcut menu, clicking Axis Options in the Format Axis pane if necessary, then entering values in the Minimum and Maximum boxes. To change the number format of the values on an axis, scroll down in the Axis Options, click Number to display the options if necessary, then select from the available number formats. In the Number area, you can also create a number format code by typing a code in the Format Code box and clicking Add. In addition to these axis options, you can work with axis text by clicking the Text Option button at the top of the pane, then clicking the Textbox button [A≡]. The Text Box group includes options for changing the vertical alignment of the data labels on the axis and the text direction of axis data labels from horizontal to stacked or rotated.

Format a Chart

Learning
Outcomes
• Change the fill of
a data series
• Apply a style to a
data series

Formatting a chart can make it easier to read and understand. You can make many formatting enhance-ments using the Chart Tools Format tab. Using a shape style in the Shape Styles group on this tab, you can apply multiple formats, such as an outline, fill color, and text color, all at once. You can use other buttons and arrows in the Shape Styles group to apply individual fill colors, outlines, and effects to chart objects. **CASE** *You want to use a different color for one data series in the chart and apply a shape style to another, to enhance the look of the chart.*

STEPS

QUICK TIP

You can remove a data series from a chart by selecting the data series, then pressing DEL.

1. **With the chart selected, click the Chart Tools Format tab on the ribbon, then click any column in the Quarter 4 data series**

   Handles appear on each column in the Quarter 4 data series, indicating that the entire series is selected.

2. **Click the Shape Fill button in the Shape Styles group**

3. **Click Plum, Accent 1, Lighter 90% (second row, fifth from the left)**

   All the columns for the series change to a light shade of plum, and the legend changes to match the new color, as shown in **FIGURE 4-15**.

QUICK TIP

You can add a tex-ture fill by pointing to Texture in the Shape Fill menu and selecting a texture.

4. **Click any column in the Quarter 3 data series**

   Handles appear on each column in the Quarter 3 data series.

5. **Click the More button ⤓ on the Shape Styles gallery, then click the Subtle Effect – Pink, Accent 3 (fourth row, fourth from the left) shape style under Theme Styles**

   The style is applied to the data series, as shown in **FIGURE 4-16**.

QUICK TIP

You can change the colors used in a chart by clicking the Chart Tools Design tab, clicking the Change Colors button in the Chart Styles group, then clicking a color palette in the gallery.

6. **Click the Insert tab on the ribbon, click the Text button, click the Header & Footer button, click Custom Footer, type your name in the center section, click OK, then click OK again**

7. **Save your work**

Working with WordArt

You can insert WordArt into a worksheet or a chart. To insert WordArt in a worksheet, click the Insert tab on the ribbon, click the Text button in the Text group, click WordArt, then click a style in the gallery. You can change a WordArt style by clicking the WordArt to select it, clicking the WordArt Styles More button ⤓ on the Drawing Tools Format tab, then selecting a new WordArt style. You can change the fill color of the WordArt by clicking the Text Fill button in the WordArt Styles group and choosing a fill color, texture, gradient, or picture. You can change the outline of selected WordArt text by clicking the Text Outline button in the WordArt Styles group and choosing an outline color, weight, and/ or dashes.

FIGURE 4-15: **New shape fill applied to data series**

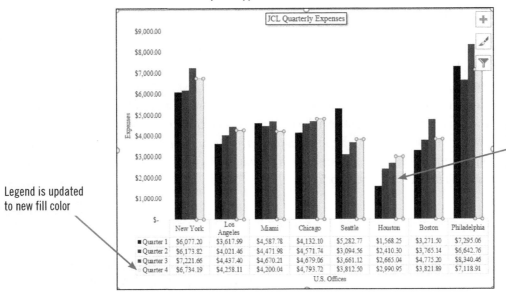

Legend is updated
to new fill color

New shape fill color
is applied to all
selected columns

FIGURE 4-16: **Style applied to data series**

Shape style applied
to selected columns

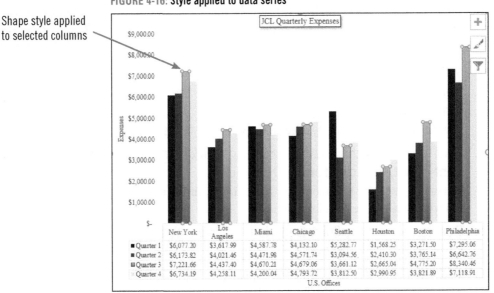

Aligning charts

If you have two or more embedded charts on a worksheet, you can line them up to make them easier to view. First, select the charts by clicking the first chart and holding CTRL, then click the other chart(s). With the charts selected, click the Drawing Tools Format tab, click the Align button in the Arrange group, then choose the alignment position for the charts. The chart shown in **FIGURE 4-17** uses the Align Top option.

FIGURE 4-17: **Charts aligned at the top**

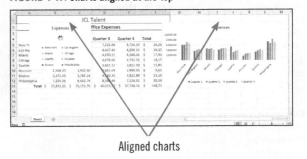

Aligned charts

Excel

Create a Pie Chart

Learning Outcomes
- Create a pie chart
- Explode a pie chart slice

You can create multiple charts based on the same worksheet data, to illustrate different aspects of the data. For example, while a column chart may reveal top performers month by month, you may want to create a pie chart to compare overall performance for the year. Depending on the type of chart you create, you have additional options for calling attention to trends and patterns. With a pie chart, for example, you can emphasize one data point by **exploding**, or moving one slice, as if someone were taking a piece away from the pie. **CASE** *At an upcoming meeting, Ellie plans to discuss the total expenses and identify offices that need to economize more in the future. You want to create a pie chart she can use to compare spending between the different offices.*

STEPS

QUICK TIP

You can insert a 3-D pie chart by choosing 3-D Pie from the chart gallery.

1. **Click the** U.S. sheet tab **to select it, select the range** A5:A12, **press and hold** CTRL, **select the range** F5:F12, **click the** Insert tab **on the ribbon if necessary, click the** Insert Pie or Doughnut Chart button 🥧▾ **in the Charts group, then click the first** 2-D Pie **in the chart gallery**

2. **Click the** Move Chart button **in the Location group, click the** New sheet option button, **type** Pie **in the New sheet box, then click** OK
   The chart is placed on a new worksheet named Pie.

3. **Select the** Chart Title placeholder, **click the** Chart Tools Format tab, **click the** WordArt Styles More button ▼, **click the** Fill: Pink, Accent Color 3; Sharp Bevel (second row, first from the right), **type** JCL Total Expenses, by Office, **then click the** Enter button ✓ **on the formula bar**
   The formatted WordArt title is added, as shown in **FIGURE 4-18**.

4. **Click the slice for the** Houston data point, **click it again so it is the only slice selected, right-click it, then click** Format Data Point
   You can use the Point Explosion slider to control the distance a pie slice moves away from the pie, or you can type a value in the Point Explosion box.

5. **Double-click** 0 **in the Point Explosion box, type** 10, **then click the** Close button ⊠
   Compare your chart to **FIGURE 4-19**.

QUICK TIP

You can change the number format of the data labels by clicking the Label Options button in the Format Data Labels pane if necessary, clicking Number to show the Number options, and choosing the desired category or entering a format code. Also in this pane are options under Label Position to change the position of the data labels to Center, Inside End, and Best Fit.

6. **Click the** Chart Elements button ⊞, **click the** Data Labels arrow ▶, **click** Outside End, **click** More Options, **in the Format Data Labels pane click the** Percentage check box **to add a checkmark, then click the** Values box **to deselect it**
   The data labels identify the pie slices by percentage.

7. **Click** ⊞, **point to** Data Labels, **click** ▶, **click** Data Callout, **click the** Legend check box **to deselect it, then click** ⊞
   The data is labeled using percentage callouts, as shown in **FIGURE 4-20**.

8. **Click the** Insert tab **on the ribbon, click the** Text button, **click the** Header & Footer button **in the Text group, click the** Custom Footer button, **enter your name in the center section, click** OK, **click** OK **again, then save your work**

FIGURE 4-18: Title formatted using WordArt

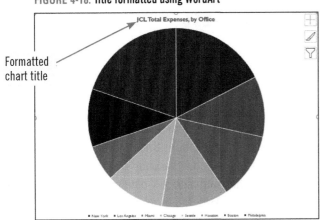

Formatted
chart title

FIGURE 4-19: Exploded pie slice

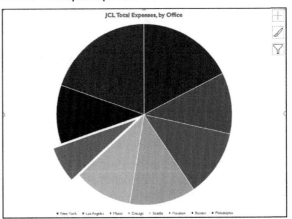

FIGURE 4-20: Pie chart with percentages

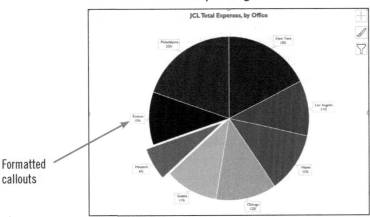

Formatted
callouts

Working with other chart types

Excel includes chart types that are useful for illustrating highly specific types of data. These include Waterfall, Histogram, Pareto, Box & Whisker, Treemap, Scatter, and Sunburst. A **treemap chart** is a hierarchy chart in which each category is placed within a rectangle and subcategories are nested as rectangles within those rectangles. A **sunburst chart** is also a hierarchy chart, but it groups categories within a series of concentric rings, with the upper levels of the hierarchy placed in the innermost rings. To insert one of these chart types, click the Insert tab, click the Insert Hierarchy Chart button ▦▾ in the Charts group, then click the chart type. **Waterfall charts** are used to track the addition and subtraction of values within a sum. To insert a Waterfall chart, click the Insert tab, click the Insert Waterfall, Funnel, Stock, Surface, or Radar Chart button ▦▾ in the Charts group, then click Waterfall. A **histogram chart** shows the distribution of data grouped in bins.

These charts look similar to column charts, but each column (or bin) represents a range of values. To insert a histogram chart, click the Insert tab on the ribbon, click the Insert Statistic Chart button ▦▾ in the Charts group, then click the Histogram chart button. You can edit the bins in a histogram chart by double-clicking the x-axis, clicking to expand the Axis Options group on the Format Axis pane, then choosing options under Bins.

A **scatter chart** displays the correlation between two numeric variables. It is a type of **XY scatter chart**, which shows the pattern or relationship between two or more sets of values. Scatter charts look similar to line charts but have two value axes. The data points on a scatter chart show the intersection of the horizontal and vertical axes values. To insert a scatter chart, select the data you want to chart, click the Insert tab, click the Insert Scatter (X,Y) or Bubble Chart button ▦▾ in the Charts group, then choose a scatter chart type.

Summarize Data with Sparklines

You can create a quick overview of your data by adding sparklines to the worksheet cells. A **sparkline** is a small, simple chart located within a worksheet cell that serves as a visual indicator of data trends. Sparklines usually appear close to the data they represent. Any changes that you make to a worksheet are reflected in the sparklines that represent the data. After you add sparklines to a worksheet, you can change the sparkline style and color, and you can format their high and low data points in special colors.

CASE ▶ As a supplement to the charts, Ellie wants the U.S. worksheet to illustrate the expense trends for the year. You decide to add sparklines to tell a quick visual story within the worksheet cells.

STEPS

QUICK TIP
If you have an empty cell directly to the right of a range, you can use the Quick Access Toolbar to insert a sparkline into the empty cell.

1. **Click the** U.S. sheet tab, **click cell** G5, **click the** Insert tab **on the ribbon if necessary, click the** Column button **in the Sparklines group, verify that the insertion point is in the Data Range box, select the range** B5:E5 **on the worksheet, then click** OK

   Columns showing the expense trend for New York appear in cell G5.

2. **With cell G5 selected, drag the** fill handle ✛ **to fill the range** G6:G12

   The sparkline is copied, and column sparklines reflecting the data for each office are added, as shown in FIGURE 4-21.

QUICK TIP
To insert Win/Loss sparklines, which show upward column symbols for positive values and downward symbols for negative values, click the Win/Loss button in the Type group.

3. **Click cell** G5, **then click the** Line button **in the Type group on the Sparkline Tools Design tab**

   When sparklines are copied they become a group, so all the sparklines in this group change to the Line sparkline type. When any sparkline type in a group is changed, the other sparklines in the group change to match the new type. You can ungroup and group sparklines using the Group and Ungroup buttons in the Group group.

4. **Click the** Sparkline Color button **in the Style group, then click** Plum, Accent 1, Lighter 10% **(last row, fifth color from the left)**

5. **Click the** More button ▾ **in the Style group, then click** Plum, Sparkline Style Accent 3, Darker 50% **(third from the left in the first row)**

   The sparkline colors and styles are consistent with the colors on the worksheet.

6. **Click the** Marker Color button **in the Style group, point to** High Point, **select** Plum Accent 2, Darker 50% **(sixth from left, sixth row), click the** Marker Color button **in the Style group, point to** Markers, **select** Blue-Gray, Accent 6 **(last in Theme Colors), then click the** Markers check box **in the Show group to add a checkmark if necessary**

   Data markers indicate each quarter's expenses, with the highest quarter value in a different color.

QUICK TIP
To clear sparklines, select the sparklines, then click the Clear button in the Group group.

7. **Click cell** C5, **type** 6,742.13, **click the** Enter button ✓, **then compare your screen to** FIGURE 4-22

   The sparklines update to reflect the new worksheet data.

8. **Click the** Insert tab **on the ribbon, click the** Text button, **click the** Header & Footer button **in the Text group, click the** Go to Footer button **in the Navigation group, enter your name in the** center footer section, **click** any cell on the worksheet, **click the** Normal button ▦ **on the status bar, then press** CTRL+HOME

9. **Save your changes**

FIGURE 4-21: Expense trend sparklines

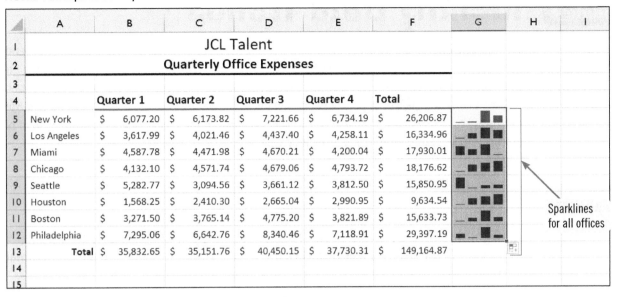

	A	B	C	D	E	F	G	H	I
1				JCL Talent					
2				**Quarterly Office Expenses**					
3									
4		**Quarter 1**	**Quarter 2**	**Quarter 3**	**Quarter 4**	**Total**			
5	New York	$ 6,077.20	$ 6,173.82	$ 7,221.66	$ 6,734.19	$ 26,206.87			
6	Los Angeles	$ 3,617.99	$ 4,021.46	$ 4,437.40	$ 4,258.11	$ 16,334.96			
7	Miami	$ 4,587.78	$ 4,471.98	$ 4,670.21	$ 4,200.04	$ 17,930.01			
8	Chicago	$ 4,132.10	$ 4,571.74	$ 4,679.06	$ 4,793.72	$ 18,176.62			
9	Seattle	$ 5,282.77	$ 3,094.56	$ 3,661.12	$ 3,812.50	$ 15,850.95			
10	Houston	$ 1,568.25	$ 2,410.30	$ 2,665.04	$ 2,990.95	$ 9,634.54			
11	Boston	$ 3,271.50	$ 3,765.14	$ 4,775.20	$ 3,821.89	$ 15,633.73			
12	Philadelphia	$ 7,295.06	$ 6,642.76	$ 8,340.46	$ 7,118.91	$ 29,397.19			
13	Total	$ 35,832.65	$ 35,151.76	$ 40,450.15	$ 37,730.31	$ 149,164.87			
14									
15									

Sparklines for all offices

FIGURE 4-22: Formatted sparklines

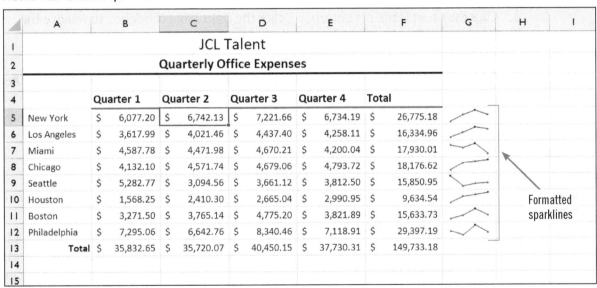

	A	B	C	D	E	F	G	H	I
1				JCL Talent					
2				**Quarterly Office Expenses**					
3									
4		**Quarter 1**	**Quarter 2**	**Quarter 3**	**Quarter 4**	**Total**			
5	New York	$ 6,077.20	$ 6,742.13	$ 7,221.66	$ 6,734.19	$ 26,775.18			
6	Los Angeles	$ 3,617.99	$ 4,021.46	$ 4,437.40	$ 4,258.11	$ 16,334.96			
7	Miami	$ 4,587.78	$ 4,471.98	$ 4,670.21	$ 4,200.04	$ 17,930.01			
8	Chicago	$ 4,132.10	$ 4,571.74	$ 4,679.06	$ 4,793.72	$ 18,176.62			
9	Seattle	$ 5,282.77	$ 3,094.56	$ 3,661.12	$ 3,812.50	$ 15,850.95			
10	Houston	$ 1,568.25	$ 2,410.30	$ 2,665.04	$ 2,990.95	$ 9,634.54			
11	Boston	$ 3,271.50	$ 3,765.14	$ 4,775.20	$ 3,821.89	$ 15,633.73			
12	Philadelphia	$ 7,295.06	$ 6,642.76	$ 8,340.46	$ 7,118.91	$ 29,397.19			
13	Total	$ 35,832.65	$ 35,720.07	$ 40,450.15	$ 37,730.31	$ 149,733.18			
14									
15									

Formatted sparklines

Identify Data Trends

Learning Outcomes
- Compare chart data using trendlines
- Format a trendline
- Forecast future trends using trendlines

To emphasize trends and patterns that occur over a period of time, you can add one or more trendlines to a chart. A **trendline** is a series of data points on a line that shows data values representing the general direction of a data series. In some business situations, you can use trendlines to project future data based on past trends. **CASE** As part of her presentation, Ellie wants to compare the New York and Houston expenses. You decide to use trendlines to highlight spending at these offices over the past year and project expenses for the next six months, if past trends continue.

STEPS

1. **Right-click the** Column sheet tab, **click** Move or Copy **on the shortcut menu, click** (move to end) **in the Before sheet box, click the** Create a copy check box **to add a checkmark, then click** OK

   The new worksheet Column (2) is a copy of the Column sheet.

2. **Right-click the** Column (2) sheet tab, **click** Rename **on the shortcut menu, type** Trends, **click the** Chart **to select it, click the** Chart Tools Design tab, **then click the** Switch Row/Column button **in the Data group**

   The chart displays quarters, a time measure, on the x-axis.

3. **Click the** Chart Elements button ⊞, **click the** Data Table check box **to remove the checkmark, click the** Legend arrow, **then click** Bottom

   The data table is removed and a legend is added.

4. **Click** Trendline, **verify that** New York **is selected in the Add Trendline dialog box, then click** OK

   A linear trendline identifying the New York expense trend in the past year is added to the chart, along with an entry in the legend identifying the line.

QUICK TIP

To ensure that a chart element is not selected, simply click away from the element.

5. **Make sure the New York trendline is not selected, click** ⊞ **if necessary, click the** Trendline arrow, **click** Linear, **click** Houston **in the Add Trendline dialog box, then click** OK

   The chart now has two trendlines, making it easy to compare the expense trends of the New York and Houston offices, as shown in **FIGURE 4-23**.

6. **Double-click the** New York data series trendline, **in the Format Trendline pane click the** Trendline Options button 📊 **if necessary, select** 0.0 **in the Forward box, type** 1, **press** ENTER, **click the** Fill & Line button 🖎, **select** 1.5 **in the Width box, type** 2.5, **then close the Format Trendline pane**

   Trendlines are often used to project future trends. The formatted New York trendline projects an additional quarter of future expenses trends for the office, assuming past trends continue.

7. **Double-click the** Houston data series trendline, **select** 0.0 **in the Forward box, type** 1, **press** ENTER, **click** 🖎, **select** 1.5 **in the Width box, type** 2.5, **then close the Format Trendline pane**

   The formatted Houston trendline also projects an additional quarter of future expenses, if past trends continue.

8. **sam↑ Save your work, preview the Trends sheet, compare your chart to** FIGURE 4-24, **close the workbook, submit the workbook to your instructor, then close Excel**

FIGURE 4-23: Chart with two trendlines

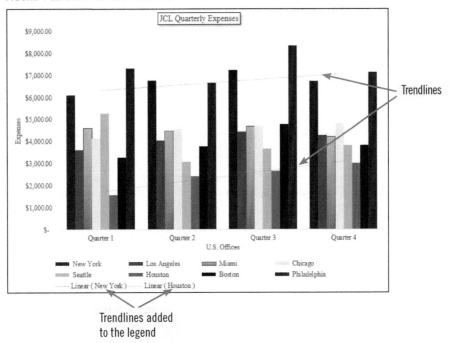

Trendlines

Trendlines added
to the legend

FIGURE 4-24: Expense chart with trendlines for New York and Houston data

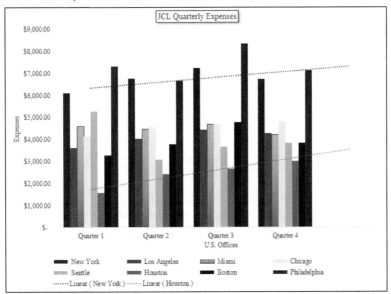

Choosing the right trendline options for your chart

When choosing a trendline, it is important to know which one is best for the information you want to communicate. If the data progression follows a straight line, using a linear trendline helps to emphasize that. If the pattern of a chart's data is linear but the data points don't follow a straight line, you can use a linear forecast trendline to chart a best-fit straight line. When data values increase or decrease in an arc shape, consider using an exponential or power trendline to illustrate this. A two-period moving average smooths out fluctuations in data by averaging the data points.

Practice

Skills Review

1. Create a chart.

a. Start Excel, open IL_EX_4-2.xlsx from the location where you store your Data Files, then save it as **IL_EX_4_FoodServices**.

b. In the worksheet, select the range containing all the sales data and headings. Do not include the totals.

c. Use the Quick Analysis tool to create a Clustered Column chart. Use the first Clustered Column option, placing the months on the x-axis.

d. Add the chart title **Brand Sales, by Month** above the chart.

e. Save your work.

2. Move and resize a chart.

a. Make sure the chart is still selected and close any open panes if necessary.

b. Move the chart beneath the worksheet data so its upper-left corner is at the upper-left corner of cell A11.

c. Widen the chart so it extends to the right edge of column H.

d. Use the Quick Layout button in the Chart Layouts group on the Chart Tools Design tab to move the legend to the right of the charted data. (*Hint*: Use Layout 1.)

e. Move the chart to a new worksheet that you name **Column**.

f. Save your work.

3. Change the chart design.

a. Activate the Q1 & Q2 sheet, then change the value in cell B4 to **80,000.00**. Activate the Column sheet and verify that the value for the Classic brand for January is $80,000.00.

b. Select the chart if necessary.

c. Use the Change Chart Type button on the Chart Tools Design tab to change the chart to a Clustered Bar chart, then change it back to a Clustered Column chart.

d. Apply Chart Style 6 to the chart.

e. Save your work.

4. Change the chart layout.

a. Use the Chart Elements button to remove the gridlines in the chart.

b. Change the font used in the horizontal and vertical axis labels to Times New Roman.

c. Change the chart title's font to Times New Roman with a font size of 20 point.

d. Insert **Sales** as the primary vertical axis title.

e. Change the font size of the vertical axis title to 16 point and the font to Times New Roman.

f. Add a solid line border to the chart title, using the default color and a (preset) shadow of Outer Offset: Bottom Right.

g. Add a data table to the chart with a legend key.

h. Save your work.

5. Format a chart.

a. Use the Chart Tools Format tab to change the shape fill of the Classic data series to Olive Green, Accent 3, Darker 50% (last row of the theme colors, seventh from the left).

b. Change the shape style of the Classic data series to Intense Effect – Blue, Accent 1 (sixth row, second from the left), then click the chart area to deselect the Classic data series.

c. Save your work.

Skills Review (continued)

6. Create a pie chart.

   a. Switch to the Q1 & Q2 sheet, then select the range A4:A8 and H4:H8. (*Hint*: Holding CTRL allows you to select multiple nonadjacent ranges.)

   b. Create a 2-D pie chart and move the chart beneath the worksheet data so the upper-left corner is at the upper-left corner of cell A11.

   c. Add data callout labels and do not display the legend.

   d. Change the chart title to **Q1 & Q2 Sales** and format the title using the WordArt style Fill: Blue, Accent color 1, Shadow (second style in the first row).

   e. Explode the Artisan slice from the pie chart at **20%**.

   f. Enter your name in the center footer section of the worksheet, then save your work.

7. Summarize data with sparklines.

FIGURE 4-25

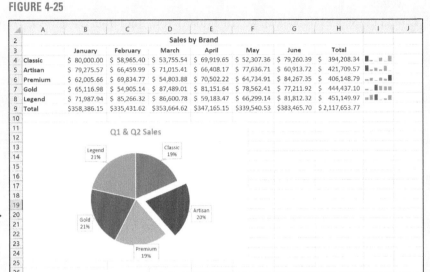

   a. Add a Line sparkline to cell I4 that represents the data in the range B4:G4.

   b. Copy the sparkline in cell I4 into the range I5:I8.

   c. Change the sparklines to columns.

   d. Apply the Sparkline style Blue Sparkline Style Dark #1 (fifth row, first column) to the group.

   e. Add high point markers with the color of Red, Accent 2 (first row, sixth from the left).

   f. Preview the worksheet and compare it to FIGURE 4-25.

   g. Save the workbook.

8. Identify data trends.

   a. Switch to the Column sheet.

   b. Add linear trendlines to the Premium and Gold data series.

   c. Set the forward option to 2 periods for both trendlines.

   d. Change the width of both trendlines to 3, then compare your screen to FIGURE 4-26.

   e. Add your name to the center footer section of the Column sheet, save the workbook, close the workbook, then submit the workbook to your instructor.

   f. Close Excel.

FIGURE 4-26

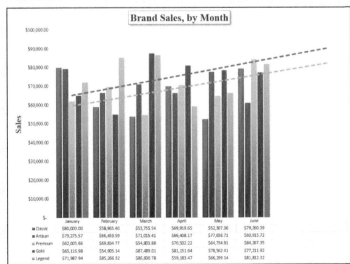

Independent Challenge 1

As an insurance manager for Riverwalk Medical Clinic, you have been asked to review the reimbursements for the clinic's departments. You will create a chart showing the insurance reimbursement over the past four quarters and predict future trends based on this history.

a. Start Excel, open IL_EX_4-3.xlsx from the location where you store your Data Files, then save it as **IL_EX_4_Reimbursements**.

b. Create a Clustered Column chart using the reimbursement amounts for the quarters and departments. (*Hint:* Do not include the totals.)

c. Switch the placement of the rows and columns, if necessary, to place the quarters on the x-axis.

d. Remove the chart gridlines.

e. Change the fill of the Psychology data series to Orange, Accent 6, Darker 50% (last row, last column of the Theme colors).

f. Add the Subtle effect – Red, Accent 2 (fourth row, third from the left) shape style to the Psychology data series.

g. Move the chart so the upper-left corner is at the upper-left corner of cell G2.

h. Change the fourth-quarter psychology reimbursement amount in cell E10 to **$60,254.20**.

i. Add the chart title **Reimbursements** and format the title with a solid line blue border from the Standard Colors.

j. Move the bottom chart border to the top of row 20, add a data table, then remove the chart legend.

k. Add trendlines to the cardiology and orthopedics department data forecasting 2 periods ahead.

l. Change the chart to a line chart, apply the Style 12 Chart Style to the chart, then compare your worksheet to FIGURE 4-27.

m. Enter your name in the center section of the worksheet footer, then save your work.

n. Submit your work to your instructor as directed.

o. Close the workbook, then close Excel.

FIGURE 4-27

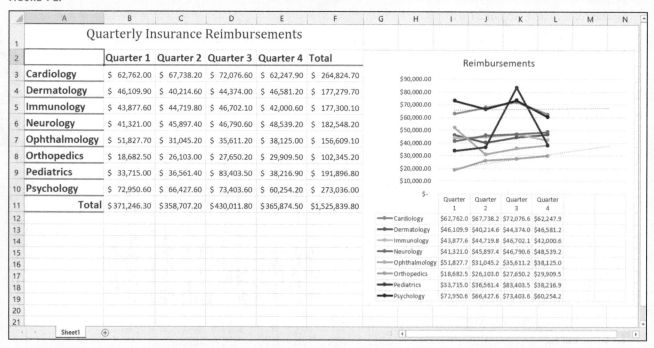

Independent Challenge 2

One of your responsibilities as the director of enrollment at Oceanview College is to present enrollment data to the executive staff at the end of the academic year. Your assistant has organized the college's enrollment data by division in a worksheet. You will review the data and create charts to visually represent the enrollment for the year.

a. Start Excel, open IL_EX_4-4.xlsx from the location where you store your Data Files, then save it as **IL_EX_4_Enrollments**.

b. Create a 3-D Clustered Column chart in the worksheet showing the enrollment data for all four terms. (*Hint*: The divisions, such as STEM, Business, and so forth, should appear on the x-axis.)

c. Add the chart title **Enrollment, by Division**, then format the title with the WordArt style of Fill: Blue, Accent color 1; Shadow (first row, second from left).

d. Move the chart so its upper-left corner is at the upper-left corner of cell H3.

e. On the worksheet, type **Average** in cell F3, then enter a formula in cell F4 to calculate the average STEM enrollment for the year.

f. Copy the average formula in cell F4 to the range F5:F9.

g. Add the average data from column F to the chart. (*Hint*: Use the Select Data button on the Chart Tools Design tab to select the new chart data, including the average data.)

h. Change the chart type to Combo Clustered Column - Line chart (first option of combo charts) with the average data series charted as a line. (*Hint*: After selecting the chart type in the Change Chart Type dialog box, scroll down to make sure the Fall, Spring, Summer, and Intersession series are charted as clustered columns and the Average data series is charted as a line. You may need to change the Intersession chart type. Do not use the secondary axis options.)

i. Add data labels to the Average data series only. (*Hint*: Select the Average data series on the chart before adding data labels.)

j. Save your work, then compare your worksheet to FIGURE 4-28.

k. Enter your name in the center footer section of the chart sheet, then preview the worksheet.

l. Submit your work to your instructor as directed, close the workbook, then close Excel.

FIGURE 4-28

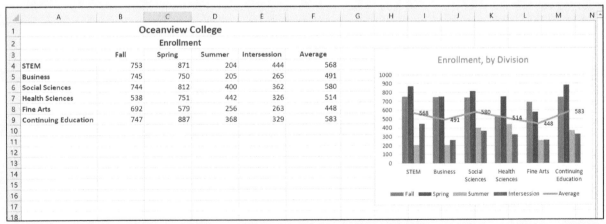

Visual Workshop

Open IL_EX_4-5.xlsx from the location where you store your Data Files, then save it as **IL_EX_4_Insurance**. Create, modify, and position the two charts, as shown in FIGURE 4-29. (*Hint*: Use the CTRL key as needed to select nonadjacent ranges.) You will need to make formatting, layout, and design changes once you create the charts. (*Hints*: The WordArt used in the pie chart title is Fill: Orange, Accent color 4: Soft Bevel. The WordArt used in the column chart title is Fill: Turquoise, Accent color 1: Shadow. The Life data point in the pie chart is exploded 30 degrees.) Enter your name in the center section of the footer, then save and preview the worksheet. Submit your work to your instructor as directed, then close the workbook and close Excel.

FIGURE 4-29

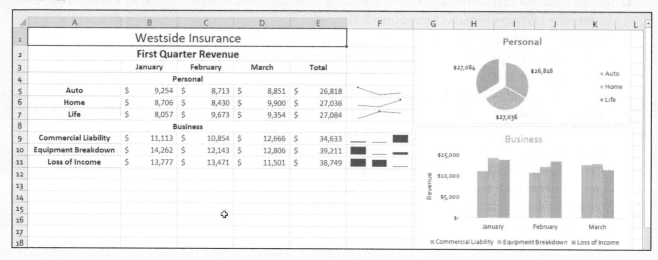

Integrating Word and Excel

CASE ▶ You are working with Lydia Snyder, the vice president of Operations for JCL Talent, Inc. Lydia has asked you to explore the integration capabilities of Microsoft Office. First, you create a report in Word that includes values and a chart created in Excel, and then you embed a paragraph of text created in Word into an Excel worksheet.

Module Objectives

After completing this module, you will be able to:

- Integrate data between Word and Excel
- Copy data from Excel to Word
- Copy a chart from Excel to Word
- Create linked objects
- Embed a Word file in Excel

Files You Will Need

IL_INT_1-1.xlsx	IL_INT_1-8.docx
IL_INT_1-2.docx	IL_INT_1-9.xlsx
IL_INT_1-3.xlsx	IL_INT_1-10.docx
IL_INT_1-4.docx	IL_INT_1-11.docx
IL_INT_1-5.xlsx	IL_INT_1-12.xlsx
IL_INT_1-6.docx	IL_INT_1-13.xlsx
IL_INT_1-7.xlsx	IL_INT_1-14.docx

Learning Outcome
• Define copy/paste, link, and embed integration options

Integrate Data between Word and Excel

Office programs are designed to work together through a process called integration. **Integration** is the combining of objects and data from two or more applications using linking or embedding. When you integrate data from multiple Office programs, you work with both a source file and a destination file. The **source file** is the file in which you create an object that you will place in a destination file. The **destination file** is the file that displays an object from a source file. You can choose from three integration methods: pasting, linking, and embedding. **CASE** *Your work in the Operations division of JCL Talent often requires you to create documents such as reports and price lists that include data from both Word and Excel. You decide to review some of the ways in which you integrate data between the two programs.*

DETAILS

You can integrate Word and Excel by:

• **Copying and pasting data from the Clipboard**

You use the Copy and Paste commands to duplicate objects such as text selections, numbers (called values in Excel), and pictures from one program and place them into another program. An **object** is the data to be exchanged between another document or program. After you copy and paste an object, changes that you make to the object in the source file do not appear in the destination file. The report shown in FIGURE 1-1 was created in Word and includes two objects that were copied from Excel—the photograph that appears to the right of the document title and the shaded table under the document subtitle.

• **Linking data**

Sometimes you want to connect the data that is included in two or more files. For example, suppose you copy the contents of a cell containing a formula from an Excel worksheet and paste it into a Word document. When you change the formula values in Excel, you want the corresponding values to change in the Word document. To create a **link**, or a connection you can create between a source file and a destination file, between data in two files, you select one of the link options that appears when you either click the Paste button arrow or view options in the Paste Special dialog box. You use the term **linked object** to refer to a text selection, value, or picture that is contained in a destination file and linked to a source file. In the report shown in FIGURE 1-1, the value "90%" is a linked object. If this percentage changes in the Excel worksheet, the linked percentage in the Word document also changes.

• **Copying and pasting charts**

When you copy a chart from Excel and paste it into Word using the Paste command, Word automatically creates a link between the pasted chart and the original chart. In the report shown in FIGURE 1-1, the column chart was copied from Excel and pasted into the Word document. When the chart values are updated in Excel, the same chart values are updated in the chart copied to Word. You can also copy a chart from the source file and then paste it into the destination file as an object that is not linked.

• **Embedding a Word file in Excel**

You can **embed**, or place an unlinked copy of, the contents of a Word file into an Excel worksheet. You edit the embedded object by double-clicking it and using Word program tools to change text and formatting. This process changes the embedded copy of the Word object in Excel, but does not affect the original source document you created in Word. Similarly, any changes to the source Word document are not reflected in the embedded copy in Excel. In the list shown in FIGURE 1-2, the text that describes current job trends was inserted in Excel as an embedded Word file.

FIGURE 1-1: Word report with objects copied from Excel

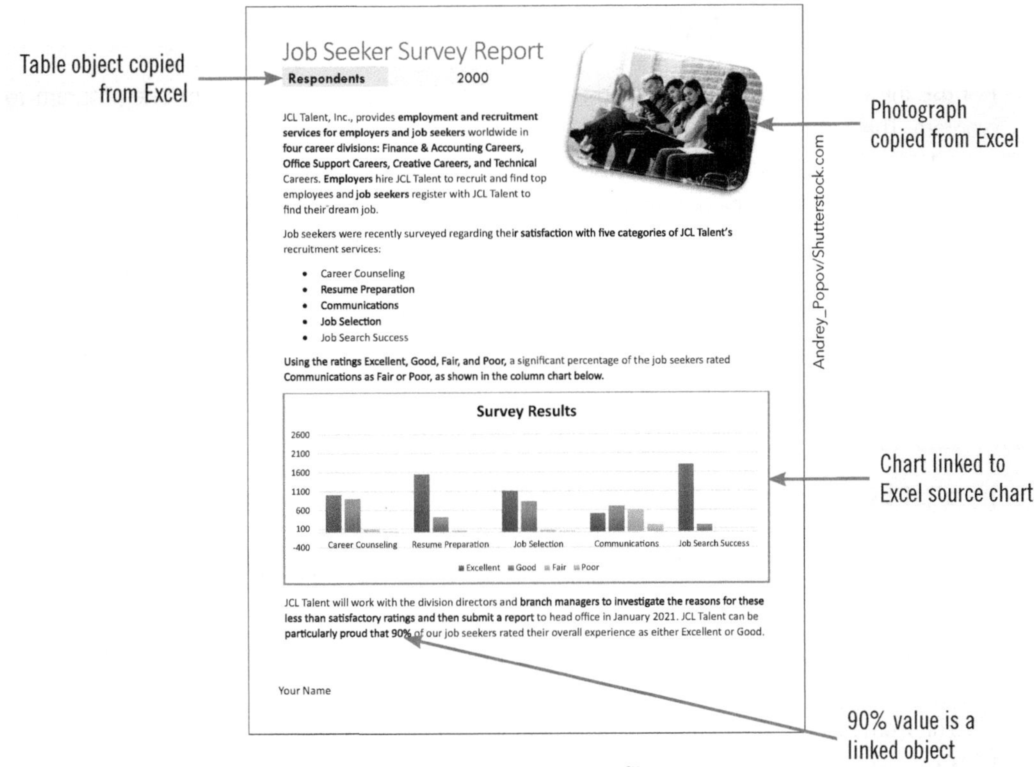

Table object copied from Excel →

← Photograph copied from Excel

Andrey_Popov/Shutterstock.com

Chart linked to Excel source chart →

90% value is a linked object →

FIGURE 1-2: Price list with embedded Word file

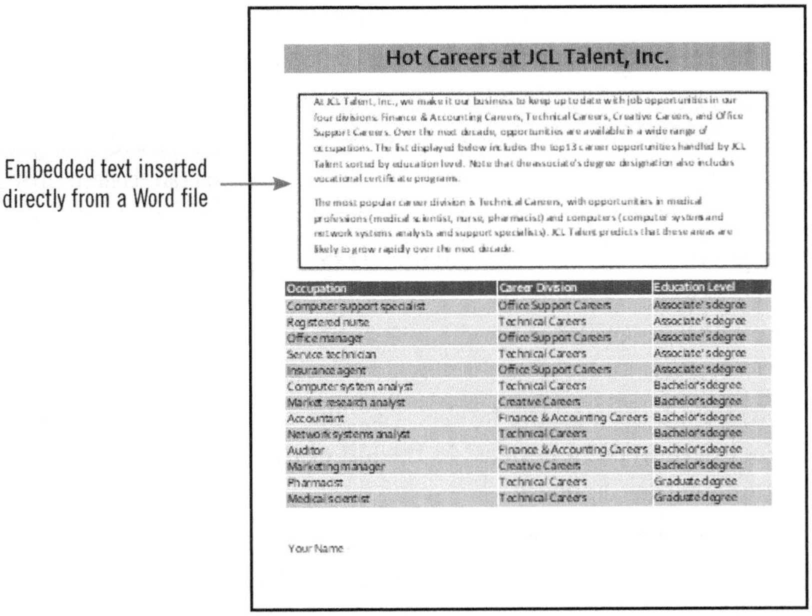

Embedded text inserted directly from a Word file →

Understanding object linking and embedding (OLE)

The term **object linking and embedding (OLE)** refers to a technology that lets you share information among the Office programs. You create an object in one program, and then you can choose to either link the object to or embed it in another program. The difference between linking and embedding relates to where the object is stored and how you update the object after you place it in a document. A linked object in a destination file is an image of an object contained in a source file, not a copy of it. Both objects share a single source, which means you make changes to an object only in the source file.

When you embed an object that you created in another program, you include a copy of the object in a destination file. To update the object, you double-click it in the destination file and then use the tools of the source program to make changes. You cannot edit the source object using the tools of the destination program.

Copy Data from Excel to Word

Learning Outcomes
- Switch between Word and Excel
- Copy objects to the clipboard
- Paste Excel objects into Word

You use the Copy and Paste commands when you want to copy an item from one program to another program. The item might be a line of text, a selection of cells, or an object such as a chart or a picture. The procedure is the same as the one you use to copy and paste an object from one location in a document to another location in the same document. By default, an object copied from one program to another program retains the formatting of the original object and is not linked to the original object. The exception occurs when you copy and paste a chart, which you will learn about in the next lesson. **CASE** ▶ *Lydia Snyder, the vice president of Operations at JCL Talent, has provided you with an Excel worksheet containing survey data gathered from job seekers about their experience with JCL Talent and created a report in Word that describes the survey results. She asks you to copy two objects from the Excel worksheet and paste them into the Word report.*

STEPS

1. **Start Excel, open IL_INT_1-1.xlsx from the location where you store your Data Files, then save it as IL_INT_1_JobSeekerSurveyResults**

   The values in the range B7:F10 represent the total number of responses in each of the four rating categories for five ways in which job seekers interacted with JCL Talent.

2. **Start Word, open IL_INT_1-2.docx from the location where you store your Data Files, then save it as IL_INT_JobSeekerSurveyReport**

   The Word report contains text that describes the results of the survey.

3. **Move the mouse pointer over the Excel program button on the taskbar, as shown in FIGURE 1-3, then click the Excel program button to switch to Excel**

   When you point to the Excel program button, a picture of the worksheet and the filename appear.

TROUBLE
If items already appear in the Clipboard pane, click Clear All.

4. **On the Home tab, click the Clipboard Dialog Box Launcher 🔲**

   The Clipboard pane opens to the left of the worksheet window. You use the Clipboard when you want to copy and paste more than one item from one program to another program. You can "collect" up to 24 items on the Clipboard and then switch to the other program to paste them.

5. **Click the photograph, click the Copy button in the Clipboard group, select the range A4:B4, then click the Copy button**

   Both items now appear on the Clipboard, as shown in FIGURE 1-4. When you place multiple items on the Clipboard, newer items appear at the top of the list and older items move down.

6. **Click the Word program button on the taskbar, click the Clipboard dialog box launcher 🔲, verify that the Insertion point appears to the left of the title in the document, then click the photograph on the Clipboard**

7. **Click in the blank space below the title Job Seeker Survey Report, click Respondents 2000 on the Clipboard, then click the Close button ✕ on the Clipboard pane**

   You pasted the object as a table below the document title. When you use the Copy and Paste commands, the default setting is for the copied object to retain the formatting applied to it in the source file.

8. **Click the photograph in the Word document, click the Layout Options button 🔼 in the upper-right corner of the photograph, click the Square option 🔲, close the Layout Options window, then drag the photograph to the right of the first paragraph using the green alignment guides, as shown in FIGURE 1-5**

9. **Click anywhere in the document to deselect the photograph, then save the document**

FIGURE 1-3: Word and Excel on the taskbar

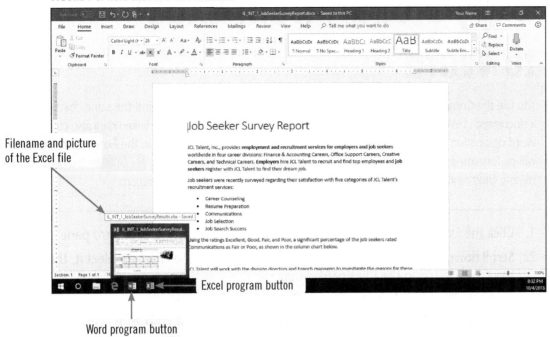

Filename and picture of the Excel file

Excel program button

Word program button

FIGURE 1-4: Two items collected on the Clipboard

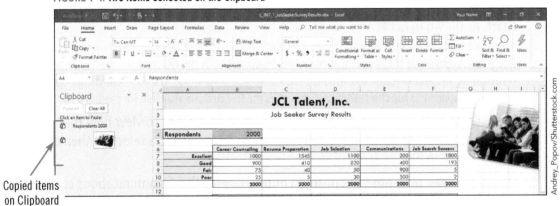

Copied items on Clipboard

Andrey_Popov/Shutterstock.com

FIGURE 1-5: Picture positioned in the Word report

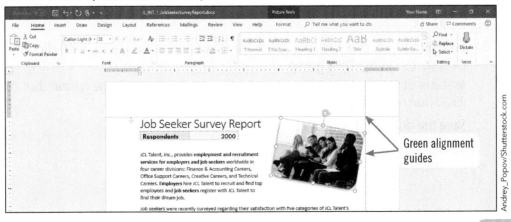

Green alignment guides

Andrey_Popov/Shutterstock.com

Copy a Chart from Excel to Word

**Learning
Outcomes**
• Copy a chart
• View Paste options
• Update a linked
  chart

You use the Copy and Paste tools to create a link between a chart in Excel and the same chart pasted into a document in Word. When you change the data in the Excel source file, the linked data also changes in the Word destination file. By default, the copied chart will be linked to the chart in the Excel report. However, it will be formatted with the same theme applied to the destination document. **CASE ▶** *You need to copy a column chart representing survey results from Excel and paste it into the Word report.*

STEPS

1. **Click the** Excel program button **on the taskbar, then close the Clipboard pane**

2. **Scroll down to view the column chart, click an edge of the chart to select it, then click the** Copy button **in the Clipboard group**

   Notice that the chart in Excel is formatted with the colors of the Circuit theme.

3. **Switch to Word, click below the second paragraph (which ends with "column chart below"), then click the** Paste button **in the Clipboard group**

   The chart appears in the Word document formatted with the colors of the Celestial theme, because this theme was already applied to the Word document. The Paste Options button appears in the lower-right corner of the chart.

4. **Click the** Paste Options button 🗋(Ctrl) ▾ **outside the lower-right corner of the pasted chart, as shown in** FIGURE 1-6

   A selection of paste options appears. By default, the option Use Destination Theme & Link Data is selected. The Word document is the destination file and is formatted with the Celestial theme. The Excel document is the source file and is formatted with the Circuit theme. As a result, the Celestial theme applied to the Word file is applied to the chart. TABLE 1-1 describes the five options available for pasting a copied chart.

5. **Move the mouse over each of the five Paste Options buttons to view how the formatting of the chart changes depending on which button is selected, then click the** Use Destination Theme & Link Data button 🗋

6. **Switch to Excel, then note the position of the bars for the Communications category in the column chart**

   At present, the Poor column (purple) is quite high compared to the Poor columns for the other categories.

7. **Scroll up, click cell E8, type 700, press** ENTER, **click cell E10, type 200, then press** ENTER **and scroll down to the chart**

   In the chart, the Good column (orange) in the Communications category has grown, and the Poor column has shrunk.

TROUBLE
You may not need
to refresh the
chart data.

8. **Switch to Word, click the** chart, **click the** Chart Tools Design tab, **then click the** Refresh Data button **in the Data group**

   As shown in FIGURE 1-7, the bars for the Communications category in the column chart change in the linked chart to reflect the changes you made to the chart in Excel.

9. **Save the document, switch to Excel, then save the workbook**

FIGURE 1-6: Paste Options

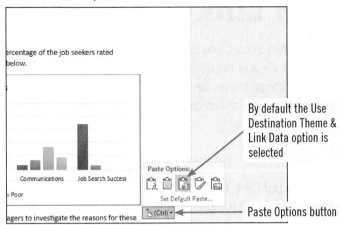

FIGURE 1-7: Linked chart updated in Word

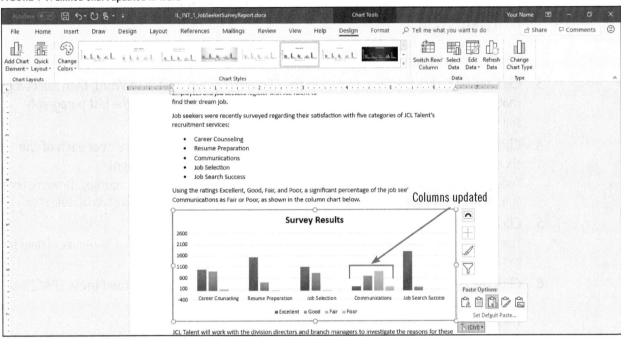

TABLE 1-1: Paste options for charts

Paste Options button	button name	description
	Use Destination Theme & Embed Workbook	The pasted chart is not linked to the source document, and the pasted chart assumes the formatting of the destination document
	Keep Source Formatting & Embed Workbook	The pasted chart is not linked to the source document, and the pasted chart keeps the same formatting as the source document
	Use Destination Theme & Link Data	This button is selected by default when a chart is pasted into the destination document; the theme of the destination document is applied to the chart, and the chart is linked to the object in the source document
	Keep Source Formatting & Link Data	The pasted chart is linked to the source document, so any changes made to the chart in the source document will be made to the copied chart in the Word document; in addition, the formatting of the source document is retained
	Picture	The chart is pasted as a picture that cannot be modified, and uses the same formatting as the chart in the source document

Create Linked Objects

To link data other than a chart, you use the Copy button and the Paste Special command to create a link between the source file and the destination file. **CASE** ▸ *You need your report to include a value that represents average ratings. You decide to link the report to the source file data so you can update the data in both files when new information becomes available.*

STEPS

1. **In Excel, click cell G14, type the formula =AVERAGE(B14:F14), press ENTER, click cell G14, then drag its fill handle to cell G17 to enter the remaining three percentages**

   The value "56%" appears in cell G14. This value indicates that, on average, 56% of the responses were Excellent. Only 3% of the responses were Poor.

2. **Click cell F18, type Good/Excellent, press TAB, type the formula =G14+G15 in cell G18, then press ENTER**

   The value "87%" appears in cell G18, indicating that 87% of job seekers rated their experience with JCL Talent as Good or Excellent.

3. **Click cell G18, click the Copy button in the Clipboard group, switch to Word, then select XX that appears following the phrase "can be particularly proud that" in the last paragraph**

   You will paste the contents of cell G18 from Excel over the "XX" in Word.

4. **Click the Paste arrow in the Clipboard group, then move your mouse over each of the six options to view how the pasted object will appear in the document**

   Two options allow linking—Link & Keep Source Formatting and Link & Merge Formatting. However, both options also insert a line break, so you look for additional paste options in the Paste Special dialog box.

5. **Click Paste Special**

   The Paste Special dialog box opens, as shown in FIGURE 1-8. In this dialog box, you have more options for pasting the value and for controlling its appearance in the destination file.

6. **Click the Paste link option button, click Unformatted Text, click OK, then press SPACEBAR once to add a space after "87%" if necessary**

   The percentage, 87%, appears in the Word document. You decide to test the link.

7. **Switch to Excel, click cell E7, type 500, press ENTER, click cell E9, type 600, then press ENTER**

   The Good/Excellent rating in cell G18 is now 90%.

8. **Switch to Word, right-click 87%, then click Update Link**

   The value 90% appears. The final document is shown in FIGURE 1-9.

9. **Type your name where indicated in the Word footer, save the document, switch to Excel, type your name where indicated in cell A37, save the workbook, submit your files to your instructor, then close the files**

   If you print the Excel workbook, make sure you fit it on one page.

FIGURE 1-8: Paste Special dialog box

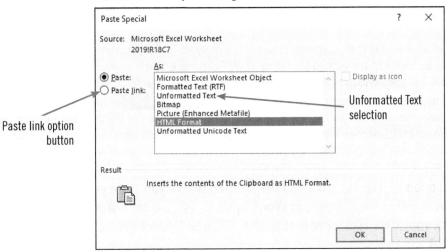

Paste link option button

Unformatted Text selection

FIGURE 1-9: Completed report

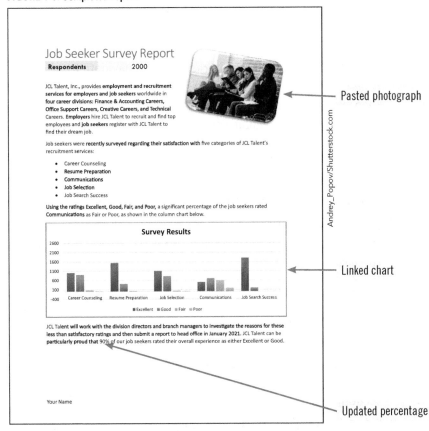

Pasted photograph

Andrey_Popov/Shutterstock.com

Linked chart

Updated percentage

Opening linked files and reestablishing links to charts

When you open a Word file that contains links from an Excel file, a dialog box opens with a message telling you that the document contains links that may refer to other files. The message also asks if you want to update this document with the data from the linked file. Click Yes to update the document with data from the linked file. If you want to change information in both the Excel file and the Word file, you need to open the Excel workbook first, followed by the Word document.

If you make a change to a linked chart in the Excel file, you need to refresh the chart data in Word. To do so, click the chart in Word, click the Chart Tools Design tab, then click the Refresh Data button in the Data group. You also need to manually update any other links by right-clicking the link in Word and then clicking Update Link.

Embed a Word File in Excel

Learning Outcomes
• Insert a Word file as an object
• Edit the Word file in Excel

You can embed an entire file that you create in one Office program into a document created in another Office program. You can then edit the embedded file by double-clicking it in the destination program to open the source program. You use the tools of the source program to make changes. TABLE 1-2 summarizes the four ways in which you integrated data between Word and Excel in this module. **CASE** ▶ *You have created a list in Excel that includes hot career opportunities currently handled by JCL Talent. Before you distribute the list at an upcoming meeting, you decide to include some explanatory text that you have stored in a Word document.*

STEPS

1. **In Excel, open IL_INT_1-3.xlsx from the location where you store your Data Files, then save it as IL_INT_1_HotCareers; in Word, open IL_INT_1-4.docx from the location where you store your Data Files, save it as IL_INT_1_CareerOpportunities, then close the document**

2. **In Excel, click cell E3, click the Insert tab, click the Text button to display the selection of Text objects, if necessary, then click the Object button** 🗐
   The Object dialog box opens. Here you can choose to either create a new object or insert an object from a file.

3. **Click the Create from File tab, click Browse, navigate to where you stored the IL_INT_1_CareerOpportunities file if necessary, double-click IL_INT_1_CareerOpportunities, then click OK**
   The text from the Word document appears in a box that starts in cell E3. When you insert an object from another program such as Word, you sometimes need to reposition the current worksheet contents to accommodate the inserted object.

4. **Select the range A4:C20, move the mouse pointer over any border of the selection to show the ⁺⃗ₖ, then drag the selection down to cell A15**

5. **Move the mouse pointer over the border of the box containing the Word text to show the ⁺⃗ₖ pointer, drag the selection to cell A3, click a blank cell, then compare your screen to FIGURE 1-10**

TROUBLE
If your embedded Word document opens in a separate window, proceed with the steps, and at the end of Step 8, close the Word window.

6. **Double-click the box containing the Word text**
   Because the object is embedded, the Word Ribbon and tabs appear within the Excel window. As a result, you can use the tools from the source program (Word) to edit the text. The title bar shows "Document in IL_INT_1_HotCareers.xlsx - Excel" because you are working within the destination file to edit the embedded object.

7. **Click the Select button in the Editing group, click Select All, in the Paragraph group, click the Dialog Box Launcher 🗔, select the contents of the Left box in the Indentation section, type .2, press TAB, type .2 in the Right box, then click OK**

8. **Select 10 in the fourth line of paragraph 1, type 13, compare the edited object to FIGURE 1-11, then click outside the object to return to Excel**
   The embedded object is updated in Excel. The text in the source file is not updated because the source file is not linked to the destination file.

9. **Click the File tab, click Print, click Page Setup, (you may need to scroll down the Print dialog box), click the Margins tab, click the Horizontally check box, click OK, then click ⬅ to return to the workbook**
   The embedded Word object and Excel data are centered between the left and right margins of the page.

10. **Type your name where indicated in cell A31, save the workbook, submit your files to your instructor, then close the workbook and close Word and Excel**

FIGURE 1-10: Embedded Word file positioned in Excel

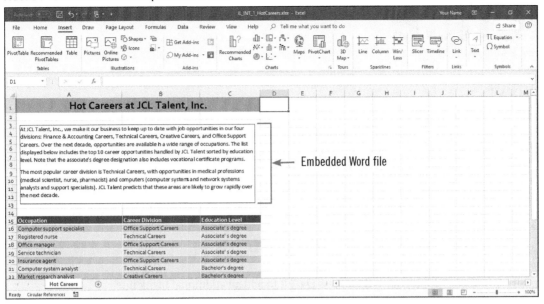

Embedded Word file

FIGURE 1-11: Embedded object updated in Excel

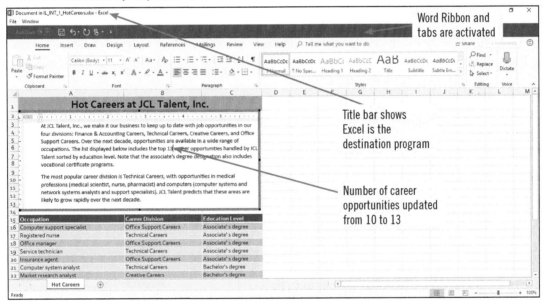

Word Ribbon and tabs are activated

Title bar shows Excel is the destination program

Number of career opportunities updated from 10 to 13

TABLE 1-2: Module 1 integration tasks

object	command	source program	destination program	result	connection	page no.
Cells	Copy/Paste	Excel	Word	Object with Excel formatting	Pasted: no link	4
Chart	Copy/Paste	Excel	Word	Object with Word formatting	Linked	6
Cell	Copy/Paste Special/Paste link	Excel	Word	Formatting varies depending on the formatting option chosen in the Paste Special dialog box	Linked	8
File	Insert/Object/ Create from File	Word	Excel	Text box containing the Word file: to update, double-click and use Word tools within the Excel destination file	Embedded: no link	10

Integration

Practice

Skills Review

1. **Copy data from Excel to Word.**
   a. Start Excel, open the IL_INT_1-5.xlsx from the location where you store your Data Files, then save it as **IL_INT_1_SciencesData**.
   b. Start Word, open IL_INT_1-6.docx from the location where you store your Data Files, then save it as **IL_INT_SciencesReport**.
   c. Switch to Excel, open the Clipboard pane, then, if there are items on the Clipboard, click Clear All.
   d. Copy the contents of cell A1 to the Clipboard.
   e. Select the range A4:A7, then copy the contents to the Clipboard.
   f. Switch to Word, open the Clipboard pane, paste the Sciences object at the top of the document (at the current position of the insertion point), then press ENTER to add an additional blank line.
   g. Paste the subject areas object on the blank line below the first paragraph.
   h. Close the Clipboard pane, then save the document.

2. **Copy a chart from Excel to Word.**
   a. Switch to Excel, close the Clipboard pane, then copy the bar chart.
   b. Switch to Word, then paste the bar chart below the second paragraph of text (which ends with "and State scores").
   c. Switch to Excel, then note the position of the bars for Physics.
   d. Change the value in cell C4 to **70**, then switch to Word.
   e. Click the chart, refresh the data, if necessary, then save the document.
   f. Switch to Excel, then save the workbook.

3. **Create linked objects.**
   a. In Excel, enter the formula **=B4-C4** in cell D4.
   b. Use the Fill handle to copy the formula to the range D5:D7.
   c. Select the range A3:D7, copy it, switch to Word, then use the Paste Special command to paste the cells as a link below paragraph 3 (which ends with "state-wide"), using the Formatted Text (RTF) selection in the Paste Special dialog box.
   d. In Excel, copy cell D7, switch to Word, then use Paste Special to paste the cell over "XX" in the last paragraph as a link using the Unformatted Text option in the Paste Special dialog box. Add a space after the linked object if necessary.
   e. In Excel, change the value in cell B7 to **90**.
   f. In Word, refresh the chart if necessary.
   g. Update the link in the table and the link in the last paragraph so that "20" appears in both places.
   h. Enter your name where indicated in the footer in Word, save the Word report, compare your document to **FIGURE 1-12**, submit your file to your instructor, then close the document.
   i. In Excel, enter your name in cell A26, save the workbook, submit the file to your instructor, then close the workbook.

FIGURE 1-12

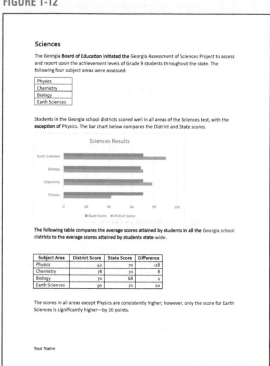

Integrating Word and Excel

Skills Review (continued)

4. Embed a Word file in Excel.

a. In Excel, open IL_INT_1-7.xlsx from the location where you store your Data Files, then save it as **IL_INT_1_LanguageCourseRevenue**.

b. In Word, open IL_IN_1-8.docx from the location where you store your Data Files, save it as **IL_INT_1_LanguageCourses**, then close it.

c. In Excel, in cell H4, insert the Word file IL_INT_1_LanguageCourses.docx as an embedded file.

d. Select the range A6:F16, then move it to cell A12.

e. Position the box containing the Word text so its upper-left corner is in cell A3.

f. Change "XX" to **$65** in paragraph 1, then change "ZZ" in paragraph 1 to **80%**.

g. Click outside the embedded object to return to Excel, adjust the size of the embedded file if necessary, compare your screen to FIGURE 1-13, enter your name in cell A22, save the workbook, submit the file to your instructor, then close the workbook and close Word and Excel.

FIGURE 1-13

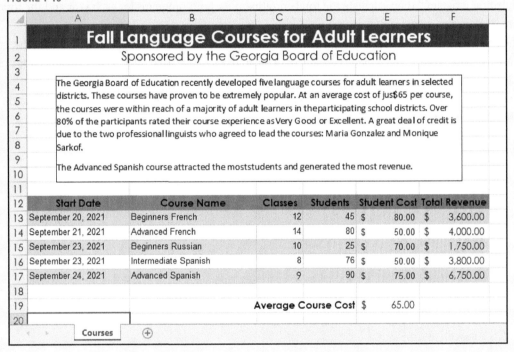

Integration

Independent Challenge 1

You assist the office manager at Riverwalk Medical Clinic, a large outpatient medical facility that provides a wide range of medical and health services and programs to community members. One of the programs trains young volunteers to assist with patient care. You have collected data about two volunteer programs from 2016 to 2021 in an Excel workbook. Now you need to prepare the workbook for distribution at an upcoming meeting of management staff at the clinic who are interested in expanding the programs. You want to include text in the workbook that you have stored in a Word document.

    a. Start Excel, open IL_INT_1-9.xlsx from the location where you store your Data Files, then save it as **IL_INT_1_RiverwalkClinicVolunteerProgram**.

    b. Start Word, open IL_INT_1-10.docx from the location where you store your Data Files, save it as **IL_INT_1_VolunteerInformation**, then close it.

    c. In a blank area of the Excel worksheet, insert the Volunteer Information file as an embedded object.

    d. Adjust the positions of the Excel data and the box containing the Word text so the Word text appears above the Excel data and below the title.

    e. In Excel, calculate the total enrollment for the Patient Care and Nutrition programs in the appropriate cells.

    f. To the right of "Nutrition Program," enter and format **Total** to match the formatting for "Patient Care Program" and "Nutrition Program," then calculate the total enrollment for both programs for each year and the total for all programs in all years.

    g. Copy the Total enrollment value, edit the embedded Word document so the text is indented by .3" from the left and right margins, then paste the correct total enrollment figure to replace "XX" using the Keep Text Only paste option. Adjust the size and position of the embedded object as necessary.

    h. Enter your name in the cell indicated in Excel, save the Excel workbook, submit the file to your instructor, then close the workbook and close Excel.

Independent Challenge 2

As a member of the Beaver Island Arts Commission in Washington State, you are responsible for compiling the minutes of the commission's quarterly meetings. You have already written most of the text required for the minutes. Now you need to insert data from Excel that shows how much money was raised from various fund-raising activities.

a. Start Word, open IL_INT_1-11.docx from the location where you store your Data Files, save it as **IL_INT_1_BeaverIslandArtsCommissionMinutes**, start Excel, open IL_INT_1-12.xlsx from the location where you store your Data Files, then save it as **IL_INT_1_BeaverIslandData**.

b. In Excel, open the Clipboard pane, clear all items if necessary, then copy the photograph and cell A2.

c. In Word, open the Clipboard pane, paste the photograph at the top of the Word document, change the text wrapping of the picture to Square, then position the photograph to the right of the first paragraph, keeping within the green guidelines.

d. Click to the left of "Approval of Minutes," then paste cell A2.

e. Copy the Fundraising Revenue chart from Excel, then paste it in the appropriate area in the Word document.

f. In Excel, change the number of participants in the bake sale to **1000**; then in Word, refresh the data in the chart if necessary. The Bake Sale slice should be 60%.

g. In Excel, copy the contents of cell E7, switch to Word, select "XX" in the paragraph below the chart, view the paste options, then paste the value as a link using the Unformatted Text selection in the Paste Special dialog box. Add a space if necessary.

h. In Excel, click cell G7, then calculate the total funds raised by adding the contents of the range B7:F7.

i. In cell B8, enter the formula **=B7/G7**, use [F4] to make cell G7 absolute, then copy the formula to the range C8:F8.

j. Copy cell E8, switch to Word, select "ZZ" in the paragraph below the chart, then paste the value as a link using the Unformatted Text selection, adding a space if necessary.

k. In Excel, change the number of participants in the bake sale to **1200**; then in Word, verify the Bake Sale slice changed to 64% and the links updated to $60,000 and 64%. If the links do not update automatically, right-click them and click Update Link in the Word document.

l. Type your name in the Word footer, then save the Word document and Excel workbook, submit the files to your instructor, then close them.

Visual Workshop

Using the Data Files IL_INT_1-13.xlsx and IL_INT_1-14.docx, create the price list shown in FIGURE 1-14. Use formulas to calculate the prices for two-packs and four-packs. Save the workbook as **IL_INT_1_GardenGourmetPriceList**, and save the Word document as **IL_INT_1_GardenGourmetInformation**. Embed the Word document into the Excel worksheet, position the inserted file and the price list in Excel as shown in FIGURE 1-14, then format the embedded Word object as shown in FIGURE 1-14. (*Hint*: The indentation on both sides of the text is .3, and the font size is 12 point.) Add your name to the Excel worksheet in the cell indicated, save all files, submit them to your instructor, then close all files.

FIGURE 1-14

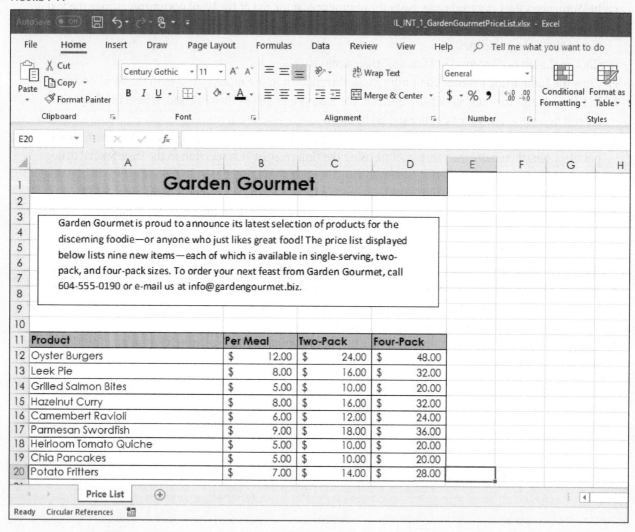

Getting Started with Access

Lydia Snyder is the vice president of operations for JCL Talent, a company that provides recruitment and employment services for employers and job seekers. You will work with Lydia to use Microsoft Access 2019 to store, maintain, and analyze job placement data.

Module Objectives

After completing this module, you will be able to:

- Understand relational databases
- Open and explore a database
- Navigate and enter data
- Edit existing data
- Create a table
- Modify fields
- Create a query
- Create a form
- Create a report
- Save and share a database with OneDrive
- Create a new database
- Compact and back up a database

Files You Will Need

IL_AC_1-1.accdb
Support_IL_AC_1_Employees.xlsx
IL_AC_1-2.accdb

Support_IL_AC_1_StatesAndProvs.xlsx
IL_AC_1-3.accdb
IL_AC_1-4.accdb

Understand Relational Databases

Learning
Outcomes
• Describe relational
database concepts
• Explain when to
use a database
• Compare a
relational database
to a spreadsheet

Microsoft Access 2019 is relational database software that runs on the Windows operating system. You use **relational database software** to manage data organized into lists, such as information about customers, products, vendors, employees, projects, or sales. Some companies track lists of information in a spreadsheet program such as Microsoft Excel. Although Excel offers some list management features, Access provides many more tools and advantages for managing data. Access uses a relational database model to manage data, whereas Excel manages data as a single list. TABLE 1-1 compares the two programs. **CASE** *Lydia has noticed that JCL Talent manages multiple copies of several lists of data in Excel. She asks you to help her review the advantages of managing data in a relational database model used by Access as compared to the single list spreadsheet approach used by Excel.*

DETAILS

The advantages of using Access for database management include the following:

- **Duplicate data is minimized**

  FIGURES 1-1 and 1-2 compare how you might store data in a single list in an Excel spreadsheet versus managing the same data using three tables in an Access relational database. With Access, you enter company data only once no matter how many jobs that company has to offer.

- **Information is more accurate, reliable, and consistent because duplicate data is minimized**

  When data is not duplicated, it is more accurate, reliable, and consistent.

- **Data entry is faster and easier using Access forms**

  Data entry forms (screen layouts) make data entry faster, easier, and more accurate than entering data in a spreadsheet.

- **Information can be viewed and sorted in many ways using Access queries, forms, and reports**

  In Access, you can save multiple queries (questions about the data), data entry forms, and reports, allowing different users to view the same data in different ways.

- **Information is more secure using Access forms, passwords, and security features**

  Access databases can be encrypted and password protected. Forms can be created to protect and display specific data.

- **Several users can share and edit information at the same time**

  Unlike spreadsheets or word-processing documents, more than one person can enter, update, and analyze data in an Access database at the same time. This also means that you are not tempted to create copies that inevitably become inaccurate because of the difficulties of updating multiple copies of the same data. Having all users work on the same, single set of data at the same time is enormously accurate and reliable.

FIGURE 1-1: Using a spreadsheet to organize data

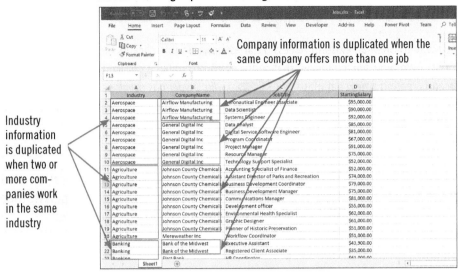

Industry information is duplicated when two or more companies work in the same industry

Company information is duplicated when the same company offers more than one job

FIGURE 1-2: Using a relational database to organize data

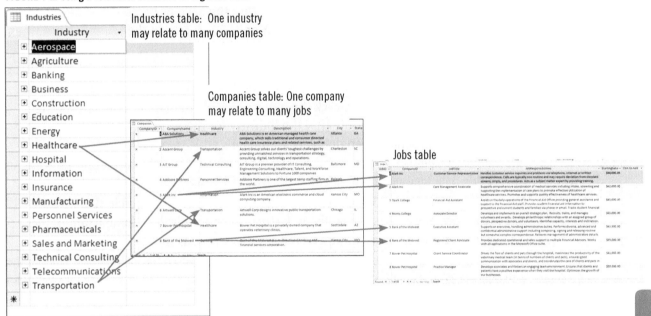

Industries table: One industry may relate to many companies

Companies table: One company may relate to many jobs

Jobs table

TABLE 1-1: Comparing Excel with Access

feature	Excel	Access
Data entry	Provides only one spreadsheet layout	Provides the ability to create an unlimited number of data entry forms
Storage	Restricted to a single file's limitations	Virtually unlimited when coupled with the ability to use Microsoft SQL Server to store data
Data model	Manages single lists of information	Manages data in a relational database with related tables, which tremendously reduces data redundancy and improves data integrity
Reporting	Provides a printout of the spreadsheet	Provides the ability to create and save an unlimited number of reports that summarize and organize data in different ways
Security	Limited to file security options such as marking the file "read-only" or protecting a range of cells	When used with SQL Server, provides extensive security down to the user and data level
Multiuser capabilities	Limited to one user at a time	Allows multiple users to simultaneously enter and update data

Open and Explore a Database

The fastest way to open an existing Access database is to double-click its file or shortcut icon. If you start Access on its own, you see a window that requires you to make a choice between opening an existing database and creating a new database. **CASE** *Lydia Snyder has developed a research database containing information about previous job opportunities that JCL Talent has managed. She asks you to start Access 2019 and review this database.*

STEPS

1. **sam↓ Start Access, click the Open Other Files link, navigate to the location where you store your Data Files, double-click the IL_AC_1-1.accdb database to open it, then click the Maximize button ▣ if the Access window is not already maximized**

   The IL_AC_1-1 database contains three tables of data named Companies, Industries, and Jobs. It also includes two queries, three forms, and one report. Each of these items (table, query, form, and report) is a different type of **object** in an Access database application and is displayed in the **Navigation Pane**. The purpose of each object is defined in TABLE 1-2.

TROUBLE
If a yellow Security Warning bar appears below the ribbon, click Enable Content.

2. **Click the File tab on the ribbon, click Save As, click the Save As button, navigate to the folder where you want to save your work, enter IL_AC_1_Jobs in the File name box, then click Save**

   If you need to redo the exercises, return to this step to make another copy of the IL_AC_1-1.accdb starting Data File.

TROUBLE
If the Navigation Pane is not open, click the Shutter Bar Open/Close button « to open it and view the database objects.

3. **In the Navigation Pane, double-click the Industries table to open it, double-click the Companies table to open it, note that the Industry for the Airflow Manufacturing company is Construction, then double-click the Jobs table to open it**

   The Industries, Companies, and Jobs tables each open in Datasheet View to display the data they store. An Access **table** is the fundamental building block of a relational database because tables store all the data.

4. **In the Navigation Pane, double-click the JobsByIndustry query to open it, double-click any occurrence of Construction in the Industry column for Airflow Manufacturing, click Aerospace in the drop-down list, then click any other row, as shown in FIGURE 1-3**

   An Access **query** selects a subset of data from one or more tables. Given the Industry field value for the Airflow Manufacturing company is stored only once in the Airflow Manufacturing record in the Companies table, changing one occurrence of that value in the query changes all records that select that company.

5. **Double-click the CompanyEntry form in the Navigation Pane to open it, then click the Next button in the upper-right corner of the form three times**

   An Access **form** is a data entry screen that often includes command buttons to make common tasks such as moving between records easy to perform. Forms are the most common way to enter and edit data. Note that Airflow Manufacturing's Industry value is Aerospace, which reflects the change you made to Airflow Manufacturing in the JobsByIndustry query.

6. **Double-click the JobsByHighestSalary report in the Navigation Pane to open it, then scroll down to see Airflow Manufacturing**

   An Access **report** is a professional printout that can be distributed electronically or on paper. The Aerospace update to Airflow Manufacturing carried through to the report, demonstrating the power and productivity of a relational database.

7. **Right-click each object tab (except for the Companies table), click Close on the shortcut menu, notice that the Industry for Airflow Manufacturing is now set to Aerospace in the Companies table, then close it**

   Changes to data are automatically saved as you work.

FIGURE 1-3: IL_AC_1_Jobs.accdb database

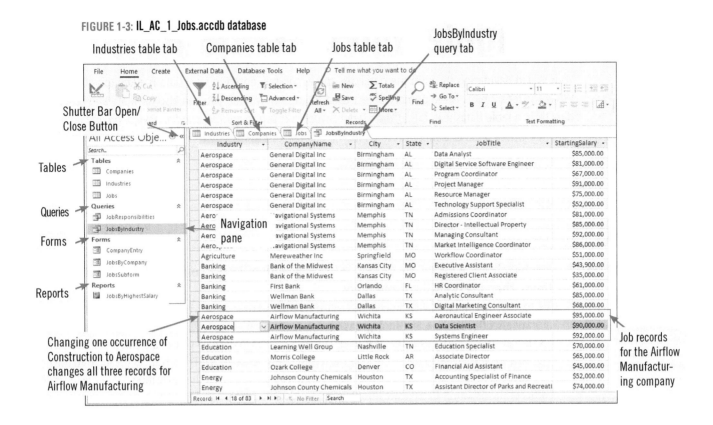

TABLE 1-2: Access objects and their purpose

object	icon	purpose
Table		Contains all the data within the database in a spreadsheet-like view called **Datasheet View**; tables are linked with a common field to create a relational database
Query		Allows you to select a subset of fields or records from one or more tables; create a query when you have a question about the data
Form		Provides an easy-to-use data entry screen
Report		Provides a professional presentation of data with headers, footers, graphics, and calculations on groups of records

Access

Navigate and Enter Data

- Navigate records in a datasheet
- Enter records in a datasheet
- Define essential database terminology

Your skill in navigating through the database and accurately entering new data is a key to your success. While the form object is the primary object used to enter new data, you can also navigate and enter data directly in a table datasheet. **CASE** *Lydia Snyder asks you to master essential navigation and data entry skills by entering another company record into the Companies table.*

STEPS

QUICK TIP

Access databases are multiuser, which means that more than one person can enter and edit data in the same database at the same time!

1. **Double-click the** Companies table **in the Navigation Pane to open it, press** TAB **three times, then press** ENTER **three times**

   A table datasheet presents data in columns called **fields** and rows called **records**. See TABLE 1-3 for a summary of essential database terminology. As you navigate through the records, note that both the TAB and ENTER keys move the focus to the next field. The **focus** refers to the data you would edit if you started typing. When you navigate to the last field of the record, pressing TAB or ENTER advances the focus to the first field of the next record. You can also use the **navigation buttons** on the navigation bar in the lower-left corner of the datasheet to navigate through the records. The **Current record box** on the navigation bar tells you the number of the current record as well as the total number of records in the datasheet. You use the navigation bar to practice record navigation.

2. **Click the** Next record button ▶ **on the navigation bar, click the** Previous record button ◀, **click the** Last record button ▶|, **click the** First record button |◀, **then click the** New (blank) record button ▶* **on the navigation bar to move to a new record**

   You navigate to and enter new records at the end of the datasheet. A complete list of navigation keystrokes is shown in TABLE 1-4.

QUICK TIP

Press TAB in the CompanyID AutoNumber field.

3. **At the end of the datasheet, enter the new record, as shown in** FIGURE 1-4
   The CompanyName is Jigsaw Company, **the Industry is** Information, **the Description is** Jigsaw provides big data mining, analytics, and forecasting tools and services, **the City is** Dayton, **and the State is** OH

   The **edit record symbol** 🖉 appears to the left of the record you are currently editing. When you move to a different record, Access automatically saves the data.

   Your CompanyID value might differ from the one in FIGURE 1-4. The CompanyID field is an **AutoNumber** field, which means that Access automatically enters the next consecutive number into the field as it creates the record. If you delete a record or are interrupted when entering a record, Access discards the value in the AutoNumber field and does not reuse it. Therefore, AutoNumber values do not represent the number of records in your table. Instead, they only provide a unique value per record.

Changing from Navigation mode to Edit mode

If you navigate to another area of the datasheet by clicking with the mouse pointer instead of pressing TAB or ENTER, you change from Navigation mode to Edit mode. In Edit mode, Access assumes that you are making changes to the current field value, so keystrokes such as CTRL+END, CTRL+HOME, ◀—, and —▶ move the insertion point within the field. To return to Navigation mode, press TAB or ENTER (thus moving the focus to the next field), or press ↑ or ↓ (thus moving the focus to a different record).

FIGURE 1-4: Adding a new record to the Companies table

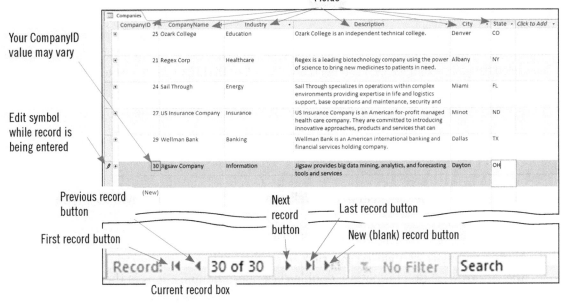

Fields

Your CompanyID value may vary

Edit symbol while record is being entered

Previous record button

First record button

Next record button

Last record button

New (blank) record button

Current record box

Record: 30 of 30   No Filter   Search

TABLE 1-3: Essential database terminology

term	description
Field	A specific piece or category of data such as a company name, first name, last name, city, state, or phone number
Record	A group of related fields that describes a person, place, thing, or transaction such as a company or job
Primary key field	A field that contains unique information for each record, such as a CompanyID value for a company
Table	A collection of records for a single subject such as Industries, Companies, or Jobs
Relational database	Multiple tables that are linked together to address a business process such as managing industries, companies, and jobs at JCL Talent
Objects	The parts of an Access database that help you view, edit, manage, and analyze the data; Access has six major objects: tables, queries, forms, reports, macros, and modules

TABLE 1-4: Navigation mode keyboard shortcuts

shortcut key	moves to the
TAB, ENTER, or →	Next field of the current record
SHIFT+TAB or ←	Previous field of the current record
HOME	First field of the current record
END	Last field of the current record
CTRL+HOME or F5	First field of the first record
CTRL+END	Last field of the last record
↑	Current field of the previous record
↓	Current field of the next record

Resizing and moving datasheet columns

You can resize the width of a field in a datasheet by dragging the column separator, the thin line that separates the field names to the left or right. The pointer changes to ↔ as you make the field wider or narrower. Release the mouse button when you have resized the field. To adjust the column width to accommodate the widest entry in the field, double-click the column separator. To move a column, click the field name to select the entire column, then drag the field name left or right.

Edit Existing Data

Learning Outcomes
- Edit data in a datasheet
- Delete records in a datasheet
- Preview and print a datasheet

Updating existing data in a database is another critical database task. To change the contents of an existing record, navigate to the field you want to change and type the new information. You can delete unwanted data by clicking the field and using BACKSPACE or DELETE to delete text to the left or right of the insertion point. Other data entry keystrokes are summarized in TABLE 1-5. **CASE** *Lydia Snyder asks you to correct two records in the Companies table and delete a record in the Jobs table.*

STEPS

1. **Select Dallas in the City field of the Wellman Bank record (CompanyID 29), type Fort Worth, then press ENTER**

   You'll also update the Description and City for CompanyID 28, CellFirst Inc.

2. **Find CompanyID 28, CellFirst Inc, click Telecommunications in the Industry field, click the list arrow, click Information, double-click telecommunications in the Description field, then type media as shown in FIGURE 1-5**

   While editing a field value, you press ESC once to remove the current field's editing changes, and twice to remove all changes to the current record. When you move to another record, Access saves your edits, so you can no longer use ESC to remove editing changes to the current record. You can, however, click the Undo button ↺ on the Quick Access Toolbar to undo the last saved action.

3. **Double-click the Jobs table in the Navigation Pane to open it in Datasheet View, click the record selector for the second record (JobID 2, Alark Inc, Care Management Associate), click the Delete button in the Records group, then click Yes**

   A message warns that you cannot undo a record deletion. The Undo button ↺ is dimmed, indicating that you cannot use it. The Jobs table now has 82 records. The first four are shown in FIGURE 1-6.

4. **Click the File tab, click Print, then click Print Preview to preview the printout of the Jobs table before printing**

5. **Click the Close Print Preview button, then right-click each table tab and click Close**

FIGURE 1-5: Editing records in the Companies table

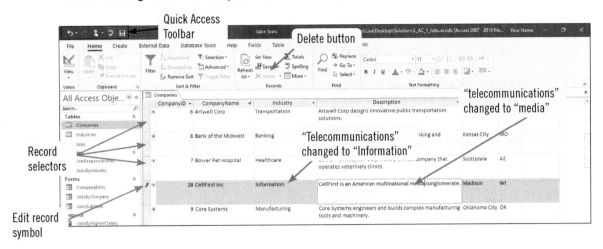

FIGURE 1-6: Deleting a record in the Jobs table

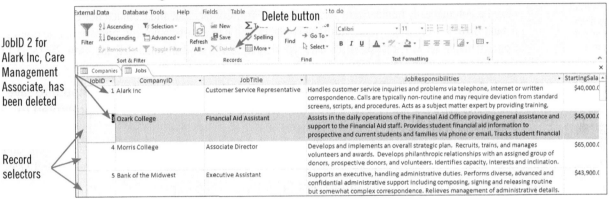

TABLE 1-5: Edit mode keyboard shortcuts

editing keystroke	action
BACKSPACE	Deletes one character to the left of the insertion point
DELETE	Deletes one character to the right of the insertion point
F2	Switches between Edit and Navigation mode
ESC	Undoes the change to the current field
ESC, ESC	Undoes all changes to the current record
F7	Starts the spell-check feature
CTRL+'	Inserts the value from the same field in the previous record into the current field
CTRL+;	Inserts the current date in a Date field

Access

Create a Table

Creating a table consists of these essential tasks: naming the fields in the table, selecting an appropriate data type for each field, naming the table, and determining how the table will participate in the relational database. **CASE** *Lydia Snyder asks you to create another table to store information about people JCL regularly communicates with at each company. Together you have decided what fields of information to track and to name the table Contacts. The Contacts table will be connected to the Companies table in the next module so that each record in the Companies table may be related to many records in the Contacts table.*

STEPS

1. **Click the** Create tab **on the ribbon, then click the** Table Design button **in the Tables group**

   You can create a table in either Datasheet View or Design View, but **Design View** gives you more control over the characteristics called **field properties** of each field in the table.

2. **Enter the Field Names and Data Types for each field as shown in** FIGURE 1-7

   The Contacts table will contain five fields. ContactID is set with an **AutoNumber** data type so each record is automatically numbered by Access. ContactFirst, ContactLast, and ContactPhone are set with the default **Short Text** data type to store the contact's first name, last name, and primary phone number. ContactEmail is set with a **Hyperlink** data type that helps you send an email to that person. See TABLE 1-6 for more information on field data types.

3. **Click the** View button ▦ **to switch to Datasheet View, click** Yes **when prompted to save the table, type** Contacts **as the table name, click** OK, **then click** No **when prompted to create a primary key**

   A **primary key field** contains unique data for each record. You'll identify a primary key field for the Contacts table in the next module. For now, you'll enter the first record in the Contacts table in Datasheet View.

4. **Press** TAB **to move to the ContactFirst field, type** Douglas, **press** TAB, **type** Griffey **in the ContactLast field, type** 5554443333 **in the ContactPhone field, press** TAB, **then type** dgriffey@accentgroup.com

   Right now, you have not identified Douglas Griffey's company affiliation. After you relate the tables in the next module, Access will make it easy to relate each contact to the correct company.

5. **Point to the** divider line **after the ContactEmail field name, then double-click the column resize pointer** ↔ **to widen the ContactEmail field to read the entire email value, as shown in** FIGURE 1-8

6. **Right-click the** Contacts table tab, **then click** Save **to save the table**

Creating a table in Datasheet View

You can also create a new table in Datasheet View using the commands on the Fields tab of the ribbon. However, if you use Design View to design your table before entering data, you will probably avoid some common data entry errors because Design View helps you focus on the appropriate data type for each field.

Selecting the best data type for each field before entering any data into that field helps prevent incorrect data and unintended typos. For example, if a field has a Number, Currency, or Date/Time data type, you will not be able to enter text into that field by mistake.

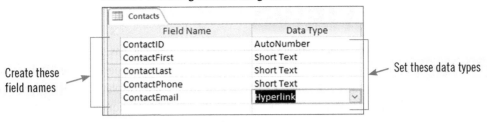

FIGURE 1-7: Creating a table in Design View

Create these field names →

Set these data types ←

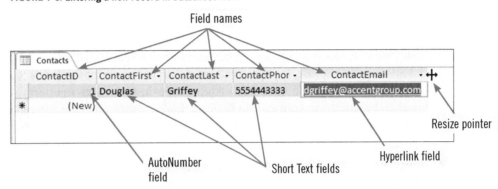

FIGURE 1-8: Entering a new record in Datasheet View

Field names

Resize pointer

Hyperlink field

AutoNumber field

Short Text fields

TABLE 1-6: Data types

data type	description of data
Short Text	Text or numbers not used in calculations such as a name, postal code, or phone number fewer than 255 characters
Long Text	Lengthy text greater than 255 characters, such as comments or notes
Number	Numeric data that can be used in calculations, such as quantities
Large Number	Provides additional analytical capability and deepens the integration experience when users are importing or linking to BigInt data
Date/Time	Dates and times
Currency	Monetary values
AutoNumber	Sequential integers controlled by Access
Yes/No	Yes or No or Null (neither Yes nor No)
OLE Object	OLE (Object Linking and Embedding) objects such as an Excel spreadsheet or Word document
Hyperlink	Web and email addresses or links to local files
Attachment	Files such as .jpg images, spreadsheets, and documents
Calculated	Result of a calculation based on other fields in the table
Lookup Wizard	The Lookup Wizard is not a data type even though it is on the Data Type list. It helps you set Lookup properties, which display a drop-down list of values for the field. After using the Lookup Wizard, the final data type for the field is either Short Text or Number depending on the type of data in the drop-down list.

Object views

Each object has a number of views that allow you to complete different tasks. For example, to enter and edit data into the database using a table or query, use Datasheet View. To enter and edit data in a form, use Form View. To see how a report will appear on a physical piece of paper, use Print Preview. To see all the available views for an object, click the arrow at the bottom of the View button 🔲 on the Home tab.

Modify Fields

Field properties are the characteristics that describe each field, such as the Field Name, Data Type, Field Size, Format, Input Mask, Caption, or Default Value. These properties help ensure database accuracy and clarity because they restrict the way data is entered, stored, and displayed. You can modify most field properties in Table Datasheet View and all field properties in Table Design View. **CASE** ▶ *After reviewing the Contacts table with Lydia Snyder, you decide to change several Short Text field properties.*

STEPS

1. **Click the Design View button** ☑ **on the ribbon**

   Field properties appear on the General tab on the lower half of the Table Design View window called the **Field Properties pane**. Field properties change depending on the field's data type. For example, when you select a field with a Short Text data type, you see the **Field Size property**, which determines the number of characters you can enter in the field. However, when you select a Hyperlink or Date/Time field, Access controls the size of the data, so the Field Size property is not displayed. Many field properties are optional, but for those that require an entry, Access provides a default value.

2. **Press the DOWN ARROW to move through each field while viewing the field properties in the lower half of the window**

   The **field selector** button to the left of the field indicates which field is currently selected.

3. **Click the ContactFirst field name, double-click 255 in the Field Size property text box, type 20, right-click the Contacts tab, click Save on the shortcut menu, then click Yes**

   The default value for the Field Size property for a Short Text field is 255, but you want to make the Field Size property for Short Text fields only as large as needed to accommodate the longest reasonable entry. In some cases, shortening the Field Size property helps prevent typographical errors. For example, you should set the Field Size property for a State field that stores two-letter state abbreviations to 2 to prevent typos such as TXX.

4. **Click the ContactLast field name, double-click 255 in the Field Size property text box, type 20, right-click the Contacts tab, click Save on the shortcut menu, then click Yes**

   No existing entries are greater than the new Field Size values, so no data is lost. Table Design View of the Contacts table should look like FIGURE 1-9.

5. **Right-click the Contacts table tab, then click Close**

FIGURE 1-9: Modifying field properties

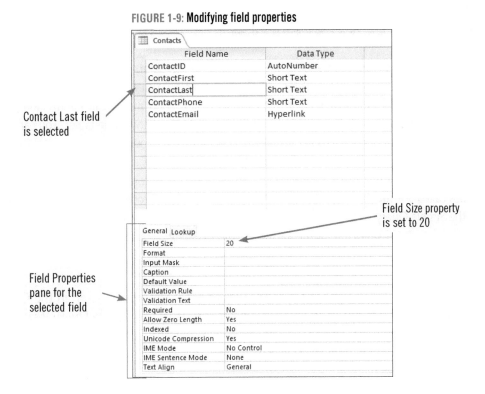

Contact Last field is selected

Field Size property is set to 20

Field Properties pane for the selected field

Field properties

Properties are the characteristics that define the field. Two properties are required for every field: Field Name and Data Type. Many other properties, such as Field Size, Format, Caption, and Default Value, are defined in the Field Properties pane in the lower half of a table's Design View. Many common properties can also be accessed on the Fields tab of the ribbon in Table Datasheet View. As you add more property entries, you are generally restricting the amount or type of data that can be entered in the field, which increases data entry accuracy. For example, you might change the Field Size property for a State field to 2 to eliminate an incorrect entry such as FLL. Field properties change depending on the data type of the selected field. For example, Date/Time, Currency, and Yes/No fields do not have a Field Size property because Access controls the size of fields with those data types.

Access

Create a Query

A **query** answers a question about the information in the database by selecting a subset of fields and records from one or more tables and presenting the selected data as a single datasheet. A major benefit of working with data through a query is that you can focus on only the specific information you need, rather than navigating through all the fields and records from one or more large tables. You can enter, edit, and navigate data in a query datasheet just like a table datasheet. However, keep in mind that Access data is physically stored only in tables, even though you can select, view, and edit it through other Access objects such as queries and forms. Because a query doesn't physically store the data, a query datasheet is sometimes called a **logical view** of the data. Access provides several tools to create a new query, one of which is the Simple Query Wizard. **CASE** *Lydia Snyder asks for a listing of jobs and starting salaries sorted in ascending order by state. You will use the Simple Query Wizard to create a query to select and display this data.*

STEPS

1. **Click the** Create tab **on the ribbon, click the** Query Wizard button **in the Queries group, then click** OK **in the New Query dialog box to start the Simple Query Wizard**

   The **Simple Query Wizard** prompts you for the information it needs to create the query. You can select fields from one or more existing tables or queries. The fields you want for this query are in the Companies and Jobs tables.

2. **Click the** Tables/Queries list arrow, **click** Table: Companies, **double-click** State **in the Available Fields list to move it to the Selected Fields list, click the** Tables/Queries list arrow, **click** Table: Jobs, **double-click** JobTitle, **then double-click** StartingSalary **as shown in** FIGURE 1-10

   You've selected three fields for this query from two different tables.

3. **Click** Next, **click** Next **to select Detail, select** Companies Query **in the title text box, type** JobsByState **as the name of the query, then click** Finish

   The JobsByState datasheet opens, displaying one field from the Companies table (State) and two from the Jobs table (JobTitle and StartingSalary). To sort the records by JobTitle within State, you'll select those two fields and use the Ascending button on the Home tab.

4. **Use the column selector pointer ↓ to drag across the field names of** State **and** JobTitle **to select both columns, click the** Home tab **on the ribbon, then click the** Ascending **button in the Sort & Filter group**

   The JobsByState datasheet is sorted in ascending order by the State field, and then in ascending order by the JobTitle field within each state, as shown in FIGURE 1-11.

5. **Right-click the** JobsByState tab, **click** Close, **then click** Yes **when prompted to save the query**

Simple Query Wizard

The **Simple Query Wizard** is a series of dialog boxes that prompt you for the information needed to create a Select query. A **Select query** selects fields from one or more tables in your database and is by far the most common type of query.

The other query wizards—Crosstab, Find Duplicates, and Find Unmatched—are used to create queries that do specialized types of data analysis and are covered in Module 5.

FIGURE 1-10: **Using the Simple Query Wizard**

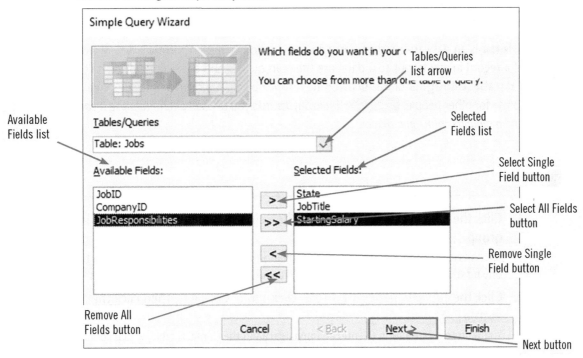

Available Fields list

Tables/Queries list arrow

Selected Fields list

Select Single Field button

Select All Fields button

Remove Single Field button

Remove All Fields button

Next button

FIGURE 1-11: **Sorting a query datasheet**

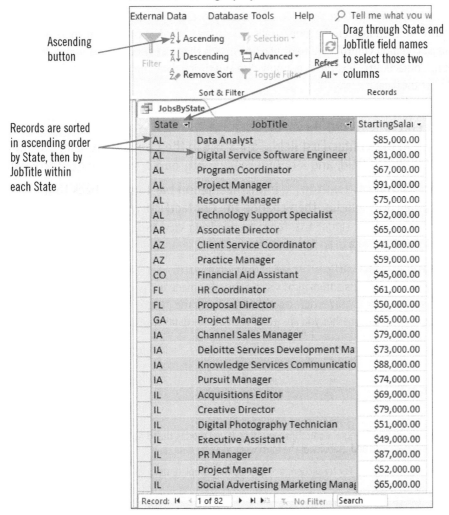

Ascending button

Drag through State and JobTitle field names to select those two columns

Records are sorted in ascending order by State, then by JobTitle within each State

Access

Create a Form

Learning
Outcomes
• Create a form with
the Form Wizard
• Sort data in a form
• Describe form
terminology and
views

A **form** is an easy-to-use data entry and navigation screen. A form allows you to arrange the fields of a record in any layout so a database user can quickly and easily find, enter, edit, and analyze data. A **database designer** or **application developer** builds and maintains forms to make the database easy to use for other people. **CASE** ▶ *Lydia Snyder asks you to build a form to make it easy for others to enter and maintain contact information.*

STEPS

1. **Click the** Create tab **on the ribbon, then click the** Form Wizard button **in the Forms group**

   The **Form Wizard** prompts you for information it needs to create a form, such as the fields, layout, and title for the form. You want to create a form to enter and update data in the Contacts table.

2. **Click the** Tables/Queries list arrow, **click** Table: Contacts, **then click the** Select All Fields button `>>`

   You want to create a form to enter and update data in the Contacts table, which contains five fields.

TROUBLE
To rename a form,
or any object, close
it, right-click it in
the Navigation
Pane, and then click
Rename.

3. **Click** Next, **click the** Columnar option button, **click** Next, **modify** Contacts **to** ContactEntry **for the title, then click** Finish

   The ContactEntry form opens in **Form View**. Access provides three different views of forms, as summarized in TABLE 1-7. Each item on the form is called a **control**. A **label** control is used to describe the data, and the most common control used to display the data is the **text box**. A label is also used for the title of the form, ContactEntry. Text boxes not only display existing data, they are also used to enter, edit, find, sort, and filter the data.

QUICK TIP
Tab through the
AutoNumber
ContactID field,
which automatically
increments.

4. **Click the** New (blank) record button `▶⃰` **in the navigation bar to move to a new, blank record and enter the record shown in** FIGURE 1-12
   Enter Kristen **in the ContactFirst field,** Fontanelle **in the ContactLast field,** 5556667777 **in the ContactPhone field, and** kfontanelle@accentgroup.com **as the ContactEmail value**

TROUBLE
If you click an email
hyperlink in the
form, Outlook starts.
Close Outlook or
click Cancel to stop
the process.

5. **Click the** Previous record button `◀` **in the navigation bar to move back to the first record, double-click** Douglas, **then change the ContactFirst value to** Doug

   Your screen should look like FIGURE 1-13. Forms open in Form View are the primary tool for database users to enter, edit, and delete data in an Access database.

6. **Right-click the** ContactEntry form tab, **then click** Close

   When a form is closed, Access automatically saves any edits made to the current record. As you have experienced, Access automatically saves new records entered into the database as well as any edits you make to existing data regardless of whether you are working in a table datasheet, query datasheet, or form.

TABLE 1-7: Form views

view	primary purpose
Form	To find, sort, enter, and edit data
Layout	To modify the size, position, or formatting of controls; shows data as you modify the form, making it the tool of choice when you want to change the appearance and usability of the form while viewing data
Design	To modify the Form Header, Detail, and Footer section, or to access the complete range of controls and form properties; Design View does not display data

FIGURE 1-12: **Entering a new record in a form**

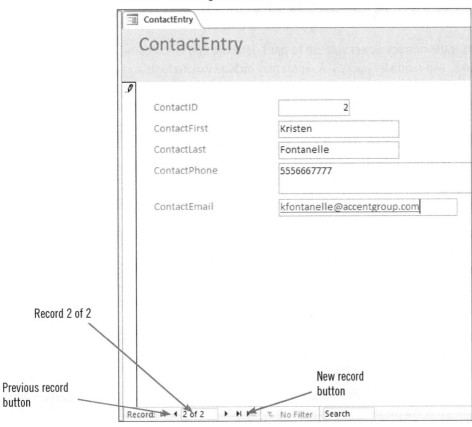

Record 2 of 2

Previous record
button

New record
button

FIGURE 1-13: **Editing an existing record in a form**

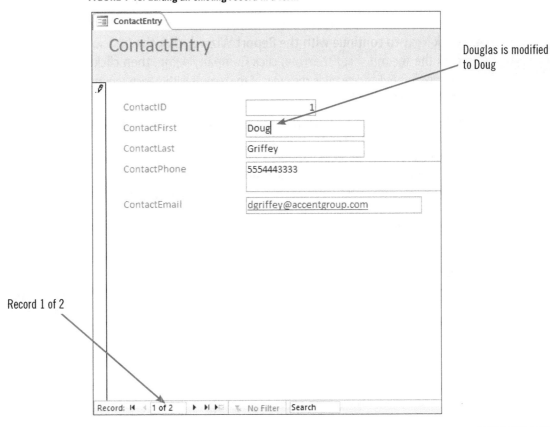

Douglas is modified
to Doug

Record 1 of 2

Access

Create a Report

Learning Outcomes
• Create a report with the Report Wizard
• Change page orientation

A **report** is the primary object you use to print database content because it provides the most formatting, layout, and summary options. A report may include various fonts and colors, clip art and lines, and multiple headers and footers. A report can also calculate subtotals, averages, counts, and other statistics for groups of records. You can create reports in Access by using the **Report Wizard**, a tool that asks questions to guide you through the initial development of the report. Your responses to the Report Wizard determine the record source, style, and layout of the report. The **record source** is the table or query that defines the fields and records displayed on the report. The Report Wizard also helps you sort, group, and analyze the records. **CASE** ▶ *Lydia Snyder asks you to use the Report Wizard to create a report to display company information within each industry.*

STEPS

1. **Click the** Create tab **on the ribbon, then click the** Report Wizard button **in the Reports group**

   The Report Wizard starts, prompting you to select the fields you want on the report. You can select fields from one or more tables or queries.

2. **Click the** Tables/Queries list arrow, **click** Table: Companies, **double-click the** State field, **double-click the** Industry field, **double-click the** CompanyName field, **then double-click the** Description field

   As you have experienced, the first step of creating a new query, form, or report using the Simple Query Wizard, Form Wizard, or Report Wizard is to select the desired fields for the new object.

   QUICK TIP
   Click Back to review previous dialog boxes within a wizard.

3. **Click** Next **to advance to the report grouping options, as shown in** FIGURE 1-14

   The Report Wizard automatically wants to group the records by Industry and gives you the opportunity to specify additional grouping levels if desired. Given you are creating a report displaying the State, CompanyName, and Description within each Industry, you do not need to add or change the existing grouping level.

4. **Click** Next **to continue with the Report Wizard, click the** first sort list arrow, **click** State, **click the** second sort list arrow, **click** CompanyName, **then click** Next

   The two sort orders determine the order of the records within each Industry group. The last questions in the Report Wizard deal with report appearance and the report title.

5. **Click** Next **to accept the Stepped Layout and Portrait orientation, modify Companies to** IndustryList **for the report title, then click** Finish

   The IndustryList report opens in **Print Preview**, which displays the report as it appears when printed, as shown in FIGURE 1-15. The records are grouped by Industry, the first one being Aerospace, and then sorted in ascending order by the State. If there were two companies in the same state and industry, they would be further ordered by CompanyName. Reports are **read-only** objects, meaning you can use them to read and display data but not to change (write to) data. As you change data using tables, queries, or forms, reports constantly display those up-to-date edits just like all the other Access objects.

6. **Right-click the** IndustryList report tab, **then click** Close

---

Changing page orientation

To change page orientation from **portrait** (8.5" wide by 11" tall) to **landscape** (11" wide by 8.5" tall) and vice versa, click the

Portrait button or Landscape button on the Print Preview tab when viewing the report in Print Preview.

FIGURE 1-14: **Setting report grouping fields**

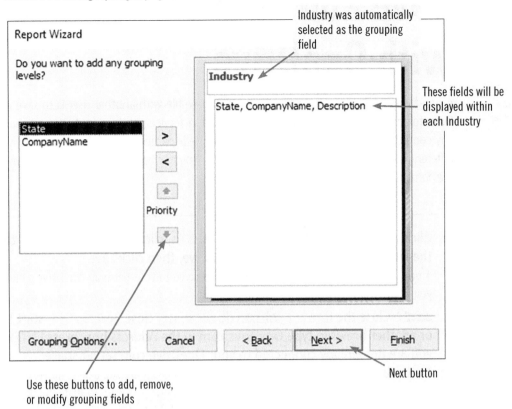

Industry was automatically selected as the grouping field

These fields will be displayed within each Industry

Next button

Use these buttons to add, remove, or modify grouping fields

FIGURE 1-15: **Previewing a report**

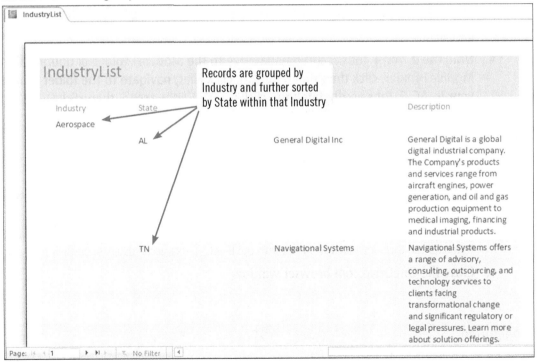

Records are grouped by Industry and further sorted by State within that Industry

Save and Share a Database with OneDrive

Learning Outcomes
• Create a OneDrive folder
• Save a file to a OneDrive folder
• Share a file in a OneDrive folder

A good way to share a copy of an Access database file with another user is to save it to a shared One-Drive folder, a cloud-based storage and file-sharing service provided by Microsoft that is accessible from any computer connected to the Internet. OneDrive is particularly handy for students who work on many different computers. **CASE** ➤ *Lydia Snyder asks you to create a folder on your OneDrive to save and share the database.*

STEPS

TROUBLE
You must be signed in to your Microsoft account to access your OneDrive.
If you do not see OneDrive in Step 1, continue to Step 2 to access it directly and sign in.

1. **Click the** File tab **on the ribbon, click** Save As, **click the** Save As button, **click** OneDrive **in the left pane or navigate to your OneDrive, then click** Save

   A **copy** of the IL_AC_1_Jobs.accdb database is saved to your personal OneDrive. OneDrive is available to you on any computer connected to the Internet.

2. **sam̓⬆ Close the** IL_AC_1_Jobs.accdb database, **close** Access 2019, **start** Microsoft Edge **or another browser, type** OneDrive.com **in the Address box, press** ENTER, **then sign in if you are not already connected to your OneDrive.com server space**

   The contents of your OneDrive appear. From here, you can upload, delete, move, download, or copy files, similar to how you work with files on your local computer. You want to share the IL_AC_1_Jobs.accdb database with your instructor. You decide to first create a folder for the database. That way, your OneDrive will stay more organized.

3. **Click the** New button, **click** Folder, **type** Module1 **as the new folder name, then press** ENTER **to create the folder, as shown in** FIGURE 1-16

   Now you're ready to open the Module1 folder and then upload or move the IL_AC_1_Jobs.accdb database file into it.

4. **Drag the** IL_AC_1_Jobs.accdb database file **to the** Module1 folder *or* **double-click the** Module1 folder, **click the** Upload button, **click** Files, **navigate to the folder that contains your** IL_AC_1_Jobs.accdb database, **click** IL_AC_1_Jobs.accdb, **then click** Open

   With the IL_AC_1_Jobs.accdb database moved or uploaded to the Module1 folder in OneDrive, you're now ready to invite your instructor to have access to the IL_AC_1_Jobs.accdb database.

5. **If it is not open, double-click the** Module1 folder **to open it, right-click the** IL_AC_1_Jobs.accdb database, **click** Share, **click** Email, **enter the** email address of your instructor, **enter the message** Sharing the IL_AC_1_Jobs.accdb database **as shown in** FIGURE 1-17, **then click** Share

   Your instructor will receive an email with your message and a link to the IL_AC_1_Jobs.accdb database. Your instructor can then download and work with the IL_AC_1_Jobs.accdb database on their local computer.

6. **Close the OneDrive.com browser window**

Cloud computing

Cloud computing means you are using an Internet resource to complete your work. Using **OneDrive**, a free service from Microsoft, you can store files in the "cloud" and retrieve them anytime you are connected to the Internet. Saving your files to the OneDrive is one example of cloud computing.

FIGURE 1-16: Creating a new folder in OneDrive

New button   Upload button

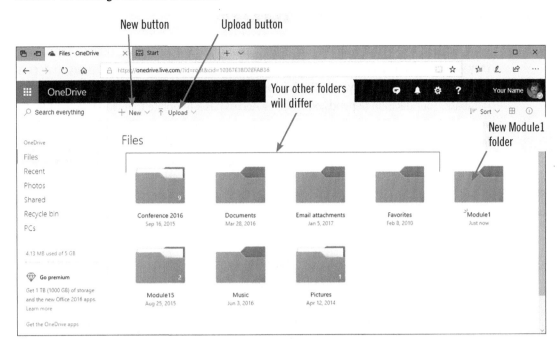

Your other folders will differ

New Module1 folder

FIGURE 1-17: Sharing a database with OneDrive

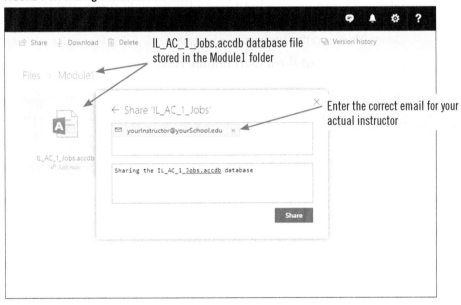

IL_AC_1_Jobs.accdb database file stored in the Module1 folder

Enter the correct email for your actual instructor

Access is a local application

Unlike Word and Excel, Access does not have an online version of itself. Access is a **local application** that runs from the hard drive of a local Windows machine. You can share a copy of a database with others using OneDrive, but remember that saving a database to OneDrive creates a **copy** of the database. For multiple people to work in the same database at the same time, the database must be located in a shared folder on a local file server.

Access

Create a Database

Learning
Outcomes
• Create a database
• Import data from
  Excel

Now that you are familiar with the four main objects of a database (tables, queries, forms, and reports), you may want to create a database from scratch. You can create a new database using an Access **template**, a sample database provided within the Microsoft Access program, or you can start with a completely blank database. Your decision depends on whether Access has a template that closely resembles the type of data you plan to manage. Regardless of which method you use, you can always add, delete, or modify objects in the database later, tailoring it to meet your specific needs. **CASE** *Lydia Snyder sees another opportunity to use Access and asks you to create a new database to track JCL technical support calls from employees.*

STEPS

1. **Start Access**

2. **Click the** Blank database icon, **click the** Browse button ⬜, **navigate to the location where you store your Data Files, type** IL_AC_1_TechSupport **in the File name box, click** OK, **then click the** Create button

   A new database file with a single table currently named Table1 is created. To create the first table needed for this database, the Employees table, you will import the data from an existing Excel spreadsheet.

3. **Right-click the** Table1 tab, **click** Close, **click the** External Data tab **on the ribbon, click the** New Data Source button **in the Import & Link group, point to** From File, **click** Excel, **click** Browse, **navigate to the location where you store your Data Files, click** Support_IL_AC_1_Employees.xlsx, **then click** Open

   You want to import the data in the file Support_IL_AC_1_Employees.xlsx into a new table.

4. **Click** OK **to accept the import option, click** Next **to import Sheet1, click the** First Row Contains Column Headings check box, **then click** Next

   The Import Spreadsheet Wizard allows you to specify information about each field that you are importing as shown in **FIGURE 1-18**. You do not need to make any modifications at this time.

5. **Click** Next

   The Import Spreadsheet Wizard is now prompting you to define a primary key field which contains unique information for each row. Accept the default option.

6. **Click** Next, **type** Employees **as the new table name, click** Finish, **click** Close, **then double-click the** Employees table **in the Navigation Pane to open it**

   As shown in **FIGURE 1-19**, you have imported 60 records, each with nine fields of data from the Support_IL_AC_1_Employees.xlsx spreadsheet into the Employees table in the IL_AC_1_TechSupport.accdb Access database.

7. **Right-click the** Employees table tab, **then click** Close **to close the Employees table**

FIGURE 1-18: Using the Import Spreadsheet Wizard

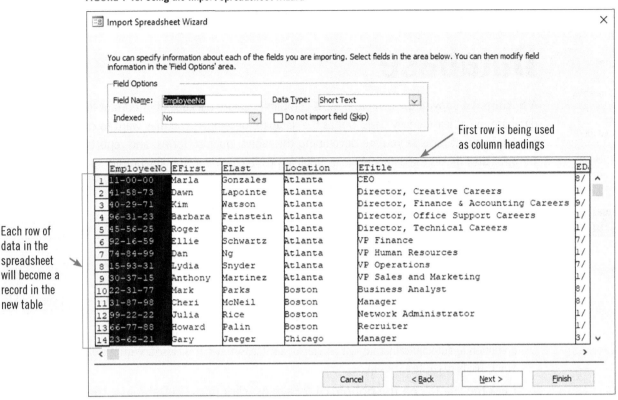

First row is being used as column headings

Each row of data in the spreadsheet will become a record in the new table

FIGURE 1-19: Employees table in Datasheet View

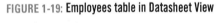

New Data Source button

External Data tab

The first row in the spreadsheet became the field names for the table in Access

Employees table tab

Employees table is the only object in the IL_AC_1_TechSupport database at this point

60 records

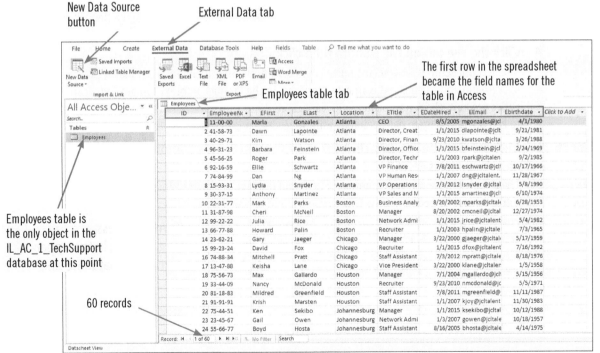

Access

Compact and Back Up a Database

Learning Outcomes
- Compact and repair a database
- Back up a database
- View Account settings
- Use the Tell Me box

A **backup** is a copy of the database. Most companies create backups of important files such as Access databases on at least a daily basis, but as the database developer, you may want to create a backup on a more frequent basis as you are developing the tables, queries, forms, and reports in the database. **Compacting** makes the database file as small as possible by removing any unused space that is created when you delete data or an object. **CASE** ▶ *Lydia Snyder would like you to frequently back up the new database as you make significant enhancements.*

STEPS

1. **Click the Database Tools tab on the ribbon, then click the Compact and Repair Database button in the Tools group**

   When you compact the database, an automatic **repair** feature is also initiated, which helps keep hidden system files up to date. It is a good idea to regularly compact and repair your databases. **Access Options**, default application settings, which you access using the Options command on the File tab, allow you to set an option to automatically compact and repair a database when it is closed. With the database compacted, you're ready to create a backup.

2. **Click the File tab on the ribbon, click Save As, click Back Up Database, then click the Save As button**

   Although any copy of the database can serve as a backup, when you use the Back Up Database option, the database file is automatically saved with a filename that includes the date the backup was made.

3. **Navigate to the folder where you want to store the backup, then click Save in the Save As dialog box**

   Now that you have a backup copy of your database, it's also a good idea to make sure that you have installed the latest Office updates to keep Access up to date.

4. **Click the File tab on the ribbon, then click Account**

   The Account settings let you customize your user information including your name, photo, email, Office background and theme, and connected services. In the Product Information area, you can manage your Office account, check for updates, and learn more about your application and recent updates. In addition to keeping Access up to date, you may want to read what is new with the latest updates.

   TROUBLE
   Click the Learn more link in the What's New in Access window if a browser doesn't open.

5. **Click the Back button ⊖, click Tell me what you want to do on the ribbon, type what's new, then press ENTER**

   The default browser on your computer opens and displays the latest "What's new" page for Access. Microsoft is constantly updating their Office products and releasing new features with Office 365.

6. **Follow the prompts to learn more and read what's new, return to Access, close any open dialog boxes or objects, then click the Close button ☒ in the upper-right corner of the window to close the IL_AC_1_TechSupport.accdb database and Access 2019**

Practice

Concepts Review

Label each element of the Access window shown in FIGURE 1-20.

FIGURE 1-20

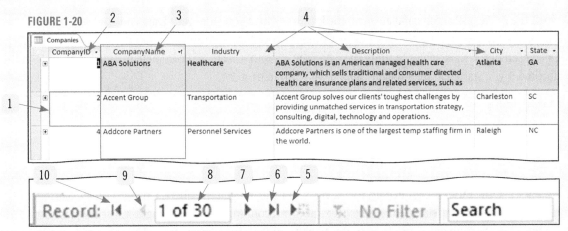

Match each term with the statement that best describes it.

11. Field   a. A subset of data from one or more tables

12. Record   b. A collection of records for a single subject, such as all the customer records

13. Table   c. A professional printout of database information

14. Datasheet   d. A spreadsheet-like grid that displays fields as columns and records as rows

15. Query   e. A group of related fields for one item, such as all the information for one customer

16. Form   f. A category of information in a table, such as a company name, city, or state

17. Report   g. An easy-to-use data entry screen

Select the best answer from the list of choices.

18. Which Access object cannot be used to enter or edit data?

   a. Report   c. Query

   b. Table   d. Form

19. Which of the following is *not* an advantage of managing data with relational database software such as Access versus spreadsheet software such as Excel?

   a. Allows multiple users to enter data simultaneously

   b. Uses a single table to store all data

   c. Reduces duplicate data entry

   d. Provides data entry forms

20. Which of the following is *not* a typical benefit of relational databases?

   a. Minimized duplicate data entry

   b. Tables automatically create needed relationships

   c. More accurate data

   d. More consistent data

Skills Review

1. **Understand relational databases.**
   a. In a Word document, enter your name and the current date.
   b. Using a bulleted list, identify five advantages of managing database information in Access versus using a spreadsheet.
   c. Write a sentence to explain how the terms *field*, *record*, *table*, and *relational database* relate to one another.
   d. Save the document with the name **IL_AC_1_Database** then close it and close Word.

2. **Open and explore a database.**
   a. Start Access.
   b. Open the IL_AC_1-2.accdb database from the location where you store your Data Files and save it as **IL_AC_1_SupportDesk**. Click Enable Content if a yellow Security Warning message appears.
   c. Open each of the three tables to study the data they contain. Create and complete the following table in the document you started in the previous step, IL_AC_1_Database.docx.

table name	number of records	number of fields

   d. Double-click the CaseListing query in the Navigation Pane to open the query. Change either occurrence of the last name of "Poole" to **Fredrick** then move to another record to save your changes. Close the CaseListing query.
   e. Double-click the EmployeeEntry form in the Navigation Pane to open the form. Use the navigation buttons to navigate through the 20 records to observe each employee's cases. When you reach the Lisa Fredrick record (record 17 of 20), change her extension value to **8686**. Close the EmployeeEntry form.
   f. Double-click the CallLog report in the Navigation Pane to open the report. The records are listed in ascending order by employee last name. Scroll through the report to find the "Fredrick, Lisa" record. Close the CallLog report. Note that both the edit to Lisa's last name and the change to her extension value in previous steps are reflected in the report.
   g. In your IL_AC_1_Database.docx document, add one more sentence to explain why the edits to Lisa's record in previous steps carried through to the CallLog report. Check the spelling, save your changes, then close the IL_AC_1_Database.docx document.

3. **Navigate and enter data.**
   a. Double-click the Employees table to open it, then enter the following record for a new employee:
      EmployeeID: (AutoNumber)
      LastName: Curtiss
      FirstName: Pamela
      Extension: 8181
      Department: Marketing
   b. Close the Employees table.

4. **Edit existing data.**
   a. Double-click the Cases table to open it, click the ResolvedDate field for CaseID 1, then enter **4/3/21**. Note that you can use the automatic Calendar Picker that assists you when you are entering or updating data in a field with a Date/Time data type. You can also type a date using a month/day/year format.
   b. Click the ResolvedDate field for the record with CaseID 5 and enter today's date. Note that you can enter today's date from the keyboard or use the CTRL+; shortcut. (*Hint*: Press and hold the CTRL key while pressing the semicolon ; key.)
   c. Edit the CaseTitle value for CaseID 23 to include the word **automatically** as in "Excel formulas are not automatically updating".
   d. Close the Cases table.

Skills Review (continued)

5. Create a table.

a. Click the Create tab on the ribbon, click the Table Design button in the Tables group, then create a new table with the following three fields and data types:

field name	data type
StateName	Short Text
StateAbbreviation	Short Text
Capital	Short Text

b. Save the table with the name **States**. Click No when asked if you want Access to create the primary key field.

6. Modify fields.

a. In Design View of the States table, change the Field Size property for the StateName and Capital fields to **25**, and the StateAbbreviation field to **2**.

b. Enter an Input Mask property of **LL;;*** for the StateAbbreviation field. (*Hint*: Do not use the Input Mask Wizard. Enter the property directly into the Input Mask property box.)

c. Change the Field Name of the StateAbbreviation field to **StateAbbrev**.

d. Save the States table, then test the Input Mask by entering the first record into the table for Alabama using the following information:

StateName	StateAbbrev	Capital
Alabama	AL	Montgomery

e. Use the Tell Me (Search) box to read about the three parts of an Input Mask property and the meaning of the L character.

f. Close the States table.

7. Create a query.

a. Use the Simple Query Wizard to create a new query with the following fields in the following order: LastName and FirstName from the Employees table, CaseTitle from the Cases table, and CallDateTime from the Calls table.

b. Select a detail query, and title the query **CallListing**.

c. Display the query datasheet, and change the last name of Mindi Meyers to **Perez**. Notice that both records that display Mindi's name change to Perez when you move to a new record. Her name was stored only once in the Employees table but selected twice for this query because she has taken two calls.

d. Save and close the CallListing query.

8. Create a form.

a. Use the Form Wizard to create a new form based on all the fields in the Employees table. Use a Columnar layout and title the form **EmployeeMaster**.

b. Use the record navigation buttons to navigate to the third record to confirm that Mindi Meyers has been changed to Mindi Perez.

c. Save and close the EmployeeMaster form.

9. Create a report.

a. Use the Report Wizard to create a new report based on all the fields of the Employees table.

b. Group the records by Department, and sort them in ascending order by LastName and then FirstName.

c. Use a stepped layout and a landscape orientation.

d. Title the report **EmployeeMasterList**, and preview it as shown in FIGURE 1-21.

e. Use the navigation buttons to locate the Mindi Perez record (in the Research department) to confirm that the report is also based on the updated data.

f. Save and close the EmployeeMasterList report.

Skills Review (continued)

FIGURE 1-21

EmployeeMasterList				

EmployeeMasterList

Department	LastName	FirstName	EmployeeID	Extension
Accounting				
	Calderon	Sean	29	6788
	Hoover	Carlos	12	3557
	Rivas	Philip	32	3322
	Serrano	Craig	24	7621
Executive				
	Carson	Victor	16	9862
	Holloway	Martin	19	9682
Human Resources				
	Fuentes	Eugene	9	2002
	Guerra	Chris	33	4411
Marketing				
	Carey	Alan	26	7958
	Mckenzie	Jesse	23	2879
	Short	Peggy	15	1366

10. **Save and share a database with OneDrive.**
    a. Close the IL_AC_1_SupportDesk.accdb database.
    b. Log into your Microsoft OneDrive.com account.
    c. Create a Module1 folder (if you have not already done so).
    d. Upload the IL_AC_1_SupportDesk.accdb database to the Module1 folder.
    e. Through email, share the IL_AC_1_SupportDesk.accdb database with your instructor.

11. **Create a new database.**
    a. Start Access and use the Blank desktop database to create a new database named **IL_AC_1_CustomerSurvey** in the folder where you store your Data Files.
    b. Close the Table1 table without saving it.
    c. Build the first table by importing a listing of states and provinces from an existing Excel spreadsheet named **Support_IL_AC_1_StatesAndProvs**.
    d. The first row contains column headings. Accept the default field options, but choose StateAbbrev as the primary key field.
    e. Name the new table **StatesAndProvs**, and do not save the import steps.
    f. Open the StatesAndProvs table in Datasheet View to confirm that 64 records were imported, then close the StatesAndProvs table.

12. **Compact and back up a database.**
    a. On the Database Tools tab, compact and repair the IL_AC_1_CustomerSurvey.accdb database.
    b. Create a backup of the IL_AC_1_CustomerSurvey.accdb database in the folder where you store your Data Files. Be sure to use the Back Up Database option so that the current date is automatically appended to the filename.
    c. View your Account settings, and in a Word document, note your existing Connected Services.
    d. Using the Tell me what you want to do feature, research Connected Services and pick one of the services to explore further. Identify which Connected Service you chose in your Word document, write at least one sentence explaining why you chose it and one sentence describing the features it offers. Save the document with the name **IL_AC_1_AccessConnectedServices**.
    e. Close the IL_AC_1_CustomerSurvey.accdb database and Access.

Independent Challenge 1

It's important to think about how to set up proper fields for a table before working in Access. Consider the following twelve subject areas:

- Contacts
- Islands of the Caribbean
- Members of the U.S. House of Representatives
- College course offerings
- Physical activities
- Ancient wonders of the world

- Restaurant menu
- Shopping catalog items
- Vehicles
- Conventions
- Party guest list
- Movie listings

a. For each subject, create a table in a single Word document named **IL_AC_1_SampleTables**. The table should contain four to seven columns and three rows. In the first row, enter appropriate field names that you would expect to see in a table used to manage that subject. Note the guidelines for proper field construction below.

b. In the second and third rows of each table, enter two realistic records. The first subject, Contacts, is completed as an example to follow.

TABLE: **Contacts**

FirstName	LastName	Street	Zip	Phone
Marco	Lopez	100 Main Street	88715	555-612-3312
Christopher	Stafford	253 Maple Lane	77824	555-612-1179

c. Use the following guidelines as you build each table in Word:

- Make sure each record represents one item in that table. For example, in the Restaurant Menu table, the following table is a random list of categories of food. These records do not represent one item in a restaurant menu.

Beverage	Appetizer	Meat	Vegetable	Dessert
Milk	Chicken wings	Steak	Carrots	Chocolate cake
Tea	Onion rings	Salmon	Potato	Cheesecake

A better example of records that describe an item in the restaurant menu would be the following:

Category	Description	Price	Calories	Spicy
Appetizer	Chicken wings	$10	800	Yes
Beverage	Milk	$2	250	No

- Do not put first and last names in the same field. This prevents you from easily sorting, filtering, or searching on either part of the name later.
- Break street, city, state, zip, and country data into separate fields for the same reasons.
- Do not put values and units of measure such as 5 minutes, 4 lbs., or 6 square miles in the same field. This also prevents you from sorting and calculating on the numeric part of the information.
- Make your field names descriptive such as TimeInMinutes or AreaInSquareMiles so that each record's entries are consistent.
- Remember that this exercise is a conceptual exercise on creating proper fields for a particular subject. Putting all these tables in one Access database would be analogous to putting a letter to your Congressman, a creative poem, and a cover letter to a future employer all in the same Word file. Use Word for this exercise to focus on the concepts of creating appropriate fields and records for a subject.

d. Save and close the IL_AC_1_SampleTables Word document.

Independent Challenge 2

You are working for a city to coordinate a series of community-wide preparedness activities. You have started a database to track the activities and volunteers who are attending them.

a. Start Access, then open the IL_AC_1-3.accdb database from the location where you store your Data Files. Save it with the name **IL_AC_1_Volunteers** and then enable content if prompted.

b. Open each table's datasheet to study the number of fields and records per table.

c. In a Word document named **IL_AC_1_VolunteerTables**, re-create the following table and fill in the blanks:

table name	number of records	number of fields

d. Close all open tables, then use the Simple Query Wizard to create a query using the following fields in the following order: FirstName and LastName from the Volunteers table, and ActivityName, ActvityDate, and ActivityHours from the Activities table. Show detail records, name the query **VolunteerActivity**, then open it in Datasheet View.

e. In the ActivityName field, change any occurrence of Shelter Fundamentals to **Outdoor Shelter Fundamentals**, then click any other record to save the change, as shown in FIGURE 1-22. Save and close the VolunteerActivity query.

f. Use the Form Wizard to create a new form based on all the fields in the Activities table. Use a columnar layout, title the form **ActivityEntry**, and view it in Form View. The Outdoor Shelter Fundamentals record should be the first record in the form. Save and close the ActivityEntry form.

FIGURE 1-22

FirstNa	LastNar	ActivityName	ActivityDate	ActivityHour
Rhea	Alman	Outdoor Shelter Fundamentals	7/31/2021	8
Micah	Ati	Managing Volunteers	8/27/2021	8
Young	Bogard	Outdoor Shelter Fundamentals	7/31/2021	8
Andrea	Collins	First Aid	8/1/2021	8
Gabriel	Hammer	Outdoor Shelter Fundamentals	7/31/2021	8
Evan	Bouchart	Forklift Training	8/14/2021	6
Ann	Bovier	Outdoor Shelter Fundamentals	7/31/2021	8
Gabriel	Hammer	Warehouse Logistics	8/19/2021	4
Forrest	Browning	Forklift Training	8/14/2021	6
Patch	Bullock	Cardiopulmonary resuscitation CPR	8/28/2021	4
Student Fi	Student La	Community Preparedness	8/7/2021	16
Denice	Custard	Water Safety	8/4/2021	6
Angela	Cabriella	Water Safety	8/4/2021	6
Gina	Daniels	Livestock in Disasters	8/22/2021	0
Quentin	Garden	Personal Safety and Security	8/15/2021	6
Heidi	Kalvert	Grief Counseling	8/6/2021	8
Helen	Hubert	Automated External Defibrillator AED	8/5/2021	4
Jeremiah	Hopper	Hurricane Preparedness	8/26/2021	6
Loraine	Goode	Outdoor Shelter Fundamentals	7/31/2021	8
Karla	Larson	Animals in Disasters	8/8/2021	4
Katrina	Margolis	Incident Management	8/11/2021	4
Harvey	McCord	Food Service	8/13/2021	6
Sally	Olingback	Community Preparedness	8/7/2021	16
Mallory	Olson	Basic Life Support BLS	8/25/2021	4

Record: 2 of 76   No Filter   Search

Getting Started with Access

Independent Challenge 2 (continued)

g. Use the Report Wizard to create a new report based on the following fields in the following order: ActivityName from the Activities table and LastName from the Volunteers table. View the data by ActivityName then sort the records in ascending order by the LastName. Use a stepped layout and a portrait orientation. Title the report **ActivityRoster** and preview the report.

h. Close the IL_AC_1_Volunteer.accdb database, then exit Access.

Visual Workshop

Open the IL_AC_1-4.accdb database from the location where you store your Data Files and save it as **IL_AC_1_CollegeCourses**, then enable content if prompted. Use the Simple Query Wizard to create the query shown in FIGURE 1-23 that contains the ClassNo, Description, and Credits fields from the Classes table, and the SectionNo, MeetingDay, and Time fields from the Sections table. Name the query **DepartmentOfferings**.

FIGURE 1-23

ClassNo	Description	Credits	SectionNo	MeetingDay	Time
ACCT109	Basics of Income Taxes	3	52	M	10:00 AM
ACCT111	Small Business Accounting	3	51	T	8:00 AM
ACCT121	Accounting I	3	48	W	10:00 AM
ACCT121	Accounting I	3	49	H	12:00 PM
ACCT121	Accounting I	3	50	M	1:00 PM
ACCT122	Accounting II	3	47	T	11:00 AM
ACCT135	Computerized Accounting Applications	3	44	W	9:00 AM
ACCT135	Computerized Accounting Applications	3	45	W	8:00 AM
ACCT135	Computerized Accounting Applications	3	46	M	9:00 AM
ACCT145	Accounting for Nonprofits	3	43	H	8:00 AM
ACCT155	Cost Accounting	3	42	T	9:00 AM
ACCT165	Managerial Accounting	3	41	W	1:00 PM
ACCT201	Fraud Examination	3	40	H	9:00 AM
BUS120	Managerial Attitudes	3	39	M	2:00 PM
BUS121	Introduction to Business	3	38	T	2:00 PM
BUS123	Personal Finance	3	37	H	1:00 PM
BUS123	Personal Finance	3	36	W	10:00 AM
BUS140	Principles of Supervision	3	34	T	9:00 AM
BUS140	Principles of Supervision	3	35	M	8:00 AM
CIS134	Programming Fundamentals	4	6	M	3:00 PM
CIS134	Programming Fundamentals	4	7	T	6:00 PM
CIS134	Programming Fundamentals	4	8	M	8:00 AM
CIS134	Programming Fundamentals	4	9	T	8:00 AM
CIS162	Database Programming	4	5	W	8:00 AM

Record: 1 of 59   No Filter   Search

Building Tables and Relationships

CASE At JCL Talent, you are working with Lydia Snyder, vice president of operations, to continue developing the Access database that tracks job placement data. You will improve the individual tables in the database and then link them together to create a relational database.

Module Objectives

After completing this module, you will be able to:

- Import data from Excel
- Modify fields in Datasheet View
- Modify Number and Currency fields
- Modify Short Text fields
- Modify Date/Time fields

- Create primary key fields
- Design related tables
- Create one-to-many relationships
- Work with subdatasheets

Files You Will Need

IL_AC_2-1.accdb	IL_AC_2-4.accdb
Support_IL_AC_2_States.xlsx	IL_AC_2-5.accdb
Support_IL_AC_2_Provs.xlsx	Support_IL_AC_2_Majors.xlsx
IL_AC_2-2.accdb	Support_IL_AC_2_Classes.xlsx
Support_IL_AC_2_Departments.xlsx	Support_IL_AC_2_Enrollments.xlsx
Support_IL_AC_2_Employees.xlsx	Support_IL_AC_2_Sections.xlsx
IL_AC_2-3.accdb	Support_IL_AC_2_Students.xlsx

Import Data from Excel

Learning Outcomes
- Import data from Excel
- Describe other file formats that work with Access

Importing enables you to quickly copy data from an external file into an Access database. You can import data from many sources, such as another Access database; Excel spreadsheet; SharePoint site; Outlook email; or text files in an HTML, XML, or delimited text file format. In a **delimited text file**, data is separated by a common character, the **delimiter**, such as a comma, tab, or dash. A **CSV (comma-separated value)** file is a common example of a delimited text file. An **XML file** contains the data surrounded by **Extensible Markup Language (XML)** tags that identify field names and data. The most common file format for importing data into an Access database is **Microsoft Excel**, the spreadsheet program in the Microsoft Office suite. **CASE** ▶ *Lydia Snyder gives you two Excel spreadsheets that list information for USA states and Canadian provinces and asks you to import the data into the database.*

STEPS

1. **sam** ↓ **Start Access, open the** IL_AC_2-1.accdb database **from the location where you store your Data Files, save it as** IL_AC_2_Jobs, **enable content if prompted, click the External Data tab, click the** New Data Source button **in the Import & Link group, point to** From File, **click** Excel, **click the** Browse button, **navigate to the location where you store your Data Files, then double-click** Support_IL_AC_2_States.xlsx

   The **Get External Data - Excel Spreadsheet** dialog box opens, as shown in FIGURE 2-1. You can **import** the records to a new table, **append** the records to an existing table, or **link** to the data source. Both importing and appending create a copy of the data in the database. **Linking** means that the data is not copied into Access; it is only stored in the original data source. See TABLE 2-1 for more information on file formats that can share data with Access.

2. **Click** OK

   The **Import Spreadsheet Wizard** helps you import data from Excel into Access and presents a sample of the data to be imported, as shown in FIGURE 2-2.

3. **Click the** First Row Contains Column Headings check box, **click** Next, **click** Next to accept the default field options, **click the** Choose my own primary key option button, **click the** StateName list arrow, **click** StateAbbrev **to choose it as the primary key field, click** Next, **type** States **as the new table name, click** Finish, **then click** Close

   The **primary key field** stores unique data for each record. The two-character state abbreviation is unique for each state and will be used later to connect to other tables. You also want to import more data that represents the 13 provinces in Canada.

4. **Click the** New Data Source button, **point to** From File, **click** Excel, **click the** Browse button, **navigate to the location where you store your Data Files, then double-click** Support_IL_AC_2_Provs.xlsx

5. **Click the** Append option button **in the Get External Data – Excel Spreadsheet dialog box, click the** Companies list arrow, **click** States, **click** OK, **click** Next, **click** Finish, **then click** Close

   In order to append data to an existing table, the column names of the Excel spreadsheet must match the field names in the Access table.

6. **Double-click the** States table **to view the imported data, note 64 in the record selector box at the bottom of the datasheet, then close the States table**

   A better name for the table would be StatesAndProvinces.

7. **Right-click the** States table **in the Navigation Pane, click** Rename, **type** StatesAndProvinces **as the new name, then press** ENTER

FIGURE 2-1: Get External Data – Excel Spreadsheet dialog box

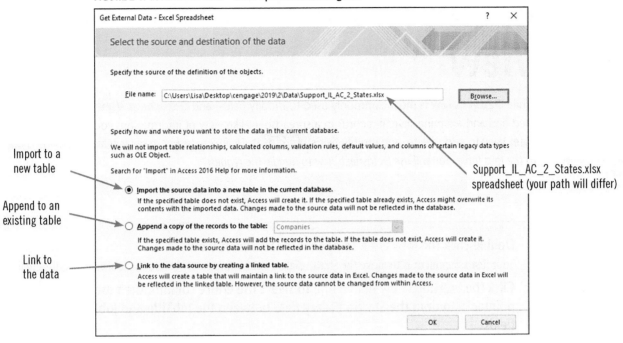

Import to a new table

Append to an existing table

Link to the data

Support_IL_AC_2_States.xlsx spreadsheet (your path will differ)

FIGURE 2-2: Import Spreadsheet Wizard

First Row Contains Column Headings check box

First row

Records of data

TABLE 2-1: File formats that Access can link to, import, and export

file format	import	link	export	file format	import	link	export
Access	✓	✓	✓	dBASE	✓	✓	✓
Excel	✓	✓	✓	HTML document	✓	✓	✓
Word			✓	PDF or XPS file			✓
SharePoint site	✓	✓	✓	Text file (delimited or fixed width)	✓	✓	✓
Email file attachments			✓	XML file	✓		✓
Outlook folder	✓	✓					
ODBC database (such as SQL Server)	✓	✓	✓				

Modify Fields in Datasheet View

Learning
Outcomes
• Move a field in
  Datasheet View
• Delete a field in
  Datasheet View
• Decrease a field's
  decimal places
• Modify the Format
  property

While **Design View** is most commonly used to modify fields, and **Datasheet View** is most commonly used find and examine several records in a spreadsheet-like view of information, you can also use Datasheet View to add, delete, and modify fields. **CASE** ▶ *Lydia Snyder has asked you to make some changes to the Jobs table. You will use Datasheet View to handle the request.*

STEPS

1. **Double-click the** Jobs table **to open it in Datasheet View**

   Your first assignment is to move the StartingSalary field immediately before the JobResponsibilties field.

2. **Click the** StartingSalary field name **to select the entire column, then use the move pointer** ⤢ **to drag the** StartingSalary field **between the JobTitle and JobResponsibilties fields**

   The StartingSalary field was created using a Number data type, but you want to display the data as a monetary value. You can use the Format property to change the appearance of data in the datasheet.

3. **With the** StartingSalary field **still selected, click the** Fields tab **on the ribbon, click the** Format list arrow **in the Formatting group, click** Currency, **then click the** Decrease Decimals button ⁰⁸⁰ **twice**

   The StartingSalary field's new position and formatting are shown in FIGURE 2-3. The last field in the table, DateFilled, was planned for the Jobs table but never used. You want to delete it.

4. **Scroll to the right to view the DateFilled field, click the** DateFilled field **to select the entire column, click the** Delete button **in the Add & Delete group, then click** Yes **when prompted**

   Given no data was entered in the DateFilled field, you are not losing any information. If you delete a field that contains data, all the values in that field for every record would be deleted. Deleting a field is an action that cannot be reversed with the Undo button ⤺.

Currency versus Number data type

In general, if a number represents a **fractional** value (such as dollars and cents, not a whole number), choose Currency for its data type. The underlying reason that all fractional values should be given a Currency data type is that a computer works with numbers using a binary system (1s and 0s), which cannot accurately store decimal fractions such as 0.1 or 0.01. The system can lead to rounding errors that all programming languages must address. In Access, the Currency data type includes special code to avoid these errors. If you are working with **integer** (a whole number, not a fraction) data, however, the Number data type provides faster performance. Whether you choose the Currency or Number data type, you can format the data to look as desired.

Modify Number and Currency Fields

Learning Outcomes
• Add a Currency field
• Add a Number field
• Modify the Field Size property for a Number field
• Modify the Decimal Places property

Number and Currency fields have similar properties because they both contain numeric values. The **Currency** data type is best applied to fractional values such as those that represent money down to the cent. The **Number** data type is best used to represent integer values, whole numbers such as quantities, measurements, and scores. **CASE** *Lydia asks you to add two new fields to the Jobs table. The first field named Fee represents money in dollars and cents, so you will use the Currency data type. The second field named Applicants represents the total number of people who applied for the job, which is never a fraction, so you will use the Number data type.*

STEPS

1. **Click the** Click to Add field name placeholder, **click** Currency, **type** Fee, **then press** ENTER

   The Fee field has been added as a new Currency field in the Jobs table. It will store monetary data in dollars and cents.

2. **Click the** Click to Add field name placeholder, **click** Number, **type** Applicants, **then press** ENTER

   The Applicants field has been added as a new Number field in the Jobs table. Test your new fields with sample data.

3. **Click the** Fee field **for the first record, type** 25.25, **press** TAB, **type** 50, **then click the second record to see the data you've entered, as shown in** FIGURE 2-4

   Access automatically formatted the value in the Fee field as $25.25. Some field properties can be set in both Datasheet View and Design View.

4. **Click the** Fee field, **click the** Fields tab **on the ribbon if not already selected, click the** Default Value button **in the Properties group, type** 50.25, **click** OK **in the Expression Builder dialog box, click the** Applicants field, **then click the** Increase Decimals button [icon] **in the Formatting group**

   The **Default Value** property automatically enters the property value, in this case 50.25, for all new records. The **Decimal Places** property displays the value with the given number of digits to the right of the decimal point. Because the Applicants field will store only whole numbers, showing the decimal place does not make good sense. You will switch to Table Design View to see how the same property can be modified in both views, then change the Decimal Places property value for the Applicants field back to 0.

5. **Right-click the** Jobs table tab, **click** Design View, **make sure the** Applicants field **is selected, click the** Decimal Places property box, **change the value to** 0, **then press** ENTER

   Table Design View gives you access to *all* field properties and as such, is generally the preferred way of changing field properties.

   The **Field Size** property determines the size or length of the maximum value for that field. Choosing the smallest Field Size for your Number fields helps improve database performance. See TABLE 2-2 for more information on Number Field Size property options. The Integer Field Size is large enough to hold any potential entry in the Applicants field.

6. **With the** Applicants field **still selected, click the** Field Size property, **click the** Field Size list arrow, **then click** Integer

   Your Table Design View should look like FIGURE 2-5.

7. **Save the** Jobs table then close it

FIGURE 2-4: Adding a Currency field and a Number field

Fee Currency field

Applicants
Number field

JobTitle	StartingSalai	JobResponsibilities	Fee	Applicants	Click to A
Customer Service Representative	$40,000	Handles customer service inquiries and problems via telephone, internet or written correspondence. Calls are typically non-routine and may require deviation from standard screens, scripts, and procedures. Acts as a subject matter expert by providing training,	$25.25	50	
Financial Aid Assistant	$45,000	Assists in the daily operations of the Financial Aid Office providing general assistance and support to the Financial Aid staff. Provides student financial aid information to prospective and current students and families via phone or email. Tracks student financial			
Associate Director	$65,000	Develops and implements an overall strategic plan. Recruits, trains, and manages volunteers and awards. Develops philanthropic relationships with an assigned group of donors, prospective donors, and volunteers. Identifies capacity, interests and inclination.			
Executive Assistant	$43,900	Supports an executive, handling administrative duties. Performs diverse, advanced and confidential administrative support including composing, signing and releasing routine but somewhat complex correspondence. Relieves management of administrative details.			

FIGURE 2-5: Modifying Number Field properties in Table Design View

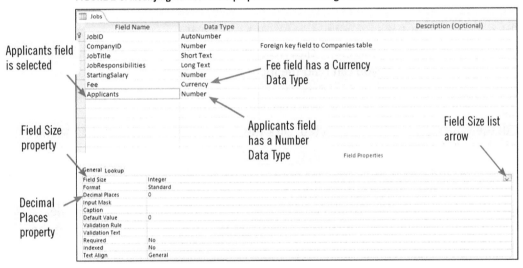

Applicants field is selected

Fee field has a Currency Data Type

Applicants field has a Number Data Type

Field Size property

Field Size list arrow

Decimal Places property

TABLE 2-2: Number Field Size property options

property	description
Byte	Stores numbers from 0 to 255 (no fractions)
Integer	Stores numbers from –32,768 to 32,767 (no fractions)
Long Integer	Stores numbers from –2,147,483,648 to 2,147,483,647 (no fractions)
Single	Stores numbers (including fractions with six digits to the right of the decimal point) times 10 to the –38th to +38th power
Double	Stores numbers (including fractions with more than 10 digits to the right of the decimal point) in the range of 10 to the –324th to +324th power

Access

Modify Short Text Fields

Learning Outcomes
• Modify the Input Mask property
• Enter data using an input mask
• Modify the Field Size property

Short Text is the most common and therefore the default field data type. Short Text is used for any field that stores letters and any field that contains numbers that do not represent quantities such as a zip code, telephone number, or product number. Short Text fields have some additional properties unique to textual data such as Input Mask. Modifying the properties of a Short Text field helps ensure database accuracy and clarity because properties can restrict the way data is entered, stored, and displayed. See TABLE 2-3 for more information on Short Text field properties. **CASE** ▶ *After reviewing the Contacts table with Lydia, you decide to modify the Input Mask and Field Size properties for the ContactCell field. You will work in Table Design View to make the changes.*

STEPS

1. **Right-click the** Contacts table **in the Navigation Pane, then click** Design View **on the shortcut menu**

   The **Input Mask** property provides a visual guide for users as they enter data. The ContactCell field is a good candidate for an Input Mask because phone numbers are consistently entered with 10 numeric characters for each record.

2. **Click** ContactCell, **click the** Input Mask property box, **click the** Build button 📋 , **click the** Phone Number input mask, **click** Next, **click** Next, **click** Finish, **then click the** ContactCell field name **so you can read the Input Mask property**

   This Input Mask will limit the number of characters the user can enter into the ContactCell field to 10, so it is a good idea to change the Field Size property from the default value of 255 to 10 as well.

3. **With the** ContactCell field **still selected, click the** Field Size property **and change the value from 255 to** 10

   Table Design View of the Contacts table should look like FIGURE 2-6, which shows the Input Mask property created for the ContactCell field as well as the updated Field Size value of 10.

4. **Right-click the** Contacts table tab, **click** Datasheet View, **click** Yes **to save the table, click** Yes **when warned that data might be lost, press TAB three times to move to the ContactCell field for the first record, type** 5553334444, **then press** ENTER

   No data was lost because no existing value in the ContactCell field is greater than 10 characters. The Input Mask property creates an easy-to-use visual guide to facilitate accurate and consistent data entry for the ContactCell field.

   Your screen should look like FIGURE 2-7.

5. **Right-click the** Contacts table tab, **then click** Close

FIGURE 2-6: Modifying the Input Mask property

ContactCell field is selected

Field Size property

Input Mask property

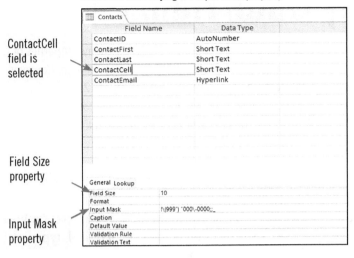

FIGURE 2-7: Entering data with an input mask

Data entered with an input mask

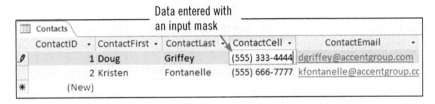

TABLE 2-3: Common Short Text field properties

property	description	sample field	sample property entry
Field Size	Controls how many characters can be entered into the field	State	2
Format	Controls how information will be displayed and printed	State	> (displays all characters in uppercase)
Input Mask	Provides a pattern for data to be entered	Phone	!(999) 000-0000;1;_
Caption	Describes the field in the first row of a datasheet, form, or report; if the Caption property is not entered, the field name is used to label the field	EmpNo	Employee Number
Default Value	Displays a value that is automatically entered in the given field for new records	City	Des Moines
Required	Determines if an entry is required for this field	LastName	Yes

Working with the Input Mask property

The Input Mask property provides a **pattern** for data to be entered, using three parts, each separated by a ; (semicolon). The first part provides a pattern for what type of data can be entered. For example, **9** represents an optional number, **0** a required number, **?** an optional letter, and **L** a required letter. The second part determines whether all displayed characters (such as dashes in a phone number) are stored in the field. For the second part of the input mask, a 0 entry stores all characters, such as 555-1199, and a 1 entry stores only the entered data, 5551199. The third part of the input mask determines which character Access uses to guide the user through the mask. Common choices are the asterisk (*), underscore (_), or pound sign (#).

Access

Modify Date/Time Fields

Learning Outcomes
- Modify the Format property
- Modify the Default Value property
- Modify the Required property

Fields with a **Date/Time** data type store dates, times, or both. Many properties of Date/Time fields work the same way as they do for Short Text or Number fields. One difference, however, is the **Format** property, which helps you format dates in various ways such as January 25, 2021; 25-Jan-21; or 01/25/2021.

CASE ▶ *Lydia asks you to add a new field to the Contacts table to track the date that the contact was added to the table. You will create a new field named EntryDate and set its properties to handle this request.*

STEPS

1. **Right-click the** Contacts table **in the Navigation Pane, click** Design View **on the shortcut menu, click the** Field Name cell **just below the ContactEmail, type** EntryDate, **press** TAB, **click the** Data Type list arrow, **then click** Date/Time

   With the field name and data type set, you use field properties to further describe the field.

2. **With the EntryDate field still selected, click the** Format property box, **click the** Format list arrow, **then click** Medium Date

   The **Format** property changes the way the data is displayed *after it is entered*. All dates in Access are *entered* in a month/day/year pattern.

3. **With the EntryDate field still selected, click the** Default Value property box, **then type** =Date()

   The Default Value property automatically enters a value in all new records. The equal sign = indicates that you are using a calculated expression, and **Date()** is an Access function that returns the current date.

   The updated Table Design View for the Contacts table is shown in FIGURE 2-8.

TROUBLE
The current date will obviously be the date you perform these steps.

4. **Right-click the** Contacts table tab, **click** Save, **right-click the** Contacts table tab **again, then click** Datasheet View

   Note that the current date is already entered in the EntryDate field for the new record. To change the value, you can enter dates from the keyboard using a month/day/year pattern or pick a date from a pop-up calendar using the **Date Picker**.

5. **Press** TAB **five times to move to the** EntryDate field, **click the** Date Picker icon ▦, **click the current date on the pop-up calendar, click the** EntryDate field **for the second record, click the** Date Picker icon ▦, **then click the current date on the calendar for the second record as well**

   With valid dates in the EntryDate field of both records, you can set the Required property to Yes for the EntryDate field.

6. **Click the** EntryDate field name, **click the** Fields tab **on the ribbon, then click the** Required check box **as shown in** FIGURE 2-9

   The **Required** property will create an error message if the user attempts to enter a record in the database without a date in the EntryDate field.

7. **Close the Contacts table**

FIGURE 2-8: **Creating a Date/Time field**

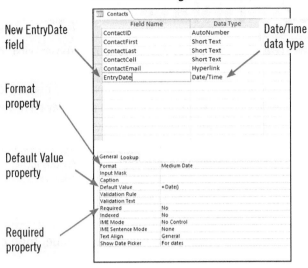

New EntryDate field

Format property

Default Value property

Required property

Date/Time data type

FIGURE 2-9: **Working with dates**

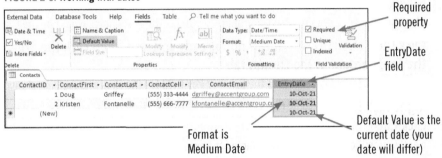

Required property

EntryDate field

Default Value is the current date (your date will differ)

Format is Medium Date

Entering dates

If you type the date for a Date/Type field instead of choosing a date from the pop-up calendar, Access assumes that years entered with two digits from 30 to 99 refer to the years 1930 through 1999, and 00 to 29 refers to the years 2000 through 2029. To enter a year before 1930 or after 2029, you must type all four digits of the year.

Using Smart Tags

Smart Tags are buttons that automatically appear in certain conditions. They provide a small menu of options to help you work with the task at hand. For example, in Table Design View, Access provides the **Property Update Options** Smart Tag to help you quickly apply property changes to other objects of the database that use the field. Another Smart Tag, the **Error Indicator** helps identify potential errors.

Create Primary Keys

The **primary key field** of a table serves two important purposes. First, it contains data that uniquely identifies each record in that table. Second, the primary key field helps relate one table to another in a **one-to-many relationship**, where one record from one table may be related to many records in the second table. For example, one record in the Companies table may be related to many records in the Jobs table. (One company may have many job openings.) The primary key field is always on the "one" side of a one-to-many relationship between two tables. **CASE** ▸ *Lydia Snyder asks you to confirm that a primary key field has been appropriately identified for each table in the new database.*

STEPS

1. **Right-click the** Companies table **in the Navigation Pane, then click** Design View

   The CompanyID AutoNumber field has been set as the primary key field as evidenced by the **key symbol** to the left of the field name. A field with the AutoNumber data type is a good candidate for the primary key field in a table because it automatically contains a unique number for each record.

2. **Right-click the** Companies table tab, **click** Close, **right-click the** Contacts table **in the Navigation Pane, then click** Design View

   The Contacts table does not have a primary key field. The best choice would be the ContactID field.

3. **Click the** ContactID field **if it is not already selected, then click the** Primary Key button **in the Tools group on the Design tab**

   The ContactID field is now set as the primary key field for the Contacts table, as shown in FIGURE 2-10.

4. **Right-click the** Contacts table, **click** Save, **right-click the** Contacts table tab **again, then click** Close

   Next, you will check the Industries table for a primary key field.

5. **Right-click the** Industries table **in the Navigation Pane, click** Design View, **observe that the Short Text Industry field is set as the primary key field, right-click the** Industries table tab, **then click** Close

   Next, check the Jobs table.

6. **Right-click the** Jobs table **in the Navigation Pane, click** Design View, **observe that the AutoNumber JobID field is set as the primary key field, right-click the** Jobs table tab, **then click** Close

   Next, check the StatesAndProvinces table.

7. **Right-click the** StatesAndProvinces table **in the Navigation Pane, click** Design View, **observe that the Short Text StateAbbrev field is set as the primary key field as shown in** FIGURE 2-11, **right-click the** StatesAndProvinces table tab, **then click** Close

   Often, the primary key field is the first field in the table, but that is not a requirement. If you do not make any design changes to an object, you are not prompted to save it when you close it.

   Now that you have confirmed that each table in the database has an appropriate primary key field, you are ready to link the tables together to create a relational database. The primary key field plays a critical role in this process.

FIGURE 2-10: Setting the primary key field in Design View of the Contacts table

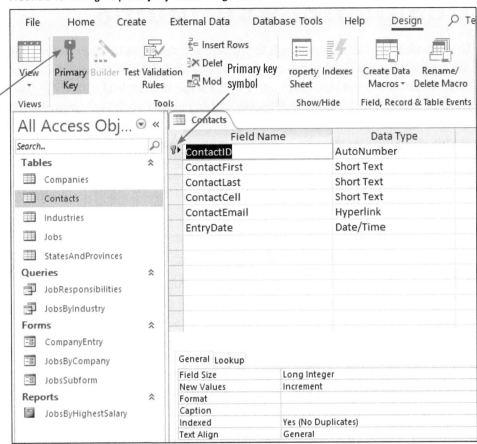

Primary Key button

FIGURE 2-11: Design View of the StatesAndProvinces table

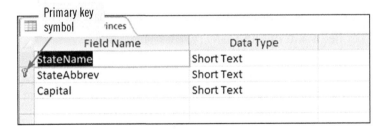

Primary key symbol

Field Name	Data Type
StateName	Short Text
StateAbbrev	Short Text
Capital	Short Text

Access

Design Related Tables

Learning
Outcomes
• Understand the
terminology used
when creating a
relational database
• Understand the
steps to create a
relational database
• Analyze one-to-
many relationships

The purpose of a relational database is to organize and store data in a way that minimizes redundancy and maximizes your flexibility when querying and analyzing data. To accomplish these goals, a relational database uses multiple related tables rather than a single large table of data. **CASE** ▶ *At one time, JCL Talent tracked information about its companies and jobs using a single Excel spreadsheet. This created data redundancy problems because of the duplicate industries and companies for each job and contact. Lydia Snyder asks you to study the principles of relational database design to help JCL Talent create a proper relational database.*

DETAILS

To design a relational database, follow these steps:

- **Design each table to contain fields that describe only one subject**

  Each table in the JCL Talent database stores records that describe only one of the following subjects: Companies, Contacts, Industries, Jobs, or StatesAndProvinces. If the data for these tables was stored in a single large table, the company information would be repeated for each job and for each contact. Many problems are created when data is duplicated such as extra data entry work; additional data entry inconsistencies and errors; larger physical data storage requirements; and limitations on the ability to search for, analyze, and report on the data. A properly designed relational database minimizes these problems.

- **Identify a primary key field for each table**

  The primary key field contains unique information for each record. You have already made sure that each of the five tables has a proper primary key field. Generally the primary key field has a numeric data type such as AutoNumber (automatically increments) or Number (user controlled), but sometimes Short Text fields serve this purpose such as the StateAbbrev field in the StatesAndProvinces table. Although using a contact's last name as the primary key field might work in a very small database, names are generally a poor choice for the primary key field because two records may legitimately have the same name.

- **Build foreign key fields and one-to-many relationships**

  To tie the information from one table to another, one field must be common to each table. This linking field is the primary key field on the "one" side of the relationship and the **foreign key field** on the "many" side of the relationship. You are not required to give the primary and foreign key fields the same name, although doing so may clarify which fields are used to relate two tables.

  The current relational database design for the Jobs database is shown in FIGURE 2-12. It is only partially completed. Currently, one record in the Industries table is related to many records in the Companies table using the common Industry field. One record in the Companies table is related to many records in the Jobs tables using the common CompanyID field. The StatesAndProvinces as well as the Contacts tables are not currently participating in the relational database, but you will correct that in the next lesson. See TABLE 2-4 for a summary of important relational database terminology.

TABLE 2-4: Terminology used when creating a relational database

term	definition
Field	An individual column of information in a table. A field should not contain more than one piece of data. For example, always separate first and last names into two fields to preserve your ability to sort, filter, or find either name. Do not enter numbers and units of measurement such as *10 minutes* or *5 hours* into a single field. Doing so prevents you from easily sorting and calculating on the numeric part of the information.
Record	A group of related fields that describes a person, place, thing, or transaction such as a company or a job; a row

term	definition
Table	A collection of records for a single subject such as Industries, Companies, Jobs, Contacts, or StatesAndProvinces
Primary key field	A field that contains unique data for each record. Often an AutoNumber or Number field, a primary key field may also have a Short Text data type. The primary key field may also be used on the parent table ("one" table) side of a one-to-many relationship.
Foreign key field	A field in the child table ("many" table) that connects each record to the appropriate record in the parent table ("one" table)
Parent table	The table on the "one" side of a "one-to-many" relationship
Parent record	A record in the parent table
Child table	The table on the "many" side of a "one-to-many" relationship
Child record	A record in the child table
One-to-many relationship	A link between two tables that relates one record in the parent table to many records in the child table. For example, one record in the Industries table can be related to many records in the Companies table. One record in the Companies table can be related to many records in the Jobs table. One record in the Companies table can be related to many records in the Contacts table.
One-to-one relationship	A link between two tables that relates one record in the parent table to one record in the child table. One-to-one relationships are rare because this relationship can be simplified by moving all the fields into a single table.
Many-to-many relationship	If two tables have a many-to-many relationship, it means that one record in one table may be related to many records in the other table and vice versa. You cannot directly create a many-to-many relationship between two tables in Access. To connect two tables with this relationship, you must establish a third table called a **junction table** and create two one-to-many relationships from the original two tables using the junction table as the child table for both relationships. For example, at a school, the Students and Classes tables have a many-to-many relationship because one student can be in many classes and one class can have many students. To connect the Students and Classes tables, you would have to create a third table, perhaps called Enrollments, as the junction table. One student can be enrolled in many classes. One class can have many enrollments.
Junction table	The table between two tables that have a many-to-many relationship; the junction table is a child table to both of the other two tables.
Referential integrity	A set of rules that helps eliminate the creation of orphan records in a child ("many") table. For example, with referential integrity enforced, you cannot enter a value in a foreign key field of the child ("many") table that does not have a match in the linking field of the parent ("one") table. Referential integrity also prevents you from deleting a record in the parent ("one") table if a matching entry exists in the foreign key field of the child ("many") table.
Orphan record	A record in a child ("many") table that has no match in the parent ("one") table. Orphan records cannot be created in a child table if referential integrity is enforced.
Scrubbing or data cleansing	The process of removing and fixing orphan records in a relational database

FIGURE 2-12: Initial relational design for the Jobs database

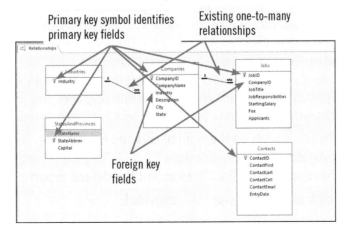

Create One-to-Many Relationships

Learning Outcomes
• Create a foreign key field
• Create one-to-many relationships
• Set referential integrity
• Create a Relationship report

You must connect the tables in your database in proper one-to-many relationships to enjoy the benefits of a relational database. You use a common field in each table to create one-to-many relationships between the tables. The common field is always the primary key field in the parent ("one") table and is called the foreign key field in the child ("many") table. TABLE 2–5 includes a few common one-to-many relationships.

CASE › *Lydia Snyder asks you to complete the relational database by connecting the StatesAndProvinces and Contacts tables with one-to-many relationships.*

STEPS

1. **Click the** Database Tools tab **on the ribbon, click the** Relationships button, **then drag the** StatesAndProvinces table **from the Navigation Pane to the Relationships window**

   Each table in the database is represented by a small **field list** window that displays the table's field names. A **key symbol** identifies the primary key field in each table. To relate the two tables in a one-to-many relationship, you connect them using a common field, which is always the primary key field on the parent ("one") side of the relationship.

2. **Drag the** StateAbbrev field **in the StatesAndProvinces table to the** State field **in the Companies table**

   The Edit Relationships dialog box opens, as shown in FIGURE 2-13, which provides information about the tables and fields that will participate in the relationship and the option to enforce referential integrity.

3. **Click the** Enforce Referential Integrity check box, **then click** Create

   A **one-to-many line** appears between the StatesAndProvinces table and the Companies table. The parent ("one") side, as indicated by the "1" symbol on the line, identifies the primary key field used in the relationship. The child ("many") side, as indicated by the **infinity symbol**, identifies the foreign key field used in the relationship.

   The Contacts table does not have a corresponding foreign key field, which you need to create a one-to-many relationship.

4. **Right-click the** Contacts table field list, **click** Table Design, **click the blank** Field Name cell **just below the EntryDate field, type** CompanyID, **click the** Data Type list arrow, **click** Number, **right-click the** Contacts table tab, **click** Save, **right-click the** Contacts table tab **again, then click** Close

   Now you are ready to connect the Contacts table to the Companies table.

5. **Drag the** CompanyID field **in the Companies table to the** CompanyID field **in the Contacts table, click the** Enforce Referential Integrity check box **in the Edit Relationships dialog box, then click** Create

   The final relational database design is shown in FIGURE 2-14.

   A printout of the Relationships window, called the **Relationship report**, includes table names, field names, primary key fields, and one-to-many relationship lines. This printout is a helpful resource as you later create queries, forms, and reports that use fields from multiple tables.

6. **Click the** Design tab **on the ribbon, click the** Relationship Report button **in the Tools group, right-click the** Relationships for IL_AC_2_Jobs report tab, **click** Close, **click** Yes **to save the report, then click** OK **to accept the default report name**

7. **Right-click the** Relationships tab **then click** Close

FIGURE 2-13: Edit Relationships dialog box

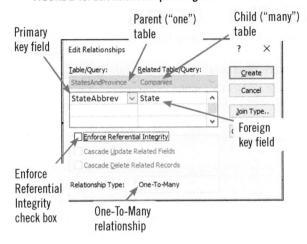

FIGURE 2-14: Final Relationships window

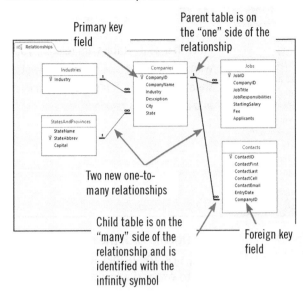

TABLE 2-5: Common one-to-many relationships

table on "one" side	table on "many" side	linking field	description
Products	Sales	ProductID	A ProductID field must have a unique entry in a Products table, but it is listed many times in a Sales table
Students	Enrollments	StudentID	A StudentID field must have a unique entry in a Students table, but it is listed many times in an Enrollments table as the student enrolls in multiple classes
Employees	Promotions	EmployeeID	An EmployeeID field must have a unique entry in an Employees table, but it is listed many times in a Promotions table as the employee is promoted to new job positions over time

Specifying the data type of the foreign key field

The foreign key field in the child table must have the same data type (Short Text or Number) as the primary key it is related to in the parent table. An exception to this rule is when the primary key field in the parent table has an AutoNumber data type. In this case, the linking foreign key field in the child table must have a Number data type. Also note that a Number field used as a foreign key field must have a Long Integer Field Size property to match the Field Size property of the AutoNumber primary key field.

Cascade options

Cascade Update Related Fields means that if a value in the primary key field (the field on the "one" side of a one-to-many relationship) is modified, all values in the foreign key field (the field on the child ("many") side of a one-to-many relationship) are automatically updated as well. **Cascade Delete Related Records** means that if a record on the parent ("one") side of a one-to-many relationship is deleted, all related records in the child ("many") table are also deleted. Because both of these options automatically change or delete data in the child ("many") table behind the scenes, they should be used with caution.

Access

Work with Subdatasheets

Now that all the tables are related, you can start enjoying the benefits of a relational database by working with subdatasheets. A **subdatasheet** shows the child records connected to each parent record in a datasheet. **CASE** *You and Lydia explore the subdatasheet feature that is provided when two tables are related in a one-to-many relationship.*

STEPS

1. **Double-click the** Industries table **to open it in Datasheet View, click the** Select All button ☐ **in the upper-left corner of the Industries datasheet, then click any** Expand button ⊞ **to expand all subdatasheets at the same time, as shown in** FIGURE 2-15

    The Industries and Companies tables are linked in a one-to-many relationship, so the subdatasheet for each industry record displays related child records from the Companies table.

    Note that the records in the subdatasheet also have Expand buttons.

2. **Click the** Expand button ⊞ **to the left of the Navigational Systems record (the second record in the Aerospace subdatasheet)**

    The Companies table participates as the parent table in two different one-to-many relationships, so you are presented with the Insert Subdatasheet dialog box, asking which child table you want to select.

3. **Click** Jobs **in the Insert Subdatasheet dialog box**

    Notice that the CompanyID field is automatically added to the Link Child Fields and Link Master Fields boxes, as shown in FIGURE 2-16, because it is the field that connects the Companies and Jobs tables.

4. **Click** OK **in the Insert Subdatasheet dialog box**

    The four records in the Jobs table are linked to the Navigational Systems record in the Companies table and are now displayed in the Navigational Systems subdatasheet. You can use subdatasheets to enter and edit data.

5. **Enter** 50.25 **as the Fee field value for each of the four job records in the Navigational Systems subdatasheet, click the** Select All button ☐ **in the upper-left corner of the Industries datasheet, click the** Collapse button ⊟ **to the left of the Aerospace record, right-click the** Industries table tab, **click** Close, **then click** No **when asked to save changes to the Companies table**

6. **Double-click the** Jobs table **to open it in Datasheet View, scroll down to the records for the Navigational Systems company (JobIDs 23 through 26), then scroll to the right to view the 50.25 entries you previously made to the Fee field in a subdatasheet**

    When working with data in Datasheet View, subdatasheets make it easy to view child records.

    As you are working with Access, you may notice messages and indicators that appear in the status bar, the bottom bar in the application window. See TABLE 2-6 for information on status bar indicators. You may turn these indicators on and off by right-clicking the status bar and selecting the indicator that you want to change. Most of the indicator messages appear in the right corner of the status bar.

7. **sam⬆** Right-click the Jobs table tab, **click** Close, **click the** Database Tools tab, **click the** Compact and Repair Database button, **then close Access**

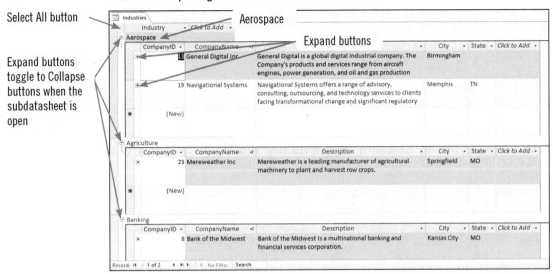

FIGURE 2-15: Expanding subdatasheets for the Industries table

Select All button

Aerospace

Expand buttons

Expand buttons toggle to Collapse buttons when the subdatasheet is open

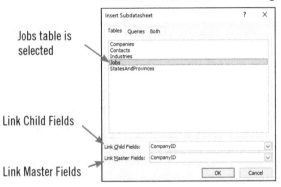

FIGURE 2-16: Insert Subdatasheet dialog box

Jobs table is selected

Link Child Fields

Link Master Fields

TABLE 2-6: Status bar indicators

status bar indicator	displays
Caps Lock	**Caps Lock** in the status bar when the Caps Lock is toggled on
Kana Mode	Short for Katakana, which is a Japanese language; you must have a special installation of Access to enter these characters
Num Lock	**Num Lock** in the status bar when the Num Lock is toggled on.
Scroll Lock	**Scroll Lock** in the status bar when the Scroll Lock is toggled on
Overtype	**Overtype** in the status bar when Overtype mode (vs. Insert mode) is toggled on
Filtered	**Filtered** in the status bar when using the filter features
Move Mode	**Move Mode** in the status bar when using customized insertion point and key behaviors
Extended Selection	**Extended Selection** in the status bar when using extend mode, a feature that allows you to more easily select text without using a mouse
View Shortcuts	**View shortcut icons**

Access

Practice

Concepts Review

Identify each element of the Relationships window shown in FIGURE 2-17.

FIGURE 2-17

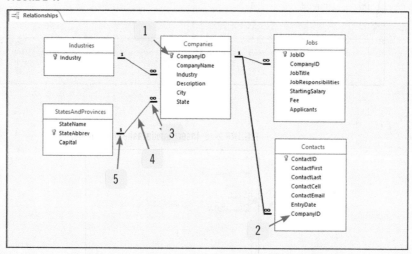

Match each term with the statement that best describes its function.

6. Subdatasheet
7. Currency data type
8. Importing
9. Foreign key field
10. Referential integrity
11. Primary key field
12. Number data type
13. Integer
14. Linking

a. Field used in a child ("many") table to establish a one-to-many relationship
b. Use this with fields that store fractional values.
c. A whole number
d. A way to copy information from another database, spreadsheet, or file format into an Access database
e. Use this with fields that store integers.
f. A way to connect to data in an external source without copying it
g. A field that contains unique information for each record in that table
h. Shows related records from a child ("many") table
i. A set of rules that prevent the creation of orphan records in the child ("many") table

Select the best answer from the list of choices.

15. **What would be the best data type for a field that stores prices in dollars and cents?**
    a. Short Text
    b. Currency
    c. Number
    d. AutoNumber

16. **What would be the best data type for a field that stores the quantity of various car parts in inventory?**
    a. Short Text
    b. Currency
    c. Number
    d. AutoNumber

17. **Which of the following is *not* a file format that Access can import?**
    a. Access
    b. Word
    c. Excel
    d. HTML

18. **Which of the following properties would you use to create a visual guide for data entry?**
   a. Format
   b. Default Value
   c. Field Size
   d. Input Mask

19. **Which is *not* true about enforcing referential integrity?**
   a. It is required for all one-to-many relationships.
   b. It prevents orphan records.
   c. It prevents records from being deleted on the "one" side of a one-to-many relationship that have matching records on the "many" side.
   d. It prevents records from being created on the "many" side of a one-to-many relationship that do not have a matching record on the "one" side.

20. **Which of the following is *not* true about linking?**
   a. Access can link to data in an Excel spreadsheet.
   b. Linking copies data from one data file to another.
   c. Access can link to data in an HTML file.
   d. You can edit linked data in Access.

Skills Review

1. **Import data from Excel.**
   a. Start Access.
   b. Open the IL_AC_2-2.accdb database from the location where you store your Data Files and save it as **IL_AC_2_SupportDesk**. Click Enable Content if a yellow Security Warning message appears.
   c. Import the **Support_IL_AC_2_Departments.xlsx** spreadsheet, located where you store your Data Files, to a new table in the current database using the Import Spreadsheet Wizard. Make sure that the first row is specified as a column heading, and do not create or select a primary key field. Name the table **Departments** and do not save the import steps.
   d. Open the Departments table in Table Datasheet View to confirm that the import worked properly. The Departments table should have seven records. Close the Departments table.
   e. Append the records from the **Support_IL_AC_2_Employees.xlsx** spreadsheet, located where you store your Data Files, to the existing Employees table. (*Hint*: If a "Subscript out of range" error appears, close the database, reopen it, then repeat Step 1e.)
   f. Open the Employees table in Table Datasheet View to confirm that the append process worked properly. The Employees table should have 26 records. Close the Employees table.

2. **Modify Datasheet View.**
   a. Open the Calls table in Datasheet View and delete the last field, CallPriority, which currently has no data.
   b. Move the CallMinutes field between the CallDateTime and CallNotes fields.
   c. Decrease decimals on the CallMinutes field to **0** and make sure the Format property is set to **Standard**.
   d. Save and close the Calls table.

3. **Modify Number and Currency fields.**
   a. Open the Employees table in Datasheet View and after the Department field, add a new field named **Salary** with a Currency data type.
   b. After the Salary field, add another field named **Dependents** with a Number data type.
   c. Enter **55000** for the Salary field and **3** for the Dependents field for the first employee (Aaron Cabrera, EmployeeID 3).
   d. Decrease the decimals for the Salary field to **0**.
   e. Make the Default Value for the Dependents field **1**.
   f. Save and close the Employees table.

4. Modify Short Text fields.

    a. Open the Employees table in Design View and after the Dependents field, add a new field named **EmergencyPhone** with a Short Text data type.

    b. Use the Input Mask Wizard to add a Phone Number input mask. Use the asterisk (*) as the Placeholder character and accept the other default settings.

    c. Change the Field Size property of the EmergencyPhone field to **10**.

    d. Change the Field Size property of the Department field to **15**.

    e. Save the Employees table and click **Yes** when prompted. No data will be lost because no existing entries exceed the new Field Size property limits you have set.

    f. Display the Employees table in Datasheet View, tab to the EmergencyPhone field for the first record (Aaron Cabrera EmployeeID 3), then type **5552227777** to experience the value of the Input Mask property.

    g. Close the Employees table.

5. Modify Date/Time fields.

    a. Open the Cases table in Design View and change the Format property for both the OpenedDate and the ResolvedDate fields to **Short Date**.

    b. Change the Default Value for the OpenedDate field to **=Date()** to provide today's date.

    c. Change the Required Value for the OpenedDate field to **Yes**.

    d. Save the table, click Yes when prompted to test the data, then close the Cases table.

6. Create primary key fields.

    a. Open the Departments table in Table Design View and set the Department field as the primary key field. Save and close the Departments table.

    b. Open each of the other tables, Calls, Cases, and Employees, in Design View to view and confirm that they have a primary key field. In each case, the first field is designated as the primary key field and has an AutoNumber data type. A field with an AutoNumber data type will automatically increment to the next number as new records are entered into that table.

7. Design related tables.

    a. Open the Relationships window to study the existing relationships between the tables.

    b. Drag the edges of the field lists so that all fields are clearly visible and drag the field list title bars as needed to clearly position the tables so that the Calls table is to the right of the Cases table and the Cases table is to the right of the Employees table.

    c. Be ready to discuss these issues in class or in an online discussion thread.
- Why is it important to relate tables in the first place?
- What relationships exist in this database?
- What role does the primary key field in each table play in the relationships identified in Step 7a?
- What is the foreign key field in each of the relationships?
- What parent ("one") tables exist in this database?
- What child ("many") tables exist in this database?
- What do the "1" and infinity symbols tell you about the relationship?

    d. Save the Relationships window.

8. Create one-to-many relationships.

    a. Add the Departments table to the Relationships window. Position it to the left of the Employees table.

    b. Create a one-to-many relationship between the Departments table and the Employees table using the common Department field.

    c. Enforce referential integrity on the relationship.

    d. Save the Relationships window, as shown in FIGURE 2-18, then close it.

Skills Review (continued)

9. Work with subdatasheets.

FIGURE 2-18

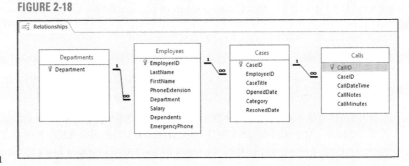

a. Open the Departments table in Datasheet View. Expand the Accounting Department's subdatasheet to display the employees who work in that department.

b. Change the Extension value of EmployeeID 24 (Craig Serrano) from 7621 to **7766** in the subdatasheet.

c. Expand the subdatasheet for EmployeeID 24 (Craig Serrano) to see the cases that are linked to that employee.

d. Expand the subdatasheet for CaseID 22 (Email attachment problem) to see what calls are linked to that case.

e. Collapse all subdatasheets and close the Departments table.

f. Compact and repair the database and close Access.

Independent Challenge 1

As the manager of Riverwalk, a multi-specialty health clinic, you have created a database to manage the schedules that connect each healthcare provider with the nurses that provider needs to efficiently handle patient visits. In this exercise, you create the primary keys and relationships required to create a relational database.

a. Start Access. Open the IL_AC_2-3.accdb database from the location where you store your Data Files and save it as **IL_AC_2_Riverwalk**. Click Enable Content if a yellow Security Warning message appears.

b. Open the Relationships window. Drag the ScheduleItems table from the Navigation Pane to the Relationships window, positioning it between the existing four tables. (*Hint*: You can also add tables to the Relationships window by clicking the Show Table button in the Relationships group on the Design tab.)

c. Now that all four tables are in the Relationships window, notice that each table has a primary key field except for the ScheduleItems table. Open the ScheduleItems table in Design View, set the TransactionNo field as the primary key field, then save and close the table to return to the Relationships window.

d. To connect the tables, you have to decide how "one" record in a parent table relates to "many" records in a child table. In this case, the ScheduleItems table is the child table to each of the four other tables. Therefore, build four one-to-many relationships with referential integrity as follows:

- Drag the ScheduleNo field from the ScheduleDate table to the ScheduleNo field of the ScheduleItems table.
- Drag the LocationNo field from the Locations table to the LocationNo field of the ScheduleItems table.
- Drag the DoctorNo field from the Providers table to the DoctorNo field of the ScheduleItems table.
- Drag the NurseNo field from the Nurses table to the NurseNo field of the ScheduleItems table.

e. Be sure to enforce referential integrity on each relationship. Doing so will add the "1" and "infinity" symbols to the relationship line. If they are missing, double-click the relationship line to open the Edit Relationships dialog box, where you can check the Enforce Referential Integrity check box.

f. Click the Relationship Report button in the Tools group on the Design tab to create a relationships report, as shown in FIGURE 2-19.

FIGURE 2-19

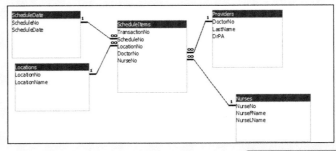

g. Save and close the report with the default name of **Relationships for IL_AC_2_ Riverwalk**, then save and close the Relationships window.

h. Compact and repair the database then close Access.

Independent Challenge 2

You are working for a city to coordinate a series of community-wide preparedness activities. You have started a database to track the activities and volunteers who are attending the activities.

a. Start Access. Open the IL_AC_2-4.accdb database from the location where you store your Data Files and save it as **IL_AC_2_Volunteers**. Click Enable Content if a yellow Security Warning message appears.

b. To best manage this relational database, start at the table level and review the table relationships. Open the Relationships window and drag the tables from the Navigation Pane to the Relationships window in this order: Zipcodes, Volunteers, Attendance, and Activities. (*Hint:* You can also add tables to the Relationships window by clicking the Show Table button in the Relationships group on the Design tab.)

c. Some of the relationships are more obvious than others. For example, one record in the Zipcodes table may be related to many records in the Volunteers table. To establish this relationship, drag the Zip field from the Zipcodes table to the Zipcode field in the Volunteers table and enforce referential integrity on the relationship.

d. The Volunteers, Attendance, and Activities tables are more difficult to analyze because one volunteer may be related to many activities and one activity may have many volunteers. This many-to-many relationship is resolved with the Attendance table, which serves as the junction table between the Volunteers and Activities tables. Open the Attendance table in Design view and add two foreign key fields named **VolunteerID** and **ActivityID**, each with a Number data type. Save and close the Attendance table and return to the Relationships window.

e. With the foreign key fields in the Attendance table established, you are ready to link the Volunteers, Attendance, and Activities tables by building these two relationships:
   - Drag the VolunteerID field from the Volunteers table to the VolunteerID field in the Attendance table. Enforce referential integrity on the relationship.
   - Drag the ActivityID field from the Activities table to the ActivityID field in the Attendance table. Enforce referential integrity on the relationship.

f. The final Relationships window should look like FIGURE 2-20. Save and close the Relationships window.

g. Open the Zipcodes table to review its one-to-many relationship with the Volunteers table by working in Table Datasheet View.

h. Expand the subdatasheet for the 64145 Springfield KS record, change Micah Ati's name to *your name*, then close the Zipcodes table.

i. Compact and repair the database and close Access.

FIGURE 2-20

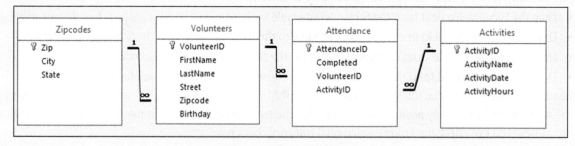

Visual Workshop

Open the IL_AC_2-5.accdb database from the location where you store your Data Files and save it as **IL_AC_2_CollegeCourses**, then enable content if prompted. Import the **Support_IL_AC_2_Majors.xlsx** Excel spreadsheet and append the records to the Departments table. Do not save the import steps.

Import the following spreadsheets as new tables with the following names. For each import, use the first row as the column headings and other default options of the Import Spreadsheet Wizard. Do not save the import steps.

Import **Support_IL_AC_2_Classes.xlsx** as **Classes** and set ClassNo as the primary key field.

Import **Support_IL_AC_2_Enrollments.xlsx** as **Enrollments** and set EnrollmentID as the primary key field.

Import **Support_IL_AC_2_Sections.xlsx** as **Sections** and set SectionNo as the primary key field.

Import **Support_IL_AC_2_Students.xlsx** as **Students** and set StudentID as the primary key field.

In the Relationships window, relate the tables in one-to-many relationships using FIGURE 2-21 as a guide. Enforce referential integrity on each relationship. Save and close the Relationships window.

FIGURE 2-21

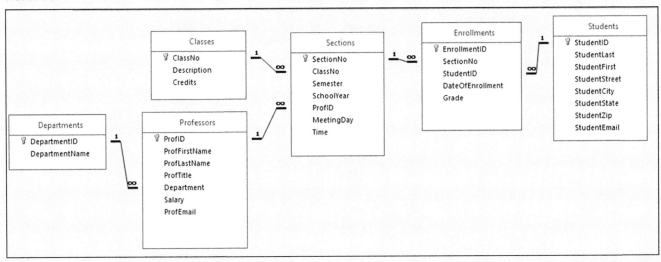

Creating Queries

CASE   Now that you've updated the tables in the database for JCL Talent and linked them in one-to-many relationships to create a relational database, you're ready to mine the data for information. You'll develop queries to provide Lydia Snyder, vice president of operations, with fast and accurate answers.

Module Objectives

After completing this module, you will be able to:

- Work in Query Datasheet View
- Work in Query Design View
- Work in SQL View
- Sort data
- Find and replace data
- Filter data
- Enter and save criteria
- Apply AND criteria
- Apply OR criteria
- Create calculated fields
- Format a datasheet

Files You Will Need

IL_AC_3-1.accdb

IL_AC_3-2.accdb

IL_AC_3-3.accdb

IL_AC_3-4.accdb

IL_AC_3-5.accdb

Work in Query Datasheet View

Learning
Outcomes
• Edit and delete
  records
• Hide and unhide
  columns
• Freeze and
  unfreeze columns

A **query** answers a question about the information in the database by allowing you to select a subset of fields and records from one or more tables and present them in a single datasheet. You can enter, edit, and navigate data in **Query Datasheet View**, which displays each field as a column and each record as a row just like Table Datasheet View. Given all data is stored only in tables, any edits, additions, or deletions made in Query Datasheet View are automatically reflected elsewhere in the database. **CASE** ▶ *Lydia asks you to change some data that is currently organized in a query. You'll work in Query Datasheet View to make the updates.*

STEPS

1. **som↓** Start Access, open the IL_AC_3-1.accdb database **from the location where you store your Data Files, save it as** IL_AC_3_Jobs, **enable content if prompted, then double-click the** JobsByIndustry query **to open it in Datasheet View**

   Each time a query is opened, it shows a current view of the data. Notice that the datasheet displays one record for every job and that one company may be connected to many jobs.

   The records for General Digital Inc in Birmingham do not have a value in the State field. Although data is stored in tables, you can edit data in Query Datasheet View.

2. **Click the** State field cell **for any General Digital Inc record, type** AL, **then click any other record**

   All records for General Digital Inc in this query update to show AL (Alabama) in the State field because General Digital Inc is related to six records in the Jobs table.

3. **Click the** record selector **to the left of the twelfth record (CompanyID 8 and JobTitle of Executive Assistant), click the** Delete button **in the Records group, then click** Yes

   You can delete records from a query datasheet the same way you delete them from a table datasheet. Notice that the navigation bar now indicates that you have 81 records in the datasheet as shown in FIGURE 3-1.

   In large datasheets, you may want to freeze certain fields so that they remain on the screen at all times.

QUICK TIP
To unfreeze a field, right-click any field name, then click Unfreeze All Fields on the shortcut menu.

4. **Right-click the** CompanyName field name **to select the entire column, click** Freeze Fields **on the shortcut menu, press** TAB **as needed to move to the** Applicants field **for the first record, then type** 15

   Notice that the CompanyName field is now positioned as the first field in the datasheet and doesn't scroll off the screen as you press TAB.

   In large datasheets, you may also want to hide fields.

QUICK TIP
To unhide a field, right-click any field name, click Unhide Fields on the shortcut menu, click the check box beside the field that you want to unhide, then click Close.

5. **Press** TAB **as needed to move to the** Description field, **right-click the** Description field name **to select the entire column, as shown in** FIGURE 3-2, **then click** Hide Fields **on the shortcut menu**

   Hiding a field in a query datasheet doesn't remove it from the query, it merely hides it on the datasheet.

6. **Right-click the** JobsByIndustry tab, **click** Save, **right-click the** JobsByIndustry tab, **then click** Close

   Saving your changes to this query saves the changes you made to freeze the CompanyName field and to hide the Description field. Edits to data are automatically saved as you work.

FIGURE 3-1: Editing data in Query Datasheet View

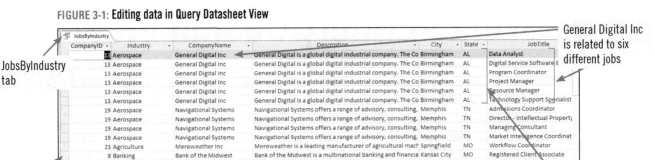

JobsByIndustry tab

Record selector button (previous record has been deleted)

81 records in the datasheet

General Digital Inc is related to six different jobs

Because of relationships, updating the State field for General Digital Inc updates every record in this datasheet related to General Digital Inc

FIGURE 3-2: Freezing and hiding columns in Query Datasheet View

Freeze the CompanyName field

Description field name

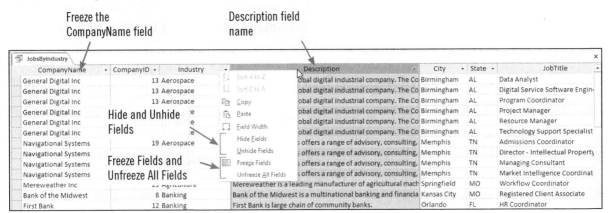

Hide and Unhide Fields

Freeze Fields and Unfreeze All Fields

Work in Query Design View

Learning
Outcomes
• Create a query
in Query Design
View
• Add, remove,
and move fields
in Query Design
View

You use **Query Design View** to modify an existing query or to create a new query. In the upper pane, Query Design View presents the fields you can use for that query in small windows called **field lists**. If you use the fields from two or more related tables in the query, the relationship between two tables is displayed with a **join line** (also called a **link line**) that identifies the fields that are used to establish the relationship. **CASE** *Lydia Snyder asks you to produce a list of jobs and salaries. You use Query Design View to modify the JobSalaries query to meet her request.*

STEPS

QUICK TIP
You can toggle the
Table row on and
off in the query grid
by clicking the Table
Names button on
the ribbon.

1. **Double-click the** JobSalaries query **in the Navigation Pane to open it in Datasheet View to review the data, then click the** View button **to switch to Query Design View**

   Query Design View displays table field lists in the upper pane of the window. The link line shows that one record in the Companies table is related to many records in the Jobs table. The lower pane of the window, called the **query design grid** (also called the **QBE**, **query by example grid**, or **query grid** for short), displays the field names, sort orders, and criteria used within the query. The JobSalaries query selects the Industry and CompanyName fields from the Companies table and three fields from the Jobs table. You want to add the StartingSalary field to the query, delete the CompanyID field, and move the CompanyName field.

QUICK TIP
You can also click
a field name in the
first row of the grid,
click the arrow, then
select a new field
from the list.

2. **Double-click the** StartingSalary field **in the Jobs field list to add it to the next available column of the query grid, click the** CompanyID field **in the query grid, click the** Delete Columns button **in the Query Setup group, click the** CompanyName field selector, **then use the arrow pointer ⬚ to drag the** CompanyName field **to the first column of the grid**

   Your screen should look like FIGURE 3-3. Removing a field from the query grid does not delete the field from its table. It simply removes the field from this query.

QUICK TIP
To add another table
to Query Design
View, drag it from
the Navigation Pane
to Query Design
View or click the
Show Table button
in the Query Setup
group.

3. **Click the** View button **to switch to Datasheet View, right-click the** JobSalaries tab, **click** Close, **then click** Yes **to save changes**

   You can also create a query from scratch using Query Design View.

4. **Click the** Create tab **on the ribbon, click the** Query Design button **in the Queries group, double-click** Jobs **in the Show Table dialog box, double-click** Companies, **then click** Close

   For this query, you want to include three fields. You can drag fields from the field lists to any column to position them in the query. Any existing fields will move to the right to accommodate the new field.

QUICK TIP
You can also add
a new column to
the grid by clicking
the Insert Columns
button in the Query
Setup group.

5. **Drag the** StartingSalary field **to the first column of the grid, drag the** JobTitle field **to the first column of the grid, then drag the** CompanyName field **to the first column of the grid**

   Your screen should look like FIGURE 3-4.

6. **Click the** Datasheet View button **to run the query**

   For a **select query**, a query that selects fields and records, you can **run** the query by clicking either the Datasheet View button or the Run button. In an **action query**, clicking the Run button starts a process that modifies all of the selected records. Because the Datasheet View button never changes data regardless of what type of query you are building, it is a safe way to run a select query or view selected fields and records for an action query. In later modules, you will learn about action queries that change data.

7. **Right-click the** Query1 tab, **click** Save, **type** CompanyJobs **as the new query name, then click** OK

FIGURE 3-3: Adding and removing fields in Query Design View

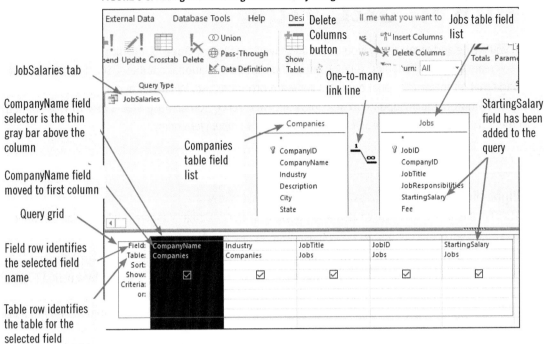

- JobSalaries tab
- CompanyName field selector is the thin gray bar above the column
- CompanyName field moved to first column
- Query grid
- Field row identifies the selected field name
- Table row identifies the table for the selected field
- Delete Columns button
- One-to-many link line
- Jobs table field list
- StartingSalary field has been added to the query
- Companies table field list

FIGURE 3-4: Creating a new query in Query Design View

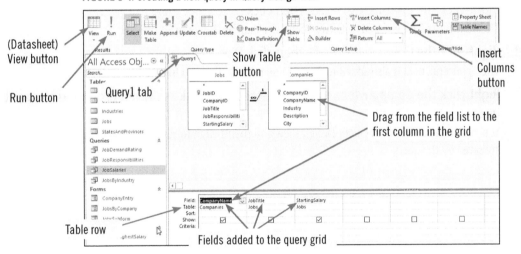

- (Datasheet) View button
- Run button
- Query1 tab
- Table row
- Show Table button
- Fields added to the query grid
- Insert Columns button
- Drag from the field list to the first column in the grid

Adding or deleting a table in Query Design View

You might want to add a table's field list to the upper pane of Query Design View to select fields from that table for the query. To add a new table to Query Design View, drag it from the Navigation Pane to Query Design View, or click the Show Table button in the Query Setup group on the Design tab. To delete an unneeded table from Query Design View, click its title bar, then press DELETE.

Linking tables in Query Design View

If tables are joined in the Relationships window, they are automatically joined in Query Design View. If tables are not joined in the Relationships window, you can join them in Query Design View by dragging the linking field from one field list to another. However, you cannot enforce referential integrity on a relationship created in Query Design View. Also, a relationship created in Query Design View is established for that query only. Creating one-to-many relationships for the database in the Relationships window provides tremendous productivity and application performance benefits over relating tables within individual queries.

Work in SQL View

Learning
Outcomes
• Modify a query in
  SQL View
• Learn common
  SQL keywords

When you create and save a query, you create and save **Structured Query Language (SQL)**, a language used to create and modify tables, relationships, and data in a relational database. SQL is a standardized language that all major relational database software programs use. Whatever actions you take in Query Design View automatically update in SQL View and vice versa. You can use **SQL View** to work directly with the SQL. **CASE** *You use SQL View to update the CompanyJobs query.*

STEPS

1. **Right-click the** CompanyJobs tab, **then click** SQL View

   The SQL statements that were created when working in Query Design View are displayed. You can directly enter SQL statements into this window to modify your query.

2. **Click to the right of Jobs.StartingSalary in the first line, then type** , Jobs.Applicants

   Your screen should look like FIGURE 3-5. Note that table and field names are separated by a period (.) and multiple fields are separated by a comma (,). Although SQL is not case sensitive, it is customary to write the SQL keywords in all capital letters and to start each statement with an SQL keyword in order to make the SQL easier to read.

   A select query starts with the SQL keyword **SELECT**. Some of the most common SQL keywords are shown in TABLE 3-1.

TROUBLE
If you receive an
error message,
make sure you have
used a comma
(,) to separate the
new field name and
spelled the table and
field name correctly.

3. **Right-click the** CompanyJobs tab, **then click** Datasheet View

   The Applicants field is added to Query Datasheet View as shown in FIGURE 3-6.

4. **Right-click the** CompanyJobs tab, **then click** Design View

   The Applicants field is also added to Query Design View as shown in FIGURE 3-7.

5. **Right-click the** CompanyJobs tab, **click** Close, **then click** Yes **when prompted to save the query**

   You can open any query in Query Design View and then switch to SQL View to see the SQL statements that are saved by the query.

FIGURE 3-5: Adding the Applicants field in SQL View

CompanyJobs
tab

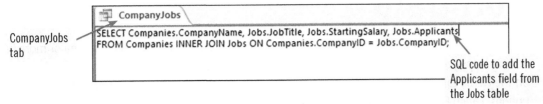

SELECT Companies.CompanyName, Jobs.JobTitle, Jobs.StartingSalary, Jobs.Applicants
FROM Companies INNER JOIN Jobs ON Companies.CompanyID = Jobs.CompanyID;

SQL code to add the
Applicants field from
the Jobs table

FIGURE 3-6: Viewing the Applicants field in Query Datasheet View

CompanyName	JobTitle	StartingSalai	Applicants
ABA Solutions	Project Manager	$65,000	31
Accent Group	Customer Service	$65,000	4
Accent Group	Operations Project Specialist	$69,000	25
Accent Group	Client Product Support Associate	$72,000	31
AIT Group	Microsoft PowerPoint specialist	$49,000	22
Addcore Partners	Program Manager	$72,000	16

Applicants field from
the Jobs table added to
the datasheet

FIGURE 3-7: Viewing the Applicants field in Query Design View

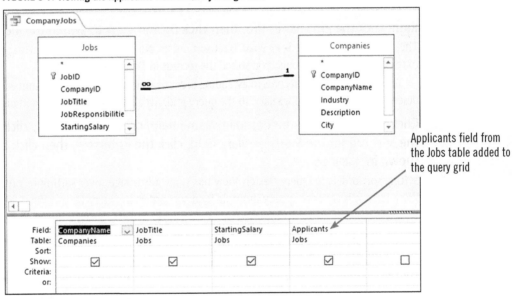

Applicants field from
the Jobs table added to
the query grid

TABLE 3-1: Common SQL keywords

keyword	identifies...
SELECT	which fields you want to include in a select query
FROM	what tables contain the fields you have selected
WHERE	criteria used to limit the number of records selected
ORDER BY ... ASC (DESC)	sort order for the records; **ASC** means ascending, **DESC** means descending
INNER JOIN ... ON	which records will be selected when choosing fields from more than one table (there must be a match in both tables)
INSERT	the data and fields used when adding a new record
UPDATE...SET	the data and fields used when updating specific records
DELETE	records to delete

Access

Creating Queries

Sort Data

Learning
Outcomes
• Sort records in
  Query Datasheet
  View
• Sort records in
  Query Design
  View

Sorting means to order records in ascending or descending order based on values in one or more fields. Sorting helps you organize records to quickly find and analyze data. TABLE 3-2 describes the Sort buttons on the Home tab. In Datasheet View, you can also click the list arrow beside a field name to access sort options. Query Design View helps you add and save sort orders and is especially useful when you want to sort on multiple fields. **CASE** *Lydia Snyder asks you to sort the JobSalaries query to more clearly show the records with a high starting salary.*

STEPS

QUICK TIP
Double-click the
column resize
pointer ++ to
widen a field to
display the widest
entry.

1. **Double-click the** JobSalaries query **in the Navigation Pane to open it in Datasheet View, click the** StartingSalary field, **click the** Descending button **in the Sort & Filter group, then use the column resize pointer ++ to widen the StartingSalary field as shown in** FIGURE 3-8

   The JobSalaries query now displays the records from highest StartingSalary to lowest, and the StartingSalary field displays a small descending sort indicator by the field name. Sort orders applied to Datasheet View, however, are not automatically added to Design View.

2. **Right-click the** JobSalaries tab, **then click** Design View **to switch to Query Design View**

   The query grid provides a **Sort row** to set sort orders. No sort orders are currently specified in the Sort row of the query grid even though you sorted the records in Datasheet View.

   You decide to sort the records in ascending order by CompanyName, and within each CompanyName, in descending order by StartingSalary. In the query grid, Access evaluates multiple sort orders from left to right.

3. **Click the** Sort cell for the CompanyName field, **click the** list arrow, **click** Ascending, **click the** Sort cell for the StartingSalary field, **click the** list arrow, **then click** Descending **as shown in** FIGURE 3-9

   Setting sort orders in Query Design View has some advantages over sorting records in Query Datasheet View. First, it is easier to specify multiple field sort orders in Query Design View. Sort orders set in Query Design View are also clearly displayed in the query grid and are reflected in SQL View.

4. **Right-click the** JobSalaries tab, **then click** Datasheet View **to view the resorted records as shown in** FIGURE 3-10

   The first, or primary, sort order is ascending by CompanyName. When two or more records have the same CompanyName value, the records are further sorted in descending order based on the StartingSalary field.

5. **Right-click the** JobSalaries tab, **click** Close, **then click** Yes **when prompted to save changes**

   Sort orders set in Query Design View are always saved with the query.

FIGURE 3-8: Sorting in Query Datasheet View

Ascending button   Descending button

Remove Sort button

JobSalaries tab

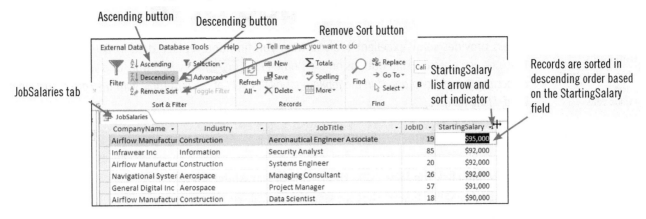

Records are sorted in descending order based on the StartingSalary field

StartingSalary list arrow and sort indicator

FIGURE 3-9: Sorting by multiple fields in Query Design View

Sort row

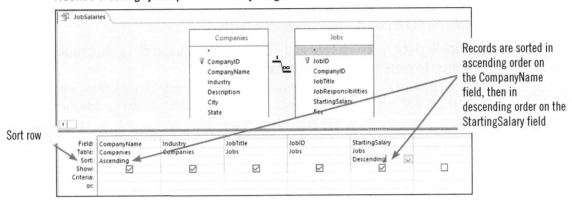

Records are sorted in ascending order on the CompanyName field, then in descending order on the StartingSalary field

FIGURE 3-10: Final JobSalaries datasheet

Records are first sorted in ascending order based on the CompanyName field

Records with the same CompanyName are further sorted in descending order on the StartingSalary field

Access

TABLE 3-2: Datasheet View Sort buttons

name	button	purpose
Ascending	⬆️	Sorts records based on the selected field in ascending order (0 to 9, A to Z)
Descending	⬇️	Sorts records based on the selected field in descending order (Z to A, 9 to 0)
Remove Sort		Removes the current sort order

Find and Replace Data

Access provides some excellent tools to help you find and replace data in Query Datasheet View. TABLE 3-3 describes the Find buttons on the Home tab. **CASE** ▶ *Lydia Snyder asks you to find and replace all occurrences of "longrange" in the JobResponsibilities field of the Jobs table with the correct spelling of the word, "long-range".*

STEPS

1. **Double-click the** Jobs table **to open it in Datasheet View**

   The sort and find features work the same way in Table and Query Datasheet View.

2. **Click** any value in the JobResponsibilities field, **click the** Replace button **in the Find group, type** longrange **in the Find What box, click in the** Replace With box, **type** long-range, **click the** Match button, **then click** Any Part of Field

   The Find and Replace dialog box is shown in FIGURE 3-11.

3. **Click** Replace All **in the Find and Replace dialog box, click** Yes **to continue, then click** Cancel **to close the Find and Replace dialog box**

   Access replaced all occurrences of "longrange" with "long-range" in the JobResponsibilities field, as shown in FIGURE 3-12. Note that you cannot undo *all* of the changes made by the find and replace feature, but if you click the Undo button ↶ on the Quick Access toolbar, you can undo the last replacement.

4. **Double-click** overall **in the JobResponsibilities field of the JobID 4 record, press** DELETE, **press** ENTER, **then click the** Undo button ↶ **on the Quick Access toolbar**

   You can reverse single edits to data using the Undo button ↶. After you click it once, the Undo button ↶ is dim, indicating it is no longer available. When working in Datasheet View, you can undo only the *most recent* edit. Use the Find feature to find and review all of the replacements that were made with the find and replace process.

5. **Click** any value in the JobResponsibilities field, **click the** Find button **in the Find group, type** long-range **in the Find What box, click** Find Next, **click** Find Next **two more times to find the three occurrences of "long-range," then click** Cancel **to close the Find and Replace dialog box**

   If you wanted to search the entire datasheet versus the current field, you could use the Look In option, which allows you to check values in every field in the entire datasheet.

6. **Right-click the** Jobs tab, **click** Close, **then click** Yes **if prompted to save changes**

   All updates to data made in Query Datasheet View are automatically updated in all objects.

FIGURE 3-11: Find and Replace dialog box

FIGURE 3-11: **Find and Replace dialog box**

Find What box

Replace With box

Look In Current Field

Match Any Part of Field

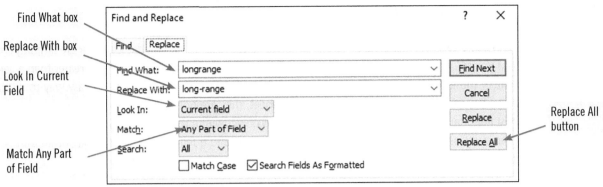

Replace All button

FIGURE 3-12: **Jobs table in Datasheet View**

Jobs tab

Find button

Replace button

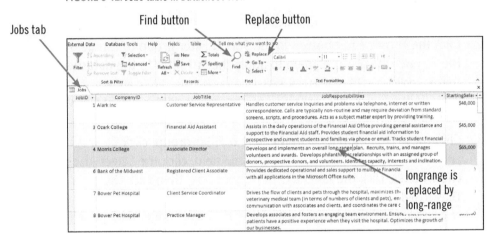

longrange is replaced by long-range

TABLE 3-3: **Find buttons**

Find		Opens the Find and Replace dialog box to find data
Replace		Opens the Find and Replace dialog box to find and replace data
Go To		Helps you navigate to the first, previous, next, last, or new record
Select		Helps you select a single record or all records in a datasheet

Access

Filter Data

**Learning
Outcomes**
• Apply and clear
  filters
• Use Filter by
  Selection and Filter
  by Form

Filtering a datasheet *temporarily* displays records that match given criteria. **Criteria** are limiting conditions you set. For example, you might want to show only jobs with a starting salary greater than a certain value or those companies in a particular state. Although filters provide a quick and easy way to display a temporary subset of records in the current datasheet, they are not as powerful or flexible as queries. The most important difference is that a query is a saved object within the database, whereas a filter is removed when you close the datasheet. TABLE 3-4 compares filters and queries. **CASE** ▶ *Lydia Snyder asks several questions about the JobsByIndustry query. You will use filters to answer these questions.*

STEPS

QUICK TIP
Filters work the same
way in Table and
Query Datasheet
Views.

1. **Double-click the** JobsByIndustry query **to open it, click any occurrence of** Energy **in the** Industry field, **click the** Selection button **in the Sort & Filter group, then click** Equals "Energy"

   Nine records from two companies are selected, as shown in FIGURE 3-13. A filter icon appears to the right of the Industry field name. Filtering by the selected field value, called **Filter By Selection**, is a fast and easy way to filter records for an exact match.

QUICK TIP
The Filtered button
to the right of the
navigation buttons
also toggles the
filter.

2. **Click the** Toggle Filter button **in the Sort & Filter group to toggle off the filter, then click the** Toggle Filter button **again to apply the last filter to the datasheet**

   You can apply a new filter in several ways. One way is to use the list arrow to the right of each field name to filter data. Before applying a new filter, however, you should clear the last filter to make sure you are working with all of the records in the datasheet.

3. **Click the** Advanced button **in the Sort & Filter group, click** Clear All Filters, **click the list arrow to the right of the CompanyName field, click the** Select All check box **to clear all check boxes, click the** Accent Group check box, **then click** OK

   Three records match the criteria of *Accent Group* for the CompanyName field. To filter for multiple criteria or comparative data, you might use the **Filter By Form** feature, which provides maximum flexibility for specifying criteria. Filter buttons and features are summarized in TABLE 3-5.

4. **Click the** Advanced button **in the Sort & Filter group, click** Clear All Filters, **click the** Advanced button **again, then click** Filter By Form

   After clearing all filters, the Filtered/Unfiltered button to the right of the navigation buttons at the bottom of the datasheet displays "No Filter" to indicate that all previous filters have been cleared. The Filter by Form window opens.

QUICK TIP
You can clear the
Filter by Form grid
by clicking the
Advanced button,
then clicking Clear
Grid.

5. **Scroll to the right, click the** StartingSalary cell, **type** >=50000, **click the** Applicants cell, **then type** <=10 **as shown in** FIGURE 3-14

   If more than one criterion is entered, a record must satisfy the requirements for each criterion to be selected.

6. **Click the** Toggle Filter button **in the Sort & Filter group**

   The datasheet selects 14 records that match both of the filter criteria, as shown in FIGURE 3-15. Note that filter icons appear next to the StartingSalary and Applicants field names.

7. **Right-click the** JobsByIndustry tab, **click** Close, **then click** Yes **if prompted**

   Filters are *temporary* views of the data. Filters are *not* saved with a table or query datasheet after you close the datasheet even if you save the datasheet. If you want to save criteria, create a query.

FIGURE 3-13: Filtering the JobsByIndustry query

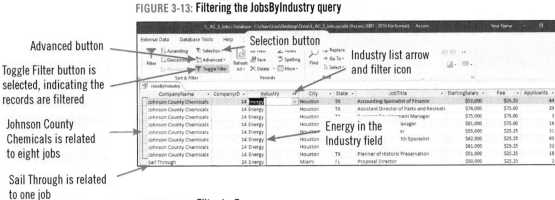

Advanced button

Toggle Filter button is selected, indicating the records are filtered

Selection button

Industry list arrow and filter icon

Johnson County Chemicals is related to eight jobs

Energy in the Industry field

Sail Through is related to one job

FIGURE 3-14: Filter by Form

JobsByIndustry: Filter by Form						
CompanyName	City	State	JobTitle	StartingSalary	Fee	Applicants
				>=50000		<=10

StartingSalary values must be greater than or equal to 50000

Applicants values must be less than or equal to 10

FIGURE 3-15: Filtering by form with two fields

Filter icons

JobsByIndustry								
CompanyName	CompanyID	Industry	City	State	JobTitle	StartingSalary	Fee	Applicants
General Digital Inc	13	Aerospace	Birmingham	AL	Resource Manager	$75,000	$75.00	3
Airflow Manufacturing	17	Construction	Wichita	KS	Aeronautical Engineer Associate	$95,000	$100.00	5
Airflow Manufacturing	17	Construction	Wichita	KS	Data Scientist	$90,000	$100.00	4
Morris College	26	Education	Little Rock	AR	Associate Director	$65,000	$25.25	3
Johnson County Chemicals	14	Energy	Houston	TX	Business Development Manager	$75,000	$75.00	3
Sail Through	24	Energy	Miami	FL	Proposal Director	$50,000	$25.25	2
Regex Corp	21	Healthcare	Albany	NY	Technology Quality Specialist	$69,000	$25.25	8
CellFirst Inc	28	Information	Madison	WI	Proposal Writer	$71,000	$75.00	10
Infrawear Inc	20	Information	Minneapolis	MN	Security Analyst	$92,000	$100.00	10
Core Systems	9	Manufacturing	Oklahoma City	OK	Computer Support Specialist	$51,000	$25.25	9
Military Grade Steel	18	Manufacturing	Las Vegas	NV	Information Technology Specialist	$65,000	$25.25	3
Denman LLC	11	Technical Consulting	Des Moines	IA	Channel Sales Manager	$79,000	$75.00	10
Accent Group	2	Transportation	Charleston	SC	Customer Service	$65,000	$25.25	4
Artwell Corp	6	Transportation	Chicago	IL	PR Manager	$87,000	$75.00	6
*	(New)							

StartingSalary is greater than or equal to 50000

Applicants are less than or equal to 10

TABLE 3-4: Filters vs. queries

characteristic	filters	queries
Are saved as an object in the database		•
Can be used to select a subset of records in a datasheet	•	•
Can be used to select a subset of fields in a datasheet		•
Resulting datasheet used to enter and edit data	•	•
Resulting datasheet used to sort, filter, and find records	•	•
Commonly used as the source of data for a form or report		•
Can calculate sums, averages, counts, and other types of summary statistics across records		•
Can be used to create calculated fields		•

TABLE 3-5: Filter buttons

name	button	purpose
Filter	▼	Provides a list of values in the selected field that can be used to customize a filter
Selection	▼	Filters records that equal, do not equal, or are otherwise compared with the current value
Advanced	▼	Provides advanced filter features such as Filter By Form, Save As Query, and Clear All Filters
Toggle Filter	▼	Applies or removes the current filter

Access

Enter and Save Criteria

Query Design View allows you to select fields, add sort orders, or add criteria to limit the number of records selected for the resulting datasheet. **Criteria** are tests, or limiting conditions, for which the record must be true to be selected for the query datasheet. Fields, sort orders, and criteria are all saved with the query object. This means that once you create and save a query, you can easily analyze the selected data later by double-clicking the query to open it. **CASE** ▸ *Lydia Snyder asks some questions about the data that you suspect will be reviewed on a regular basis. You create queries for these questions in order to save the criteria.*

STEPS

1. **Click the Create tab on the ribbon, click the Query Design button, double-click Companies, double-click Jobs, then click Close in the Show Table dialog box**

   This query will select one field from the Companies table and three from the Jobs table.

2. **Double-click CompanyName in the Companies field list, then in the Jobs field list double-click JobTitle, Fee, and FirstPosted**

   Criteria are limiting conditions you set in the query design grid.

3. **Click the Criteria cell for the CompanyName field, type Artwell Corp, then click any other location in the query grid as shown in FIGURE 3-16**

   Access assists you with **criteria syntax**, rules that specify how to enter criteria. Criteria for fields with a Short Text data type are surrounded by "quotation marks" though you do not need to type them. Access automatically adds the quotation marks for you.

4. **Click the View button ▦ in the Results group to switch to Datasheet View**

   Eight records match the criterion of Artwell Corp in the CompanyName field.

5. **Click the View button ⊠ to switch to Design View, delete the "Artwell Corp" criterion in the CompanyName field, click the Fee Criteria cell, type 75, then click the View button ▦**

   Criteria in Number, Currency, and Yes/No fields are not surrounded by any characters. Thirty records are selected where the Fee field equals 75.

6. **Click the View button ⊠, delete the 75 criterion in the Fee field, click the FirstPosted Criteria cell, type 1/4/21, then click in any other location in the query grid as shown in FIGURE 3-17**

   Criteria for fields with a Date/Time data type are surrounded by #pound signs# though you do not need to type them. The pound sign symbol (#) is also known as the number sign, hashtag, and octothorpe.

7. **Click the View button ▦**

   Seven records are selected where the FirstPosted field equals 1/4/21.

8. **Right-click the Query1 tab, click Save, type FirstPostedJan4, click OK, right-click the FirstPostedJan4 tab, then click Close**

   The query is saved with the new name, FirstPostedJan4, as a new query object in the database. Criteria entered in Query Design View are saved with the query.

FIGURE 3-16: **Entering text criteria**

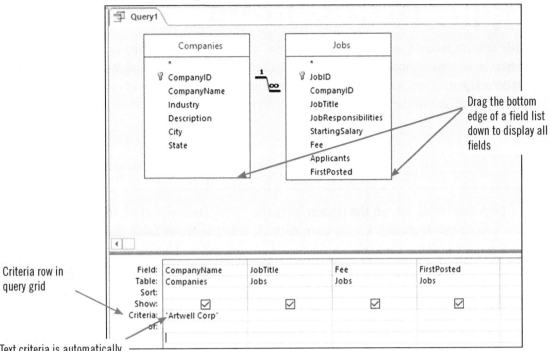

Criteria row in query grid

Text criteria is automatically surrounded by "quotation marks"

FIGURE 3-17: **Entering date criteria**

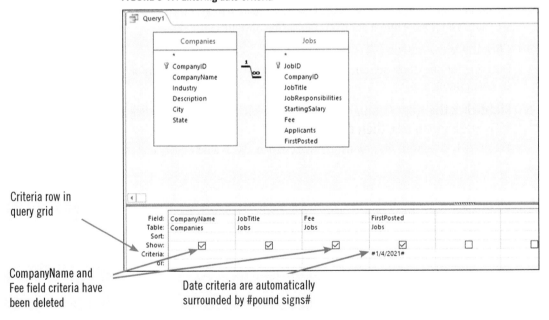

Criteria row in query grid

CompanyName and Fee field criteria have been deleted

Date criteria are automatically surrounded by #pound signs#

Apply AND Criteria

**Learning
Outcomes**
• Enter AND criteria
  in a query
• Use comparison
  operators

AND criteria means that *all* criteria must be true for a record to be selected in a query. To create AND criteria, enter two or more criteria on the *same* Criteria row of the query design grid. **CASE** ▶ *Lydia Snyder asks you a question about the data that meets multiple conditions. You will use Query Design View with AND criteria to give her the answer.*

STEPS

1. **Click the** Create tab **on the ribbon, click the** Query Design button, **double-click** Companies, **double-click** Jobs, **then click** Close **in the Show Table dialog box**

   This query will select two fields from the Companies table and two from the Jobs table.

QUICK TIP
Drag the bottom
edge of a field list to
resize it to display all
fields.

2. **Double-click** CompanyName **and** State **in the Companies field list, then double-click** JobTitle **and** StartingSalary **in the Jobs field list**

   Enter AND criteria, where each criterion must be true for the record to be selected, on the *same* row. For every new criterion on the same row, you potentially *reduce* the number of records that are selected because the record must be true for *each* criterion.

3. **Click the** Criteria cell for the State field, **type** MO, **click in the** Criteria cell for the StartingSalary field, **type** <50000, **then click in any other location in the query grid as shown in** FIGURE 3-18

   The less than symbol (<) is a **comparison operator** that compares the criterion to the values in the StartingSalary field. In this case, it selects all records with a StartingSalary less than 50,000. If no comparison operator was entered, Access would assume an equal sign (=) and select those records equal to 50,000. See TABLE 3-6 for more information on comparison operators.

TROUBLE
If your datasheet
doesn't match
FIGURE 3-19,
return to Query
Design View and
compare your
criteria with that of
FIGURE 3-18.

4. **Click the** View button 🗔

   Querying for only those jobs in the state of Missouri (state abbreviation of MO) selects two records as shown in FIGURE 3-19.

5. **Right-click the** Query1 tab, **click** Save, **type** MOLessThan50K, **click** OK, **right-click the** MOLessThan50K tab, **then click** Close

   The query is saved with the new name, MOLessThan50K, as a new query object in the database.

FIGURE 3-18: Query Design View with AND criteria

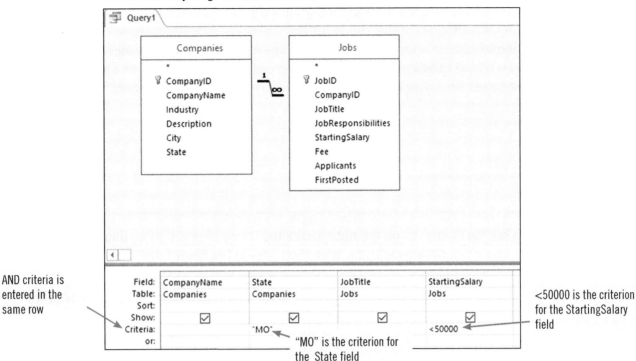

AND criteria is entered in the same row

"MO" is the criterion for the State field

<50000 is the criterion for the StartingSalary field

FIGURE 3-19: Final datasheet of MOLessThan50K query

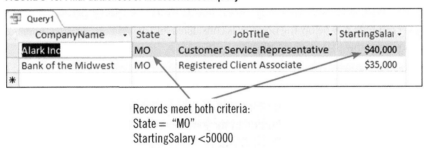

Records meet both criteria:
State = "MO"
StartingSalary <50000

TABLE 3-6: Comparison operators

operator	description	expression	meaning
>	Greater than	>500	Numbers greater than 500
>=	Greater than or equal to	>=500	Numbers greater than or equal to 500
<	Less than	<"Elder"	Names from A to Elder, but not Elder
<=	Less than or equal to	<="Langguth"	Names from A through Langguth, inclusive
<>	Not equal to	<>"Fontanelle"	Any name except for Fontanelle
=	Equal to	="Eagan" =500	Equal to Eagan Equal to 500. Note that the equal sign is assumed when no other comparison operator is used.

Searching for blank fields

Is Null and Is Not Null are two other types of common criteria. The **Is Null** criterion finds all records where no entry has been made in the field. **Is Not Null** finds all records where there is any entry in the field, even if the entry is 0. Primary key fields cannot have a null entry.

Access

Apply OR Criteria

Learning
Outcomes
• Enter OR criteria in
a query
• Enter criteria with
a wildcard
• Enter both AND
and OR criteria in
a query

You use **OR criteria** when *any one row* must be true in order for the record to be selected. Enter OR criteria on *different* Criteria rows of the query design grid. **CASE** *Lydia Snyder asks you more questions about the jobs. You will use Query Design View with OR criteria to give her the answers.*

STEPS

1. **Click the Create tab on the ribbon, click the Query Design button, double-click Companies, double-click Jobs, then click Close in the Show Table dialog box**

   Again select two fields from the Companies table and two from the Jobs table.

2. **Double-click CompanyName and State in the Companies field list, then double-click JobTitle and StartingSalary in the Jobs field list**

   Enter OR criteria on *different* rows. Access selects a record if it matches the criteria for *any row* that contains criteria. Therefore, for every new row of criteria, you potentially *increase* the number of records that are selected.

QUICK TIP
The query grid
provides eight
criteria rows by
default, but you can
add more by clicking
the Insert Rows
button in the Query
Setup group on the
Design tab.

3. **Click the Criteria cell for the State field, type MO, click the or Criteria cell for the State field, type TX, then click any other location in the query grid as shown in** FIGURE 3-20

   Every Criteria row below the first row is considered an "or" row. Access selects records that match the criterion in *any* row that contains criteria.

4. **Click the View button**

   Fourteen records meet the State criteria of MO or TX. In addition, you want to select only those records with the word "Manager" in the JobTitle field. You use asterisk characters (*) to help select records that have the word "Manager" in any position in the JobTitle field value.

5. **Click the View button, click the Criteria cell for the JobTitle field, type *Manager*, then click**

   Twelve records meet the State criteria of MO with the word "Manager" in the JobTitle field or the State criteria of TX. But *all* TX records are still selected.

6. **Click , click the second Criteria cell for the JobTitle field, type *Manager*, then click any other location in the query grid as shown in** FIGURE 3-21

   Access adds the **Like** keyword to criteria that contain the asterisk (*) wildcard character.

7. **Click to switch to Datasheet View**

   Three records meet the State criteria of MO or the State criteria of TX with the word "Manager" in the JobTitle field, as shown in FIGURE 3-22.

8. **Right-click the Query1 tab, click Save, type MOTXManager, click OK, right-click the MOTXManager tab, then click Close**

   You can also use **AND OR** SQL keywords in your criteria. But a simpler approach is to remember these rules: Criteria on a *single row must all be true* for a record to be selected. Criteria on *different rows constitute separate tests* that the record may satisfy in order to be selected.

FIGURE 3-20: **Query Design View with OR criteria**

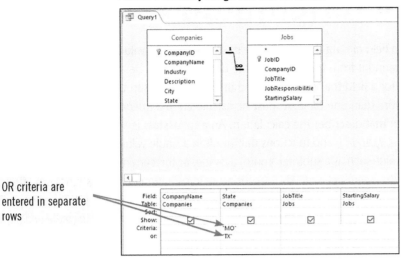

OR criteria are entered in separate rows

FIGURE 3-21: **Query Design View with AND and OR criteria**

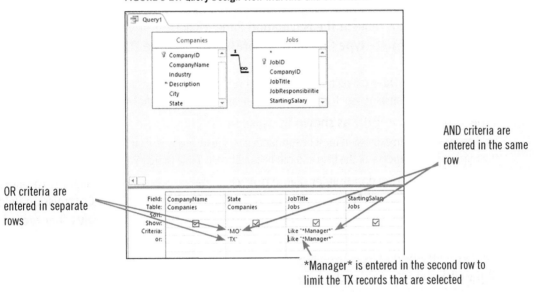

AND criteria are entered in the same row

OR criteria are entered in separate rows

Manager is entered in the second row to limit the TX records that are selected

FIGURE 3-22: **Final datasheet of MOTXManager query**

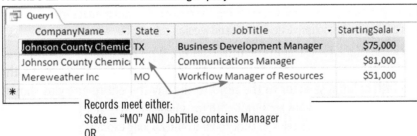

CompanyName	State	JobTitle	StartingSalar
Johnson County Chemic	TX	Business Development Manager	$75,000
Johnson County Chemic	TX	Communications Manager	$81,000
Mereweather Inc	MO	Workflow Manager of Resources	$51,000

Records meet either:
State = "MO" AND JobTitle contains Manager
OR
State = "TX" AND JobTitle contains Manager

Using wildcard characters

To search for a pattern, you can use a wildcard character to represent any character in the condition entry. Use a question mark (?) to search for any single character and an asterisk (*) to search for any number of characters. Access uses the **Like** keyword when your criterion contains wildcard characters. For example, the criterion Like "12/*/21" finds all dates in December of 2021, and the criterion Like "F*" finds all values that start with the letter F.

Create a Calculated Field

A **calculated field** is a field of data that can be created based on the values of other fields. By calculating the data versus entering it from the keyboard, the data will always be accurate. Access provides the **Calculated** data type for a field that can be defined using other fields in the *same* table. If the calculation uses fields from more than one table, it must be calculated in a query. To create a calculated field, you enter an expression that describes the calculation. An **expression** is a combination of field names, **operators** (such as +, –, /, and *), and functions that result in a single value. A **function** is a predefined formula that returns a value such as a subtotal, count, average, or the current date. See TABLE 3-7 for more information on arithmetic operators and TABLE 3-8 for more information on Access functions. **CASE** Lydia Snyder asks you to calculate a job placement commission for each position that JCL Talent helps fill. You will create a Calculated field in the Jobs table to satisfy this request. Lydia also asks you to create an internal job rating calculation based on the job's starting salary and an industry demand index. Given that data is stored in two different tables, you will create a calculated field in a query for this answer.

STEPS

1. **Right-click the** Jobs table **in the Navigation Pane, click** Design View, **click the** Field Name **cell below FirstPosted, type** Commission, **press TAB, click the** Data Type **list arrow, then click** Calculated

   The **Expression Builder** dialog box opens to help you build expressions by providing information about built-in functions, constants (such as True and False), and operators in the bottom half of the window.

2. **Type [StartingSalary]*0.1 as shown in** FIGURE 3-23

   Field names used in an expression must be surrounded by square brackets. [StartingSalary]*0.1 is now entered in the **Expression property** of the field and can be modified in Table Design View.

3. **Click** OK **in the Expression Builder dialog box, click the** View button 📊, **click** Yes **to save the table, press TAB enough times to view both the StartingSalary and new Commission fields, change the StartingSalary value for the first record to** 47000, **then click any other record**

   The Commission value for the first record correctly updates to 4700 as shown in FIGURE 3-24. The second calculation involves data from multiple tables, so you will use a query.

4. **Right-click the** Jobs tab, **click** Close, **right-click the** JobDemandRating query, **then click** Design View

   The Job Index calculation is defined as the starting salary divided by 1000 times the job demand index, which is a value from 1 to 5 that estimates the relative strength of that industry. To create a calculated field, you enter a new descriptive field name and a colon followed by an expression.

5. **Click the** blank Field cell **in the fifth column, type** JobIndex: [StartingSalary] /1000*[JobDemandIndex], **then drag the column resize pointer** ↔ **on the right edge of the fifth column selector to the right to display the entire entry as shown in** FIGURE 3-25

   Field names in expressions are surrounded by [square brackets] not {curly braces} and not (parentheses). You can also right-click a cell and click Zoom to enter a long expression.

6. **Click the** View button 📊, **edit the JobDemandIndex value for any record with the Industry value of Personnel Services from 3 to 4, then click any other record**

   The JobIndex value for all jobs within the industry of Personnel Services automatically recalculated when you changed the JobDemandIndex value used in the expression for that calculated field.

7. **Click the** Save button 💾 **on the Quick Access toolbar, right-click the** JobDemandRating tab, **then click** Close

   Some database experts encourage you to create all calculations using queries because the Calculated field data type doesn't convert well to other relational database systems.

FIGURE 3-23: Creating a Calculated field in Table Design View

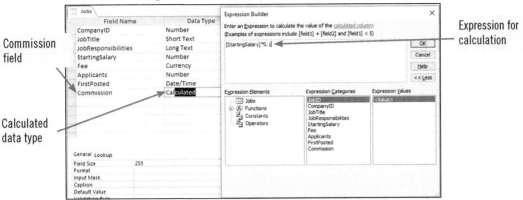

FIGURE 3-24: Calculated field in Table Datasheet View

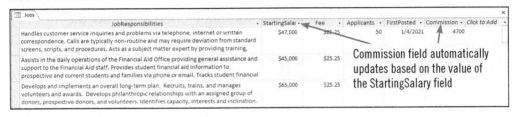

FIGURE 3-25: Creating a calculated field in Query Design View

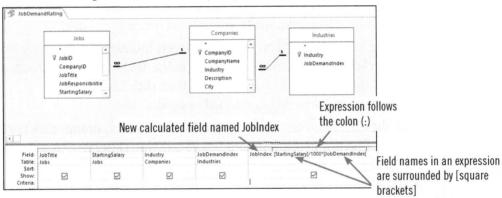

TABLE 3-7: Arithmetic operators

operator	description
+	Addition
–	Subtraction
*	Multiplication
/	Division
^	Exponentiation

TABLE 3-8: Common functions

function	sample expression and description
DATE	DATE()-[BirthDate] Calculates the number of days between today and the date in the BirthDate field; Access expressions are not case sensitive, so DATE()-[BirthDate] is equivalent to date()-[birthdate] and DATE()-[BIRTHDATE]; therefore, use capitalization in expressions in any way that makes the expression easier to read
PMT	PMT([Rate],[Term],[Loan]) Calculates the monthly payment on a loan where the Rate field contains the monthly interest rate, the Term field contains the number of monthly payments, and the Loan field contains the total amount financed
LEFT	LEFT([LastName],2) Returns the first two characters of the entry in the LastName field
RIGHT	RIGHT([PartNo],3) Returns the last three characters of the entry in the PartNo field
LEN	LEN([Description]) Returns the number of characters in the Description field

Access

Format a Datasheet

Learning Outcomes
- Change page orientation
- Change margins
- Format a datasheet

In a datasheet, you can apply basic formatting modifications such as changing the font size, font face, colors, and gridlines. Formatting in a datasheet applies to every record and works the same way in Table and Query Datasheet Views. See TABLE 3-9 for common formatting commands. **CASE** *Lydia Snyder asks you to prepare a printout of the companies list. You format the Companies table datasheet for her.*

STEPS

1. **Double-click the Companies table to open it in Datasheet View**
   Before applying new formatting enhancements, preview the default printout.

2. **Click the File tab, click Print, click Print Preview, then click the Next Page button ▶ in the navigation bar five times to move to the last page of the printout**
   Currently, the printout is six pages, but you can reduce that number by changing the page orientation and margin.

3. **Click the Landscape button in the Page Layout group on the Print Preview tab to switch the report to landscape orientation, click the Margins button in the Page Size group, click Narrow, then click the Previous Page button ◀ twice to display the first page**
   The datasheet is now only three pages. You return to Datasheet View where you can make font face, font size, font color, gridline color, and background color choices.

4. **Click the Save button 🖫 on the Quick Access toolbar, click the Close Print Preview button, click the Font arrow Calibri (Body) ▼ in the Text Formatting group, click Arial Narrow, click the Font Size arrow 11 ▼, then click 12**
   You also decide to change the font color and background color.

5. **Click the Font Color arrow 🗛 ▼ in the Text Formatting group, click Dark Blue (fourth column, first row in the Standard Colors palette), click the Alternate Row Color arrow 🖽 ▼ in the Text Formatting group, then click White (first column, first row in the Standard Colors palette)**

6. **Click the File tab, click Print, click Print Preview, then click the preview to zoom in and out**
   Your Companies datasheet should look like FIGURE 3-26. The preview is three pages, and in landscape orientation, it is easier to read.

7. **sam ⬆ Right-click the Companies tab, click Close, click Yes when prompted to save changes, then click the Close button ⊠ on the title bar to close the database and Access 2019**

FIGURE 3-26: Formatted Companies datasheet

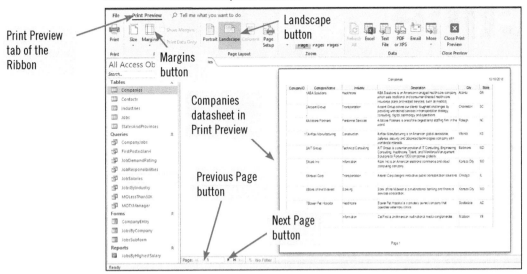

Print Preview tab of the Ribbon

Landscape button

Margins button

Companies datasheet in Print Preview

Previous Page button

Next Page button

TABLE 3-9: Useful formatting commands

button	button name	description
Calibri (Body)	Font	Changes the font face of the data
11	Font Size	Changes the font size of the data
B	Bold	Toggles bold on or off
I	Italic	Toggles italic on or off
U	Underline	Toggles underline on or off
A	Font Color	Changes the font color of the data
(icon)	Background Color	Changes the background color
(icon)	Align Left	Left-aligns the data
(icon)	Center	Centers the data
(icon)	Align Right	Right-aligns the data
(icon)	Alternate Row Color	Changes the background color of alternate records
(icon)	Gridlines	Changes the gridlines

Access

Practice

Concepts Review

Label each element of the Access window shown in FIGURE 3-27.

FIGURE 3-27

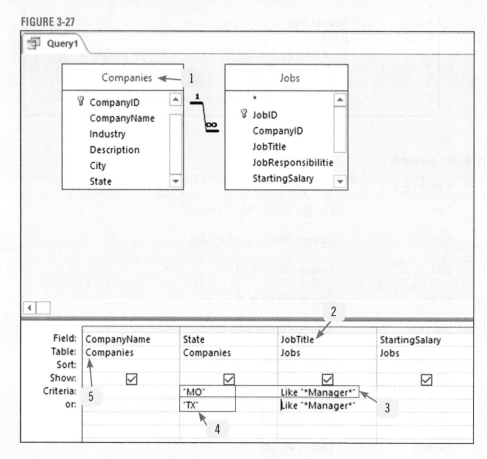

Match each term with the statement that best describes it.

6. Query grid   a. A fast and easy way to filter the records for an exact match
7. Field selector   b. Limiting conditions used to restrict the number of records that are selected in a query
8. Filter   c. The thin gray bar above each field in the query grid
9. Filter By Selection   d. Creates a temporary subset of records
10. Field lists   e. Small windows that display field names
11. Sorting   f. Rules that determine how criteria are entered
12. Join line   g. Used to search for a pattern of characters
13. Criteria   h. The lower pane in Query Design View
14. Syntax   i. Identifies which fields are used to establish a relationship between two tables
15. Wildcard   j. Putting records in ascending or descending order based on the values of a field

Select the best answer from the list of choices.

16. AND criteria:

   a. Determine sort orders.

   b. Help set link lines between tables in a query.

   c. Must all be true for the record to be selected.

   d. Determine fields selected for a query.

17. SQL stands for which of the following?

   a. Simple Query Listing

   b. Structured Query Language

   c. Standard Query Language

   d. Special Query Listing

18. Which of the following is *not* true about a calculated field?

   a. You can create some calculated fields in a table.

   b. You can create all calculated fields in a query.

   c. Some database experts encourage all calculated fields be created in a query.

   d. Once the expression for a calculated field is created, it cannot be changed.

19. Which of the following describes OR criteria?

   a. Use two or more rows of the query grid to select only those records that meet given criteria.

   b. Select a subset of fields and/or records to view as a datasheet from one or more tables.

   c. Reorganize the records in either ascending or descending order based on the contents of one or more fields.

   d. Use multiple fields in the query design grid.

20. Which of the following is *not* true about a query?

   a. A query can select fields from one or more tables in a relational database.

   b. A query is the same thing as a filter.

   c. A query can be used to enter and edit data.

   d. An existing query can be modified in Query Design View.

Skills Review

1. Work in Query Datasheet View.

   a. Open the IL_AC_3-2.accdb database from the location where you store your Data Files and save it as **IL_AC_3_SupportDesk**. Click Enable Content if a yellow Security Warning message appears.

   b. Open the CaseDetails query in Datasheet View and change Cabrera to **Douglas** in the LastName field of either the first or second record.

   c. Delete the third record (EmployeeID 6, Tony Roth).

   d. Hide the Dependents field.

   e. Freeze the first three fields: EmployeeID, FirstName, and LastName in their current positions in the datasheet. (*Hint*: Select all three fields by dragging through their field names before selecting the Freeze Fields option.)

   f. Save and close the CaseDetails query.

2. Work in Query Design View.

   a. Create a new query in Query Design View. Add the Cases and Calls tables.

   b. Select the CaseTitle and Category fields from the Cases table. Select the CallDateTime and CallNotes from the Calls table.

   c. Save the query with the name **CallListing**, then view it in Datasheet View to observe that one case may have many calls over a period of several dates in the CallDateTime field.

3. Work in SQL View.

a. Open the CallListing query in SQL View.

b. Add the CallMinutes field to the query after the CallNotes field.

c. Save the query then view it in Datasheet View to make sure your SQL statement was entered correctly. Save and close the CallListing query.

4. Sort data.

a. Open the EmployeeCalls query in Datasheet View, sort the records in ascending order by the LastName field, then save and close the query.

b. Open the EmployeesByDepartment query in Design View, then add an ascending sort order to the Department, LastName, and FirstName fields.

c. Save the EmployeesByDepartment query, then view it in Datasheet View.

d. Be prepared to discuss this question in class on in a discussion thread: Were all three sort fields used to determine the order of the records? If so, where?

e. Close the EmployeesByDepartment query.

5. Find and replace data.

a. In Datasheet View of the Cases table, click any value in the Category field, then search for all occurrences of "Office" and replace it with **Microsoft Office** using the Whole Field match.

b. Click the Undo button on the Quick Access toolbar and note that you can undo your last replacement, but not all replacements.

c. Edit the Category entry in the last record (CaseID 23) to be **Microsoft Office** versus Office.

d. Save and close the Cases table datasheet.

6. Filter data.

a. Open the CaseDetails query and filter for all records where the Department is **Accounting** and the CallMinutes is **greater than or equal to 30**. Your datasheet should show five records that meet this criteria.

b. There are several ways to apply a filter, including the filter buttons in the Sort & Filter group of the ribbon, the Filter by Form feature, and the options listed in the sort and filter menu when you click the list arrow to the right of the field name in the datasheet. In class or in a discussion group, be prepared to explain which technique you chose to apply the filter.

c. Save and close the CaseDetails query. Reopen it to see that all records are shown. In class or in a discussion group be prepared to explain why the filter criteria was not reapplied to the query.

7. Enter and save criteria.

a. Create a query in Query Design View with the Cases and Employees tables.

b. Add the following fields, in this order: CaseID and Category from the Cases table, LastName and FirstName from the Employees table.

c. Add criteria to select only those records with **Internet** in the Category field.

d. Save the query with the name **InternetCases**, display it in Datasheet View to make sure you have selected the correct records, and then close the InternetCases query.

8. Apply AND criteria.

a. Right-click the InternetCases query, copy it, and then paste it as **InternetAccountingCases**.

b. Add the Department field to the InternetAccountingCases query, then add criteria to select all of the records **Internet** in the Category field and **Accounting** in the Department field.

c. Display the results in Datasheet View as shown in **FIGURE 3-28**, then save and close the query.

FIGURE 3-28

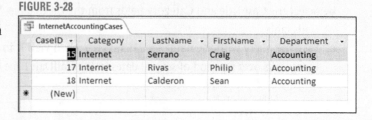

Skills Review (continued)

9. Apply OR criteria.

a. Copy the InternetAccountingCases, then paste it as **InternetAccountingProductionCases**.

b. Open the InternetAccountingProductionCases query in Design View, then add criteria to select the records in either the Departments of **Accounting** or **Production** with a Category value of **Internet**.

c. Display the results in Datasheet View as shown in FIGURE 3-29, then save and close the query.

FIGURE 3-29

CaseID	Category	LastName	FirstName	Department
15	Internet	Serrano	Craig	Accounting
17	Internet	Rivas	Philip	Accounting
18	Internet	Calderon	Sean	Accounting
20	Internet	Clayton	Shawn	Production
* (New)				

10. Create Calculated fields.

a. Open the Employees table in Design View then add field named **Monthly** with a Currency format and Calculated data type.

b. Use the expression **[Salary]/12** to calculate the values for the new Monthly field.

c. Save the Employees table and display it in Datasheet View.

d. Change the salary for Mindi Perez from $70,000 to **80000** then click anywhere else in the datasheet to observe the automatic update to the Monthly field.

e. Save and close the Employees table.

f. Create a new query in Query Design View with the Employees, Cases, and Calls tables.

g. Add the LastName field from the Employees table, the CaseTitle field from the Cases table, and the CallMinutes field from the Calls table.

h. Add a calculated field to the fourth column of the query grid with the following field name and expression: **TotalTime: [CallMinutes]+10** which estimates the total time required per call for assuming a five-minute gap before and after each call.

i. Save the query with the name **TotalCallMinutes** and display the datasheet. Change the CallMinutes value for the first "Google doesn't look right" record from 40 minutes to 45 minutes, then click anywhere else in the datasheet. The TotalTime value should automatically update to 55.

j. Save and close the TotalCallMinutes datasheet.

k. In class or in a discussion group, be prepared to discuss the TotalTime calculated field in the TotalCallMinutes query. What are the advantages and disadvantages of creating this field in a query versus in the Calls table?

11. Format a datasheet.

a. In the Cases table datasheet, apply the Georgia font and a **12**-point font size.

b. Change the alternate row color to Light Blue 1 (fifth column, second row in the Standard Colors palette), and the gridlines to None.

c. Display the Cases datasheet in Print Preview, then switch the orientation to Landscape, and the margins to Narrow. The datasheet should now fit on a single sheet of paper.

d. Save the Cases datasheet, and then close it.

e. Close Access 2019.

Independent Challenge 1

As the manager of Riverwalk, a multi-specialty health clinic, you have created a database to manage the schedules that connect each healthcare provider with the nurses that provider needs to efficiently handle patient visits. In this exercise, you will create a query to answer a special scheduling question at the clinic.

a. Start Access. Open the IL_AC_3-3.accdb database from the location where you store your Data Files and save it as **IL_AC_3_Riverwalk**. Click Enable Content if a yellow Security Warning message appears.

b. Create a new query in Query Design View with the Locations, ScheduleItems, ScheduleDate, and Nurses tables.

Independent Challenge 1 (continued)

c. Add the following fields to the query in this order: LocationName from the Locations table, ScheduleDate from the ScheduleDate table, and NurseLName and NurseFName from the Nurses table.

d. Sort the records in ascending order by ScheduleDate, then NurseLName.

e. Save the query with the name **NorthSouth**.

f. Add criteria to select only the records for a LocationName of **North** or **South**, a NurseLName value of **Washington** or **Fredrick**, and a ScheduleDate **on or after 12/1/2021** as shown in FIGURE 3-30.

g. Close the NorthSouth query, then close the database and exit Access 2019.

FIGURE 3-30

LocationNam	ScheduleDat	NurseLName	NurseFNam
North	12/6/2021	Fredrick	Sam
South	12/6/2021	Washington	Dana
North	12/9/2021	Fredrick	Sam
South	12/9/2021	Washington	Dana
North	12/10/2021	Fredrick	Sam
South	12/10/2021	Washington	Dana
North	12/11/2021	Fredrick	Sam
North	12/11/2021	Washington	Dana
North	12/12/2021	Fredrick	Sam
South	12/12/2021	Washington	Dana
North	12/13/2021	Fredrick	Sam
South	12/13/2021	Washington	Dana
North	12/16/2021	Fredrick	Sam
South	12/16/2021	Washington	Dana

Independent Challenge 2

You are working for a city to coordinate a series of community-wide preparedness activities. You have created a database to track the activities and volunteers who are attending the activities. In this exercise you will create a query to answer a special activities question at the city.

a. Start Access. Open the IL_AC_3-4.accdb database from the location where you store your Data Files and save it as **IL_AC_3_Volunteers**. Click Enable Content if a yellow Security Warning message appears.

b. Create a new query in Query Design View with the Volunteers, Attendance, and Activities tables.

c. Add the following fields to the query in this order: FirstName and LastName from the Volunteers table, Completed field from the Attendance table, ActivityName and ActivityHours from the Activities table.

d. Sort the records in ascending order on LastName.

e. Add criteria to select only those records with **CPR** anywhere in the ActivityName field and an ActivityHours value **greater than or equal to 7**.

f. Add a calculated field with the following name and expression to estimate the value of the volunteer's time within that activity: **Labor: [ActivityHours]*15**

g. Save the query with the name **LaborCalculation**, display it in Datasheet View, then change the record for William Wilberforce to have your first and last names, as shown in FIGURE 3-31.

h. Close the database and exit Access 2019.

FIGURE 3-31

FirstNa	LastNar	Completed	ActivityName	ActivityHou	Labor
Rhea	Alman	☑	First Aid and CPR	8	120
Young	Bogard	☑	First Aid and CPR	8	120
Forrest	Browning	☑	First Aid and CPR	8	120
Patch	Bullock	☑	First Aid and CPR	8	120
Angela	Cabriella	☑	First Aid and CPR	8	120
Herman	Cain	☑	First Aid and CPR	8	120
Gina	Daniels	☑	First Aid and CPR	8	120
Quentin	Garden	☑	First Aid and CPR	8	120
Loraine	Goode	☑	First Aid and CPR	8	120
Loraine	Goode	☑	CPR and Automated External Defibrillator AED	7	105
Karla	Larson	☑	First Aid and CPR	8	120
Karla	Larson	☑	CPR and Automated External Defibrillator AED	7	105
Aaron	Love	☑	CPR and Automated External Defibrillator AED	7	105
Aaron	Love	☑	First Aid and CPR	8	120
Katrina	Margolis	☑	CPR and Automated External Defibrillator AED	7	105
Katrina	Margolis	☑	First Aid and CPR	8	120
Jaye	Mati	☑	First Aid and CPR	8	120
Jaye	Mati	☑	CPR and Automated External Defibrillator AED	7	105
Jon	Maxim	☑	First Aid and CPR	8	120
Jon	Maxim	☑	CPR and Automated External Defibrillator AED	7	105
Sindy	Russo	☑	First Aid and CPR	8	120
StudentFi	StudentLa	☑	First Aid and CPR	8	120

Record: I◄ ◄ 1 of 22 ► ►I ► No Filter   Search

Visual Workshop

Open the IL_AC_3-5.accdb database from the location where you store your Data Files and save it as **IL_AC_3_CollegeCourses**, then enable content if prompted. Create a query in Query Design View based on the Classes, Professors, Sections, Enrollments, and Students tables with the fields shown in FIGURE 3-32. Add criteria to select only those records where Grade field value is **A** or **B** and the Credits field value equals **4**. Display the query in Datasheet View, widen the columns to display all of the data, and save it with the name **4CreditsAB**. Close the 4CreditsAB query then exit Access 2019.

FIGURE 3-32

StudentLast	StudentFirst	Description	Credits	Grade	ProfLastName
Mitchell	Irma	Programming Fundamentals	4	B	Zimmerman
Davis	Timothy	Programming Fundamentals	4	A	Zimmerman
Bennet	Domenico	Programming Fundamentals	4	A	Zimmerman
Snow	Frederick	Programming Fundamentals	4	A	Zimmerman
Gregory	Roger	Programming Fundamentals	4	A	Zimmerman
Simmons	Michael	Programming Fundamentals	4	B	Zimmerman
Owen	Leo	Programming Fundamentals	4	B	Zimmerman
Amstell	Mark	Database Programming	4	B	Quinn
Willis	Carl	Database Programming	4	A	Douglas
Cooper	Yehudah	Mobile Application Development	4	B	Quinn
Gallow	Taiichi	Mobile Application Development	4	B	Quinn
Noble	Hector	Database Management	4	B	Zimmerman
Noble	Hector	Engineering Graphics	4	B	Rosenbaum
Cooper	Yehudah	Engineering Graphics	4	B	Rosenbaum
Bennet	Domenico	Engineering Graphics	4	A	Rosenbaum
Dow	Johann	Engineering Graphics	4	A	Rosenbaum
Gregory	Roger	Engineering Graphics	4	A	Rosenbaum
Gallow	Taiichi	Engineering Graphics	4	B	Rosenbaum
Owen	Leo	Engineering Graphics	4	B	Rosenbaum

Record: 1 of 19   No Filter   Search

Working with Forms and Reports

CASE ▶ Lydia Snyder, vice president of operations at JCL Talent, asks you to create forms to make job and company information easier to access, enter, and update. She also wants you to create some reports that will provide a professional presentation and analysis of selected data.

Module Objectives

After completing this module, you will be able to:

- Work in Form View
- Work in Form Layout View
- Work in Form Design View
- Work in Report Layout View
- Work in Report Design View
- Add conditional formatting
- Use the Format Painter and themes

Files You Will Need

IL_AC_4-1.accdb
IL_AC_4-2.accdb
IL_AC_4-3.accdb

IL_AC_4-4.accdb
IL_AC_4-5.accdb

Work in Form View

Learning Outcomes
- Navigate records in a form
- Enter records in a form

A form allows you to arrange the fields of a record in any layout so a database **user** can quickly and easily find, enter, edit, and analyze data. You can use several different tools to create forms, as shown in TABLE 4-1. Each form has three views, and each view has a primary purpose, as described in TABLE 4-2, although you can complete some tasks in multiple views. **Form View** gives a user an easy-to-use data entry and navigation screen. **CASE** ▶ *Lydia Snyder asks you to find and enter company data in the database. You will use a form to complete the work.*

STEPS

1. **sanf ↓ Start Access, open the** IL_AC_4-1.accdb database **from the location where you store your Data Files, save it as** IL_AC_4_Jobs, **enable content if prompted, then double-click the** CompanyEntry form **to open it in Form View**

   The CompanyEntry form organizes all the fields of the Companies table to clearly display the data from one record at a time. Forms contain **controls** such as labels to describe information, text boxes and combo boxes to help you enter information, and command buttons to help you work with the form. Forms also provide **navigation buttons** in the lower-left corner, which help you navigate through the data.

2. **Click the** Next record button ▶ **in the navigation bar three times to navigate to the fourth record**

   The **Current Record box** identifies what record you are currently viewing as well as the total number of records. The navigation buttons also provide a way to move to the first or last record in the form very quickly.

3. **Click the** Last record button ▶| **in the navigation bar**

   To move to a prior record, you use the Previous record and First record buttons.

4. **Click the** Previous record button ◀ **in the navigation bar, then click the** First record button |◀ **to return to the first record**

   In addition, you can type any number in the Current Record box to quickly move to that record.

5. **Click the** Current Record box, **type 17, press ENTER, then change the Industry field value to** Aerospace

   Changes are saved as you move from record to record and new records are always entered at the end.

6. **Click the** New (blank) record button ▶▥, **then enter a new company record, as shown in** FIGURE 4-1 **and described below**

Company ID:	TAB (AutoNumber field that automatically increments)
Company Name:	Heritage Computing Inc
Industry:	Information
Description:	Database modeling, management, warehousing and analytics.
City:	Springfield
State:	MO

7. **Right-click the** CompanyEntry tab, **then click** Close

   When you close a form, Access automatically saves data in the current record.

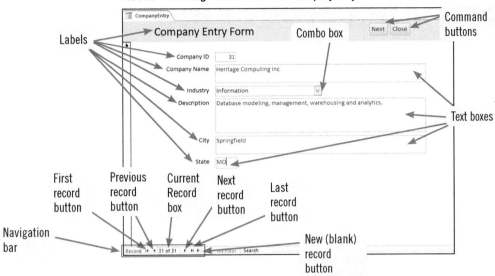

FIGURE 4-1: Adding a new record to the CompanyEntry form in Form View

TABLE 4-1: Form creation tools

tool	icon	creates a form
Form		with one click based on the selected table or query
Form Design		from scratch in Form Design View
Blank Form		from scratch in Form Layout View
Form Wizard		by answering a series of questions provided by the Form Wizard dialog boxes
Navigation		to navigate or move between different areas of the database
More Forms		for Multiple Items, Datasheet, Split Form, or Modal Dialog arrangements
Split Form		with two panes, the upper showing one record at a time and the lower displaying a datasheet of many records

TABLE 4-2: Form views

view	primary purpose
Form	To find, sort, enter, and edit data
Layout	To modify the size, position, or formatting of controls; shows data as you modify the form, making it the tool of choice when you want to change the appearance and usability of the form while viewing data
Design	To modify the Form Header, Detail, and Footer section, to work with form rulers and gridlines, or to access the complete range of controls and form properties; Design View does not display data

Use Form Layout View

Learning
Outcomes
• Format controls in
Form Layout View
• Edit labels in Form
Layout View

Form Layout View and Form Design View may both be used to create and modify a form. The most important benefit of **Form Layout View** is that it lets you make design changes to the form while browsing the data. This helps you productively resize and format the controls on the form. Although you can see the data in Form Layout View, you cannot enter or edit it in this view. TABLE 4-3 lists several of the most popular formatting commands on the Format tab of the ribbon that help you work in Layout View.

CASE *Lydia asks you to make several design changes to the CompanyEntry form. You make these changes in Form Layout View.*

STEPS

1. **Right-click the** CompanyEntry form **in the Navigation Pane, then click** Layout View
   Layout View opens and looks very similar to Form View. In Layout View, you can move through the records, but you cannot enter or edit the data as you can in Form View. You decide to enhance the Company Entry Form label at the top of the form.

QUICK TIP
You can also apply formatting commands in Form Design View.

2. **Click the** Company Entry Form label **in the Form Header section, click the** Format tab **on the ribbon, click the** Bold button B, **click the** Font Color list arrow A ·, **click** Dark Blue **(fourth column, first row of the Standard Colors palette), click the** Font Size arrow 11 ·, **then click** 24
   You often use Layout View to make minor design changes, such as editing labels and changing formatting characteristics.

3. **Click the** Industry label **to select it, click the** Industry label **again to position the insertion point within the label, edit the text to be** Primary Industry, **then press** ENTER
   Your users do not need the Next button because they use the buttons in the navigation bar, so you can delete the Next command button.

4. **Click the** Next command button, **then press** DELETE
   You change the style, shape, and outline of the Close button.

QUICK TIP
You can undo multiple formatting actions by clicking the Undo button ↺ on the Quick Access toolbar.

5. **Click the** Close command button, **click the** Quick Styles button, **click the** Colored Fill – Blue, Accent 1 option **(second column, second row), click the** Change Shape button, **click the** Oval shape, **click the** Shape Outline button, **then click** Transparent **near the bottom of the menu**
   You decide to make one other small change. You feel that the data in the Company ID text box would be easier to read if it were centered.

TROUBLE
Be sure to modify the text box instead of the Company ID label on the left.

6. **Click** 1 **in the box to the right of the Company ID label, then click the** Center button ≡
   Your CompanyEntry form should look like FIGURE 4-2. The form label is more pronounced, the Close button is styled, and the Company ID data is easier to read.

FIGURE 4-2: Modifying controls in Form Layout View

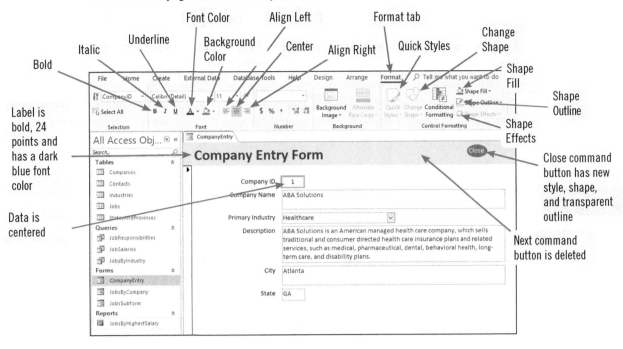

TABLE 4-3: Useful formatting commands

button	button name	description
B	Bold	Toggles bold on or off for the selected control(s)
I	Italic	Toggles italic on or off for the selected control(s)
U	Underline	Toggles underline on or off for the selected control(s)
A	Font Color	Changes the text color of the selected control(s)
◢	Background Color or Shape Fill	Changes the background color of the selected control(s)
≡	Align Left	Left-aligns the selected control(s) within its own border
≡	Center	Centers the selected control(s) within its own border
≡	Align Right	Right-aligns the selected control(s) within its own border
⊞	Alternate Row Color	Changes the background color of alternate records in the selected section
◩	Shape Outline	Changes the border color, thickness, or style of the selected control(s)
◔	Shape Effects	Changes the special visual effect of the selected control(s)

Work in Form Design View

Most form developers prefer to use Form Design View to add, move, and resize controls because **Form Design View** provides tools such as rulers and gridlines to help make precise changes to the position of controls. TABLE 4-4 shows the mouse pointer shapes that help you work in Form or Report Design View to select, resize, and move controls. **CASE** *Lydia Snyder asks you to modify the CompanyEntry form by placing controls in precise positions. You respond to her request by working in Form Design View.*

STEPS

1. **Right-click the** CompanyEntry **tab, click** Design View, **click the** Design tab **on the ribbon, then click** Add Existing Fields button **in the Tools group to open the Field List**
   The **Field List** opens, which lists the fields available for this form. You can drag the title bar of the Field List to move it, and double-click the title bar of the Field List to dock it to the right.

2. **Drag the** ZipCode field **to the form, then use the move pointer ⁺ₖ to drag the new** ZipCode text box and label **below the State text box, as shown in** FIGURE 4-3
   When you add the ZipCode field to the form, two controls are added: a label and a text box. The **label** on the left describes the data. By default, the label displays the field name, though you can modify it as desired. The **text box** on the right displays the data from the field. It *must* contain the actual field name to stay connected (also called "**bound**") to the data.

3. **Click the** ZipCode label, **click the** ZipCode label **a second time to place the insertion point in the text, modify the text to be** ZIP, **press** ENTER, **click the** Format tab **on the ribbon, click the** Font Color arrow Ⓐ⁻, **then click** Automatic
   You also want to align and format the new controls.

4. **Click the** ZIP label, **click the** Align Right button ≡, **press and hold** CTRL, **click the** State label **to select both labels at the same time, click the** Arrange tab **on the ribbon, click the** Align button, **then click** Right
   You right-aligned the ZIP text within the label, then you right-aligned the right edges of the ZIP label with the State label above it. Now left-align the edges of the State and ZipCode text boxes.

5. **Click the** State text box, **press and hold** CTRL, **click the** ZipCode text box, **click the** Align button, **then click** Left
   The new controls for the ZipCode field are now added, moved, and aligned on the form. As a final touch, you want to add a label to the Form Footer section with the text "JCL Talent".

6. **Drag the bottom of the** Form Footer bar **down about 0.5", click the** Design tab **on the ribbon, click the** Label button Aa, **click at about the 1" mark in the Form Footer section, type** JCL Talent, **then press** ENTER
   You are ready to review the final CompanyEntry form in Form View.

7. **Right-click the** CompanyEntry **tab, click** Save, **right-click the** CompanyEntry **tab again, then click** Form View **as shown in** FIGURE 4-4
   In general, it is common to use Form Layout View for formatting changes and Form Design View to add and position new controls. However, much of the functionality between the two views overlaps.

8. **Right-click the** CompanyEntry **tab, then click** Close

FIGURE 4-3: Adding, moving, and aligning controls in Form Design View

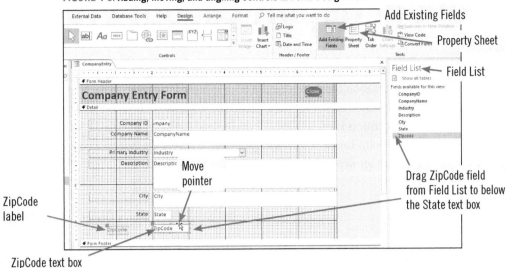

FIGURE 4-4: Final CompanyEntry form in Form View

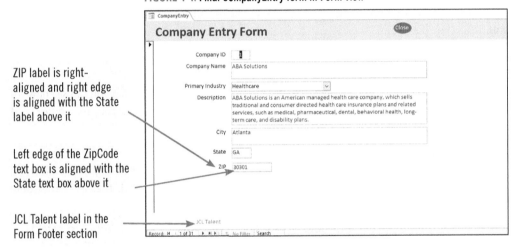

TABLE 4-4: Mouse pointer shapes in Form or Report Design View

shape	when does this shape appear?	action
↖	When you point to any unselected control on the form (the default mouse pointer)	Single-clicking with this mouse pointer selects a control
↖⁺	When you point to the upper-left corner or edge of a selected control in Form Design View or the middle of the control in Form Layout View	Dragging with this mouse pointer moves the selected control(s)
↕ ↔ ↗ ↙	When you point to any sizing handle (except the larger one in the upper-left corner in Form Design View)	Dragging with one of these mouse pointers resizes the control

Bound versus unbound controls

Controls are either bound or unbound. **Bound controls** display values from a field such as text boxes and combo boxes. The most common bound control is the text box. **Unbound controls** describe data or enhance the appearance of the form. Labels are the most common type of unbound control, but other types include lines, images, tabs, and command buttons. Another way

to distinguish bound from unbound controls is to observe the form as you move from record to record. Because bound controls display data, their contents change as you move through the records, displaying data from the field of the current record. Unbound controls such as labels, lines, and command buttons do not change as you move through the records in a form.

Access

Work in Report Layout View

Learning
Outcomes
• Create a report
  with the Report
  tool
• Move, resize, and
  format controls
  in Report Layout
  View
• Change page
  orientation

Reports allow you to organize, group, sort, and subtotal records for professional presentations of data. Reports can be created with multiple tools and have multiple views just like forms. See TABLE 4-5 for more information on report creation tools and TABLE 4-6 for more information on report views. Although you use forms for data entry and reports for data distribution, many of the same tasks such as formatting, moving, and resizing controls work similarly between the two objects. For example, **Report Layout View** is very similar to Form Layout View. **CASE** *Lydia Snyder asks you to create a specific report. You create the report and then use Report Layout View to modify it.*

STEPS

1. **Click the** JobSalaries query, **click the** Create tab **on the ribbon, then click the** Report button

    A report opens in Report Layout View, which displays data and allows you to move, resize, and format controls.

2. **Click any value in the** Industry column, **then use the two-headed arrow pointer** ↔ **to narrow the column to about half its size, as shown in** FIGURE 4-5

    A benefit of resizing controls in Report Layout View versus Report Design View is that you can see how the data fits as you resize the control. The report is still too wide to fit on a standard piece of paper in **portrait orientation** (8.5" wide by 11" tall), as indicated by the dashed lines.

3. **Click the** Page Setup tab, **then click the** Landscape button

    Landscape orientation switches the orientation of the paper to 11" wide by 8.5" tall, which allows for more columns across the page. You also want to change the font color of the labels that serve as column headings.

4. **Click the** Industry label, **press and hold** SHIFT, **then click the** Applicants label **to select all column heading labels in that row, click the** Format tab **on the ribbon, click the** Font Color arrow ![A▾], **then click** Automatic

    Your last change is to move the StartingSalary column to the far right.

5. **Click the** StartingSalary label, **press and hold** SHIFT, **click** any value **in the StartingSalary column, then use the move pointer** ⁛ **to drag the column to the right of the Applicants column**

    The final JobSalaries report is shown in FIGURE 4-6.

6. **Right-click the** JobSalaries tab, **click** Save, **click** OK **to accept the default name, right-click the** JobSalaries tab, **click** Print Preview **to preview the report as it would fit on a piece of paper, right-click the** JobSalaries tab, **then click** Layout View **to return to Layout View**

FIGURE 4-5: Resizing a column in Report Layout View

Resizing
the Industry
column

Dashed line indicates
the right edge of the
paper

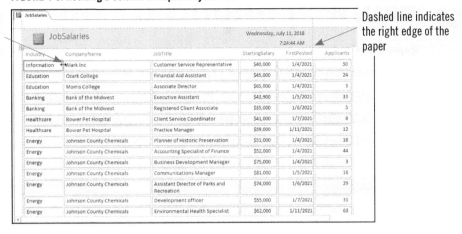

FIGURE 4-6: Final JobSalaries report in Report Layout View

Labels used as column headings
have an Automatic font color

StartingSalary column
moved to the end

Dashed line
in landscape
orientation

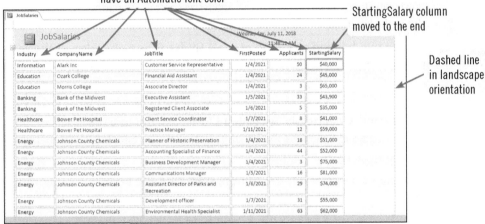

TABLE 4-5: Report creation tools

tool	icon	creates a report
Report		with one click based on the selected table or query
Report Design		from scratch in Report Design View
Blank Report		from scratch in Report Layout View
Report Wizard		by answering a series of questions provided by the Report Wizard dialog boxes
Labels		by answering a series of questions provided by the Label Wizard dialog boxes

TABLE 4-6: Report views

view	primary purpose
Report View	To quickly review the report without page breaks
Print Preview	To review each page of an entire report as it will appear if printed
Layout View	To modify the size, position, or formatting of controls; shows live data as you modify the report, making it the tool of choice when you want to change the appearance and positioning of controls on a report while also reviewing live data
Design View	To work with report sections or to access the complete range of controls and report properties; Design View does not display data

Work in Report Design View

Learning Outcomes

- Modify controls in Report Design View
- Group and ungroup controls in Report Design View
- Change report width

Report Design View gives you maximum control over all report modifications by providing extra design tools such as rulers and section bars. Report **sections** determine where and how often controls in that section print in the final report. For example, controls in the Report Header section print only once at the beginning of the report, but controls in the Detail section print once for every record the report displays. TABLE 4-7 describes report sections. **CASE** *Lydia Snyder asks you to modify the JobSalaries report. You use Report Design View to make the changes.*

1. **Right-click the** JobSalaries tab, **then click** Design View

   Five report **section bars** are displayed that identify the report sections. The **horizontal ruler** is also shown, which helps you precisely move and resize controls. To narrow the entire report, you drag the right edge to the left in Report Design View.

   QUICK TIP
   If a report is too wide to fit on a piece of paper, a green error indicator appears in the upper-left corner of the report.

2. **Use the two-headed arrow pointer ↔ to drag the** right edge of the report **as far left as possible, then click the** Control Selection button ⊞ **in the upper-left corner of the Report Header section to select the controls**

   The controls in the Report Header section are arranged in a **control layout**, a grid of cells that help organize the controls they contain. See TABLE 4-8 for buttons that help you modify control layouts. You want to move the date and time boxes to the right, but to move or resize individual controls in a layout, you must first remove the layout.

3. **Click the** Arrange tab **on the ribbon, then click the** Remove Layout button

   Now you can work with the individual controls.

4. **Click the** =Date() text box, **press and hold** CTRL, **click the** =Time() text box, **click the** Size/Space button, **click** Group, **then press** RIGHT ARROW **enough times to position the right edge of the controls at the 9" mark on the horizontal ruler**

   Your screen should look like FIGURE 4-7. You can also use the mouse to move controls in Report or Form Design View, though the arrow keys allow you to precisely position the selected controls. You also want to make some formatting changes to the title of the report.

5. **Click the** JobSalaries label **in the Report Header, click the** Format tab **on the ribbon, click the** Font Color arrow ▲ ▾ **click** Automatic, **click the** Font Size arrow ⏧ ▾, **click** 24, **click the** JobSalaries label **again to place the insertion pointer in the text, then add a space so that the label reads** Job Salaries

   Your final modification will be to change the background color of the StartingSalary data.

   QUICK TIP
   Labels are edited and controls are formatted the same way in Form Design View and Form Layout View.

6. **Click the** StartingSalary text box **in the Detail section, click the** Background Color arrow ▨ ▾, **then click the** Green 2 box **(seventh column, third row in the Standard Colors palette)**

   The final Report Design View should look like FIGURE 4-8. To review your modifications, show the report in Print Preview.

7. **Right-click the** JobSalaries tab, **click** Save, **right-click the** JobSalaries tab, **click** Print Preview, **click the** Next Page button ▶ **to navigate through the pages of the report, right-click the** JobSalaries tab, **then click** Close

   Previewing each page of the report helps you confirm that no blank pages are created and allows you to examine how the different report sections print on each page.

FIGURE 4-7: Working in Report Design View

Report Header section bar
Page Header section bar
Detail section bar
Page Footer section bar
Report Footer section bar

Horizontal ruler

9" mark on horizontal ruler

Selected controls are grouped together and moved

FIGURE 4-8: Final JobSalaries report in Report Design View

Font Color   Background Color   Font Size   Arrange tab   Format tab   Text boxes have been moved to the right

Job Salaries label is modified with Automatic font color and 24-point font size

Right edge of the report has been moved to the left

Green 2 background color applied to the StartingSalary text box

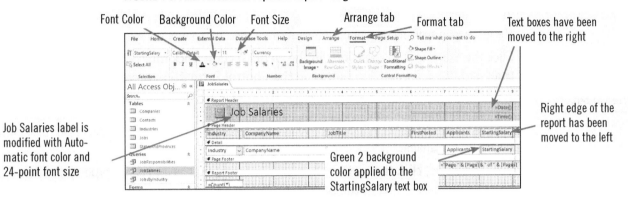

TABLE 4-7: Report sections

section	where does this section print?
Report Header	At the top of the first page
Page Header	At the top of every page (but below the Report Header on the first page)
Detail	Once for every record
Page Footer	At the bottom of every page
Report Footer	At the end of the report

TABLE 4-8: Control layout buttons

button		description	button		description
Gridlines		Applies gridlines in different colors, widths, and borders to the cells of the control layout	Select Layout		Selects the entire layout
			Select Column		Selects a single column of a layout
Stacked		Applies a vertical layout with labels on the left and text boxes on the right	Select Row		Selects a single row of a layout
			Merge		Merges cells in a layout
Tabular		Applies a horizontal layout similar to a spreadsheet	Split Vertically		Splits cells into two rows
Remove Layout		Removes a layout	Split Horizontally		Splits cells into two columns
Insert Above		Inserts a row above the layout	Move Up		Moves cells into the section above the current section
Insert Below		Inserts a row below the layout	Move Down		Moves cells into the section below the current section
Insert Left		Inserts a column to the left of the layout			
Insert Right		Inserts a column to the right of the layout			

Apply Conditional Formatting

Conditional formatting allows you to change the appearance of a control on a form or report based on criteria you specify. Conditional formatting helps you highlight important or exceptional data on a form or report. **CASE** ▶ *Lydia Snyder wants you to format the salary data in the JobsByHighestSalary report to emphasize different starting salary levels.*

STEPS

1. **Right-click the** JobsByHighestSalary report **in the Navigation Pane, then click** Design View

   The first step in applying conditional formatting is to select the control you want to format.

TROUBLE
Be sure to select the
StartingSalary text
box (not the label).

2. **Click the** StartingSalary text box **in the Detail section, click the** Format tab, **then click the** Conditional Formatting button **in the Control Formatting group**

   The Conditional Formatting Rules Manager dialog box opens, asking you to define the conditional formatting rules. You want to format StartingSalary values between 0 and 49,999 with a yellow background, those between 50,000 and 69,999 with a light green background, and those equal to or greater than 70,000 with a light blue background.

QUICK TIP
Between . . . and
criteria include both
values in the range.

3. **Click** New Rule, **click the** text box to the right of the between arrow, **type** 0, **click the** and box, **type** 49999, **click the** Background color arrow 🖌 ▾, **click the** Yellow box **on the bottom row, then click** OK

   You add the second conditional formatting rule.

4. **Click** New Rule, **click the** text box to the right of the between arrow, **type** 50000, **click the** and box, **type** 69999, **click the** Background color arrow 🖌 ▾, **click the** Light Green box **on the bottom row, then click** OK

   You add the third conditional formatting rule.

5. **Click** New Rule, **click the** between arrow, **click** greater than or equal to, **click the** value box, **type** 70000, **click the** Background color arrow 🖌 ▾, **click the** Light Blue box **on the bottom row, then click** OK

   The Conditional Formatting Rules Manager dialog box with two rules should look like FIGURE 4-9.

QUICK TIP
Conditional
formatting works the
same way in Form
and Report Layout
and Design Views.

6. **Click** OK **in the Conditional Formatting Rules Manager dialog box, right-click the** JobsByHighestSalary tab, **then click** Print Preview

   Conditional formatting rules applied a yellow, light green, or light blue background color to the StartingSalary text box for each record, as shown in FIGURE 4-10.

7. **Right-click the** JobsByHighestSalary tab, **click** Save, **right-click the** JobsByHighestSalary tab, **then click** Close

FIGURE 4-9: Conditional Formatting Rules Manager dialog box

Rule 1 for values
between 0 and 49999

Rule 2 for values between
50000 and 69999

Rule 3 for values greater
than or equal to 70000

Yellow background

Light green background

Light blue background

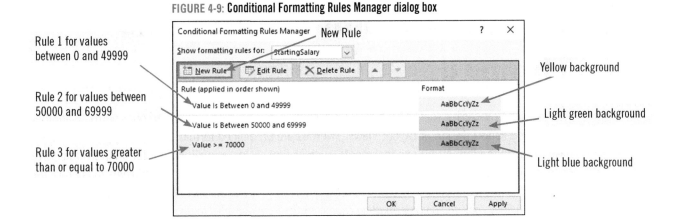

FIGURE 4-10: Conditional formatting applied to the JobsByHighestSalary report

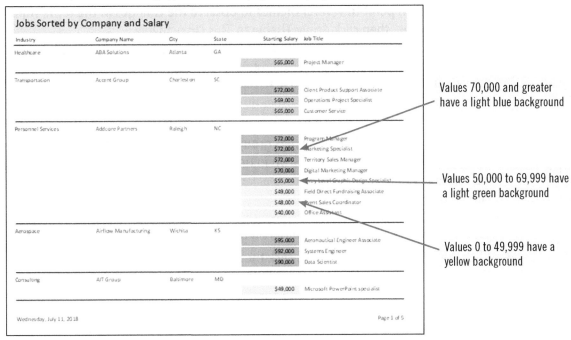

Values 70,000 and greater
have a light blue background

Values 50,000 to 69,999 have
a light green background

Values 0 to 49,999 have a
yellow background

Use the Format Painter and Themes

The **Format Painter** is a tool you use to copy multiple formatting properties from one control to another in Form and Report Design or Layout Views. **Themes** are predefined formats that you apply to the database to set all the formatting enhancements, such as font, color, and alignment for an individual form or report or for all the forms and reports in the database. **CASE** *Lydia Snyder wants to improve the appearance of the JobsByCompany form. You apply a built-in theme to the entire form and then use the Format Painter to quickly copy and paste formatting characteristics from one label to another.*

STEPS

1. **Right-click the** JobsByCompany form **in the Navigation Pane, click** Design View, **click the** Themes button, **point to several themes to observe the changes in the form, right-click the** Facet theme, **then click** Apply Theme to This Object Only

   If you click (versus right-click) a theme, it is applied to all the forms and reports in the database. This keeps the look and feel of the entire application consistent. In this case, however, you want to apply the theme to this form only to test it before applying it to all objects.

   A theme applies new colors, fonts, alignment, and other formatting options. You can also choose to change only the colors or only the fonts.

QUICK TIP
You can apply themes, theme fonts, or theme colors in Form and Report Layout and Design views.

2. **Click the** Fonts button **in the Themes group, right-click** Arial, **then click** Apply Font Scheme to This Object Only **as shown in** FIGURE 4-11

   The current theme fonts change for the current form. The Colors button works in a similar way, changing only the current theme's colors.

   The Print command button was formatted previously and does not look the same as the Close button. To copy formats quickly, you use the Format Painter.

3. **Click the** Close command button, **click the** Home tab, **click the** Format Painter button, **then click the** Print command button **in the Form Header section**

   The Print command button is now formatted just like the Close command button. You can double-click the Format Painter button to copy formatting to more than one control.

QUICK TIP
The Format Painter works the same way in Form and Report Layout and Design Views.

4. **Right-click the** JobsByCompany tab, **click** Save, **right-click the** JobsByCompany tab, **then click** Form View **to review the changes shown in** FIGURE 4-12

5. **Click the** Close command button **to close the** CompanyJobs form, **click the** Database Tools tab, **then click the** Compact and Repair Database button

6. **sam** ⬆ Close the database and exit Access 2019

FIGURE 4-11: Applying themes

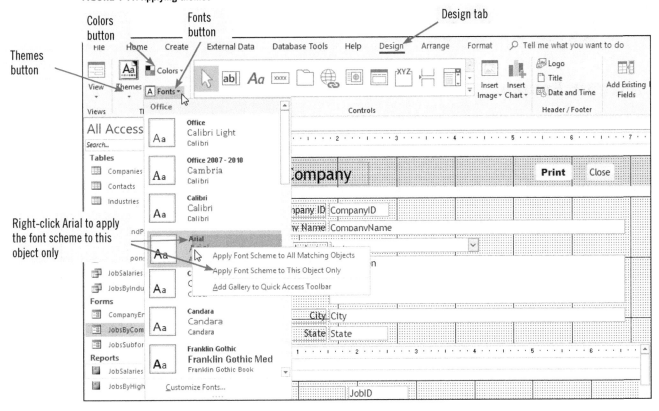

FIGURE 4-12: Final CompanyJobs form

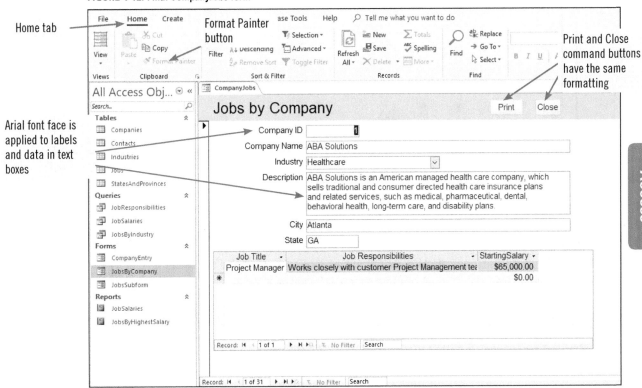

Practice

Concepts Review

Label each element of Form Design View shown in FIGURE 4-13.

FIGURE 4-13

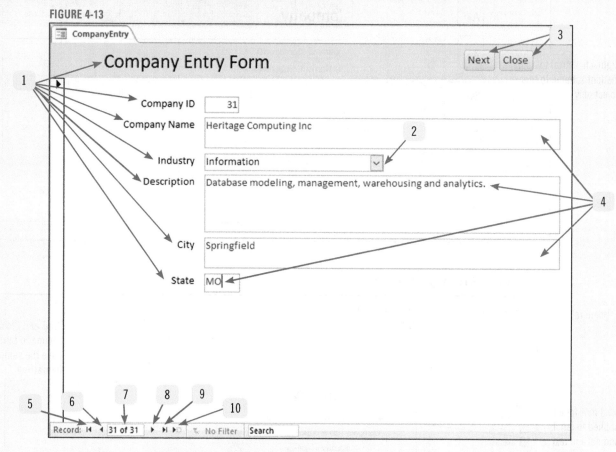

Match each term with the statement that best describes it.

11. **Form View**
12. **Detail section**
13. **Report Footer section**
14. **Bound control**
15. **Landscape orientation**

a. Controls placed here print once for every record
b. Used on a form to display data from a field
c. Controls placed here print only once at the end of the report
d. Most commonly used to find, enter, and edit data
e. A printout that is 11" wide by 8.5" tall

Select the best answer from the list of choices.

16. **Every element on a form is called a(n):**
    a. Property.
    b. Item.
    c. Control.
    d. Tool.

17. **Which of the following may *not* be used to format controls?**
    a. Form View
    b. Form Layout View
    c. Report Design View
    d. Report Layout View

18. The most common bound control is the:

   a. Combo box.

   b. Label.

   c. List box.

   d. Text box.

19. The most common unbound control is the:

   a. Text box.

   b. Combo box.

   c. Label.

   d. Command button.

20. Which view does not show data?

   a. Form Layout View

   b. Form Design View

   c. Print Preview

   d. Report Layout View

Skills Review

1. Work in Form View.

   a. Start Access, open the IL_AC_4-2.accdb database from the location where you store your Data Files, save it as **IL_AC_4_SupportDesk**, then enable content if prompted.

   b. Open the EmployeeMaster form in Form View.

   c. Find the record for Peggy Short and change the LastName value to **Hopper**

   d. Add a new record with your name in the LastName and FirstName fields, and **Executive** in the Department field.

   e. Save the EmployeeMaster form.

2. Work in Form Layout View.

   a. Open the EmployeeMaster in Layout View.

   b. Modify the label in the Form Header section to have a space between the words to read: **Employee Master**

   c. Modify the labels on the left in the Detail section to have spaces between the words to read: **Employee ID**, **Last Name**, and **First Name**

   d. Modify the labels on the left in the Detail section to be right-aligned.

   e. Change the font color for all labels to Automatic (black).

   f. Save the EmployeeMaster form.

3. Work in Form Design View.

   a. Open the EmployeeMaster form in Design View.

   b. Move the Department label and Department combo box up to fill the blank space after the FirstName controls.

   c. Open the Field List, then add the Salary field to the form.

   d. Align the right edge of the Salary label with the labels above it and change the font color for the Salary label to Automatic (black).

   e. Align the left edge of the Salary text box with the combo box and text boxes above it.

   f. Save the EmployeeMaster form and open it in Form View as shown in FIGURE 4-14.

   g. Close the EmployeeMaster form.

4. Work in Report Layout View.

   a. Use the Report tool to create a new report on the Cases table.

   b. In Layout View of the new report, resize the Category column to be about half of its current size.

   c. In Layout View of the new report, expand the CaseTitle column to be about 50 percent wider than its current size.

   d. Switch the report to landscape orientation.

   e. Move the OpenedDate column, both the label and the text box, to be the third column in the report.

FIGURE 4-14

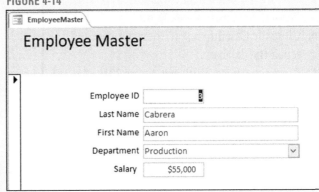

Access

Skills Review (continued)

    f. Modify the font color of the Cases label in the Report Header section to Dark Blue (second to the last button in the last row of the Standard Colors palette) and the font size to **24**.

    g. Delete the date and time controls in the Report Header section.

    h. Modify the font color of the labels that identify every column heading to also be Dark Blue.

    i. Save the report with the name **CaseInfo**.

5. **Work in Report Design View.**

    a. Switch the CaseInfo report to Report Design View.

    b. Narrow the report to the 10" mark on the horizontal ruler.

    c. Remove the control layout from the controls in the Page Header, Detail, Page Footer, and Report Footer sections. (*Hint*: Click the Control Selection button in the upper-left corner of the section to select the control layout.)

    d. Resize the =Count(*) text box in the Report Footer to be tall enough so that the entire expression is shown. (*Hint*: This expression was created by the Report tool when the report was initially created. It calculates the total number of records in the report.)

    e. Move and align the =Count(*) text box in the Report Footer section so that its top edge is touching the Report Footer section bar and its left edge is aligned with the left edge of the text box in the Page Footer section that contains the page number expression.

    f. Delete any extra space in the Report Footer section by dragging the bottom of the report up as far as possible.

    g. Select all the labels in the Page Header section and group them together so that they will move as a group should you want to reposition them later.

    h. Save the CaseInfo report.

6. **Add conditional formatting.**

    a. With the CaseInfo report still in Report Design View, add a conditional formatting rule to the Category text box. If the field value is equal to **"MS Office"** change the font color to Red (second column, last row of Standard Colors palette).

    b. Add a second conditional formatting rule to the Category text box. If the field value is equal to **"Internet"** change the font color to Green (sixth column, last row of Standard Colors palette).

    c. Save the CaseInfo report, switch to Print Preview to make sure the conditional formats are applied correctly, then return to Report Design View.

7. **Use the Format Painter and themes.**

    a. In Report Design View, use the Format Painter to copy the format from the page expression text box in the Page Footer section to the =Count(*) control in the Report Footer section.

    b. Apply the Franklin Gothic theme font to the CaseInfo report object only.

    c. Apply the Blue Warm theme color to the CaseInfo report object only.

    d. Save the CaseInfo report and switch to Print Preview, as shown in **FIGURE 4-15**.

    e. Close the CaseInfo report, then compact and repair the database.

    f. Close the database and exit Access 2019.

FIGURE 4-15

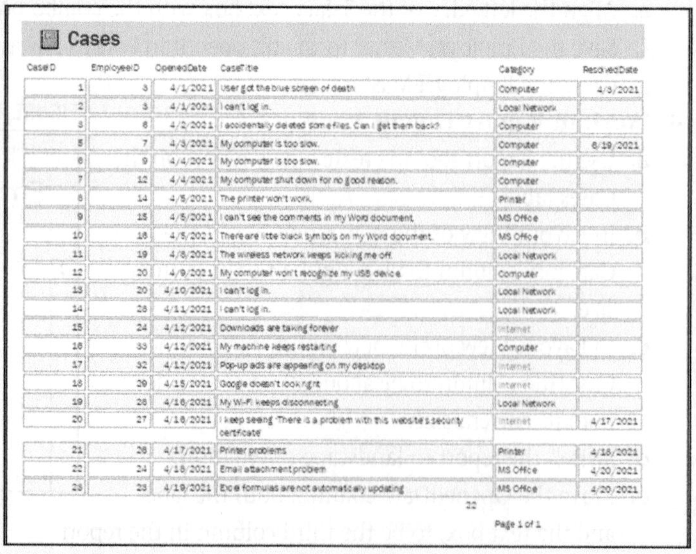

Independent Challenge 1

As the manager of Riverwalk, a multispecialty health clinic, you have created a database to manage the schedules that connect each healthcare provider with the nurses that provider needs to efficiently handle patient visits. In this exercise, you will modify a form to help users find, enter, and edit data.

a. Start Access. Open the IL_AC_4-3.accdb database from the location where you store your Data Files and save it as **IL_AC_4_Riverwalk**. Click Enable Content if a yellow Security Warning message appears.

b. Open the ScheduleDate form in Form Design View.

c. Change the font face for all controls in the Detail section, including those in the subform, to Calibri (Detail) and a **10**-point font size. (*Hint:* This form contains a subform, the ScheduleItemsSubform. You can change the font face and font size for the controls directly in Form Design View of the ScheduleDate form, or you can close the ScheduleDate form and apply the formats to the ScheduleItemsSubform in Form Design View.)

d. Modify the Work Schedule label in the Form Header section to read **Doctor and Nurse Schedule**. Change the font size to be **16** and resize the label as needed to display it clearly.

e. There are four command buttons in the Detail section with the following Captions: Day, Nurse, by Location, and by Nurse. Format the Day command button with the Rectangle: Rounded Corners shape, and the Colored Fill – Olive Green, Accent 3 quick style.

f. Use the Format Painter to copy the formatting from the Day command button to the Nurse, by Location, and by Nurse command buttons.

g. Save the ScheduleDate form and switch to Form View.

h. Click the Nurse command button, then click the New (blank) record button to position your insertion point at a new record at the end of the form. Enter your name as a new record.

i. Close the Nurse Entry form, then reopen the ScheduleDate form.

j. Move to the first record in the ScheduleDate form, then add a new record in the subform for LocationNo **East**, DoctorNo **Samuelson**, and your name in the NurseNo field, as shown in FIGURE 4-16.

k. Save and close the ScheduleDate form, and compact and repair the database.

l. Close the database, then exit Access 2019.

FIGURE 4-16

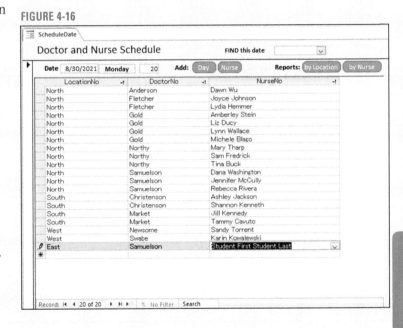

Independent Challenge 2

You are working for a city to coordinate a series of community-wide preparedness activities. You have created a database to track the activities and volunteers who are attending the activities. In this exercise, you will create and modify a report to analyze data.

a. Start Access, open the IL_AC_4-4.accdb database from the location where you store your Data Files, save it as **IL_AC_4_Volunteers**, then enable content if prompted.

b. Use the Report tool to create a new report on the Volunteers table.

c. In Report Layout View, resize the FirstName and LastName columns to be about half as wide.

d. In Report Layout View, resize the Street column to be slightly narrower so that the entire report fits within the dashed line that indicates the right side of the paper in portrait orientation.

Independent Challenge 2 (continued)

e. Switch to Report Design View and remove the control layout from the controls in the Report Header section.

f. Select and then delete the report image to the left of the Volunteers label in the Report Header section. Select and then delete the =Time() text box in the Report Header section.

g. Group the remaining two controls in the Report Header section, then move them to the left edge of the report.

h. Delete the =Count(*) text box in the Report Footer section.

i. Move the text box that contains the page number expression to the left edge of the report.

j. Drag the right edge of the report as far to the left as possible to narrow the report.

k. Apply the Century Schoolbook theme font to this report only.

l. Save the report with the name **VolunteerList**, then display it in Print Preview, as shown in FIGURE 4-17.

m. Save and close the VolunteerList report, then compact and repair the database.

n. Close the database and exit Access 2019.

FIGURE 4-17

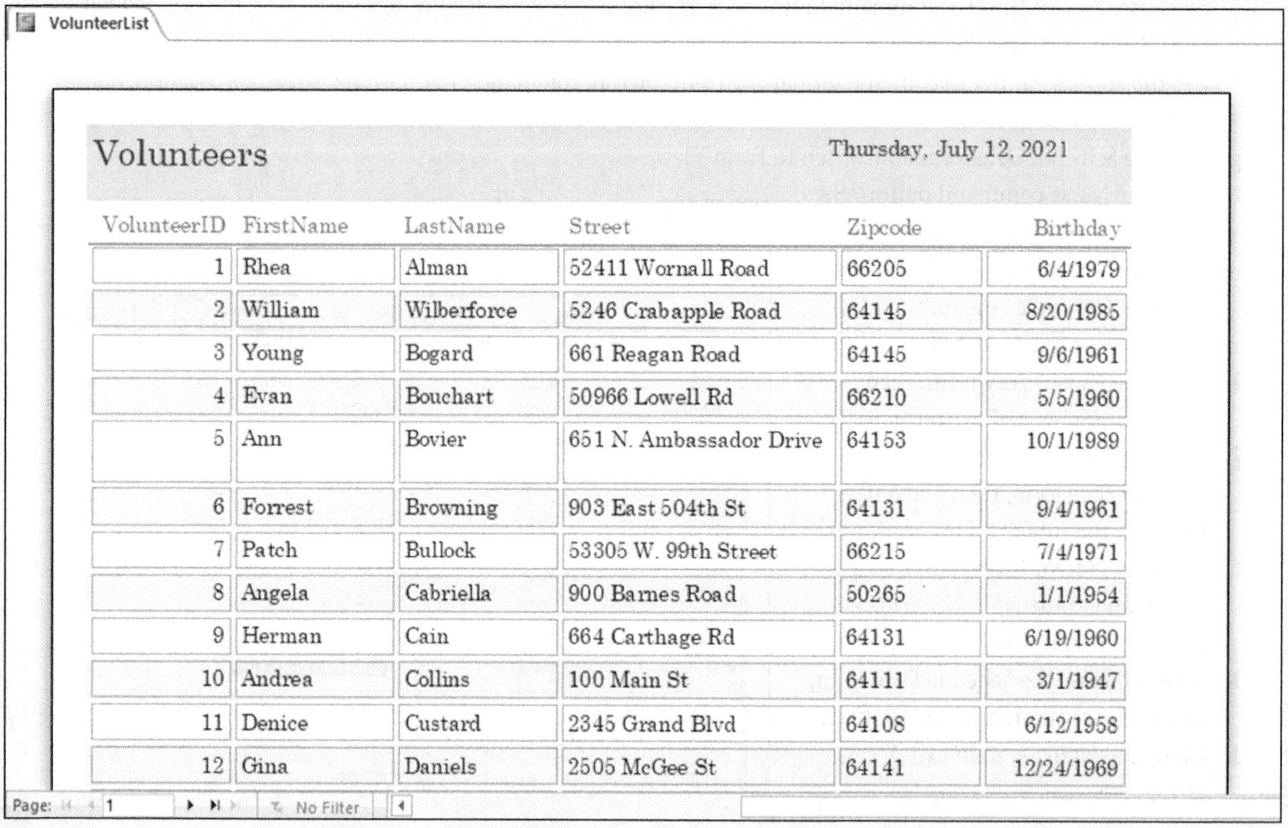

VolunteerID	FirstName	LastName	Street	Zipcode	Birthday
1	Rhea	Alman	52411 Wornall Road	66205	6/4/1979
2	William	Wilberforce	5246 Crabapple Road	64145	8/20/1985
3	Young	Bogard	661 Reagan Road	64145	9/6/1961
4	Evan	Bouchart	50966 Lowell Rd	66210	5/5/1960
5	Ann	Bovier	651 N. Ambassador Drive	64153	10/1/1989
6	Forrest	Browning	903 East 504th St	64131	9/4/1961
7	Patch	Bullock	53305 W. 99th Street	66215	7/4/1971
8	Angela	Cabriella	900 Barnes Road	50265	1/1/1954
9	Herman	Cain	664 Carthage Rd	64131	6/19/1960
10	Andrea	Collins	100 Main St	64111	3/1/1947
11	Denice	Custard	2345 Grand Blvd	64108	6/12/1958
12	Gina	Daniels	2505 McGee St	64141	12/24/1969

Volunteers   Thursday, July 12, 2021

Page: 1 ► ►| ⊺ No Filter ◄

Visual Workshop

Start Access, open the IL_AC_4-5.accdb database from the location where you store your Data Files, save it as **IL_AC_4_CollegeCourses**, then enable content if prompted.

In Query Design View, create a query with the following fields from the following tables:

- Description from the Classes table
- ClassNo from the Sections table
- Grade from the Enrollments table
- StudentFirst and StudentLast from the Students table

Save the query with the name **StudentGrades**, display it in Datasheet View, change any occurrence of Carl Willis to *your name*, then close the StudentGrades query.

Use the Report tool to create a report on this query.

Use Report Layout View to narrow the ClassNo, Grade, StudentFirst, and StudentLast columns. Move the Grade column to be the last. Modify the report title to be **Student Grade Listing**.

Use Report Design View to delete all the controls in the Page Footer and Report Footer sections. Delete the text boxes in the Report Header section that calculate the current date and the current time. Also use Report Design View to narrow the width of the report to 8" or less. Save the report with the name **StudentGradeListing** and preview it in Print Preview, as shown in FIGURE 4-18. Compact and repair the database, then close the database and exit Access 2019.

FIGURE 4-18

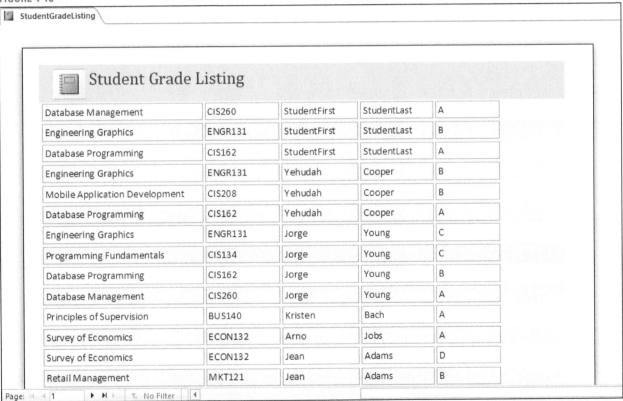

Integrating Word, Excel, and Access

CASE ▸ Anthony Martinez, vice president of Sales and Marketing at the head office of JCL Talent, Inc., in Atlanta, GA, asks you to use Word, Excel, and Access in Office to organize and process data related to the company's top corporate clients.

Module Objectives

After completing this module, you will be able to:

- Integrate data among Word, Excel, and Access
- Import an Excel worksheet into Access
- Copy a Word table to Access
- Link an Access table to Excel and Word
- Copy an Access table to Word

Files You Will Need

IL_INT_2-1.xlsx

Support_INT_2_SalesInformation.docx

IL_INT_2-2.docx

IL_INT_2-3.xlsx

Support_INT_2_EventPlanning.docx

IL_INT_2-4.docx

Support_INT_2_AppsPriceList.docx

IL_INT_2-5.xlsx

Support_INT_2_TimeWiseConsultants.docx

Support_INT_2_ProjectManagerTravel.docx

Integrate Data Among Word, Excel, and Access

You can increase efficiency by integrating the information you create in Word, Excel, and Access so it works together. For example, you can enter data into an Access database, make calculations using that data in Excel, and then create a report in Word that incorporates the Excel data and the Access table. You can also import data from an Excel spreadsheet into Access and copy a table created in Word into an Access table. **CASE** ▶ *Anthony Martinez asks you to create a report in Word to describe the company's top corporate clients. The information you need for this report is contained in Excel, Access, and Word files. Before you create the report, you decide to review some of the ways in which information can be shared among Word, Excel, and Access.*

DETAILS

You can integrate Word, Excel, and Access by:

- **Importing an Excel worksheet into Access**

  You can enter data directly into an Access database table, or you can import data from other sources such as an Excel workbook, another Access database, or even a text file. You use the Get External Data command in Access to import data from an outside source. **FIGURE 2-1** shows how data entered in an Excel file appears when imported into a new table in an Access database. During the import process, you can change the field names and the data types of selected fields.

- **Copying a Word table into Access**

  You can also create a table in Word that contains data you want to include in an Access database. To save time, you can copy the table from Word and paste it into a new or existing Access table. By doing so, you save typing time and minimize errors.

- **Linking an Access table to Excel and Word**

  You link an Access table to Excel and then to Word when you want the data in all three applications to always remain current. First, you use the Copy and Paste Special commands to copy an Access table and paste it into Excel as a link. You can then make calculations using Excel tools that are not available in Access. Any changes you make to the data in Access are also reflected in the linked Excel copy. However, you cannot change the structure of the linked Access table in Excel. For example, you cannot delete any of the columns or rows that contain copied data. The data used in the Excel calculations is linked to the source file in Access. When the data in Access is changed, the results of the formulas in Excel also change.

  Once you have made calculations based on the data in Excel, you can then copy the data from Excel and paste it as a link into Word. When you change the data in Access, the data in both the Excel and the Word files also changes. **FIGURE 2-2** shows a Word document that contains two tables. The top table is linked to both Excel and Access. The table was copied from Access and pasted as a link into Excel, additional calculations were made in Excel, and then the table was copied to the Word report and pasted as a link.

- **Copying an Access table to Word**

  You can use the Copy and Paste Special commands to copy a table from Access and then paste it into a Word document. You can then format the table attractively. In **FIGURE 2-2**, the bottom table was copied from Access, pasted into Word, and then reformatted.

FIGURE 2-1: Excel data imported to an Access table

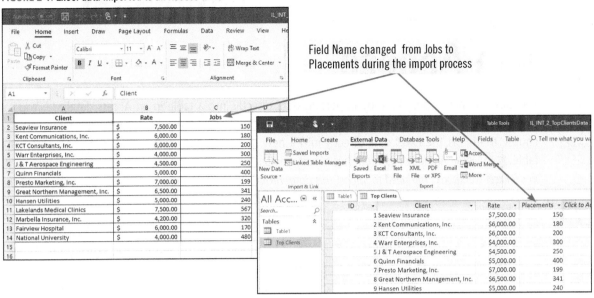

Field Name changed from Jobs to
Placements during the import process

FIGURE 2-2: Word report with links to Excel and Access

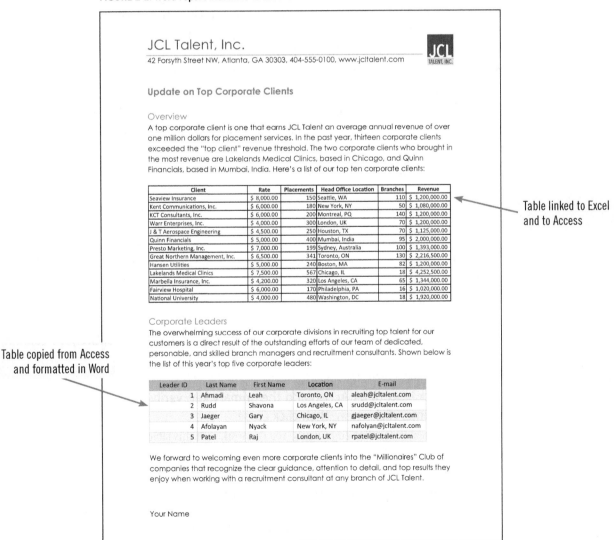

Table linked to Excel
and to Access

Table copied from Access
and formatted in Word

Integration

Import an Excel Worksheet into Access

Learning
Outcomes
- Prepare an Excel table for export to Access
- Import an Excel table to Access
- Rename imported field names

You can minimize typing time by importing data directly into a table in an Access database. You can then delete field names and data you do not need and add additional records to the table. You can choose to import the Excel data directly into a new table, or you can append the data to an existing table. **CASE** *Anthony's assistant has already compiled data about the company's top ten corporate clients in an Excel workbook. You need to import this data into a new Access database. First, you open the report that will eventually contain the data compiled from Word, Excel, and Access.*

1. **Start Excel, open the file IL_INT_2-1.xlsx from the location where you store your Data Files, then save it as IL_INT_2_TopClients**

   The Top Clients sheet of the Excel workbook contains a list of the company's top corporate clients. A workbook that you plan to export from Excel into Access must contain only the data that you want to appear in the Access table; you need to remove titles, subtitles, charts, and any other extraneous data.

2. **Move the mouse pointer to the left of row 1, click and drag to select rows 1 and 2, click the right mouse button, click Delete, then save and close the workbook**

3. **Start Access, click Blank database, replace the current filename with IL_INT_2_TopClientsData in the File Name box, click the Browse button [image], navigate to the location where you store your Data Files, click OK, then click Create**

   A new database opens in Access.

4. **Click the External Data tab, click New Data Source in the Import & Link group, point to From File, click Excel, click Browse, then navigate to the location where you stored the IL_INT_2_TopClients.xlsx file**

5. **Click IL_INT_2_TopClients.xlsx, then click Open**

   In the Get External Data - Excel Spreadsheet dialog box shown in FIGURE 2-3, you can choose from among three options. When you select the first or second option, any change you make to the data in the Excel source file will not be made to the data imported to Access. If you choose the third option, the imported Excel source file is linked to the data imported to Access. You want to import, rather than link, the data.

6. **Click OK to accept the default option and start the Import Spreadsheet Wizard, then verify the First Row Contains Column Headings check box is selected**

   The column headings in the Excel spreadsheet become field names in the Access table. A preview of the Access table appears, with the column names shown in gray header boxes.

7. **Click Next, click the Jobs column in the Table Preview to select the entire Jobs column, then type Placements as shown in FIGURE 2-4**

   The field name changes in the Field Name text box and in the table preview.

8. **Click Next, click Next to let Access add the primary key, verify that Top Clients appears as the table name, click Finish, then click Close**

   Access creates a new table called Top Clients. You can work with this table in the same way you work with any table you create in Access.

9. **Double-click Top Clients in the list of tables, widen the Client column, click below "National University", then compare the table to FIGURE 2-5**

   The imported Excel data now appears in a new Access table. You chose to import the data without links, so any changes you make to the Excel source data will not be reflected in the Access table.

FIGURE 2-3: Selecting a data source in the Get External Data dialog box

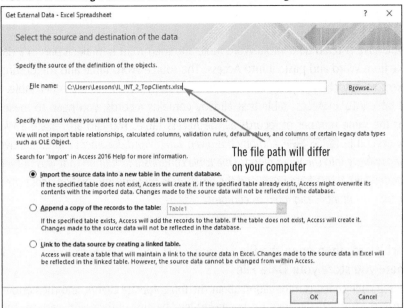

The file path will differ on your computer

FIGURE 2-4: Changing a field name in an imported table

Placements entered in the Field Name box

Field name changes in column heading

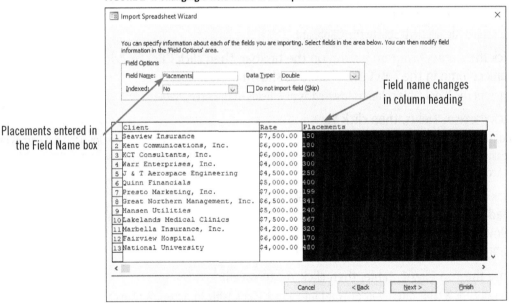

FIGURE 2-5: Excel data imported to an Access table

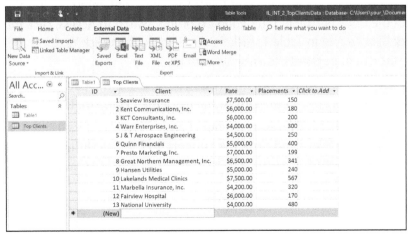

Integration

Copy a Word Table to Access

Learning Outcomes
• Copy a Word table to an existing Access table
• Copy a Word table to a new Access table

When you have entered data into a Word table and then want to make it part of a database, you can copy the table from Word and paste it into Access. The source Word table and the destination Access table are not linked, so any change you make to one table does not affect the other table. If you want to paste a Word table into an Access table that already contains records, you need to make sure the Word table contains the same number of records as the Access table. You can also paste a Word table into a new, blank Access table. **CASE** *Anthony has given you a Word document containing two tables that he wants you to incorporate into the Word report. One table contains information that was not included in the client list you imported into Access from Excel, and the other table contains information about the branch managers and recruitment consultants designated as corporate leaders.*

STEPS

1. **Start Word, then open the file Support_INT_2_SalesInformation.docx from the location where you store your Data Files**

   The top table contains information about the top corporate clients, and the bottom table lists the branch managers who are designated "Corporate Leaders" because of their work with the top clients.

2. **Click Client in the top table, click the table select button ⊞, then click the Copy button in the Clipboard group**

   You copied the selected table to the Clipboard.

QUICK TIP
If you want to import additional records to an existing database, make sure the imported Excel data contains the same number of fields (columns) as the database.

3. **Click the Access program button on the taskbar, then click Click to Add at the top of the blank column in the Top Clients table as shown in FIGURE 2-6**

   You want the Word table columns inserted as new fields in the Access table.

4. **Click Paste as Fields, then click Yes**

   Additional data for the 13 records is pasted into the Top Clients table in Access. You do not need the names of the clients to appear twice in the database table. When you copy data from another source and paste it into an Access table, you can delete fields and records in the same way you normally do in Access.

5. **Click anywhere in the table, right-click Client1, click Delete Field, click Yes, widen the Head Office Location field so all the records are visible, then click in the blank field below National University**

   The Top Clients table appears as shown in FIGURE 2-7.

6. **Close the Top Clients table, then click Yes to save it**

   You can copy a table directly from Word into a new blank table in Access. A blank table called Table1 was automatically created when you created the database, so you can place the copied information there.

7. **Switch to Word, scroll down and select the table containing the list of corporate leaders, click the Copy button in the Clipboard group, switch to Access, click the Home tab, click Click to Add in Table 1, click Paste as Fields, then click Yes**

   The five records are pasted into a new Access table.

8. **Double-click ID, type Leader ID, press ENTER, widen the Location and E-mail columns, click below Record 5 in the Last Name field, then compare the table to FIGURE 2-8**

9. **Close the table, click Yes to save your changes, type Leaders as the table name, click OK, then switch to Word and close the Support_INT_2_SalesInformation.docx**

   You created a new table using data imported from a Word table and named it Leaders.

FIGURE 2-6: Selecting the location for copied data

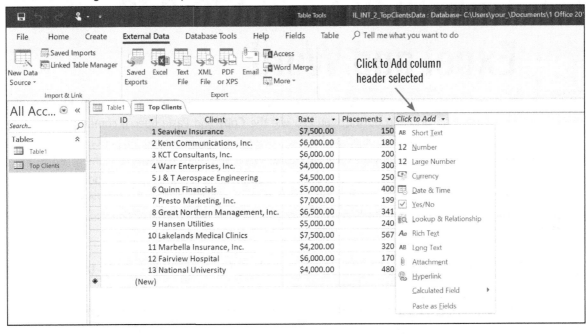

FIGURE 2-7: Table containing data copied from Word

FIGURE 2-8: Renaming the ID field

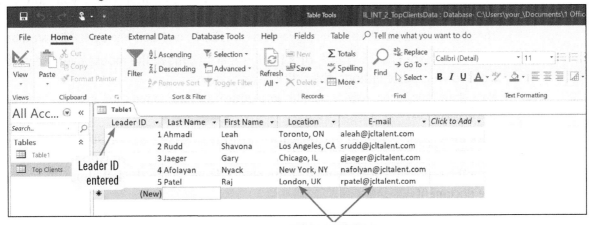

Location and E-mail
columns widened

Link an Access Table to Excel and Word

Learning Outcomes
- Use Copy and Paste Special to create links
- Update linked data

You can link data among three programs to increase efficiency and to reduce the need to enter the same data more than once. To do this, you can use the Copy and Paste Special commands to create a link between an Access database object and an Excel destination file, where you can perform calculations and create charts. You can then copy the Excel data, calculations, and charts to a Word document. When you change the data in the source Access database, the linked data in both Excel and Word are updated to reflect the new information. **CASE** ▶ *You want your report to include revenue information. You link the Access Top Clients table to an Excel worksheet, calculate the revenue using Excel tools, then link the calculation results to the report in Word.*

STEPS

1. **In Access, click the Top Clients table in the list of tables if necessary, then click the Copy button in the Clipboard group**

> **QUICK TIP**
> Click cell A1 if necessary to select it before pasting. If you do not see the Paste Link button, return to Access and copy the table again.

2. **In Excel, create a new blank workbook, click the Paste arrow in the Clipboard group, then click the Paste Link button 📋 (the second of the three Paste options)**

   The Top Clients table appears in Excel. You cannot delete any of the rows or columns in the pasted data in Excel because it is linked to the Access source table. However, you can modify cell formatting, and you can perform calculations based on the pasted data.

3. **With all the data still selected, click the Format button in the Cells group, then click AutoFit Column Width**

   In the copied table, you can make calculations based on the linked data.

4. **Click cell G1, type Revenue, press ENTER, type the formula =C2*D2, press ENTER, then copy the formula to the range G3:G14**

5. **With the range G2:G14 still selected, press and hold CTRL, select the range C2:C14, release CTRL, click the Accounting Number Format button $ in the Number group, click cell A15, increase column widths if needed, then save the workbook as IL_INT_2_TopCorporateRevenue**

   The values in columns C and G are formatted in the Accounting format as shown in **FIGURE 2-9**.

6. **Select the range B1:G14, then click the Copy button in the Clipboard group**

7. **Switch to Word, open the file IL_INT_2-2.docx from the location where you store your Data Files, then save it as IL_INT_2_TopCorporateClientsReport**

   The report contains text about the top corporate clients. Placeholders show where you will paste two tables.

8. **Select the text CLIENTS TABLE, click the Paste arrow, move the mouse over the paste icons to view paste options, then click Paste Special**

   None of the Paste options provide you with appropriate formatting, so you select an option from the Paste Special dialog box.

9. **Click the Paste link option button, click Microsoft Excel Worksheet Object, click OK, press ENTER to add a blank line below the object, click the pasted worksheet object, drag the top-right corner handle of the object down and to the left about 1", then save the document**

   The table appears as shown in **FIGURE 2-10**. This table is linked to the table you copied from Excel, which, in turn, is linked to the table you copied from Access. **TABLE 2-1** describes the differences between the three Paste options you have used in these lessons.

FIGURE 2-9: Copied data formatted in Excel

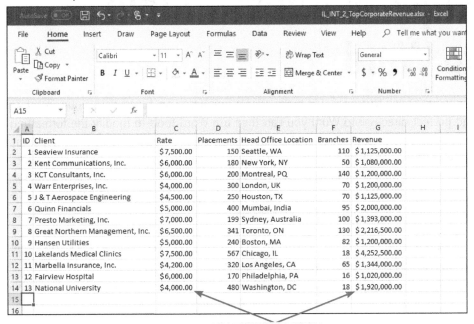

Accounting style applied

FIGURE 2-10: Excel data pasted and linked in Word

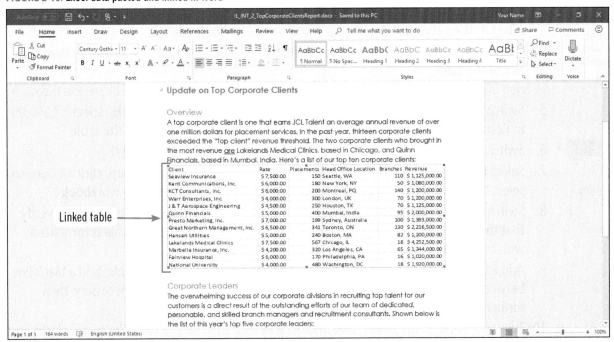

Linked table

TABLE 2-1: Paste options

command	location	use to
Paste	Paste button in Word and Excel	Paste an object without creating a link; the exception is a chart—when you copy a chart from Excel and paste it into Word, the chart is, by default, linked to the source file in Excel
Paste Special	Paste button list shows Paste Special selection in Word and Excel	Paste an object when you want to create a link or you want to select from a variety of formatting options for the pasted object, whether linked or not
Paste Link	Paste button list shows Paste Link button in Excel	Paste an object such as a copied table from Access into Excel as a link

Copy an Access Table to Word

If you don't need to use Excel to make calculations based on Access data, you can copy an Access table and paste it directly into Word you can then use Word tools to modify the formatting of the pasted table so the table communicates the data clearly. TABLE 2-2 summarizes the integration tasks you performed in this module. **CASE** ▶ *The Word report needs to contain a list of the top branch managers and recruitment consultants who have been designated "Corporate Leaders." You copy the Leaders table from Access and paste it into Word, then test the links you created in the previous lesson.*

STEPS

1. Switch to Access, click Leaders in the list of tables to select it, click the Copy button in the Clipboard group, then switch to Word

2. Select the text LEADERS TABLE below paragraph 2, click the Paste arrow, click Paste Special, click Formatted Text (RTF), then click OK

   The Leaders table is pasted as formatted text in Word and is not linked to the Access database. You can format the table using Word table tools.

QUICK TIP
You must always close the table in Access before you check if linked data has been updated in Excel and Word.

3. Click the pasted table, click the table select button ⊞ to select the table, click the Table Tools Design tab, click the Header Row check box in the Table Style Options group to select it, then click the Banded Columns check box to deselect it

4. Click the More button in the Table Styles group, click Grid Table 4 - Accent 4, then click below the table

   Now that you have formatted the table, you decide to test the links you created in the previous lesson.

5. Switch to Access, double-click Top Clients to open the Top Clients table, select $7,500.00 in Record 1 (Seaview Insurance), type 8000, press ENTER, then close the table

6. Switch to Excel, then verify the rate for Seaview Insurance is $8,000.00

TROUBLE
You may need to wait about two minutes for the data to be updated in Excel.

7. Select the range A1:G14, click the Borders arrow ⊞ ▾ in the Font group, click All Borders, select the range A1:G1, apply bold and center the data, then save the workbook

8. Switch to Word, scroll up and right-click the Clients table, click Update Link, then verify that the revenue from Seaview Insurance is now $1,200,000.00, the table is formatted with border lines, and the text in row 1 is bold and centered

9. Add a blank line between the "Overview" paragraph and the Clients table, add a blank line between the "Corporate Leaders" paragraph and the Leaders table, if necessary, then further adjust spacing as needed (see FIGURE 2-11)

10. Type your name in the footer, save and close all files, then submit your files to your instructor

Opening linked files and enabling content

When you open files created in different applications, you need to create them on the same computer logged in as the same user. Open them in the order in which they were created. For example, if you want to change the Word report and need to maintain links, open the Access database first, followed by the Excel workbook. When you open a linked Excel file, click Enable Content if prompted, click Update in response to the message, then, if prompted, click Yes. The exact order of these steps varies depending on how often you have opened the files. In Word, click Yes in response to the message. If all the files were created on the same computer by the same user, the links will all update.

When you email your files to another user, such as your instructor, the links will not work. However, the new user may view the files. After opening the workbook in Excel, they click No, close the workbook without saving it, then reopen the workbook and click Don't Update. In Word, they click No to update links.

FIGURE 2-11: **Completed Word report**

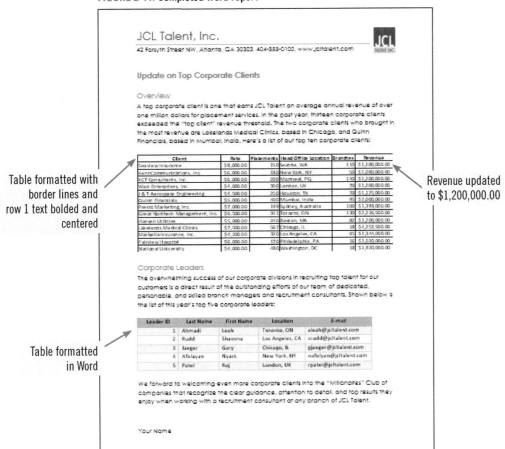

Table formatted with border lines and row 1 text bolded and centered

Revenue updated to $1,200,000.00

Table formatted in Word

TABLE 2-2: **Module 2 integration tasks**

object	commands	source program(s)	destination program	result	connection	page no.
Excel file	External Data/Excel	Excel	Access	Excel spreadsheet is imported into a new table in Access; the spreadsheet must contain only the rows and columns required for the Access table	None	4
Word table	Copy/Paste	Word	Access	Word table is pasted in a new or existing table in Access; if an existing table, the Word table should contain the same number of records as the Access table	None	6
Access table	Copy/Paste Special/ Paste Link	Access	Excel	Access table is pasted into Excel as a link; the linked data can be formatted in Excel and included in formulas but cannot be modified or deleted	Linked	8
Linked Access table in Excel	Copy/Paste Link in Excel Copy/Paste Special/ Paste Link in Word	Access and Excel	Word	Access table is linked to Excel and then to Word; changes made in Access appear in Excel and Word	Linked	8
Access table	Copy/Paste Special	Access	Word	Access table is pasted in Word and can be formatted using Word tools	None	10

Practice

Skills Review

1. **Import an Excel worksheet into Access.**
   a. Start Excel, open the file IL_INT_2-3.xlsx from the location where you store your Data Files, then save it as **IL_INT_2_SummerEvents**.
   b. Delete rows 1 and 2, then save and close the workbook.
   c. Start Access, then create a new blank database called **IL_INT_2_Events** in the location where you store your Data Files.
   d. In Access, import the file **IL_INT_2_SummerEvents.xlsx** file from Excel as external data. In the Import Spreadsheet wizard, change the name of the People field to **Attendees**, then name the new table **Events**.
   e. Close the wizard, open the Events table, then widen columns as necessary.

2. **Copy a Word table to Access.**
   a. Start Word, open the file Support_INT_2_EventPlanning.docx from the location where you store your Data Files.
   b. Select the top table (which contains the list of events), copy it, then switch to Access.
   c. Paste the table in the Events table, delete the duplicate column, widen columns as needed, then save and close the table. *Note*: Don't worry if no data appears in the duplicate column.
   d. In Word, select the table containing the list of event services, copy the table, then paste it as a new table in Access.
   e. Change the ID field to **Services ID**, widen columns, then close the table and name it **Services**.
   f. In Word, close the EventPlanning file.

3. **Link an Access table to Excel and Word.**
   a. In Access, copy the Events table.
   b. Create a new Excel workbook, paste the Events table as a link in cell A1, save the workbook as **IL_INT_2_EventsData**, then adjust column widths where necessary.
   c. Enter **Total Revenue** in cell G1, adjust the column width, then in cell G2, enter a formula to multiply the Per Person Rate by the Attendees.
   d. Copy the formula to the range G3:G16, then format the values in columns C and G in the Accounting Number format.
   e. Copy the range B1:G16, switch to Word, open the file IL_INT_2-4.docx from the location where you store your Data Files, then save it as **IL_INT_2_SummerEventsOverview**.
   f. In the Word document, select the text EVENT LIST, paste the copied data as a linked Microsoft Excel Worksheet Object, add a blank line below the table if necessary, reduce the width of the table to match the line width, then save the document.

4. **Copy an Access table to Word.**
   a. In Access, copy the Services table, switch to Word, then select the SERVICES LIST placeholder.
   b. Paste the copied table as a Formatted Text (RTF) object, then format the table with the Grid Table 2 - Accent 1 table design with the Header Row selected and the Banded Columns deselected.
   c. In Access, open the Events table, change the number of attendees at the Hospital Gala (Record 3) to **700**, then close the table.
   d. In Excel, verify the total revenue value for the Hospital Gala is $560,000.00. You may need to wait a few minutes.
   e. Select the range A1:G16, add border lines to all cells, select the range A1:G1, then apply bold and centering.

Skills Review (continued)

f. In Word, update the link to the table that lists the events, then verify the Hospital Gala total changes to $560,000.00 and the header formats change to the new format.

g. Compare the completed report to FIGURE 2-12, make any necessary spacing adjustments, type your name where indicated in the footer, save and close all open files and programs, then submit your files to your instructor.

Independent Challenge 1

Riverwalk Medical Clinic in San Antonio, TX, has partnered with a local software developer to create apps that help patients monitor their health and well-being. The demand for the apps is growing rapidly, and you need to develop a system for keeping track of the apps sold. You have a price list saved in a Word document. You transfer the price list into an Access database, then add some new records. You then perform calculations on the data in Excel and verify that when you update data in the Access database, the data in Excel also changes.

a. Start Word, open the file Support_INT_2_AppsPriceList. docx from the location where you store your Data Files.

b. Copy the table, create a new database in Access called **IL_INT_2_RiverwalkApps** in the location where you store your Data Files, then paste the copied table into a new table named **Products**.

c. Add two new records to the Products table with the following information:

App	Category	Price
Blood Sugar Monitor	Medical	$7.00
Yoga for Seniors	Fitness	$5.00

d. Close the table, copy it and paste it as a link into a new Excel workbook, then add a new column in Excel called **Sales**.

e. Enter **200** as the number of sales for the first four products and **300** as the number of sales for the last eight products.

f. Add a new column called **Revenue**, calculate the total revenue for each app, then save the workbook as **IL_INT_2_RiverwalkAppsSales**.

g. Format the Price and Revenue values with the Accounting Number format, then adjust column widths as necessary.

h. Note the current revenue amount for the Heart Health and Fitness Buddy apps ($800 and $1,050).

i. In the Access Products table, change the price of the Heart Health app to $5.00 and the price of the Fitness Buddy app to $4.00, then close the table.

j. In Excel, verify the values have been updated to $1,000 and $1,200. You may need to wait a few minutes.

FIGURE 2-12

Independent Challenge 1 (continued)

k. Bold and center the labels in row 1, insert a new row 1, enter **Riverwalk Apps Sales**, merge and center it across the range A1:F1, increase the font size to 16 point, apply bold formatting, then apply the Blue, Accent 5, Lighter 60% fill color.

l. Type your name in cell A16, compare the completed workbook to FIGURE 2-13, save and close all open files and programs, then submit your files to your instructor.

FIGURE 2-13

	A	B	C	D	E	F	G
1		**Riverwalk Apps Sales**					
2	ID	App	Category	Price	Sales	Revenue	
3	1	Tracking Nutrition	Nutrition	$ 7.00	200	$1,400.00	
4	2	Heart Health	Medical	$ 5.00	200	$1,000.00	
5	3	Meditation Helper	Wellness	$ 1.50	200	$ 300.00	
6	4	Meal Planning Pal	Nutrition	$ 6.00	200	$1,200.00	
7	5	First Aid	Emergency	$ 2.00	300	$ 600.00	
8	6	My Records	Medical	$ 3.00	300	$ 900.00	
9	7	Fitness Buddy	Fitness	$ 4.00	300	$1,200.00	
10	8	Rx Helper	Medical	$ 5.50	300	$1,650.00	
11	9	Doctor on Call	Medical	$ 4.50	300	$1,350.00	
12	10	Med Pulse	Medical	$ 3.00	300	$ 900.00	
13	11	Blood Sugar Monitor	Medical	$ 7.00	300	$2,100.00	
14	12	Yoga for Seniors	Fitness	$ 5.00	300	$1,500.00	
15							
16	Your Name						
17							
18							

Independent Challenge 2

Time Wise Media provides social media services to small business owners. You have been asked to build a database that the owner can use to keep track of contracts. The owner would also like you to create a report that analyzes sales trends.

a. Start Excel, open the file **IL_INT_2-5.xlsx** from the location where you store your Data Files, then save it as **IL_INT_2_TimeWiseContracts**.

b. Delete any rows and objects that cannot be imported into Access, then save and close the workbook.

c. Create a database in Access called **IL_INT_2_TimeWiseMedia**, and save it in the location where you store your Data Files.

d. Import the Excel file IL_INT_2_TimeWiseContracts.xlsx into the Access database, change the Description field name to **Service**, and accept **Contracts** as the table name.

e. Start Word, open the file Support_INT_2_TimeWiseConsultants.docx from the location where you store your Data Files, copy the table, close the document, then paste the table into the Contracts table in Access.

f. Delete the Client Name1 column from the pasted information, widen columns as needed, then save and close the table.

g. Copy the Contracts table, paste it as a linked file into cell A1 of a new Excel workbook, then adjust the column widths.

h. Calculate the total revenue from each contract total based on an hourly rate of $110. (*Hint*: Add two new columns—one called "Rate" with "110" entered for each record and one called "Total" with the formula entered for each record.)

i. Format the values in columns G and H with the Accounting Number format, then save the Excel workbook as **IL_INT_2_TimeWiseRevenue**.

j. In Word, open a new document and enter the text shown in the completed document in FIGURE 2-14, then save it as **IL_INT_2_TimeWiseSpringContracts**. Format the title in 22 point, bold and the subtitle in 14 point, bold.

k. Copy cells B1 to H11 from Excel, paste them as a link using the Microsoft Excel Worksheet Object option in the Paste Special dialog box below the text paragraph in the IL_INT_2_TimeWiseSpringContracts document, resize the object so it fits into the Word document (*Hint*: Drag the bottom left corner sizing handle up), then save the document.

l. In the Contracts table in Access, change the number of hours for Isabel Cox to **35**, close the table, then verify the revenue for Isabel Cox has changed from $2,200 to $3,850 in the Excel file. Remember, you may need to wait a few minutes for the values to update.

m. Format the range A1:H11 with border lines around all cells, and bold and center column titles.

n. Update the worksheet object in the Word file.

o. Add your name below the worksheet object, compare the completed document to FIGURE 2-14, save all files and close all programs, then submit your files to your instructor.

FIGURE 2-14

Time Wise Media

Spring Contracts

Time Wise Media provides small businesses with a one-stop shop for social media and Web marketing services. The table below lists the clients serviced by Time Wise Media in March and April.

Client Name	Service	Hours	Consultant	Location	Rate	Total
Marsha Platt	Instagram Setup	12	Mitsuko Haraki	Head Office	$ 110.00	$ 1,320.00
Wendell McNair	Facebook Ads	15	Rebecka Tapia	Client's Office	$ 110.00	$ 1,650.00
Olive Ng	Twitter Expansion	10	Josie Pike	Client's Home	$ 110.00	$ 1,100.00
Isabel Cox	Website Optimization	35	Corrin Macon	Head Office	$ 110.00	$ 3,850.00
Joanna Roy	Facebook Ads	15	Jamee Sweitz	Kansas Branch	$ 110.00	$ 1,650.00
Avery Burks	Podcast Development	25	Mitsuko Haraki	Client's Home	$ 110.00	$ 2,750.00
Hye Cano	YouTube Channel Setup	25	Felicity Vasquez	Nevada Branc	$ 110.00	$ 2,750.00
Tari Prater	Email Marketing	10	Josie Pike	Head Office	$ 110.00	$ 1,100.00
Vincenza Morelli	Twitter Expansion	15	Rebecka Tapia	Head Office	$ 110.00	$ 1,650.00
Ivy Florez	Instagram Setup	10	Jason Bahn	Client's Home	$ 110.00	$ 1,100.00

Your Name

Visual Workshop

Create a new database called **IL_INT_2_BentonEngineering** in the location where you store your Data Files, then copy the table from the Word file **Support_INT_2_ProjectManagerTravel.docx** into the database as a new table. Name the table **Manager Travel**. Copy the table, then paste it as linked data in a new Excel workbook. Save the workbook as **IL_INT_2_BentonEngineeringTravelExpenses**. Refer to FIGURE 2-15 to add two new columns, enter a per diem rate of **$300**, and calculate the total expenses for each staff person. Calculate the total expenses in cell G12. In the Access source table, change the number of days that Jill Zimmerman was away to **20** and the number of days that Alonzo Peters was away to **22**, then close the table. In Excel, verify that the appropriate values are updated, then as shown in FIGURE 2-15, add and format a title and subtitle. (*Hint*: The font size of the title is 20 point, and the font size of the subtitle is 16 point.) Format data as shown in the figure. Include your name under the table, save and close all open files and programs, then submit your files to your instructor.

FIGURE 2-15

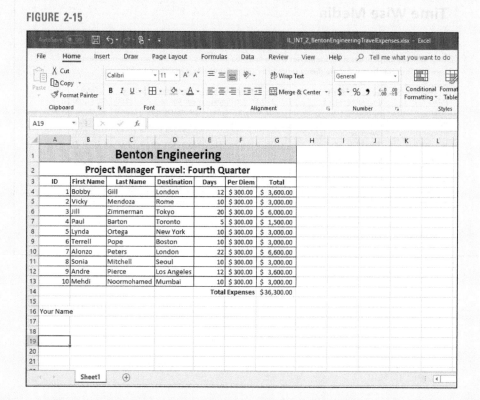

ID	First Name	Last Name	Destination	Days	Per Diem	Total
1	Bobby	Gill	London	12	$ 300.00	$ 3,600.00
2	Vicky	Mendoza	Rome	10	$ 300.00	$ 3,000.00
3	Jill	Zimmerman	Tokyo	20	$ 300.00	$ 6,000.00
4	Paul	Barton	Toronto	5	$ 300.00	$ 1,500.00
5	Lynda	Ortega	New York	10	$ 300.00	$ 3,000.00
6	Terrell	Pope	Boston	10	$ 300.00	$ 3,000.00
7	Alonzo	Peters	London	22	$ 300.00	$ 6,600.00
8	Sonia	Mitchell	Seoul	10	$ 300.00	$ 3,000.00
9	Andre	Pierce	Los Angeles	12	$ 300.00	$ 3,600.00
10	Mehdi	Noormohamed	Mumbai	10	$ 300.00	$ 3,000.00
					Total Expenses	$ 36,300.00

Benton Engineering — Project Manager Travel: Fourth Quarter

Your Name

Creating a Presentation in PowerPoint

CASE JCL Talent, based in Atlanta, Georgia, is a company that provides comprehensive recruitment and employment services for employers and job seekers worldwide. You work for Dawn Lapointe in the Technical Careers division. You have been asked to help her create a presentation on global workforce trends that she will give at an upcoming recruiters convention. Use PowerPoint 2019 to create the presentation.

Module Objectives

After completing this module, you will be able to:

- Define presentation software
- Plan an effective presentation
- Examine the PowerPoint window
- Enter slide text
- Add a new slide
- Format text

- Apply a design theme
- Compare presentation views
- Insert and resize a picture
- Check spelling
- Print a PowerPoint presentation

Files You Will Need

Support_PPT_1_Woman.jpg
IL_PPT_1-1.pptx
Support_PPT_1_Group.jpg
IL_ PPT_1-2.pptx
IL_ PPT_1-3.pptx

Define Presentation Software

Presentation software (also called presentation graphics software) is a computer program you use to organize and present information to others. Presentations are typically in the form of a slide show. Whether you are explaining a new product or moderating a meeting, presentation software can help you effectively communicate your ideas. You can use PowerPoint to create informational slides that you print or display on a monitor, share in real time on the web, or save as a video for others to watch. **CASE** *You need to start working on the global workforce presentation. Because you are only somewhat familiar with PowerPoint, you get to work exploring its capabilities.* FIGURE 1-1 *shows how a presentation looks printed as handouts.* FIGURE 1-2 *shows how the same presentation might look saved as a video.*

DETAILS

You can easily complete the following tasks using PowerPoint:

- **Enter and edit text easily**

  Text editing and formatting commands in PowerPoint are organized by the task you are performing at the time, so you can enter, edit, and format text information simply and efficiently to produce the best results in the least amount of time.

- **Change the appearance of information**

  PowerPoint has many effects that can transform the way text, graphics, and slides appear. By exploring some of these capabilities, you discover how easy it is to change the appearance of your presentation.

- **Organize and arrange information**

  Once you start using PowerPoint, you won't have to spend much time making sure your information is correct and in the right order. With PowerPoint, you can quickly and easily rearrange and modify text, graphics, and slides in your presentation.

- **Include information from other sources**

  Often, when you create presentations, you use information from a variety of sources. With PowerPoint, you can import text, photographs, videos, numerical data, and other information from files created in programs such as Adobe Photoshop, Microsoft Word, Microsoft Excel, and Microsoft Access. You can also import information from other PowerPoint presentations as well as graphic images from a variety of sources such as the Internet, storage devices, computers, a camera, or other graphics programs. Always be sure you have permission to use any work that you did not create yourself.

- **Present information in a variety of ways**

  With PowerPoint, you can present information using a variety of methods. For example, you can print handout pages or an outline of your presentation for audience members. You can display your presentation as an on-screen slide show using your computer, or if you are presenting to a large group, you can use a video projector and a large screen. If you want to reach an even wider audience, you can broadcast the presentation or upload it as a video to the Internet so people anywhere in the world can use a web browser to view your presentation.

- **Collaborate with others on a presentation**

  PowerPoint makes it easy to collaborate or share a presentation with colleagues and coworkers using the Internet. You can use your email program to send a presentation as an attachment to a colleague for feedback. If you have a number of people that need to work together on a presentation, you can save the presentation to a shared workspace such as a network drive or OneDrive so authorized users in your group with an Internet connection can access the presentation.

FIGURE 1-1: **PowerPoint handout**

7/11/2021

Asier Romero/Shutterstock.com

FIGURE 1-2: **Presentation saved as a video**

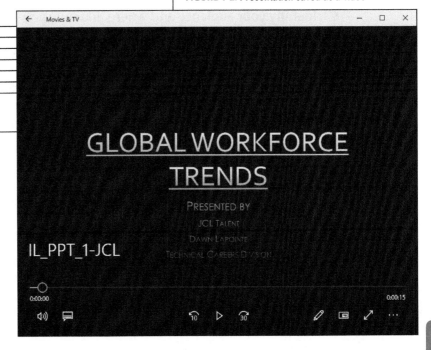

Using PowerPoint on a touch screen

You can use PowerPoint 2019 on a Windows computer with a touch-enabled monitor or any other compatible touch screen, such as a tablet computer. Using your fingers, you can use typical touch gestures to create, modify, and navigate presentations. To enable touch mode capabilities in PowerPoint, you need to add the Touch Mode button to the Quick Access toolbar. Click the Customize Quick Access Toolbar button, click Touch/Mouse Mode, click the on the Quick Access toolbar, then click Touch. In Touch mode, additional space is added around all of the buttons and icons in the Ribbon and the status bar to make them easier to touch. Common gestures that you can use in PowerPoint include double-tapping text to edit it and tapping a slide then dragging it to rearrange it in the presentation.

Plan an Effective Presentation

Before you create a presentation, you need to have a general idea of the information you want to communicate. PowerPoint is a powerful and flexible program that gives you the ability to start a presentation simply by entering the text of your message. If you have a specific design in mind that you want to use, you can start the presentation by working on the design. In most cases you'll probably enter the text of your presentation into PowerPoint first and then tailor the design to the message and audience. When preparing your presentation, you need to keep in mind not only who you are giving it to, but also how you are presenting it. For example, if you are giving a presentation using a projector, you need to know what other equipment you will need, such as a sound system. **CASE** *Use the planning guidelines below to help plan an effective presentation.* FIGURE 1-3 *illustrates a storyboard for a well-planned presentation.*

DETAILS

In planning a presentation, it is important to:

• **Determine and outline the message you want to communicate**

The more time you take developing the message and outline of your presentation, the better your presentation will be in the end. A presentation with a clear message that reads like a story and is illustrated with appropriate visual aids will have the greatest impact on your audience. Start the presentation by providing a general description of the global workforce trends. See FIGURE 1-3.

• **Identify your audience and where and how you are giving the presentation**

Audience and delivery location are major factors in the type of presentation you create. For example, a presentation you develop for a staff meeting that is held in a conference room would not necessarily need to be as sophisticated or detailed as a presentation that you develop for a large audience in an auditorium. Room lighting, natural light, screen position, and room layout all affect how the audience responds to your presentation. You might also broadcast your presentation over the Internet to several people who view the presentation on their computers in real time. This presentation will be broadcast over the Internet.

• **Determine the type of output**

Output choices for a presentation include black-and-white or color handouts for audience members, an on-screen slide show, a video, or an online broadcast. Consider the time demands and computer equipment availability as you decide which output types to produce. Because this presentation will be broadcast over the Internet, the default output settings work just fine.

• **Determine the design**

Visual appeal, graphics, and presentation design work together to communicate your message. You can choose one of the professionally designed themes that come with PowerPoint, modify one of these themes, or create one of your own. You decide to choose one of PowerPoint's design themes for your presentation.

FIGURE 1-3: **Storyboard of the presentation**

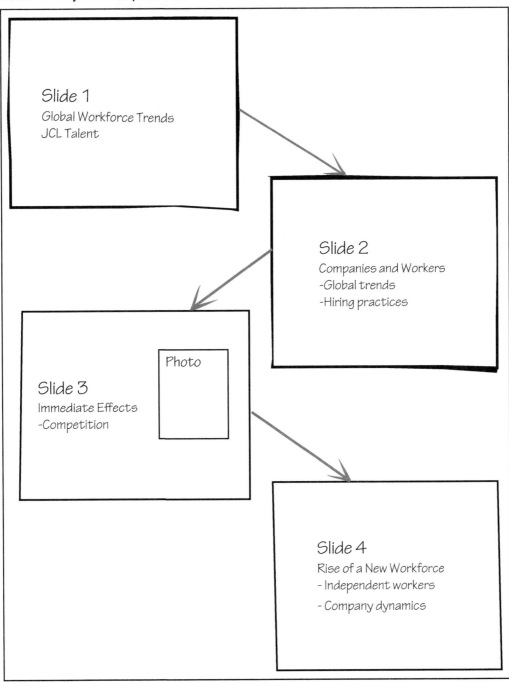

Understanding copyright

Intellectual property is any idea or creation of the human mind. Copyright law is a type of intellectual property law that protects works of authorship, including books, web pages, computer games, music, artwork, and photographs. Copyright protects the expression of an idea, but not the underlying facts or concepts. In other words, the general subject matter is not protected, but how you express it is, such as when several people photograph the same sunset. Copyright attaches to any original work of authorship as soon as it is created; you do not have to register it with the Copyright Office or display the copyright symbol, ©. Fair use is an exception to copyright and permits the public to use copyrighted material for certain purposes without obtaining prior consent from the owner. Determining whether fair use applies to a work depends on its purpose, the nature of the work, how much of the work you want to copy, and the effect on the work's value. Unauthorized use of protected work (such as downloading a photo or a song from the web) is known as copyright infringement and can lead to legal action.

Examine the PowerPoint Window

When you first start PowerPoint, you have the ability to choose what kind of presentation you want to use to start—a blank one, or one with a preformatted design. You can also open and work on an existing presentation. PowerPoint has different **views** that allow you to see your presentation in different forms. By default, the PowerPoint window opens in **Normal view**, which is the primary view that you use to write, edit, and design your presentation. Normal view is divided into areas called **panes**: the pane on the left, called the **Slides tab**, displays the slides of your presentation as small images, called **slide thumbnails**. The large pane is the Slide pane where you do most of your work on the slide. **CASE** ▶ *The PowerPoint window and the specific parts of Normal view are described below.*

STEPS

1. **sam** ✦ Start PowerPoint 2019

   PowerPoint starts and the PowerPoint start screen opens, as shown in FIGURE 1-4.

2. **Click the** Blank Presentation slide thumbnail

   The PowerPoint window opens in Normal view, as shown in FIGURE 1-5.

DETAILS

Using Figure 1-5 as a guide, examine the elements of the PowerPoint window, then find and compare the elements described below:

- The **Ribbon** is a wide band spanning the top of the PowerPoint window that organizes all of PowerPoint's primary commands. Each set of primary commands is identified by a **tab**; for example, the Home tab is selected by default, as shown in FIGURE 1-5. Commands are further arranged into **groups** on the Ribbon based on their function. So, for example, text formatting commands such as Bold, Underline, and Italic are located on the Home tab, in the Font group.

- The Slides tab is to the left. You can navigate through the slides in your presentation by clicking the slide thumbnails. You can also add, delete, or rearrange slides using this pane.

- The **Slide pane** displays the current slide in your presentation.

- The **Quick Access toolbar** provides access to common commands such as Save, Undo, Redo, and Start From Beginning. The Quick Access toolbar is always visible no matter which Ribbon tab you select. Click the Customize Quick Access Toolbar button to add or remove buttons.

- The **View Shortcuts** buttons on the status bar allow you to switch quickly between PowerPoint views.

- The **Notes button** on the status bar opens the Notes pane and is used to enter text that references a slide's content. You can print these notes and refer to them when you make a presentation or use them as audience handouts. The Notes pane is not visible in Slide Show view.

- The **status bar**, located at the bottom of the PowerPoint window, shows messages about what you are doing and seeing in PowerPoint, including which slide you are viewing and the total number of slides. In addition, the status bar displays the Zoom slider controls, the Fit slide to current window button ⊞, and other functionality information.

- The **Zoom slider** on the lower-right corner of the status bar is used to zoom the slide in and out.

FIGURE 1-4: **PowerPoint start screen**

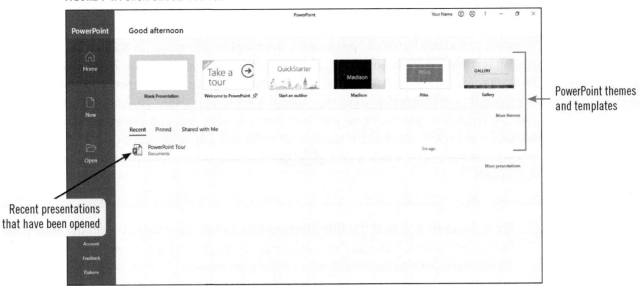

Recent presentations that have been opened

PowerPoint themes and templates

FIGURE 1-5: **PowerPoint window in Normal view**

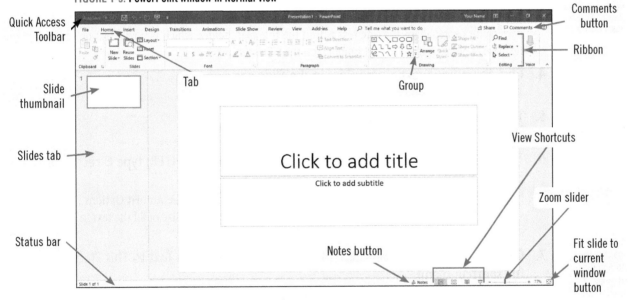

Quick Access Toolbar

Slide thumbnail

Slides tab

Status bar

Tab

Group

Click to add title

Click to add subtitle

Comments button

Ribbon

View Shortcuts

Zoom slider

Notes button

Fit slide to current window button

Creating a presentation using a template

PowerPoint offers you a variety of ways to create a presentation, including starting with a blank presentation, a theme, a template, or an existing presentation. A **template** is a type of presentation that contains design information on the slide master and often includes text and design suggestions for information you might want to include in the presentation. You have access to sample templates in PowerPoint and online at the Microsoft.com website. To create a presentation using a template, click the File tab on the Ribbon, click the New tab, locate the template, then click Create.

Enter Slide Text

Learning Outcomes
• Enter slide text
• Change slide text

When you start a blank PowerPoint presentation, an empty title slide appears in Normal view. The title slide has two **text placeholders**—boxes with dotted borders—where you enter text. The top text placeholder on the title slide is the **title placeholder**, labeled "Click to add title". The bottom text placeholder on the title slide is the **subtitle text placeholder**, labeled "Click to add subtitle". To enter text in a placeholder, click the placeholder and then type your text. After you enter text in a placeholder, the placeholder becomes a text object. An **object** is any item on a slide that can be modified. Objects are the building blocks that make up a presentation slide. **CASE** ▶ *Begin working on your presentation by entering text on the title slide.*

STEPS

1. **Move the pointer ⇦ over the title placeholder labeled** Click to add title **in the Slide pane**

   The pointer changes to ⊺ when you move the pointer over the placeholder. In PowerPoint, the pointer often changes shape, depending on the task you are trying to accomplish.

2. **Click the** title placeholder **in the Slide pane**

   The **insertion point**, a blinking vertical line, indicates where your text appears when you type in the placeholder. A **selection box** with a dashed line border and **sizing handles** appears around the placeholder, indicating that it is selected and ready to accept text. When a placeholder or object is selected, you can change its shape or size by dragging one of the sizing handles. See FIGURE 1-6.

3. **Type** Global Workforce Trends

   PowerPoint center-aligns the title text within the title placeholder, which is now a text object. Notice the text also appears on the Slide 1 thumbnail on the Slides tab.

4. **Click the** subtitle text placeholder **in the Slide pane**

   The subtitle text placeholder is ready to accept text.

5. **Type** Presented by, **then press** ENTER

   The insertion point moves to the next line in the text object.

6. **Type** JCL Talent, **press** ENTER, **type** Dawn Lapointe, **press** ENTER, **type** Director, **press** ENTER, **then type** Technical Careers Division

   Notice the AutoFit Options button ⊞ appears near the text object. The AutoFit Options button on your screen indicates that PowerPoint has automatically decreased the font size of all the text in the text object so it fits inside the text object.

7. **Click the** AutoFit Options button ⊞, **then click** Stop Fitting Text to This Placeholder **on the shortcut menu**

   The text in the text object changes back to its original size and no longer fits inside the text object.

8. **In the subtitle text object, position** ⊺ **to the right of** Director, **drag left to select the whole word, press** BACKSPACE, **then click outside the text object in a blank area of the slide**

   The Director line of text is deleted and the AutoFit Options button menu closes, as shown in FIGURE 1-7. Clicking a blank area of the slide deselects all selected objects on the slide.

9. **Click the** Save button 🖫 **on the Quick Access toolbar to open Backstage view, then save the presentation as** IL_PPT_1_JCL **in the location where you store your Data Files**

   In Backstage view, you have the option of saving your presentation to your computer or OneDrive. Notice that PowerPoint automatically entered the title of the presentation as the filename in the Save As dialog box.

FIGURE 1-6: **Title text placeholder selected**

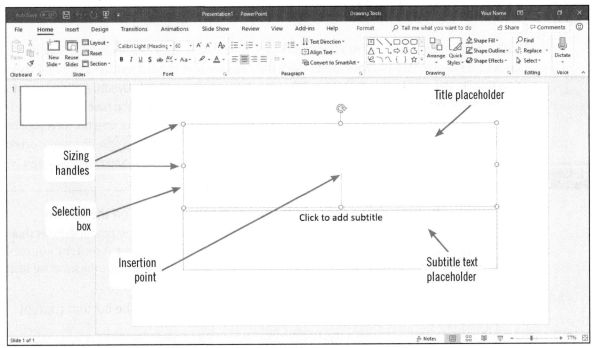

FIGURE 1-7: **Text on title slide**

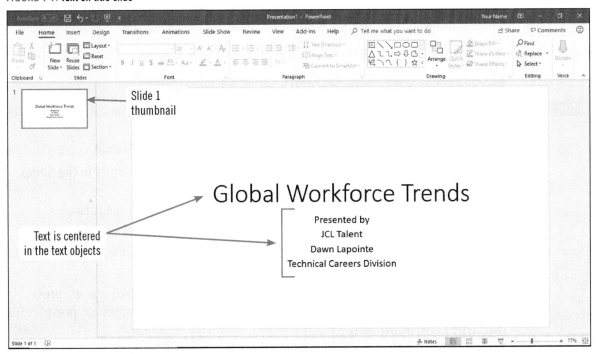

Inking a slide

In Slide View, you can add freehand pen and highlighter marks, also known as **inking**, to the slides of your presentation to emphasize information. To begin inking, go to the slide you want to mark up, click the Review tab, then click the Start Inking button in the Ink group. The Pens tab appears on the Ribbon, and the Pen tool appears on the slide ready for you to draw using your mouse. To customize your pen, select a different pen color, style, or thickness from options in the Pens group. Click the Highlighter button in the Write group to insert highlighter strokes on your slide. To erase inking on the slide, click the Eraser button in the Write group.

PowerPoint

Add a New Slide

Usually when you add a new slide to a presentation, you have a pretty good idea of what you want the slide to look like. For example, you may want to add a slide that has a title over bulleted text and a picture. To help you add a slide like this quickly and easily, PowerPoint provides many standard slide layouts. A **slide layout** contains text and object placeholders that are arranged in a specific way on the slide. You have already worked with the Title Slide layout in the previous lesson. In the event that a standard slide layout does not meet your needs, you can modify an existing slide layout or create a new, custom slide layout. **CASE** ▶ *To continue developing the presentation, you create a slide that explains the changing relationship between companies and workers.*

STEPS

1. **Click the** New Slide button **in the Slides group on the Home tab on the Ribbon**

   A new blank slide (now the current slide) appears as the second slide in your presentation, as shown in FIGURE 1-8. The new slide contains a title placeholder and a content placeholder. A **content placeholder** can be used to insert text or objects such as tables, charts, videos, or pictures. Notice the status bar indicates Slide 2 of 2 and the Slides tab now contains two slide thumbnails.

2. **Type** Relationship Between Companies and Workers, **then click the** bottom content placeholder

   The text you typed appears in the title placeholder, and the insertion point is now at the top of the bottom content placeholder.

3. **Type** Global trends, **then press** ENTER

   The insertion point appears directly below the text when you press ENTER, and a new first-level bullet automatically appears.

4. **Press** TAB

   The new first-level bullet is indented and becomes a second-level bullet.

5. **Type** Hiring practices since 2009, **press** ENTER, **then click the** Decrease List Level button ⊞ **in the Paragraph group**

   The Decrease List Level button changes the second-level bullet into a first-level bullet.

6. **Type** Reduction of full-time employees, **then click the** New Slide arrow **in the Slides group**

   The Office Theme layout gallery opens. Each slide layout is identified by a descriptive name.

7. **Click the** Two Content slide layout, **then type** Immediate Effects

   A new slide with a title placeholder and two content placeholders appears as the third slide. The text you typed is the title text for the slide.

8. **Click the left content placeholder, type** Independent workers — free agents, **press** ENTER, **click the** Increase List Level button ⊞, **type** Increase competition, **press** ENTER, **then type** Drive down costs

   The Increase List Level button moves the insertion point one level to the right.

9. **Click a blank area of the slide, then click the** Save button 🖫 **on the Quick Access toolbar**

   The Save button saves all of the changes to the file. Compare your screen with FIGURE 1-9.

FIGURE 1-8: **New blank slide in Normal view**

New Slide button

New slide thumbnail added to Slides tab

New Slide button arrow

Title text placeholder

Content placeholder

Current slide number

Total number of slides

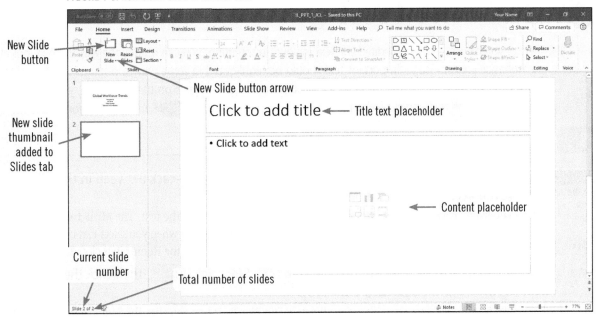

FIGURE 1-9: **New slide with Two Content slide layout**

Decrease List Level button

Increase List Level button

First-level bullet

Second-level bullet

Two content placeholders based on the slide layout

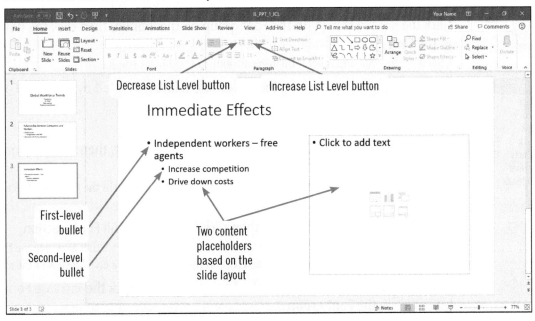

Viewing your presentation in grayscale or black and white

Viewing your presentation in grayscale (using shades of gray) or pure black and white is very useful when you are printing a presentation on a black-and-white printer and you want to make sure your presentation prints correctly. To see how your color presentation looks in grayscale or black and white, click the View tab, then click either the Grayscale or Black and White button in the Color/Grayscale group. Depending on which button you select, the Grayscale or the Black and White tab appears, and the Ribbon displays different settings that you can customize. If you don't like the way an individual object looks in black and white or grayscale, you can change its color. Click the object while still in Grayscale or Black and White view, then choose an option in the Change Selected Object group on the Ribbon.

Format Text

Once you have entered and edited the text in your presentation, you can modify the way the text looks to emphasize your message. Important text should be highlighted in some way to distinguish it from other text or objects on the slide. For example, if you have two text objects on the same slide, you could draw attention to one text object by changing its color, font, or size. **CASE** ▶ *You decide to format the text on two slides of the presentation.*

STEPS

1. **Click the Slide 2 thumbnail in the Slides tab, then double-click Between in the title text object**

   The word "Between" is selected, and a Mini toolbar appears above the text. The **Mini toolbar** contains basic text-formatting commands, such as bold and italic, and appears when you select text using the mouse. This toolbar makes it quick and easy to format text, especially when the Home tab is closed.

2. **Move ⌖ over the Mini toolbar, click the Font Color arrow A ▾, then click the Dark Red color box in the Standard Colors row**

   The text changes color to dark red, as shown in FIGURE 1-10. When you click the Font Color arrow, the Font Color gallery appears showing the Theme Colors and Standard Colors. ScreenTips help identify font colors. Notice that the Font Color button on the Mini toolbar and the Font Color button in the Font group on the Home tab change color to reflect the new color choice, which is now the active color.

3. **Click the Bold button B in the Font group on the Ribbon, then click the Italic button I in the Font group**

   Changing the color and other formatting attributes of text helps emphasize it.

4. **Click the Slide 1 thumbnail in the Slides tab, select Presented by, click the Font Size arrow 11 ▾ in the Mini toolbar, then click 28**

   The text increases in size to 28.

5. **Select the text Global Workforce Trends in the title object, then click the Font arrow in the Font group**

   A list of available fonts opens with Calibri Light, the current font used in the title text object, selected at the top of the list in the Theme Fonts section.

6. **Scroll down the alphabetical list, then click Corbel in the All Fonts section**

   The Corbel font replaces the original font in the title text object. Notice that as you move the pointer over the font names in the font list, the selected text on the slide displays a Live Preview of the available fonts.

7. **Click the Underline button U in the Font group, then click the Increase Font Size button A˄ in the Font group**

   All of the text now displays an underline and increases in size to 66.

8. **Click a blank area of the slide outside the text object to deselect it, then save your work**

   Clicking a blank area of the slide deselects all objects that are selected. Compare your screen to FIGURE 1-11.

FIGURE 1-10: Selected word with Mini toolbar open

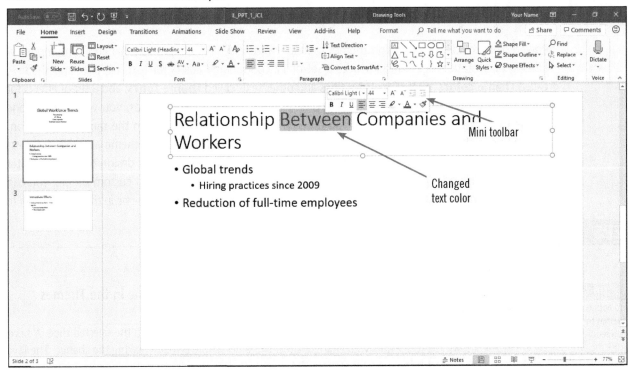

FIGURE 1-11: Formatted text

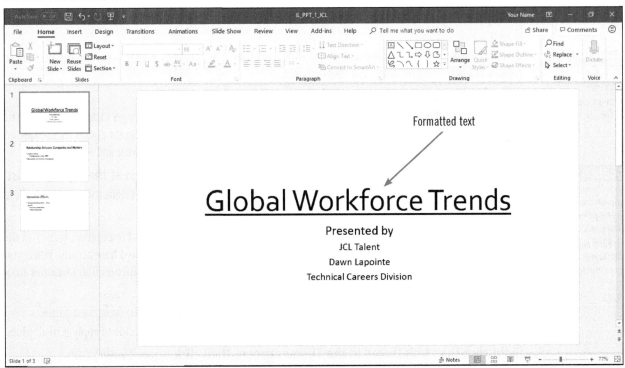

Adding bullets to paragraphs

In PowerPoint, paragraph text is often preceded by either a number or some kind of bullet. Common bullets include graphic images such as arrows, dots, or blocks. To add or change bullets, select the text or text object, click the Bullets arrow in the Paragraph group on the Ribbon, then select a bullet.

Apply a Design Theme

PowerPoint provides many design themes to help you quickly create a professional and contemporary-looking presentation. A **theme** includes a set of 12 coordinated colors for text, fill, line, and shadow, called **theme colors**; a set of fonts for titles and other text, called **theme fonts**; and a set of effects for lines and fills, called **theme effects** to create a cohesive look. In most cases, you would apply one theme to an entire presentation; you can, however, apply multiple themes to the same presentation. You can use a design theme as is, or you can alter individual elements of the theme as needed. Unless you need to use a specific design theme, such as a company theme or product design theme, it is faster and easier to use one of the themes supplied with PowerPoint. If you design a custom theme, you can save it to use in the future. **CASE** ▶ *You decide to change the default design theme in the presentation to a new one.*

STEPS

1. **Click the** Slide 1 thumbnail **on the Slides tab**

2. **Click the** Design tab **on the Ribbon, then point to the** Gallery theme **in the Themes group, as shown in** FIGURE 1-12

    The Design tab appears, and a Live Preview of the Gallery theme is displayed on the selected slide. A **Live Preview** allows you to see how your changes affect the slides before actually making the change. The Live Preview lasts about 1 minute, and then your slide reverts back to its original state. The first (far-left) theme thumbnail identifies the current theme applied to the presentation, in this case, the default design theme called the Office Theme.

3. **Slowly move your pointer** ⬚ **over the other design themes, then click the** Themes group down scroll arrow

    A Live Preview of the theme appears on the slide each time you pass your pointer over the theme thumbnails, and a ScreenTip identifies the theme names.

4. **Move** ⬚ **over the** design themes, **then click the** Slice theme

    The Slice design theme is applied to all the slides in the presentation and the Design Ideas pane opens. The Design Ideas pane provides additional customized design themes based on the current design theme applied to your presentation. Notice the new slide background color, graphic elements, fonts, and text color.

5. **Scroll down and back up the Design Ideas pane, then click the design at the top of the list**

    The presentation displays the suggested design theme. You decide this theme isn't right for the presentation.

6. **Click the** More button ⬚ **in the Themes group**

    The Themes gallery window opens. At the top of the gallery window in the This Presentation section is the current theme applied to the presentation. Notice that just the Slice theme is listed here because when you changed the theme, you replaced the default theme with the Slice theme. The Office section identifies all of the standard themes that come with PowerPoint.

7. **Right-click the** Mesh theme **in the Office section, then click** Apply to Selected Slides

    The Mesh theme is applied only to Slide 1. You like the Mesh theme better, and decide to apply it to all slides.

8. **Right-click the** Mesh theme **in the Themes group, then click** Apply to All Slides

    The Mesh theme is applied to all three slides. Preview the next slide in the presentation to see how it looks.

9. **Click the** Next Slide button ⬚ **at the bottom of the vertical scroll bar, click the** Close button ⬚ **in the Design Ideas pane, then save your changes**

    Compare your screen to FIGURE 1-13.

FIGURE 1-12: Slide showing a different design theme

Current theme applied

Office theme

Design tab

Screentip

Gallery theme

More button

Themes group down scroll arrow

Variants

New graphic elements

New font type

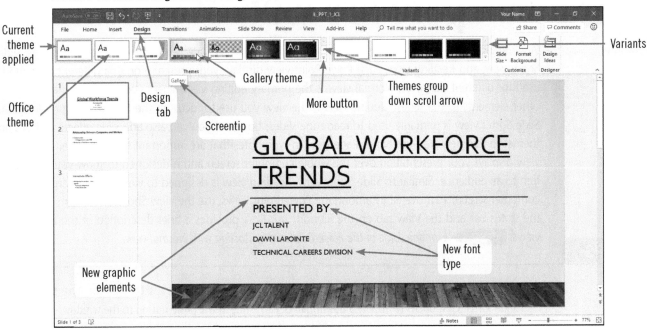

FIGURE 1-13: Presentation with Mesh theme applied

Slide appearance will depend on Design Idea selected

Mesh theme applied to all three slides

Previous slide button

Next slide button

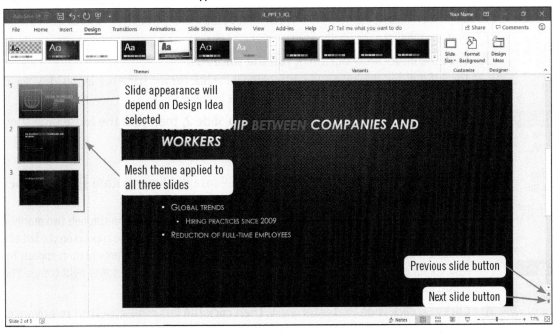

Changing theme colors

You are not limited to using the standard theme colors PowerPoint provides; you can also modify theme colors or create your own custom theme. For example, you might want to incorporate your school's or company's colors on the slide background of the presentation. To change existing theme colors, click the Design tab on the Ribbon, click the More button in the Variants group, point to Colors then select a color theme. You also have the ability to create a new color theme from scratch by clicking the More button in the Variants group, pointing to Colors, then clicking Customize Colors. The Create New Theme Colors dialog box opens where you can select the theme colors you want and then save the color theme with a new name.

PowerPoint

Compare Presentation Views

PowerPoint has six primary views: Normal view, Outline view, Slide Sorter view, Notes Page view, Slide Show view, and Reading view. Each PowerPoint view displays your presentation in a different way and is used for different purposes. Normal view is the primary editing view where you add text, graphics, and other elements to the slides. Outline view is the view you use to focus on the text of your presentation. Slide Sorter view is primarily used to rearrange slides; however, you can also add slide effects and design themes in this view. You use Notes Page view to type notes that are important for each slide. Slide Show view displays your presentation over the whole computer screen and is designed to show your presentation to an audience. Similar to Slide Show view, Reading view is designed to view your presentation on a computer screen. To move easily among the PowerPoint views, use the View Shortcuts buttons located on the status bar and the View tab on the Ribbon. TABLE 1-1 provides a brief description of the PowerPoint views. **CASE** ▶ *Examine some of the PowerPoint views, starting with Normal view.*

STEPS

1. **Click the** View tab **on the Ribbon, then click the** Slide Sorter button ⊞ **on the status bar**
   Slide Sorter View opens to display a thumbnail of each slide in the presentation in the window, as shown in FIGURE 1-14. You can examine the flow of your slides and drag any slide or group of slides to rearrange the order of the slides.

2. **Double-click the** Slide 1 thumbnail, **then click the** Notes button **on the status bar**
   The first slide appears in Normal view, and the Notes pane opens. The status bar controls at the bottom of the window make it easy to move between slides in this view. You can type notes in the Notes pane to guide your presentation.

3. **Click the** Slide Show button ⊡ **on the status bar**
   The first slide fills the entire screen now without the title bar and status bar. In this view, you can practice running through your slides as they would appear in a slide show.

4. **Click the** left mouse button **to advance to Slide 2, then click the** More slide show options button ⊝ **on the Slide Show toolbar**
   The slide show options menu opens.

5. **Click** Show Presenter View, **then click the** Pause the timer button ▮▮ **above the slide, as shown in** FIGURE 1-15
   Presenter view is a view that you can use when showing a presentation through two monitors; one that you see as the presenter and one that your audience sees. The current slide appears on the left of your screen (which is the only object your audience sees), and the next slide in the presentation appears in the upper-right corner of the screen. Speaker notes, if you have any, appear in the lower-right corner. The timer you paused identifies how long the slide has been viewed by the audience.

6. **Click** ⊝, **click** Hide Presenter View, **then click the** left mouse button **to advance through the slide show until you see a black slide, then press** SPACEBAR
   At the end of a slide show, you return to the slide and view you were in before you ran the slide show, in this case Slide 1 in Normal view.

7. **Click the** Home tab **on the Ribbon**

FIGURE 1-14: Slide Sorter view

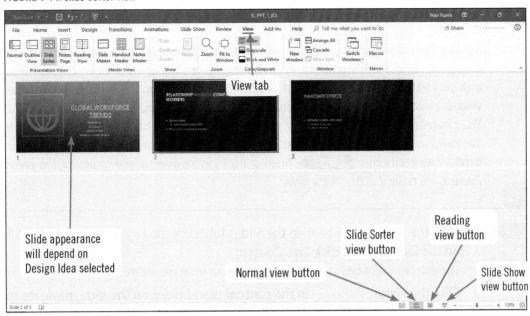

Slide appearance will depend on Design Idea selected

View tab

Normal view button

Slide Sorter view button

Reading view button

Slide Show view button

FIGURE 1-15: Slide 2 in Presenter view

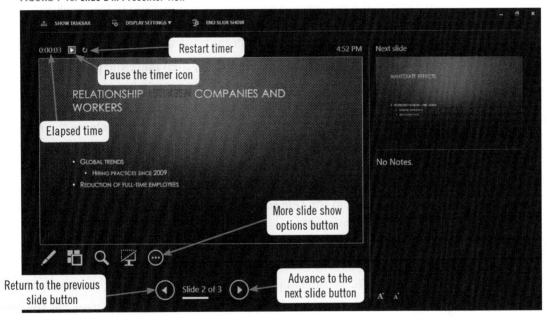

Restart timer

Pause the timer icon

Elapsed time

More slide show options button

Return to the previous slide button

Advance to the next slide button

TABLE 1-1: PowerPoint views

view name	button	button name	displays
Normal	🖼	Normal	The Slide pane and the Slides tab at the same time
Outline View	(no View Shortcuts button)		An outline of the presentation and the Slide pane at the same time
Slide Sorter	⊞	Slide Sorter	Thumbnails of all slides
Slide Show	🖵	Slide Show	Your presentation on the whole computer screen
Reading View	📖	Reading View	Your presentation in a large window on your computer screen
Notes Page	(no View Shortcuts button)		A reduced image of the current slide above a large text box

PowerPoint

Insert and Resize a Picture

Learning Outcomes
• Insert a picture
• Resize and move a picture

In PowerPoint, a **picture** is defined as a digital photograph, a piece of line art or clip art, or other artwork that is created in another program. PowerPoint gives you the ability to insert different types of pictures, including JPEG File Interchange Format and BMP Windows Bitmap files into a PowerPoint presentation. As with all objects in PowerPoint, you can format and resize inserted pictures to help them fit on the slide. You can resize pictures proportionally, which keeps changes to height and width relative to each other. You can also resize a picture non-proportionally, which allows the height and width to change independently from each other. **CASE** ▶ *Insert a stock picture given to you to use for this presentation. Once inserted, you resize it to best fit the slide.*

STEPS

QUICK TIP
You can also insert a picture by clicking the Pictures button in the Images group on the Insert tab.

1. **Click the Slide 2 thumbnail in the Slides tab, click the Layout button in the Slides group on the Ribbon, then click Two Content**
   The slide layout changes to the Two Content layout to accommodate a new picture.

2. **Click the Pictures icon in the content placeholder on the slide, navigate to the location where you store your Data Files, select the picture file Support_PPT_1_Woman.jpg, then click Insert**
   The Insert Picture dialog box opens displaying the pictures available in the default Pictures folder. The newly inserted picture fills the content placeholder on the slide, and the Picture Tools Format tab opens on the Ribbon. The Design Ideas pane also opens offering you design suggestions for the slide.

QUICK TIP
To select all the objects on a slide, click the Home tab on the Ribbon, click the Select arrow in the Editing group, then click Select All.

3. **Click the Close button in the Design Ideas pane, then place the pointer over the middle-left sizing handle on the picture**
   The pointer changes to ⟺.

4. **Drag the sizing handle to the left as shown in FIGURE 1-16, then release the mouse button**
   Dragging any of the middle sizing handles resizes the picture non-proportionally, whereas dragging one of the corner sizing handles resizes the picture proportionally. The picture would look better if it was resized proportionally.

5. **Click the Undo button in the Quick Access Toolbar on the title bar**
   The picture reverts to its original size.

QUICK TIP
You can also resize a picture proportionally by entering specific height or width values in the Height or Width text boxes in the Size group on the Picture Tools Format tab.

6. **Place the pointer over the top-left sizing handle, then drag to the left until the picture edge is just under the word "Between" in the title**
   The picture is now resized proportionally. To see a portion of a slide close up, you can zoom in.

7. **Drag the Zoom slider in the status bar to the right until the picture fills the screen**
   The selected picture fills the screen.

8. **Click the Fit slide to current window button in the status bar, click a blank area of the slide, then save your work**
   The zoom setting returns to its previous position and the slide fits in the PowerPoint window. Compare your screen to FIGURE 1-17.

9. **Click the File tab on the Ribbon, then click Close**
   The presentation file closes.

FIGURE 1-16: Picture sized non-proportionally

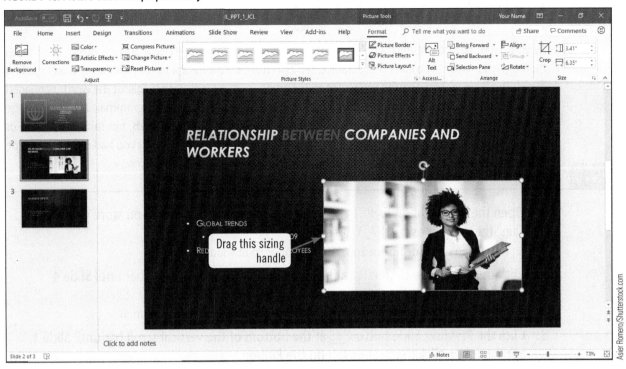

Asier Romero/Shutterstock.com

FIGURE 1-17: Picture sized proportionally

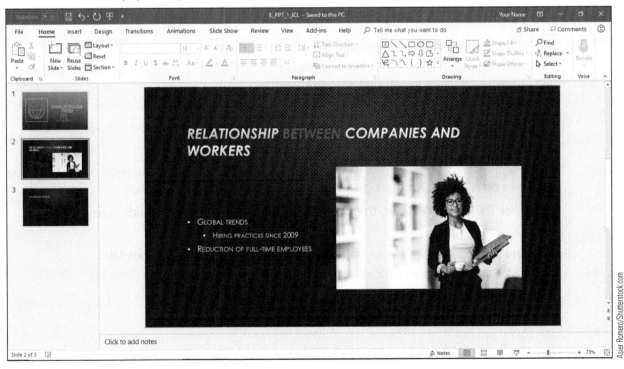

Asier Romero/Shutterstock.com

Check Spelling

As your work on the presentation file nears completion, you need to review and proofread your slides thoroughly for errors. You can use the Spell Checker feature in PowerPoint to check for and correct spelling errors. This feature compares the spelling of all the words in your presentation against the words contained in the dictionary. You still must proofread your presentation for punctuation, grammar, and word-usage errors because the Spell Checker recognizes only misspelled and unknown words, not misused words. For example, the spell checker would not identify the word "last" as an error, even if you had intended to type the word "past." **CASE** *You've been given a presentation by a colleague to review.*

STEPS

1. **Open the presentation IL_PPT_1-1.pptx from the location where you store your Data Files, then save it as IL_PPT_1_Interview**

   A presentation with a new name appears in the PowerPoint window.

2. **Click the Next Slide button ⬇ at the bottom of the vertical scroll bar until Slide 4 appears**

   You notice some spelling errors and decide to check the spelling of the presentation.

3. **Click the Previous Slide button ⬆ at the bottom of the vertical scroll bar until Slide 1 appears, then click the Review tab on the Ribbon**

4. **Click the Spelling button in the Proofing group**

   PowerPoint begins to check the spelling in your presentation. When PowerPoint finds a misspelled word or a word that is not in its dictionary, the Spelling pane opens, as shown in **FIGURE 1-18**. In this case, the Spell Checker identifies a name on Slide 1, but it does not recognize that it's spelled correctly and suggests some replacement words.

5. **Click Ignore Once in the Spelling pane**

   PowerPoint ignores this instance of the word and continues to check the rest of the presentation for errors. PowerPoint finds the misspelled word "professional" on Slide 2.

6. **Click the Change All button in the Spelling pane**

   All instances of this misspelled word are corrected. The word "settings" on Slide 3 is also misspelled.

7. **Click the Change button in the Spelling pane**

   The misspelled word is corrected. When the Spell Checker finishes checking your presentation, the Spelling pane closes, and an alert box opens with a message stating the spelling check is complete.

8. **Click OK in the Alert box, then click the Slide 4 thumbnail in the Slides tab**

   The alert box closes.

9. **Drag the Slide 4 thumbnail between Slide 1 and Slide 2 in the Slides tab.**

   Slide 4 moves and becomes the second slide in the presentation. Compare your screen to **FIGURE 1-19**.

FIGURE 1-18: Window with Spelling pane open

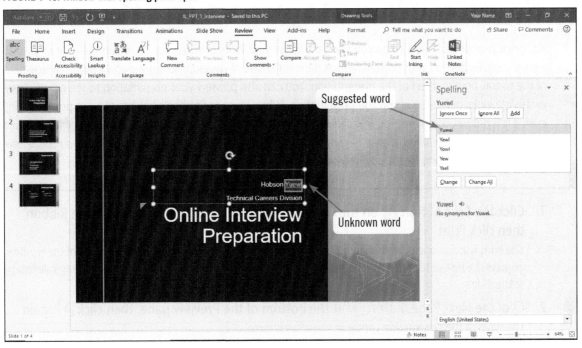

FIGURE 1-19: Moved slide

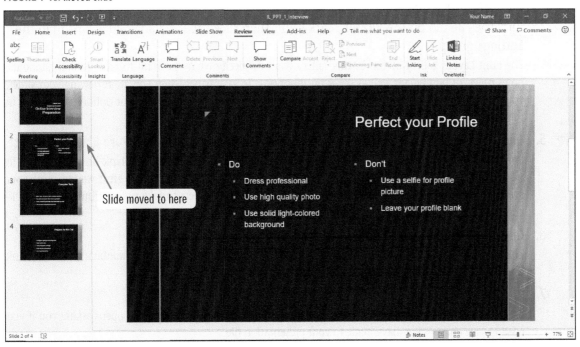

Checking spelling as you type

By default, PowerPoint checks your spelling as you type. If you type a word that is not in the dictionary, a wavy red line appears under it. To correct an error, right-click the misspelled word, then review the suggestions, which appear in the shortcut menu. You can select a suggestion, add the word you typed to your custom dictionary, or ignore it. To turn off automatic spell checking, click the File tab, then click Options to open the PowerPoint Options dialog box. Click Proofing in the left column, then click the Check spelling as you type check box to deselect it. To temporarily hide the wavy red lines, click the Hide spelling and grammar errors check box to select it. Contextual spelling in PowerPoint identifies common grammatically misused words; for example, if you type the word "their" and the correct word is "there," PowerPoint will identify the mistake and place a wavy red line under the word. To turn contextual spelling on or off, click Proofing in the PowerPoint Options dialog box, then click the Check grammar with spelling check box.

Print a PowerPoint Presentation

**Learning
Outcomes**
• Print a
presentation
• Set print settings
• Modify color
settings

You print your presentation when you want to review your work or when you have completed it and want a hard copy. Reviewing your presentation at different stages of development gives you a better perspective of the overall flow and feel of the presentation. You can also preview your presentation to see exactly how each slide looks before you print the presentation. When you are finished working on your presentation, even if it is not yet complete, you can close the presentation file and exit PowerPoint. **CASE** *You save and preview the presentation, then you print the slides and notes pages of the presentation so you can review them later. Before leaving for the day, you close the file and exit PowerPoint.*

STEPS

1. **Click the Save button 🖫 on the Quick Access toolbar, click the File tab on the Ribbon, then click Print**

   The Print window opens, as shown in FIGURE 1-20. Notice the preview pane on the right side of the window displays the first slide of the presentation. If you do not have a color printer, you will see a grayscale image of the slide.

2. **Click the Next Page button ▶ at the bottom of the Preview pane, then click ▶ again**

   The slides of the presentation appear in the preview pane.

3. **Click the Print button**

   Each slide in the presentation prints.

4. **Click the File tab on the Ribbon, click Print, then click the Full Page Slides button in the Settings group**

   The Print Layout gallery opens. In this gallery you can specify what you want to print (slides, handouts, notes pages, or outline), as well as other print options. To save paper when you are reviewing your slides, you can print in handout format, which lets you print up to nine slides per page. The options you choose in the Print window remain there until you change them or close the presentation.

5. **Click 3 Slides, click the Color button in the Settings group, then click Pure Black and White**

   PowerPoint removes the color and displays the slides as thumbnails next to blank lines, as shown in FIGURE 1-21. Using the Handouts with three slides per page printing option is a great way to print your presentation when you want to provide a way for audience members to take notes. Printing pure black-and-white prints without any gray tones can save printer toner.

6. **Click the Print button**

   The presentation prints one page showing all the slides of the presentation as thumbnails next to blank lines.

7. **Click the File tab on the Ribbon, then click Close**

   If you have made changes to your presentation, a Microsoft PowerPoint alert box opens asking you if you want to save changes you have made to your presentation file.

8. **Click Save, if necessary, to close the alert box**

   Your presentation closes.

9. **sam⁷⬆ Click the Close button ✕ in the Title bar**

   The PowerPoint program closes, and you return to the Windows desktop.

FIGURE 1-20: Print window

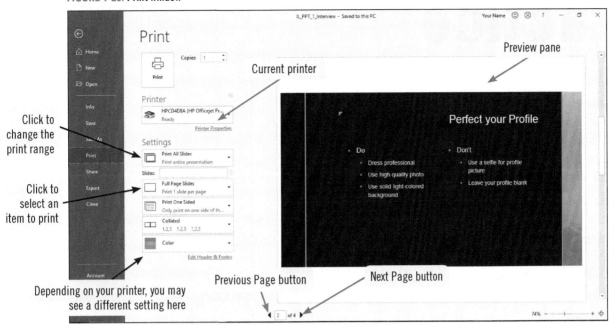

Preview pane

Current printer

Click to change the print range

Click to select an item to print

Depending on your printer, you may see a different setting here

Previous Page button

Next Page button

FIGURE 1-21: Print window with changed settings

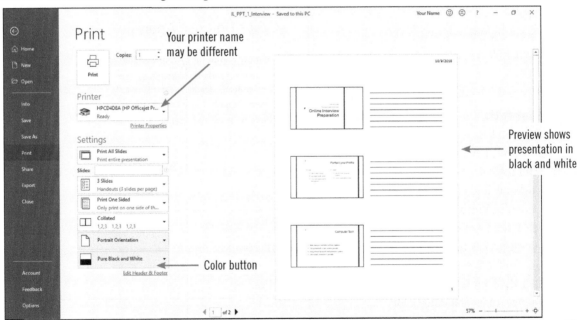

Your printer name may be different

Preview shows presentation in black and white

Color button

Microsoft Office Online Apps

Some Office programs, PowerPoint for example, include the capability to incorporate feedback—called online collaboration—across the Internet or a company network. Using **cloud computing** (work done in a virtual environment), you can take advantage of web programs called Microsoft Office Online Apps, which are simplified versions of the programs found in the Microsoft Office 2019 suite. Because these programs are online,

they take up no computer disk space and are accessed using Microsoft OneDrive, a free service from Microsoft. Using Microsoft OneDrive, you and your colleagues can create and store documents in the "cloud" and make the documents available to whomever you grant access. To use Microsoft OneDrive, you need to create a free Microsoft account, which you obtain at the Microsoft website.

Practice

Skills Review

1. **Examine the PowerPoint window.**
   a. Start PowerPoint, if necessary then open a new blank presentation.
   b. Identify as many elements of the PowerPoint window as you can without referring to the lessons in this module.
   c. Be able to describe the purpose or function of each element.
   d. For any elements you cannot identify, refer to the lessons in this module.

2. **Enter slide text.**
   a. In the Slide pane in Normal view, enter the text **TC Insurance Services** in the title placeholder.
   b. In the subtitle text placeholder, enter **Company Security Division**.
   c. On the next line of the placeholder, enter your name.
   d. Deselect the text object.
   e. Save the presentation using the filename **IL_PPT_1_Analysis** to the location where you store your Data Files.

3. **Add a new slide.**
   a. Create a new slide using the Title and Content layout.
   b. Using FIGURE 1-22, enter text on the slide.
   c. Create another new slide.
   d. Using FIGURE 1-23, enter text on the slide.
   e. Save your changes.

FIGURE 1-22

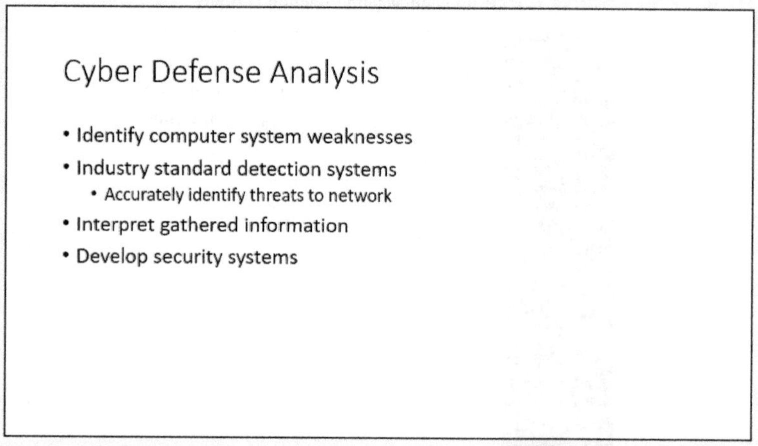

Cyber Defense Analysis

- Identify computer system weaknesses
- Industry standard detection systems
  - Accurately identify threats to network
- Interpret gathered information
- Develop security systems

4. **Format text.**
   a. Go to Slide 1, select the text TC Insurance Services, then move the pointer over the Mini toolbar.
   b. Click the Bold button, then click the Underline button.
   c. Select the text Company Security Division, click the Italic button, then click the Increase Font Size button.
   d. Go to Slide 2, select the word Accurately, click the Font Color arrow, then click Orange under Standard Colors.

FIGURE 1-23

Cyber Infrastructure Support

- Apply cybersecurity principles
- Knowledge of computer networking
- Understanding of common regulations
  - Laws, policies, and procedures
- Secure network communications

   e. Go to Slide 3, select the word common in the third bullet point, click the Font Size arrow, then click 32.
   f. Click the Font button, click Algerian, then save your changes.

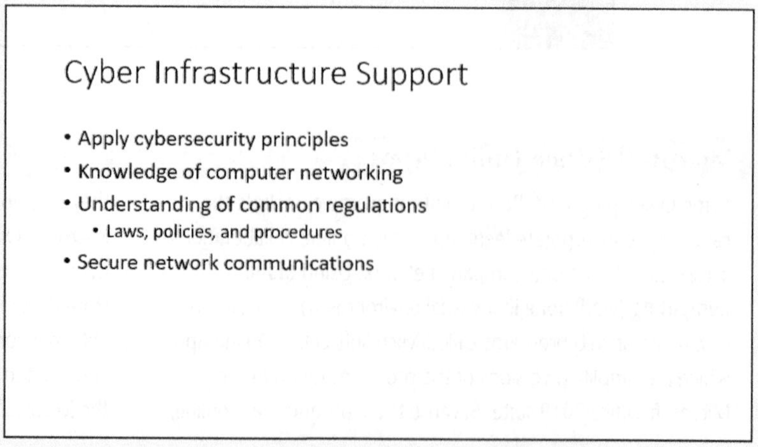

Skills Review (continued)

5. Apply a design theme.

    a. Click the Design tab.

    b. Click the Themes group More button, then point to all of the themes.

    c. Locate the Madison theme, then apply it to the selected slide.

    d. Go to Slide 1, click the Themes group More button, locate the Parallax theme, then apply it to Slide 1.

    e. Apply the Parallax theme to all of the slides in the presentation.

    f. Click the first design in the Design Ideas pane, then close the Design Ideas pane.

    g. Use the Next Slide button to move to Slide 3, then save your changes.

6. Compare presentation views.

    a. Click the View tab, then click the Slide Sorter button in the Presentation Views group.

    b. Click the Normal button in the Presentation Views group, then click the Notes button in the status bar.

    c. Click the Notes button, then click the Next button on the status bar.

    d. Click the Slide Show button on the status bar.

    e. Click the More slide show options button, click Show Presenter View, then click the Pause button.

    f. Click the More slide show options button, then click Hide Presenter View.

    g. Advance the slides until a black screen appears, then click to end the presentation.

    h. Save your changes.

7. Insert and resize a picture.

    a. Select Slide 2 in the Slides tab, then click the Home tab.

    b. Click the Layout button, change the slide layout to Two Content, then insert the picture **Support_PPT_1_Group.jpg** from the location where you store your Data Files.

    c. Close the Design Ideas pane, then drag the left-middle sizing handle to the left.

    d. Click the Undo button, then drag the bottom-left corner sizing handle down to the left to increase the picture size.

    e. Drag the Zoom Slider in the status bar to the right until 100% appears next to the Zoom Slider.

    f. Click the Fit slide to current window button in the status bar, save your changes, then close the presentation.

8. Check Spelling.

    a. Open the presentation IL_PPT_1-2.pptx from the location where you store your Data Files, then save it as **IL_PPT_ 1_Emergency**.

    b. Click the Next Slide button at the bottom of the vertical scroll bar.

    c. Click the Previous Slide button at the bottom of the vertical scroll bar until Slide 1 appears, then click the Review tab.

    d. Click the Spelling button in the Proofing group. The word incident is misspelled on Slide 2.

    e. Make sure the word incident is selected in the Spelling pane, then click the Change All button. The word Responsibilities is also misspelled.

    f. Click the Change button in the Spelling pane. A correctly spelled abbreviation appears in the Spelling pane.

    g. Click the Ignore All button.

    h. Click OK in the alert box, then save your changes.

9. Print a PowerPoint presentation.

    a. Print all the slides as handouts, 3 Slides, in color.

    b. Close the file, saving your changes.

    c. Exit PowerPoint.

Independent Challenge 1

You work for Riverwalk Medical Clinic (RMC), a large medical facility in Cambridge, Massachusetts. You have been asked to put together a presentation on the hospital's internship program. The presentation will be used to recruit interns from local colleges.

a. Start PowerPoint, then open a new blank presentation.

b. In the title placeholder on Slide 1, type **Riverwalk Medical Clinic**.

c. In the subtitle placeholder, type Medical Internship Program, press ENTER, then type your name.

d. Underline the text Medical Internship Program, then italicize your name.

e. Apply the Wood Type design theme to the presentation, click the third design theme from the top in the Design Ideas pane, then close the Design Ideas pane.

f. Save your presentation with the filename **IL_PPT_1_Intern** to the location where you store your Data Files.

g. Use FIGURE 1-24 and FIGURE 1-25 to add two more slides to your presentation.

h. On Slide 3 format the color, font type, and font size of the words Oral interview to Red, 24 pt, Arial Black.

i. Use the buttons on the View tab to switch between PowerPoint's views, then open and close Presenter View.

j. Print the presentation using handouts, 3 Slides, in black and white.

k. Save and close the file, then exit PowerPoint.

FIGURE 1-24

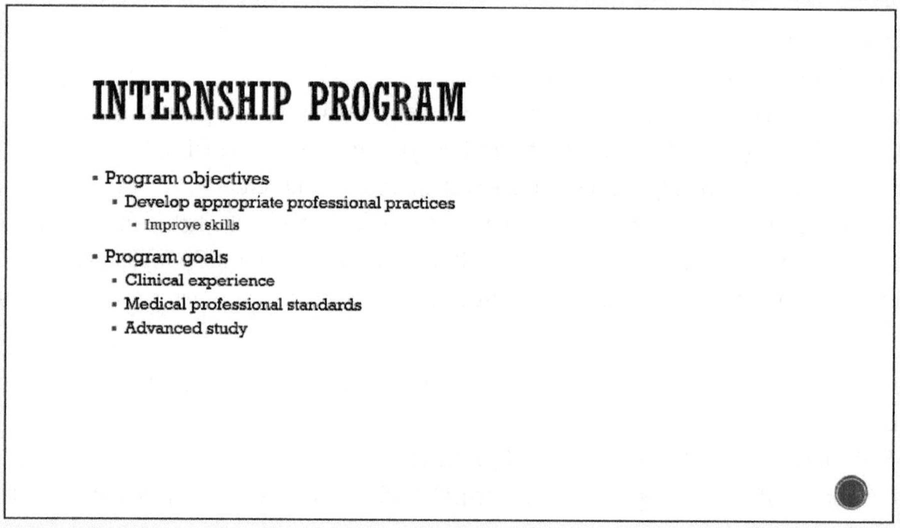

INTERNSHIP PROGRAM

- Program objectives
  - Develop appropriate professional practices
    - Improve skills
- Program goals
  - Clinical experience
  - Medical professional standards
  - Advanced study

FIGURE 1-25

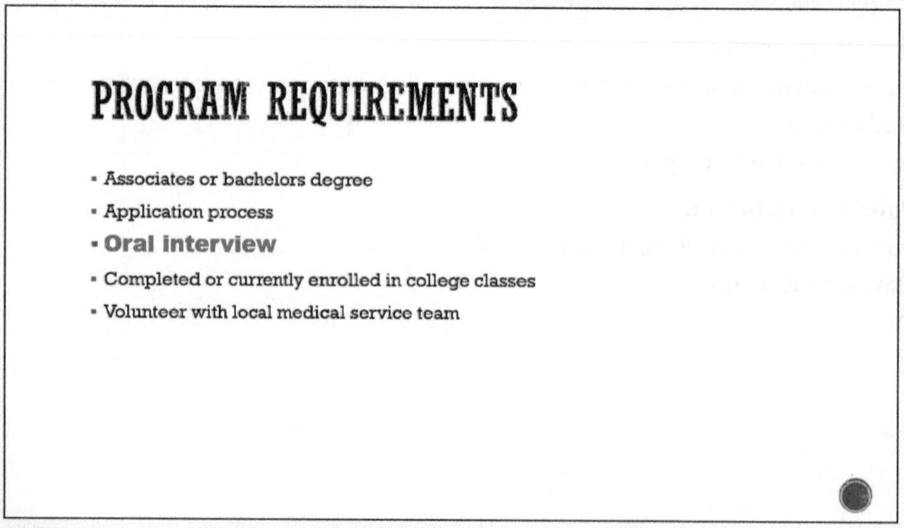

PROGRAM REQUIREMENTS

- Associates or bachelors degree
- Application process
- **Oral interview**
- Completed or currently enrolled in college classes
- Volunteer with local medical service team

Independent Challenge 2

You are an assistant in the Computer Science Department at City College and you have been asked to create a presentation on a new course being offered on artificial intelligence (AI). AI is a fast-growing industry and the Computer Science Dept. wants to have relevant classes for students to better prepare them for future jobs. You have already started working on the presentation and now you add and resize a picture, add a design theme, and run a spell check.

a. Start PowerPoint, open the presentation IL_PPT_1-3.pptx from the location where you store your Data Files, and save it as **IL_PPT_1_AI400**.

b. Apply the Circuit design theme to all the slides, apply a design theme from the Design Ideas pane similar to one shown in FIGURE 1-26, then close the Design Ideas pane.

FIGURE 1-26

c. Spell check the presentation. There is a misspelled word on Slide 3.

d. Drag Slide 3 above Slide 2 in the Slides tab, then change the slide layout to Two Content.

e. Insert the picture Support_PPT_1_Group.jpg from the location where you store your Data Files into the right content placeholder.

f. Resize the picture using a middle sizing handle, then undo the action by clicking the Undo button.

g. Resize the picture using a corner sizing handle, click the first design in the Design Ideas pane, then close the Design Ideas pane.

h. Switch views. Run through the slide show at least once.

i. Open and close Presenter view.

j. Close the presentation and exit PowerPoint.

Visual Workshop

Create the presentation shown in FIGURE 1-27 and FIGURE 1-28. Make sure you include your name on the title slide. Save the presentation as **IL_PPT_1_Allesco** to the location where you store your Data Files. Print the slides.

FIGURE 1-27

FIGURE 1-28

Modifying a Presentation

CASE You continue working on your global workforce presentation. In this module, you'll create a SmartArt graphic, draw and work with shapes, add slide footer information, and set slide transitions and timings in the presentation.

Module Objectives

After completing this module, you will be able to:

- Convert text to SmartArt
- Insert and style shapes
- Rotate and modify shapes
- Rearrange and merge shapes

- Edit and duplicate shapes
- Align and group objects
- Add slide footers
- Set slide transitions and timings

Files You Will Need

IL_PPT_2-1.pptx	IL_PPT_2-4.pptx
IL_PPT_2-2.pptx	IL_PPT_2-5.pptx
IL_PPT_2-3.pptx	

Convert Text to SmartArt

Learning
Outcomes
• Create a SmartArt
  graphic
• Modify the
  SmartArt design

Sometimes when you are working with text it just doesn't capture your attention. The ability to convert text to a SmartArt graphic provides a creative way to convey a message using text and graphics. A **SmartArt** graphic is a professional-quality diagram that graphically illustrates text. For example, you can show steps in a process or timeline, show proportional relationships, or show how parts relate to a whole. You can create a SmartArt graphic from scratch or create one by converting existing text you have entered on a slide. **CASE** *You want the presentation to appear visually dynamic, so you convert the text on Slide 4 to a SmartArt graphic.*

STEPS

1. **sam↓ Start PowerPoint, open the presentation IL_PPT_2-1.PPTX from the location where you store your Data Files, then save it as IL_PPT_2_JCL**
   A presentation with the new filename appears in the PowerPoint window.

2. **Click the Slide 4 thumbnail in the Slides tab, click Service in the text object, then click the Convert to SmartArt Graphic button in the Paragraph group**
   A gallery of SmartArt graphic layouts opens. As with many features in PowerPoint, you can preview how your text will look prior to applying the SmartArt graphic layout by using PowerPoint's Live Preview feature. You can review each SmartArt graphic layout and see how it changes the appearance of the text.

3. **Move ⌖ over the SmartArt graphic layouts in the gallery**
   Notice how the text becomes part of the graphic and changes each time you move the pointer over a different graphic layout. SmartArt graphic names appear in ScreenTips.

4. **Click the Vertical Block List layout in the SmartArt graphics gallery**
   A SmartArt graphic appears on the slide in place of the text object, and the SmartArt Tools Design tab opens on the Ribbon, as shown in **FIGURE 2-1**. A SmartArt graphic consists of two parts: the SmartArt graphic and a Text pane where you type and edit text.

5. **Click the SmartArt Tools Design tab on the Ribbon, click the More button ⊽ in the Layouts group, click More Layouts to open the Choose a SmartArt Graphic dialog box, click Pyramid, click the Pyramid List layout icon, then click OK**
   The SmartArt graphic changes to the new graphic layout. You can change how the SmartArt graphic looks by applying a SmartArt Style. A **SmartArt Style** is a preset combination of simple and 3-D formatting options that follows the presentation theme.

6. **Move ⌖ slowly over the styles in the SmartArt Styles group, then click the More button ⊽ in the SmartArt Styles group**
   A Live Preview of each style is displayed on the SmartArt graphic. The SmartArt styles are organized into sections; the top group offers suggestions for the best match for the document, and the bottom group shows you all the possible 3-D styles that are available.

7. **Move ⌖ over the styles in the gallery, click Inset Effect in the 3-D section, then click in a blank area of the slide outside the SmartArt graphic**
   Notice how the Inset style adds a shadow and an edge to achieve a 3-D effect. Compare your screen to **FIGURE 2-2**.

8. **Click the Slide 4 thumbnail in the Slides tab, then save your work**

FIGURE 2-1: Text converted to a Vertical Block List layout SmartArt graphic

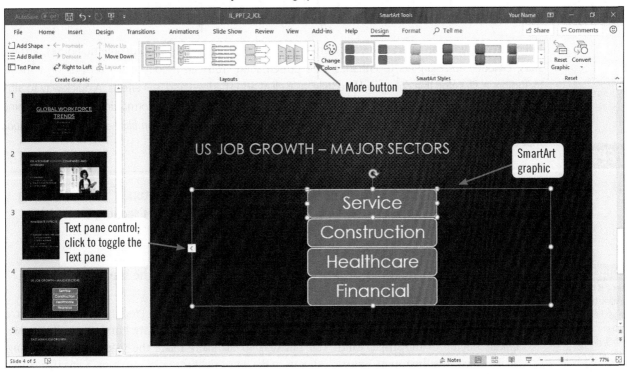

FIGURE 2-2: Final Pyramid List with Inset 3-D effect SmartArt graphic

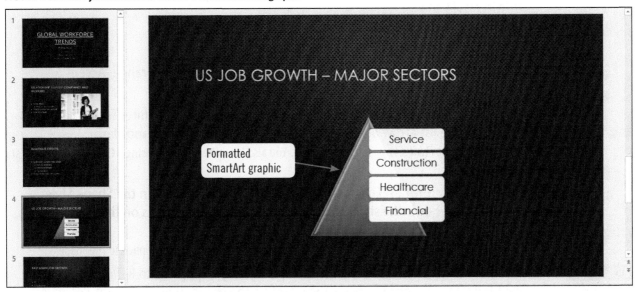

Entering and printing notes

You can add notes to your slides when there are certain facts you want to remember during a presentation or when there is additional information you want to hand out to your audience. Notes do not appear on the slides when you run a slide show. Use the Notes pane in Normal view or Notes Page view to enter notes for your slides. To open or close the Notes pane, click the Notes button on the status bar. To enter text notes on a slide, click in the Notes pane, then type the note. If you want to insert graphics as notes, you must use Notes Page view. To open Notes Page view, click the View tab on the Ribbon, then click the Notes Page button in the Presentation Views group. You can print your notes by clicking the File tab on the Ribbon to open Backstage view. Click Print, click the Full Page Slides list arrow in the Settings group (this button retains the last setting for what was printed previously so it might differ) to open the gallery, and then click Notes Pages. Once you verify your print settings, click the Print button. If you don't enter any notes in the Notes pane and print the notes pages, the slides print as large thumbnails with blank space below the thumbnails to handwrite notes.

Insert and Style Shapes

Learning Outcomes
- Create a shape
- Modify a shape's style

In PowerPoint you can insert many different types of shapes, including lines, geometric figures, arrows, stars, callouts, and banners to enhance your presentation. You can modify many aspects of a shape, including its fill color, line color, and line style, as well as add shadows and 3-D effects. A quick way to alter the appearance of a shape is to apply a Quick Style. A **Quick Style** is a set of formatting options, including line style, fill color, and effects. **CASE** ▸ *You decide to draw some shapes on Slide 3 of your presentation that complement the slide content.*

STEPS

1. **Click the** Slide 3 thumbnail **in the Slides tab, click the** More button ⏷ **in the Drawing group, click the** Arrow: Pentagon button ▷ **in the Block Arrows section, then position** ╪ **in the blank area of Slide 3**

   ScreenTips help you identify the shapes.

TROUBLE

If your shape is not approximately the same size as the one shown in FIGURE 2-3, drag one of the corner sizing handles to resize the object.

2. **Press and hold** SHIFT, **drag** ╪ **down and to the right to create the shape, as shown in** FIGURE 2-3, **release the mouse button, then release** SHIFT

   A block arrow shape appears on the slide, filled with the default theme color. Pressing SHIFT while you create the object maintains the object proportions as you change its size. A **rotate handle**—circular arrow—appears on top of the shape, which you can drag to manually rotate the shape. An yellow-orange circle—called an **adjustment handle**—appears in the upper-right corner of the shape. Some shapes have an adjustment handle that can be moved to change the most prominent feature of an object, in this case the shape of the arrow.

3. **Drag the** adjustment handle **left over the middle sizing handle**

   The tip of the arrow changes shape.

4. **Click the** Shape Fill list arrow **in the Drawing group, then click** Orange, Accent 6

   An orange fill color is applied to the shape.

5. **Click the** Shape Outline list arrow **in the Drawing group, click** White, Text 1, **click the** Shape Outline list arrow **again, point to** Dashes, **then click the** Long Dash

   The shape outline changes to a long white dash. You also have the option of using a Quick Style to format a shape.

6. **Click the** Drawing Tools Format tab **on the Ribbon, click the** ⏷ **in the Shape Styles group, move** ⧄ **over the styles in the gallery to review the effects on the shape, then click** Intense Effect—Gold, Accent 4

   A gold Quick Style with coordinated gradient fill, line, and shadow color is applied to the shape.

QUICK TIP

To change the transparency of a shape or text object filled with a color, right-click the object, click Format Shape, click Fill, then move the Transparency slider.

7. **Click the** Shape Effects button **in the Shape Styles group, point to** Reflection, **move** ⧄ **over the effect options to review the effect on the shape, then click** Tight Reflection: Touching

   A short faded reflection of the shape appears below the shape, as shown in FIGURE 2-4.

8. **Click a blank area of the slide, then save your work**

   Clicking a blank area of the slide deselects all selected objects.

FIGURE 2-3: Arrow shape added to slide

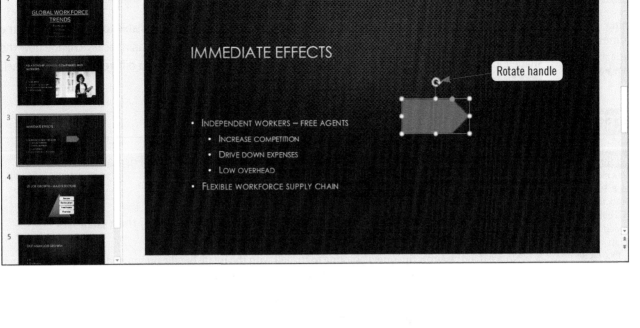

FIGURE 2-4: Styled arrow shape

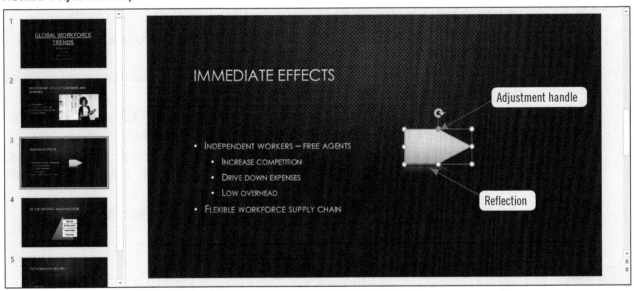

Using the Eyedropper to match colors

As you develop your presentation and work with different shapes and pictures, sometimes from other sources, there may be a certain color that is not in the theme colors of the presentation that you want to capture and apply to objects in your presentation. To capture a color on a specific slide, select any object on the slide, click any button arrow with a color feature, such as the Shape Fill button or the Shape Outline button on the Drawing Tools Format tab, then click Eyedropper. Move the 🖊 over the color you want to capture and pause, or hover. As you hover over a color, a Live Preview of the color appears and the RGB (Red Green Blue) values, called coordinates, appear in a ScreenTip. Click when you see the color you want to capture. The new color now appears in any color gallery under Recent Colors. If you decide not to capture a new color, press ESC to close the Eyedropper without making any change.

PowerPoint

Modifying a Presentation

Rotate and Modify Shapes

Learning
Outcomes
• Rotate a shape
• Change a shape

Once you have created a shape, you have a number of formatting options available to you to enhance the shape. Some of these options include flipping and rotating the shape, which can radically change how the shape looks. Or, if a shape doesn't meet your needs, you can easily change to a different shape altogether. **CASE** ▶ *You continue to work on the shape on Slide 3.*

STEPS

QUICK TIP
To apply a picture fill to a shape, select the shape, click the Shape Fill button on the Drawing Tools Format tab, click Picture, then locate and insert a picture.

1. **Select the** Block arrow shape **on Slide 3, click the** Drawing Tools Format tab **on the Ribbon, then click the** Rotate button **in the Arrange group**
   The Rotate menu appears with two rotate options and two flip options.

2. **Move** ⍾ **over all of the options to review the effect on the shape, then click** Flip Horizontal
   Notice that the arrow tip is now pointing to the left with the rotate handle on top, indicating that the shape has flipped horizontally, or rotated 180 degrees, as shown in FIGURE 2-5.

3. **Click the** rotate handle **on the shape, then drag to the right until the shape is approximately 45 degrees from where it started**
   The shape is now pointing toward the top of the slide and the reflection is under the shape. You decide to rotate the shape by a specific amount.

4. **Click the** Undo button ↶ **on the Quick Access Toolbar, click the** Rotate button, **then click** Rotate Right 90
   The shape is now pointing up. It is 90 degrees from where it was just pointing and the rotate handle is to the right. It is easy to change the shape to any other shape in the shapes gallery.

5. **Click the** Edit Shape button **in the Insert Shapes group, point to** Change Shape **to open the shapes gallery, then click the** Frame button ▣ **in the Basic Shapes section**
   The block arrow shape changes to a frame shape. Notice that even though the shape has changed, it is still rotated 90 degrees from its original position and maintains the formatting changes you have already applied. You decide to rotate it back to its original position.

6. **Click the** Rotate button, **then click** Rotate Left 90, **click a blank area of the slide, then save your work**
   The shape is rotated back to its original position, as shown in FIGURE 2-6.

QUICK TIP
You can also use the Cut button in the Clipboard group on the Home tab to delete a slide.

7. **Right-click the** Slide 5 thumbnail **in the Slides tab**
   A shortcut menu appears with common slide commands. This slide is not needed, so you delete it from the presentation.

8. **Click** Delete Slide, **click the** Slide 3 thumbnail **in the Slides tab, then save your work**
   The fifth slide is deleted and Slide 3 appears in the Slide pane.

FIGURE 2-5: **Flipped arrow shape**

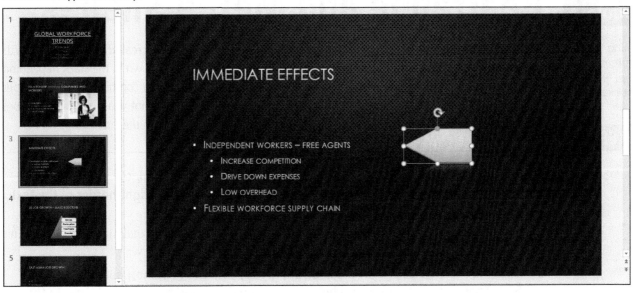

FIGURE 2-6: **Frame shape**

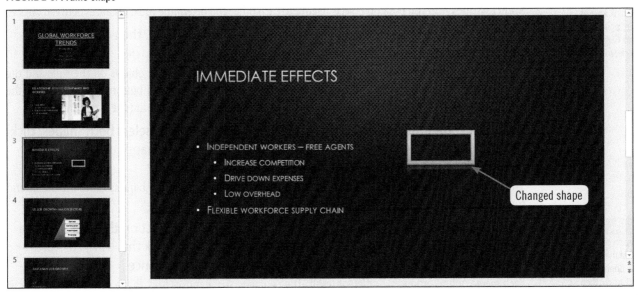

Aligning paragraph text

PowerPoint offers six ways to align paragraph text within a text object: Top, Middle, Bottom, Top Centered, Middle Centered, and Bottom Centered. To change paragraph text alignment, click the Home tab on the Ribbon, select the text you want to change, then click the Align Text button in the Paragraph group to open the Align Text menu. To see all the alignment options, click More Options in the Align Text menu, then click the Vertical alignment arrow.

PowerPoint

Rearrange and Merge Shapes

Every object on a slide is placed, or stacked, on the slide in the order it was created, like a deck of cards placed one on top of another. Each object on a slide can be moved up or down in the stack depending on how you want the objects to look on the slide. **Merging** shapes, which combines multiple shapes together, provides you the potential to create unique geometric shapes not available in the shapes gallery. **CASE** *You create a pentagon shape on Slide 3, then merge it with the frame shape.*

STEPS

1. **Click Independent in the text object, position ◌ over the right-middle sizing handle, ◌ changes to ↔, then drag the sizing handle to the left until the right border of the text object is next to the word "agents" in the text object**

   The width of the text object decreases. When you position ◌ over a sizing handle, it changes to ↔. This pointer points in different directions depending on which sizing handle it is over.

2. **Click the More button ⊟ in the Drawing group, click the Pentagon button ⬠ in the Basic Shapes section, press and hold SHIFT, drag down and to the right to create the shape, then release SHIFT**

   Compare your screen to FIGURE 2-7. A pentagon shape appears on the slide, filled with the default theme color. You can move shapes by dragging them on the slide.

3. **Drag the pentagon shape over the frame shape, then use the Smart Guides that appear to position the pentagon shape in the center of the frame shape where the guides intersect**

   Smart Guides help you position objects relative to each other and determine equal distances between objects.

4. **Click the Select button in the Editing group, click Selection Pane, then click the Send Backward button ⊟ in the Selection pane once**

   The Selection pane opens on the right side of the window showing the four objects on the slide and the order they are stacked on the slide. The Send Backward and Bring Forward buttons let you change the stacking order. The pentagon shape moves back one position in the stack behind the frame shape.

5. **Press SHIFT, click the frame shape on the slide, release SHIFT to select both shapes, click the Drawing Tools Format tab on the Ribbon, click the Merge Shapes button in the Insert Shapes group, then point to Union**

   The two shapes appear to merge, or combine, to form one shape. The merged shape assumes the theme and formatting style of the pentagon shape because it was selected first.

6. **Move ◌ over the other merge shapes options to review the effect on the shape, click a blank area of the slide twice, click the pentagon shape, then click the Bring Forward button in the Arrange group on the Drawing Tools Format tab once**

   Each merge option produces a different result. The pentagon shape moves back to the top of the stack. Now, you want to see what happens when you select the frame shape first before you merge the two shapes together.

7. **Click the frame shape, press SHIFT, click the pentagon shape, release SHIFT, click the Merge Shapes button in the Insert Shapes group, then point to Union**

   The merged shape adopts the theme and formatting style of the frame shape.

8. **Point to each of the merge shapes options, then click Subtract**

   The two shapes merge into one shape. This merge option deletes the area of all shapes from the first shape you selected, so in this case the area of the pentagon shape is deleted from the frame shape. The merged shape is identified as a sequentially numbered Freeform in the Selection pane. See FIGURE 2-8.

9. **Click the Selection Pane button in the Arrange group, click a blank area of the slide, then save your work**

FIGURE 2-7: Pentagon shape added to slide

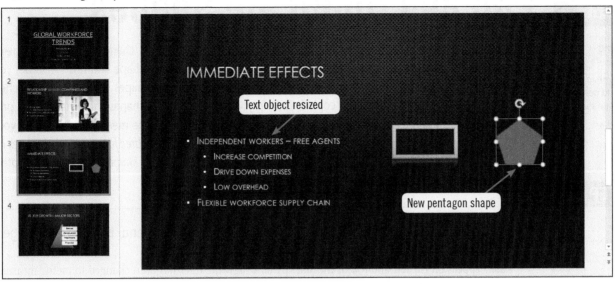

FIGURE 2-8: New Merged shape

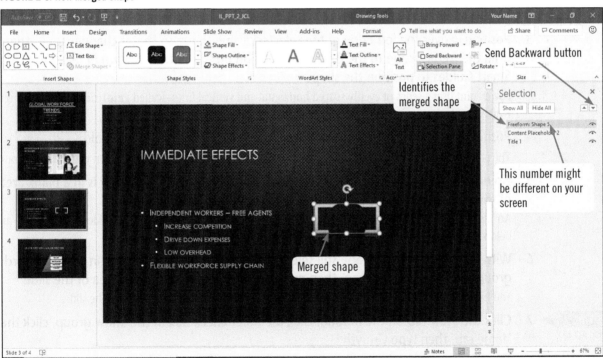

Changing the size and position of shapes

Usually when you resize a shape proportionally you can simply drag one of the corner sizing handles on the outside of the shape, but sometimes you may need to resize a shape more precisely. When you select a shape, the Drawing Tools Format tab appears on the Ribbon, offering you many different formatting options, including some sizing commands located in the Size group. The Width and Height commands in the Size group allow you to change the width and height of a shape. You also have the option to open the Format Shape pane, which allows you to change the size of a shape, as well as the rotation, scale, and position of a shape on the slide.

Edit and Duplicate Shapes

Once you have created a shape you still have the ability to refine its basic characteristics, which helps change the size and appearance of the shape. For example, if you create a shape and it is too large, you can reduce its size by dragging any of its sizing handles. Most PowerPoint shapes can have text attached to them. All shapes can be moved and copied. To help you resize and move shapes and other objects precisely, PowerPoint has rulers you can add to the Slide pane. Rulers display the measurement system your computer uses, either inches or metric measurements. **CASE** ▸ *You want three identical frame shapes on Slide 3. You first add the ruler to the slide to help you change the size of the frame shape you've already created, then you make copies of it.*

STEPS

1. **Right-click a blank area of Slide 3, click Ruler on the shortcut menu, then click the edge of the frame shape to select it**

   Rulers appear on the left and top of the Slide pane. Unless the ruler has been changed to metric measurements, it is divided into inches with ½" and ⅛" marks. Notice the current location of the ⬉ is identified on both rulers by a small dotted red line.

2. **Drag the middle-right sizing handle on the frame shape to the right approximately ½", then release the mouse button**

   The frame shape is now slightly wider.

3. **Position ⬉ over the left edge of the selected frame shape so that it changes to ⤧, then drag the frame shape to the 0.00 ruler position on the slide, as shown in FIGURE 2-9 using Smart Guides to position the shape**

   PowerPoint uses a series of evenly spaced horizontal and vertical lines—called **gridlines**—to align objects, which force objects to "snap" to the grid.

4. **Position ⤧ over the bottom part of the frame shape, then press and hold CTRL**

   The pointer changes to ⬉, indicating that PowerPoint makes a copy of the shape when you drag the mouse.

5. **Holding CTRL, drag the frame shape down until the frame shape copy is in a blank area of the slide, release the mouse button, then release CTRL**

   An identical duplicate copy of the frame shape appears on the slide and Smart Guides appear above and below the shape as you drag the new shape, which helps you align shapes.

6. **With the second frame shape still selected, click the Copy button ▦ ▾ in the Clipboard group, click the Paste button, then move the new shape to a blank area of the slide**

   You have duplicated the frame shape twice and now have three identical shapes on the slide.

7. **Click the View tab on the Ribbon, click the Ruler check box in the Show group, click the Home tab, then type Growth**

   The ruler closes, and the text you type appears in the selected frame shape and becomes a part of the shape. Now if you move or rotate the shape, the text moves with it. Compare your screen with FIGURE 2-10.

8. **Click the middle frame shape, type Supply, click the top frame shape, type Trends, click in a blank area of the slide, then save your work**

   All three frame shapes include text.

FIGURE 2-9: Merged shape moved on slide

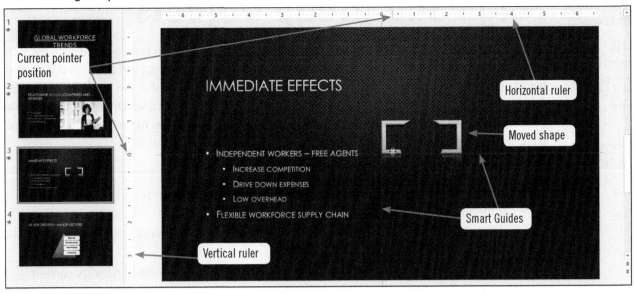

FIGURE 2-10: Duplicated shapes

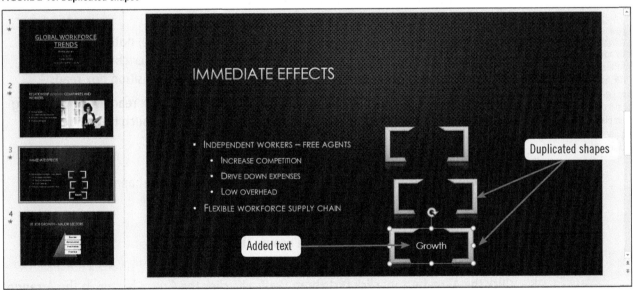

Editing points of a shape

If you want to customize the form (or outline) of any shape in the shapes gallery, you can modify its edit points. To display a shape's edit points, select the shape you want to modify, click the Drawing Tools Format tab on the Ribbon, click the Edit Shape button in the Insert Shapes group, then click Edit Points. Black edit points appear on the shape. To change the form of a shape, drag a black edit point. When you click a black edit point, white square edit points appear on either side of the black edit point, which allow you to change the curvature of a line between two black edit points. When you are finished with your custom shape, you can save it as a picture and reuse it in other presentations or other files. To save the shape as a picture, right-click the shape, then click Save as Picture.

Align and Group Objects

Learning
Outcomes
• Move shapes using
  guides
• Align and group
  shapes

After you are finished creating and modifying your objects, you can position them accurately on the slide to achieve the look you want. Using the Align commands in the Arrange group, you can align objects relative to each other by snapping them to the gridlines on a slide or to guides that you manually position on the slide. The Group command groups two or more objects into one object, which secures their relative position to each other and makes it easy to edit and move them. **CASE** *You are ready to position and group the frame shapes on Slide 3 to finish the slide.*

STEPS

1. **Right-click a blank area of the slide, point to the Grid and Guides arrow on the short-cut menu, then click Gridlines**

   Gridlines appear on the slide as a series of evenly spaced vertical and horizontal dotted lines. Gridlines can help you position objects on the slide.

2. **Drag the Trends shape until it snaps into place on a set of gridlines near its current position, click the View tab, then click the Gridlines checkbox to remove the gridlines**

   The shape snaps into place using gridlines.

3. **Right-click a blank area of the slide, point to Grid and Guides arrow on the shortcut menu, then click Guides**

   The guides appear as dotted lines on the slide and usually intersect at the center of the slide. Guides help you position objects precisely on the slide.

4. **Position ⌖ over the horizontal guide in a blank area of the slide, notice the pointer change to ⇕, press and hold the mouse button until the pointer changes to a measurement guide box, then drag the guide up until the guide position box reads 1.83**

5. **Drag the vertical guide to the right until the guide position box reads 1.83, then drag the Trends shape so that the top and left edges of the shape touch the guides, as shown in FIGURE 2-11**

   The Trends shape attaches or "snaps" to the guides.

6. **Press and hold SHIFT, click the Supply shape, click the Growth shape, release SHIFT, then click the Drawing Tools Format tab on the Ribbon**

   All three frame shapes are now selected.

7. **Click the Align button in the Arrange group, then click Align Right**

   The two lower frame shapes move to the right and align with the top frame shape along their right edges.

8. **Click the Align button, click Distribute Vertically, click the Group button in the Arrange group, then click Group**

   The shapes are now distributed evenly among themselves and are grouped together to form one object without losing their individual attributes. Notice that the sizing handles and rotate handle now appear on the outer edge of the grouped object as shown in FIGURE 2-12, not around each individual object.

9. **Drag the horizontal guide to the middle of the slide until its guide position box reads 0.00, then drag the vertical guide to the middle of the slide until its guide position box reads 0.00**

10. **Click the View tab on the Ribbon, click the Guides check box in the Show group, click a blank area of the slide, then save your work**

    The guides are no longer displayed on the slide.

FIGURE 2-11: **Repositioned shape**

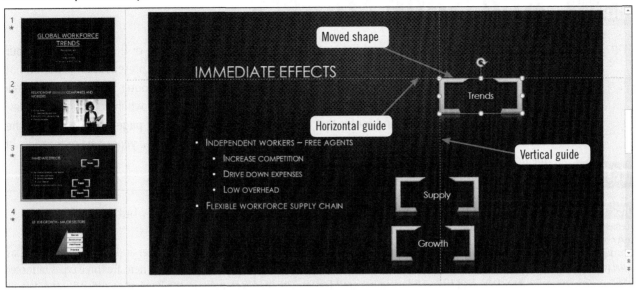

FIGURE 2-12: **Grouped shapes**

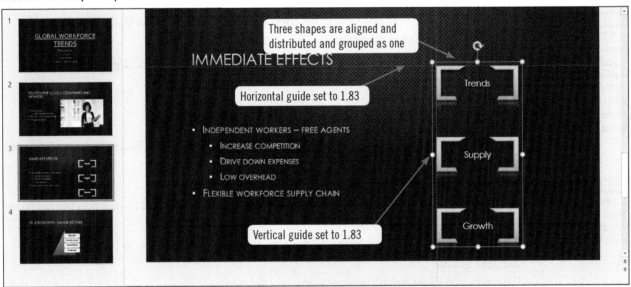

Distributing objects

There are two ways to distribute objects in PowerPoint: relative to each other and relative to the slide edge. If you choose to distribute objects relative to each other, PowerPoint evenly divides the empty space between all of the selected objects. When distributing objects in relation to the slide, PowerPoint evenly splits the empty space from slide edge to slide edge between the selected objects. To distribute objects relative to each other, click the Align button in the Arrange group on the Drawing Tools Format tab, then click Align Selected Objects. To distribute objects relative to the slide, click the Align button in the Arrange group on the Drawing Tools Format tab, then click Align to Slide.

PowerPoint

Add Slide Footers

Learning Outcome
• Add footer text to slides

Footer text, such as a company, school, or product name, the slide number, or the date, can give your slides a professional look and make it easier for your audience to follow your presentation. Slides do not have headers. However, notes or handouts can include both header and footer text. You can review footer information that you apply to the slides in the PowerPoint views and when you print the slides. Notes and handouts header and footer text is visible when you print notes pages, handouts, and the outline. **CASE** ▶ *You add footer text that includes the date, slide number, and your name to the slides of the presentation to make it easier for the audience to follow.*

STEPS

QUICK TIP
The placement of the footer text objects on the slide is dependent on the presentation theme.

1. **Click the** Insert tab **on the Ribbon, then click the** Header & Footer button **in the Text group**

   The Header and Footer dialog box opens, as shown in **FIGURE 2-13**. The Header and Footer dialog box has two tabs: a Slide tab and a Notes and Handouts tab. The Slide tab is selected. There are three types of footer text, Date and time, Slide number, and Footer. The bold rectangles in the Preview box identify the default position of the three types of footer text placeholders on the slides.

2. **Click the** Date and time check box **to select it**

   The date and time options are now available to select. The Update automatically date and time option button is selected by default. This option updates the date and time to the date and time set by your computer every time you open or print the file.

QUICK TIP
If you want a specific date to appear every time you view or print the presentation, click the Fixed date option button, then type the date in the Fixed text box.

3. **Click the** Update automatically arrow, **then click the** fourth option **in the list**

   The month is spelled out in this option.

4. **Click the** Slide number check box, **click the** Footer check box, **click the** Footer text box, **then type your name**

   The Preview box now shows all three footer placeholders are selected.

5. **Click the** Don't show on title slide check box

   Selecting this check box prevents the footer information you entered in the Header and Footer dialog box from appearing on the title slide.

TROUBLE
If the grouped shapes cover the footer text, drag them up out of the way.

6. **Click** Apply to All

   The dialog box closes, and the footer information is applied to all of the slides in your presentation except the title slide. Compare your screen to **FIGURE 2-14**.

7. **Click the** Slide 1 thumbnail **in the Slides tab, then click the** Header & Footer button **in the Text group**

   The Header and Footer dialog box opens again.

8. **Click the** Don't show on title slide check box **to deselect it, click the** Footer check box, **then select the text in the Footer text box**

TROUBLE
If you click Apply to All in Step 9, click the Undo button on the Quick Access toolbar and repeat Steps 7, 8, and 9.

9. **Type** Always Looking Forward, **click** Apply, **then save your work**

   The text in the Footer text box appears on the title slide. Clicking Apply applies this footer information to just the current slide.

FIGURE 2-13: Header and Footer dialog box

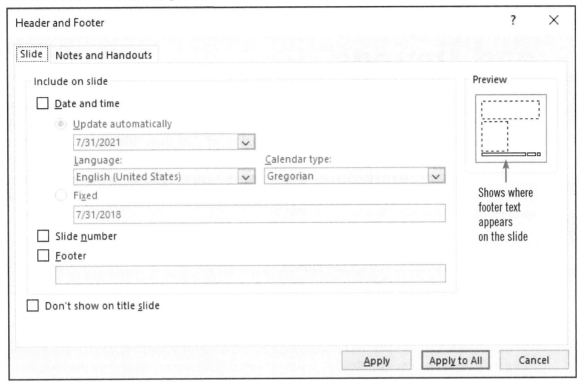

FIGURE 2-14: Footer information added to presentation

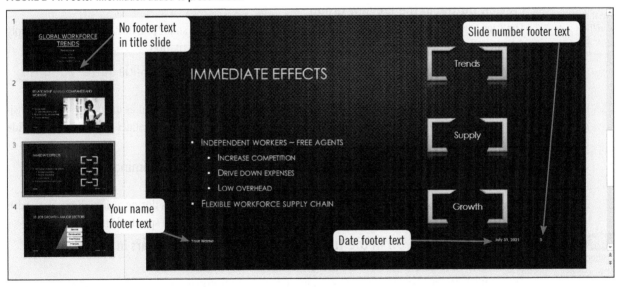

Creating superscript and subscript text

Superscript or subscript text is a number, figure, symbol, or letter that appears smaller than other text and is positioned above or below the normal line of text. A common superscript in the English language is the sign indicator next to a number, such as 1st or 3rd. Other examples of superscripts are the trademark symbol™ and the copyright symbol©. To create superscript text in PowerPoint, select the text, number, or symbol, then press CTRL SHIFT + at the same time. Probably the most familiar uses of subscript text are the numerals in chemical compounds and formulas, for example, H_2O and CO_2. To create subscript text, select the text, number, or symbol, then press CTRL = at the same time. To change superscript or subscript text back to normal text, select the text, then press CTRL SPACEBAR.

Set Slide Transitions and Timings

Learning
Outcomes
• Apply and modify
a transition
• Modify slide
timings

In a slide show, you can determine how each slide advances in and out of view and how long each slide appears on the screen. **Slide transitions** are the visual and audio effects you apply to a slide that determine how each slide moves on and off the screen during the slide show. **Slide timing** refers to the amount of time a slide is visible on the screen. Typically, you set slide timings only if you want the presentation to automatically progress through the slides during a slide show. Each slide can have a different slide transition and different slide timing. **CASE** *You decide to set slide transitions and 7-second slide timings for all the slides.*

STEPS

1. **Click the** Transitions tab **on the Ribbon**

   Transitions are organized by type into three groups: Subtle, Exciting, and Dynamic Content.

2. **Click the** More button ⊽ **in the Transition to This Slide group, then click** Page Curl **in the Exciting section**

   The new slide transition plays on the slide, and a transition icon ⭐ appears next to the slide thumbnail in the Slides tab as shown in FIGURE 2-15. You can change the direction and speed of the slide transition.

3. **Click the** Effect Options button **in the Transition to This Slide group, click** Double Right, **click the** Duration up arrow **in the Timing group until** 2.00 **appears, then click the** Preview button **in the Preview group**

   The Page Curl slide transition now plays double from the left on the slide for 2.00 seconds. You can apply this transition with the custom settings to all of the slides in the presentation.

4. **Click the** Apply To All button **in the Timing group, then click the** Slide Sorter button ▦ **on the status bar**

   All of the slides now have the customized Page Curl transition applied to them as identified by the transition icons located below each slide. You also have the ability to determine how slides progress during a slide show—either manually by mouse click or automatically by slide timing.

5. **Click the** On Mouse Click check box **under Advance Slide in the Timing group to clear the check mark**

   When this option is selected, you have to click to manually advance slides during a slide show. Now, with this option disabled, you can set the slides to advance automatically after a specified amount of time.

6. **Click the** After up arrow **in the Timing group until** 00:07.00 **appears in the text box, then click the** Apply To All button

   The timing between slides is 7 seconds as indicated by the time under each slide thumbnail in FIGURE 2-16. When you run the slide show, each slide will remain on the screen for 7 seconds. You can override a slide's timing and speed up the slide show by using any of the manual advance slide commands.

7. **Click the** Slide Show button 🖵 **on the status bar**

   The slide show advances automatically. A new slide appears every 7 seconds using the Page Curl transition.

8. **sam'**✦ **When you see the black slide, press** SPACEBAR, **save your changes, submit your presentation to your instructor, then exit PowerPoint**

   The slide show ends, and you return to Slide Sorter view with Slide 1 selected.

FIGURE 2-15: **Applied slide transition**

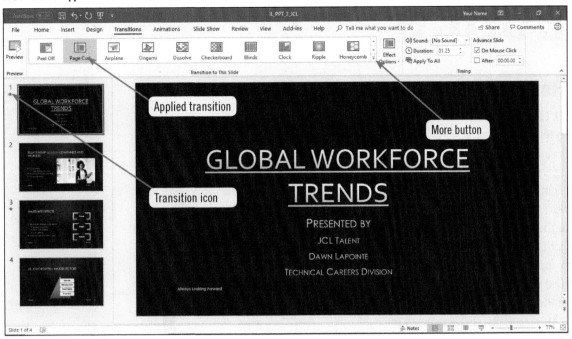

FIGURE 2-16: **Slide sorter view showing applied transition and timing**

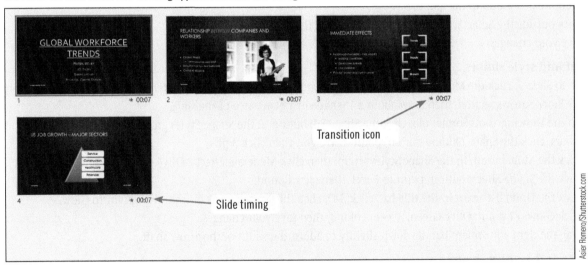

Asier Romero/Shutterstock.com

Inserting hyperlinks in a webpage

While creating a presentation there may be information on the Internet you want to reference or view during a slide show. Instead of re-creating the information in PowerPoint, you can insert a hyperlink on a slide that when clicked during a slide show will open the webpage directly from the Internet. To insert a hyperlink, select an object on the slide, such as a picture or text object, then click the Insert tab on the Ribbon. Click the Link button in the Links group to open the Insert Hyperlink dialog box. Click the Existing File or Web Page button in the link to section, then locate the webpage you want to link. Use the Address bar in the dialog box to insert the webpage address, then click OK. Now during a slide show, click the object with the hyperlink and you will view the linked webpage.

Practice

Skills Review

1. Convert text to SmartArt.

a. Open the presentation IL_PPT_2-2.pptx from the location where you store your Data Files, then save it as **IL_PPT_2_Broker**. The completed presentation is shown in FIGURE 2-17.

FIGURE 2-17

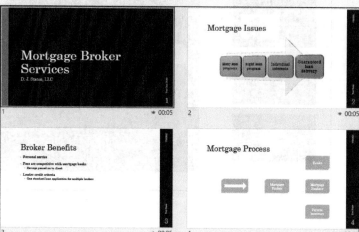

b. Click the text object on Slide 2.

c. Click the Convert to SmartArt Graphic button, then apply the Basic Cycle graphic layout to the text object.

d. Click the More button in the Layouts group, click More Layouts, click Process in the Choose a SmartArt Graphic dialog box, click Continuous Block Process, then click OK.

e. Click the More button in the SmartArt Styles group, then apply the Metallic Scene style from the 3-D group to the graphic.

f. Click outside the SmartArt graphic in a blank part of the slide.

g. Save your changes.

2. Insert and style shapes.

a. Go to Slide 5, click the More button in the Drawing group to open the Shapes gallery, click the Arrow: Right button in the Block Arrows section, then draw about a 1" shape in a blank area of the slide.

b. On the Drawing Tools Format tab, click the Shape Fill button in the Shape Styles group, click yellow under Standard Colors, click the Shape Outline button, point to Weight, then click 3 pt.

c. Click the More button in the Shape Styles group, then click Moderate Effect—Olive Green, Accent 3.

d. Click the Shape Effects button, point to Bevel, then click Round.

e. Click the Undo list arrow in the title bar, click 3-D, click the Shape Effects button, then point to Glow.

f. Click Glow: 11 point; Olive Green, Accent color 3, then save your changes.

g. Drag the right adjustment handle down slightly to adjust the width of the arrow shaft.

3. Rotate and modify shapes.

a. Click the arrow shape on the slide, click the Rotate button in the Arrange group, then click Flip Horizontal.

b. Drag the Rotate handle to the left until the arrow is pointing to the bottom of the slide, click the Undo list arrow, then click Rotate Object.

c. Click the Rotate button, then click Flip Horizontal.

d. Click the Edit Shape button in the Insert Shapes group, point to Change Shape, then click Arrow: Notched Right in the Block Arrows section.

e. Right-click the Slide 4 thumbnail in the Slides tab, click Delete Slide, then save your work.

4. Rearrange and merge shapes.

a. Click the green arrow shape on Slide 4, then click the Drawing Tools Format tab.

b. Drag the arrow shape over the top of the blank rectangle shape, center it on the rectangle shape using the SmartGuides, then adjust the shape if needed to make it fit in the space as shown in FIGURE 2-18.

Modifying a Presentation

Skills Review (continued)

c. Send the arrow shape back one level, press SHIFT, click the rectangle shape, then click the Merge Shapes button in the Insert Shapes group.

d. Point to each of the merge shapes options, click a blank area of the slide twice, then click the rectangle shape.

e. Send the rectangle shape back one level, then click a blank area of the slide.

f. Press SHIFT, click the arrow shape, click the rectangle shape, click the Merge Shapes button, click Combine, then save your work.

FIGURE 2-18

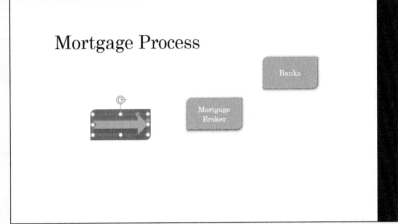

5. **Edit and duplicate shapes.**
   a. Show Rulers, select the Banks shape, then using CTRL make one copy of the shape.
   b. Using the ruler, move the new shape to approximately 3.5 (right of 0) on the vertical ruler, then close the rulers.
   c. Click the new shape, click the Copy button in the Clipboard group, then click the Paste button in the Clipboard group.
   d. Move the new square shape to a blank area at the bottom of the slide, then select the text in the shape.
   e. Type **Private Investors**, select the text in the other new rectangle shape, then type **Mortgage Bankers**.
   f. Click the arrow shape, then drag the right-middle sizing handle to the right ¼".
   g. Click a blank area of the slide, add the gridlines to the Slide pane, then save your changes.

6. **Align and group objects.**
   a. Drag the Mortgage Broker rectangle shape down until its bottom edge snaps to a horizontal gridline, then click the Drawing Tools Format tab.
   b. Press CTRL, click the arrow shape, click the Mortgage Bankers shape, release CTRL, then click the Align button in the Arrange group.
   c. Click Align Middle, click the Align button, then click Distribute Horizontally.
   d. Hide the gridlines, display the guides, then move the vertical guide to the right until 3.00 appears.
   e. Move the Private Investors shape to the left until it is centered over the vertical guide, move the vertical guide back to 0.00, then hide the guides.
   f. Select the three rectangle shapes on the right, click the Align button, then click Align Right.
   g. Select all five square shapes, click the Group button in the Arrange group, click Group, then save your work. Your screen should look similar to FIGURE 2-19.

FIGURE 2-19

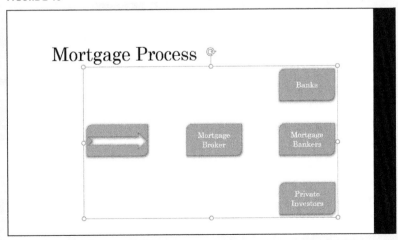

PowerPoint

Skills Review (continued)

7. Add slide footers.

   a. Open the Header and Footer dialog box.

   b. On the Slide tab, click the Date and time check box to select it, then click the Fixed option button.

   c. Add the slide number to the footer, then type your name in the Footer text box.

   d. Apply the footer to all of the slides except the title slide.

   e. Click the Slide 1 thumbnail in the Slides tab, open the Header and Footer dialog box again, then click the Don't show on title slide check box.

   f. Click the Footer check box, then type your class name in the text box.

   g. Click the Slide number check box, then click Apply.

   h. Save your changes, submit your presentation to your instructor, close the presentation, then exit PowerPoint.

8. Set slide transitions and timings.

   a. Go to Slide Sorter view, click the Slide 1 thumbnail, click the Transition tab, then apply the Wind transition to the slide.

   b. Change the effect option to Left, change the duration to 2.75, then apply to all the slides.

   c. Change the slide timing to 5 seconds, then apply to all of the slides.

   d. Switch to Normal view, view the slide show, then save your work.

Independent Challenge 1

Riverwalk Medical Clinic (RMC) is a large medical facility in Cambridge, Massachusetts. You have been asked to create a presentation on the latest emergency response procedures for a staff training later in the week.

   a. Start PowerPoint, open the presentation IL_PPT_2-3.pptx from the location where you store your Data Files, and save it as **IL_PPT_2_ERP**.

   b. Display the guides to the Slide pane, move the horizontal guide down to 2.00, then move the vertical guide left to 5.00.

   c. Drag the rectangle shape so its top and left edges snap into the guides, then move both guides back to 0.00 and hide the guides.

   d. Move the left adjustment handle on the rectangle shape slightly to the right to change the shape of the rectangle.

   e. Change the shape fill color to Rose, Accent 6, then change the shape outline to solid 1 ½ point black.

   f. Duplicate the shape twice, align the shapes along their bottom edges across the slide, distribute the space horizontally between the shapes, then group the shapes.

   g. Type **CPR** in the left shape, type **Airway kits** in the middle shape, then type **Crash cart** in the right shape.

   h. Apply the Reveal transition to all the slides with a 4.50 duration time.

   i Change the bulleted text on Slide 4 to the Trapezoid List SmartArt Graphic, then apply the Inset SmartArt style.

   j. Add your name and slide number as a footer on all the slides except the title slide, then save your changes. Your completed presentation might look similar to FIGURE 2-20.

   k. Submit your presentation to your instructor, close your presentation, then exit PowerPoint.

FIGURE 2-20

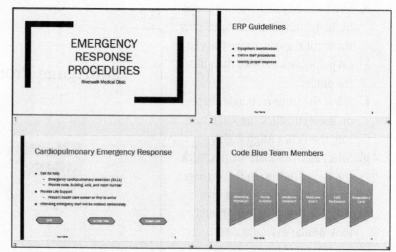

Independent Challenge 2

You are one of the assistants to the Career and Intern Program manager at Delvall Corp., a large engineering and manufacturing company. You have been asked by your manager to develop a new presentation outlining the details of the career and intern leadership program offered by Delvall. You continue working on the presentation you have already started.

a. Start PowerPoint, open the presentation IL_PPT_2-4.pptx from the location where you store your Data Files, and save it as **IL_PPT_2_Delvall**.

b. Go to Slide 4, show the rulers in the Slide pane, then drag the lower-right sizing handle on the shape down and to the right until the pointer reaches the 3 in the horizontal ruler.

c. Draw a 1" proportional chevron shape from the Block Arrows section of shapes. (*Hint:* to draw a specific size shape, position your pointer on the 0 of a ruler and drag until your pointer reaches the size you want on the ruler.)

d. Click the Drawing Tools Format tab, flip the shape horizontal, then drag the shape's rotate handle until the arrow is pointing up.

e. Select both shapes, then apply Intense Effect—Orange, Accent 2 from the Shape Styles group.

f. Apply the Preset 1 shape effect, then merge the two shapes together using the Union option, as shown in FIGURE 2-21.

g. Show gridlines in the Slide pane, drag the merged shape to the left until the shape's left and bottom edges are touching gridlines, then hide the gridlines.

h. Apply to all the slides the transition Random Bars with a duration of 2.00, then change the effect option to horizontal.

i. Delete Slide 2 from the presentation, add the slide number and your name as a footer on the slides, then save your changes.

j. Run a slide show, submit your presentation to your instructor, close your presentation, then exit PowerPoint.

FIGURE 2-21

Visual Workshop

Open the presentation IL_PPT_2-5.pptx from the location where you store your Data Files, and save it as **IL_PPT_2_LaSalle**. Create the presentation shown in FIGURE 2-22 and FIGURE 2-23. Add today's date as the date on the title slide. Create and duplicate the merged shape, which is made with an Arrow: Bent-Up shape and a Rectangle: Rounded Corners shape. The shapes are 1 ½" proportional shapes with the Subtle Effect—Dark Purple, Accent 2 applied to them. (*Hint:* The arrow shape is rotated 90 degrees before it's merged with the square shape.) Set the horizontal guide to 1 and the vertical guide to 3, as shown in FIGURE 2-22. The SmartArt graphic in FIGURE 2-23 is created with the Basic Matrix layout and has the Moderate Effect style applied to it. Review your slides in Slide Show view, then add your name as a footer to the slides. Submit your presentation to your instructor, save your changes, close the presentation, then exit PowerPoint.

FIGURE 2-22

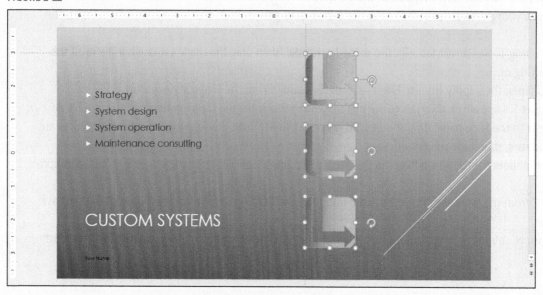

FIGURE 2-23

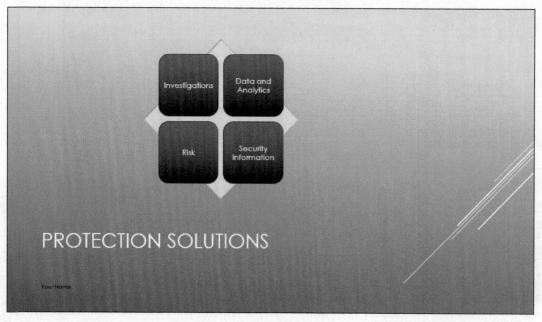

Inserting Objects into a Presentation

CASE In this module, you continue working on the JCL Talent presentation by inserting and formatting a text box and then cropping and styling a picture. You also add visual elements into the presentation, including a chart, slides from another presentation, and a table. You format these objects using the powerful object-editing features in PowerPoint.

Module Objectives

After completing this module, you will be able to:

- Insert a text box
- Crop and style a picture
- Insert a chart
- Enter and edit chart data
- Insert slides from other presentations

- Insert a table
- Insert and format WordArt
- Animate objects
- Insert and edit digital video

Files You Will Need

IL_PPT_3-1.pptx	IL_PPT_3-3.pptx
Support_PPT_3_Presentation.pptx	Support_PPT_3_ER.pptx
Support_PPT_3_Video.mp4	IL_PPT_3-4.pptx
IL_PPT_3-2.pptx	Support_PPT_3_Invest.pptx
Support_PPT_3_PMI.pptx	Support_PPT_3_Woman.jpg
Support_PPT_3_Desk.mp4	

Insert a Text Box

Learning Outcomes
- Insert a text box
- Format text in a text box
- Resize and move a text box

In most cases, you enter text on a slide using a title or content placeholder that is arranged on the slide based on a slide layout. Every so often you need additional text on a slide where the traditional placeholder does not place text. There are two types of text boxes: a text label, used for a small phrase where text doesn't automatically wrap inside the boundaries of a text box, and a word-processing box, used for a sentence or paragraph where the text wraps inside a text box. Either type of text box can be formatted and edited just like any other text object. **CASE** *You create a text box next to the SmartArt graphic on Slide 4, then edit and format the text.*

STEPS

1. **sam Start PowerPoint, open the presentation IL_PPT_3-1.pptx from the location where you store your Data Files, then save it as IL_PPT_3_JCL**
2. **Click the Slide 4 thumbnail in the Slides tab, click the Insert tab on the Ribbon, then click the Text Box button in the Text group**
   The pointer changes to ↓.
3. **Move ↓ to the blank area to the left of the SmartArt object on the slide, then drag the pointer + down and toward the right about 3" to create a text box**
   When you begin dragging, an outline of the text box appears, indicating the size of the text box you are drawing. After you release the mouse button, a blinking insertion point appears inside the text box, in this case a word-processing box, indicating that you can enter text.
4. **Type Last year's growth increased over 25% in all areas**
   Notice the text box increases in size as your text wraps to additional lines inside the text box. Your screen should look similar to FIGURE 3-1. After entering the text, you decide to edit the sentence.
5. **Drag I over the phrase in all areas to select it, position ↖ on top of the selected phrase, then press and hold the left mouse button**
   The pointer changes to ↖.
6. **Drag the selected words to the right of the word "growth", release the mouse button, then click to the left of the text box**
   A grey insertion line appears as you drag, indicating where PowerPoint places the text when you release the mouse button. The phrase "in all areas" moves after the word "growth". Notice there is no space between the words "growth" and "in" and the spelling error is identified by a red wavy underline.
7. **Right-click the red underlined words in the text box, then click "growth in" on the shortcut menu**
   Space is added between the two words in the text box.
8. **Move I to the edge of the text box, which changes to ✥, click the text box border (it changes to a solid line), then click the Drawing Tools Format tab on the Ribbon**
9. **Click the Shape Fill list arrow in the Shape Styles group, click the Gold, Accent 4 color box, click the Shape Outline list arrow in the Shape Styles group, point to Weight, then click 4½ pt**
   The text object is now filled with a gold color and has a thicker outline.
10. **Position ✥ over the text box edge, drag the text box to the Smart Guide on the slide as shown in FIGURE 3-2, then save your changes**

QUICK TIP
To create a text label, click the Text Box button, position the pointer on the slide, click once, then enter your text.

QUICK TIP
Click the Shape Effects list arrow in the Shape Styles group, then click one of the preset effects to change the style of a text object.

FIGURE 3-1: New text object

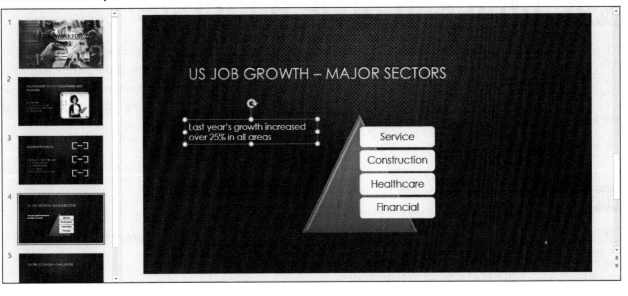

FIGURE 3-2: Formatted text object

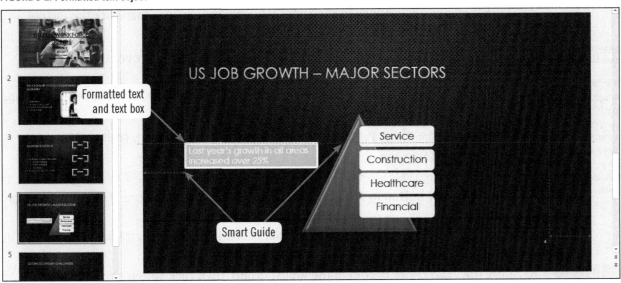

Changing text box defaults

You can change the default formatting characteristics of text boxes you create using the Text Box button on the Insert tab. To change the formatting defaults for text boxes, select an existing formatted text box, or create a new one and format it using any of the PowerPoint formatting commands. When you are ready to change the text box defaults of a text box that is not selected, press SHIFT, right-click the formatted text box, release SHIFT, then click Set as Default Text Box on the shortcut menu. Now, any text boxes you create will display the formatting characteristics of this formatted text box.

PowerPoint

Crop and Style a Picture

Learning Outcomes
- Crop a picture
- Apply a picture style
- Add effects to a picture
- Resize and move a picture

PowerPoint provides many editing tools that help you style a picture, such as transparency, sharpening or softening edges, color tone, and cropping. **Cropping** a picture hides a portion of the picture you don't want to see. The cropped portion of a picture is still available to you if you ever want to show that part of the picture again. **CASE** ▶ *In this lesson you crop and style a picture to best fit the slide, but first you format a picture you insert on the Slide Master.*

STEPS

QUICK TIP
You can also insert a picture without a content placeholder by clicking the Pictures button in the Images group on the Insert tab.

1. **Click the** Slide 1 thumbnail **in the Slides tab, right click a blank area of the slide, then click** Format Background **on the shortcut menu**
   The Format Background pane opens.

2. **Click** File **in the Format Background task pane, navigate to location where you store your Data Files, select the picture file** Support_PPT_3_Group.jpg, **then click** Insert
   The picture fills the slide.

3. **Drag the** Transparency Slider **to** 50%, **then close the Format Background pane**
   The slide background picture on Slide 1 is more transparent.

4. **Click the** Slide 2 thumbnail **in the Slides tab, click the** picture, **then click the** Picture Tools Format tab **on the Ribbon**

QUICK TIP
Click the Crop button list arrow to take advantage of other crop options, including cropping to a shape from the Shapes gallery and cropping to a common photo size or aspect ratio.

5. **Click the** Crop button **in the Size group, then place the pointer over the** middle-left cropping handle **on the picture**
   The pointer changes to ⊣. When the Crop button is active, cropping handles appear next to the sizing handles on the selected object.

6. **Drag the** middle of the picture **to the right as shown in** FIGURE 3-3, **release the mouse button, then press** ESC
   The picture would look better on the slide if it had a different color tone.

7. **Click the** Color button **in the Adjust group, then click** Temperature: 4700K **in the Color Tone row**
   The options in the Color Tone row add more blue or orange to the picture, making it appear cooler or warmer.

QUICK TIP
If you have multiple pictures on a slide, you can align them using guides or SmartGuides.

8. **Click the** Corrections button **in the Adjust group, then click** Soften: 25% **in the Sharpen/Soften section**
   The picture is slightly unclear.

9. **Click the** More button ⊡ **in the Picture Styles group, then click** Metal Rounded Rectangle **(4th row)**
   The picture now has rounded corners with a metal-looking frame. Notice the picture has an adjustment handle that you can move.

10. **Drag the** picture **to the center of the blank area of the slide to the right of the text object, click a blank area on the slide, then save your changes**
    Compare your screen to FIGURE 3-4.

FIGURE 3-3: Using the cropping pointer to crop a picture

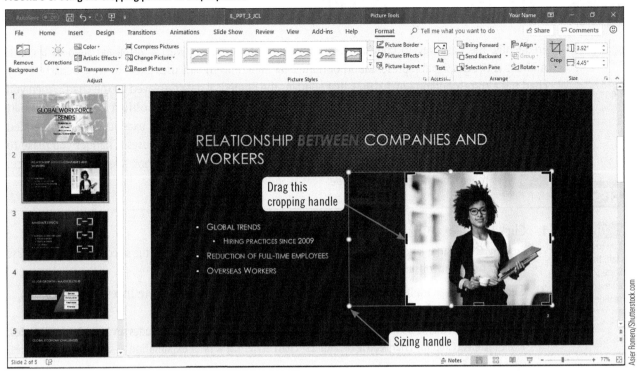

FIGURE 3-4: Cropped and styled picture

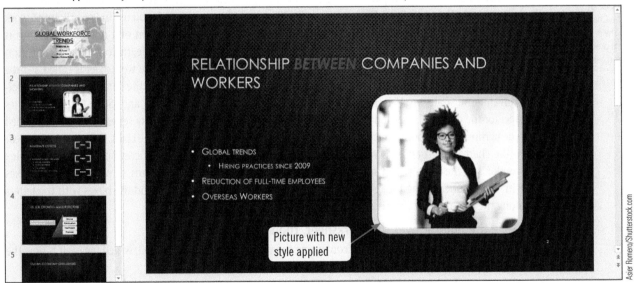

Inserting a screen recording

Using the Screen Recording button in the Media group on the Insert tab, you can record your computer screen with audio and insert the recording in a slide. For example, if you want to make a recording of an Internet video, locate and display the video on your computer screen. In PowerPoint on the slide where you want to insert the recording, click the Screen Recording button.

On the toolbar, click the Select Area button, drag a selection box around the video, click the Audio button if necessary, then click the Record button on the toolbar. Click the video play button. When finished recording, click Windows Logo+SHIFT+Q to stop recording. PowerPoint opens and the recording appears on your slide. Click the Play button to review your recording.

PowerPoint

Insert a Chart

Learning
Outcome
• Insert a new chart
  on a slide

Frequently, the best way to communicate numerical information is with a visual aid such as a chart. A **chart** is the graphical representation of numerical data. PowerPoint uses Excel to create charts. Every chart has a corresponding **worksheet** that contains the numerical data displayed by the chart. When you insert a chart object into PowerPoint, you are embedding it. An **embedded object** is one that is a part of your presentation (just like any other object you insert into PowerPoint) except that an embedded object's data source can be opened, in this case using Excel, for editing purposes. Changes you make to an embedded object in PowerPoint using the features in PowerPoint do not affect the data source.
CASE ▶ *You insert a chart on a new slide.*

STEPS

1. **Click the** Slide 4 thumbnail **in the Slides tab, then press** ENTER
   Pressing ENTER adds a new slide to your presentation with the slide layout of the selected slide, in this case the Title and Content slide layout.

2. **Click the** Title placeholder, **type** Free Agency Trends, **then click the** Insert Chart icon 📊 **in the Content placeholder**
   The Insert Chart dialog box opens as shown in FIGURE 3-5. Each chart type includes several 2D and 3D styles. The Clustered Column chart is the default 2D chart style. For a brief explanation of common chart types, refer to TABLE 3-1.

3. **Click** OK
   The PowerPoint window displays a clustered column chart below a worksheet with sample data, as shown in FIGURE 3-6. The Chart Tools Design tab on the Ribbon contains commands you use in PowerPoint to work with the chart. The worksheet consists of rows and columns. The intersection of a row and a column is called a **cell**. Cells are referred to by their row and column location; for example, the cell at the intersection of column A and row 1 is called cell A1. Each column and row of data in the worksheet is called a **data series**. Cells in column A and row 1 contain **data series labels** that identify the data or values in the column and row. "Category 1" is the data series label for the data in the second row, and "Series 1" is a data series label for the data in the second column. Cells below and to the right of the data series labels, in the shaded blue portion of the worksheet, contain the data values that are represented in the chart. Cells in row 1 appear in the chart **legend** and describe the data in the series. Each data series has corresponding **data series markers** in the chart, which are graphical representations such as bars, columns, or pie wedges. The boxes with the numbers along the left side of the worksheet are **row headings**, and the boxes with the letters along the top of the worksheet are **column headings**.

4. **Move the pointer over the worksheet, then click cell** C4
   The pointer changes to ✚. Cell C4, containing the value 1.8, is the selected cell, which means it is now the **active cell**. The active cell has a thick green border around it.

5. **Click the** Close button ✕ **on the worksheet title bar, then click the** Quick Layout button **in the Chart Layouts group**
   The worksheet window closes, and the Quick Layout gallery opens.

6. **Move** ⌖ **over the layouts in the gallery, then click** Layout 9
   This new layout moves the legend to the right side of the chart and increases the size of the data series markers.

7. **Drag the chart straight up to center it on the slide**

8. **Click in a blank area of the slide to deselect the chart, then save your changes**
   The Chart Tools Design tab is no longer active.

FIGURE 3-5: Insert Chart dialog box

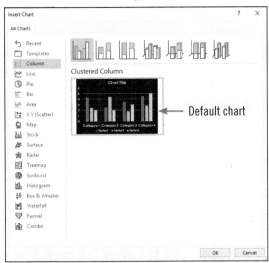

Default chart

FIGURE 3-6: Worksheet open showing chart data

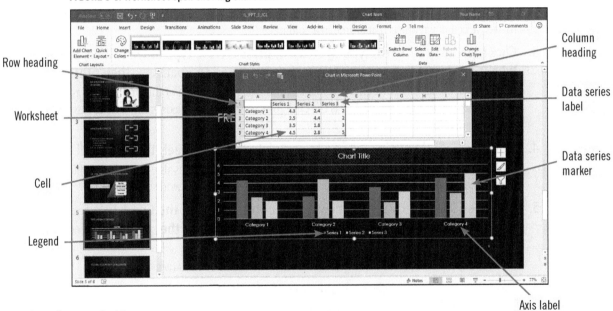

Row heading

Worksheet

Cell

Legend

Column heading

Data series label

Data series marker

Axis label

TABLE 3-1: Common chart types

chart type	icon looks like	use to
Column		Track values over time or across categories
Line		Track values over time
Pie		Compare individual values to the whole
Bar		Compare values in categories or over time
Area		Show contribution of each data series to the total over time
X Y (Scatter)		Compare pairs of values
Stock		Show stock market information or scientific data
Surface		Show value trends across two dimensions
Radar		Show changes in values in relation to a center point
Combo		Use multiple types of data markers to compare values

Enter and Edit Chart Data

Learning
Outcomes
• Change chart data
  values and labels
• Format a chart

After you insert a chart into your presentation, you need to replace the sample information with the correct data. If you have the data you want to chart in an Excel worksheet, you can import it from Excel; otherwise, you can type the data into the worksheet on the slide. As you enter data and make other changes in the worksheet, the chart on the slide automatically reflects the new changes. **CASE** *You enter and format internal company data you have gathered comparing free agency trends over the last five years.*

STEPS

1. **Click the** chart object **on Slide 5, click the** Chart Tools Design tab **on the Ribbon, then click the** Edit Data button **in the Data group**
   The chart is selected and the worksheet opens in a separate window. The information in the worksheet needs to be replaced with the correct data.

QUICK TIP
Click the chart in the PowerPoint window, then move your pointer over each bar in the chart to see the data source values.

2. **Click the** Series 1 cell, **type** Last 5 Yrs, **press** TAB, **type** Prev 10 Yrs, **press** TAB, **then type** Next 5 Yrs
   The data series labels you enter in the worksheet are displayed in the legend on the chart. Pressing TAB moves the active cell from left to right one cell at a time in a row. Pressing ENTER in the worksheet moves the active cell down one cell at a time in a column.

3. **Click the** Category 1 cell, **type** Decreased, **press** ENTER, **type** Stayed Same, **press** ENTER, **type** Increased Slightly, **press** ENTER, **type** Increased Dramatically, **then press** TAB
   These data series labels appear in the worksheet and along the bottom of the chart on the *x*-axis. The *x*-axis is the horizontal axis also referred to as the **category axis**, and the *y*-axis is the vertical axis also referred to as the **value axis**.

4. **Enter the data shown in** FIGURE 3-7 **to complete the worksheet, then click** cell E5
   Notice that the height of each column in the chart, as well as the values along the *y*-axis, adjust to reflect the numbers you typed. You have finished entering the data in the Excel worksheet.

5. **Click the** Close button ☒ **on the worksheet title bar, click the** Chart Title text box object **in the chart, click the** Home tab **on the Ribbon, then click the** A˘ Increase Font Size button **in the Font group**
   The worksheet window closes. The text in the Chart Title text box is larger.

QUICK TIP
You can also change the chart style by clicking a style option in the Chart Styles group on the Chart Tools Design tab.

6. **Type** Global Changes, **click a blank area of the chart, then click the** Chart Styles button ✎ **to the right of the chart to open the Chart Styles gallery**
   The Chart Styles gallery opens on the left side of the chart with Style selected.

7. **Scroll down the gallery, click** Style 5, **click** Color **at the top of the Chart Styles gallery, then click the** Colorful Palette 2 **in the Colorful section**
   The new chart style and color give the column data markers a professional look as shown in FIGURE 3-8.

8. **Click a blank area on the slide, then save the presentation**
   The Chart Styles gallery closes.

FIGURE 3-7: **Worksheet data for the chart**

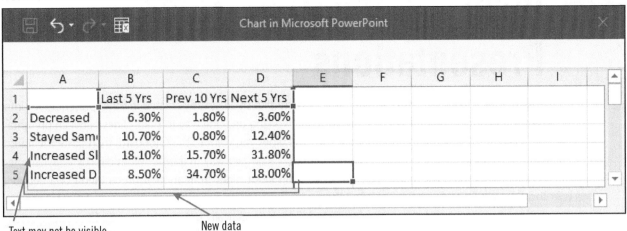

Text may not be visible
in the worksheet but
will appear in the chart

New data

FIGURE 3-8: **Formatted chart**

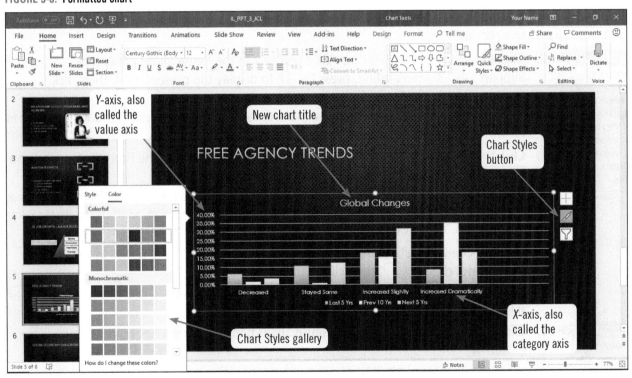

Adding a hyperlink to a chart

You can add a hyperlink to any object in PowerPoint, including a chart. Select that chart, click the Insert tab on the Ribbon, then click the Hyperlink button in the Links group. If you are linking to another file, click the Existing File or Web Page button, locate the file you want to link to the chart, then click OK. Or, if you want to link to another slide in the presentation, click the Place in This Document button, click the slide in the list, then click OK. Now, during a slide show you can click the chart to open the linked object. To remove the link, click the chart, click the Hyperlink button in the Links group, then click Remove Link.

Insert Slides from Other Presentations

To save time and energy, you can insert one or more slides you already created in other presentations into an existing presentation or one you are currently working on. One way to share slides between presentations is to open an existing presentation, copy the slides you want to the Clipboard, then paste them into your open presentation. However, PowerPoint offers a simpler way to transfer slides directly between presentations. By using the Reuse Slides pane, you can insert slides from another presentation or a network location called a Slide Library. A **Slide Library** is a folder that you and others can access to open, modify, and review presentation slides. Newly inserted slides automatically take on the theme of the open presentation, unless you decide to use slide formatting from the original source presentation. **CASE** *You decide to insert slides you created for another presentation into the JCL Talent presentation.*

STEPS

1. **Click the Slide 2 thumbnail in the Slides tab, then click the Reuse Slides button in the Slides group**

    The Reuse Slides pane opens on the right side of the presentation window and displays recently opened presentations.

TROUBLE
Be sure you have
access to the
location where you
store your Data Files
and spell the name
of the presentation
correctly when are
searching for a
specific file.

2. **Click the Search PowerPoint for slides text box in the Reuse Slides pane, type Support_PPT_3_Presentation, press ENTER to display the presentation, then click Choose Slides in the Reuse Slides pane**

    Slide thumbnails are displayed in the pane as shown in FIGURE 3-9. The slide thumbnails identify the slides in the **source presentation**, Support_PPT_3_Presentation.pptx.

3. **Click the Slide 1 thumbnail in the Reuse Slides pane, then click the Paste Options button ⬚ (Ctrl) ▾ in the Slides tab**

    The new slide appears in the Slides tab and Slide pane as the new Slide 3. Notice the new slide does not automatically assume the design style and formatting of your presentation, which is the **destination presentation**. The Paste Options button provides different methods for pasting objects and slides.

4. **Click the Use Destination Theme button ⬚, click the Slide 3 thumbnail in the Reuse Slides pane, click ⬚ (Ctrl) ▾, then click ⬚**

    The new Slide 3 assumes the design style and formatting of the destination presentation and a new Slide 4 appears.

QUICK TIP
To copy noncontigu-
ous slides, open Slide
Sorter view, click the
first slide thumbnail,
press and hold CTRL,
click each additional
slide thumbnail,
release CTRL,
then click the
Copy button.

5. **Click the Slide 2 thumbnail in the Reuse Slides pane, then click Reuse Slides pane Close button ✕**

    One more slide is inserted into the presentation with the design style and formatting of the source presentation and the Reuse Slides pane closes. You realize the last slide you inserted is not needed for this presentation.

6. **Right-click the Slide 5 thumbnail in the Slides tab, then click Delete Slide in the shortcut menu**

    Slide 5 is deleted.

7. **Click the ⬚ Slide Sorter button in the status bar, then drag Slide 4 to the right of Slide 2**

8. **Click the ⬚ Normal button in the status bar, then save the presentation**

    Slide 4 becomes Slide 3. Compare your screen to FIGURE 3-10.

FIGURE 3-9: Presentation window with Reuse Slides pane open

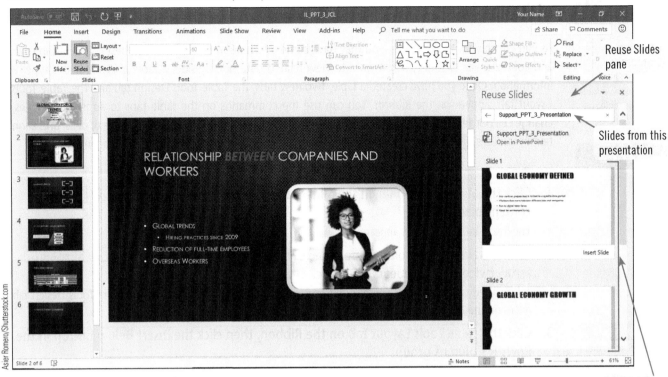

FIGURE 3-10: New slides added to presentation

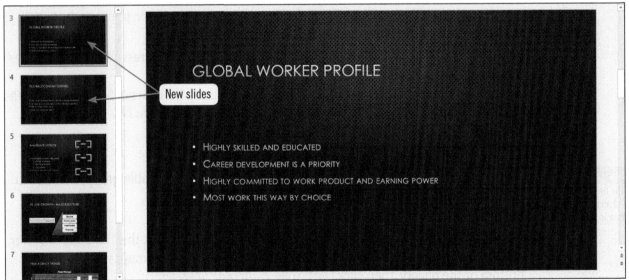

Working with multiple windows

Another way to work with information in multiple presentations is to arrange the presentation windows on your monitor so you see each window side by side. Open each presentation, click the View tab on the Ribbon in any presentation window, then click the Arrange All button in the Window group. Each presentation you have open is placed next to each other so you can easily drag, or transfer, information between the presentations.

If you are working with more than two open presentations, you can overlap the presentation windows on top of one another. Open all the presentations you want, then click the Cascade Windows button in the Window group. Now you can easily jump from one presentation to another by clicking the presentation title bar or any part of the presentation window.

Inserting Objects into a Presentation

Insert a Table

Learning Outcomes
• Insert a table
• Add text to a table
• Change table size and layout

As you create your presentation, you may have some information that would look best organized in rows and columns. For example, if you want to view related data side by side, a table is ideal for this type of information. Once you have created a table, two new tabs, the Table Tools Design tab and the Table Tools Layout tab, appear on the Ribbon. You can use the commands on the table tabs to apply color styles, change cell borders, add cell effects, add rows and columns to your table, adjust the size of cells, and align text in the cells. **CASE** ▶ *You decide a table best illustrates the challenges of using free agency workers.*

STEPS

1. **Click the** Slide 8 thumbnail **in the Slides tab, then click the** Insert Table icon ▦ **in the content placeholder**

   The Insert Table dialog box appears.

2. **Click the** Number of columns down arrow **until** 2 **appears, click the** Number of rows up arrow **twice until** 4 **appears, then click** OK

   A formatted table with two columns and four rows appears on the slide, and the Table Tools Design tab opens on the Ribbon. The table has 8 cells and you realize you need more cells.

QUICK TIP
Press TAB when the insertion point is in the last cell of a table to insert a new row.

3. **Click the** Table Tools Layout tab **on the Ribbon, then click the** Insert Below button **in the Rows & Columns group**

   A new row is added to the table below the current row.

4. **Click the** top-left cell **in the table, click the** Insert Left button **in the Rows & Columns group, then click the** top-left cell **again**

   The table has a new column to the left of the current column and the insertion point is in the first cell of the table ready to accept text.

5. **Type** Rank of Concerns, **press TAB, type** Free Agency Employer, **press TAB, type** Non-Free Agency Employer, **then press TAB**

   The text you typed appears in the top three cells of the table. Pressing TAB moves the insertion point to the next cell; pressing ENTER moves the insertion point to the next line in the same cell.

6. **Enter the rest of the table information shown in** FIGURE 3-11

   The table would look better if it were formatted differently.

QUICK TIP
Change the height or width of any table cell by dragging its borders.

7. **Click the** top-left cell **in the table, click the** Select button **in the Table group, click** Select Row, **then click the** Center button ▤ **in the Alignment group**

   The text in the top row is centered horizontally in each cell.

8. **Click the** Select button **in the Table group, click** Select Table, **click the** Table Tools Design tab **on the Ribbon, click the** More button ▾ **in the Table Styles group, scroll to the bottom of the gallery, then click** Dark Style 2 - Accent 5/Accent 6

   The table color changes to reflect the table style you applied.

QUICK TIP
To change the cell color behind text, click the Shading list arrow in the Table Styles group, then choose a color.

9. **Click the** Effects button **in the Table Styles group, point to** Cell Bevel, **click** Divot **(3rd row), click a blank area of the slide, then save the presentation**

   The 3D effect makes the cells of the table stand out. Compare your screen with FIGURE 3-12.

FIGURE 3-11: Inserted table with data

FIGURE 3-12: Formatted table

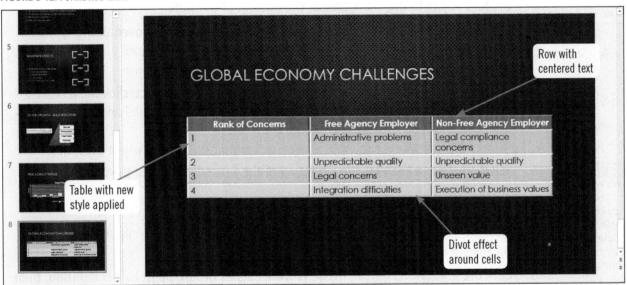

Setting permissions

In PowerPoint, you can set specific access permissions for people who review or edit your work so you have better control over your content. For example, you may want to give a user permission to edit or change your presentation but not allow them to print it. You can also restrict a user by permitting them to view the presentation without the ability to edit or print the presentation, or you can give the user full access or control of the presentation. To use this feature, you first access the information rights management services company. Then, to set user access permissions, click the File tab, click the Protect Presentation button, point to Restrict Access, then click an appropriate option.

Insert and Format WordArt

Learning Outcome
• Create, format, and resize WordArt

As you work to create an interesting presentation, your goal should include making your slides visually appealing. Sometimes plain text can come across as dull and unexciting in a presentation. **WordArt** is a set of decorative text styles, or text effects, you can apply to any text object to help direct the attention of your audience to a certain piece of information. You can use WordArt in two different ways: you can apply a WordArt text style to an existing text object that converts the text into WordArt, or you can create a new WordArt object. The WordArt text styles and effects include text shadows, reflections, glows, bevels, 3D rotations, and transformations. **CASE** ▶ *Create a new WordArt text object on Slide 3.*

STEPS

QUICK TIP

To convert any text or text object to WordArt, select the text or text object, click the Drawing Tools Format tab on the Ribbon, then click a WordArt style option in the WordArt Styles group.

1. **Click the Slide 3 thumbnail in the Slides tab, click the Insert tab on the Ribbon, then click the WordArt button in the Text group**
   The WordArt gallery appears displaying 20 WordArt text styles.

2. **Click Fill: Gold, Accent color 4; Soft Bevel (first row)**
   A text object appears in the middle of the slide displaying sample text with the WordArt style you just selected. The Drawing Tools Format tab is open on the Ribbon.

3. **Click the edge of the WordArt text object, then when the pointer changes to 🔧, drag the text object to the blank area at the bottom of the slide**

4. **Click the More button ⊽ in the WordArt Styles group, move ▷ over all the WordArt styles in the gallery, then click Fill: Tan, Accent color 3; Sharp Bevel**
   The sample text in the WordArt text object changes to the new WordArt style.

5. **Drag to select the text Your text here in the WordArt text object, click the Decrease Font Size button A˅ in the Mini toolbar so that 40 appears in the Font Size text box, then type Demand Drives Innovation**
   The text, "Demand Drives Innovation" is on the slide as WordArt. Compare your screen to FIGURE 3-13.

QUICK TIP

To convert a WordArt object to a SmartArt object, right-click the WordArt object, point to Convert to SmartArt on the shortcut menu, then click a SmartArt layout.

6. **Select the text in the WordArt object, click the Text Fill button in the WordArt Styles group, then click Tan, Accent 3, Darker 25%**
   The WordArt color is darker.

7. **Click the Text Outline button in the WordArt Styles group, then click White, Text 1**
   The WordArt outline is now white.

8. **Click the Text Effects button in the WordArt Styles group, point to 3-D Rotation, then click Perspective: Relaxed Moderately in the Perspective section (second row)**
   The off-axis effect is applied to the text object. You are unsure of this effect and apply another one.

9. **Click the Text Effects button, point to Transform, then click Triangle: Down in the Warp section (first row)**
   The effect is applied to the text object.

10. **Press SHIFT, drag the lower-right sizing handle down ½ inch, release SHIFT, click a blank area of the slide, then save your work**
    The text object is proportionally larger. Compare your screen to FIGURE 3-14.

FIGURE 3-13: WordArt inserted on slide

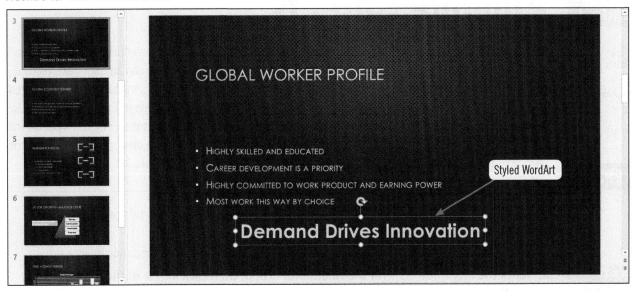

FIGURE 3-14: Formatted WordArt object

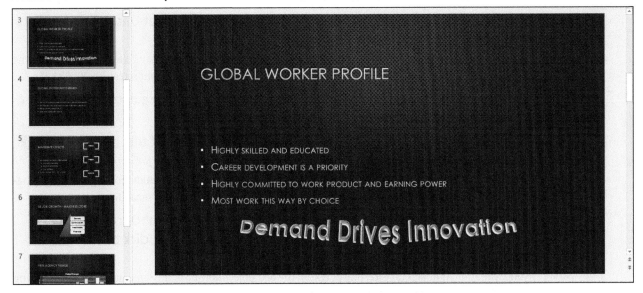

Animate Objects

Learning Outcomes
• Animate objects
• Modify animation effects

Animations let you control how objects and text appear and move on the screen during a slide show and allow you to manage the flow of information and emphasize specific facts. You can animate text, pictures, sounds, hyperlinks, SmartArt diagrams, charts, and individual chart elements. Animations are organized into four categories, Entrance, Emphasis, Exit, and Motion Paths. The Entrance and Exit animations cause an object to enter or exit the slide with an effect. An Emphasis animation causes an object visible on the slide to have an effect, and a Motion Path animation causes an object to move on a specified path on the slide. **CASE** *You animate the text and graphics on several slides in the presentation.*

STEPS

1. **Click the Slide 6 thumbnail in the Slides tab, click the Animations tab on the Ribbon, then click the SmartArt object**

   Text as well as other objects, such as a shape or picture, can be animated during a slide show.

2. **Click the More button ⋶ in the Animation group, then click Shape in the Entrance section**

   A small numeral 1, called an animation tag 1, appears on the slide. **Animation tags** identify the order in which objects are animated during a slide show.

   QUICK TIP
   There are additional animation options for each animation category located at the bottom of the animations gallery.

3. **Click the Effect Options button in the Animation group, click All at Once, click the Effect Options button, then click Out**

   Effect options are different for every animation, and some animations don't have effect options. All of the objects in the SmartArt animate together in an outward direction. Compare your screen to FIGURE 3-15.

4. **Click the Slide Show button 🖵 on the status bar, click your mouse once, then press ESC**

   The SmartArt object animates

5. **Click the Slide 4 thumbnail in the Slides tab, click the bulleted list text object, then click Fade in the Animation group**

   The text object is animated with the Fade animation. Each line of text has an animation tag with each paragraph displaying a different number. Accordingly, each paragraph is animated separately.

6. **Click the Effect Options button in the Animation group, click All at Once, click the Duration up arrow in the Timing group until 01.50 appears, then click the Preview button in the Preview group**

   Notice the animation tags for each line of text in the text object now have the same numeral (1), indicating that each line of text animates at the same time.

7. **Click Economy in the title text object, click ⋶ in the Animation group, scroll down, then click Arcs in the Motion Paths section**

   A motion path object appears over the shapes object and identifies the direction and shape, or path, of the animation. When needed, you can move, resize, and change the direction of the motion path. Notice the numeral 2 animation tag next to the title text object indicating that it is animated *after* the bulleted list text object. Compare your screen to FIGURE 3-16.

   QUICK TIP
   If you want to individually animate the parts of a grouped object, then you must ungroup the objects before you animate them.

8. **Click the Move Earlier button in the Timing group, click the Slide Show tab on the Ribbon, then click the From Beginning button in the Start Slide Show group**

   Slide 1 appears in Slide Show view.

9. **Press SPACE to advance the slides, when you see the black slide, press ENTER, then save your changes**

FIGURE 3-15: Animation applied to SmartArt object

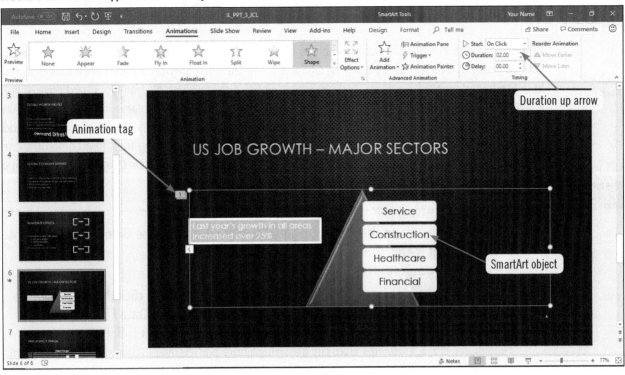

FIGURE 3-16: Motion path applied to title text object

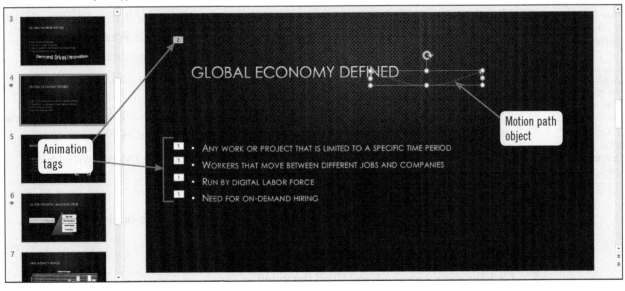

Attaching a sound to an animation

Text or objects that have animation applied can be customized further by attaching a sound for extra emphasis. First, select the animated object, then on the Animations tab, click the Animation Pane button in the Advanced Animation group. In the Animation Pane, click the animation you want to apply the sound to, click the Animation list arrow, then click Effect Options to open the animation effect's dialog box. In the Enhancements section, click the Sound list arrow, then choose a sound. Click OK when you are finished. Now, when you run the slide show, the sound you applied will play with the animation.

Insert and Edit Digital Video

Learning Outcomes
• Link a video
• Add a bookmark

In your presentation, you may want to use special effects to illustrate a point or capture the attention of your audience. You can do this by inserting digital or animated video. **Digital video** is live action captured in digital format by a video camera. You can embed or link a digital video file from your hard drive or link a digital video file from a webpage on the Internet. **Animated video** contains multiple images that stream together or move to give the illusion of motion. If you need to edit the length of a video or add effects or background color to a video, you can use PowerPoint's video-editing tools to accomplish those and other basic editing tasks. **CASE** ▶ *You continue to develop your presentation by inserting and editing a video clip.*

STEPS

1. **Click the** Home tab **on the Ribbon, right-click a blank area of the slide, point to** Layout **in the shortcut menu, then click** Two Content
   The slide layout changes and has two content placeholders.

2. **Click the** Insert Video icon 🖳 **in the new Content placeholder, click the** From a file Browse button, **navigate to the location where you store your Data Files, click** Support_PPT_3_Video.mp4, **click the** Insert list arrow, **then click** Link to File
   The Support_PPT_3_Video.mp4 video clip displaying a black preview image is linked to the slide. By linking the digital video to the presentation, you do not increase the file size of the presentation, but remember, you need direct access to the location where the video file is stored in order to play it.

3. **Click the** Play/Pause button ▷ **in the video control bar**
   The short video plays through once but does not rewind to the beginning.

4. **Click the** Video Tools Playback tab **on the Ribbon, click the** Rewind after Playing check box **in the Video Options group, then click the** Play button **in the Preview group**
   The video plays through once, and this time the video rewinds back to the beginning.

5. **Click the** video control timeline **at about** 00:06.00, **then click the** Add Bookmark button **in the Bookmarks group as shown in** FIGURE 3-17
   A yellow circle appears in the video control timeline, indicating the video has a bookmark. A **bookmark** can indicate a point of interest in a video; it can also be used to jump to a specific point in a video.

6. **Click the** Slide Show button 🖵 **on the status bar, then click the mouse twice to view the animations on the slide**
   The text object animations play.

7. **Move** ⍾ **over the video, the pointer changes to** 🖐, **then click the bookmark as shown in** FIGURE 3-18
   The video moves to the bookmarked frame.

8. **Click the** Play/Pause button ▷ **on the video**
   The video plays from the bookmarked frame to the end of the video and then rewinds to the beginning.

9. **Press** ESC, **click the** Video Tools Format tab **on the Ribbon, click the** More button ▼ **in the Video Styles group, then click** Reflected Bevel Black **in the Intense section**
   A bevel effect is added to the video.

10. **sam** ↑ **Click a blank area of the slide, save your work, submit your presentation to your instructor, then exit PowerPoint**

FIGURE 3-17: Video clip inserted on the slide

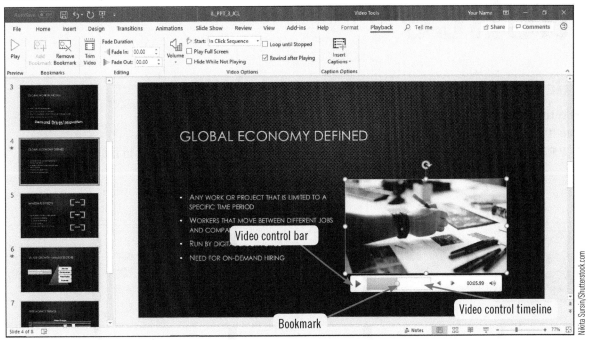

Nikita Sursin/Shutterstock.com

FIGURE 3-18: Video in Slide Show view with selected bookmark

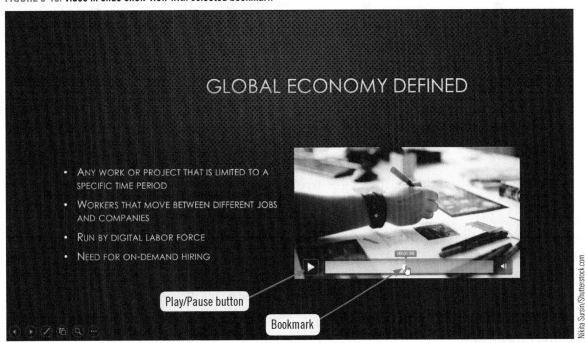

Nikita Sursin/Shutterstock.com

Saving a presentation as a video

You can save your PowerPoint presentation as a full-fidelity video, which incorporates all slide timings, transitions, animations, and narrations. The video can be distributed using a disc, the web, or email. Depending on how you want to display your video, you have three resolution settings from which to choose: Presentation Quality, Internet Quality, and Low Quality. The Large setting, Presentation Quality (1920 × 1080), is used for viewing on a computer monitor, projector, or other high-definition displays. The Medium setting, Internet Quality (1280 × 720), is used for uploading to the web or copying to a standard DVD. The Small setting, Low Quality (852 × 480), is used on portable media players. To save your presentation as a video, click the File tab, click Export, click Create a Video, choose your settings, then click the Create Video button.

Practice

Skills Review

1. Insert a text box.

a. Open IL_PPT_3-2.pptx from the location where you store your Data Files, then save it as **IL_PPT_3_Broker2.** You will work to create the completed presentation. as shown in FIGURE 3-19.

FIGURE 3-19

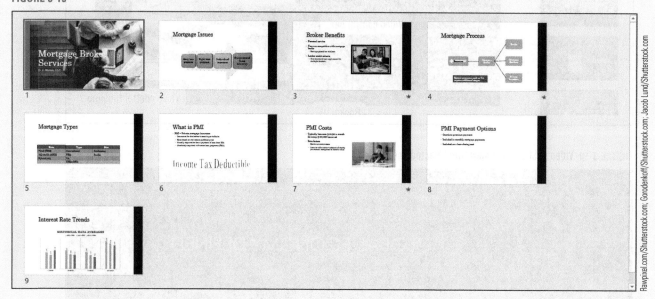

Rawpixel.com/Shutterstock.com; Gorodenkoff/Shutterstock.com; Jacob Lund/Shutterstock.com

b. On Slide 4, insert a text box below the shapes, then type **Special programs require additional stages such as VA**

c. Move the words "such as VA" after the word "programs", then add space between words as necessary.

d. Select the text object, then click the More button in the Shape Styles group on the Drawing Tools Format tab.

e. Click Moderate Effect – Purple, Accent 5, then resize the text box to fit the text on two lines by dragging its sizing handles, if necessary. The second line of text begins with the word "require".

f. Using Smart Guides, drag the text object so its right edge is centered on the slide and its bottom edge is aligned with the bottom edge of the bottom rectangle shape.

2. Crop and style a picture.

a. Select Slide 3 in the Slides tab, then crop the left side of the picture up to the right cup on the table in the background.

b. Drag the picture to the center of the blank area of the slide.

c. Click the Color button, then change the color tone to Temperature: 8800 K.

d. Click the Corrections button, then change the sharpness of the picture to Sharpen: 50%.

e. Change the picture style to Double Frame, Black.

f. Select Slide 1 in the Slides tab, open the Format Background task pane, then click the Picture or texture fill option button.

Skills Review (continued)

   g. Click the File button in the task pane, then insert the picture Support_PPT_3_Group.jpg from the location where you store your Data Files.

   h. Click the Tile picture as texture check box in the task pane, close the Format Background pane, then save your changes.

3. Insert a chart.

   a. Create a new slide after Slide 5 with a Title and Content layout and title it **Interest Rate Trends**.

   b. Insert a Clustered Column chart.

   c. Close the worksheet, drag the chart down the slide away from the title, then apply the Layout 3 quick layout to the chart.

4. Enter and edit chart data.

TABLE 3-2

   a. Show the worksheet, enter the data shown in TABLE 3-2 into the worksheet, then close the worksheet.

   b. Type **Historical Data Averages** in the chart title text object then increase the font size of the chart title using the Increase Font Size button.

   c. Click the Chart Styles button next to the chart, then change the chart style to Style 2.

	30 Yr FRM	15 Yr FRM	5/1 Yr FRM
1 Year	3.82	3.19	4.19
3 Year	4.20	3.36	3.14
5 Year	3.89	3.19	2.75
10 Year	6.32	5.79	5.45

   d. Click Color in the Charts Styles gallery, then change the color to Colorful Palette 3 in the Colorful section.

   e. Close the Charts Styles gallery, then save your changes.

5. Insert slides from other presentations.

   a. Go to Slide 5, then open the Reuse Slides pane.

   b. Open Support_PPT_3_PMI.pptx from the location where you store your Data Files.

   c. Insert the second slide thumbnail, insert the third slide thumbnail, then insert the first slide thumbnail.

   d. Close the Reuse Slides pane, then open the Slide Sorter view.

   e. Move Slide 8 between Slide 5 and Slide 6, switch to Normal view, then save your work.

6. Insert a table.

   a. Go to Slide 5, then insert a table with two columns and four rows.

   b. Add one more row and one more column to the table, then enter the information shown in TABLE 3-3.

   c. On the Table Tools Design tab, change the table style to Themed Style 1 – Accent 5.

TABLE 3-3

   d. In the Table Tools Layout tab, select the top row, then center the text.

   e. Select the whole table, open the Table Tools Design tab, click the Effects button, point to Cell Bevel, then apply the Soft Round effect.

Rate	Type	Size
Fixed (FRM)	Conventional	Conforming
Adjustable (ARM)	FHA	Jumbo
Hybrid (5/1)	VA	
	USDA/RHA	

   f. Move the table to the center of the blank area of the slide, then save your changes.

7. Insert and format WordArt.

   a. Go to Slide 6, then insert a WordArt text object using the style Gradient Fill, Gray.

   b. Type **Income Tax Deductible**, apply the Transform text effect Inflate (sixth row in the Warp section) to the text object, then move the text object to the middle of the blank area of the slide.

   c. Apply the 3-D Rotation text effect Perspective: Relaxed Moderately (second row in the Perspective section).

   d. Change the text fill color to Dark Red, then change the text outline to Black, Text 1.

   e. Apply the WordArt style Fill: Black, Text color 1; Outline: White, Background color 1; Hard Shadow: Purple, Accent color 5.

   f. Increase the size of the WordArt object proportionally, view the slide in Slide Show view, then save your changes.

8. **Animate objects.**

   a. Go to Slide 4, click the Animations tab, then select the four black arrow lines on the slide. (*Hint*: Use SHIFT to select the shapes.)

   b. Apply the Wipe effect to the objects, click the Effect Options button, then apply the From Right effect.

   c. Change the animation duration to 01.00, then preview the animations.

   d. Click the Move Earlier button in the Timing group.

   e. Go to Slide 3, click the title text object, then apply the animation Brush Color in the Emphasis section.

   f. Click the Effect Options button, click Orange in Standard Colors, then open Slide Show view.

   g. Click through the animations on Slides 3 and 4, press ESC when you see Slide 5, then save your work.

9. **Insert and edit digital video.**

   a. Go to Slide 7, change the slide layout to Two Content, then click the Insert Video icon.

   b. Locate the file Support_PPT_3_Desk.mp4 from the location where you store your Data Files, click the Insert list arrow, then click Link to File.

   c. On the Video Tools Playback tab, click the Rewind after Playing check box, then add a bookmark at about the 00:04.00 point on the video control timeline.

   d. Apply the video style Center Shadow Rectangle, then preview the video clip in Slide Show view.

   e. Switch to Normal view, then save your work.

   f. Submit your presentation to your instructor, close your presentation, then exit PowerPoint.

Independent Challenge 1

Riverwalk Medical Clinic (RMC), is a large medical facility in Cambridge, Massachusetts. You continue to work on a presentation on the latest emergency response procedures for a staff training later in the week.

   a. Start PowerPoint, open IL_PPT_3-3.pptx from the location where you store your Data Files, and save it as **IL_PPT_3_Riverwalk**. You will work to create the completed presentation as shown in FIGURE 3-20.

   b. Add your name and today's date to Slide 1 in the Subtitle text box.

   c. Go to Slide 4, change the slide layout to Two Content, click the Pictures icon in the content placeholder, then insert the file Support_PPT_3_ER.jpg from the location where you store your Data Files.

   d. Crop the right side of the picture up to the red emergency sign next to the entrance, apply the Drop Shadow Rectangle picture style to the picture, click the Color button, then change the color tone to Temperature: 5300 K.

FIGURE 3-20

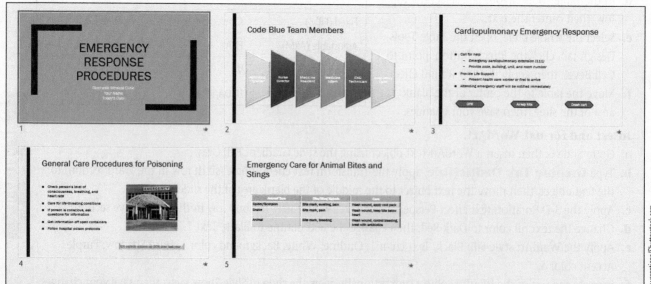

Independent Challenge 1 (continued)

e. Change the sharpness of the picture to Sharpen: 25%, then move the picture to the center of the blank area of the slide.

f. Insert a text box on the slide below the picture, type **ER walk-in volume up 20% over last year**, then change the text color to red.

g. Apply the shape style Colored Fill - Gold, Accent 2 to the text object, then apply the Preset 2 shape effect.

h. Go to Slide 5, create a new table, then enter the data in TABLE 3-4.

i. Apply the table style Medium Style 1 - Accent 2, apply the Round bevel effect, then center the text in the top row of the table.

j. Apply the Fly In animation to the SmartArt object on Slide 2, change the effect option to From Bottom-Right and the sequence to One by One, then change the duration to 01.00.

k. Add a Doors transition to all slides with a horizontal effect, and a duration time of 02.00.

l. View the final presentation in Slide Show view.

m. Save the presentation, submit the presentation to your instructor, close the file, then exit PowerPoint.

TABLE 3-4

Animal Type	Bite/Sting Signals	Care
Spider/Scorpion	Bite mark, swelling, pain	Wash wound, apply cold pack
Snake	Bite mark, pain	Wash wound, keep bite below heart
Animal	Bite mark, bleeding	Wash wound, control bleeding, treat with antibiotics

Independent Challenge 2

You are an associate at Myers Reed, a financial investment and management company, located in St. Louis, Missouri. One of your responsibilities is to create general presentations for use on the company website. As part of this presentation, you insert a chart, insert a video, add a WordArt object, and insert slides from another presentation. You finish the presentation by adding slide transitions and animations to the slides.

a. Open IL_PPT_3_4.pptx from the location where you store your Data Files, then save it as **IL_PPT_3_Reed**. You will work to create the completed presentation as shown in FIGURE 3-21.

b. Apply the Ion Design Theme, refer to Slide 1 in FIGURE 3-21 and select the thumbnail in the Design Ideas task pane, then close the task pane.

FIGURE 3-21

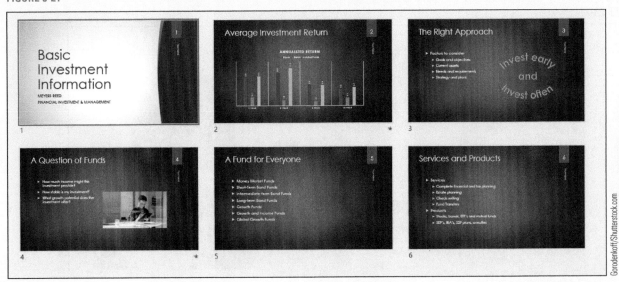

PowerPoint

Independent Challenge 2 (continued)

c. Insert a clustered column chart on Slide 2, then enter the data in TABLE 3-5 into the worksheet.

d. Close the worksheet, format the chart using Style 2, change the color to Colorful Palette 3, then move the chart to the center of the blank area of the slide.

e. Type **Annualized Return** in the chart title text object, then decrease the font size to 20 point.

TABLE 3-5

	Stocks	Bonds	Mutual funds
1 Year	8.9	2.7	9.3
3 Year	10.3	1.8	11.9
5 Year	6.6	1.3	6.4
10 Year	5.2	2.5	5.7

f. Open the Reuse Slides pane, open Support_PPT_3_Invest.pptx from the location where you store your Data Files, then insert Slides 2, 3, and 4.

g. Close the Reuse Slides pane, open Slide Sorter view, move Slide 5 between Slide 3 and Slide 4, then double-click Slide 3.

h. Insert a WordArt object using the Fill: Gold, Accent color 4; Sharp Bevel style, type **Invest early**, press ENTER, type **and**, press ENTER, then type **Invest often**.

i. Click the Text Effects button, point to Transform, apply the Button text effect from the Follow Path section, then move the WordArt object to a blank area of the slide.

j. Go to Slide 4, change the slide layout to Two Content, then link the video Support_PPT_3_Desk from the location where you store your Data Files. (*Hint*: be sure to use the Link to File option when you link the video in this step.)

k. Insert a bookmark at about 00:03.00, rewind the video after playing, then apply the Center Shadow Rectangle video style.

l. Go to Slide 2, apply the animation Float In to the chart, apply the By Element in Category effect option, then set the duration to 01.50.

m. Apply the animation Random Bars to the slide title, then reorder the animation to first in the sequence.

n. Add your name and slide number as the footer on all of the slides, view the slide show, then save your work.

o. Submit the presentation to your instructor, close the presentation, then exit PowerPoint.

Visual Workshop

Create a one-slide presentation that looks like FIGURE 3-22. To complete this presentation, insert the picture file Support_PPT_3_Woman from the location where you store your Data Files to the slide background. Change the picture transparency to 30% and then format with the tile picture as texture option. Format the text box with a 54-point, Orange, Accent 2 Calibri Light font and then apply a Tight Reflection: Touching text effect. Set the text object's top edge at 1.00 and its right edge on the slide center line. Add your name as footer text to the slide, save the presentation as **IL_PPT_3_Brookdale** to the location where you store your Data Files, then submit your presentation to your instructor.

FIGURE 3-22

Integrating Word, Excel, Access, and PowerPoint

CASE ▶ Anthony Martinez, vice president of sales and marketing at the head office of JCL Talent, Inc., in Atlanta, GA, creates presentations for clients that often include objects from Word, Excel, and Access. He asks you to explore how to use linking and embedding in Office and then how to insert linked objects from Word, Excel, and Access into a PowerPoint presentation.

Module Objectives

After completing this module, you will be able to:

- Integrate data among Word, Excel, Access, and PowerPoint
- Import a Word outline into PowerPoint
- Embed an Excel worksheet in PowerPoint
- Link Access and Excel objects to PowerPoint
- Manage links

Files You Will Need

IL_INT_3-1.docx	IL_INT_3-6.accdb
IL_INT_3-2.accdb	IL_INT_3-7.docx
IL_INT_3-3.docx	IL_INT_3-8.accdb
IL_INT_3-4.accdb	IL_INT_3-9.accdb
IL_INT_3-5.docx	

Integration
Module 3

Learning
Outcome
• Identify integration
options for Word,
Excel, Access, and
PowerPoint

Integrate Data among Word, Excel, Access, and PowerPoint

You can integrate information into a PowerPoint presentation using the linking and embedding techniques you learned with Word, Excel, and Access. As with those programs, you embed data created in other programs in PowerPoint when you want to be able to edit the data from within the destination file. You use linking when you want the linked data in the destination file to be updated when you change the data in the source file. In addition, you can import a Word outline into PowerPoint to automatically create slides without having to reenter information. The PowerPoint presentation in FIGURE 3-1 includes information originally created in Word, Excel, and Access. **CASE** ▸ *Before you create the presentation, you review some of the ways you can integrate information among Word, Excel, Access, and PowerPoint.*

DETAILS

You can integrate Word, Excel, Access, and PowerPoint by:

• **Importing a Word outline into PowerPoint**

  In the course of your work, you may create Word documents that contain information that you also want to use in a PowerPoint presentation. Instead of retyping the information in PowerPoint, you can save time by importing it directly from Word into PowerPoint. FIGURE 3-1 shows how a Word outline appears before and after it is imported into a PowerPoint presentation. Each Level 1 heading in the outline becomes a slide, and the Level 2 headings become bullets on the slides. Before you import a Word outline, you need to make sure all the headings and subheadings are formatted with heading styles. When you import an outline from Word to PowerPoint, you cannot create a link between the two files.

• **Embedding objects**

  Recall that when you embed an object, you do not create a link to the source file. However, you can use the source program tools to edit the embedded object within the destination file. An embedded object becomes a part of the PowerPoint file, which means that the file size of the PowerPoint presentation increases relative to the file size of the embedded object; a large embedded object, such as a graphic, will increase the size of the PowerPoint presentation considerably. To embed an object in a PowerPoint presentation, you use the Object command in the Text group on the Insert tab. In FIGURE 3-1, the table on Slide 3 is an embedded Excel worksheet object.

  To edit an embedded object, you double-click it. The source program starts, and the Ribbon and tabs of the source program appear inside the PowerPoint window.

• **Linking objects**

  When you link an object to a PowerPoint slide, a picture of the object is placed on the slide instead of the actual object. This representation of the object is connected, or linked, to the original file. The object is still stored in the source file in the source program, unlike an embedded object, which is stored directly on the PowerPoint slide. Any change you make to a linked object's source file is reflected in the linked object. The pie chart shown on Slide 4 of the presentation in FIGURE 3-1 is linked to values entered in an Excel worksheet, which is, in turn, linked to data entered in an Access database. The differences between embedding and linking are summarized in TABLE 3-1.

  You can open the source file and make changes to the linked object as long as all files remain on your computer. When you move files among machines or transmit files to other people, the links will not be maintained. However, recipients can open and view the linked files. After opening the workbook in Excel, they need to click No, close the workbook without saving it, then reopen the workbook and click Don't Update. In Word, they click No to update links.

FIGURE 3-1: PowerPoint presentation with integrated objects

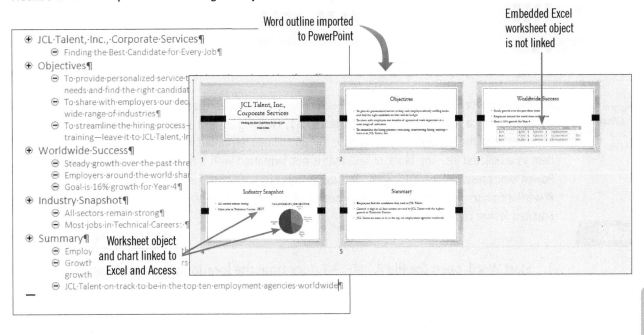

TABLE 3-1: Embedding vs. linking

	Embed	Link
User	You are the only user of an object and you want the object to be a part of your presentation	The object's source file is shared on a network or other users have access to the file and can change it
Availability	You want to open the object in its source program, even when the source file is not available	You are able to open the source file
Timeliness	Information does not change over time	You always want the object to include the latest information
Updating	You want to update the object manually while working in PowerPoint	You want the object to update automatically
File size	File size is not an issue	You want to keep the file size of the presentation small

Import a Word Outline into PowerPoint

Learning
Outcomes
• Prepare a Word
outline for
PowerPoint
• Import a Word
outline into
PowerPoint

Before you import a Word outline into PowerPoint, you should ensure that each Word outline heading is formatted with a heading style such as Heading 1, Heading 2, and so on. PowerPoint imports all text formatted with the Heading 1 style as a slide title and all text formatted with the Heading 2 style as a Level 1 item in a bulleted list. Any block of text that is not formatted with a heading style is not included in the PowerPoint presentation. **CASE** *You use information included in a Word document as the basis of a PowerPoint presentation about the services offered by JCL Talent to employers looking to find candidates to fill positions in their companies.*

STEPS

1. **Start Word, open the file IL_INT_3-1.docx from the location where you store your Data Files, save it as IL_INT_3_CorporateOutline, click the View tab, then click the Outline button in the Views group**

   The document appears in Outline view. Each Level 1 heading will become a slide title in PowerPoint, and each Level 2 heading will become a bulleted item. Before you import a Word outline into a PowerPoint presentation, you check that all the headings and subheadings are positioned at the correct levels.

2. **Click Finding the Best Candidate for Every Job (the second line), then click the Demote button → in the Outline Tools group once**

   The text moves to the right one tab stop and changes from body text to a Level 2 heading. In PowerPoint, this text will appear as a bulleted item under the slide title "JCL Talent, Inc., Corporate Services."

3. **Click Worldwide Success (the fourth bullet below the Objectives heading), click the Promote button ← in the Outline Tools group, click All sectors remain strong, press TAB, then compare your Word outline to FIGURE 3-2**

4. **Save and close the document**

5. **Start PowerPoint, create a blank presentation, then save it as IL_INT_3_ CorporatePresentation in the location where you store your Data Files**

6. **Click the New Slide arrow in the Slides group, click Slides from Outline, navigate to the location where you stored IL_INT_3_CorporateOutline, then double-click IL_INT_3_CorporateOutline.docx**

   The Thumbnails pane and the status bar indicate the presentation now contains six slides. Slide 1 is blank, and Slides 2 through 6 represent the Level 1 headings in the Word outline.

7. **Click Slide 1 in the Thumbnails pane, press DELETE, click the Layout button in the Slides group, click Title Slide, click the View tab, click the Outline View button in the Presentation Views group, click after Finding the Best Candidate for Every Job on Slide 1, press ENTER, then type your name**

   You change the slide layout for the first slide so the title and subtitle of the presentation and your name appear in the middle of the slide.

8. **Click the Design tab, click the More button ▼ in the Themes group, then click the Organic theme**

9. **Click the View tab, click the Slide Sorter button in the Presentation Views group, press CTRL+A to select all the slides, click the Home tab, click the Reset button in the Slides group, then save the presentation**

   The formatted presentation appears as shown in FIGURE 3-3.

FIGURE 3-2: Edited outline in Word Outline view

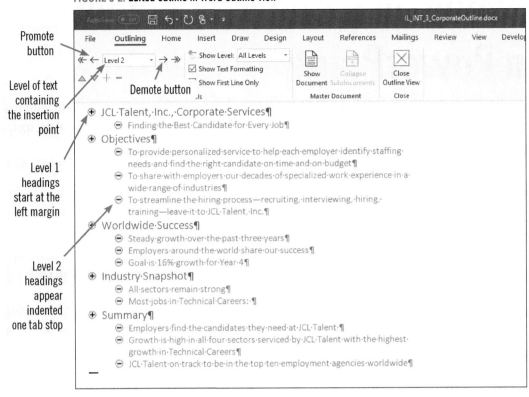

Promote button

Level of text containing the insertion point

Demote button

Level 1 headings start at the left margin

Level 2 headings appear indented one tab stop

FIGURE 3-3: Formatted presentation in Slide Sorter view

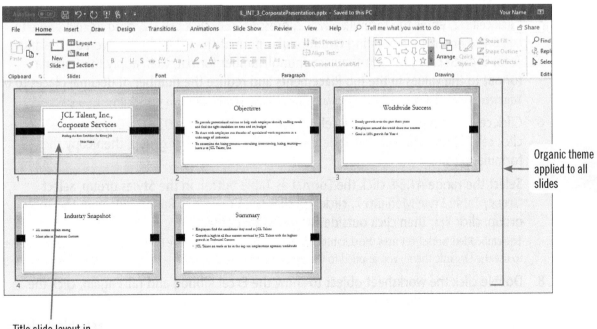

Organic theme applied to all slides

Title slide layout in the Organic theme

Integration

Embed an Excel Worksheet in PowerPoint

Learning Outcomes
- Embed a Worksheet object in PowerPoint
- Edit an embedded worksheet

You can use the Object command to embed Excel objects such as worksheets and charts into both Word and PowerPoint documents. When you double-click the embedded object, you can then use the tools of the source program to edit the object. **CASE** *You want Slide 3 to include a worksheet with calculations that you can edit from within PowerPoint when you obtain new data. You create an Excel worksheet on the slide, and then edit it using Excel tools.*

STEPS

1. **Click the** View tab, **click the** Normal button **in the Presentation Views group, click** Slide 3 **in the Thumbnails pane to move to Slide 3, click the** Insert tab, **click the** Object button ▣ **in the Text group, verify the** Create new option button **is selected, scroll to and click** Microsoft Excel Worksheet, **then click** OK

   An Excel worksheet appears on the PowerPoint slide, and the Excel Ribbon and tabs appear. The PowerPoint title bar and menu bar, above the Excel tools, indicate that Excel is operating within PowerPoint. When you embed a worksheet object in a PowerPoint slide, you generally want to show only the cells that contain data.

TROUBLE
You move the mouse over the bottom-right corner of the embedded worksheet to show the resize pointer ⬉, then drag up and to the left until you see columns A to E and rows 1 to 4. You may need to adjust the view by dragging again.

2. **Drag the lower-right** corner handle **of the worksheet object up so only columns A to E and rows 1 to 4 are visible, as shown in** FIGURE 3-4

   You want to clearly see the data you need to enter into the worksheet object.

3. **Click the** Select All button ◢ **in the upper-left corner of the embedded worksheet to select all the worksheet cells, change the font size to** 24 point, **then click cell** A1

TROUBLE
Press the arrow keys, use the scroll bars, or press CTRL+HOME to move to the top of the embedded worksheet.

4. **Enter the labels and values in the range A1:D4 as shown in** FIGURE 3-5, **widening columns as needed**

5. **Click cell** D2, **enter the formula** =B2*C2, **press** ENTER, **click cell** D2, **drag its** fill handle **to cell D4 to enter the remaining two formulas, format the values in the Average Fee and Total Growth columns with the Accounting Number format, then apply the Comma format to the values in the Job Placements and reduce the number of decimal places to 0**

   You need to calculate the percentage change in revenue over the past two years.

6. **Click cell** E1, **type** Change, **click cell** E3, **enter the formula** =(D3-D2)/D3, **press** ENTER, **click cell** E3, **click the** Percent Style button ▣ **in the Number group, then copy the formula to cell** E4

TROUBLE
To set the width of column E, you will need to widen the worksheet object, double-click the column divider between columns E and F, then decrease the width of the workshop object so only columns A to E are visible.

7. **Select the range** A1:E4, **click the** Format as Table button **in the Styles group, select** Green, Table Style Medium 7, **click** OK, **click the** Convert to Range button **in the Tools group, click** Yes, **then click outside the worksheet object**

   The embedded worksheet uses the default Office theme, and you want the fonts and colors of the worksheet to use the Organic theme you applied to the PowerPoint slide.

8. **Double-click the worksheet object to show the Excel Ribbon and tabs again, click the** Page Layout tab, **click the** Themes button **in the Themes group, then click** Organic

9. **Change the value in cell** C4 **to** 6300, **press** TAB, **click outside the worksheet object, drag the object below the text as shown in** FIGURE 3-6, **then save the presentation**

   The percentage growth for 2021 is now 25%.

FIGURE 3-4: Resizing the worksheet object

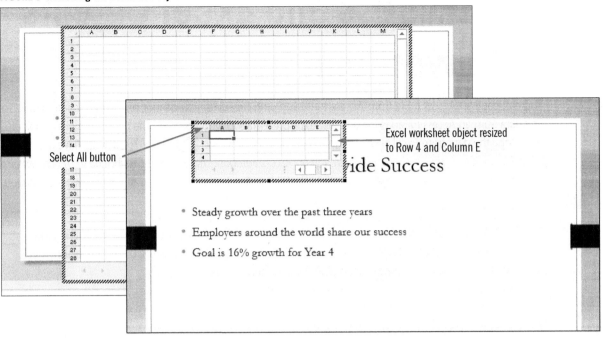

Select All button

Excel worksheet object resized to Row 4 and Column E

Steady growth over the past three years

Employers around the world share our success

Goal is 16% growth for Year 4

FIGURE 3-5: Labels and values entered in the Excel worksheet object

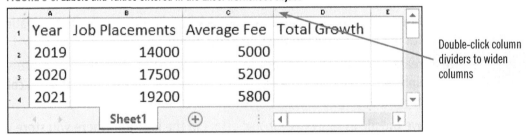

	A	B	C	D	E
1	Year	Job Placements	Average Fee	Total Growth	
2	2019	14000	5000		
3	2020	17500	5200		
4	2021	19200	5800		

Sheet1

Double-click column dividers to widen columns

FIGURE 3-6: Completed Excel worksheet object

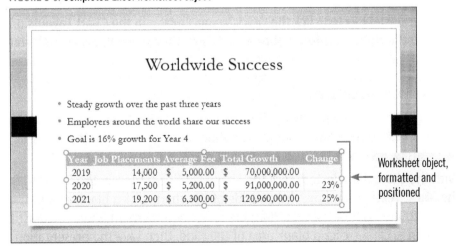

Worksheet object, formatted and positioned

Link Access and Excel Objects to PowerPoint

Learning
Outcomes
• Link an Access
  table to Excel
• Link an Excel chart
  to PowerPoint

You can copy an Access table from Access to PowerPoint; however, you cannot paste the table as a link. To link data from an Access database to a PowerPoint presentation, you first copy the data to Excel as a link and then copy the data from Excel and paste it as a link into PowerPoint. **CASE** ▶ *You already have data about available position and average salaries stored in an Access database that you want to include in the PowerPoint presentation. You want any changes you make to the table in Access also to appear in the PowerPoint presentation.*

STEPS

QUICK TIP
To save the database
with a new name,
click the File tab,
click Save As, click
the Save As button,
navigate to the loca-
tion where you store
your Data Files, type
the new filename,
then click Save.

1. **Start Access, open the file** IL_INT_3-2.accdb **from the location where you store your Data Files, save the database as** IL_INT_3_JobsData, **click** Enable Content, **double-click the** Positions table, **then review the Sector field**

   You need to sort the Positions table alphabetically by Sector so you can use the data in a chart you create in Excel. You create a query to sort the data so the sorting is maintained when you copy the data to Excel.

2. **Close the Positions table, click the** Create tab, **click the** Query Wizard button **in the Queries group, click** OK, **click the** Select All Fields button `>>` **to add all the fields in the Positions table to the query, click** Next, **click** Next, **then click** Finish

3. **Click the** Home tab, **click the** View button **in the Views group to go to Design view, click the** blank line below "Positions" in the [Sector] column, **click the** Sector Sort arrow, **then select** Ascending **as shown in** FIGURE 3-7

4. **Close and save the Positions query, click** Positions Query **in the Navigation pane, then click the** Copy button **in the Clipboard group**

5. **Create a new blank workbook in Excel, click cell** A1, **click the** Paste arrow **in the Clipboard group, click the** Paste Link button 📋, **format the values in column E with the Accounting Number format, then widen columns as necessary**

6. **Save the file as** IL_INT_3_JobsbySectors **in the location where you store your Data Files, click cell** C23, **then enter the labels and formulas as shown in** FIGURE 3-8

7. **Select the range** C23:F24, **click the** Insert tab, **click the** Insert Pie or Doughnut Chart button 🥧▾ **in the Charts group, click the** top-left pie style, **change the chart title to** Vacancies by Job Sector, **click the** Quick Layout button **in the Chart Layouts group, select** Layout 6 (far right selection in the second row), **then move the chart so it starts in cell G1**

   The total number of job vacancies in the Creative sector is 16% of total vacancies, the vacancies for Finance & Accounting jobs are 17%, vacancies for Office Support jobs are 18% and the vacancies in the Technical Sector comprise 49% of the total salaries.

QUICK TIP
The chart you copied
from Excel is linked
by default to the
source file but takes
on the theme of the
destination file.

8. **Click the** border of the pie chart, **click the** Home tab, **click the** Copy button **in the Clipboard group, switch to the PowerPoint presentation, show** Slide 4, **click the** Home tab, **click the** Paste arrow, **then click the** Use Destination Theme & Link Data button 📋

9. **With the chart still selected, click the** Shape Outline button **in the Drawing group, click the** Black, Text 1 color box, **click outside of the chart, click a blank area of the chart, drag it to the right of the text, drag the lower right corner handle to adjust the size as shown in** FIGURE 3-9, **click a blank area of the slide, then save the presentation**

   The chart is linked to the Excel worksheet and the Positions Query datasheet in Access. You will improve the chart's readability in the next lesson.

FIGURE 3-7: Sorting the Season field in Query Design view

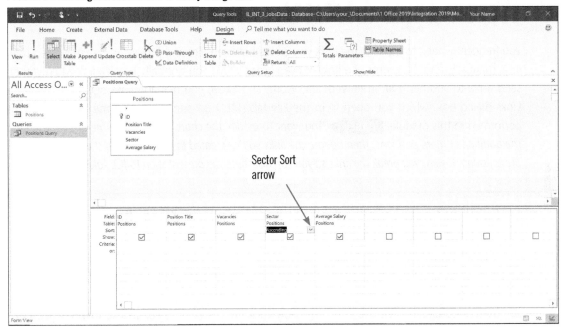

Sector Sort arrow

FIGURE 3-8: Formulas to calculate total tours by Category

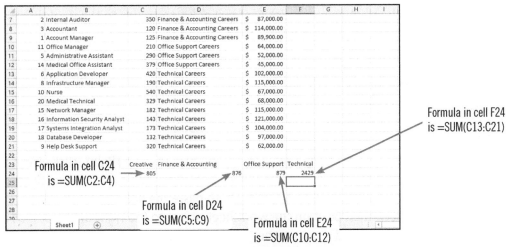

	A	B	C	D	E	F	G	H	I
7		2 Internal Auditor	350	Finance & Accounting Careers	$ 87,000.00				
8		3 Accountant	120	Finance & Accounting Careers	$ 114,000.00				
9		1 Account Manager	125	Finance & Accounting Careers	$ 89,900.00				
10		11 Office Manager	210	Office Support Careers	$ 64,000.00				
11		5 Administrative Assistant	290	Office Support Careers	$ 52,000.00				
12		14 Medical Office Assistant	379	Office Support Careers	$ 45,000.00				
13		6 Application Developer	420	Technical Careers	$ 102,000.00				
14		8 Infrastructure Manager	190	Technical Careers	$ 115,000.00				
15		10 Nurse	540	Technical Careers	$ 67,000.00				
16		20 Medical Technical	329	Technical Careers	$ 68,000.00				
17		15 Network Manager	182	Technical Careers	$ 115,000.00				
18		16 Information Security Analyst	143	Technical Careers	$ 121,000.00				
19		17 Systems Integration Analyst	173	Technical Careers	$ 104,000.00				
20		18 Database Developer	132	Technical Careers	$ 97,000.00				
21		9 Help Desk Support	320	Technical Careers	$ 62,000.00				
22									
23			Creative	Finance & Accounting		Office Support Technical			
24			805		876	879	2429		
25									

Formula in cell C24 is =SUM(C2:C4)

Formula in cell D24 is =SUM(C5:C9)

Formula in cell E24 is =SUM(C10:C12)

Formula in cell F24 is =SUM(C13:C21)

FIGURE 3-9: Linking a copied chart to PowerPoint

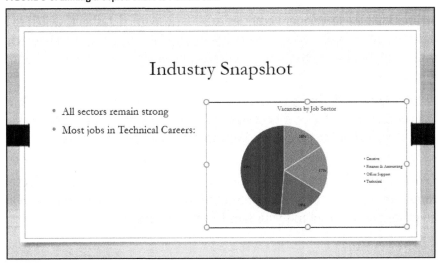

Manage Links

Learning Outcomes
- Manually update links
- Break links

You frequently need to manage the links you create between files and programs. You may need to update links manually, find the source of a link, or even break a link. You normally break a link when you need to send a file to another user. In PowerPoint, Word, and Excel, you manage links between files in the Edit Links dialog box, which you open from the File tab. TABLE 3-2 summarizes all the integration tasks you performed in this module. **CASE** *You want to modify the chart on Slide 4 of the presentation to reflect the addition of more positions, then update the links you've created in the database, the spreadsheet, and the presentation. Finally, you break the links so you can distribute the presentation to JCL Talent's branch managers.*

STEPS

1. **Switch to Access, open the** Positions Query datasheet, **change the number of job vacancies for the Help Desk Support position (last entry) to** 400, **press ENTER, then close the Positions Query datasheet**

   When you change data in the Positions Query datasheet, the corresponding data in the Positions table also changes.

2. **Switch to Excel, click the** File tab, **then click** Edit Links to Files **in the lower-right corner of the screen, as shown in** FIGURE 3-10

   The Edit Links dialog box opens.

3. **Click** Update Values, **click** Close, **click** 🔙 **to return to the worksheet, verify that the Technical slice is now 50%, then save the workbook**

4. **Switch to PowerPoint, then verify that the Technical slice is now 50%**

5. **Click the** pie chart, **click the** Chart Tools Design tab, **click the** More button ⊡ **in the Chart Styles group, then select** Style 9

   When you insert an Excel chart into a PowerPoint presentation, you usually need to select a new chart style so the data is easy to read on a slide.

6. **Switch to Excel, copy cell** F24, **switch back to PowerPoint, click after Careers: in the second bulleted item, press SPACEBAR, click the** Paste arrow, **click** Paste Special, **click the** Paste link option button, **click** OK **to paste the link as a Microsoft Excel Worksheet Object, then position the worksheet object to the right of "Most jobs in Technical Careers:," and drag a corner handle to increase its size slightly**

   The copied object appears as 2509.

7. **Switch to Access, open the** Positions Query datasheet, **change the Nurse vacancies to** 700 **and the Database Developer vacancies to** 300, **close the datasheet, switch to Excel and open the Edit Links dialog box on the File tab, update the link in Excel, switch to PowerPoint, then verify the worksheet object in PowerPoint is now** 2837 **and the Technical pie slice is** 53%

8. **In PowerPoint, click the** File tab, **click** Edit Links to Files, **click the** top link, **click** Break Link, **confirm the deletion if necessary, click the** remaining link, **click** Break Link, **click** Close, **then repeat the process in Excel to break the link to Access**

   Now when you change data in the Access file, the linked Excel chart in PowerPoint will not be updated.

9. **In PowerPoint, click the** View tab, **click the** Slide Sorter button **in the Presentation Views group, compare the completed presentation to** FIGURE 3-11, **save and close all open files and programs, then submit your files to your instructor**

FIGURE 3-10: Updating links using the File tab

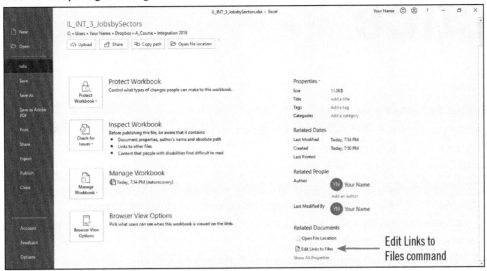

FIGURE 3-11: Completed presentation in Slide Sorter view

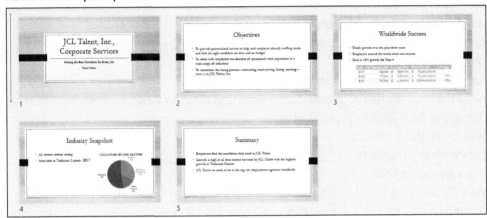

TABLE 3-2: Module 3 integration tasks

object	commands	source program(s)	destination program	result	connection	page no.
Word outline	In PowerPoint: New Slide/Slides from Outline	Word	PowerPoint	Word outline inserted into PowerPoint; Level 1 headings are slide titles, and Level 2 headings are text items	None	4
Excel worksheet	In PowerPoint: Insert/Object/ Create New	Excel	PowerPoint	Excel worksheet created in PowerPoint, then updated by double-clicking and using Excel tools	Embedded	6
Access query	Copy/Paste Link button	Access	Excel	Access query is pasted into Excel as a link; linked data can only be formatted in Excel	Linked	8
Excel chart	Copy/Paste Link using the Use Destination Themes and Link Data button	Access/Excel	PowerPoint	Chart created from linked Access query is pasted into PowerPoint as a link; when Access data changes, Excel and PowerPoint data is updated	Linked	8

Integration

Practice

Skills Review

1. Import a Word outline into PowerPoint.

 a. Start Word, then open the file IL_INT_3-3.docx from the location where you store your Data Files, then save it as **IL_INT_3_MiracleEventsOutline**.

 b. Switch to Outline view, then demote the body text "Your Vision, Our Plan" to Level 2.

 c. Demote the three subheadings: "Private," "Nonprofit," and "Corporate" to Level 3.

 d. Promote the Six-Month Revenue subheading to Level 1, then save and close the document.

 e. Open a blank presentation in PowerPoint, then save it as **IL_INT_3_MiracleEventsPresentation** in the location where you store your Data Files.

 f. Import the IL_INT_3_MiracleEventsOutline document as slides into PowerPoint.

 g. Delete the blank Slide 1, apply the Title Slide layout to the new Slide 1, then add your name after the subtitle on Slide 1.

 h. Apply the Vapor Trail theme with the pink variant (third variant from the left).

 i. Switch to Slide Sorter view, select all the slides, reset the layout, then save the presentation.

2. Embed an Excel worksheet in PowerPoint.

 a. Switch to Normal view, move to Slide 4, delete the blank text placeholder, then insert a Microsoft Excel Worksheet object.

 b. Resize the object so only columns A to D and rows 1 to 5 are visible.

 c. Change the font size of all the cells to 28 point, enter labels and values as shown in FIGURE 3-12, then adjust column widths and the size of the worksheet object as needed.

 d. Enter a formula in cell D2 to multiply the number of events by the average revenue for the first quarter, then copy the formula to the range D3:D5 and widen columns as needed.

FIGURE 3-12

	A	B	C	D
1	QTR	Events	Average Revenue	Total
2	Q1	10	40000	
3	Q2	8	24000	
4	Q3	12	38000	
5	Q4	20	42000	

Sheet1

 e. Apply the Vapor Trail theme to the embedded workbook, apply the Table Style Bright Green Medium 13 style, convert the table to a range, format the dollar values in columns C and D with the Accounting Number format, then widen columns as needed.

 (*Hint:* To widen column D, resize the object to show column E, widen Column D, then reduce the object size again.)

 f. Right-align the worksheet object below the slide title.

 g. In the worksheet object, change the number of events in the third quarter to **15**, then save the presentation.

3. Link Access and Excel objects to PowerPoint.

 a. Start Access, open the file IL_INT_3-4.accdb from the location where you store your Data Files, save it as **IL_INT_3_MiracleEventsData**, then enable the content.

 b. Create a query called **Events Query** from the Events table, that contains all fields and that sorts the contents of the Category field in ascending order. (*Hint:* Remember to sort the Category field in Design view.)

 c. Close and save the query, copy it, create a new workbook in Excel, then paste the query datasheet as a link into cell A1.

Skills Review (continued)

d. Format the values in column F using the Accounting Number format, widen columns as necessary, enter **Total** in cell G1, enter the formula in cell G2 to multiply the Participants by the Per Person cost, then copy the formula to the range G3:G16 and widen the column as necessary.

e. In the range B18:D19, enter labels and formulas to calculate the total revenue from all the events in each of the three categories: Corporate, Nonprofit, and Private, widen columns as needed, then save the workbook as **IL_INT_3_MiracleEventsRevenue**.

f. Create a pie chart in the first 2D style from the range B18:D19, then apply Quick Layout 1 and move the chart to the right of the data.

g. Change the chart title to **Revenue by Event Category**, copy the chart, then paste it on Slide 5 in the PowerPoint presentation using the Use Destination Theme & Link Data option.

h. Move the worksheet object below the bullet point, then add a black outline.

4. Manage links.

a. In the Access query, change the per person cost for the Product Launch to **$150.00**, then close the query.

b. Switch to Excel, then update the link in the Edit Links dialog box if the value in cell F2 does not automatically update to $150.00.

c. Switch to PowerPoint, then update the link, if necessary, and verify that the Corporate wedge is now 80%.

d. Size and position the pie chart so it fills the blank area on the slide attractively, then apply Chart Style 11.

e. In Excel, copy cell B19, then paste it as a linked worksheet object on Slide 5 in PowerPoint.

f. Position the Excel object after "is" and resize it so its font size is comparable to the bullet text.

g. In the Events Query datasheet in Access, change the number of participants in the Opening Gala to 2000, then close the datasheet.

h. Update the link in Excel, switch to PowerPoint, then, if necessary, update the links to the chart and the worksheet object. The worksheet object is now $1,880,200.00 and the Corporate slice is 77%.

i. Break the links to the Excel chart and worksheet, break the link from Excel to Access, view the presentation in Slide Sorter view, compare the presentation to FIGURE 3-13, save and close all open files and programs, then submit your files to your instructor.

FIGURE 3-13

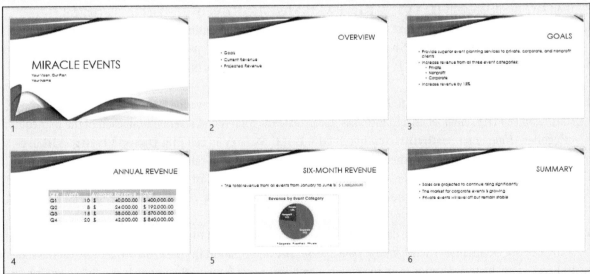

Independent Challenge 1

Riverwalk Medical Clinic in Cambridge, Massachusetts, operates a "Med Shed" that loans and rents medical equipment to patients. You have collected data about recent loans and rentals in an Access database, and now you need to create a presentation in PowerPoint that contains links to the loan and rental figures. You also need to import some of the slides needed for the presentation from a Word outline.

a. In Word, open the file IL_INT_3-5.docx from the location where you store your Data Files, then save it as **IL_INT_3_RiverwalkMedShedOutline**.

b. In Outline view, demote the subtitle text to Level 2, then demote the list of the four equipment categories (from "Ambulatory Equipment" to "Daily Living Aids") to Level 3.

c. Save and close the document.

d. Start a blank presentation in PowerPoint, then save it as **IL_INT_3_RiverwalkMedShedPresentation** in the location where you store your Data Files.

e. Insert the RiverwalkMedShed Outline document into PowerPoint, delete Slide 1, apply the Title Slide layout to the new Slide 1, then add your name after the subtitle on Slide 1.

f. In Slide Sorter view, reset the layout of all the slides, then apply the View theme with the variant that includes a red stripe along the right edge (third from the left in the selection of variants in the Variants group).

g. In Normal view on the new Slide 2 (Average Monthly Loans), embed an Excel Worksheet object resized to column B and row 6 with a 22 pt font size and containing the information and formatted as shown in FIGURE 3-14.

h. Calculate the total number of monthly loans in cell B6.

i. Apply the View theme to the Excel worksheet, select the range A1:B6, apply the Brown, Table Style Medium 7, convert the table to a range, then left align worksheet object with the title and bulleted item on the slide.

FIGURE 3-14

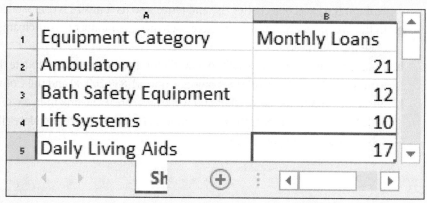

j. Start Access, open the file IL_INT_3-6.accdb the location where you store your Data Files, then save the database as **IL_INT_3_RiverwalkMedShedInventory** and enable content.

k. Create a query called **Equipment Query** from the Equipment table, using all fields, that sorts the contents of the Category field in ascending order. Save and close the query, copy the query, paste it as a link into a new Excel workbook, then save the workbook as **IL_INT_3_RiverwalkMedShedRentals** in the location where you save your Data Files.

l. Enter **Total Rental Revenue** in cell H1, then calculate the total revenue from rentals only in column H, then starting in cell D18, enter labels and formulas to calculate the total rental revenue from each of the four equipment categories. (*Hint:* Enter **Ambulatory** in cell D18, **Bath Safety** in cell E18, **Daily Living Aid** in cell F18, and **Lift System** in cell G18, then enter the required calculations in cells D19:G19.)

m. Format all dollar amounts with the Accounting Number format and adjust column widths as needed, then use the data in the range D18:G19 to create a 2D pie chart entitled **Rental Revenue by Category** using Quick Layout 6 and Chart Style 3.

n. Move the chart to the right of the data, copy the pie chart, then paste it on the appropriate slide in the presentation using the Use Destination Theme & Link Data option. Size and position the pie chart attractively on the slide.

o. In Excel, copy the total revenue from the rental of ambulatory equipment, then paste it as a linked worksheet object in the appropriate location on the slide containing the chart.

p. Size and position the worksheet object attractively, then enclose the chart in a black outline.

Independent Challenge 1

q. In Access, change the rental rate for Forearm Crutches to **$20.00** and the quantity rented to **25**, then update the links in Excel and PowerPoint. The slice for Ambulatory equipment should be 53% as shown in FIGURE 3-15.

r. Break the links in Excel and PowerPoint, view the presentation in Slide Sorter view, compare it to FIGURE 3-15 save and close all open files and programs, then submit your files to your instructor.

FIGURE 3-15

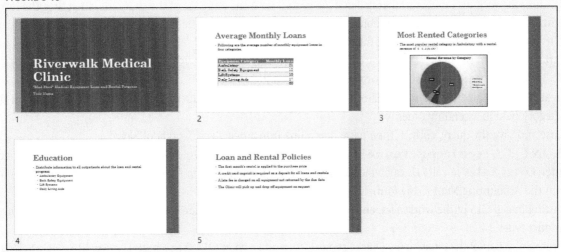

Independent Challenge 2

You are the Assistant Manager at Green Tech, a company that distributes eco-friendly products such as solar-powered battery chargers and energy-efficient appliances. To assist your customers, you have created a database of product information they can access online. You have also decided to create a short PowerPoint presentation from information you have stored in Word. The presentation will include data from the database, an embedded worksheet, and a linked chart.

a. Start Word, open the file IL_INT_3-7.docx from the location where you store your Data Files, in Outline view, demote the subtitle to Level 2 and promote "Product Sales" to Level 1.

b. Save the document as **IL_INT_3_GreenTechOutline**, and close the document.

c. Start a new PowerPoint presentation, save it as **IL_INT_3_GreenTechPresentation**, then import the IL_INT_3_GreenTechOutline document into the presentation.

d. Delete the blank Slide 1, apply the Title Slide layout to the new Slide 1, add your name below the subtitle on Slide 1, then apply the Metropolitan theme. Select the green variant in the Variants group to change the colors of the theme.

e. In Slide Sorter view, reset the layout of all the slides.

f. On Slide 2, embed an Excel Worksheet object displaying five columns and four rows, apply the 28-point font size so the cells are visible, then enter the information shown in FIGURE 3-16 and adjust column widths.

g. Calculate the savings per product in cells D2 by subtracting the values in the Green Tech Cost column from the values in the Conventional Cost column.

h. In cell E2, enter the formula **=D2/B2** to calculate the percent savings on monthly power costs when using Green Tech products.

FIGURE 3-16

Product	Conventional Cost	Green Tech Cost	Savings	Percent
LED Light Bulbs	30	20		
Smart Power Strips	25	20		
Solar Panels	120	80		

Sheet1

Independent Challenge 2

i. Copy the formulas for the other two product categories, format values with the Accounting Number and Percent formats, then widen columns, as necessary.

j. Apply the Metropolitan theme, select the range A1:E4, apply Olive Green, Table Style Medium 10, then convert the table to a range.

k. Make sure the completed table displays all five columns (you may need to re-adjust the width of the worksheet object).

l. Position the worksheet object so that its left edge is even with the left edge of the slide title, then drag the lower-right sizing handle of the worksheet object in PowerPoint down and to the right to increase the width of the object so its right edge is even with "top" in the second bulleted item.

m. Start Access, open the file IL_INT_3-8.accdb the location where you store your Data Files, save the database as **IL_INT_3_GreenTechInventory**, then enable content.

n. Create a query called **Products Query** from all the fields in the Products table that sorts the contents of the Category field in ascending order.

o. Close and save the query, copy it, then paste it as a link into a new Excel workbook saved as **IL_INT_3_GreenTechRevenue** in the location where you store your Data Files. Widen columns as needed. Enter **Total Sales** in cell G1, calculate total sales for each product, then format the values in Columns F and G with the Accounting Numbering format.

p. Starting in cell C15 of the worksheet, enter labels and formulas to calculate the total revenue from each of the four product types.

q. Create a pie chart of the totals, apply Quick Layout 1, then add a chart title: **Revenue by Product Category**.

r. Copy the chart, then paste it using the Use Destination Theme & Link Data paste option on the appropriate slide in the presentation. Add a black border, then resize and reposition the pie chart to fit the space attractively.

s. Apply Chart Style 12 to the chart and remove the legend. (*Hint*: Click the Add Chart Element button in the Chart Layouts group, point to Legend, then click None.)

t. Copy cell F16 in the source workbook, then paste it as a linked worksheet object in the appropriate place following the colon in the bulleted item.

u. In the Access query, change the Price of the Air Purifier to **1200**, the price of Low Power Air Conditioner to **2000** and the price of the solar panels to **5000**, then close the query.

v. Update links in Excel and PowerPoint. Verify that the value of the worksheet object is now $1,668,600.00 as shown in FIGURE 3-17.

w. In Excel and PowerPoint, break the links, view the presentation, save and close all open files and programs, then submit your files to your instructor.

FIGURE 3-17

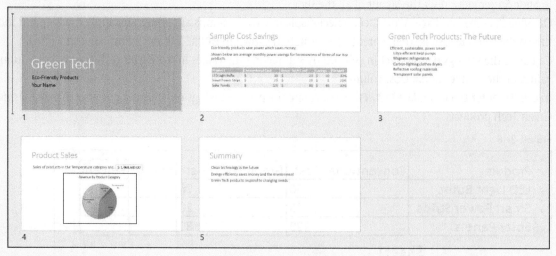

Visual Workshop

For a college course on tourism in New Zealand at Memorial University in Arizona, you have decided to create a presentation that focuses on popular hotels in various locations. The presentation will contain one slide displaying a pie chart showing the breakdown of hotel guests by location. In Access, open the file IL_INT_3-9.accdb from the location where you store your Data Files, then save the database as **IL_INT_3_NewZealandHotels**. Create a query called **Hotels Query** that includes all fields and that sorts the Hotels table in ascending order by Location. Copy the query, paste it as a link into Excel, then create the 2D pie chart similar to the one shown in FIGURE 3-18, and save the Excel workbook as **IL_INT_3_NewZealandHotelsData**. As shown in the figure, create a one-slide PowerPoint presentation called **IL_INT_3_NewZealandHotelsPresentation**, apply the Title Only slide layout, then copy the pie chart from Excel and paste it onto the slide using the Use Destination Theme & Link Data option. Format the slide as shown: add the slide title, apply the Dividend slide design with the Green variant (third from the left), apply a black border, format the chart with Quick Layout 6 and Style 9, then remove the chart title from the chart. Switch to Access, open the Hotels query, change the number of guests who stayed at the Lakeview Resort in Queenstown to **150**, close the query, update the links in Excel and PowerPoint, then enter your name in the slide footer. Break the link to the Excel workbook and PowerPoint presentation, save and close all open files and programs, then submit your files to your instructor.

FIGURE 3-18

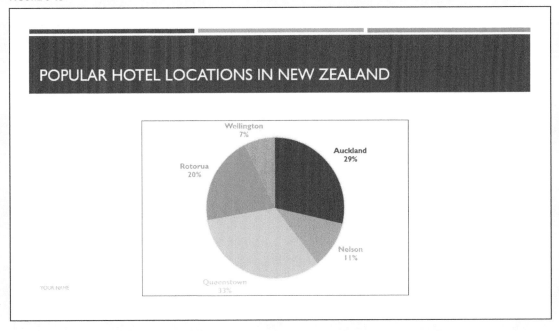

Index

Special Characters

+ (addition), AC 3-21, EX 1-11
' (apostrophe), EX A-10
* (asterisk), AC B-10, EX B-7
^ (caret), EX 1-11, EX B-7
/ (division), AC 3-21, EX 1-11
$ (dollar sign), EX C-2
= (equal to), AC 3-17, EX B-6, EX 3-5
^ (exponentiation), AC 3-21
> (greater than), AC B-15, AC 3-17, EX 3-5
>= (greater than or equal to operator), AC B-15, AC 3-17
(hash mark; pound sign), AC B-10, EX C-8
< (less than operator), AC B-15, AC 3-17, EX 3-5
<= (less than or equal to operator), AC B-15, AC 3-17
- (minus sign), EX B-7
* (multiplication), AC 3-21, EX 1-11
<>/≠ (not equal to operator), AC B-15, AC 3-17
% (percent sign), EX B-7
% (percent), EX 1-11
+ (plus sign), EX B-7
? (question mark), AC B-10
/ (slash), EX B-7
- (subtraction), AC 3-21, EX 1-11

A

Access. *See* Microsoft Access 2019
absolute cell references, EX 1-14–EX 1-15
Access Options, AC 1-24
accessibility, EX 2-13
Accessibility Checker, WD 3-19
action query, AC 3-4
absolute references, CC 5-17
active cell, PPT 3-6
access password, CC 6-16
active window, CC 4-12
adjustment handle, PPT–4
address bar, CC 2-4
add-ins, WD 2-9
addition operator (+), AC 3-21, EX 1-11
address spoofing, CC 6-11
administrative tools, CC 4-13–4-15
   customizing operating system, CC 4-14–4-15
   power settings, CC 4-13–4-14
   user accounts, CC 4-15
   using utilities, CC 4-14
   virtual machine, CC 4-15

administrator account, CC 4-15
Adobe Premiere Clip, CC 5-31
AI. *See* artificial intelligence (AI)
Alexa (Amazon), CC 1-8
aligning
   objects, PPT 2-12–PPT 2-13
   paragraph text, PPT 2-7
alignment, EX 2-6–EX 2-7
all-in-one computer, CC 3-8
alternative text (alt text), CC 1-11
Alt Text command, WD 3-19
Americans with Disabilities Act (ADA), CC 1-10
anchored, WD 3-14
AND Criteria, AC 3-16–AC 3-17
AND function, EX 3-6–EX 3-7
AND OR SQL keyword, AC 3-18
Android, CC 4-5
animations
   attaching sound, PPT 3-17
   defined, CC 5-21
   objects in presentation, PPT 3-16–PPT 3-17
   in presentation, CC 5-21–5-22
   to SmartArt object, PPT 3-17
animation tags, PPT 3-16
Apache OpenOffice, CC 5-11
append, AC 2-2
Apple iWork, CC 5-10
Apple-Pay, CC 2-13
application developer, AC 1-16
apps
   defined, CC 2-8, CC 5-2
   common features of, CC 5-4
   development, CC 1-14
   purpose of, CC 5-3
   types of, CC 5-3–5-4
app store, CC 5-6
area chart, EX 4-3, PPT 3-7
arguments, EX 1-10
argument of function, CC 5-17
arithmetic logic unit (ALU), CC 3-3
arithmetic operators, AC 3-21, EX 1-10, EX 1-11
artificial intelligence (AI), CC 1-6
Artistic Effects command, WD 3-18
ASCII, CC 3-6
Ask a Librarian, CC 2-18
ATMs. *See* automated teller machines (ATMs)
Attachment data type, AC 1-11
attackers, computer security, CC 6-3